D0679656

THE BEST PLAYS OF 1999–2000

THE OTIS GUERNSEY BURNS MANTLE THEATER YEARBOOK

THE BEST PLAYS OF 1999–2000

EDITED BY OTIS L. GUERNSEY JR.

Illustrated with photographs and
with drawings by HIRSCHFELD

LIMELIGHT EDITIONS

ISBN: 0-87910-955-6

ISSN: 1071-6971

Printed in the United States of America

EDITOR'S NOTE

AS FAR as the theater is concerned, the 20th century came to an end on May 31, 2000, the turning-point of its seasons and the cut-off point of this, the 81st annual edition of the *Best Plays* series of theater yearbooks started by Burns Mantle at Dodd, Mead and Company with the 1919–1920 season. That first volume's ten Best Plays were all Broadway productions, of course (this year, four of our six cited scripts premiered off Broadway, and one came from off off). One of the 1919–1920 bests was a ringer from the previous season (Sem Benelli's *The Jest),* and the list included Eugene O'Neill's *Beyond the Horizon* and the Ethel Barrymore vehicle *Declassée* by Zoe "Atkins" (even *Best Plays* editors sometimes make mistakes). The 20th century theater surged onward from there, recorded in *Best Plays* by five editors—Mantle, John Chapman, Louis Kronenberger, Henry Hewes and the undersigned—and our coverage also looked back over its shoulder in two retrospective volumes, *The Best Plays of 1899–1909* and *1909–1919,* so that we have the entire 100 years on our record. As the century's curtain falls, our final featured play is Wallace Shawn's *The Designated Mourner,* which opened in New York on May 13 in a tiny OOB venue. It is a most appropriate representative of end-of-the-century American theater, which is busily expanding the vocabulary of the stage as we've known it, not only in experimental-sized productions everywhere but also in large ones like another of this season's prize plays, *Contact.*

Editing *Best Plays* is an ideal job for a theater lover, as it concentrates the much greater portion of its attention and energy on the plus side, emphasizing our wonderful theater's major achievements. But it is far from being a solo show. With Jonathan Dodd's eagle eye (for the last half of the century) on details of text and publication, and Dorianne D. Guernsey's painstaking review of the content, there have been very, very few Atkinses where Akins should be. The *Best Plays* series as a whole is an album of Al Hirschfeld's drawings of the theater and its personalities; in this 1999–2000 volume he shows us with his caricatures how the theater's final 20th century season and its performers really looked. The distinguished playwrights Jeffrey Sweet and Sally Dixon Wiener have contributed synopses of prizewinning plays. Our off-off-Broadway critic Mel Gussow has outlined the shape of the season on the glowing fringes of the New York stage, and Rue E. Canvin has provided her usual portion of the Facts and Figures listing, including necrology and published plays.

Our comprehensive factual coverage of the off-off-Broadway and cross-country scenes in this book published by Melvyn B. Zerman's Limelight Editions are the result of the diligent ministrations of our associate editor, Camille Dee, who also processed the material provided by Lawrence Bommer for the American Theater Critics Association in our Theater Around the United States section. This text is embellished with introductory reviews of ATCA's cited plays by Richard Christiansen, Alice T. Carter and Rosalind Friedman. Under the chairmanship of Jeffrey Eric Jenkins, this year ATCA members voted their selections of the most significant American plays and musicals of the 20th century (the composite results appear in the ATCA section of this volume), and their organization enhanced its annual citations of outstanding cross-country plays with substantial cash awards to the winners provided by the Harold and Mimi Steinberg Charitable Trust. In honor of this development, we have augmented our coverage of the ATCA/Steinberg New Play Award winner in that section. And ATCA Chairman Jenkins, New York critic for the Seattle *Post-Intelligencer* and a visiting assistant professor of drama at N.Y.U., is the author of our Season in New York essay covering all the year's major Broadway and off-Broadway developments and achievements.

Once again, the Jeffrey Finn Productions staff has prepared the list of major cast replacements in Broadway and off-Broadway holdovers, together with the casts of the first class touring companies of New York shows. And there are scores of other theater folk and theater aficionados who help with the details of *Best Plays* coverage, starting with the generous and indispensable cooperation of the press agents in New York and across the country, and including former *Best Plays* editor Henry Hewes (Theater Hall of Fame data), Michael Kuchwara (details of the Critics' voting for their bests), Thomas T. Foose (historical footnotes), Tish Dace (Hewes Design Awards), Ralph Newman of the Drama Book Shop, Markland Taylor (New England theater information), David Rosenberg (Connecticut Critics), Caldwell Titcomb (Elliot Norton Awards) and Joshua Crouthamel (program listings assistant).

It is putting it mildly to say that we are grateful for all the helping hands—we have depended on them year after year for the very essence of this project. And we extend our most particular gratitude to the producers who supply us with our graphics illustrating the art of the stage—the examples of the prizewinning *Kiss Me, Kate* costume designs of Martin Pakledinaz and *Aida* set designs of Bob Crowley, as well as of many of the 1999–2000 theater's onstage scenes as depicted in the photos of David Allen, Tina Barney, Chris Bennion, Michael Brosilow, Marc Bryan-Brown, Barry Burns, Susan Cook, Paula Court, Whitney Cox, Shannon Donahue, Mark Douet, T. Charles Erickson, Eric Y. Exit, Rainer Fehringer, Gerry Goodstein, Michelle Hollberg, Ken Howard, Paul Kolnik, James J. Kriegsman Jr., Ivan Kynel, Liz Lauren, Gary Mamay, Joan Marcus, Eduardo Patino, Carol Rosegg, Craig Schwartz, Dixie Sheridan, Diane Sobole, Richard Trigg, Jay Westhauser and Rich Wilson.

In this connection, we extend our special thanks to Sherman Howe Jr. for converting color slides to black-and-white photographs for several of our recent volumes. Kronenberger introduced photography to *Best Plays* in his 1956–57 edition, but the insidious intrusion of color into coverage of the theater, even in the New York *Times,* has begun to create a shortage of those black-and-whites which can so effectively portray the moods, the darker and lighter passions, the contrasting extravagancies of the theater art. The focus of the black-and-white illusion matches the focus of stage illusion caught in the act, while color photography diffuses its impact with many visual statements in the same package. To serve the purposes of the record, the conversion of color slides does the job, but for the most part the trendy gravitation towards color threatens to dilute future illustration of theater activity.

Both the 20th century theater and the readers of 20th century *Best Plays* owe their greatest debt of gratitude to our dramatists. We salute the authors of 1999–2000's prizewinning and specially cited plays—John Weidman and Susan Stroman *(Contact),* Richard Nelson and Shaun Davey *(James Joyce's The Dead),* Donald Margulies *(Dinner With Friends),* Michael Frayn *(Copenhagen),* August Wilson *(Jitney)* and Wallace Shawn *(The Designated Mourner).* We salute those dramatists revived this season—among them Irving Berlin, Cole Porter, Eugene O'Neill, Meredith Willson, Stephen Sondheim, John Kander & Fred Ebb, Arthur Miller, Sam Shepard and David Mamet—and all the others alive and dead who have created plays and musicals which, in their revival mode, have made Broadway and off Broadway into a sparkling American repertory theater. And we most respectfully salute all the unsung playwrights, composers and lyricists who have risen again and again from their own ashes in dedication and service to our stage. As the 20th century comes to a close, this is the last volume to be edited by Jonathan Dodd and the undersigned. All of us at *Best Plays* hope that our series of yearbooks on the library shelves promises, at the very least, that theater lovers will never forget any of them.

OTIS L. GUERNSEY JR.

September 1, 2000

CONTENTS

Drawings by HIRSCHFELD

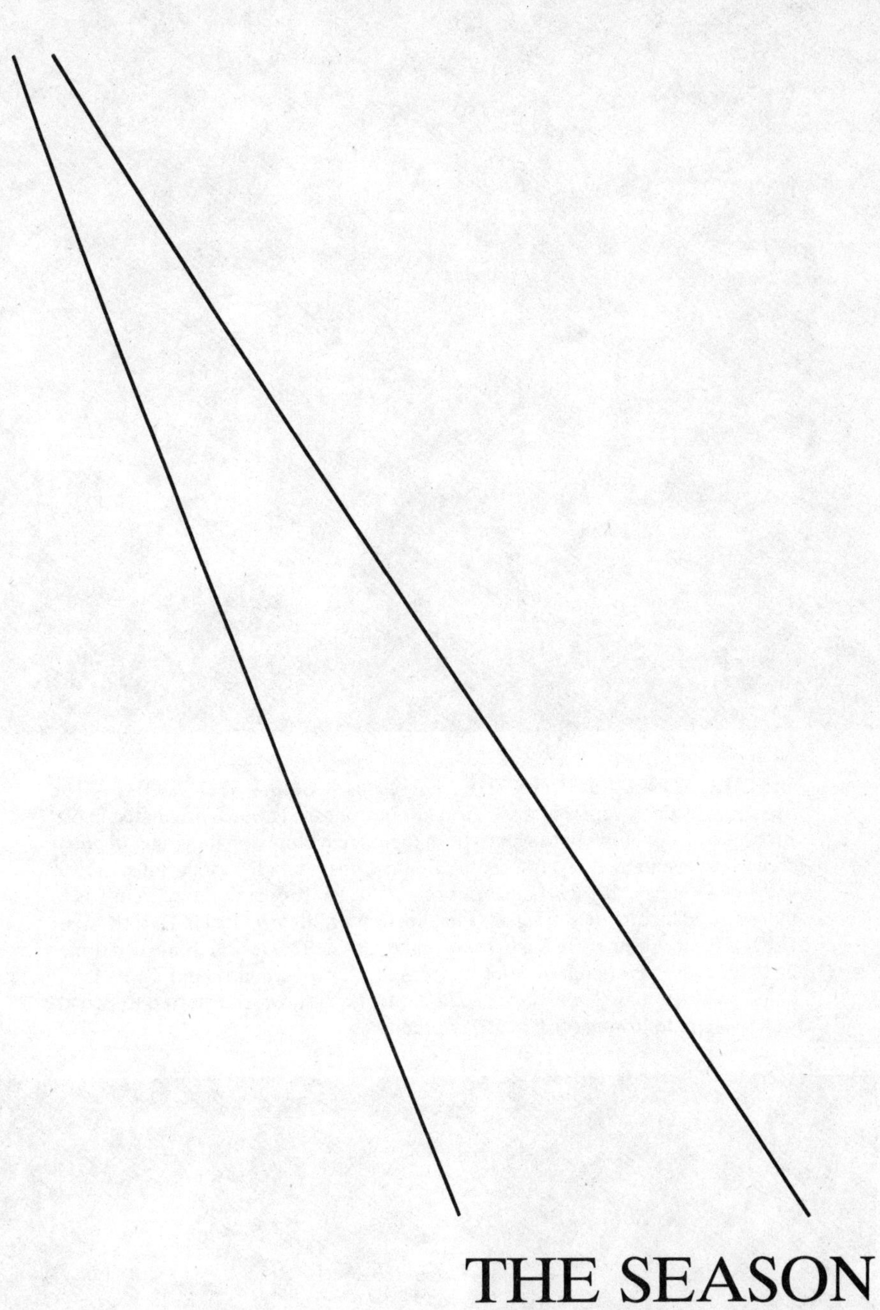

THE SEASON ON AND OFF BROADWAY

OFF BROADWAY STEALS THE 1999–2000 MUSICAL SPOTLIGHT—The two shows which swept this season's major best-musical awards originated in off-Broadway productions, and scenes from them are pictured on this page. *In photo above,* the company of Tony-winning *Contact* (including Deborah Yates, *center,* and Boyd Gaines, *far right*) performs one of Susan Stroman's dance numbers in the swing dance club setting at Lincoln Center. *Below,* Brian Davies, Blair Brown, Emily Skinner (*in background*) and Dashiell Eaves celebrate Christmas in Playwrights' Horizons' Lortel and Critics Award-winning and Tony-nominated production of *James Joyce's The Dead.* Both shows transferred to Broadway theaters following off-Broadway premieres

BROADWAY AND OFF BROADWAY

By Jeffrey Eric Jenkins

IF there is one thing that is certain in New York theater, it is that nothing is certain. Except, perhaps, that each season will give way to the next.

While much of the globe marked the end of 1999 with massive celebrations to herald the end of the millennium (yes, we know the millennium actually ends on New Year's Eve 2000), *Variety* reported that Broadway producers saw New Year's week grosses decline by 13 percent from the previous year's take. With throngs filling Times Square hotels and angling for a view of the big ball-drop at midnight on December 31, theater had taken to the streets. And, of course, there were those feared millennial glitches that kept many people close to home. Remember the dreaded Y2K computer bug?

Still, though, New York theater artists and their audiences had their own milestones to celebrate. The 1999–2000 theater season observed important anniversaries of two quite different icons of the stage. Noel Coward's centenary saw several of his shows revived during the season. *If Love Were All*, *Sail Away*, *Waiting in the Wings* and *Suite in 2 Keys* were the major productions. *Wings*, a 40-year-old sentimental comedy with no previous American productions of record, twisted logic in a way that is unique to theater and qualified as a "new" play.

Stephen Sondheim's 70th birthday was commemorated with highs and lows that seemed taken from one of his musicals. A long-awaited musical with book writer John Weidman, *Wise Guys*, ground to a halt after a semi-secretive development process at New York Theater Workshop. Based on the lives of the Mizner brothers, a pair of sharpies who got rich in the Florida land boom of the early 20th century, the piece had been in development for years. Sondheim fans were disappointed, but other productions (*Putting It Together*, *Saturday Night*, a *Sweeney Todd* concert) helped salve their wounds.

As time passes, torches also pass from one generation to another. After more than 30 years at the helm of the Brooklyn Academy of Music, Harvey Lichtenstein retired as president and executive producer and passed his mantle onto two of his longtime associates. Karen Brooks Hopkins, long the driving force behind BAM's successful fundraising efforts, now serves as president. Joseph V. Melillo, the visionary responsible for many of BAM's forays onto the artistic cutting-edge, is now executive producer.

Ordinarily, this sort of shared power might signal future trouble. But Brooks Hopkins and Melillo have worked together for many years, so they have probably already smoothed out the kinks. However it falls out, there was no noticeable shift in artistic vision as BAM presented a typically stunning visual feast by Ingmar Bergman before Lichtenstein's departure and continued with lively, edgy works from abroad as the new leaders moved forward.

Bergman's *The Image Makers*, like much of the great director's work for both film and theater, focused on the moments of consciousness that fix ideas and anchor the roots of creative inspiration. As BAM's Next Wave Festival got underway, productions of *The Whiteheaded Boy* and *Life Is a Dream* showed that Melillo plans to continue finding fresh, new interpretations of theater. The London group Shared Experience—whose artistic director, Nancy Meckler, staged the Broadway production of *Rose*—returned to BAM with another magical literary adaptation, *Jane Eyre*.

Later in the season, the Royal Shakespeare Company took up residence at BAM for three productions. T.S. Eliot's *The Family Reunion*, Friedrich Schiller's *Don Carlos* and Shakespeare's *A Midsummer Night's Dream* demonstrated the range of interest and risk that artistic director Adrian Noble is willing to undertake as he attempts to reinvigorate the company's fortunes. Although there was critical disagreement over the RSC's artistic success during this stand, no one can argue that the company and its directors lack theatrical imagination. Indeed, Gale Edwards, who directed the season's Broadway production of *Jesus Christ Superstar* as well as *Don Carlos*, showed ability beyond the banal work demonstrated in *Superstar*.

During the 1999–2000 season it became clear that "forever" is just less than two decades, that the finest new American plays continue to skip Broadway, that the much-lamented state of Broadway choreography is in the midst of a renaissance and that we should never underestimate the attraction of the wonderful world of Disney.

It also became obvious that the old definitions for "play" and "musical" will continue to evolve (as will notions of "new" and "revival" for Tony Awards administrators). Plays that stretched boundaries included Claudia Shear's tribute to society's outsiders, *Dirty Blonde*, and Julie Taymor's inventive adaptation of Carlo Gozzi's *The Green Bird*, each of which contained nearly enough music and musical staging to be considered musical works. Richard Nelson and Shaun Davey's *James Joyce's The Dead*—featuring Irish folk songs performed at a remembered Christmas party—was subtitled A New Musical Play and gingerly crossed the play-musical border. Due to the festive context of the performance, the singers often gave the theater audience a generous view of their backsides as they performed for the party guests. Nonetheless, *The Dead*, which premiered at off-Broadway's Playwrights Horizons before moving to the Belasco Theater, was a poignant addition to the season and was named best musical by the New York Drama Critics Circle and the Lortel Awards Committee.

There was controversy elsewhere on the musical front as the awards season drew near. When Susan Stroman and John Weidman's dance play, *Contact*, was nomi-

The 1999–2000 Season on Broadway

PLAYS (5)

Voices in the Dark
Epic Proportions
Wrong Mountain
Taller Than a Dwarf
Dirty Blonde
(transfer)

FOREIGN PLAYS (2)

Waiting in the Wings
(revised version)
COPENHAGEN

MUSICALS (8)

Kat and the Kings
The Scarlet Pimpernel
(revised version)
Saturday Night Fever
Marie Christine
JAMES JOYCE'S
THE DEAD
(transfer)
Aida
The Wild Party
Meredith Willson's
The Music Man

REVUES (3)

Minnelli on Minnelli
Swing!
Riverdance on Broadway
(return engagement)

SPECIALTIES (3)

Radio City Christmas
Spectacular
Squonk
(transfer)
CONTACT
(dance play)

REVIVALS (15)

Roundabout:
The Rainmaker
Uncle Vanya
The Price
Tango Argentino
Kiss Me, Kate
Putting It Together
A Christmas Carol
Amadeus
Porgy and Bess
True West
A Moon for the
Misbegotten
The Ride Down
Mt. Morgan
Jesus Christ Superstar
The Real Thing
The Green Bird

SOLO SHOWS (3)

Dame Edna:
The Royal Tour
Much Ado About
Everything
Rose

Categorized above are all the new productions listed in the Plays Produced on Broadway section of this volume.
Plays listed in CAPITAL LETTERS were major 1999–2000 prizewinners.
Plays listed in *italics* were still running on June 1, 2000.

nated for a Tony as best musical, an uproar ensued because there was neither a book—in the conventional sense of dialogue between characters, although there was a story line told through movement—nor an original score. In *Contact*, the dancers move to recorded numbers ranging from pop to classical music, but singing is not a factor in the performance. After the Tony nominations were announced, the musicians' union filed an official objection, and a member of the Tony nominating committee resigned in protest. But the show had a powerful emotional pull on audiences, which helped it win best new musical at the Tony and Drama Desk Awards. Deborah Yates as the Girl in a Yellow Dress was a vision of physical and terpsichorean perfection. Boyd Gaines and Karen Ziemba were Tony honorees as best featured musical actor and actress, while director-choreographer Stroman received the best-choreography Tony.

Elsewhere in the redefinition sweepstakes, there was a plethora of Broadway musical entertainments ranging from a South African doo-wop revue with a thinly stretched story line (*Kat and the Kings*) to a multimedia event (*Squonk*) to a revue of hot swing dancing (*Swing!*) to a revival of a Stephen Sondheim revue (*Putting It Together*) with veteran trouper Carol Burnett and television personality Kathie Lee Gifford alternating in the lead female role. And then there was the third version—in three seasons—of *The Scarlet Pimpernel*, informally dubbed *Scarlet 3.0*. Scaled down from an earlier revision for the 1998–99 season, the 1999–2000 issue of *Scarlet Pimpernel* was created for touring.

Even the folks at Disney did a bit of downsizing when they closed *Beauty and the Beast* at the Palace Theater, fired the actors—causing consternation at Actors Equity—and then reopened several weeks later with a smaller cast at the Lunt-Fontanne. After hosting the planned short run of Liza Minnelli's *Minnelli on Minnelli* revue—celebrating the work of the singer's father, Vincente—the Palace became the home of Disney's third concurrent Broadway production, *Aida*.

Although the production—based on Verdi's opera—received unenthusiastic reviews, the lure of Elton John's familiar music and Tim Rice's vapid lyrics overcame critical gibes about the work's lack of artistic heft. From a design point of view, though, scenery and costume designer Bob Crowley created a stunning fantasia of ancient Egypt as imagined by someone digging into Disney's deep pockets. Likewise, Natasha Katz's lighting was a visual wonder. The saving grace of *Aida*, however, was the superb voice of Heather Headley in the title role. A pop diva with enormous vocal range, Headley offered to work for Disney for "forever" at an awards ceremony—she had earlier been the original Nala in *The Lion King*. The entertainment megalith may well hold her to her pledge: Headley's voice, Katz's lighting and Crowley's scenery were all honored with Tony Awards.

Throughout the performance, John's pleasant, yet unchallenging music reminded the audience that they were in the artistic presence of the man who wrote "Goodbye, Yellow Brick Road" and "Candle in the Wind." Perhaps impressed by the composer's consistency, perhaps discouraged by the quality of their other choices, Tony voters honored *Aida*'s music and lyrics. Apparently otherwise engaged, John and Rice were the only winners who failed to collect their own awards at the ceremony.

TONY AWARD-WINNING DESIGNS—*Above,* Bob Crowley's sketch for his vision of the Nile valley in *Aida* (in color the river is blue, the banks an orangey red, the foliage silhouetted in black); *below,* two of Martin Pakledinaz's costume sketches for the revival of *Kiss Me, Kate*

Doubly (or perhaps quadruply) disappointed on the big night was the man sometimes called the "next Stephen Sondheim," Michael John LaChiusa. The composer and lyricist for two new Broadway musicals in the 1999–2000 season—*Marie Christine* and *The Wild Party*—LaChiusa received Tony nominations for both. He was also nominated as the book writer of *Marie Christine* and as co-book writer (with George C. Wolfe) of New York Shakespeare Festival's *The Wild Party*.

Unfortunately though, LaChiusa seemed as cursed as the title character of his epic-themed *Marie Christine*. Written for three-time Tony winner Audra McDonald, LaChiusa's musical lacerates the Medea myth with a racist edge when a ne'er-do-well white man woos a member of Afro-Caribbean aristocracy. Although the near-operatic musical construction allowed McDonald to show her powerful singing voice and nuanced acting ability, the bleak outlook of the story combines with its tragic ending to dampen audience enthusiasm for the work.

It's hard to imagine that anyone saw the dark themes of *Marie Christine* as a possible commercial breakout from Lincoln Center's Vivian Beaumont. But LaChiusa and Wolfe's *The Wild Party* was developed for a Broadway run. It was a gutsy move for NYSF producer Wolfe because the nonprofit downtown company had suffered a huge flop in the 1998–99 Broadway season with the troubled revival of *On the Town*. Financed solely by NYSF when other producing partners dropped out amid rumors of dissension over creative decisions, *On the Town* cost NYSF millions of dollars. With this latest entry in the Broadway crapshoot, though, Wolfe and his board of directors managed to retain their outside producing partners, which reduced the company's financial exposure.

70, Sondheim's 70

As the 1999–2000 season took shape, it became obvious that this would be a year of wild parties. In addition to the LaChiusa version commissioned by Wolfe, off Broadway's Manhattan Theater Club was slated to open Andrew Lippa's take on Joseph Moncure March's 1928 epic poem about love, liquor and loss. Because most musicals are written with an eye toward a Broadway run, Times Square touts were handicapping the odds of seeing two musicals with the same theme and title running at the same time. Alas, it was not to happen. Manhattan Theater Club's production opened first and was believed by prospective producers to have too little critical support to make the commercial move. In addition, the off-Broadway production lacked Broadway stars. The NYSF production had Mandy Patinkin, Eartha Kitt and Academy Award nominee Toni Collette.

But when the LaChiusa rendering opened, the critical reception was cool. It was terrific to see Patinkin and Kitt strut their respective stuff, but overall the show lacked the heat and immediacy of Andrew Lippa's off-Broadway version. Wolfe's Broadway production also suffered from critical familiarity with the off-Broadway edition, which detracted from the show's theatrical edge. Nominated for seven Tony Awards, *The Wild Party* won none and announced its closing a few days after the ceremony. Both versions of this musical figured prominently, however, in the New York Drama Critics Circle's voting at the end of the season.

Meanwhile, the actual Stephen Sondheim was feted by a season-long celebration of his 70th birthday. In addition to having productions both on and off Broadway in the 1999–2000 season, the master of lyrical irony heard his quasi-operatic *Sweeney Todd* performed in a concert version by the New York Philharmonic at Avery Fisher Hall. Lucky concertgoers heard a cast that blended musical theater performers and opera singers (even as the debate over whether *Sweeney* is theater or opera continued to swirl with Sondheim and composer Ned Rorem discussing the issue in the pages of The New York *Times*). Musical theater was represented in the performance by George Hearn, Patti LuPone, Audra McDonald, Davis Gaines and Neil Patrick Harris. The opera performers included Heidi Grant Murphy, Paul Plishka, John Aler and Stanford Olsen.

But the Sondheim celebration got off to a rocky start with the Broadway production of his revue *Putting It Together*. A flaccid exercise that lacked the right context to capture the verve and intensity of Sondheim's work, the show probably could have done with a leading lady whose characterizations shaded more darkly. Carol Burnett and her alternate, Kathie Lee Gifford, both seem cut from the same bright fabric. The wounded female creatures in Sondheim don't bubble, they don't do Tarzan yells and they don't pull on an ear lobe to say "hi" to Grandma back home.

Just three days after *Putting It Together* closed at the Ethel Barrymore, Second Stage premiered Sondheim's *Saturday Night*. Written in the 1950s, it was not performed until 1997 in England. The 45-year-old musical then had its American premiere in Chicago in 1999, fulfilling its promise to give an early peek at the Sondheim we now know. Based on the play *Front Porch in Flatbush* by the Epstein brothers, who collaborated on the screenplay for *Casablanca*, it featured music and lyrics by Sondheim and a book by Julius J. Epstein. The story focused on the seemingly timeless tale of young Brooklynites looking across the East River toward Manhattan and the Main Chance.

Directed by the extremely talented choreographer Kathleen Marshall, who is also artistic director of the *Encores! Great American Musicals in Concert* series at City Center, Sondheim's 45-year-old essay in 1920s nostalgia was part of the backward-looking musical trend off Broadway and on. Off-Broadway audiences saw celebrations of Noel Coward's musical work and life (*If Love Were All* and *Sail Away*); a musicalization of the late 1960s entitled *Summer 69*; a retrospective of Frank Sinatra songs in *Our Sinatra*; the York Theater Company's season-long look at music and musicals of the past (*Jolson & Co.*, *Taking a Chance on Love*, *Kean*, *Wish You Were Here*, and *70, Girls, 70*); as well as the aforementioned *James Joyce's The Dead* and *The Wild Party*.

As Marshall prepared *Saturday Night* for its New York bow, Mark Brokaw, better known for his work on new plays (*As Bees in Honey Drown*, *How I Learned to Drive*), directed the *Encores!* production of *On a Clear Day You Can See Forever* with the delicious Kristin Chenoweth as Daisy Gamble and Peter Friedman as Dr. Mark Bruckner in the 1965 Alan Jay Lerner and Burton Lane musical. The founding artistic director of *Encores!*, Walter Bobbie, returned to stage Jerry Bock and Sheldon Harnick's 1960 musical, *Tenderloin*—sometimes called a downtown version of *Guys and Dolls*. David Ogden Stiers starred as the crusading Reverend Brock. For the final production of the *Encores!* season, Marshall returned to direct the 1953

Leonard Bernstein, Betty Comden and Adolph Green musical, *Wonderful Town*. Donna Murphy, player of dreary women in Sondheim's *Passion* and the recent revival of *The King and I*, surprised audiences with her spark-plug intensity as Ruth. Laura Benanti, while keeping her day job in the musical *Swing!*, played her sister Eileen. Other notables in the cast included Richard Muenz, Lewis J. Stadlen, Gregory Jbara, Raymond Jaramillo McLeod and Alix Korey. The artistic excellence of the *Encores!* series was honored by a special 2000 Tony Award presented to City Center president and executive director Judith Daykin.

Arguably the biggest splash among off-Broadway musicals, though, was made by *The Bomb-itty of Errors*, which was also the most successful adaptation of Shakespeare in the 1999–2000 season. The creation of a group of former New York University drama students who developed the work while still in school, *Bomb-itty* is a hip-hop version of *The Comedy of Errors*. Unusually popular with late-teens and twentysomethings, the adaptation appalled some Shakespeareans and thrilled others. Although some theatergoers were concerned about a group of young white men appropriating African-American cultural expression through hip-hop and rap lyrics, others argued that appropriation is the name of the game in all of Shakespeare. However people felt about the political underpinnings of the show, it was impossible not to enjoy its infectious (and occasionally offensive) humor.

Although off Broadway can be a safe harbor for artistic risk, it is worth remembering that long-running off-Broadway productions are not so different from those on the Great White Way. That is, the long-runners in both areas tend to be "event theater." Who can say whether *The Fantasticks* continues to run on its artistic strength or on its record of more than 16,500 performances, which makes it a kind of international must-see musical. Warren Manzi's *Perfect Crime*, at more than 5,400 performances, holds a similar distinction among dramatic plays.

Indeed, a quick perusal of long runs confirms the hold of event theater on off Broadway's consciousness. *Tony 'n' Tina's Wedding*, *Tubes*, *Stomp* and *De La Guarda* all transcend (or transgress) the borders that mark traditional theater. And yet these borders continued to stretch in the 1999–2000 season with shows such as *Naked Boys Singing!* (a title that needs no further explication).

So when we worry over the Disneyfication of Broadway—a concern that loomed larger after the House of Mickey settled into three concurrent runs by season's end—we need to remember that the theater is an art form constantly changing to survive. If event theater is certain to be part of the theatrical future, it is also only part of the theatrical mosaic. In the near term, though, some of the big-event Broadway productions of the 1980s have finally begun to wind down.

End of an Era?

The big news from the 1999–2000 Broadway theater season—besides records set in box office sales and ticket prices—was the announcement in February that *Cats* would close after a run of nearly 19 years. The announcement gave ticket sales a bounce that encouraged producers to extend the run for an additional 11 weeks. At

DIRTY BLONDE—Claudia Shear in the play she wrote about Mae West that "stretched boundaries"

press time, the final meow was to be September 10 and would mark 7,485 performances. After years of a "now and forever" marketing strategy, it seemed as though the fat kitty would finally sing his last.

In a *Variety* article about media coverage of Broadway theater, press agent Bill Evans told reporter Robert Hofler that the *Cats* closing announcement sparked a "phenomenal" 395 mentions in television coverage. Evans compared that with 175 placements when *Cats* surpassed *A Chorus Line* as the long-running champ in June 1997. Why were media outlets so much more interested in the closing than the extension of a record? At a time when "millennium" mentions had just begun to abate, media types found themselves with a new topic for the old "end of an era" angle. But the ubiquitous quality of *Cats*—is there any medium-to-large city that has not seen a touring production several times?—undoubtedly lent heat to the story.

Consider the affect of *Cats* on Broadway musicals today. When it first premiered, there was nothing quite like it. A middlebrow cartoon come to life, it deconstructed the traditional commercial theater space and connected with its audience in one-on-one interactions. As a pure spectacle, with little story line and often garbled lyrics, *Cats* aimed at enfolding its audience in a fantasy world. Following this production, other musicals began to emulate *Cats*'s emphasis on pure theater, which led to a gradual diminishment of plot and text.

Successful shows that followed relied more and more on spectacular effects—eyepopping bits of theatrical magic. There was the turntable and massive barricade in *Les Misérables*, the chandelier in *The Phantom of the Opera*, the helicopter in *Miss Saigon*. As ticket prices rose, of course, it became difficult to justify *not* having the big effect.

A few weeks after the *Cats* closing announcement, Cameron Mackintosh announced that he would close the helicopter musical, *Miss Saigon*, on New Year's Eve 2000 after 4,063 performances. Was "a new era," indeed, at hand? Considering the spectacle in this season's *Aida*, it is highly unlikely. It is more probable that both *Cats* and *Miss Saigon* merely ran out of gas—after making a dozen or so people very wealthy and providing steady (if, as in *Cats*, body punishing) work for many theater artists.

Even shows without Disney's resources rely heavily on spectacle and minimize text and plot. Such is the case with *Saturday Night Fever*, the latest example of what happens when theater people run out of ideas. The 1977 film *Saturday Night Fever* gave shape and voice to the struggles of a generation of young people when it appeared. Viewers needn't have lived in Bay Ridge, Brooklyn to appreciate the aspirations of kids grasping for the next rung on society's ladder while seeking release through dance. When the Broadway musical version appeared, however, the humanity of the story was traded for thrusting male pelvises, lusty female ciphers and musical numbers that were not so much performed as wielded like assault weapons—loud, sharp and painful.

After nearly universal pans by the critics, the producers of *Saturday Night Fever* jubilantly announced a $20 million advance sale. One producer told the *Daily News* that people were rushing to "buy repeat tickets at intermission time so they can come back and see the show all over again." While the show's marketing seemed to have circumvented the critics, it received no Tony nominations and sales figures near season's end were down sharply. By the end of the 1999–2000 season, it seemed as though *Saturday Night Fever* was beginning to get the wrong kind of word-of-mouth.

The retreading of shows such as *Scarlet Pimpernel* and the film version of *Saturday Night Fever* also extends to the occasional play. For many years, shows traditionally have been considered new until they opened on Broadway. A play such as Sam Shepard's *True West* may have had hundreds of productions, following controversial premieres 20 years ago in New York and San Francisco theaters. But if it didn't open in a theater of more than 500 seats in New York City, the general definition of a Broadway house, it was still a "new" play to the Tony nominators—but not to *Best Plays*. According to the longstanding policy of *Best Plays*, a script that has had an off-Broadway production of record—commercial or nonprofit— is considered "frozen" in its final form. Future productions, such as this year's *True West*, are considered revivals. Of course there are individual cases of revisions that need to be reconsidered, but they are few and far between. Off-off-Broadway productions are, with rare exceptions, classed as works-in-progress.

True West had its New York premiere of record in 1980 at New York Shakespeare Festival. It was a post-premiere production mounted off-Broadway in the 1982–83 season by Chicago's Steppenwolf Theater, however, that made stars of Gary Sinise and John Malkovich as a pair of dysfunctional brothers who battle over that most contested of territories: the borders between family and self. Even with the celebrated Malkovich and Sinise production, though, the 1999–2000 Broadway production of *True West*—starring blossoming film stars Philip Seymour Hoffman and John C. Reilly—was judged eligible for the best new play Tony and was duly nominated. Indeed, the stars and the director, Matthew Warchus, were also nominated but no Tony laurels were bestowed. The gimmick of this *True West*, performed in some prior productions, was that the main actors switched roles for alternating performances. Several critics (and audience members) who did not see both versions of this production were heard to remark, "I must have seen the wrong pairing of the roles." More likely is that director Warchus's facile style—which served his 1997–98 Broadway production of Yasmina Reza's *Art* so well—skimmed over the deeper, more compelling emotional elements in Shepard's best-known play.

This was not the first time that Shepard has had an older play revivified as a new work for Tony consideration. The 1995–96 Broadway production of *Buried Child* was similarly declared eligible for new play consideration. In that case, though, Shepard had made textual revisions that helped the "new play" argument.

New Plays on Broadway

True West aside, there were plays in the 1999–2000 Broadway season that could honestly claim to be new. In the early months of the season, though, there was little to cheer. John Pielmeier's *Voices in the Dark*, which premiered at Seattle's A Contemporary Theater in 1994, is the sort of thriller that was once a Broadway staple. Judith Ivey offered her usual solid work—this time as a radio psychologist stalked by a psycho—and audiences gasped in surprise at the plot's twists and turns. But reviews were unenthusiastic and attendance dwindled until the show closed.

Larry Coen and David Crane's *Epic Proportions* limped along for nearly two months before its producers mercifully pulled the plug. Even the considerable charms of star Kristin Chenoweth could not overcome Coen and Crane's sophomoric attempt at spoofing the heyday of epic Hollywood films. The production also marked the passing of the fine comic character actor Richard B. Shull. Playing the filmmaker D.W. DeWitt, Shull died during the show's run and was replaced by Larry Cahn.

As the season wore on, there was little of note in the category of new plays on Broadway. Noel Coward's *Waiting in the Wings*, a decidedly lesser work of the author's canon, survived mainly on the strength of several *grande dames* of the stage in the cast. Rosemary Harris, Lauren Bacall, Elizabeth Wilson, Helen Stenborg, Dana Ivey and others propped up a creaky tale about retired actresses who find themselves thrust together in a retirement home called the Wings. Although the play was 40 years old, it had no other American performances of record, which made it a "new play."

David Hirson's *Wrong Mountain*, which opened in January, was dutifully (and unnecessarily) pummeled by the critical community for creating a thoroughly unpleasant character (played by Ron Rifkin) who is transformed by theatrical success. At least one critic wrote that Hirson's play was better suited to off Broadway, implying that artistically risky works need not apply to the big houses.

The Broadway new play malaise continued apace until April when Arthur Miller's *The Ride Down Mt. Morgan* and Michael Frayn's *Copenhagen* opened. Both of these plays found their legs in London; *Mt. Morgan* in 1991, *Copenhagen* more recently. The Miller play indulges in a kind of free-form speculation regarding a man's duty to himself (read: his libido) as opposed to others (his loved ones). Miller's testosterone-influenced argument frequently causes wincing pain due to his main character's callous treatment of women as objects. But Patrick Stewart, as bigamist Lyman Felt—an interesting progression from Loman—charmed away audience concerns about his character's sexual politics. Then, in a spectacular display of hubris worthy of his character, the actor chose to denounce Gerald Schoenfeld and the Shubert Organization, in a curtain speech, for failing to properly promote the production. After a few tense days of accusations flying in the media, Stewart was ordered by Actors Equity to apologize for his remarks. The play was nominated for a Tony Award, as was co-star Frances Conroy; Stewart was not.

Departing theatergoers interviewed on television about *Copenhagen* demonstrated the curiosity of Frayn's play. While most thought that it was a very good play, these same people also attested that they weren't sure they understood it—a brave admission in competitive New York City. Essentially, Frayn's play is a tale of male friendship and its many complexities. Set against the backdrop of the labyrinthine relationship between two theoretical physicists—Niels Bohr (Philip Bosco) and Werner Heisenberg (Michael Cumpsty)—and their respective contributions to nuclear warfare, the playwright attempts to draw parallels between nuclear physics and human interaction. He is largely successful, although the physics becomes a kind of smoke screen behind which a rather simple story hides.

Although the play won the Tony Award for best new play and the Drama Critics Circle Award for best foreign play—and helped Michael Blakemore win two directing Tonys (he also won for the musical revival of *Kiss Me, Kate*)—neither of the actors who played the physicists was even nominated. The third player, Blair Brown, who played Bohr's wife and "interpreter," Margrethe, was nominated for featured actress and won. She had also received acclaim earlier in the season for her leading role in *James Joyce's The Dead*.

Olympia Dukakis returned to the New York stage in the Broadway production of Martin Sherman's one-woman play, *Rose*. Developed in London with director Nancy Meckler, this intermissionless production concerned a Zelig-like Jewish

WRONG MOUNTAIN—Daniel Davis and Ron Rifkin in David Hirson's play

woman who not only survived the Holocaust but also wound up a potsmoking hippie in middle age. Watching this wide-ranging show, audience members might have thought that they had wandered into Jackie Mason's solo comedy performance, *Much Ado About Everything*—except that Mason is much funnier and his tales ring truer.

The best of the solo performances on Broadway in the 1999–2000 season, though, was Barry Humphries's turn as Dame Edna Everage in *Dame Edna: The Royal Tour*. Bedecked in sequins, mauve hair and huge owlish spectacles, Dame Edna chatted with the audience about her life as a megastar and asked them about their own lives. In the course of a performance she telephoned babysitters at home, brought a couple onstage who seemed "a bit peckish" and fed them a meal, and costumed a group of good natured theatergoers so that they could become her entourage. All the while she referred to the audience as "possums," demonstrated the striations of class that still exist in American society and received huge gales of laughter. It was the funniest show of the season—on Broadway or off.

Elaine May's *Taller Than a Dwarf* had audiences scratching their heads and wondering how so much talent could go so wrong. Directed by Alan Arkin and featuring Matthew Broderick, Parker Posey, Jerry Adler, Joyce Van Patten and Micheal McShane, *Taller* could have been called *Prisoner of Queens Boulevard*. It was strikingly similar to Neil Simon's *Prisoner of Second Avenue* yet misfired repeatedly as it attempted to drag Broadway comedy 30 years backwards. Broadway wasn't going along.

The final new play of the Broadway season was Claudia Shear's *Dirty Blonde*, which first appeared at New York Theater Workshop. Co-conceived with director

James Lapine, Shear's play is a tribute to society's outsiders filtered through the life of Mae West and a couple who are enraptured with her legend. After the bad taste left in many critical mouths by the Broadway new play offerings in the 1999–2000, the New York *Times* seemed to mount a campaign aimed at helping Shear and her show win a Tony Award. Critic Ben Brantley was quoted as calling *Dirty Blonde* "The best new American play of the season." Articles appeared that lauded Shear's struggles as an uncompromising artist and celebrating the work of her co-stars, Kevin Chamberlin and Bob Stillman. Indeed, Chamberlin's portrayal of a heterosexual man who seeks comfort by dressing as Mae West was one of the more subtle and carefully nuanced performances of the year. Unfortunately, the production suffered from the author's own dead-on portrayal of West in her decrepitude. It sagged under the weight of West's pathetic visage as she attempted to maintain the illusion of her sex appeal—and the author's final reconciliation of her oddball devotees with one another seemed hollow and forced.

Providing more food for dramatic thought were four major Brian Friel productions, presented in a festival at Lincoln Center and in an off-Broadway run at Roundabout Theater Company's Gramercy Theater space. The Lincoln Center Festival included an adaptation of Anton Chekhov's *Uncle Vanya*, the Chekhovian (by way of the mythical town of Ballybeg) *Aristocrats* and the fact-based *The Freedom of the City*. Friel and his collaborators demonstrated the playwright's fascination with how "truth" resides at the intersection of many truths. His *Vanya* and *Aristocrats* both showed a loving care for the lugubrious, inexorable unraveling (financial, political, cultural) of the landed gentry. In the 1973 play *Freedom*, Friel reminded 1999 audiences how the "troubles" in Ireland continued to spin amid a climate of official distortion, oppression and anger.

Friel's new play for the Roundabout, *Give Me Your Answer, Do!*, centered on the many compromises writers make as they attempt to live their lives and ply their crafts. Featuring the terrific cast of John Glover, Kate Burton, Joel Grey, Lois Smith and Michael Emerson, *Give Me* forces a writer to answer to himself when he has an opportunity to make his family more financially secure. Taken together, Friel's productions in the 1999–2000 season reiterate his position as one of the finest writers of drama in the English language.

Off-Broadway Identities

Off Broadway's season saw a fair amount of diversity among new play offerings. Indeed, off Broadway is the arena where the current interest in identity and sexual politics can find sharper expression. The best of these encompass middle-class angst (*Dinner With Friends*, *The Tale of the Allergist's Wife*); female sexuality (*The Vagina Monologues*); modern Jewish identity (*The Gathering*); the enigma of hate crimes (*The Laramie Project*); working-class tragedy (*The Trestle at Pope Lick Creek*); and the struggles of being black, female or a black female (*Jitney*, *Fuddy Meers*, *Proof*, *Two Sisters and a Piano*, *The Exact Center of the Universe*, *Jar the Floor*, *In the Blood*).

And then there was Anna Deavere Smith's *House Arrest* at the Joseph Papp Public Theater, which attempted to chronicle the U.S. Presidency while including all of the identities and voices mentioned above and more. Unfortunately, the breadth of points of view with regard to our nation's highest office defies the sort of definition to which Smith seems drawn. *House Arrest*, while having much to recommend it, overreached its grasp.

Among the off-Broadway offerings, Donald Margulies's *Dinner With Friends* and August Wilson's *Jitney* were justly singled out for honors by, respectively, the Pulitzer Prize jury and the New York Drama Critics Circle. *Dinner With Friends* sharply delineates the existential terror induced when a married couple watches as their closest friends divorce. Margulies is deliciously funny and insightful when it comes to chronicling the relationships men and women navigate today.

Wilson's *Jitney*, originally written in the 1970s, follows the trajectory of a group of black men trying to make their own way as independent drivers for a car service in Pittsburgh. In the Second Stage production, the men battled the forces of urban renewal while facing the limited choices offered by the dominant white society—which remains an unseen presence. With this play, audiences witnessed the young Wilson's voice beginning to emerge. The playwright's keen ear for dialogue and his cutting sense of humor made this production one of the high points of the theater season. It was certainly one of the finest acting ensembles seen in several seasons.

Charles Busch's *The Tale of the Allergist's Wife* marked a solid step into the theatrical mainstream for the crossdressing actor-playwright. His story of a neurotic Upper West Side Jewish matron was an audience-pleasing exercise in its Manhattan Theater Club bow. At press time, Busch's play was slated to move to Broadway with stars Linda Lavin (she's the wife), Tony Roberts and Michele Lee.

Eve Ensler's *Vagina Monologues* explored and celebrated the nether regions of female sexuality. After an initial run with Ensler performing the piece, the production began to use three well-known women to do the show as a reading—and the performers changed from week to week. For instance, one such grouping included Diahann Carroll, Judith Ivey and Marisa Tomei. Mostly attended by women, the performance was a delightfully funny survey of female sexuality in its many incarnations.

Marion McClinton emerged as a star-caliber director in the 1999–2000 season with productions of Cheryl West's *Jar the Floor* and *Jitney*. The director, who has long labored in the theatrical vineyards, demonstrated an uncanny knack for creating superb acting ensembles and getting at the heart of a text.

David Lindsay-Abaire's *Fuddy Meers* marked the appearance of a terrific new playwriting talent. In *Fuddy Meers* (an important malapropism uttered by a lively stroke victim in the play), the author presents time-worn tales of family abuse and dysfunction with a twist and a razor-sharp edge. The play's dark undercurrent about good women and their relationships with bad men was presented with a cartoonish quality that made the piece hilarious (if a bit painful) from start to finish. After its premiere at the Manhattan Theater Club, the play moved to a commercial run.

Near season's end, Manhattan Theater Club pulled another rabbit from its overstuffed hat with the premiere of *Proof* by David Auburn. Yet another play with

The 1999–2000 Season Off Broadway

PLAYS (30)

Roundabout:
  Hurrah at Last
  Give Me Your Answer, Do!
NYTW:
  The Trestle at Pope Lick Creek
  Dirty Blonde
The Gathering
Second Stage:
  Jar the Floor
  JITNEY
The Exact Center of the Universe
The Countess
Playwrights Horizons:
  Lobster Alice
  The Moment When
MTC:
  Fuddy Meers
  Y2K
  The Tale of the Allergist's Wife
  Proof
DINNER WITH FRIENDS
Maybe Baby, It's You
Last Train to Nibroc
NY Shakespeare:
  In the Blood
  Space
  Two Sisters and a Piano
Jolson & Co.
If Memory Serves
Panache
Joyful Noise
The Waverly Gallery
Family Week
Suite in 2 Keys
Hansen's Cab
The Laramie Project

REVUES (6)

If Love Were All
Naked Boys Singing!
A Good Swift Kick
Y2K, You're OK
Our Sinatra
Taking a Chance on Love

MUSICALS (8)

Summer 69
After the Fair
Stars in Your Eyes
JAMES JOYCE'S THE DEAD
Inappropriate
Saturday Night
The Wild Party
The Big Bang

FOREIGN PLAYS (6)

BAM:
  The Image Makers
  Jane Eyre
MTC:
  La Terrasse
  Experiment Air Pump
Shockheaded Peter
What You Get

SPECIALTIES (2)

CONTACT (dance play)
Bomb-itty of Errors
Thwak

REVIVALS (25)

Gemini
NY Shakespeare:
  The Taming of the Shrew
  Tartuffe
  Hamlet
Lincoln Ctr. Fest:
  Uncle Vanya
  Freedom of the City
  Aristocrats
NYTW:
  A Streetcar Named Desire
  Lydie Breeze, I & II
Arms and the Man
BAM:
  The Family Reunion
  Don Carlos
  A Midsummer Night's Dream
Sail Away
York:
  Kean
  Wish You Were Here
  70, Girls, 70
Encores!:
  On a Clear Day You Can See Forever
  Tenderloin
  Wonderful Town
The Time of the Cuckoo
American Buffalo
Acting Company:
  The Rivals
  Macbeth
Sweeney Todd

SOLO SHOWS (6)

Vagina Monologues
Chesapeake
Fully Committed
Elsa Edgar
House Arrest
Wake Up and Smell the Coffee

Categorized above are all new productions listed (with some titles abbreviated) in the Plays Produced Off Broadway section of this volume.
Play listed in CAPITAL LETTERS were major 1999–2000 prizewinners.
Plays listed in *italics* were in a continuing run June 1, 2000.

science at its core—added to *Copenhagen* and Tina Landau's *Space* in the Broadway and off-Broadway realms—*Proof* follows the difficulties suffered by a woman who has abandoned her own life to care for her eccentric mathematician father. Sharing her father's interest in math, she begins to explore the work and eventually develops a tenuous connection with one of her father's former graduate students. Featuring a superb performance by Mary-Louise Parker, *Proof* was filled with wit, warmth and humanity. As *Best Plays* goes to press, producers seek a Broadway home for the play.

Proof also marked another in a string of successes for director Daniel Sullivan. Sullivan returned to the itinerant director's life a few years ago after 17 years at the Seattle Repertory Theater, where he was artistic director. Besides *Proof*, Sullivan helmed the Pulitzer Prize-winning *Dinner With Friends*, the Broadway revival of *A Moon for the Misbegotten* and A. R. Gurney's *Ancestral Voices* during the 1999–2000 season. In addition, the director also teaches theater at a university in Illinois.

Eileen Heckart gave what was reported to be her valedictory performance in Kenneth Lonergan's off-Broadway production of *The Waverly Gallery*. Lonergan's story of an enfeebled grandmother who was once a font of artistic life and lively intellect is a sad but funny reminder of what may await us all—if we're lucky and we live that long. Heckart, brilliant as the grandmother sinking into dementia, was honored with a special Tony Award for lifetime achievement.

John Ruskin fans had much to discuss with the production of Gregory Murphy's *The Countess*. The play is based on the true story of John Ruskin's tortured relationship with his wife, Effie, who left him for another man—and with very good reason. *The Countess* found a following among art history buffs and Ruskin aficionados, which allowed it to move to an off-Broadway theater for an extended run. An interesting story, its dramaturgy never quite rose above its Victorian soap-opera leanings or its arty aspirations.

Mark Setlock gave a bravura performance of what seemed to be dozens of characters in the deliciously funny *Fully Committed* by Becky Mode. Armed only with a headset telephone, Sam negotiates the various ids, egos and superegos he encounters in his day job as a reservations clerk for a four-star restaurant. It is pure pleasure to watch Sam's growth from a timid, out-of-work actor into someone who knows how to work the system. Mode's play is clever work—and pinpoint accurate to anyone who's been in the food business, they say—but the kudos go to Setlock, who plays all of the characters with clarity and precision.

Elsewhere, Mark Linn-Baker and Eric Bogosian also trod the boards in solo performances. Linn-Baker played a performance artist who imagines that he is reincarnated as the pet of an anti-arts Southern senator in *Chesapeake*, by Lee Blessing, a twisted tale of kidnapping, metamorphosis and deliverance into the corridors of power. Opening around the time of the censorship debate surrounding the Sensation exhibit at the Brooklyn Museum of Art, *Chesapeake* had a certain political currency. Unfortunately for the talented playwright, the arguments in this play are relatively pat and predictable.

Bogosian's *Wake Up and Smell the Coffee* ranges widely through the satirist's fantasies about God, the devil, airline disasters, cell phones, overworked father-

THE COUNTESS—Jennifer Woodward as Effie Ruskin and Jy Murphy as John Everett Millais in Gregory Murphy's play

husbands, the Hollywood talent grinder and various other stresses that face millennial middle-agers. Even though the performance artist managed to craft the work into a neat circle, his postmodern reluctance to tell longer stories (that is, to write more plays) confirms his position as a kind of Will Rogers for our age. Unlike Rogers, though, we can be pretty sure that Bogosian has met more than a few men that he "didn't like."

In a completely different vein, the new play season off Broadway drew to a close with *The Laramie Project*, a collective performance piece created by Moisés Kaufman and the Tectonic Theater Project. In the wake of the murder of Matthew Shepard, a young gay man in Laramie, Wyoming, Kaufman and his company asked local residents, friends of Shepard and religious leaders to discuss what happened. The result is a delicate and often powerful examination of the irrational roots of hate. As performed by the company members, the brilliance of *The Laramie Project* is in its careful and deeply nuanced acting. Missing from the touching tale, however, is a needed dramatic edge. When a company performs characters whom they have interviewed in depth and with whom they sympathize, it is difficult to retain objectivity and provide perspective. Given the subject matter, though, perhaps the softer outlines of *The Laramie Project* allow for more careful audience introspection about these awful incidents.

Shticky Business

It was the season of shtick for the New York Shakespeare Festival as the company stumbled in the presentation of its signature works. Mel Shapiro returned to the festival after a long absence to direct *The Taming of the Shrew* at the Delacorte. With the gifted Allison Janney and Jay O. Sanders as Kate and Petruchio, Shapiro had a pair of strapping leads with almost no chemistry between them. The director's reliance on his trademark vaudevillian shtick—much of it having little to do with telling the story—turned the production into a postmodern jokebook that delivered few genuine laughs.

Mark Brokaw's production of *Tartuffe*, with a stellar cast of Dylan Baker, Charles Kimbrough, Dana Ivey, J. Smith-Cameron and Mary Testa, was a similarly facile production of classic Molière that relied on a broad playing of the text. Director Brokaw and his cast were largely unable to mine and exploit the darker elements of the comedy. Incidentally, our historian, Thomas T. Foose, reminds us that the last three major American productions of *Tartuffe*—one in San Francisco and two in New York including this one—have used the Richard Wilbur translation, as did the 1977 production starring John Wood. "Seldom has a single English translation so dominated a play," reports Foose. "The world premiere of the Wilbur translation was in January 1964 at Milwaukee's Fred Miller Theater. It was heard for the first time in New York City in the Lincoln Center Repertory staging January 14, 1965, with Michael O'Sullivan as Tartuffe."

Not even the direction of Andrei Serban could avoid getting stuck in shtick with his odd take on *Hamlet*, featuring Liev Schreiber as the Danish prince. One observer said it seemed like Serban made it "six weeks into a six-month workshop." Many of the ideas seemed half-baked—for instance, having Hamlet retch into a pile of rocks at centerstage—others appeared kitschy for the sake of kitsch. Why, for instance, was Claudius a knock-off of Mussolini? Is Hamlet a victim of fascism? What underpinned the imagery of multiple ghosts of the dead king? Chaos? Multiple points of view? Or was is it simply an attempt to be "magical"? Theater should evoke the mysteries of life and cling to us as we depart, but Serban's *Hamlet* was shed at the door.

The Atlantic Theater Company tipped its cap to founding inspiration David Mamet with an off-Broadway production of *American Buffalo*. It featured longtime

Mamet actor William H. Macy as the unctuous Teach opposite Philip Baker Hall as Don, the junk dealer. Mamet's signature work, *American Buffalo*, didn't fare well in the Atlantic production. Although the losers in *Buffalo* are meant to lose, the audience shouldn't know it from the first moment. In this production, there was no suspense, and we're left thinking the ending might as well have been the beginning. This undramatic approach undermines the power of Mamet's tale of futility and leaves us waiting for a sharper production. That asserted, however, it is worth noting that the show was well received by audiences and the run was extended.

The final production of note among off-Broadway revivals included an American classic directed by a European. Ivo van Hove's production of Tennessee Williams's *A Streetcar Named Desire* for New York Theater Workshop raised more than a few hackles when it opened. The Dutch director deconstructed the play's text and shoved the actors out of the comfort zone of naturalism. Dialogue was often spoken in a monotone or in a high-pitched shriek, which accented some of Williams's own expressionistic impulses. Although the approach was unsettling at first, audience members who allowed the experience to wash over them found a kind of renewal for the convention-bound text. Elizabeth Marvel as Blanche and Christopher Evan Welch as Mitch were particularly engaging as two pieces of damaged goods. Van Hove's imagery, which made innovative use of an old-fashioned bathtub filled with water—where Blanche takes long and frequent baths, to Stanley's consternation—was stunning and effective.

Broadway Revival

More than six decades after George S. Kaufman and Moss Hart dubbed Broadway theater "The Fabulous Invalid," the creaky creature continues to limp along. As attendance and box office income figures ascend to dizzying heights, though, it's awfully hard to view commercial theater as something tottering on its last legs.

From an all-time attendance peak of 11,605,278 in the 1998–99 season, according to *Variety*'s end of season reports, 1999–2000 declined slightly (about 2 percent) to 11,365,309. With a record-breaking Broadway box office total of $602,596,528, however, it was clear that higher overall ticket prices probably weren't keeping the audiences away. But these figures also came just as the financial markets were in the midst of a downward adjustment after years of what Federal Reserve chairman Alan Greenspan called "irrational exuberance." A huge question looms. Will those 11 million keep coming if the economy turns a bit stale? Or has Broadway simply found the key to keep the "invalid" zipping around in a fancy electric wheelchair?

Broadway revivals of plays and musicals represented less than half of all shows that opened in the 1999–2000 season. New dramatic and musical material accounted for 22 productions during this season; revivals and return engagements came to 17. But if we look closely at this year's offerings, it is interesting to note that revivals often succeeded artistically and generated more interest than new works. Others, of course, may not rise to these lofty heights but remain mass-appeal attractions (producers hope) aimed at a well-heeled audience.

The finest work on any Broadway stage this season was Michael Blakemore's production of *Kiss Me, Kate* at the Martin Beck Theater. Brian Stokes Mitchell and Marin Mazzie combined to make a romantic and comic duo that hadn't been seen in years. John Guare's work as "doctor" of Sam and Bella Spewack's book was virtually unnoticeable, yet gave the show a gentle lift. Busy Kathleen Marshall oversaw a rebirth of Broadway choreography with her staging of "Too Darn Hot." But the best-kept secret was Mazzie's superb comic acting skills, which should propel her to the next level of her career. It was a revival 50 years coming, but worth the wait. Hopefully, Cole Porter's score and the Spewacks' book will encourage some new talents to emulate their work.

Any other year, Susan Stroman's production of *The Music Man* would have been a shoo-in for numerous Tony Awards. That it was blanked is partly due to Stroman's own choreography for *Contact*—she beat the versatile Marshall for *Kate* and herself for *Music Man*. Craig Bierko's turn as Harold Hill seemed, at times, to channel Robert Preston's work in the film—which was not necessarily a bad thing. But Bierko's boyish charm never completely convinced that he was scoundrel enough to engineer this sort of con game. Stroman's *Music Man*, however, got the grins (and toe tapping) going early, and it never let go.

These two revivals gave a kind of glow to the Broadway musical season. Others, such as *Tango Argentino*, *Riverdance on Broadway* and *Jesus Christ Superstar*, were amorphous entities that never seemed to connect with their audiences on emotional or spiritual levels the way great theater does.

On the whole, play revivals also accounted for many of the artistic strengths of the past Broadway season. N. Richard Nash's *The Rainmaker* brought Woody Harrelson to Broadway for a respectable run. The cast of Jayne Atkinson, Jerry Hardin, John Bedford Lloyd, David Aaron Baker and Randle Mell—a fine ensemble—overmatched the Hollywood star a bit, and it seemed as though Harrelson needed a bit more stage seasoning.

Arthur Miller's *The Price* was directed by actor James Naughton with a fine cast that included Jeffrey DeMunn, Harris Yulin, Bob Dishy and Lizbeth Mackay. This taut, engaging production reminded audiences why Miller is a writer of Olympian magnitude: even his lesser plays are fine works. Nominated for a best play revival Tony Award, Miller became the first playwright of record to receive nominations in the same year for a new play as well as a revival. The secret? Longevity and productivity.

David Suchet introduced a charmingly new and improved Salieri in the revival of Peter Shaffer's *Amadeus* as stylishly directed by Peter Hall. Michael Sheen created a fizzy, but not unsympathetic Mozart, and David McCallum was sharp as Emperor Joseph II. Unfortunately, though, there seemed no good reason to do the play other than that some producer must have sat up in the middle of the night and said, "I know! I'll revive *Amadeus*!" There was little about the show that compelled attention—other than Suchet and Sheen's lively performances.

Daniel Sullivan's production of Eugene O'Neill's *A Moon for the Misbegotten* started at the Goodman Theater in Chicago. Starring Cherry Jones, Gabriel Byrne

A MOON FOR THE MISBEGOTTEN—Roy Dotrice, Cherry Jones and Gabriel Byrne under Daniel Sullivan's direction in the revival of Eugene O'Neill's play

and Roy Dotrice, the show offered flashes of brilliance punctuated by stretches of ennui. This listlessness is a key characteristic of many of O'Neill's dramatic creations, but the pairing of Jones and Byrne was too often without a driving force. Byrne, especially, seemed to just bounce along until his big confessional scene late in the play. Dotrice's Tony Award-winning performance nearly stole the show with his appropriately antic behavior as the acid-tongued farmer, Phil Hogan.

David Leveaux's production of *The Real Thing*, with Stephen Dillane and Jennifer Ehle as the lead pair of lovers, walked away with best revival and best acting Tonys for the leads. A delightfully funny and honest look at the negotiations we undergo in modern relationships, Tom Stoppard's play scrutinizes the emotional price we often pay for happiness with his usual insight and intelligence. Strangely, though, the director himself was shut out of the Tony Awards in favor of Michael Blakemore (*Copenhagen*). Perhaps sorting out the strands of a tightly wound love story seemed less challenging to Tony voters than Blakemore's staging of a play with nuclear physics among its topics.

Finally, a pair of play revivals near the season's end surprised many observers when they fell short of their perceived potential. Julie Taymor's production of Carlo Gozzi's *The Green Bird* was filled with inventive masks, costumes and other bits of theatrical magic. It was the sort of thing for which Taymor became famous with her production of *The Lion King*. By mining the elements of *commedia dell'arte*, the director offered a lively production of a classic tale. Complete with text updated by Eric Overmyer and music by Elliot Goldenthal, the piece simmered with invention. Oddly, though, beneath all of the cleverness and dramatic artifice there was an emotional coolness, a disappointing distance that was impossible to surmount. Foose, our historian, reminds us that "The two stagings of Julie Taymor's production of *The Green Bird* March 7, 1996 at the New Victory and April 18, 2000 at the Cort Theater account for most of the stage history of this play in New York City. I have no record of any other New York productions."

Similarly, the Roundabout Theater Company production of Chekhov's *Uncle Vanya* was eagerly awaited. Directed by *wunderkind* Michael Mayer, with a cast that included Roger Rees, Derek Jacobi, Brian Murray, Laura Linney, Anne Pitoniak and Rita Gam, the Broadway production promised to blend culture and commerce on the Brooks Atkinson stage. Unfortunately, though, Mayer never had control of his material or his cast. The very talented actors seemed to be playing several different versions of the play at once. An emphasis on a kind of slapstick comedy undermined the work of all concerned, but the most glaring stylistic blunder was the employment of several different types of accents. Was no one listening in rehearsal? Tony Walton's lovely scenery and Amy Ryan's plain-Jane portrayal of Sonya were the pleasures of the production.

The theater community bade farewell to many fine talents during the 1999–2000 season. Among them were Richard B. Shull, mentioned above, and the gifted director Mike Ockrent—husband to Tony Award-winning choreographer Susan Stroman—who lost his battle with leukemia.

When David Merrick and Alexander H. Cohen died a few days apart during the season, it marked the passing of two great showmen who helped to define Broadway theater in the 20th century. Although Merrick was the more successful producer, Cohen was unquestionably more a part of the Broadway community. Merrick was a consummate promoter well known for his outlandish publicity stunts. He once hired people who had the same names as important critics and then ran their "quotes" in newspaper advertisements. When director and choreographer Gower Champion died on the opening night of *42nd Street* in 1980, Merrick held the announcement until the curtain call. There is a classic photograph of the actors onstage reacting in horror as he has just given them (and the audience) the news.

In addition to his theater work, Cohen produced many Tony Awards broadcasts and television specials over the years with his wife, Hildy Parks, who survives him. Opinionated, funny and always ready to discuss any theatrical topic, he even headlined a one-man show about his life in show business, *Star Billing* (1998). Cohen and Merrick represent the time when a single producer could raise the money for a Broadway show. Those days are gone forever with deep-pocket corporate funding now ruling the theater district.

Each season, the theater of old gives way to the new. Boundaries expand and contract, borders are crossed and the liveliest art form continues to transcend (and occasionally transgress) everyday life. As we mourn the passing of Alex Cohen, David Merrick and their ilk, we also honor a new generation of artists and leaders who will take us into the theatrical future. At the end of each season, a new one stands ready, and to lovers of theater the time to come always looks bright.

A GRAPHIC GLANCE

1999–2000
Drawings
By Hirschfeld

Barry Humphries as Dame Edna Everage in *Dame Edna: The Royal Tour*

Members of the large cast of dancers in the imported *Riverdance on Broadway*

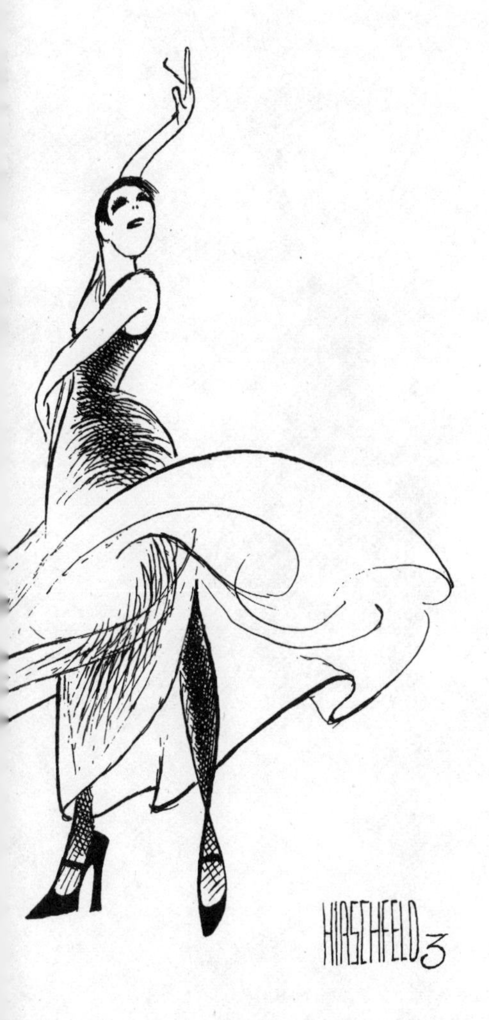

Boyd Gaines, Deborah Yates and Karen Ziemba in the Tony-winning (for best musical) dance play *Contact*

Twiggy (as Gertrude Lawrence) and Harry Groener
(as Noel Coward) in the revue *If Love Were All*

Blair Brown, Philip Bosco and Michael Cumpsty in the multi-award-winning *Copenhagen*

Elizabeth Wilson, Rosemary Murphy, Helena Carroll, Rosemary Harris (in glasses), Lauren Bacall, Patricia Conolly and Betty Henritze in Noel Coward's *Waiting in the Wings*

HIRSCHFELD 3

Olympia Dukakis in *Rose*

Brian Stokes Mitchell and Marin Mazzie in *Kiss Me, Kate*

Clockwise from The Green Bird *(at top)*: Bruce Turk, Reg E. Cathey, Edward Hibbert, Derek Smith, Kristine Nielsen, Ned Eisenberg, Didi Conn, Sebastian Roché, Andrew Weems and Katie MacNichol in *The Green Bird*

HIRSCHFELD 5

Liza Minnelli in *Minnelli on Minnelli*

Below, Paige Price and James Carpinello *(in foreground)* with members of the company in *Saturday Night Fever*

Dana Ivey, Wendell Pierce, J. Smith-Cameron, Dylan Baker, Mary Testa and Charles Kimbrough in *Tartuffe*

Parker Posey and Matthew Broderick in *Taller Than a Dwarf*

Below, Roy Dotrice, Gabriel Byrne and Cherry Jones in the revival of O'Neill's *A Moon for the Misbegotten*

THE PLAYWRIGHT—Fount and origin of the theater. The distinguished individual celebrated *above* in a Hirschfeld drawing is Wendy Wasserstein

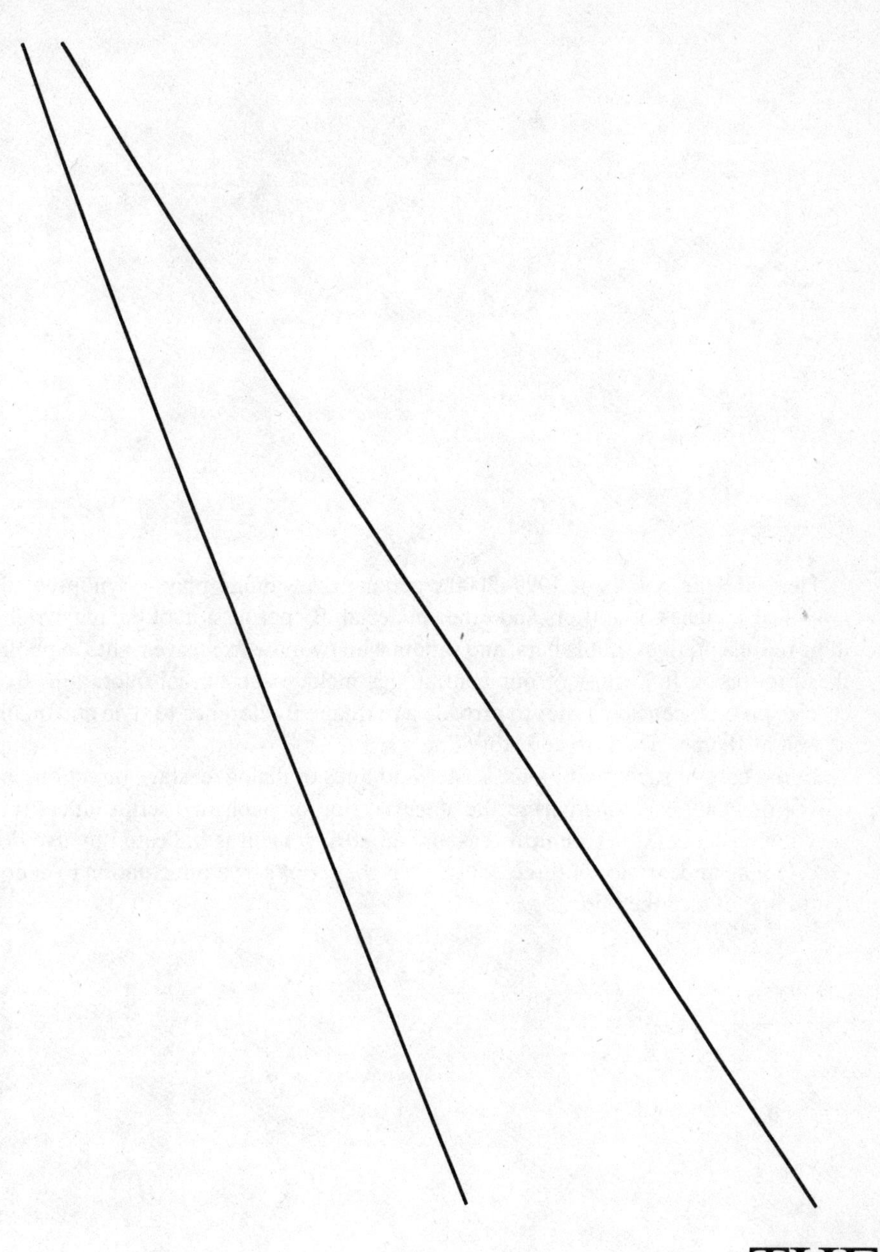

THE PRIZEWINNING PLAYS

Here are the details of 1999–2000's major prizewinning plays—synopses, biographical sketches of authors and other material. By permission of the playwrights, their representatives, publishers, and others who own the exclusive rights to publish these scripts in full, most of our continuities include substantial quotations from crucial/pivotal scenes in order to provide a permanent reference to style and quality as well as theme, structure and story line.

In the case of such quotations, scenes and lines of dialogue, stage directions and descriptions appear *exactly* as in the stage version or published script unless (in a very few instances, for technical reasons) an abridgement is indicated by five dots (. . . . .). The appearance of three dots (. . .) is the script's own punctuation to denote the timing of a spoken line.

Tony Award

CONTACT

A Dance Play With Music in Three Short Stories

BY SUSAN STROMAN AND JOHN WEIDMAN

WRITTEN BY JOHN WEIDMAN

DIRECTION AND CHOREOGRAPHY BY
SUSAN STROMAN

Cast and credits appear on pages 187, 189 and 220–221

JOHN WEIDMAN (co-author) was born in New York City in 1946, the son of the distinguished novelist and dramatist Jerome Weidman. He was educated in public schools when his family moved to Westport, Conn., then back in New York at Collegiate School, graduating in 1964. He went on to Harvard where he wrote for the unversity's humor magazine Lampoon *and graduated in 1968. He continued to contribute to the* National Lampoon *after it was founded in 1970 as an offshoot of the undergraduate publication.*

Weidman went on to Yale Law School and graduated from there in 1974. His father expected that John would pursue a career in either law or politics and never pushed his son toward or away from writing. But on January 11, 1976 there appeared at Broadway's Winter Garden the first work of any size that Weidman ever set out to write: Pacific Overtures, *the Stephen Sondheim musical for which Weidman wrote the Tony-nominated book. It ran for 193 performances, was named a Best Play of its season and won the Critics Award for best musical.*

Weidman turned to musical book writing again with a revision of Anything Goes *(in collaboration with Timothy Crouse) for a Broadway revival October 19, 1987 that ran for 804 performances and won the best-revival Tony. He worked with Sondheim again, providing the book for the short-lived but sharp-edged* Assassins *off Broadway at Playwrights Horizons. He adapted his father's memorable* Fiorello! *for Encores concert performances in February 1994 and contributed the Tony-nominated book for the David Shire-Richard Maltby Jr. musical* Big *which premiered on Broadway November 28, 1996. His second* Best Plays-*cited work is this season's* Contact, *described in the original credits as "a dance play by Susan Stroman and John Weidman, written by John Weidman, directed and choreographed by Susan Stroman." This high-spirited work, with a recorded score, opened in an off-Broadway production October 7 at Lincoln Center's Newhouse Theater, ran there for 101 performances, then was moved by Lincoln Center to its Broadway-sized Vivian Beaumont Theater for a continuing run. In its Broadway mode it won the best-musical Tony.*

Weidman has also contributed to the multi-award-winning Sesame Street *on TV and has recently been working on two other musicals, one for Sondheim and one for Lynn Ahrens and Stephen Flaherty. He is the president of The Dramatists Guild, the professional association of playwrights, book writers, composers and lyricists, and he lives in New York City with his wife Lila and their two children, Laura and Jonathan.*

SUSAN STROMAN (co-author, director, choreographer) was born in Wilmington, Del., where her father was a salesman. After her graduation from the University of Delaware, her first choreography credits listed in Best Plays *were for* Sayonara *at Millburn, N.J. in 1987 and two years later for* Rhythm Ranch *at the same place. Her first New York choreography credit of record coincided with her first authorship credit, as co-conceiver and choreographer of the Kander & Ebb musical* And the World Goes 'Round *off Broadway in 1991. She also co-conceived and choreographed the musical* Steel Pier *on Broadway in 1997, and she is fully billed in the* Contact *playbill as a co-author as well as the creator of the choreography, for which she has won the 1999–2000 Tony, Drama Desk, Outer Critics and Astaire Awards. She also won the Outer Critics Award for her direction—and her direction and choreography of the revival of* The Music Man *were Tony-nominated this year.*

Stroman's long list of other choreographic achievements on the New York stage have included Crazy for You *(1992, Tony),* 110 in the Shade *(1992 for New York City Opera),* Picnic *(1994, musical interludes and choreography),* Show Boat *(1994, Tony and* Big *(1996, Tony-nominated). Stroman also choreographed the Madison Square Garden productions* A Christmas Carol *and* The Wizard of Oz *which her late husband, Mike Ockrent, directed. Among her recent accolades was the Olivier Award for choreographing the Royal National Theater's* Oklahoma!

PART I: SWINGING

A Forest Glade, 1767

> *Spotlight on a painting: Fragonard's* The Swing *(1767), a sensuous image of a flirtatious young Girl in silks and petticoats swinging on a swing in a sylvan glade. In the shadows of a tree behind her, an impassive Servant*

CONTACT—Seán Martin Hingston as the Servant and Stephanie Michels as the Girl in *Swinging*

pushes the swing. Reclining on the lawn in front of her, a dandified Aristocrat, clearly enjoying himself, looks up her skirts. In the background, a statue of Cupid looks on, a finger to his lips.

The scene comes to life to the music of Stephane Grapelli's "My Heart Stood Still." The Girl jumps from the swing into the Aristocrat's arms. They dance, after which the Aristocrat delights her with gifts and a champagne picnic. Surreptitiously, the Girl pours out the bottle of champagne.

The Aristocrat moves in to kiss her, but she pushes him away and pouts at the empty bottle. He beams and dashes off to get a refill.

As soon as he's gone, the Girl removes her hat and drifts up beside the impassive Servant. She shoots him a flirtatious look, sits on the swing and clears a space for him.

The Servant joins the Girl on the moving swing where the two make energetic, acrobatic love. He jumps off the swing to give it another push.

She stands on the swing. He grabs the ropes and leaps forward, feet first, thrusting himself between her legs. She lowers herself onto him, and they twist the swing into a final, spinning, groaning climax.

The Girl slides off the swing, retrieves her hat and moves back toward the picnic basket. The Servant returns to his spot behind the swing, as the Aristocrat returns with another bottle of champagne. The Girl refuses him again when he tries to kiss her. She returns to the swing which the Servant at first resumes pushing then he *"suddenly claps his hands."* Servant and Aristocrat immediately reveal their true identities: the "Servant" (the Real Aristocrat, whose fantasy game this has all been) rewards the "Aristocrat" (the Real Servant) with a purse of coins and the Girl with a kiss. The Real Servant doffs and returns to the Real Aristocrat his silk frock coat.

The Girl applauds and, at the apex of her swing, kicks off one of her satin shoes.

REAL ARISTOCRAT *(catches it, inhales its aroma and reclines in front of her):* Well played!

Fragonard's image has been perfectly restored. The game is finished. Everyone is happy. Blackout.

PART II: DID YOU MOVE?

An Italian Restaurant, Queens, 1954

Outside the restaurant, "Santa Lucia" is the background music for a Husband waiting for his Wife. He's had a tough day. She hurries in and bumps into him.

WIFE: Oops! Sorry! I don't know what's the matter with me. Maybe it's the music. I start to hear those crazy mandolins. I just get so excited when you take me out like this—

HUSBAND *(cutting her off):* You know, I had a bad day—

WIFE: I know, I'm sorry, I—

HUSBAND: Slow down.

WIFE: Absolutely. It's just—

HUSBAND: Calm down.

WIFE: Calm. Right—

HUSBAND: You look good.

WIFE *(pleased):* Yeah?

HUSBAND: Let's eat.

Inside the restaurant, the decoration includes the Fragonard Cupid wearing leis of peppers and garlic. The Headwaiter is busily and graciously hovering about other couples at their tables, while a Busboy is using a knife as a mirror to admire himself.

The Husband and Wife enter from the buffet carrying their plates of dinner.

The Headwaiter turns, sees the Husband and instantly flashes an unctious smile.

HEADWAITER: Ah! Signor! Signora! Tonight my humble restaurant is truly blessed. To have you honor us with your presence once again, what can I say, but—welcome back to buffet night at the Cafe Vesuvio!

HUSBAND *(pointing at an empty bread basket on the table):* There's no fuckin' rolls.

HEADWAITER: I will attend to it immediately, Signor. *(Snapping his fingers at the Busboy.)* Tony. Rolls.

The Busboy nods and heads into the kitchen. The Husband sits, as the Headwaiter pulls out the Wife's chair. She smiles at him, pleased, the Husband pays no attention. The Headwaiter snaps open a gold tasseled wine list.

HEADWAITER: May I recommend tonight, a very excellent Soave—

HUSBAND: Gimme a double bourbon.

HEADWAITER: And for the signora?

HUSBAND: She's fine.

WIFE *(smiling pleasantly):* I'm fine.

HEADWAITER: Va bene! Buon appetito!

He moves away. The Husband lowers his head and digs into his food.

The Waterboy comes to the table with a pepper mill. When the Husband sees the Waterboy smiling at his wife, he drives him away with "What are you lookin' at?" The bourbon arrives. The Wife tries to make conversation about their new TV, which was delivered to the house that day, but the Husband has his nose in his dish. Only when the Busboy crosses with a tray of cannelloni for the buffet table in the next room does the Husband take notice. He tells the Wife, "I'm gettin' some cannelloni. Don't talk to the waiter. Don't smile at the busboy. Don't fuckin' move."

As the Husband exits, the wife closes her eyes, the lighting softens and Grieg's "Anitra's Dance" is heard. Soon the wife is dancing around the room—an elegant, classical ballet performed with conviction and abandon—which no one in the restaurant notices.

She spots a particularly handsome waiter taking an order, wraps her arms around him from behind and lets him drag her across the room as he heads for the bar. She releases him and leaps onto the shoulder of the Man sitting at the downstage table as he stands to go get more food. He drops his napkin, and when he bends to pick it up, she steps gracefully off of him, spins him toward the buffet room and continues to dance. She steals a forkful of pasta from the Man at the upstage table, then—as the music builds to a climax—spins dizzily across the room.

The fantasy ends as the Husband returns with his cannelloni and notices that there are still no rolls. When the Busboy comes out of the kitchen again, not with rolls but with a tray of manicotti, the Husband orders him, "Come outta there again, you better come out with a fuckin' roll, O.K?" He decides on another visit to the buffet, telling his wife, "Don't talk. Don't smile. Don't fuckin' move."

Tchaikovsky's "Waltz From *Eugene Onegin*," Opus 24, is heard, and the Wife is again up and dancing, throwing herself into the arms of the Headwaiter.

CONTACT—Karen Ziemba in her Tony-winning performance as the Wife in *Did You Move?*

He swings her up into an exhilarating lift, the beginning of a passionate, romantic dance which carries them around the restaurant . . . Winded, the Wife leans against the upstage table, as the Headwaiter does a series of masterful leaps downstage. Behind his back, the Wife ducks playfully under the table. The Headwaiter frowns—where did she go? She reaches out, grabs his leg and pulls him under the table after her.

When they emerge from under the table, their dalliance continues, as a Waiter removes the Husband's bourbon glass, an ancient busboy passes with a basket of rolls and the restaurant Photographer snaps their picture. The Headwaiter takes the Wife on a romantic ride in a sports car made of chairs, and their dance is punctuated with a kiss as, finally, *"He carries her back to her table, returns her to her seat and does a somersault back to his station as the music, and the fantasy, come to an end."*

The Husband returns with his plate of manicotti. Not until *"he puts his plate down with a bang"* does the Wife come out of her reverie. His rolls have not yet arrived, yet others seem to have an abundance, and the Busboy comes in carrying a basket full. The Busboy plants himself behind the Husband and waits till he turns. "Fuckin' rolls!", he announces, and then exits. The Husband follows him off.

The Wife rises as Bizet's "Farandole From L'Arlesienne Suite No. 2" is heard. She makes "*several rude Italian gestures*" at her departing husband's back and begins to dance. This time all the others in the restaurant join her.

The music cuts off, and the Husband comes back in, carrying two rolls.

HUSBAND: Forgot my fuckin' bread pla—

He stops in his tracks and stares at his wife, who stares back, terrified. He drops the rolls.

You moved.

He strides toward her. She backs away.

I told you not to fuckin' move . . . !

He swings at her. One of the waiters tries to grab him. He hurls him aside. The Wife screams and flees. He follows her around the restaurant. Waiters and patrons shout and call for help. One or two try to tackle him. He shoves them out of his way. The Wife picks up the rolls and throws them at him. He closes in on her, as the Busboy rushes on and grabs him. He throws the Busboy aside, draws a gun and aims it at the Wife. Shrieks, then silence.

The Wife manages to wrestle the gun away from her husband and toss it to a trio of waiters, who hide it from him with their trays in what resembles a game of three-card monte. When he menaces her once again, it turns out she has the gun, and she shoots him in the chest. He staggers offstage into the buffet room, mortally wounded: "*A final crash. A roll flies out onto the stage. A breathless pause.*"

The music sends the Wife into "*a defiant dance of liberation and celebration.*" Restaurant patrons and employees join in with enthusiasm culminating in a final tableau with the Wife in the center clutching a rose. After she is returned to her seat, a bit disheveled and breathless, the Husband walks in carrying his plate of rolls, sits down and starts to eat.

The Wife looks at him and does a double take. A long beat, then she reaches out and touches him with the rose. He stops eating, takes the flower—stares at it—and throws it away.

HUSBAND: Did you fuckin' move?

WIFE *(smiling nervously):* Me? No. *(Brushing at his lapel.)* Oops, you've got a couple of breadcrumbs on your—

He slaps her hand away, hard; she jumps up.

Stop it!

HUSBAND: What? Stop what?

A long beat.

WIFE: Nothing.

She sits. He starts to eat again.

HUSBAND: You wait twenty minutes for a fuckin' roll, maybe it could be fuckin' hot.

He keeps eating. She stares at him and closes her eyes, defeated. Music starts—the last phrases from Puccini's "O Mio Babbino Caro" from Gianni Schicchi. *Lights fade . . .*

PART III: CONTACT

Scene 1: New York City, 1999

Lights come up on an answering machine, on which a woman is trying to reach one Michael Wiley, while Dean Martin is heard singing "You're Nobody Till Somebody Loves You." Then the lights come up on an awards ceremony at which Michael Wiley is receiving an award, a statuette version of the Fragonard Cupid, for *"best direction of a major brand name television spot of sixty seconds or less."* Michael, in his tuxedo, is at the podium giving his acceptance speech for this, his fifth such award in a row. But there is as much irony as gratitude in his manner: "You know, I don't know about the rest of you, but the older I get, the more it feels to me like life is getting away from me somehow. Like for a long time it was, 'what's coming next?' and suddenly 'this is it!' So when you're given a moment like this one, a moment where you can actually pick something up, and hold it in your hand, and say this is what I've done with my life, this is what my life is all about—well, I think those moments are pretty special. *(Applause.)* Yeah! Because what could be more special than knowing that you'd focused all your energies on one thing and that you'd achieved it? What could be more special than this gold statue—" *(Pause. He looks at it.)* "Although it isn't really gold, is it? It's more of a gold plate, or a 'gold tone.' And I guess it's not really a statue either."

Michael suddenly remembers that he is supposed to thank people—his agent, his business manager, his psychiatrist, his art director—and finally his cat. Lights fade as he waves and makes his way unsteadily from the podium.

Scene 2

The atmosphere of Michael's apartment is bleak, with bare floors, a row of windows and a large multipurpose unit which doubles as seating and a coffee table. As Michael enters, the red light is flashing on his answering machine. He lights up a cigarette, takes out and lines up his several bottles of prescription pills, opens one of the windows, fixes himself a drink and turns on the machine. The first message is from a neighbor, Gina Minetti, who has turned in a complaint about Michael to the board of this co-op. He has failed to put in a rug as per the building's rules, and she had to do something about it. She lives in the apartment below him, and the noise caused by his bare floor prevents her from sleeping.

The next message is from an associate who congratulates Michael on his award and wants to talk to him about a new ad campaign. Michael drops his statuette into the waste basket and hears the next caller, his psychiatrist Dr. Kaufman, warn him that he should come have a talk before terminating therapy. Then his agent Marty wants to know why he didn't join them for a celebration after the ceremony. They're all going downtown to this swing dancing club called Vinnie's, where "It's like a pool hall during the day, then at night they push the tables back—" Dr. Kaufman calls him again, and then Marty calls again to say they're not going swing dancing after all, they're going to Clarke's.

Michael pours the contents of all the pill bottles into his hand. He is about to swallow them when the open window comes down with a crash, startling him into spilling the pills all over the floor. He races to the window, but now it is stuck shut. He throws the window cord over a light fixture and makes a noose at the other end, but, standing on the coffee table part of the unit, he can't quite reach it.

He piles two books on the unit—still not high enough. The phone rings. The answering machine answers. It's Miss Minetti again, complaining that the noise he has been making woke her up.

Michael stamps back to the coffee table, slams a third book down on the first two, and, as the message continues, climbs back up on the unit.

WOMAN'S VOICE *(on the machine):* O.K., Mr. Wiley. You obviously have not gotten a rug yet, so until you do, which had better be the first thing tomorrow morning, would you please, *please,* stop making noise?

Michael reaches up, grabs the noose, and—finally—slides it over his head.

Because if I don't get some sleep I'm going to kill myself!

MICHAEL: Good luck.

The answering machine clicks off. Michael takes a deep breath, closes his eyes, and steps off the unit. The rope breaks, and he hits the floor. He gags and struggles to his feet. As he does, we hear the metallic sound of someone banging on a pipe and the voice of the woman downstairs, as if from a distance.

VOICE FROM DOWNSTAIRS *(off):* Mr Wiley? . . . Mr. Wiley? . . . I know you're there, Mr. Wiley . . . Mr. Wiley . . .

Michael curses, hurls the noose onto the desk, grabs his coat and slams out the door. Blackout.

Scene 3

The sound of a break shot on a pool table, as lights come up on Michael, in limbo. He starts to walk, aimlessly wandering the streets of New York. The sound of pool balls being banged togther keeps time with his steps. Shadowy figures fall in line behind him, silently, one at a time.

He passes a sign: "Vinnie's." Suddenly he stops. Music starts: "Put a Lid on It" by The Squirrel Nut Zippers. A Man in a Silk Shirt throws open a door, and Michael finds himself in a smoke-filled Club, where couples are dancing energetically.

The room is bare, except for a nondescript, slightly shabby bar upstage and a couple of pool tables and a pinball machine pushed aside to create dance space. A Bartender stands behind the bar, emptying ashtrays and racking glasses. Michael watches the dancers in a kind of daze—then heads across the dance floor towards the bar. The couples swirl around him. He tries to avoid them, to stay out of their way. But he is awkward and ungainly, his rhythms out of sync with theirs.

In addition to the Man in the Silk Shirt, two other male dancers are particularly prominent. Together they form a group: Johnny, Jack and Joe. As Michael makes his way clumsily across the floor, they observe him with something more than casual interest.

Michael arrives at the bar to the sound of "Sweet Lorraine" played by Stephane Grappelli. Listlessly, he orders a beer and asks the Bartender about this place and what people are doing there. The Bartender shows him a writeup in *New York Magazine:* It's a pool hall by day and a swing dance palace by night. Michael inquires about the people who come there, "the regulars."

BARTENDER *(a shrug):* They don't talk about themselves much. They just dance.

Michael considers this, turns his attention back to the dancers. A long beat. One of the men lowers one of the women in a dip right in front of him.

How 'bout you?

MICHAEL: What?

BARTENDER: You gonna dance?

MICHAEL: Me? I don't dance.

BARTENDER: Just gonna hang. That's cool. *(Smiling.)* But you know, my friend, the night is young.

"Sweet Lorraine" ends. The dancers, who have finished in a cluster in front of the door, begin to drift apart, revealing a Girl, wearing a yellow dress, carrying a yellow handbag. She is stunning—beautiful and sexy, but in a distant, slightly unsettling way. Michael stares at her . . .

And God said . . . *(He puts on a pair of dark glasses.)* Let there be light.

MICHAEL: Who is she?

BARTENDER: Someone who likes to dance.

MICHAEL: You mean she's a regular?

BARTENDER: I mean she likes to dance. I'm not sure there's anything about her I'd call regular.

Now the music is "Runaround Sue" sung by Dion, as the Girl in the Yellow Dress makes her way to the bar, brushing Joe aside, sitting next to Michael but paying him no attention and adjusting her makeup while the Bartender pours her a glass of champagne. When she takes out a cigarette, the Bartender gives Michael a broad hint by handing him a book of matches, but Michael, staring at the Girl, doesn't get it. When he finally does, it's too late—she's lit her own cigarette.

CONTACT—Jason Antoon as the Bartender, Boyd Gaines as Michael (a Tony winner), Deborah Yates as the Girl in the Yellow Dress (Tony-nominated) and Seán Martin Hingston as Johnny in Part III of the best musical Tony-winning John Weidman-Susan Stroman dance show

The music changes to the Royal Crown Revue performing "Beyond the Sea." The Girl puts out her cigarette and starts to cross the room.

Michael follows, nervously. He is summoning up the courage to try to speak to her when Jack takes her hand and pulls her out onto the floor. The other dancers groan in mock sympathy.

Michael watches as Jack dances her smoothly around the floor. One time around, however, and one sexy lift, and she abandons him. He slaps the floor in frustration, as Johnny seizes his opportunity, and her. They dance. Then Joe moves in and takes her over. He partners with her briefly, then she deserts him too, moves out on the floor, and, in effect, dances with all the men at once.

Michael watches from the sidelines, mesmerized, but too timid to approach her. In subtle ways, she indicates that she's available to him—a

> *look, a smile—but that he has to come and get her. She is a challenge to which he has to rise.*

Michael mounts a bar stool to get a better view. The Bartender diverts his attention for a moment, and when he turns back the Girl is gone. He tries to find her, burying himself in the group of dancers. They open up to disclose Michael sitting in his office chair, and the scene changes.

Scene 4

Michael is sitting at the desk in his apartment listening to the messages on his answering machine. His agent is at Clarke's and has signed him up for a three-day photo shoot at Montego Bay for a shampoo named Yellow Bird, and Michael gets to pick the model. Dr. Kaufman offers words of sympathy and understanding for what he's sure Michael must be feeling: "the anguish and despair of loneliness . . . . . some shameful deficiency in us that dooms us to be alone forever, incapable of loving or being loved." And a salesman is offering him the opportunity of a lifetime, urging him not to delay.

Michael takes a book of matches from his pocket to light a cigarette and realizes that they are the ones he got from the Bartender. He turns off the machine and hurries out.

Scene 5

When Michael arrives at the Club, the music is "See What I Mean" played by Al Cooper. Couples are dancing or standing around, but the Girl in the Yellow Dress is not present. The Bartender is surprised to see Michael. He'd labeled him as "a guy who'd given up." He offers Michael words of sympathy for his apparently lonely state, in terms indentical to Dr. Kaufman's message on the answering machine. "Simply Irresistible" sung by Robert Palmer begins.

> *Michael moves downstage and stares up at the door. It bangs open, and the Girl in the Yellow Dress enters and strides downstage toward him. Just as she's about to reach him, Johnny leaps in front of her and grabs her. The song erupts, and everyone but Michael starts to dance.*
>
> *Michael stares, following the Girl around the floor, as if he can't help himself. Johnny grins and, as he dances with her, pushes him away.*

The Bartender keeps urging Michael to talk to the Girl, but each time he tries he is tongue-tied. Finally the Bartender picks up a couple of pool balls and *"clicks them together."* "Balls . . . !" he says. But even when the Girl comes to sit beside Michael at the bar, he can't make a move. Finally, she gives up and joins Jack out on the floor. The Bartender gives Michael a shove, and he lands in front of the Girl. He starts to dance, "*clumsily and awkwardly,*" but suddenly the music ends. The three men give Michael mock applause, and Jack *"drags his hand across the Girl's bare shoulder,"* sending Michael a humiliating message.

Now the music is "Do You Wanna Dance?" sung by the Beach Boys, as the Girl comes over to the bar to sit beside Michael. The male dancers form a line and one by one try to entice her with a special turn. She turns them all down until the last in line, Jack, offers her his arm. *"She stares at him, then stares at Michael. He stares back, then looks away."*

The Girl steps out onto the floor, looks Jack in the eye, but rejects him. She goes to the bar to get her handbag and is about to exit when Michael slaps the bar. The music stops, then changes to "Topsy" performed by the Royal Crown Revue, as Michael heads out onto the floor, fortified by tossing off a shot glass of whisky provided by the Bartender. The men make fun of Michael's attempt to dance, but they stop when the Girl joins him.

> *Finally, Michael and the Girl are dancing. A beat, then the others join them. Michael, feeling cocky, swings the girl around like she was Ginger Rogers and he was Fred Astaire. They get hopelessly tangled up. Jack, Johnny and Joe sneer, as Michael tries to untangle them. He fails. He tries again and fails. Then, finally, triumphantly, he succeeds. He and the Girl beam, and dance for joy. Their eyes meet, the beginning of a real connection.*
>
> *The other dancers divide into two groups and form lines behind them. They grab them, dancing with them—then start to pull them apart. Michael, completely focused on the Girl, looks surprised, then horrified. He struggles, lunging for the Girl, as they are separated, violently. The Girl is pulled offstage. Michael is pulled back towards the door, then hurled to the floor by Jack. Michael howls and slams the floor, cutting off the music. Silence, as he finds himself . . .*

Scene 6

Back in his apartment, Michael sits at his desk—*"mortified and in despair."* The answering machine seems to take on a life of its own, playing the music of "You're Nobody Till Somebody Loves You," moving toward him when he's not looking at it, flashing a yellow light instead of a red one. Michael comes to a decision, turns off the machine and exits.

Scene 7

At the Club the music is "Sing Sing Sing" played by Benny Goodman, and *"the mood has intensified to suit the music. Everyone is dancing, and the dancing is hot, tense and very sexy."* Michael comes in and frantically looks around for the Girl. She comes in, and Johnny grabs her and takes her out onto the floor. For a time, her presence is obscured by the movements of the dancers. Michael finally sees her but can't reach her, and again she disappears from his view amid the tumult of the dancing. In his efforts to find her, he accidentally bumps into Jack. Jack takes it as a deliberate challenge, and Joe and Johnny help him to grab Michael and isolate him on top of the pinball machine.

From this perch Michael can see the Girl on top of the bar, transported by the female dancers downstage to one of the pool tables, where she starts to dance a solo which grows hotter and sexier, attracting the attention of all the male dancers. They all try to reach her, and it is Jack who succeeds in lifting her down. But Michael steps between them, *"grabs Jack and hurls him upstage . . . . . slugs him and slams his head down on the bar. Jack collapses behind the bar."* The other couples exit, *"slowly and sensuously,"* leaving Michael and the Girl alone to dance.

> *And with Michael leading, they begin to dance—a dance which builds slowly and passionately, becoming more and more intense. This is what Michael wanted, although he couldn't get it. This is what Michael needed, although he didn't know it. All his desperate neediness and longing escape from him in a final, wracking sob, as the dance turns into an embrace . . .*
>
> *And suddenly the dancers are back, filling the room, as the Club is transformed into Michael's apartment. Johnny and Joe lift Michael out of the Girl's arms and put him on the coffee table, where Jack slips the noose around his neck. The music hits its climax and ends abruptly, as everybody disappears except the Girl in the Yellow Dress. She stares at Michael, hanging, and moves slowly and sadly past him, upstage, and out the door.*

Scene 8

> *Michael hangs, lifeless and limp. Lights begin to fade. The stage is slowly blacking out—when suddenly he twitches, reaches up, grabs the noose and with a final, convulsive effort tears it down and crashes to the floor.*

The phone rings. The machine answers. It's Miss Minetti, now truly furious about the noise. Michael struggles to answer the phone but doesn't quite make it before she hangs up. Suddenly she's knocking at his door. Michael realizes the room is a mess and rushes to tidy it up before he lets her in. Finally he opens the door and is astonished to see that she is *"the Girl from the Club, looking pretty but terminally frazzled in a rumpled yellow bathrobe."* Michael has ridden the elevator with her and jostled her at the mail boxes (she tells him), but he has never actually met her. She has brought him a page torn from the Yellow Pages, listing a company which delivers rugs 24 hours a day.

Michael interrupts her; he's not going to put down a rug in this apartment. "What I *am* going to do is put in carpeting. Wall-to-wall—with pile so deep I'll have to have it mowed instead of vacuumed. With plush so thick the Jets could play the Giants in my living room, and you wouldn't hear so much as a thud." But he insists on something in return: she has to dance with him.

MISS MINETTI: Mr Wiley, I don't even know you.

MICHAEL: Hey, I've been on this earth for forty-three years, and I just realized I don't know *anybody. (He holds out his arm.)* Come on. Come on.

MISS MINETTI: I'm sorry, no.

MICHAEL: No? *(A resigned sigh.)* No . . . ?

He sits heavily in the desk chair and starts to roll it noisily across the floor, stamping his feet. A beat, then Miss Minetti follows.

MISS MINETTI: Mr. Wiley—

MICHAEL: Miss Minetti—

MISS MINETTI: Mr. Wiley—

MICHAEL: Miss Minetti—

MISS MINETTI *(losing it):* Mr. Wiley, please! I've got to go to work! It's late!

MICHAEL *(stops rolling, sincere):* I know it is. And I can't waste any more time.

He stands, grabs the remote control and aims it at the stereo. Music starts: "Sweet Lorraine."

One dance. Please.

MISS MINETTI *(a long beat):* What about the carpet?

MICHAEL: First thing tomorrow morning. Promise!

He crosses his heart. Another beat, then she gives up.

MISS MINETTI: O.K.

MICHAEL: O.K.

He holds out his arm again. Gingerly, keeping her distance, she steps into his arms, and they begin to dance . . . As he spins her gently around, she takes in the disorder in the room.

MISS MINETTI *(frowning):* What went on in here tonight?

MICHAEL: Nothing. I was just helping somebody move out . . .

She looks at him; he smiles and spins her happily around the room—as lights fade to black.

ooo
ooo
ooo
ooo
ooo
ooo

JAMES JOYCE'S THE DEAD

A Full-Length Musical in One Act

BOOK BY RICHARD NELSON

LYRICS BY RICHARD NELSON AND SHAUN DAVEY

MUSIC BY SHAUN DAVEY

BASED ON THE STORY BY JAMES JOYCE

Cast and credits appear on pages 193–194 and 223–224

RICHARD NELSON (book and lyrics) was born in Chicago, where his father was a business man and his mother a dancer and housewife, on October 7, 1950. He graduated from Hamilton College in 1972 and has pursued a long and fruitful career in New York and regional theater. He has served as literary manager of the Brooklyn Academy of Music Theater Company (1979–81), as associate director of Chicago's Goodman Theater (1980–83) and as dramaturge of Minneapolis's Tyrone Guthrie Theater (1981–82). Meanwhile, he has been writing plays. His first New York production was Conjuring an Event *at American Place March 10, 1978, two years after its first production in cross-country theater. According to the* Best Plays *record, there have followed an adaptation of Dario Fo's* Accidental Death of an Anarchist *(1984) and Beaumarchais's* The Marriage of Figaro *(1985), both on Broadway;* The Vienna Notes *(1985) at Second Stage;* Principia Scriptoriae *(1986) at Manhattan Theater Club; the one-acter* The Return of Pinocchio *(1986) off Broadway; the book of the Broadway musical* Chess *(1988);* Some Americans Abroad *(1990) off Broadway and* Two Shakespearean Actors *on (1992, Tony-nominated for best play), both at Lincoln Center theaters;* Misha's Party *(1993), co-authored with Alexander Gelman, in a Read-*

ing Room Reading; Life Sentences *(1993) at Second Stage;* New England *(1995) a Best Play of its season, commissioned and produced in London by the Royal Shakespeare Company before coming to New York at MTC; an adaptation of Strindberg's* The Father *(1996) at the Roundabout; and* Goodnight Children Everywhere *(1999) at the Roundabout, directed by Nelson himself and the winner of a 2000 Olivier Award in its Royal Shakespeare Company production in London.*

Nelson's second musical to reach Broadway and second work to receive a Best Plays *citation is this season's* James Joyce's The Dead, *adapted like John Huston's movie from the Joyce story, with Nelson sharing the lyric authorship with composer Shaun Davey and the director's credit with Jack Hofsiss, opening off Broadway at Playwrights Horizons October 28. After 38 performances there, it moved up to the Belasco Theater on Broadway January 11 for an additional 112 performances, with Nelson the sole director of this version. In its off-Broadway incarnation, it won the Lucille Lortel Award for the best musical of the season. The New York Drama Critics voted it best musical, and as a Broadway show it was Tony-nominated.*

Nelson's long list of other stage works produced in regional theater or abroad includes Columbus and the Discovery of Japan, Jungle Coup, Bal, Rip Van Winkle or The Works, An American Comedy, Roots in Water, Between East and West *and* The General From America *and translations of* Three Sisters, Il Campiello *and* Jungle of Cities. *He is also the author of the screen play for* Ethan Frome *and has written extensively for radio and TV, both in the U.S. and for the B.B.C.*

Nelson has received Thomas J. Watson, NEA Creative Writing, Guggenheim and NEA Playwriting Fellowships and has been awarded grants from the Office of Advanced Drama Research, the Rockefeller Foundation and the Lila Wallace Fund. He lives in Rhinebeck, N.Y., and he and his wife Cynthia have two children, Zoe and Jocelyn.

SHAUN DAVEY (music and lyrics) was born in Belfast in Northern Ireland, where his father was a bank manager. He was educated at Campbell College in Belfast, Trinity College in Dublin and The Courtauld Institute in London. He has been a professional composer since 1977, and his work has been presented at least twice before in New York as a part of visiting English productions: the music for the Royal Shakespeare Company's The Winter's Tale *in 1994 and for Out of Joint's* The Steward of Christendom *in 1997, both at the Brooklyn Academy of Music. His credits on his home stages have included* Catchpenny Twist, Fanny Hawke, Observe the Sons of Ulster Marching Towards the Somme, Well of the Saints *and* The Crucible *at the Abbey Theater;* The Steward of Christendom *at the Royal Court;* Fair Maid of the West, Mary and Lizzie, Troilus and Cressida, A Winter's Tale, King Lear, The Tempest, Romeo and Juliet, Columbus and the Discovery of Japan *(written by his present collaborator Richard Nelson), and* The Lion, the Witch and the Wardrobe *at Royal Shakespeare; and* Peer Gynt *at the Gate Theater.*

Davey's musical contributions to the large and small screen media have often been cited: Ivor Novello Award for The Hanging Gale, *Ivor Novello nomination for* Twelfth Night, *BAFTA nominations for* The Hanging Gale *and* Ballykissangel,

Golden Reel Award nomination for Waking Ned Devine*; Tric Award for* Ballykissangel. *The Lortel and Critics Awards to* James Joyce's The Dead *as the best musical of the season is his first formal accolade on this side of the Atlantic. Davey is married, with five children, and lives in Dublin.*

Time: Near the turn of the century

Place: The Misses Morkans' Annual Christmas Party, Dublin

Scene l: The drawing room of the Misses Morkans' Flat

SYNOPSIS: Along with the chairs and tables in the Morkans' drawing room is a piano with an assortment of family pictures. In the adjoining hallway downstage, Gabriel Conroy, the Morkan sisters' nephew, in his 40s, speaking to the audience as a narrator, explains that friends—"and the occasional musical celebrity who happens to be visiting Dublin"—are here this evening for annual Christmas festivities, which will include entertainment by some of the Morkans' music students. As family members (Aunt Julia, Aunt Kate, Mary Jane and the maid Lily) enter with friends (Mr. Browne, Mrs. Malins and Miss Ivors), the celebrity (Bartell D'Arcy, an opera singer) and young music students (Michael, Rita and two musicians), Gabriel elucidates further.

GABRIEL: For thirty years there was a party.

They all begin to mingle and socialize. Music continues.

Ever since leaving the house in Stony Batter, after the death of their brother Pat, the Aunts took with them Pat's daughter, Mary Jane . . .

Mary Jane comes around the group, smiling, greeting.

. . . to live here in this dark gaunt house on Usher's Island. The upper part they rent from Mr. Fulham—the cornfactor on the ground floor. He *(Three stage thumps.)* was never invited. Mary Jane is now the main prop of the household, she has the organ in Haddington Road. She has been through the Academy and gives the pupils' concert each year in the upper room of the ancient concert rooms. Many of her pupils belong to the better class families—those on the Kingstown And Dalkey line! But old as they are, the aunts still do their share.

We see Kate and Julia handing out drinks, greetings, etc.

Aunt Julia, until quite recently, had been lead soprano at the Church of the Immaculate Conception or—Adam and Eve's, as it's generally known. Her retirement was—how should one put it?—not without tears. And Aunt Kate will continue to give lessons here in this room until her dying day.

Music stops.

An angel passed.

Music starts again.

The world, I've come to think, is like the surface of a frozen lake. We walk along, we slip, we try to keep our balance and not to fall. One day there's a crack, and so we learn that underneath us—is an unimaginable depth. According to the newspapers that night, snow would be general all over Ireland. For thirty years the Misses Morkan gave their party. And for thirty years—everyone sang and everyone danced.

Music and guests' chatter get louder. Gabriel's wife Gretta joins him in the hallway—they are nearly the last to arrive. Aunts Kate and Julia enter the hallway and escort Gretta into the drawing room, leaving Gabriel behind to fuss over the speech he is going to give. Lily enters, reluctantly accepts the coin Gabriel offers her as a Christmas present, then exits. Molly Ivors enters—she's not staying for dinner so will miss his speech, but she has something else on her mind.

IVORS: I have a crow to pluck with you, Mr. Conroy.
GABRIEL: With me?
IVORS: Yes. Who is G.C.?
GABRIEL: What do you mean?
IVORS: ..... I have found out you are the G.C. writing for the Daily Express. Now, aren't you ashamed of yourself? Writing for a rag like that.
GABRIEL: I write book reviews—
IVORS: I didn't think, Gabriel Conroy, that you were a West Briton.
GABRIEL: I'm not a West Briton!

This quiets the drawing room. From the drawing room we hear:

BROWNE: I'm trying to get Mr. Bartell D'Arcy to to sing later on. All Dublin is raving about him.
KATE: Shouldn't we begin the singing? Gabriel and Gretta have arrived, so we're mostly here.
MALINS: My son isn't here.
MARY JANE: He'll be here, Mrs. Malins.
MALINS: And he'll be screwed.

Ivors suggests the Conroys might like to join her on an excursion to the Aran Islands this summer. But Gabriel already has plans for a bicycling trip to the continent. Ivor suggests he might do better to explore his own country. Gabriel blurts out, "To tell you the truth, I'm sick of my own country!!!", loudly enough to be heard in the other room, briefly interrupting Mary Jane's announcement of a song, "Killarney's Lakes," written by the poet Michael William Balfe. Gabriel and Ivors move into the drawing room as Ivors exclaims, "West Briton!!" Rita joins Mary Jane and Kate for the song.

MARY JANE, KATE, RITA *(sing):*
By Killarney's lakes and fells,
Em'rald Isles and winding bays,
Mountain paths, and woodland dells,

Mem'ry ever fondly strays,
Bounteous nature loves all lands . . . . .

Gabriel joins Mrs. Malins in the hallway. Gretta follows. In the drawing room, the song ends to applause, and the three women take their bow.

Gabriel tells Gretta of Ivors's invitation.

GABRIEL: Why do I let someone like Molly Ivors bother me so?

GRETTA: I don't know, Gabriel.

GABRIEL: She is so—what's the word? Confident. It's her confidence that's . . . How can she be so damn sure she's right?

GRETTA: She's young.

GABRIEL: When I was young I respected my elders. I didn't make fun of them.

GRETTA: And she's just teasing you. So, tease her back, Gabriel.

Gabriel goes back into drawing room.

(To Mrs. Malins): He'll be here any minute, Mrs. Malins. (*Goes into drawing room.)*

MARY JANE: Now Michael here. Is in truth from the Killarncy Lakes! And a fine student as well. Don't go blushing now, Michael. *(To Gretta.)* Is Gabriel all right? We heard voices.

GRETTA: It wasn't a thing, Mary Jane, not a thing.

MARY JANE: We're getting hungry, and when we're hungry we're quarrelsome.

D'ARCY: And when we're thirsty we are also quarrelsome.

GRETTA: And when we have quenched that thirst—we are sometimes also quarrelsome too.

MARY JANE: This is true. *(To Michael.)* So tell us what you're going to sing?

MICHAEL: This is a . . .

MARY JANE: No, rather—shall it be a surprise? But let it be said that it was Michael's own idea. And he thought it might be especially poignant after what's just been sung.

MICHAEL *(to the Musicians):* Now I once knew a girl like this. *(Sings "Kate Kearney"):*

Oh did you ever hear of Kate
Wait till I tell you, wait till I tell you
She'll get you in a terrible state
Should you ever visit the banks of Killarney.
Gentlemen, beware the smile
For many's the wile lies hid in the smile
Of lovely Kate, just you wait
Till you visit the banks of Killarney.

Browne remarks, "That sounds like Molly Ivors," as the song continues. Lily enters and whispers something to Kate and Julia. Julia whispers to Gabriel. Gabriel exits, and we can hear him shshing Freddy Malins, who has arrived and is joining in the song offstage.

JAMES JOYCE'S THE DEAD—Stephen Spinella as Freddy, Alice Ripley as Ivors and Emily Skinner as Mary Jane in a scene from the Richard Nelson-Shaun Davey musical

COMPANY *(sing):*

She lives on the banks of Killarney
From the glance of her eye
Shun the dangers and fly, for
Fatal's the glance of Kate Kearney . . . . .

FREDDY *(sings offstage):*

That eye so modestly beaming
You'd never think of the mischief
She's dreaming
Wait till I tell you . . .

MALINS: He's screwed. I knew he'd be screwed.

FREDDY *(sings):*

Wait till I tell you, wait till I . . .

Freddy follows shortly after Gabriel, who goes back into the drawing room.

MALINS: Don't let him in if he's screwed!

KATE *(turning to Gabriel):* He's not bad, is he?

GABRIEL: Oh, no. Hardly noticeable.

Freddy enters the drawing room, sees that his mother is already here and apologizes for his own late arrival. Browne suggests a glass of lemonade might "buck him up," and Kate observes that Freddy's mother has recently made him take the pledge. And Mrs. Malins goes out of her way to praise her daughter and son-in-law in Scotland, whom she is soon to visit.

Gretta calls for another song by Michael.

MARY JANE: The Parnell song.

JULIA: Oh not that song!

KATE *(at the same time):* Please, Mary Jane.

MARY JANE: It's a lovely song.

GABRIEL: Aren't we tired of simplistic patriotism? I hate this song. It's mindless.

IVORS: I love it.

GABRIEL: Do you now? What a surprise!

MICHAEL *(sings "Parnell's Plight"):*

Who fears to speak of Parnell's plight?

MICHAEL & IVORS *(sing):*

Who blushes at the name?
When cowards mock our patriot's fight
Who hangs his head in shame?
Who hangs his head in shame?

IVORS *(sings):*

He's all a knave and half a slave
Who slights his country thus.
But a true man
Like you man
Will fill your glass with us!
Will fill your glass with us!

FREDDY: She pinched your song!

IVORS *(sings):*

Some on the shores of distant lands
Their weary hearts have laid
And by the strangers' heedless hands
Their lonely graves were made

IVORS & MICHAEL *(sing):*

Their lonely graves were made.

IVORS *(sings):*

But though their clay be far away

Beyond the Atlantic foam
To you men, say men—

Gabriel suddenly jumps in, topping Michael.

GABRIEL *(sings):*

For Christ sake don't come home!

Laughter at this interruption and deflating of this song. These "other" lyrics have gone around the Dublin pubs, etc.

GRETTA: Gabriel.

BROWNE & GABRIEL *(sing):*

For Christ sake don't come home!

MEN *(sing):*

We owe our duty to Ireland and
We hold her honor in our hand.

They hold up their drinks, the "honor" they hold in their hand. Laughter.

Through low and high land
Come all free men make a stand

IVORS *(sings):*

They rose in dark and evil days
To right their native soil

GABRIEL *(sings):*

They rose in dark and evil ways
And avoided work and toil

GABRIEL & MEN *(sing):*

And avoided work and toil

More laughter, as the song continues with its contrast between the lyrics and the mocking parody. As the song comes to an end, Ivors calls out, "Six hand jig!" and the company chooses partners and goes into a changing-partners-down-a-line dance. Freddy *"goes across the room to his mother, gets on his knees and finally she relents and takes his hand and the two begin to dance together."* During the dance Gretta seems to be reacting particularly to Michael. And the sportive mood of the party has made Ivors decide to stay for dinner.

It's Gabriel and Gretta's turn to do a number, the same one as last Christmas, "Adieu to Ballyshannon."

GABRIEL *(sings):*

Adieu to Ballyshannon where I was bred and born
Go where I may, I'll think of you, as sure as
Night and morn
I'll leave my warm heart with you although
My back I'm forced to turn—
And so adieu to Ballyshannon.
And the winding banks of Erne .....

GABRIEL & GRETTA *(sing):*

Adieu to evening dances, where merry neighbors meet
And the fiddle says to boys and girls,
"Get up and shake your feet."
The mournful song of exile now
Is all that's left for me to learn
And so adieu my dear companions
And the winding banks of Erne.

The Conroys receive compliments on their performance. Freddy, trying to be ingratiating, calls for a song from Julia, proclaims that he loves her voice, it gets better every year, and the choir is lucky to have her as a member. But he has put his foot in it, because, as Mary Jane quickly interposes, Julia has "retired" from the choir. The Aunts are forthright in their comments.

KATE: I don't think it is at all honorable to turn out women out of choirs who have slaved there all their lives and put those little whipper-snappers in their place. It's not right. Is what I think. It's not just.

FREDDY: Well then—we are the more fortunate to have Julia Morkan sing for us.

JULIA: I don't have much of a voice any more. You all know that. But I'll sing if you insist.

FREDDY: I insist!

JULIA: I did have a nice voice when I was young. *(Sings "When Lovely Lady.")*

When lovely lady stoops to folly
And finds too late that men betray
What charms can soothe her melancholy,
What art can wash her grief away?

The only art her guilt to cover
To hide her shame from every eye,
To give repentance to her lover,
And wring his bosom is—to die.

As sung in Julia's weakened voice, the lyric is particularly touching. Julia ends by telling the group, "As I said, I used to have a nice voice." Freddy tells her, "That was so—lovely Julia," and then agrees to do the next number whose title is the name of a pub, "The Three Jolly Pigeons."

FREDDY *(sings):*

Let school masters puzzle
Their brains with grammar
And nonsense and learning
I stoutly maintain

Good liquor gives genius
A better discerning.
Folderol-dee, folderol-dae . . . . .

Freddy goes on in this vein, joined by Browne and others, celebrating the joys of drinking, to the amusement of the crowd, and in the end to their slight sense of guilt at having applauded what they know is Freddy's weakness.

Gretta surprises Gabriel by coming forward and offering to do a song without him. She hopes that Michael will know it and join her. But Michael is sent off by Mary Jane to see how dinner is coming. Gabriel addresses the audience.

GABRIEL: And then she sang. A song I'd never heard. In a voice I'd never known.

GRETTA *(sings "Goldenhair):*

Lean out of the window Goldenhair
I heard you singing a merry air

My book was closed I read no more
Watching the fire dancing on the floor.

I left my book
I left my room
I heard you singing
Through the gloom
Singing and singing. A merry air
Lean out of the window Goldenhair

Arise my beautiful one
Arise arise . . . . .

The night dew lies
Upon my lips and eyes.

GABRIEL: A song I'd never heard her sing. In a voice I'd never known. When she'd finished I noticed her face flush a bright red and her hands tremble. And she sighed—like a girl. That's what I remember thinking—like a girl. And I was so pleased to be her boy . . . . . The Misses Morkan's party continued that year. Other songs were sung, others danced as we waited for dinner. But all I remember—is my wife. My children's mother appearing to me again as the girl of our youth. Gretta—as if pulled back through the dull existence that is time, and back toward the lost moments that are ecstasy. How I desired her. My soul's tender fire was heartier than I'd feared. Children, writing, household cares had not smothered the coals . . . . . Nor shall I forget that love in her eyes. And the need. It simply did not occur to me at the time, that it wasn't for me.

As the tables are readied for Christmas dinner, Gabriel remembers that they were loaded with goose, ham and multiple side dishes, with an abundance of sherry, port, stout and ale arrayed on the closed piano. As Gabriel takes his place at the table to carve, he comments, "The ever rising small talk and conviviality returned my mind back to this world."

Scene 2: The drawing room arranged for dinner

The family and guests sit around the table, attended by Lily and two students, Michael and Rita. They are discussing a performance at the Theater Royal, but Freddy brings up a pantomime at the Gaiety, where "a Negro chieftain" with a fine tenor voice leads every chorus. The diners chat about the great singers they have heard and admired in days of yore. D'Arcy observes that today's singers, Caruso for example, are the equal of any in the past. Kate remembers an English tenor named Parkinson who had the purest voice she's ever heard.

Julia rises to begin clearing the table, but Mary Jane stops her, reminding her that Lily and her helpers will attend to that. Gabriel asks for the diners' attention to something he has prepared for this occasion, as he has done on Christmases past, but he is interrupted when Julia drops her glass and is helped from the room to get a breath of air by Mary Jane and Kate. Browne pours a drink for himself and one for Freddy—"For the toast," he explains to Mrs. Malins, who nods her consent. Mrs. Malins talks about her son's scheduled visit to a monastery, where the monks sleep in their coffins and take people in for visits without charge.

The three women return to the table, Julia recovered from her spell. Gabriel rises to praise the annual hospitality of the good ladies of this house, in the unique tradition of Irish hospitality, which some consider a failing—"a princely failing," he insists, which he hopes will endure far into the future. As for the present, "We are living in a skeptical age . . . . . a less beautiful time," he says, and Browne applauds, "Here! Here!"

> *"Three Graces" instrumental begins to play, and Gabriel steps back from the table. Though everyone else continues to watch "Gabriel" give his speech, Gabriel wanders around the table, watching the others watching and listening.*

GABRIEL *(to the audience):* As I spoke that evening, I found my mind constantly wandering, drifting—first it was upon people who might be passing in the snow on the quay just outside. I imagined them gazing up at our lighted, beckoning window, then drifted back upon all of us together, around this table. I found myself watching each face, each a map of life in flesh. Which chart our days, our pains and joys, our losses, our loves. Each face listening to the words I had so cautiously collected and now—released.

BROWNE: Hear! Hear!

GABRIEL *(still to audience):* Second-hand, third-hand thoughts these were. Words as overused by time as to have had their meanings beaten out of them, much as an old sofa loses its stuffing. But no one seemed to mind. Where are the words which can express one's heart; I have not heard them. So they listened, as family and friends must do, with good humor and bright attention: those twin threads that keep us together, keep us from splitting apart, keep us out of the dark that lies everywhere else. They watched. They listened. They smiled, and if a mind drifted—she tried to hide this from the rest of us.

The instrumental ceases, and Gabriel returns to the head of the table to end his speech, declining to dwell on the past, he says, which holds so many bad memories. "Here we are gathered together for a brief moment from the bustle and rush of our everyday routine. We are met here as friends, in the spirit of good fellowship, as colleagues, as family, and as the guests of—what shall we call them?—the Three Graces of the Dublin musical world!!"

The "Three Graces" music starts again.

GABRIEL *(sings):*

I shall make a toast
A blessing on this house.
Timeless beauties each
And everyone God's gift to us . . . . .

First there is Julia
Her face a candle
Lighting our way into the dark.

Next is Aunt Kate.
With a heart as large
As a full moon over Dublin.

And Mary Jane
With heaven's smile
Sent to warm us on winter's night.

Health and good cheer to
Our Three Graces
And every blessing be upon this house.

The toast continues in song, with others joining in and with Browne pouring more drinks for himself, Freddy and D'Arcy. When the toast ends, to applause, Gretta reaches over and touches Gabriel's hand, commenting, "That was lovely." Even Ivors approves.

Freddy loudly demands a speech in response to the toast. Julia declares, somewhat gravely, that the Morkan ladies have prepared a little something. Solemnly, Julia and Kate stand and Mary Jane takes her place at the piano. Suddenly they burst into the song "Naughty Girls," surprising and delighting their audience.

JULIA *(sings):*

I'm an imp on mischief bent

Emily Skinner, Sally Ann Howes and Marni Nixon as the Morkan sisters performing their "Naughty Girls" number in *James Joyce's The Dead*

Only feeling quite content
When doing wrong
At the Roman clubs, no doubt
Funny tales you hear about
My goings on.
Sometimes when I've had the fun
I repent on what I've done
But not for long
No, I break back into song.

GRETTA: Oh Aunt Julia,

JULIA *(sings):*

I'm a naughty girl
Naughty girl
And Rome is in a whirl
Because I'm a naughty girl.

FREDDY: Julia Morkan . . . . .

JULIA *(sings):*

If some youth with manners free
Dares to snatch a kiss from me,
Do we ask him to explain?

JULIA, KATE & MARY JANE *(sing):*
No! We kiss him back again!
We are naughty girls
Naughty girls
And Rome is in a whirl
Because we're naughty girls

The three ladies start a snake-like train around the table.

We are naughty girls
Naughty girls
Because they're all afraid
Of this naughty little maid.

Freddy joins the ladies, then one by one the table gets up and joins the singing and dancing, soon holding hands and making a snake-like chain. The entire party (except for Lily, Michael and Rita who come in and clean up the tables and chairs) begins to move around the room, then out the door and back, etc., singing.

All at once, Julia has to break away from the chain and sit down, soon attended by Gretta, Gabriel and Kate. The others hardly notice as the singing and dancing continues. Suddenly a banging can be heard—the resident of the floor below, Mr. Fulham, is banging on his ceiling to let them know that the sound of the revelry is annoying him. This infuriates Freddy, who stomps on the floor to answer Mr. Fulham's banging, while expressing his anger in the song "Wake the Dead."

FREDDY *(sings)*
It's him we have to shsh whom I should have shshed
Him we have to shsh all along.
It's him we have to shsh to hear the singer
It's him we have to shsh to hear the song.
You don't shsh the singer, you let the singer sing
Who cares if you wake the neighbors.

FREDDY & BROWNE *(sing):*
You don't shsh the singer you let the singer sing
Who cares if we wake the dead

IVORS *(sings):*
So why can't we have a voice too
Why can't he have a voice or him or him?

FREDDY, D'ARCY & LILY: *(sing):*
How would they like it if we went

Five stomps followed by seven bangs.

Challenging the neighbor's interference, Freddy cries "Dance!!" The furnishings, including the carpet, are set aside to make room. Michael calls for a Highland Fling. *"Dance break—the young ones dance and the others cheer them on with the rhythmic 'Wake the dead/They've slept long enough/And they'll soon be asleep again/Wake the dead!/they've slept long enough/And they'll soon be asleep again/Wake the dead!!' "*

Scene 3: Aunt Julia's bedroom

Gabriel watches the scene being changed while he shares some of his family memories with the audience. While he is speaking, Mary Jane is at the piano playing "her Academy piece—full of runs and difficult passages." As Aunt Julia gets into bed, Gabriel studies a photo of his late mother, remarking, "Gretta nursed her during her last long illness in our house. Gretta—who once she had called 'country cute.' "

The piano piece ends. Kate enters with a hot water bottle for her sister, who refuses it. Gabriel comes into the room with Mary Jane, and when Gabriel offers Julia the hot water bottle she accepts it gratefully. Browne comes in as Kate exits, fighting back tears.

JULIA: She's getting old. She cries like that all the time. It gets tiring, if the truth be told.

BROWNE: The Misses Morkan! Dublin's—naughty girls! If I had only known I could have been booking you for years!

JULIA: I said to Kate . . . when chosing which song to sing. I said this year haven't we heard enough of the church's music? After all, hasn't the church heard enough of me?

MARY JANE: Why do you say that? Aunt Julia, you know that's not true.

JULIA: You're leaving.

BROWNE: Soon. It was a glorious evening.

JULIA: I don't envy you your journey home at this hour.

BROWNE: I'd like nothing better this minute than a rattling fine walk in the country or a fast drive with a good spanking goer between the shafts.

JULIA: We used to have a very good horse and trap at home.

MARY JANE: The never-to-be-forgotten Johnny.

JULIA: You remember.

BROWNE: Well now, what was so wonderful about Johnny?

JULIA: The late lamented Patrick Morkan—their grandfather, he was a glue-boiler.

GABRIEL: He had a starch mill.

JULIA: He had a horse by the name of Johnny. And Johnny used to work in the mill, walking round and round in order to drive the mill. Which was all very well, but now comes the tragic part. One fine day the old gentleman thought he'd like to drive out to the park.

MARY JANE: Lord have mercy on his soul.

JULIA: Amen. As I said, so the old gentleman harnessed Johnny, put on his very best tall hat and very best stock collar and drove out in grand style.

GABRIEL: This was in Back Lane.

JULIA: Oh, Gabriel, he didn't live in Back Lane. Only the mill was there. So out he drove with Johnny. And everything went beautifully until Johnny comes in sight of King Billy's statue. Now whether he falls in love with the horse King Billy sits on or whether he thought he was back again in the mill, anyhow he began to walk round and round the statue! To walk round and round the statue! *(Laughing.)* With the old gentleman pompous like shouting . . . *(Coughing fit. Everyone quiets down.)*

The sound of the party in the drawing room has died down. Kate comes in with D'Arcy, followed by Gretta, Ivors and Mrs. Malins. D'Arcy favors Julia with an aria, beautifully rendered, from the Italian opera *Le Droghe D'Amore.* He had previously told the company he couldn't sing tonight because of a bad cold.

The men now gather to serenade Julia with a lullaby they've been practicing.

MEN *(sing "Queen of Our Hearts"):*

Goodnight, sleep tight
You queen of our hearts
Cuddle in your bed tonight
Goodnight, goodnight . . . . .

Your pillow he's a lucky fellow
His hand upon your head
All alone with you in bed
May your dreams be always dreamy
May your sleep be always sleepy
May you slumber, may you snooze
The night away and never lose
Your zest for rising up tomorrow morning
As the sun comes up
May your toes be warmed forevermore

Goodnight

The guests prepare to take their leave. Gabriel and Gretta offer to see Ivors home "two steps up the quay," but Ivors declines: "I'm quite well able to take care of myself, and besides, Michael has already offered." She leaves arm in arm with Michael. Lily has managed to flag one cab which Gabriel leaves to Freddy and his mother—and Browne, who hitches a ride with them.

Gabriel and Gretta are spending the night at the Gresham Hotel, and they make their goodbyes, Julia thanking Gabriel for his speech and Gabriel promising, "I'll come by on Saturday."

Young Julia enters and sits on the bed.

JULIA *(startled):* Oh, who are you? Me. I was talking about you just tonight. Now what was I saying? I was telling them when I was young, my voice wasn't too bad, was it? When I was young, some people thought it quite a lovely voice. It was lovely, wasn't it?

YOUNG JULIA *(sings):*

When lovely lady stoops to folly
And finds too late that men betray
What charms can soothe her melancholy
What art can wash her grief away?

JULIA: Yes. That is exactly how I used to sing it. Not so sad.

Kate comes in to search her coin purse for Freddy, who lacks change. Kate assures Julia the musicians have been taken care of—they are being given their pies. Kate exits, and Gabriel enters in his role as narrator. Gabriel tells the audience, "She slept peacefully that night. And the next. And a third. And as promised I returned on Saturday, but dressed now in black, with a band about my arm, seeking words to express our loss and finding none."

The two Julias reprise the first verse of "When Lovely Lady" and exit, leaving Gabriel to be joined by Gretta as the lights fade and the scene changes.

Scene 4: A room in the Gresham Hotel

The intrumental of "Michael Furey" is heard while Gabriel watches his wife undress. He remembers some of the most vibrant incidents in their marriage. Then he observes, "I could hear the falling of the candle's molten wax into the tray and the thumping of my own heart. She said to the porter that she didn't want any light. That there was light enough from the street. It could have been our honeymoon. But it wasn't."

As Gretta heads for bed, Gabriel tries to get her attention but soon realizes that she is not herself, something is amiss. He hopes he has done nothing to upset her, and she assures him he has not. But she is in tears and blames "that silly song" and the young student Michael for reminding her of a lad she once knew when she was spending the summer with her grandmother in Galway. He used to sing that song, and his name was Michael too—Michael Furey.

Gabriel suggests, "You were in love with him," and that perhaps Gretta considered going to Galway with Molly Ivors in order to see him again. Gretta denies this. He misunderstands, she tells him. He agrees, feeling that if that lad was all that meaningful in her life she'd have told him about him before. Gretta sees she must explain, doing so with the song "Michael Furey": "He was very delicate/Such eyes he had, big dark eyes/I used to walk with him/He died." He was only 17 (the song lyrics continue their explanation), and when the time came for her to leave her grandmother's Gretta wrote to him promising to come back the next summer. That night he awoke her by throwing stones at her window.

GRETTA *(sings):*

I can see his eyes
As he shivered in the rain
I implored him to go home again
That he would catch his death,
But he said
I do not wish to live
And when I was only a week up here
I heard Michael Furey was dead.

Michael Furey
He was very delicate
Such eyes he had
Big dark eyes
I think he died for me
For me.

Gabriel sees that it was Michael Furey she was thinking about when she sang "Goldenhair," and that Gretta loved the boy "more than—anything." Here, he realizes, is that world "like the surface of a frozen lake" he cited previously: "We walk along, we slip, we try to keep our balance and not to fall, but then one day there's a crack—and so we learn that underneath us is an unimagined depth just below." Gretta sobs her apology.

GABRIEL *(sings "The Living and the Dead"):*

Snow will be general
All over Ireland
Falling on every part
Of the dark central plain . . . . .

Snow will be general
All over Ireland
Falling on the churchyard
Where lies Michael Furey's grave.
Lying thickly upon the crooked crosses
And on the headstones,
On the spears of the gate,
On the barren stones . . . . .

All enter.

GABRIEL & COMPANY *(sing):*

Snow will be falling,
Falling softly,
Faintly falling,
All over Ireland,
Snow will be falling

Snow will be falling
Snow will be falling
Upon the living and the dead.

GABRIEL *(sings):*

Upon the living and the dead.

Curtain.

Pulitzer Prize, Lortel Award

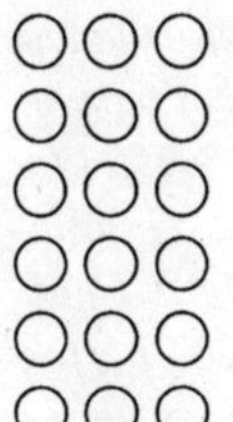

DINNER WITH FRIENDS

A Play in Two Acts

BY DONALD MARGULIES

Cast and credits appear on page 229

DONALD MARGULIES was born in Brooklyn September 2, 1954. His father was a salesman in a store selling wallpaper, and the future playwright showed an early interest, not in writing, but in the visual arts. After attending public school and John Dewey High School, he studied graphic design at Pratt Institute and proceeded to SUNY Purchase where he received his BFA in visual arts in 1977. But at SUNY he began to take an interest in playwriting—for no particular reason he can put his finger on now—and approached Julius Novick, who was teaching the subject there. Novick asked Margulies if he'd ever written a play, and Margulies replied frankly, "No." Novick nevertheless agreed to sponsor the young man in a playwriting tutorial, "a life-changing event," as Margulies looks back on it.

The first Margulies scripts were put on at SUNY, and in New York City he first surfaced off off Broadway with Luna Park, *a one-act adaptation of a Delmore Schwartz short story, commissioned by Jewish Repertory Theater and staged by them February 5, 1982. There followed* Resting Place *OOB at Theater for the New City (1982),* Gifted Children *at JRT (1983) and finally the full-fledged off-Broadway production of* Found a Peanut *at New York Shakespeare Festival June 17, 1984 for 33 performances.*

Later that season, Manhattan Theater Club produced Margulies's What's Wrong With This Picture? *in previews, but this one was withdrawn before opening and wasn't officially presented until 1988 in a revised version at the Back Alley Theater in Los Angeles (and it was produced on Broadway December 8, 1994 for 13 performances). Los Angeles was also the site of Margulies's* The Model Apartment *in 1989, winning its author an Obie and a New York State arts grant (its New York appearances took place OOB at JRT in 1990 and at Primary Stages in 1995). JRT also staged his* Zimmer *in 1987.*

Margulies's The Loman Family Picnic *ran for only 16 off-Broadway performances when first produced by MTC June 20, 1989, but Jeffrey Sweet enthusiastically designated it a Best Play of its season; and indeed, MTC revived it November 18, 1993 for a 62-performance run. Margulies's second Best Play,* Sight Unseen, *was commissioned by and first produced in 1991 at South Coast Repertory in Costa Mesa, Calif., after which MTC provided its New York debut on January 20, 1992 for 263 performances. It won Margulies an Obie for playwriting and was nominated for many major awards including the New York Drama Critics Circle, Pulitzer, Outer Critics Circle, Hull-Warriner and Drama Desk best-play citations.*

In 1994 the Williamstown Theater Festival presented Margulies's Broken Sleep: Three Plays, *and in 1995 Actors Theater of Louisville premiered Margulies's* July 4, 1994 *in its Humana Festival of New American Plays. Louisville did the same for his* Dinner With Friends *at the 1998 Humana Festival, winning Margulies an ATCA citation as one of the cross-country year's best scripts. This season* Dinner With Friends *arrived in New York under Daniel Sullivan's direction on November 4, to receive the millennial Pulitzer Prize, plus the Lucille Lortel Award for best off-Broadway play.*

On May 20, 1997 Margulies came back to MTC with Collected Stories *for an 80-performance run.This play returned to off Broadway in an independent revival production August 13, 1998 for a run of 232 performances. Margulies is also the author of* Women in Motion, *commissioned by the Lucille Ball Festival;* Pitching to the Star, *presented OOB at the West Bank Cafe; and an adaptation of Sholem Asch's* God of Vengeance, *produced April 13 by Seattle's A Contemporary Theater. Margulies has received National Endowment for the Arts, Guggenheim and New York Foundation of the Arts grants and is a member of both New Dramatists and the Dramatists Guild. He lives with his wife and son in New Haven, Conn. where he is a visiting lecturer at the Yale School of Drama.*

The following synopsis of Dinner With Friends *was prepared by Jeffrey Sweet.*

ACT I

Scene 1: Karen and Gabe's kitchen in Connecticut

SYNOPSIS: Outside, it's a snowy winter evening in New England. Inside, in their impressive eat-in kitchen, Gabe and Karen are telling their friend Beth of their recent trip to Italy. Apparently, Gabe and Karen are food writers, and their trip included a visit to an 86-year-old Roman chef named Emelia who took them to an extraordinary market and did amazing things with amazing ingredients. Only gradually do they begin to notice that Beth isn't entirely there.

One of the four kids upstairs (two of them belonging to Beth) calls down about a VCR emergency threatening their viewing of *The Aristocats*. Gabe heads up to deal with the problem, telling Karen, "Don't talk about Florence without me." Karen, sensing that something is wrong, tries to open the door for Beth to say what's on her mind, but Beth doesn't respond. Karen suggests that maybe the next time she and Gabe go to Italy, Beth and her husband Tom might go with them. (Tom was apparently unable to join them for dinner tonight because of some business down in Washington. Karen doesn't envy him the flight in this weather.) Karen suddenly remembers a present they brought back from Italy for Beth and Tom: placemats. Looking at them seems to sadden Beth.

Gabe returns, thrilled by the sight of the four children lined up "like four little Raphael cherubs" watching TV. He wishes there were film left in the camera so he could get that picture. *"Beth suddenly breaks down and sobs."* And now the story comes out. Tom is leaving her. He's involved with a stewardess named Nancy. Has been for a few months. Beth found out last week, while Karen and Gabe were away, in the middle of an argument.

BETH: He told me he was miserable, that he's always been miserable . . .

GABE: What?

BETH *(continuous):* . . . he's been miserable for so long he doesn't remember what it was like to be happy.

GABE: *Tom* said that?

BETH *(nods, then):* He said this isn't the life he had in mind for himself, that if he were to stay married to me, it would kill him, he would die young.

GABE: Jesus.

BETH *(to Gabe):* Did you know about this?, did he say anything to you?

GABE *(over "to you?"):* No! This is totally . . . I didn't have a *clue* . . .

KAREN: We all just went out to eat together.

BETH: I know.

KAREN: Right before we left. That Indian place in Branford. We loved their chicken tikka masala.

BETH: I know; that's right.

KAREN: You seemed fine; both of you did. He didn't seem "miserable" at all.

BETH: I know.

KAREN: You mean to tell me we were sitting there having a wonderful time and he was not only miserable but in love with someone else?!

BETH: I know, isn't that . . . ?

KAREN: Oh, sweetie, I'm so sorry, this can't be happening . . . How could he do this to you? I just can't believe it.

To Gabe, off his silence.

Feel free; jump in any time.

GABE *(defensively):* What. *(She gives him a look.)* I'm listening.

KAREN *(to Beth):* So, are you getting some counseling or something?

BETH *(shakes her head, then):* He doesn't want to.

KAREN: Come on! Twelve years, two kids: he doesn't *want* to?

GABE: What *does* he want? A trial separation or something?

BETH: No, no, he wants a divorce.

GABE: A divorce?!

KAREN: Oh, that's ridiculous.

BETH: That's what he *says* . . . He says he's tried for *years* to work it out . . .

KAREN: *How*? *How* did he try?

BETH *(continuous):* He's had it, he's spent, he can't give it anymore.

GABE: I don't get it; this just doesn't sound like Tom. It's like his body's been snatched and he's been replaced by a pod.

BETH: I know. You should have seen him. The rage! I didn't recognize him. I've never seen that kind of rage in him before! He *hates* me.

KAREN *(soothing):* No . . .

BETH: He does. He says I've ruined his life.

KAREN: Well, this sounds like something else is going on.

BETH: Doesn't it?

KAREN: Some kind of life-crisis thing. God, I wish you guys had come with us to Italy!

BETH: I think he's really in trouble. I tried telling him that, but that only made him angrier.

KAREN: Oh, this is classic. We've got to get him some help.

BETH: Good luck. You know Tom: he's suspicious of every kind of therapy you can think of. I'm just worried he's headed for some kind of breakdown.

KAREN: Do you think it's drugs?

GABE: Karen . . .

KAREN: How else do you account for something like this? It's a total personality transformation.

BETH: Karen, I've been racking my brain, playing back every little tiff, every long-distance phone conversation . . .

KAREN: He's crazy about you, Beth! I know it! I've seen it! You can't fake something like that.

BETH *(over "something like that"):* Karen. The things he said to me . . . This is not a man who's crazy about me, believe me. He's in love with this person. He *is*. He says she's everything I'm not.

KAREN: What is that supposed to mean?

BETH: He says she's completely devoted to him. She hangs on his every word. She's "there" for him.

KAREN: Oh, God, such bullshit.

BETH: Really. The stuff pouring out of his mouth . . . It's like bad greeting cards. He says *I* gave him seventy-five percent, she gives him a hundred and twenty.

KAREN: He said that? A hundred and twenty percent?

Beth nods.

He's into percentages? What's that extra twenty percent supposed to be?

Beth and Gabe look at her.

GABE: Karen.

KAREN: Oh. *(To Beth.)* What, you didn't go for that extra twenty percent?
BETH: Apparently not like *she* does.

Beth had noticed his moods, but she figured this probably had something to do with his job or his traveling. And there has been some odd sexual behavior, a sort of test which apparently she failed.

Upstairs, the kids cry out that the VCR is acting up again. (No, Beth hasn't told the kids.) Karen decides it's her turn to attend to the machine, leaving Gabe and Beth alone in awkwardness. Gabe drinks a little more wine and reminisces about the Vineyard, where Beth and her husband Tom met, and the two couples had such wonderful times together.

A cheer from upstairs; Karen has fixed things. Beth starts to collect her kids' stuff in preparation for going home, but when Karen comes back she persuades Beth to stay for dessert. Gabe does the honors with the dessert, which Karen made. It's very fancy, with vanilla and eggs. They all comment appreciatively on its excellence, discussing the ingredients and preparation. Then—

BETH *(sighs)*: I feel so much better now that I told you. All night long, sitting here, I thought I was gonna burst. You're my closest friends, you know.
KAREN: Of course we are.
GABE: Of course.
BETH: My closest friends in the world.
They eat in silence.
Mm, this is so good.
Karen and Gabe are pensive. End of scene.

Scene 2: Tom and Beth's bedroom later that night

Later. "*Beth, seeming vulnerable and bereft in her own home, disrobes and, wearing a tee-shirt and panties, gets into bed. Somewhere in the house, a dog barks.*" She shouts for the dog to be quiet. Then the bedroom door opens and Tom enters, dressed for winter, his boots tracking snow into the room. He has startled her. She didn't expect him here tonight. "You can't just come and go as you please anymore, Tom . . . " He apologizes. His flight to D.C. was cancelled, there wasn't a room to be had in a hotel, and he couldn't face sleeping on the airport floor. And no, his girlfriend Nancy (who, by the way, is a travel agent, not the stewardess Beth wants to believe she is) couldn't help. So he came back to what he can't keep from calling "home." And, of course, he'll sleep in the den, but he wanted to say hi.

He sits down to take off his boots and asks questions about the kids. She tells him that Sam is coming down with a cold, but that she had him take Tylenol before they left Gabe and Karen's. Tom is impressed that she was able to get him to swallow the medicine. Beth isn't happy talking domestic talk with Tom and asks him to leave. Oh, and he'll probably want to take an extra blanket to the den. Tom opens a chest to get the blanket and sees the new placemats—a gift from Gabe and Karen, Beth explains and tells him the dinner was "fabulous," as usual at their house, this time with new recipes picked up on their trip to Italy.

Tom tries to maintain a matter-of-fact tone as he quizzes her about what she told their friends about the reason for his absence. Beth tries to cover. They were sorry he wasn't there but, no, they didn't think anything particular of it. The conversation? The usual stuff. But Tom keeps pushing. "You mean to tell me the whole evening went by without a word about us?" She tries to evade, but he senses the truth. She spilled it, didn't she? She told them about the breakup. He's very upset. This isn't what they agreed. "We were gonna get a sitter and tell them together, face to face, remember?! That's all I asked: Wait for me to get back, we'll tell them together."

He questions her on the circumstances of the revelation. No, she assures him, the kids weren't present. No, it wasn't in the living room. It was over dessert. He wants to know what the dessert was. "Some kind of lemon-almond cake, made with polenta." And yes, since he asks, it was great. And yes, she cried. This upsets him even more.

BETH: So what? So what if they know? So they know! They were bound to find out!

TOM: That's not the point! *You've* got the advantage now!

BETH: What?! I do not!

TOM: Of course you do! You got to them first!

BETH: Tom . . .

TOM *(continuous):* They heard your side of the story first! Of *course* they're gonna side with you, it's only natural!

BETH: Oh, come on, nobody's taking sides.

TOM: Don't be naive! You know how it is! I'm not gonna let you get away with this . . .

BETH: What?!

TOM *(continuous):* Gabe and Karen mean too much to me, I'm not gonna let you turn them against me!

BETH: Tom, you're overreacting.

TOM: Don't tell me I'm overreacting! You've prejudiced my case!

BETH: I have not, Tommy. I was very even-handed.

TOM: How can you say that?! You're sitting there turning on the tears . . .

BETH: I wasn't turning on anything! Fuck you, I stated the facts. They were very sympathetic.

TOM: Of course they were sympathetic. You won them over.

BETH: I did not. Stop saying that.

TOM: You *intended* to tell them.

BETH: That is not true! I tried, I really did. I couldn't help it! Everything just spilled out!

Tom wants to know how their friends reacted to this news. They were sad, Beth tells him, shocked and sad. And now it's evidently into the routine they've been going through a lot lately. He accuses her of being deaf to his needs, of undermining him. She accuses him of undermining her, of not taking her art seriously. He antes up the evidence that he was supportive, even as he takes shots at her illusions of artistry.

TOM: Do you know what it's like having to support something you don't believe in? Do you, Beth? Do you? It's exhausting . . . . . What was I supposed to tell you, that I thought your "art" sucked?

BETH: Bastard . . .

TOM *(continuous):* Huh? Is that what I was supposed to say? That it was just an excuse not to get a fucking job just like everybody else . . .

BETH: You are such a fucking bastard.

TOM *(continuous):* . . . and really *do* something with your life?!

BETH: How dare you! How *dare* you!

TOM *(continuous):* I couldn't do that; how could I? Everything depended on perpetuating this myth of talent!

She strikes him. He grabs her wrists.

You wanna fight? Huh? You wanna hit me?

He gets into the bed, straddles her.

BETH *(overlap):* Let go of me! Let *go* of me!

TOM *(overlap):* Hit me! Hit me! Go ahead and hit me!

BETH: Prick!

TOM: Bitch!

She spits in his face. They wrestle, roll around on the bed, inflaming their conflicted passions.

Ballbreaker!

BETH: Liar!

TOM: Dilettante!

BETH: You fuck!

TOM: Look at me! Look what you've done to me!

BETH: Look what you've done to *me*!

TOM: I could kill you! Right now, I could fucking kill you!

BETH: Try it. I dare you.

They're looking at one another. He suddenly kisses her hard on the mouth. Pause. Equally aroused, she quickly undoes his pants as lights fade.

Scene 3: Karen and Gabe's living room, later still

Gabe and Karen are still digesting Beth's disturbing news as they drink the last of a bottle of wine. "*Their banter is edgy but always affectionate.*" Their dismay is compounded by the fact that they introduced Beth and Tom in the first place.

While Gabe is inclined to withhold his judgment until he hears both sides, Karen is utterly disillusioned by and disgusted with Tom. As far as she's concerned, Tom is an imposter, a con artist. Gabe can't see abandoning a friend in trouble, and from what he can tell Tom is indeed in trouble. Karen has little patience for this. Gabe can do as he likes, but she will never again be able to treat Tom as a friend; he has proved himself to be not worthy of trust.

GABE: You are so strict.

KAREN: I am not "strict"—I resent that, that's one of those words . . .

GABE: Okay; I'm sorry.

KAREN *(continuous):* I'm principled. You can't fault me for being principled . . .

GABE: But doesn't forgiveness enter into it for you, or are you too principled for that?

KAREN: Some things are not forgivable; this is *not* forgivable.

GABE: Boy . . .

KAREN *(continuous):* That's too easy. I'm sorry: Actions have consequences.

GABE: Remind me not to get on your bad side.

KAREN: You do something like this, I'm telling you right now, you are outta here.

GABE: Really?

KAREN: You better believe it. None of that sleeping-in-the-den shit.

GABE: It's for the kids' sake; that's what she said; I can understand that.

KAREN: If he's gonna decimate his family, he doesn't deserve to sleep under the same roof, I'm sorry.

GABE: But it's for the kids!

KAREN: That's a privilege; he's *lost* that privilege.

GABE: Wow. You are really tough.

KAREN: Don't be facetious! There has got to be a price for doing what he did; this neither/nor situation just won't do. I don't know how she can tolerate that. I would just throw him the hell out.

GABE: So, if in a moment of weakness, I sleep with a check-out girl or something, and am foolish enough to confess to you and beg for your forgiveness, you'd tell me, what, to go fuck myself?

KAREN: That's right.

GABE: You mean we couldn't still be friends?

KAREN: No way. Are you kidding?

GABE: You mean we wouldn't even be civil with one another?

She shakes her head as if to say, What are you crazy?

At least now I know where you stand.

KAREN: As if you had any doubt.

She pulls him closer; he rests his head on her lap.

GABE: The thing is, you never know what couples are like when they're alone; you never do. You know *that*: There's no way of knowing. It's all very mysterious.

KAREN: There goes the Vineyard.

GABE: Oh, God, you're right. How would we work that?

KAREN: We couldn't. What, we'd have Beth come with the kids for two weeks, then she would go and Tom would take over? That's ridiculous.

GABE: It sounds awful.

KAREN: What a mess.

GABE: It's like a death, isn't it?

She nods.

Gabe says he didn't talk much tonight because he was too stunned. Besides, he suggests, isn't that their dynamic? "You generally have more to say on any given subject than I do. That's why we work well together: you talk, I write, you edit me." But Karen thinks there was more to his silence than habit. Something about what Beth told them made him very uncomfortable. Gabe is very uncomfortable talking about what Karen thinks makes him uncomfortable. Karen suggests that he has a habit of evading the important stuff. Now Gabe escalates from uncomfortable to agitated. Is she trying to pick a fight?

Headlights signal the arrival of—oh God, could it be? yes—Tom. Unheralded. He's coming up their driveway now. Karen heads for the stairs. She doesn't want to see him. Gabe can deal with him; after all, Tom is *his* friend. Gabe pleads with Karen not to leave him alone. She relents, as Gabe goes to the door and Tom enters a little sheepishly. He hugs Tom. When he moves to hug Karen, she hesitates before letting him embrace her. He apologizes for dropping in on them unannounced, but the phone in his car isn't working. Gabe offers to fix Tom a plate of food (over Karen's silent objection). Tom wonders if there is any of the lemon-almond-polenta cake left. Karen is surprised to hear Tom mention it; it suggests that Beth told Tom about it. The idea that in the middle of the breakup of their marriage Beth and Tom would talk about *cake* . . . Tom tells them he's very upset. He can sense that Karen is angry at him. He can sense that what Beth said has colored their opinion of him.

TOM: I wanted us to tell you together. I knew this would happen. And so did she. It was really vindictive of her, it really was.

KAREN *(over "it really was"):* I don't feel like getting into this with you right now. You drop in, unannounced . . .

GABE: Karen . . .

TOM: I said I was sorry about that; my car phone was dead . . .

KAREN: Yeah, well, I'm going to bed.

Turns to go.

GABE *(surprised by her behavior):* Honey!

TOM: I didn't want a night to go by without seeing you guys.

KAREN: Good night.

TOM: Hey. Aren't you even willing to hear me out?

She stops.

I came here . . . I mean, really, Karen, don't you think you owe it to me? Owe it to our friendship? You guys mean too much to me to just . . .

GABE *(over "You guys," gently):* He's right.

KAREN: Okay, you made your point, Tom; you drove all the way over here in a snowstorm to lobby for our support. That's very politic of you.

TOM: I'm not lobbying for anything. I just think you've got to hear me out. You can't just go by what Beth says.

KAREN: It's pretty unambiguous, isn't it, Tom?

TOM: No. It's not. I'm not the villain here.

She laughs scoffingly.

If you insist on seeing me as the villain . . . I could tell you things about Beth . . .

KAREN: Boy, there's just no end to how low you'll stoop, is there?

GABE *(over "is there?"):* Karen . . .

TOM: *(continuous)*: Things that might give you a little perspective on all this . . . Did Beth tell you how she wouldn't touch me anymore?

KAREN: I don't want to hear it.

TOM *(continuous):* Huh? She tell you how she stopped touching me?

KAREN: *I don't want to hear it!*

TOM: But, hey, if you don't want to hear it . . . If you want to just be pissed at me, fine . . .

KAREN: It's so squalid: A stewardess?!

GABE: Karen . . .

TOM *(overlap):* What?! Is that what she told you?!

KAREN *(continuous):* I mean, really, couldn't you do better than that?

TOM *(continuous):* Nancy's not a stewardess, she's a travel agent, okay?

KAREN *(over "okay?"):* I don't care *what* she is, Tom. The point is you fucked her.

GABE *(winces):* Gosh, Karen . . .

TOM *(to Karen):* What are *you* so angry about? *(To Gabe.)* Jesus, she acts as if I . . .

Gabe shrugs.

KAREN: Any man who would do that to his wife, to his family . . .

TOM: Do you think I'd do something like break up my family lightly? Do you, Karen? Is that what you think of me?

KAREN: I don't know *what* I think of you, Tom. I honestly don't.

GABE: Karen . . .

KAREN: All I know is, she'd better be worth it.

GABE *(to Karen):* Look, maybe you'd *better* go to bed.

KAREN: Maybe I should. *(A beat.)* Good night, boys.

And she goes upstairs, leaving the two men alone. Tom claims not to be surprised by Karen's reaction. Gabe, playing host, offers some wine, which Tom accepts gratefully as he begins to eat. For the moment he is distracted from his downcast state by the deliciousness of the lamb on his plate and presses Gabe for details about its preparation.

Gabe tells Tom that he's worried about him, that Beth thinks that Tom is headed for a crackup. Tom snorts that he's not going crazy, he's going sane. Gabe wishes Tom had confided in him, maybe he could have helped. Tom says that Gabe would have just put in useless effort to try to patch up a marriage that shouldn't be patched up. The impending divorce is hard, yes, but Tom sees it as a good and necessary thing. Struggling to understand, Gabe asks if this is about sex. Actually, Tom confides, the sex lately has been pretty terrific.

GABE: You mean you and Beth . . . ?
TOM: Uh huh.
GABE: You and Beth are still having sex?
TOM: Yeah. Why?
GABE: I don't know, it seems to me that given the circumstances . . . the level of hatred and animosity . . . I don't necessarily see how combat is conducive to great sex.
TOM: Oh, God, it's been so intense! If the sex had been this good when we still had a marriage . . .
GABE: I must be really out of it. I thought really good sex was the product of trust and love and mutual respect.
TOM: You're kidding, right? Don't underestimate rage; rage can be an amazing aphrodisiac.
GABE: Huh.
TOM *(tastes the cake):* Mmm! It's really polenta!
GABE: Yeah, there's no white flour in it, just polenta. So you're still making love, huh.
TOM: I wouldn't exactly call it making love. *(A beat.)* Beth really wouldn't touch me much anymore.
GABE: What do you mean?
TOM: I mean, the way someone who loved you might casually slip a hand through your arm or onto your shoulder or something. *(A beat.)* I did an experiment. I decided I wasn't going to touch *her* and see how long it would take before she touched me. I'm not talking about sex now; I'm talking about skin-to-skin contact. A simple good night kiss, holding hands. She wouldn't touch me, Gabe. At all. I gave it a week. I couldn't stand it. I broke down and cried.
GABE: Gee . . .
TOM: I don't know about you, but I'm at the point in my life where I want to enjoy myself. I don't want to go through life hoping I'm gonna get lucky with my own wife. You know? You go to bed and you think you're gonna have sex and then you say something, some kind of offhanded remark of no consequence whatsoever, and it pisses her off and the mood is gone and it's lights out and that's it. I must've masturbated more than any married man in history.

Tom isn't just talking about sex, he's talking about a sense of companionship, something which simply disappeared from his marriage to Beth. And no, he didn't screw around. He had opportunities on the road. "I'd be in a hotel bar and strike up a conversation with a female colleague, or some divorcee with big hair, and I'd make them laugh and they'd look pretty and I'd feel competent again, you know?, and think, Gee, maybe I *am* still clever and attractive after all. There'd be that

DINNER WITH FRIENDS—Matthew Arkin as Gabe, Lisa Emery as Karen, Carolyn McCormick as Beth and Jonathan Walker as Tom in Donald Margulies's play

electricity in the air, that kind of buzz I hadn't felt since college, remember?, when a single move, any move at all, and there'd be sex? But I'd get scared and say goodnight and go back to my room and call Beth out of guilt, or hope, and get some shit about *some*thing I neglected to do or did badly." He was primed for Nancy when he met her. She was the travel agent who had been booking his flights on the phone. "She had this great laugh and this flirty sense of humor, and she said, 'We've been talking for weeks, I want to meet you already!' And I began to think, Why the hell not? What am I saving myself for? This hypercritical woman waiting for me back home? Who looks at me with withering disappointment. All the time. This accusatory, How-could-you-be-so-thoughtless look. So, on one hand, there's this *delightful* woman who makes me feel worthwhile and there's this *other* woman, my wife, who makes me feel like shit. Who would *you* choose?"

Gabe asks if Tom and Beth are going to go into counseling. Tom sees that Gabe still doesn't *get* it. Counseling is for when you want to repair a relationship. The marriage is over. And no, he doesn't feel they should stay together for the kids. He's only stuck it this long for the kids' sake. Gabe still thinks that maybe Tom should be sure that this isn't some midlife thing that, when he gets to the other side, he won't regret. Tom assures him it isn't.

Tom makes it clear now he doesn't want Gabe's advice. He appreciates that Gabe has a lot of feelings about this, but that's not what Tom has come to him for. All

Tom wants is a sympathetic ear. Gabe promises to shut up and listen. With the floor now his, all that Tom can finally say is, "I . . . I hope you never know . . . the . . . *loneliness* I've known. I hope you never do." And with that, though Gabe tries to get him to stay and talk more, Tom thanks Gabe for dinner and leaves.

Gabe turns off the lamps. He sits, deep in thought, in near darkness for a moment. The stairway light comes on.

KAREN *(off, from the stairs):* Gabe?

GABE: Yeah?

KAREN *(off):* So? How was that?

GABE: Okay.

KAREN *(off):* Come to bed and tell me.

GABE: In a minute.

He lingers, looking around the dimly lit room which suddenly feels cold and strange to him.

KAREN *(off):* Honey?

GABE *(calls):* Coming.

He remains seated as the lights fade.

ACT II

Scene 1: A house on Martha's Vineyard, summer, twelve and a half years earlier

We are in the main room (used for cooking, eating and digesting) of the house on the Vineyard to which Gabe and Karen referred in the first act. It is on a hill overlooking the ocean and proclaims itself as a setting for the good life. The time is about six in the evening (the lighting will drift into dusk during the course of this scene), and Karen is at work on preparing a gourmet meal as Gabe enters with provisions to complement it. *"Everyone has more hair."* Karen's friend Beth is currently out walking, having driven up with Gabe and Karen, and Gabe's friend Tom has yet to arrive.

Karen thinks Beth and Tom might be a good match. She sees Tom as "essentially a good guy waiting-to-happen." All he needs is the right woman. Gabe isn't so sure Beth is the right woman. Tom is a down-to-earth guy and Beth?—she is a little too "new age" for Gabe's tastes (communing with nature and listening to relaxation tapes), too high strung (hence the need for relaxation tapes) and the stuff he's seen in her sketch book is off-putting. Karen thinks it can't hurt to try.

Gabe unloads the massive supply of liquor he has brought, and starts to cuddle with Karen as she tries to work. Evidently they have been married recently and the glow is still very much with them. After nibbling a bit, Gabe goes into what is apparently a standing routine for them, "*an intimate game ..... played utterly straight, i.e., no baby talk.*"

GABE: Uh oh.

KAREN: What.

GABE: You know what time it is?

KAREN: What.

GABE: It's time for me to scare you.

KAREN *(playing along.)*: Oh, no, please don't.

GABE: I do; it's time.

KAREN: No, Gabe, please?

GABE: Sorry. A man's got to do what a man's got to do.

KAREN: Please, please don't.

GABE: Sorry, Sweetie. It can happen any time now.

KAREN *(pleading)*: No . . .

GABE: Any second.

KAREN: Gabe, please . . .

GABE: Sorry, kid. That's just the way it is.

A beat. He says, "Boo!" She jumps.

Works every time.

She kisses him. Their kissing progresses. Tom, wearing a knapsack, arrives after a long bike ride. He watches them for a moment. Karen catches his eye and abruptly stops.

GABE: What.

She indicates with her eyes, he turns.

Oh. Tom. Hi.

TOM: Carry on, don't mind me, it was just getting good.

KAREN: How long have you been standing there?

TOM: Ten, fifteen minutes.

KAREN: Jerk.

She kisses Tom's cheek.

Tom has just arrived with his bicycle on the ferry. He quickly impresses as an agreeable if flip guy who tends to cut to the chase. The chase being cut to at the moment is the whereabouts of this woman he's here to be fixed up with. Karen protests that characterizing this as a set-up "sounds so cheap and scheming." Tom replies, "That's okay with me. I have no problem with cheap and scheming." It turns out that Tom has encountered Beth before—at Gabe and Karen's wedding, in fact. Beth apparently attracted some notice by dancing by herself in a vaguely Kabuki style towards the end of the reception.

Gabe continues to make jokes about Beth—including her painting which he describes as "Expressionistic, neo-psychotic." This angers Karen, and she and Gabe retreat into silence. "Gee," says Tom, "it's really generous of you guys to be setting your friends up. I guess you just want us to be as happy as *you* are, huh? That's really sweet." This raises a smile and a cheerful "screw you" from Karen.

Now Beth comes in from her walk. Purposefully oblivious to a smiling Tom, she reports on her adventure—a walk to a beach where the light on the cliffs was splendid.

BETH: And these people, these beautiful men and women, were cavorting in the clay . . .

GABE: Oh, yeah.

BETH *(continuous):* . . . and the *light* on their bodies . . .

TOM: Were they naked?

BETH *(a beat, looking at him for the first time):* Excuse me?

TOM: I was just wondering if they were naked.

BETH: Some of them.

GABE: I'm sorry; Beth, this is Tom. Tom . . .

TOM: Hi.

He extends his hand; they shake hands.

BETH: I remember you. *(To Karen.)* I do remember him.

KAREN: I knew you would.

TOM: Wait wait: I don't think we ever . . .

BETH: At the wedding. I talked a lot to the woman you were with. She was a public defender.

TOM: Not anymore. I mean, she's still a public defender, I'm just not with her anymore.

BETH: Oh, that's too bad.

TOM: Not necessarily.

BETH: She seemed great.

TOM *(equivocally):* Uh . . .

BETH: As I recall, *I* talked to her a lot more than you did. Maybe if you paid more attention to her . . .

GABE: Moving right along . . .

The getting-to-know-you phase continues, helped along by some drinks. Beth says, yes, this is her first visit to the Vineyard. Tom says he's been coming here for years as Gabe's guest (the house is in Gabe's family). He and Gabe met during freshman orientation in college and they stayed friends, even though, according to Gabe, Tom had a habit of hitting on the women with whom Gabe was speechlessly infatuated. Tom protests this is an exaggeration, but Gabe cites chapter and verse. Tom pretends to make a pass at Karen, saying, "He can't give you what I can give you, Karen. I *know*; I've seen him naked." Karen, to Gabe's gratification says she's not complaining.

Beth wants to know Tom's story, and he obliges, "Oh, I'm just another jaded lawyer, burnt-out at thirty-one but hanging in there for want of anything better to do." Beth and Karen tell of their days working together doing in-house promo at Doubleday (Karen writing, Beth designing) before Beth left. She's now free-lancing, doing mass market paperbacks and looking forward to even better things to come.

KAREN: Beth is really a terrific artist.

BETH: I wish you would stop saying that.

TOM: What kind of stuff do you do? Expressionistic, neo-psychotic . . . ?

BETH: Excuse me?

Gabe glares at Tom in disbelief.

TOM: I mean . . . What style? Whatayacallit, realistic . . . ?

BETH: I hate labels.

TOM: Oh, okay.

BETH: Do you know art?

TOM: Not really.

BETH: Then why ask for labels? Why not just take it at face value?

TOM *(pointing to her notebook):* Can I see?

BETH *(outraged):* No!

TOM: Oh. Okay.

BETH: Why should I let you see it?

TOM: I don't know, I just . . .

BETH: I mean, forgive me: Who are you to me, anyway?

Gabe clears his throat, for effect.

TOM: You're right, I'm nobody.

BETH: Sharing one's art . . . That comes with trust. It's a gift. I never show my art on the first date.

TOM: Oh, is this a date? *(Looking to his hosts.)* I thought this *wasn't* a date.

Looking for cover, Beth goes to help Gabe with the cooking. Tom follows, mentioning he remembers Beth from the wedding, too, particularly her dance at the end. Beth is embarrassed, but Tom insists she looked beautiful. They both agree the wedding was lovely. Karen insists she doesn't remember very much of it. Gabe verifies that she was a wreck during much of it, even insisting they do the ceremony ten minutes early. And he dutifully agreed, herding the guests so Karen's sense of the moment could be seized. Beth wonders if being married has made a difference in their relationship. "It feels . . . *calmer* than before," Gabe remarks. Karen agrees, yes, the pressures they felt while being single and living together have disappeared, and their lives and relationship seem more clearly defined. Beth and Tom agree that the marriage option is beginning to look better and better.

Beth, still helping with the food preparation, cuts herself. The others fly around trying to be useful. Tom approaches with Band-Aids and sees to the patient. Seeing that Beth and Tom have the opportunity to share a moment, Gabe and Karen decide to leave them alone by going outside to look at the sky.

And indeed they have a little moment as Tom reassures her that she has no reason to be embarrassed by her mishap. Sensing that something might happen now that she's not quite ready for, Beth heads outside to look at the colors in the sky. Tom promises to follow with her drink.

Now Karen returns. Given how beautiful the night is, she's decided to move the meal outside. As she begins to assemble stuff, Tom "*lightly touches her hair for a beat before she realizes it.*" He makes some comment about her having gotten sun, but there's an undercurrent, and he takes the opportunity to touch Karen's hair again. She short-circuits the moment by asking him to fetch something outside for her and going to the door. As she leaves, she meets Gabe in the doorway. They exchange a kiss in passing.

GABE: So, what do you think of Beth?

TOM *(equivocally):* She's nice. She's intense. Better yet, what does she think of me?

GABE: I don't know, I think she likes you.

TOM: Yeah? Then I like her.

GABE: Uh, you're so deep.

BETH *(from the deck):* Tom, get out here. You're gonna miss the sunset.

GABE *(to Tom):* Go. Destiny calls.

They join the women on the deck. Responding to the sunset.

Oh, wow . . . !

BETH *(off):* Isn't that incredible?

TOM *(off):* It is. It really is.

Scene 2: Karen and Gabe's patio, five months after the events in Act I

Karen and Beth have lunch on Karen and Gabe's garden patio. As the scene begins, Beth is complaining about Tom having missed a scheduled get-together with their daughter Laurie, who was devastated. Off running around with his girl friend, probably. Finally, late at night, a phone call of wan apology, asking Beth to tell Laurie he's sorry. Beth told him to call back when Laurie was awake and tell her himself. Karen comments, "Unbelievable. Was he always like this or is this what happens to people when they break up? Do they get stupid, or what?"

Karen feels she hasn't seen Beth in months. For a time immediately after the breakup, there was a lot of contact, and then, suddenly, Beth seemed to disappear. Beth says she was afraid of getting wearisome. Hell, she was beginning to bore herself. Karen was afraid she'd offended Beth in some way. Beth wonders how Karen could believe such a thing. Karen wonders if, on some level, Beth didn't blame her for the whole mess. After all, Karen was the one who introduced her to Tom. Beth insists she was and is fully capable of making her own decisions and mistakes and accepting responsibility for them. Regarding what went on between her and Tom, Beth assures Karen, "It was out of your control. That we came together was as much out of your control as our falling apart. You can't control everything, Karen, even though you'd like to think you can."

Karen assumes that Beth has been using some of the interim to paint, but Beth says, actually, she has pretty much stopped painting. Once Tom was gone and she no longer had to defend her painting from him, she found she didn't really need it. There were other things for her to do with her life. And besides, she has come to see she wasn't a very good painter. Karen protests, but Beth isn't interested in Karen's defense of her talent. Painting isn't important to her.

What has become important to her is someone named David. She's seeing a lot of him. He's not exactly new to her life because he and Tom used to work together, and Karen and Tom used to sometimes have dinner with David and his then-wife. So a shorthand already existed. Karen is happy to see her friend is enjoying a romantic interlude.

But Beth insists this isn't an interlude. She and David are serious. They're in love. They're going to get married. Karen is alarmed at the swiftness of the decision. Surely it's too soon after the breakup to be thinking of marriage. Wouldn't Beth like to explore her independence a little? Beth suggests it is *Karen* who would like Beth to explore her independence, but no, Beth knows what she wants and she's going after it, with or without her friend's endorsement. "I know what I'm doing, Karen. This is the man I was meant to be with. I really believe that. I had to survive Tom so I could end up with David. It was my fate."

With a flash of irritation, Beth suggests that that Karen likes seeing Beth's life in a shambles. "I'm finally feeling whole, finally feeling like I'm on the right track, for the first time in my life, and what do you do? You undermine me!" It is easy for Karen to adopt this attitude with her ostentatiously good marriage to Gabe, but Beth isn't about to blow this chance for happiness just to play the part Karen has assigned to her. Karen doesn't know what Beth is talking about.

BETH: You know what I think? I think you *love* it when I'm a mess.

KAREN: What?!

BETH: You do. You love it when I'm all-over-the-place, flailing about. I finally find someone who's like a, like an *anchor*, and you don't want to hear about it!

KAREN: That is not true.

BETH: As long as I'm artsy and incompetent, everything is fine. The minute I show any signs of being on an equal footing with you, forget it; you can't deal with it, you have to knock me over!

KAREN: How can you say that?

BETH: Come on, you *need* me to be a mess; you're *invested* in it. Every Karen needs a Beth.

KAREN: That really isn't fair.

BETH: We all play the parts we're handed. I was The Mess, The Ditz, The Comic Relief. You got to be Miss Perfect: Everything just right. Just the right wine, just the right spice, just the right husband. How was I supposed to compete with *that*?

KAREN: Nobody was asking you to compete with anything.

BETH: You're right, there was no contest; I couldn't possibly reciprocate . . . The hostess gifts you would give me! I could never tell if you were being remedial or just plain hostile.

KAREN: I had no idea you felt this way . . .

BETH: We can't all be like you, Karen. God knows I've tried. No matter how much *I* stir, *my* soup still sticks to the pot.

Pause. In a conciliatory gesture, Beth takes Karen's hand.

KAREN: We loved nothing more than having you in our home and cooking you meals.

BETH: We loved it, too.

KAREN: You're my family.

BETH: I know.

KAREN: I spent my *first* twenty years doing whatever the hell I could do to get *away* from my family and my *second* twenty years doing everything I could to cobble together a family of my own. I thought if I could *choose* my family this time, if I could make my friends my family . . .

BETH: Congratulations. The family you've chosen is just as fucked up and fallible as the one you were born into.

They resume eating in silence.

How are the boys?

Karen, distracted, nods.

And you and Gabe?

KAREN: We're good. We're fine.

Beth nods. Silence.

Scene 3: A bar in Manhattan, the same afternoon

Gabe waits, drinking Pellegrino. Tom enters, looking fit in a smart summer suit, and hugs Gabe with enthusiasm, apologizing for being late. He and Nancy are in New York for a couple of days to see some shows and frolic. No, in answer to Gabe's question, he won't be up to see the kids. It's not his weekend, and Beth is pretty by-the-book on the scheduling stuff.

Tom is bubbling with enthusiasm about his new life. Up at six with Nancy, they run every morning. He's lost a lot of weight and he's in great shape. And yes, having an uninhibited sexual partner is part of the fun of it. Nancy is such a contrast to Beth. They make love every morning in the shower, and Nancy actually makes the first move a lot. Total contrast to Beth, who always acted as if sex were one of the duties that came with marriage. Not that the relationship with Nancy is only sexual. They talk, they really talk. And, unlike Beth, Nancy *hears* him. He truly believes that Nancy has saved his life.

Tom can't help noticing that Gabe has been restrained throughout this. He wants Gabe to share what's on his mind. Gabe wonders if he really wants that. That night last winter (in Act I, Scene 3), Tom was insistent that all he wanted from Gabe was someone to listen. Have the rules changed? Can it be that Tom actually wants to know what Gabe thinks?

"Okay, you want to know what I'm thinking? I'm thinking: I hear you *talk*ing, Tom, I hear these *words* coming out, and you sound like a fucking *moonie* to me, Tom, you really do . . . "

Tom protests that when he was with Beth he was in a state of living death, buried under the crap of domestic life—who picks up the kids, who runs this errand, who does that chore. The final straw was the dog. The dog that Beth insisted the kids had to have because Beth had had one when she was a kid. "I'd spent my entire adult life cleaning up one form of shit or another, now I was on to *dog* shit. I should've gone into waste management. How do you keep love alive when you're shovelling shit all day long?"

Gabe insists that this is part of what you do to get the other stuff—the family. Tom agrees that it might be worth it if a family is what you want. One of the things he has discovered is that he didn't. Not really. He only thought he did because it was one of the things you were supposed to want. But honestly, it was against his nature, as imposed on him as the law career he embarked on because his family expected it. But Tom has realized that giving into those pressures led him to leading what he can only call an "inauthentic life."

GABE: What, you were a party boy trapped in the body of a family man? Tommy, I could swear I actually saw you *enjoy*ing yourself on a number of occasions in the last decade or so.

TOM: Well, sure. But, honestly?, most of the time I was just being a good sport.

GABE: A good sport?!

TOM: You know what I mean . . .

GABE *(continuous):* Wait a minute. You were faking it?! You mean to tell me that all those years—all those *years*, Tom!—the four of us together, raising our *kids* together, the dinners, the vacations, the hours of videotape, you were just being a good sport?

TOM: No . . .

GABE: Then what, Tom, I don't get it. I was there, as well as you. This *misery* you describe, the agony. Gee, I thought we were all just living our lives, you know? Sharing our humdrum little existences. I *thought* you were there, wholeheartedly there. And now you're saying you had an eye on the clock and a foot out the door?!

TOM: You've got to stop taking this so personally.

GABE: How would *you* take it? You say you were wasting your life, that's what you've said.

TOM *(over "that's what you've said"):* I don't mean you and Karen. I don't mean *you*, I'd never mean *you*; you're my best friend, I've got to be able to say this stuff to you. I'm talking about my marriage.

GABE: But it's not that simple, Tom. We were there. Karen and Danny and Isaac and I, we were all there, we were all a big part of that terrible life you had to get the hell away from. Isaac's totally freaked out by this, by the way. So when you repudiate your entire adult life . . .

TOM: That's not what I've done . . .

GABE: That's essentially what you've done. And I can understand how you might find it necessary to do that: It must be strangely *exhilarating* blowing everything to bits.

TOM: Gabe . . .

GABE: I mean it. You build something that's precarious in even the best of circumstances and you succeed, or at least you make it *look* like you've succeeded, your *friends* think you have, you had *us* fooled, and then, one day, you blow it all up! It's like, I watch Danny and Isaac sometimes, dump all their toys on the floor, Legos and blocks and train tracks, and build these elaborate cities together. They'll spend hours at it, they'll plan and collaborate, and squabble and negotiate, but they'll do it. And *then* what do they do? They wreck it! No pause to revel in what they accomplished, no sigh of satisfaction, they just launch into a full-throttle attack, bombs bursting, and tear the whole damn thing apart.

Pause.

TOM: I just want you to be my friend. That's all. I want you to be happy for me.

GABE: Happy for you.

TOM: Happy I turned my life around.

GABE: Sure, Tom. I'm happy for you.

A smug response, Tom feels, and he warns Gabe that his marriage could wind up in the doldrums too. Gabe admits that he and Karen have had their rough spots, but he believes that "the key to civilization" is finding a way to get through them and go on. Tom for one is not going to suffer as their parents did, plodding through fifty-year marriages with no hope of relief, no chance to show their children that if you make a mistake, you can change your life for the better. And he doesn't want to see Gabe suffer either.

TOM: I'm your friend. I'd hate for you to wake up at fifty and . . .

GABE: You don't get it: I cling to Karen; I *cling* to her. Imagining a life without her doesn't excite me, it just makes me anxious.

TOM *(backing off):* Okay. . . .

GABE: It all goes by so fast, Tom, I know. The hair goes, and the waist. And the stamina; the capacity for staying up late, to read or watch a movie, never mind sex. Want to hear a shocker? Karen is pre-menopausal. That's right: my sweetheart, my lover, that sweet girl I lolled around with on endless Sundays, is getting hot flashes. It doesn't seem possible.

A beat.

We spend our youth unconscious, feeling immortal, then we marry and have kids and awaken with a shock to mortality, theirs, ours, that's all we see. We worry about them, *their* safety, our *own*, air bags, plane crashes, pederasts, and spend our middle years wanting back the dreamy, carefree part, the part we fucked and pissed away; now we want that back, 'cause now we know how fleeting it all is, now we know, and it just doesn't seem fair that so much is gone when there's really so little left. So, some of us, try to regain unconsciousness. Some of us blow up our homes . . . And others of us . . . take up piano; I'm taking piano.

From Gabe's perspective, when Tom bailed out on his marriage, he bailed out on another important commitment — the commitment to grow old with Gabe and Karen in coupledom, attend all of each other's family rituals, be a constant part of each other's lives. Tom protests that he's still there and he still intends to make good on all that, just not in tow with Beth. Gabe doesn't appear to be convinced.

Matthew Arkin and Jonathan Walker in *Dinner With Friends*

Tom asks if there's anything new with Beth. How are things going with her and David, the guy she's seeing. Evidently, David is news to Gabe, too. Also news to him is the implicit background that ten years or so ago, Beth and David had an affair. Tom sort of wishes that the marriage had busted up then. That way Beth and David could have gotten together sooner, and, of course, Tom would have gotten his freedom sooner.

Tom has to take off now. Grabbing the bill, he talks about introducing Gabe and Karen to Nancy (who is now thinking of becoming a nutritionist) and offers to walk Gabe to his train. But Gabe isn't taking the train home. He's catching a flight to the Vineyard where he's meeting Karen and the boys to open up the house for the summer. Tom is nostalgic about his visits to Gabe's Vineyard place. "I wish I was going with you." Gabe is non-commital and says goodbye. Tom and Gabe "*hug for the last time.*"

TOM: I'll call you.

Gabe nods. Tom starts to go.

Say hi to Karen if you think she'd be glad to hear from me. And send my love to the boys. Tell Isaac everything's gonna be okay.

GABE *(nods, then):* Bye.

Tom waves and goes. Gabe's smile fades as he watches him walk away. He smiles and waves again; Tom has looked back one last time.

Scene 4: Karen and Gabe's bedroom, that night

Karen and Gabe first make, then get into their bed in the Martha's Vineyard house. They can't help discussing Tom's revelation of Beth's earlier affair with

David. Karen is suspicious about Tom telling Gabe this, but Gabe insists that Tom seemed to assume that they already knew about it from around when it happened, ten years ago.

Karen does the math: ten years ago Beth and Tom were newly married and the two couples saw each other constantly. And yet neither Karen nor Gabe sensed that anything was going on. How was that possible? They seemed to be such happy days.

Both Karen and Gabe are shocked by the implications of this information. It means that the woman Karen thought was her best friend never confided in her. Even today, at lunch, when Beth could have told her about her real history with David, she didn't. "How could she?" Gabe replies. "She's spent all these months portraying herself as the wronged woman, she couldn't drop a bombshell like that. Her credibility would've been shot to hell."

Gabe admits to Karen that he didn't pick up on the revelation about David when Tom and he were talking in the bar. He couldn't muster the will to do so. Tom seemed to grow smaller and smaller, and Gabe felt increasingly detached from this man. "And I realized . . . I don't love him anymore."

With their understanding of their past with Tom and Beth invalidated, both Gabe and Karen feel as if there's no chance of making a future with them. Gabe tells Karen about Tom's desire to introduce them to Nancy. Karen winces. Gabe assures her it won't happen. The friendships are over. But each has to admit that both Tom and Beth look good. Gabe jokes that it must be all that high-quality sex.

For a second, they talk family business, then they turn to the books they've brought to bed. But, unable to read, Karen turns to Gabe. She wants to share a dream she had. They were in this bed, making love in the simple and effortless way they used to (and yes, sometimes still do). But Karen was aware of another couple in bed with them. No, not Tom and Beth. Themselves—Karen and Gabe. Middle-aged. Commenting and bickering as they watched their younger selves. Gabe initially doesn't have any comment, which irritates Karen.

KAREN: How come the minute the conversation turns to us you're struck mute? Huh, Gabe?

GABE: Uh . . . I don't know . . .

KAREN: Why is that?

He shrugs, shakes his head.

We can sit here and go on and on about everyone we know and all the problems of the world and the minute I . . . You know?, for a guy who's pretty damn articulate about a number of things . . . Do you ever wonder about it, Gabe, do you ever wonder why that is?

GABE: Uh, yeah, sometimes . . .

KAREN: And?

He shrugs.

I tell you, I *confide* in you this dream I had . . .

GABE: Uh huh.

KAREN *(continuous):* This revealing dream I had about us and you have nothing to say?

GABE: Well, sure I do.

KAREN: What. Speak.

GABE *(a beat):* It's . . . It obviously . . . I think it's about what happens to couples.

KAREN: What.

GABE: I think . . . it's the inevitable . . . evolution.

KAREN: Inevitable?

GABE *(considers this):* Yes. I think it is.

KAREN: And what is it?

GABE: What.

KAREN: The evolution. Define it.

GABE: You want me to . . . ?

KAREN: Yes! Talk to me, Gabe. Goddamn it, you have got to talk to me!

GABE: Okay.

A beat.

It's . . . I think it's what happens when . . . when practical matters begin to outweigh . . . abandon. You know?

KAREN: Abandon?

GABE: Uh huh.

KAREN: Is that it?

Gabe nods.

Do they have to?

GABE: I think so. *(A beat.)* I *think* so.

KAREN: Why?

GABE *(shrugs):* It's . . . I think it's . . . *You* know: Having kids . . . having to pay the mortgage . . . making the deadline . . . marinating the snapper . . .

KAREN *(tears in her eyes):* Don't you ever miss me, Gabe?

GABE *(surprised by her sudden emotion):* What?

KAREN: Don't you ever miss me?

GABE: Oh, God, honey, yes. Yes. Sure I miss you. I miss you a lot.

KAREN *(almost childlike):* How do we not get lost?

Gabe shakes his head. He takes her hand. They're both frightened. Silence. He begins to play their intimate game from long ago.

GABE *(softly):* Uh oh.

KAREN: What.

GABE: You know what time it is?

KAREN: What.

GABE: It's that time again.

KAREN *(catching on):* Oh, no . . .

GABE: Yup, I'm afraid so . . .

KAREN: Not tonight, Gabe, really . . .

GABE: It's time for me to scare you.

KAREN: Oh, no, Gabe, please don't scare me . . .

GABE: Sorry, kid, that's just the way it is . . .

KAREN: Please please don't?

GABE: It can happen any time now . . .

KAREN: Please, Gabe?

GABE: Any second.

KAREN: No . . .

GABE: Sorry, kid . . .

KAREN: No . . . Please . . .

GABE: A man's got to do what a man's got to do. *(A beat. Softly)* Boo!

Startled, she gasps. They hold each other as lights fade. Curtain.

Critics, Tony Awards

○○○
○○○
○○○
○○○
○○○
○○○

COPENHAGEN

A Play in Two Acts

BY MICHAEL FRAYN

Cast and credits appear on page 199

MICHAEL FRAYN was born August 9, 1933 (not 1925, as erroneously reported in previous Best Plays *volumes) in northwest London, the son of a sales representative. He attended Kingston Grammar School but left in 1952 and went into the Army, which assigned him to train for the job of interpreter studying Russian at Cambridge and in Moscow. He received a commission as an intelligence officer before his discharge in 1954, when he returned to Cambridge to study philosophy and—in 1957—to co-author* Zounds!, *a college-produced musical comedy.*

Frayn worked for the Manchester Guardian *as reporter and satirical columnist until 1962 and for the London* Observer *until 1968, the year in which his first dramatic work,* Jamie on a Flying Visit, *was televised on the BBC. His London stage debut took place in 1970 at the Garrick Theater with* The Two of Us, *a program of four short works:* Black and Silver, The New Quixote, Mr Foot *and* Chinamen. *There followed* The Sandboy *(produced in 1971 at the Greenwich Theater);* Alphabetical Order *(1975 in London and later in the U.S.A. at the Long Wharf Theater in New Haven, Conn.);* Donkey's Years *(1976);* Clouds *(1976);* Balmoral *(1979), which was revised as* Liberty Hall *(1980); and* Make and Break *(1980).*

Four of the five Frayn plays which have come to New York have been prizewinners. His first Best Play, Noises Off, *had its premiere at the Lyric Theater, Hammersmith, February 11, 1982 and soon transferred to the Savoy Theater in the heart of London, where it continued as a long-run hit while its American production was being staged on Broadway December 11, 1983 for 553 performances. His second Best Play,* Benefactors, *opened at the Vaudeville Theater in London April 4, 1984 and was presented on Broadway December 22, 1985 for 217 performances. His third was* Wild Honey, *his adaptation of Anton Chekhov's first, untitled, playscript, which premiered at the*

National Theater in London July 19, 1974 and opened on Broadway December 18, 1986. Like too many other plays of exceptional quality, it failed to find an audience in New York and closed after a run of only 28 performances, having made its mark, however, as a Best Play of the 1986–87 season.

Frayn's fourth New York prizewinner is this season's Copenhagen, *a 1998 National Theater production in London, which opened on Broadway April 11 and was the New York Drama Critics Circle's choice as the year's best foreign play and won the Tony Award for best play. And in London Frayn's plays have won him five Evening Standard and three Olivier Awards.*

Another Frayn play, his translation and adaptation of Exchange *by Yuri Trifonov, was produced off off Broadway by Blue Heron in 1994. His stage credits include an adaptation of Jean Anouilh's* Le Nombril *(retitled* Number One), *and translations of Tolstoi's* The Fruits of Enlightenment *and Chekhov's* The Cherry Orchard, *the latter two produced by the National Theater. Among his published works are collections of his newpaper writings, a volume of philosophy* (Constructions) *and nine novels including* The Tin Men, The Russian Interpreter *(for which he won the Hawthornden Prize),* Towards the End of the Morning, A Very Private Life, Sweet Dreams *and* Headlong *(shortlisted for the Booker Prize). Among his numerous TV productions have been documentaries on Berlin, Vienna, Australia, Jerusalem and the London suburbs, where he makes his home with his wife and three daughters.*

ACT I

SYNOPSIS: Beyond the grave, Niels Bohr and his wife Margrethe are discussing a question which has puzzled them through life and into eternity: Why did their one-time very close friend and colleague, Werner Heisenberg, come to visit them in Copenhagen in September 1941 while Denmark was under German occupation, when Heisenberg was technically their enemy on the opposing side of a bitter struggle?

Heisenberg is present with them in the hereafter, represented by a stage furnished only with three chairs and with a door up left. The trio's conversation often includes statements addressed as though to an interested observer like the audience, and their perspective sometimes makes abrupt shifts in time. Heisenberg comments, "Now we're all dead and gone, yes, and there are only two things the world remembers about me. One is the uncertainty principle, and the other is my mysterious visit to Niels Bohr in Copenhagen in 1941. Everyone understands uncertainty. Or thinks he does. No one understands my trip to Copenhagen. Time and time again I've explained it. To Bohr himself, and Margrethe. To interrogators and intelligence officers, to journalists and historians. The more I've explained, the deeper the uncertainty has become. Well, I shall be happy to make one more attempt. Now we're all dead and gone. Now no one can be hurt, now no one can be betrayed."

Bohr and his wife continue their discussion as though Heisenberg were not there.

MARGRETHE: I never entirely liked him, you know. Perhaps I can say that to you now.

BOHR: Yes, you did. When he was first here in the twenties? Of course you did. On the beach at Tisvilde with us and the boys? He was one of the family.

MARGRETHE: Something alien about him, even then.

BOHR: So quick and eager.

MARGRETHE: Too quick. Too eager.

BOHR: Those bright watchful eyes.

MARGRETHE: Too bright. Too watchful.

BOHR: Well, he was a very great physicist. I never changed my mind about that.

MARGRETHE: They were all good, all the people who came to Copenhagen to work with you. You had most of the great pioneers in atomic theory here at one time or another.

BOHR: And the more I look back on it, the more I think Heisenberg was the greatest of them all.

HEISENBERG: So what was Bohr? He was the first of us all, the father of us all. Modern atomic physics began when Bohr realized that quantum theory applied to matter as well as to energy. 1913. Everything we did was based on that great insight of his.

BOHR: When you think that he first came to work here in 1924 . . .

HEISENBERG: I'd only just finished my doctorate, and Bohr was the most famous atomic physicist in the world.

BOHR: . . . and in just over a year he'd invented quantum mechanics.

MARGRETHE: It came out of his work with you.

BOHR: Mostly out of what he'd been doing with Max Born and Pascual Jordan at Göttingen. Another year or so and he'd got uncertainty.

MARGRETHE: And you'd done complementarity.

BOHR: We argued them both out together.

HEISENBERG: We did most of our best work together.

They were running atomic physics like a father-and-son business team at that time, but why did Heisenberg come to Copenhagen in 1941? Bohr asks himself again.

Heisenberg recalls that he went there with a colleague, Carl von Weizsäcker, ostensibly to give a lecture at the German Cultural Institute. But Weizäcker had notified Bohr of the real reason for the visit—to see Bohr, not only at an official luncheon, which turned out to be "a difficult occasion" for everyone, but hoping for a private visit later at the Bohrs' home.

HEISENBERG: I wonder if they suspect for one moment how painful it was to get permission for this trip. The humiliating appeals to the Party, the demeaning efforts to have strings pulled by our friends in the Foreign Office.

MARGRETHE: How did he seem? Is he greatly changed?

BOHR: A little older.

MARGRETHE: I still think of him as a boy.

BOHR: He's nearly forty. A middle-aged professor, fast catching up with the rest of us.

MARGRETHE: You still want to invite him here?

BOHR: Let's add up the arguments on either side in a reasonably scientific way. Firstly, Heisenberg is a friend . . .

MARGRETHE: Firstly, Heisenberg is a German.

BOHR: A White Jew. That's what the Nazis called him. He taught relativity, and they said it was Jewish physics. He couldn't mention Einstein by name, but he stuck with relativity, in spite of the most terrible attacks.

MARGRETHE: All the real Jews have lost their jobs. He's still teaching.

BOHR: He's still teaching relativity.

MARGRETHE: Still a professor at Leipzig.

BOHR: At Leipzig, yes. Not at Munich. They kept him out of the chair at Munich.

MARGRETHE: He could have been at Columbia.

BOHR: Or Chicago. He had offers from both.

MARGRETHE: He wouldn't leave Germany.

BOHR: He wants to be there to rebuild German science when Hitler goes. He told Goudsmit.

MARGRETHE: And if he's being watched it will all be reported upon. Who he sees. What he says to them. What they say to him.

HEISENBERG: I carry my surveillance around like an infectious disease. But then I happen to know that Bohr is also under surveillance.

MARGRETHE: And you know you're being watched yourself.

BOHR: By the Gestapo?

HEISENBERG: Does he realize?

BOHR: I've nothing to hide.

MARGRETHE: By our fellow-Danes. It would be a terrible betrayal of all their trust in you if they thought you were collaborating.

BOHR: Inviting an old friend to dinner is hardly collaborating.

MARGRETHE: It might appear to be collaborating.

BOHR: Yes. He's put us in a difficult position.

MARGRETHE: I shall never forgive him.

BOHR: He must have good reason. He must have very good reason.

Bohr resolves to avoid politics and stick to physics during the visit. Margrethe suggests the the two can go for one of their long walks together if they want to speak privately. She conjectures that Heisenberg may want to talk about fission, on which Bohr is "the acknowledged authority," that the Nazis may want to develop some kind of weapon. If so, Heisenberg, the leading German physicist, would certainly be put in charge of such a project, though fission hasn't been a special field of his. Bohr believes he helped prove in 1939 that "There's no way in the forseeable future in which fission can be used to produce any kind of weapon." But physicists around the world are still working on fission, "Because there's an element of magic in it. You fire a neutron at the nucleus of a uranium atom, and it splits into two other elements. It's what the alchemists were trying to do—to turn one element into another."

Heisenberg remembers walking up the gravel path to the Bohrs' front door and being greeted warmly by his friend and onetime surrogate father. They mutually regret the present situation and ask after each others' children, who are well. Heisenberg has been worried about the Bohrs but is told that so far "The race laws have not been enforced." Bohr hasn't been able to keep up his sailing (the waters are mined) or his skiing (Norway, where he used to ski, is occupied too). Heisenberg suggests Bohr might come to Germany, and Bohr stiffens.

BOHR: My dear Heisenberg, it would be an easy mistake to make, to think that the citizens of a small nation, of a small nation overrun, wantonly and cruelly overrun, by its more powerful neighbor, don't have exactly the same feelings of national pride as their conquerors, exactly the same love of their country.

MARGRETHE: Niels, we agreed.

BOHR: To talk about physics, yes.

MARGRETHE: Not about politics.

BOHR: I'm sorry.

HEISENBERG: No, no—I was simply going to say that I still have my old ski hut at Bayrischzell. So if by any chance . . . at any time . . . for any reason . . .

BOHR: Perhaps Margrethe would be kind enough to sew a yellow star on my ski-jacket.

HEISENBERG: Yes. Yes. Stupid of me.

Bohr is still working on fission, he tells Heisenberg, and he has a cyclotron. There are 30 in the United States but none in Germany, as the Nazis have regarded theoretical physics as a field dominated by Jewish scientists and have given it no support. Heisenberg is still teaching at Leipzig part of each week but is busy elsewhere. He feels Bohr out about contacts with British or American scientists, but Bohr says he has had none. He hints that there are those in the German Embassy who would appreciate Bohr's attending lectures and discussions there and might some day prove to be friends in need. Bohr puts his reaction in the form of questions: "Is that why you've come to Copenhagen? To invite me to watch the deportation of my fellow-Danes from a grandstand seat in the windows of the German Embassy?"

Margrethe observes that it's time for their visitor to explain why he's come here. Heisenberg suggests that one of their strolls might be in order, but Bohr tells him it's too cold for that. Heisenberg recalls their first meeting at a festival in Bohr's honor in 1922, when Bohr was one of the few who were willing to treat a defeated and devastated Germany with some respect. "We worshipped you because you held out your hand to us," Heisenberg remembers.

BOHR: As a matter of fact. You bit it.

HEISENBERG: Bit it?

BOHR: Bit my hand! You did! I held it out, in my most statesmanlike and conciliatory way, and you gave it a very nasty nip.

HEISENBERG: *I* did?

BOHR: The first time I ever set eyes on you. At one of those lectures I was giving in Göttingen.

HEISENBERG: What are you talking about?

BOHR: You stood up and laid into me.

HEISENBERG: Oh . . . I offered a few comments.

BOHR: Beautiful summer's day. The scent of roses drifting in from the gardens. Rows of eminent physicists and mathematicians, all nodding approval of my benevolence and wisdom. Suddenly, up jumps a cheeky young pup and tells me my mathematics are wrong.

HEISENBERG: They were wrong.

BOHR: How old were you?

HEISENBERG: Twenty.

BOHR: Two years younger than the century.

HEISENBERG: Not quite.

BOHR: December Fifth, yes?

HEISENBERG: 1.93 years younger than the century.

BOHR: To be precise.

HEISENBERG: No—to two places of decimals. To be *precise,* 1.928 . . . 7 . . . 6 . . . 7 . . . 7 . . . 1 . . .

BOHR: I always keep track of you, all the same. And the century.

MARGRETHE: And Niels has suddenly decided to love him again, in spite of everything. Why? What happened? Was it the recollection of that summer's day in Göttingen? Or everything? Or nothing at all? Whatever it was, by the time we've sat down to dinner the cold ashes have started into flame once again.

Bohr recalls that Heisenberg was especially combative at games and a reckless skier—and also a bit reckless in his approach to science, following mathematics to whatever result, without considering any of the philosophical implications.

HEISENBERG: The faster you ski, the better you think.

BOHR: Not to disagree, but that is most . . . most interesting.

HEISENBERG: By which you mean it's nonsense. But it's not nonsense. Decisions make themselves when you're coming downhill at seventy kilometers an hour. Suddenly there's the edge of nothingness in front of you. Swerve left? Swerve right? Or think about it and die? In your head you swerve both ways.

MARGRETHE: Like that particle.

HEISENBERG: What particle?

MARGRETHE: The one you said goes through two different slits at the same time.

HEISENBERG: Oh, in our old thought-experiment. Yes. Yes!

MARGRETHE: Or Schrödinger's wretched cat.

HEISENBERG: That's alive and dead at the same time.

COPENHAGEN—Philip Bosco as Niels Bohr, Blair Brown as Margrethe and Michael Cumpsty as Heisenberg in Michael Frayn's play

MARGRETHE: Poor beast.

BOHR: My love, it was an imaginary cat.

MARGRETHE: I know.

BOHR: Locked away with an imaginary phial of cyanide.

MARGRETHE: I know, I know.

HEISENBERG: So the particle's here, the particle's there . . .

BOHR: The cat's alive, the cat's dead . . .

MARGRETHE: You've swerved left, you've swerved right . . .

HEISENBERG: Until the experiment is over, this is the point, until the sealed chamber is opened, the abyss detoured; and it turns out that the particle has met itself again, the cat's dead . . .

MARGRETHE: And you're alive.

BOHR: Not so fast, Heisenberg . . .

HEISENBERG: The swerve itself was the decision.

BOHR: Not so fast, not so fast!

Bohr recalls an argument he once had with a colleague about which would be faster, an act or the reaction to that act. An experiment with cap pistols apparently indicated that the reactor was quicker on the draw. Heisenberg claims that playing the piano gives him a momentum that clears away all in front of him—it once led him into whirlwind courtship and marriage of a young woman he happened to glimpse while playing the Beethoven G major.

Tragic memories of two of the Bohrs' six children take over their thoughts—"Harald. Lying alone in that ward," and Christian, the oldest, knocked overboard by their sailboat's tiller, struggling toward a life preserver, "So near, so near!"; trying, almost touching but finally failing to reach it and drowning before the eyes of his father unable to save him.

Bohr decides it's warm enough for a walk with Heisenberg after all. They once went on a week's hike through Zeeland, and to Elsinore, where "The whole appearance was changed . . . . . by our knowing that Hamlet had lived there. Every dark corner there reminds us of the darkness inside the human soul." The two men have enjoyed long walks all their lives, but, Margrethe notes, "This time, in 1941, their walk takes a different course. Ten minutes after they went out . . . they're back! I've scarcely had the table cleared when there's Niels in the doorway. I see at once how upset he is—he can't look me in the eye." Nor can Heisenberg, who offers the perfunctory courtesies of departure, the thanks and good wishes.

Bohr, disturbed and talking partly to Margrethe, partly to himself, asks, "How can he possibly be right? Wheeler and I went through the whole thing in 1939." Apparently, Heisenberg had said something about fission on their short walk, because Bohr goes on reviewing this process with Margrethe, how a neutron fired at a uraniaum nucleus will split it, releasing energy, "about enough to move a speck of dust." But it also sends out two or three more neutrons, which in their turn split more and more nuclei, "doubling and quadrupling in millionths of a second from one generation to the next," until in the eightieth generation there are "enough specks of dust to constitute a city and all who live in it."

BOHR: There is a catch, thank God. Natural uranium consists of two different isotopes, U-238 and U-235. Less than one percent of it is U-235, and this tiny fraction is the only part of it that's fissionable by fast neutrons.

HEISENBERG: This was Bohr's great insight. Another of his amazing intuitions. It came to him when he was at Princeton in 1939, walking across the campus with Wheeler. A characteristic Bohr moment—I wish I'd been there to enjoy it. Five minutes deep silence as they walked, then: "Now hear this—I have understood everything."

BOHR: In fact it's a double catch. 238 is not only impossible to fission by fast neutrons—it also absorbs them. So, very soon after the chain reaction starts, there aren't enough fast neutrons left to fission the 235.

HEISENBERG: And the chain stops.

BOHR: Now, you can fission the 235 with slow neutrons as well. But then the chain reaction occurs more slowly than the uranium blows itself apart.

HEISENBERG: So again the chain stops.

BOHR: What all this means is that an explosive chain reaction will never occur in natural uranium. To make an explosion you will have to separate out pure 235. And to make the chain long enough for a large explosion . . .

HEISENBERG: Eighty generations, let's say . . .

BOHR: . . . you would need many tons of it. And it's extremely difficult to separate.

HEISENBERG: Tantalizingly difficult.

BOHR: Mercifully difficult. The best estimates, when I was in America in 1939, were that to produce even one grain of U-235 would take 26,000 years. By which time, surely, this war will be over. So he's wrong, you see, he's wrong! Or could *I* be wrong? Could I have miscalculated? Let me see . . . What are the absorption rates for fast neutrons in 238? What's the mean free path of slow neutrons in 235 . . . ?

MARGRETHE: But what exactly had Heisenberg said? That's what everyone wanted to know, then and forever after.

BOHR: It's what the British wanted to know, as soon as Chadwick managed to get in touch with me. What exactly did Heisenberg say?

HEISENBERG: And what exactly did Bohr reply? That was of course the first thing my colleagues asked me when I got back to Germany.

MARGRETHE: What did Heisenberg tell Niels—what did Niels reply? The person who wanted to know most of all was Heisenberg himself.

In 1947, after the war was over, Heisenberg returned to visit the Bohrs—this time accompanied by someone from British intelligence. The two men tried to recall and reconstruct their conversation during that brief stroll in 1941, but even then they couldn't agree on what had taken place.

HEISENBERG: There's no mystery about it. There never was any mystery. I remember it absolutely clearly, because my life was at stake, and I chose my words very carefully. I simply asked you if as a physicist one had the moral right to work on the practical exploitation of atomic energy. Yes?

BOHR: I don't recall.

HEISENBERG: You don't recall, no, because you immediately became alarmed. You stopped dead in your tracks.

BOHR: I was horrified.

HEISENBERG: Horrified. Good, you remember that. You stood there gazing at me, horrified.

BOHR: Because the implication was obvious. That you *were* working on it.

HEISENBERG: And you jumped to the conclusion that I was trying to provide Hitler with nuclear weapons.

BOHR: And you were!

HEISENBERG: No! A reactor! That's what we were trying to build! A machine to produce power! To generate electricity, to drive ships!

BOHR: You didn't say anything about a reactor.

HEISENBERG: I didn't say anything about anything! Not in so many words. I couldn't! I'd no idea how much could be overheard. How much you'd repeat to others.

BOHR: But then I asked you if you actually thought that uranium fission could be used for the construction of weapons.

HEISENBERG: Ah! It's coming back!

BOHR: And I clearly remember what you replied.

HEISENBERG: I said I now knew that it could be.

BOHR: That is what really horrified me.

In 1941 Heisenberg had realized—"based on that fundamental insight" of Bohr's at Princeton in 1939—that a reactor could turn U-238 into a new element entirely, neptunium, and then turn neptunium into plutonium, "at least as fissile as the 235 that we couldn't separate." Heisenberg had wanted to get that information across to Bohr, but Bohr had ceased listening because he was in shock at the thought of Hitler getting his hands on such a weapon, and their walk and conversation came to an end.

All of the German nuclear scientists had wanted Heisenberg to consult Bohr about this, because they considered Bohr the Pope of their profession and, in their moral quandry, wanted him to give them a sort of absolution. Heisenberg recalls that as they turned back toward the house Bohr did absolve them: "You muttered something about everyone in wartime being obliged to do his best for his own country. Yes?" Bohr doesn't remember what he said, but he doubts that the German scientific community would have immediately stopped working on fission if he had advised them against "supplying a homicidal maniac with an improved instrument of mass murder." Besides, if anything were to happen to Heisenberg, he'd be replaced as the head of the program by a Nazi named Diebner: "My one hope is to remain in control."

Heisenberg asks for Bohr's careful attention, as he explains that a nuclear weapons program would require a huge effort, so that governments will be asking the nuclear physics community whether it is worthwhile, whether it can provide effective results in time: "Sooner or later, if I manage to remain in control of our program, the German government is going to come to *me!* They will ask *me* whether to continue or not. *I* will have to decide what to tell them."

Bohr advises, "You tell them how difficult it will be. And perhaps they'll be discouraged." But Heisenberg can't make such a decision unless he can determine the state of the Allied nuclear program.

HEISENBERG: There was a report in a Stockholm paper that the Americans are working on an atomic bomb.

BOHR: Ah. Now it comes, now it comes. Now I understand everything. You think I have contacts with the Americans?

HEISENBERG: You may. It's just conceivable. If anyone in occupied Europe does, it will be you.

BOHR: So you *do* want to know about the Allied nuclear program.

HEISENBERG: I simply want to know if there is one. Some hint. Some clue. I've just betrayed my country and risked my life to warn you of the German program . . .

BOHR: And now I'm to return the compliment?

HEISENBERG: Bohr, I have to know! I'm the one who has to decide! If the Allies are building a bomb, what am I choosing for my country? You said it would be easy to imagine that one might have less love for one's country if it's small and defenseless. Yes, and it would be another easy mistake to make, to think that one loved one's country less because it happened to be in the wrong. Germany is where I was born. Germany is where I became what I am. Germany is all the faces of my childhood, all the hands that picked me up when I fell, all the voices that encouraged me and set me on my way, all the hearts that speak to my heart. Germany is my widowed mother and my impossible brother. Germany is my wife. Germany is our children. I have to know what I'm deciding for them! Is it another defeat? Another nightmare like the nightmare I grew up with? Bohr, my childhood in Munich came to an end in anarchy and civil war. Are more children going to starve, as we did? Are they going to have to spend winter nights as I did when I was a schoolboy, crawling on my hands and knees through the enemy lines, creeping out into the country under cover of darkness in the snow to find food for my family? Are they going to sit up all night, as I did at the age of seventeen, guarding some terrified prisoner, talking to him and talking to him through the small hours, because he's going to be executed in the morning?

BOHR: But my dear Heisenberg, there's nothing I can tell you. I've no idea whether there's an Allied nuclear program.

HEISENBERG: It's just getting under way even as you and I are talking. And maybe I'm choosing something worse even than defeat. Because the bomb they're building is to be used on us.

Abruptly changing his perspective from 1941 to post-war, Heidenberg goes on the say that none of the American scientists stopped to consider the consequences of what they were doing, not even Einstein when he wrote to Roosevelt in 1939 advising him to finance nuclear research, not even Bohr after he escaped from occupied Denmark and joined the others at Los Alamos. And none of them had experienced the full consequences of dropping bombs on a defenseless population, as Heisenberg had in Berlin, a whole city on fire "with people trapped, people in various stages of burning to death." Bohr claims that the Allies were going ahead with the bomb because they feared the Germans were working on it. Heisenberg believes that if Bohr had cooperated in 1941, Oppenheimer and the German physicists alike might have been discouraged from going any farther with weaponry: "Worth trying, surely! But already you're too angry to understand what I'm saying."

After the German surrender, the British collected Heisenberg and the whole team of German scientists and sequestered them in, to them, the dream world of a Huntingdonshire country house where they enjoyed formal dinners while back in shattered Germany their families were starving. It was like a house party until the day when they heard the news of Hiroshima. "I can't describe the effect it has on us. You play happily with your toy cap-pistol. Then someone else picks it up and pulls the trigger . . . and all at once there's blood everywhere and people screaming, because it wasn't a toy at all . . . We sit up half the night, talking about it, trying to take it in. We're all literally in shock."

One of them, Otto Hahn, felt some of that blood was on his hands because he discovered fission. On the other hand, the Nazi Gerlach was ashamed that his hands were clean. But, Heisenberg finishes, "You've built the bomb . . . . . and you've used it on a living target."

Margrethe wonders whether Heisenberg is implying that Bohr took part in deciding to make an atomic bomb. It was in development before Bohr arrived at Los Alamos, so he was spared any part in that decision, though he made a small contribution, putting forward an idea that helped trigger the Nagasaki bomb. Margrethe accuses Heisenberg of returning to Germany after that 1941 meeting and telling them that making an atomic bomb was possible. Heisenberg admits he told some minor officials about the possibilities of plutonium.

HEISENBERG: It might be a very different story if it's Diebner who puts the case at our meeting with Albert Speer, instead of me.

MARGRETHE: The famous meeting with Speer.

HEISENBERG: But this is when it counts. This is the real moment of decision. It's June 1942. Nine months after my trip to Copenhagen. All research cancelled by Hitler unless it produces immediate results—and Speer is the sole arbiter of what will qualify. Now, we've just got the first sign that our reactor's going to work. Our first increase in neutrons. Not much—thirteen percent—but it's a start.

BOHR: June 1942? You're slightly ahead of Fermi in Chicago.

HEISENBERG: Only we don't know that. But the RAF have been terror-bombing. They've obliterated half of Lubeck and the whole center of Rostock and Cologne. We're desperate for new weapons to strike back with. If ever there's a moment to make our case, this is it.

MARGRETHE: You don't ask him for the funding to continue?

HEISENBERG: To continue with the reactor? Of course I do. But I ask for so little that he doesn't take the program seriously.

MARGRETHE: Do you tell him the reactor will produce plutonium?

HEISENBERG: I don't tell him the reactor will produce plutonium. Not Speer, no. I don't tell him the reactor will produce plutonium.

BOHR: A striking omission, I have to admit.

HEISENBERG: And what happens? It works! He gives us barely enough money to keep the reactor program ticking over. And that is the end of the German atomic bomb. That is the end of it.

To protect it from the bombing raids, Heisenberg's group transported their reactor across Germany to a deep wine cellar in the Swabian Jura. They kept working with it until they achieved 670 percent neutron growth. But they had only a lump of cadmium, not cadmium control rods, Bohr notes, "to absorb any excess of neutrons, to slow the reaction when it overheated," a reaction which Heisenberg admits was not self-limiting. They were only two weeks away from achieving critical mass. In Bohr's opinion, "It was only the arrival of the Allies that saved you" from an uncontrollable meltdown or lethal radiation, from which they had arranged no protection. They were single-mindedly intent on getting the reactor running. Otherwise, Heisenberg recalls, it was "the last happy time in my life," relatively peaceful with the war running down and no longer any interference from the government.

Once more, Bohr asks why Heisenberg came to Copenhagen in 1941. Surely he didn't expect Bohr to tell him anything about the American atomic project, surely he intended to go back to work with his reactor whatever Bohr might say.

BOHR: Tell us once again. Another draft of the paper. And this time we shall get it right. This time we shall understand.

MARGRETHE: Maybe you'll even understand yourself.

BOHR: After all, the workings of the atom were difficult to explain. We made many attempts. Each time we tried they became more obscure. We got there in the end, however. So—another draft, another draft.

HEISENBERG: Why did I come? And once again I go through that evening in 1941. I crunch over the familiar gravel and tug at the familiar bell-pull. What's in my head? Fear, certainly, and the absurd and horrible importance of someone bearing bad news. But . . . yes . . . something else as well. Here it comes again. I can almost see its face. Something good. Something bright and eager and hopeful.

BOHR: I open the door.

HEISENBERG: And there he is. I see his eyes light up at the sight of me.

BOHR: He's smiling his wary schoolboy smile.

HEISENBERG: And I feel a moment of such consolation.

BOHR: A flash of such pure gladness.

HEISENBERG: As if I'd come home after a long journey.

BOHR: As if a long-lost child had appeared on the doorstep.

HEISENBERG: Suddenly I'm free of all the dark tangled currents in the water.

BOHR: Christian is alive, Harald still unborn.

HEISENBERG: The world is at peace again.

MARGRETHE: Look at them. Father and son still. Just for a moment. Even now we're all dead.

BOHR: For a moment, yes, it's the twenties again.

HEISENBERG: And we shall speak to each other and understand each other in the way we did before.

MARGRETHE: And from those two heads the future will emerge. Which cities will be detroyed, and which survive. Who will die, and who will live. Which world will go down to obliteration, and which will triumph.

BOHR: My dear Heisenberg!

HEISENBERG: My dear Bohr!

BOHR: Come in, come in . . .

Curtain.

ACT II

Heisenberg is thinking back to his first visit to Copenhagen in 1924 when he was 22 and Bohr was 38, and they immediately set off on their hundred-mile walk passing through Elsinore. The Bohrs had a flat at the Institute, and Heisenberg, who was giving lectures in Danish, had a little room in the servants' quarters. Margrethe claims she didn't mind being left at home during the walking trip: "I was pleased you had an excuse to get away. And you always went off hiking with your new assistants."

The two men reminisce about Bohr's previous assistant, Kramer, his "favorite son" until Heisenberg came along; about the physicists all over Europe with whom they exchanged ideas and papers; about a journey to Leiden with colleagues waiting on the platforms to ask Bohr's opinion about the spin of electrons at every stop, and then the last stop at Leiden, where, Bohr says, "I'm met at the barrier by Einstein and Ehrenfest. And I change my mind because Einstein—Einstein, you see?—I'm the Pope—he's God—because Einstein has made a relativistic analysis, and it resolves all my doubts." Bohr and Heisenberg were on the cutting edge of major developments in physics, when, in 1927, Heisenberg left to take up his position at Leipzig. The special way the two had worked on everything together in those years was in Heisenberg's mind when he came to Copenhagen in 1941.

MARGRETHE: You didn't do any of those things together.

BOHR: Yes, we did. Of course we did.

MARGRETHE: No, you didn't. Every single one of them you did when you were apart. *(To Heisenberg.) You* first worked out quantum mechanics on Heligoland.

HEISENBERG: Well, it was summer by then. I had my hay fever.

MARGRETHE: And on Heligoland, on your own, on a rocky bare island in the middle of the North Sea, you said there was nothing to distract you . . .

HEISENBERG: My head began to clear, and I had this very sharp picture of what atomic physics ought to be like. I suddenly realized that we had to limit it to the measurements we could actually make, to what we could actually observe. We can't see the electrons inside the atom . . .

MARGRETHE: Any more than Niels can see the thoughts in your head, or you the thoughts in Niels's.

HEISENBERG: All we can see are the effects that the electrons produce, on the light that they reflect . . .

BOHR: But the difficulties you were trying to resolve were the ones we'd explored together, over dinner in the flat, on the beach at Tisvilde.

HEISENBERG: Of course. But I remember the evening when the mathematics first began to chime with the principle.

MARGRETHE: On Heligoland.

HEISENBERG: On Heligoland.

MARGRETHE: On your own.

HEISENBERG: It was terribly laborious—I didn't understand matrix calculus then . . . I get so excited I keep making mistakes. But by three in the morning I've got it. I seem to be looking through the surface of atomic phenomena into a strangely beautiful interior world. A world of pure mathematical structures. I'm too excited to sleep. I go down to the southern end of the island. There's a rock jutting out into the sea that I've been longing to climb. I get up it in the half-light before the dawn and lie on top, gazing out to sea.

MARGRETHE: On your own.

HEISENBERG: On my own. And yes—I was happy.

Then along came Schrödinger's wave mechanics which put matrix mechanics somewhat in the shade (Heisenberg and Schrödinger applied the word "repulsive" to each other's systems). Schrödinger came to Copenhagen to discuss these matters, and they attacked him so fiercely they made him ill. They even pursued him into the sick room with their arguments, but by the time Schrödinger finally left, Bohr was beginning to take his side.

BOHR: Because *you'd* gone mad by this time. You'd become fanatical! You were refusing to allow wave theory any place in quantum mechanics at all!

HEISENBERG: You'd completely turned your coat!

BOHR: I said wave mechanics and matrix mechanics were simply alternate tools.

HEISENBERG: Something you're always accusing me of. "If it works it works." Never mind what it means.

BOHR: Of course I mind what it means.

HEISENBERG: What it means in language.

BOHR: In plain language, yes.

HEISENBERG: What something means is what it means in mathematics.

BOHR: You think that so long as the mathematics works out the sense doesn't matter.

HEISENBERG: Mathematics is sense! That's what sense is!

But finally they must be able to explain it to a lay person like Margrethe in language she can understand, Bohr adds.

The track of an electron in a cloud chamber brought on another argument, and Bohr went skiing in Norway to get away, "And you worked out complementarity in Norway, on your own," Margrethe reminds him. "You're a lot better apart, you two." While Bohr was away, Heisenberg thought out a principle of uncertainty leading to the understanding that what they observe in the cloud chamber is "not a continuous track but a series of glimpses—a series of collisions between the passing electron and various molecules of water vapor . . . . . not even the collisions themselves, but the water-droplets that condense around them, as big as cities around a traveler."

Heisenberg's paper on uncertainty was already in circulation by the time Bohr got back from skiing. He summarizes its theory: "You have no absolutely determi-

Blair Brown, Philip Bosco and Michael Cumpsty in a scene from *Copenhagen*

nate situation in the world, which among other things lays waste to the idea of causality, the whole foundation of science—because if you don't know how things are today you certainly can't know how they're going to be tomorrow. I shatter the objective universe around you." Heisenberg sets up an example of a wandering electron colliding with a photon, and Bohr replies, "I have to use not only your particle mechanics, I have to use the Schrödinger wave function . . . . . Particles are things, complete in themselves. Waves are disturbances in something else." This is an example of Bohr's complementarity, Heisenberg remarks, and they argue about whether or not Heisenberg has accepted this theory.

Their work has "put man back at the center of the universe," Bohr states, after centuries as "tiny figures kneeling in the great cathedral of creation"; then, after a brief period of recovery in the Renaissance, "pushed aside by our own reasoning" and governed by the laws of classical mechanics.

BOHR: Until we come to the beginning of the twentieth century, and we're suddenly forced to rise from our knees again.

HEISENBERG: It starts with Einstein.

BOHR: It starts with Einstein. He shows that measurement—measurement, on which the whole possibility of science depends—measurement is not an impersonal event that occurs with impartial universality. It's a human act, carried out from a specific point of view in time and space, from the one particular viewpoint of a possible observer. Then, here in Copenhagen in those three years in the mid-twenties, we discover that there is no precisely determinable objective universe. That the universe exists only as a series of approximations. Only within the limits determined by our relationship with it. Only through the understanding lodged inside the human head.

MARGRETHE: So this man you've put at the center of the universe—is it you, or is it Heisenberg?

BOHR: Now, now, my love.

MARGRETHE: Yes, but it makes a difference.

BOHR: Either of us. Both of us. Yourself. All of us.

MARGRETHE: If it's Heisenberg at the center of the universe, then the one bit of the universe that he can't see is Heisenberg.

HEISENBERG: So . . .

MARGRETHE: So it's no good asking him why he came to Copenhagen in 1941. He doesn't know!

HEISENBERG: I thought for a moment just then I caught a glimpse of it.

MARGRETHE: Then you turned to look.

HEISENBERG: And away it went.

MARGRETHE: Complementarity again. Yes?

BOHR: Yes, yes.

MARGRETHE: I've typed it out often enough. If you're doing something you have to concentrate on, you can't also be thinking about doing it, and if you're thinking about doing it, then you can't actually be doing it. Yes?

HEISENBERG: Swerve left, swerve right, or think about it and die.

BOHR: But *after* you've done it . . .

MARGRETHE: You look back and make a guess, just like the rest of us. Only a worse guess, because you didn't see yourself doing it, and we did. Forgive me, but you don't even know why you did uncertainty in the first place.

Publication of the paper on uncertainty led to Heisenberg's receiving the appointment at Leipzig instead of Schrödinger, so that he became Germany's youngest full professor. To give him added stature, he and Bohr agreed to endorse each other's ideas. Margrethe insists she knows why he came to them in 1941. It was to show off. He was in Copenhagen in the twenties as a humble assistant, and in 1941 he wanted to impress on his former master that he was now in charge of a project so important that the Gestapo was taking an interest in his project.

MARGRETHE: And as you frankly admit, you're going to go back and continue doing precisely what you were doing before, whatever Niels tells you.

HEISENBERG: Yes.

MARGRETHE: Because you wouldn't dream of giving up such a wonderful opportunity for research.

HEISENBERG: Not if I can possibly help it.

MARGRETHE: Also you want to demonstrate to the Nazis how useful theoretical physics can be. You want to save the honor of German science. You want to be there to reestablish it in all its glory as soon as the war's over.

HEISENBERG: All the same, I don't tell Speer that the reactor . . .

MARGRETHE: . . . will produce plutonium, no, because you're afraid of what will happen if the Nazis commit huge resources and you fail to deliver the bombs. Please don't try to tell us that you're a hero of the resistance.

HEISENBERG: I've never claimed to be a hero.

MARGRETHE: Your talent is skiing too fast for anyone to see where you are. For always being in more than one position at a time, like one of your particles.

HEISENBERG: I can only say that it worked. Unlike most of the gestures made by heroes of the resistance. It worked! I know what you think. You think I should have joined the plot against Hitler and got myself hanged like the others.

BOHR: Of course not.

HEISENBERG: You can't say it, because there are some things that can't be said. But you think it.

BOHR: No.

HEISENBERG: What would it have achieved? What would it have achieved if you had dived in after Christian and drowned as well? But that's another thing that can't be said.

BOHR: Only thought.

HEISENBERG: Yes, I'm sorry.

BOHR: And rethought. Every day.

HEISENBERG: You had to be held back, I know.

MARGRETHE: Whereas you held yourself back.

HEISENBERG: Better to stay on the boat, though, and fetch it about. Better to remain alive and throw the lifebuoy. Surely!

BOHR: Perhaps. Perhaps not.

HEISENBERG: Better. Better.

MARGRETHE: Really, it is ridiculous. You reasoned your way, both of you, with such astonishing delicacy and precision into the tiny world of the atom. Now it turns out that everything depends upon those really rather large objects on our shoulders. And what's going on in there is . . .

HEISENBERG: Elsinore.

BOHR: Elsinore.

Heisenberg points out that if the Bohrs thought that he was going to develop an atom bomb for Hitler, they should have killed him by talking about his secret decisions and plans where the Gestapo could overhear. He was the personification of complementarity, both enemy and friend, dangerous and a guest, wave and particle. Heisenberg once again "came out on top" after the war, as the head of German science under British protection, Margrethe reminds him. And in the meantime Bohr was forced to flee Denmark, "Crawling down to the beach in the darkness in 1943, fleeing like a thief in the night from his own homeland to escape being murdered," getting across to Sweden in a fishing boat just as two freighters arrived to ship out all Denmark's Jews.

"And where were you?" Margrethe asks Heisenberg. "Shut away in a cave like a savage, trying to conjure an evil spirit out of a hole in the ground," trying to create a machine that could kill the earth's whole population. But he didn't create it, Heisenberg pleads."Because you couldn't," Margrethe challenges.

Heisenberg insists that he knew perfectly well how to make a bomb, he just didn't tell anyone, and he offers proof. In England, the evening after they heard about Hiroshima, Heisenberg told Otto Hahn in detail about how the bomb had worked, even the figure on the critical mass, and this conversation was recorded by hidden microphones. The one detail he had wrong, Heisenberg admits, was the weight of the critical mass—he told Hahn it would have been about a ton, whereas it was only 50 kilograms. Heisenberg hadn't made the calculation of the diffusion equation—he thought that had been done already, in 1939, but when he finally did it himself he found his mistake. Believing that the greater mass was required, it was "plainly unimagineable" for Heisenberg to make a bomb. The Americans used the correct solution to the diffusion equation provided by Frisch and Peierls, two German Jewish refugee physicists in England, and they made the bomb.

BOHR: So, Heisenberg, tell us one simple thing: why didn't you do the calculation?

HEISENBERG: The question is why Frisch and Peierls *did* do it. It was a stupid waste of time. However much 235 it turned out to be, it was obviously going to be more than anyone could imagine producing.

BOHR: Except that it wasn't!

HEISENBERG: Except that it wasn't.

BOHR: So why . . . ?

HEISENBERG: I don't know! I don't know why I didn't do it! Because I never thought of it! Because it didn't occur to me! Because I assumed it wasn't worth doing!

BOHR: Assumed? Assumed? You never assumed things! That's how you got uncertainty, because you rejected our assumptions! You calculated, Heisenberg! You calculated everything! The first thing you did with a problem was the mathematics!

HEISENBERG: You should have been there to slow me down.

BOHR: Yes, you wouldn't have got away with it if I'd been standing over you.

HEISENBERG: Though in fact you made exactly the same assumption! You thought there was no danger for exactly the same reason as I did! Why didn't *you* calculate it?

BOHR: Why didn't *I* calculate it?

HEISENBERG: Tell us why *you* didn't calculate it, and we'll know why *I* didn't.

BOHR: It's obvious why *I* didn't.

HEISENBERG: Go on.

MARGRETHE: Because he wasn't trying to build a bomb!

HEISENBERG: Yes. Thank you. Because he wasn't trying to build a bomb. I imagine it was the same with me. Because *I* wasn't trying to build a bomb. Thank you.

Once again the question is raised: Why did Heisenberg come to Copenhagen? They review the process of his arrival, their smiles at each other, their remarks about each other's family, skiing, Elsinore; then out for the stroll and their "moment of collision" over the possible development of nuclear energy, splitting them once again as partners and as friends. But this time Bohr has a second thought.

BOHR: Let's suppose for a moment that I don't go flying off into the night. Let's see what happens if instead I remember the paternal role I'm supposed to play. If I stop, and control my anger, and turn to him. And ask him why.

HEISENBERG: Why?

BOHR: Why are you confident that it's going to be so reassuringly difficult to build a bomb with 235? Is it because you've done the calculation?

HEISENBERG: The calculation?

BOHR: Of the diffusion in 235. No. It's because you haven't calculated it. You haven't considered calculating it. You hadn't consciously realized there was a calculation to be made.

HEISENBERG: And of course now I *have* realized. In fact, it wouldn't be all that difficult. Let's see . . . The scattering cross-section's about six by ten to the 24th power, so the mean free path would be . . . Hold on . . .

BOHR: And suddenly a very different and very terrible new world begins to take shape . . .

MARGRETHE: That was the last and greatest demand that Heisenberg made on his friendship with you. To be understood when he couldn't understand himself. And that was the last and greatest act of friendship for Heisenberg that you performed in return. To leave him misunderstood.

HEISENBERG: Yes. Perhaps I should thank you.

BOHR: Perhaps you should.

MARGRETHE: Anyway, it was the end of the story.

Bohr in his turn is grateful for Heisenberg's German Embassy connection. One of the men there tipped them off that the freighters were coming to take away 8,000 Jews. When the ships arrived, almost all of the Jewish population had been hidden away by the Danes in their homes and churches. And "a whole Armada" of fishing boats carried them across the sound to Sweden and safety. Ironically, Bohr wound up at Los Alamos and participated in a small way in the bombings of Japan, while Heisenberg has not a single life on his physicist's conscience, not even that of the prisoner he once guarded. He persuaded the others to let him go.

Heisenberg tells the others how, crossing defeated and despairing Germany on foot, he was nearly shot as a deserter by an SS man. His would-be killer was in the process of opening the holster of his pistol when Heisenberg, without thinking, like skiing, held out a package of Lucky Strikes.

HEISENBERG: He closes the holster and takes the cigarettes instead . . . It had worked, it had worked! Like all the other solutions to all the other problems. For twenty cigarettes he let me live. And on I went. Three days and three nights. Past the weeping children, the lost and hungry children, drafted to fight, then abandoned by their commanders. Past the starving slave-laborers walking home to France, to Poland, to Estonia. Through Gammertingen and Biberach and Memmingen, Mindelheim, Kaufbeuren and Schöngau. Across my beloved homeland. My ruined and dishonored and beloved homeland.

BOHR: My dear Heisenberg! My dear friend!

MARGRETHE: Silence. The silence we always in the end return to.

HEISENBERG: And of course I know what they're thinking about.

MARGRETHE: All those lost children on the road.

BOHR: Heisenberg wandering the world like a lost child himself.

MARGRETHE: Our own lost children.

HEISENBERG: And over goes the tiller once again.

BOHR: So near, so near! So slight a thing!

MARGRETHE: He stands in the doorway, watching me, then he turns his head away . . .

HEISENBERG: And once again away he goes, into the dark waters.

BOHR: Before we can lay our hands on anything, our life's over.

HEISENBERG: Before we can glimpse who or what we are, we're gone and laid to dust.

BOHR: Settled among all the dust we raised.

MARGRETHE: And sooner or later there will come a time when all our children are laid to dust, and all our children's children.

BOHR: When no more decisions, great or small, are ever made again. When there's no more uncertainty, because there's no more knowledge.

MARGRETHE: And when all our eyes are closed, when even the ghosts have gone, what will be left of our beloved world? Our ruined and dishonored and beloved world?

HEISENBERG: But in the meanwhile, in this most precious meanwhile, there it is. The trees in Faelled Park. Ganmmertingen and Biberach and Mindelheim. Our children and our children's children. Preserved, just possibly, by that one short moment in Copenhagen. By some event that will never quite be located or defined. By the final core of uncertainty at the heart of things.

Curtain.

Critics Award

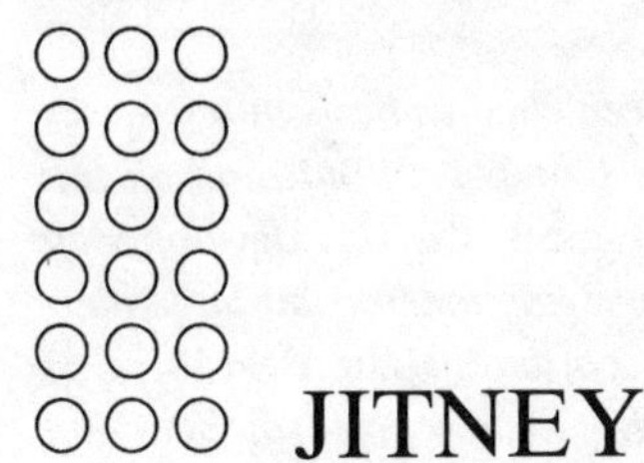

JITNEY

A Play in Two Acts

BY AUGUST WILSON

Cast and credits appear on page 246–247

AUGUST WILSON was born in 1945 in the Hill District of Pittsburgh, where his father worked as a baker and his mother determinedly introduced her son to the written word and had him reading at 4 years old. Despite his early acquaintance and continuing fascination with words, he didn't pursue a formal education, leaving Central Catholic High School before graduating. He can clearly remember when he began to approach writing as a profession: it was April 1, 1965. He had just earned $20 writing a term paper for his sister, and he bought a typewriter which, he remembers, "represented my total commitment" because it took every penny he had. Lacking bus fare, he carried it home.

Wilson started with poetry. By 1972 he was writing one-acts. His first production was the one-act Jitney, *staged in 1978 by Black Horizons Theater, a group which he himself had founded in 1968. This play, set in Pittsburgh's Hill District in 1977, rewritten as a full-length and produced June 14, 1996 at Pittsburgh Public Theater, won him an ATCA New Play Citation. In off-Broadway production this season on April 25 by Second Stage Theater in association with the Mark Taper Forum, under Marion McClinton's direction, it won the New York Drama Critics Circle Award as the year's best play. And it has a special added importance as the representative of the 1970s in Wilson's decade-by-decade chronicle of black America in the 20th century.*

The one-act version of Jitney *was repeated in 1982 by Allegheny Repertory Theater; meanwhile Wilson's* Black Bart and the Sacred Hill *was produced in 1981 by Penumbra Theater in St. Paul. Then came* Ma Rainey's Black Bottom. *After a staged reading at the O'Neill Theater Center in 1982 and production by Yale Repertory Theater April 3, 1984 (both organizations and the play itself directed by Lloyd Rich-*

ards), Ma Rainey *was brought to Broadway October 11, 1984 for 275 performances, its author's first full New York production, first Best Play, first Tony nominee and the winner of the Critics Award for best play.*

All seven of Wilson's New York productions have been cited as bests in our series of Best Plays *yearbooks, all figured prominently in the Critics citations, and all but the current* Jitney *were directed by Richards. Wilson's* Fences *was also developed at the O'Neill and premiered at Yale Rep April 25, 1985, receiving the first annual American Theater Critics Association New Play Award, as recorded in* The Best Plays of 1985–86. *It was produced on Broadway March 26, 1987 for 526 performances and carried off the Critics best-of-bests citation, the Pulitzer Prize and the Tony Awards for both play and direction. A year later,* Fences *was still running when Wilson's* Joe Turner's Come and Gone *opened on Broadway March 27, 1988 after previous stagings at Yale Rep and the Huntington Theater Company, Boston.* Joe Turner *won its author his third Best Play and third Critics Award for best-of-bests, playing 105 performances.*

During the 1987–88 season, Wilson's The Piano Lesson *received an O'Neill tryout, followed by a Goodman Theater, Chicago production cited by ATCA for its fourth New Play Award. It came to Broadway April 16, 1990 for a run of 329 performances, and in the course of its career it received its author's fourth Best Play citation, fourth Critics best-of-bests Award and second Pulitzer Prize. Wilson's* Two Trains Running *had already received the ATCA New Play Award after four regional theater productions when it arrived on Broadway April 13, 1992 for 160 performances, its author's fifth straight Best Play and Critics Award winner (for best American play).*

About the same time as its opening on Broadway March 28, 1996, Wilson's Seven Guitars *received an ATCA 1995 New Play Citation.* Seven Guitars *played 187 Broadway performances, made it an even half dozen Best Plays and Critics Awards (for best-of-bests) for Wilson. The seven full-length plays in its author's cycle about the lives of black Americans now represent their decades as follows:* Joe Turner *(the Teens),* Ma Rainey *(1920s),* Piano Lesson *(1930s),* Seven Guitars *(1940s),* Fences *(1950s),* Two Trains *(1960s) and now* Jitney *(1970s). And this season on December 15, the Pittsburgh Public Theater presented, in association with Seattle Repertory Theater, August Wilson's* King Hedley II *under Marion McClinton's direction. Its era? "The mid-1980s."*

Wilson is an alumnus of New Dramatists (which presented his The Mill Hand's Lunch Bucket *in staged readings in 1983 and 1984) and the Playwrights Center in Minneapolis. He is a Whiting Writers Award winner, a recipient of Bush, McKnight, Rockefeller and Guggenheim Fellowships and is a member of the American Academy of Arts and Sciences and the American Academy of Arts and Letters. He is married to the costume designer Constanza Romero, has one daughter and makes his home in Seattle.*

Like all the other synopses of August Wilson plays in the Best Plays *series, this synopsis of* Jitney *was prepared by Sally Dixon Wiener.*

Time: 1977

Place: Pittsburgh's Hill District

ACT I

Scene 1

SYNOPSIS: The setting is a gypsy cab station. Upstage through a large window area we see the rundown neighborhood in which it's located. The station and the buildings across the street, some of them boarded up, reflect the urban decay. Above and beyond is the sad and sooty aerial tangle of the industrial skyline of a steel mill city.Three big old ramshackle cars are parked on the uphill street outside the upstage door of the station, the only suggestion that anything is going anywhere else except downhill in this part of town—including the station itself. *"The paint is peeling off the walls, and the floor is covered with linoleum that is worn through in several areas."*

The door, upstage right, is flanked on the right by a coat rack, on the left by a blackboard. At stage right are a potbellied stove and a refuse container, at stage left a pay phone mounted on a square structural element, an ancient upholstered couch and a filing cabinet with an old-fashioned radio atop it. Upstage left a window seat runs the length of the big picture window. Downstage center is a small table with a checkerboard and unmatched chairs.

As the play begins, it is mid-morning on an early fall day, and Youngblood (whose real name is Darnell Williams), 24, a nice looking, feisty young man given to wearing a big leather cap, is playing checkers with Turnbo, 57, a lighter-skinned, baldish, stocky middle-aged man, querulous by nature. Seated nearby is Fielding, 49, tall and lean, his suit draped loosely on his lanky body, his ever-askew tie a bright flowered signal of distress.

Youngblood and Turnbo are arguing as they play, Youngblood claiming he was the checkers champ of 'Nam. Fielding, who has been ferreting about under a cushion for his bottle and finding it empty, interrupts them, trying unsuccessfully to borrow four dollars. The phone rings—a customer wants to book a ride with this jitney service. Fielding takes the job, telling the customer that a ride to East Liberty will be four dollars, despite what others may charge, and that he'll be right there.

Doub, 53, a tall, laid-back man in a plaid shirt, wearing glasses, comes in as Fielding hangs up. Fielding asks Doub for four dollars, saying he needs it for gas to make the run to East Liberty. Doub gives it to him reluctantly, telling Fielding it's the only time in his life he's to ask him—and he should pay the money back, too. After Fielding leaves, Turnbo insists Fielding will just go spend it on liquor.

There's another call for car service, to pick somebody up at a market. It's Youngblood's turn, but he won't take the job—he doesn't want his car messed up carrying groceries. Turnbo takes it.

Shealy, 43, a nice-enough-looking man in a silky-looking suit and a hat, comes in to use the phone to take bets on the numbers. Doub has seen one of Shealy's customers, Big Ben, who owns a restaurant, with a new Buick Riviera, and Doub wonders how much Big Ben hit the numbers for. Shealy isn't about to "be putting nobody's business on the street" and claims he knows nothing about that. He does know Big Ben is closing his restaurant, though. The city's going to tear down the building.

Shealy remembers a "lttle yellow gal" who used to work for Big Ben and who almost lifted the curse that he thinks a woman named Rosie put on him. Rosie didn't want him to have any other other woman, but she didn't want him.

SHEALY: She say, you a poor man. What I need with a poor man? I told her say if I make a hundred I'll give you ninety-nine. She didn't trust me on that one, but I went down to the crap game, I hit six quick licks, left with a hundred and sixty-three dollars. I went back up there. She let me in. I lay a hundred dollars down on the table and told her, now, if I can just get one of them back I'd be satisfied. She reached down and handed me a dollar, and I went on in the room and went to bed. I got up and she had my breakfast on the table. It wasn't soon long that ninety-nine dollars ran out, and next thing I knew she had barred the door. I went on and left, but I never could get her off my mind. I said I was gonna find me another woman. But every time I get hold to one . . . time I lay down with them . . . I see her face. I told myself the first time I lay down with a woman and don't see her face then that be the one I'm gonna marry. That be my little test. Now with that old yellow gal used to work down at Ben's I seen Rosie's face . . . but it was blurry. Like a cloud of something come over it. I say, "I got to try this again. Maybe next time I won't see nothing." She told me she didn't want to see me no more. She told me come back same time tomorrow, and if she changed her mind she'd leave the key in the mailbox. I went up there, and there was one man in the house and two others sitting on the doorstep. I don't know who had the key.

Shealy and Doub discuss the scheduled release from the penitentiary next month of a young man, the son of Becker, the boss of this station. The phone rings, and Doub leaves to take on a job, but not before putting down a dollar on a number with Shealy.

Philmore, in his 40s, unpretentious except for a mustache—six years working at a hotel, never missed a day, never late, due for a raise—comes in, *"obviously drunk."* He's been out all night and must get home: "My old lady gonna be mad at me." Youngblood comes in and agrees to take Philmore home. Philmore *"builds a pyramid out of dollar bills then blows them over."* He tells Youngblood, "Now when my old lady tells me I been out blowing my money . . . you can tell her it's the truth." The two go off.

Then phone rings, and Shealy takes a message for Becker from a Mr. Pease of the Pittsburgh Renewal Council.

TURNBO *(enters):* Boy, I don't know what this world's coming to. You know McNeil, don't you?

SHEALY: Who?

TURNBO: McNeil. McNeil what live up on Webster. Old lady McNeil, got them two boys and work cleaning up down at the courthouse.

SHEALY: *(trying to recognize the name):* McNeil? I don't know . . .

TURNBO *(agitated):* You know who I'm talking about. McNeil! Use to be Brownie's old lady. You know Brownie was staying up there trying to help her raise them two boys. One of them got an old funny shaped head.

SHEALY: Oh, yeah. Yeah, I know who you talking about now.

TURNBO: Well, the boy come by here a little while ago this morning. The oldest one, can't be no more than sixteen or seventeen at the most. Come by here and asked me to carry him on a trip to the Northside. Then he say he got to make a stop up on Whiteside Road. I carried him up there and he go into one of these houses and come out carrying a television. He ain't said nothing about no television now. I told him it was gonna cost him two dollars more for me to be hauling around a television. Had me carry him over on the Northside to the pawnshop. Now, I know the boy done stole the television, but I ain't said nothing. I just want my money. Come on back and stopped at Pat's Place to get me some tobacco, and the fellows standing around just happened to mention the name of this woman who done had her television stolen. Don't you know that boy done went and stole his grandmama's television! Name is Bolger. Miss Sarah Bolger. That's old lady McNeil's mother. I used to carry her to church before she got too old to go. Steal his own grandmother's television!

Becker comes on—a large heavy-set man in a hat and a blue jacket, a man of great presence, and we don't need to be told he's the boss. (Among his posted rules: "No Overcharging, Keep Car Clean, No Drinking, Be Courteous.") Turnbo tries a replay of his McNeil saga, but Becker cuts him off.

Becker gives Shealy his wife Lucille's number bets and agrees to try to find a job down at the mill, where he has some influence, for Shealy's nephew who is "trying to make something of himself." After Shealy leaves, Turnbo starts badmouthing the nephew as "a thug," but Becker cuts him off again with, "You just like an old lady, always gossiping and running off at the mouth."

The phone rings for another job, which Becker takes and exits, as Doub and Youngblood enter.

YOUNGBLOOD: Cigar Annie standing up there in the middle of Robert Street cussing out everybody.

DOUB: Oh, yeah. Who she mad at now?

YOUNGBLOOD: She started with God and went on down the list. She cussing out the mayor, Doc Goldblum, Mr. Eli, her landlord, the light man, gas man, telephone man, and everybody else she can think of. They got her furniture and everything sitting out on the sidewalk.

JITNEY—Paul Butler as Becker in August Wilson's play

TURNBO: I knew it was gonna come to that. Everbody else done move out of that place two months ago. The building has been condemned for two years.

YOUNGBLOOD: She standing up there in the middle of the street raising up her dress.

TURNBO: I bet she ain't got no draws on.

YOUNGBLOOD: She had traffic back up . . . almost got hit by a milk truck . . . the cars trying to go around her, but she won't let them. Standing there just throwing up her dress.

TURNBO: I don't know what she doing that for. She ain't got nothing nobody want. Now if Pearline get out there and raise up her dress . . . that be another thing. You have a riot on your hands. They ought to put Cigar Annie in Mayview.

DOUB: Ain't nothing wrong with Cigar Annie. They had her down in Mayview two or three times. They figure anybody cuss out God and don't care who's listening got to be crazy. They found out she got more sense than they do. That's why they let her go. She raising up her dress cause that's all anybody wanted from her since she was twelve years old. She say if that's all you want . . . here it is.

TURNBO: She sending out an S.O.S. That's what she's doing.

DOUB: Turnbo. I don't know why I try and talk with you. Next time remind me to shut up.

Youngblood asks if Peaches has come by (she hasn't) and leaves word with Doub to tell her he'll be at at Clifford's. Turnbo asks Youngblood to bring him back some coffee, but Youngblood tells him, "I ain't your slave. Walk over and get you own coffee" and exits.

Turnbo starts on Youngblood who he believes is "messing around" with Peaches, the sister of the woman Youngblood lives with and who has borne his child. Turnbo has seen them riding around in Youngblood's car. Doub warns Turnbo to stop putting his nose in everybody else's business, but Turnbo defends his right to express his opinions like anybody else: "I just talk what I know."

Turnbo gets a call and takes a job, as Youngblood returns, bringing him coffee and asks him for thirty cents. On his way out, Turnbo tells him, "You told me to get my own. How you know I ain't sent somebody else?"

The phone rings again. Youngblood answers "Car service," and then tells the caller, "I thought you was going down to the furniture store with me . . . . . Naw, I ain't told her. I'm gonna wait till everything's settled. What time you gonna be done? All right, I'll pick you up at three o'clock." He hangs up and dials again, asking a Mr. Harper about a house he's trying to buy under the G.I. Bill. He's made a down payment, but he has to come up with some more for the title search, which will take about two weeks. Youngblood promises, "I'll have it for you tomorrow," and hangs up. *"He takes out his notebook, looking to see how much money he has. It is obvious he does not have enough. He sits thinking when suddenly an idea occurs to him. He gets up and exits. The lights go down on the scene."*

Scene 2

It is early afternoon. Becker and Turnbo are in the station when Youngblood comes in, immediately demanding his thirty cents for the coffee, which is still standing there on the stove. Turnbo hasn't touched the coffee and refuses to pay for it.

BECKER: Give the man his money, Turnbo.
TURNBO: I ain't giving him nothing.
BECKER: I ain't gonna have that dissension in here. Give the man his money!
TURNBO *(goes into his poket):* Here. Here's your thirty cents.
He throws it on the floor. Youngblood crosses and stands over Turnbo, angry.
YOUNGBLOOD: Pick it up!
TURNBO: It's yours. You pick it up.
YOUNGBLOOD: I ain't throw it down there.
TURNBO: Well, let it lay there then. I'm through with it.
Turnbo goes back to reading his magazine. Youngblood backs off.
YOUNGBLOOD: Well, let it lay there then. But before this day is over you gonna pick up my thirty cents.
TURNBO *(suddenly jumps up and picks up the money):* Here! Here! Here's your thirty cents. You satisfied?
They stare at each other for a beat.

The phone rings—it's Youngblood's turn to take the job, and he leaves. Becker goes out to pick up groceries. The next phone call, answered by Turnbo, is Peaches, who wants Youngblood to pick her up at four o'clock instead of three. As Turnbo hangs up, Rena, 21, Youngblood's girl friend and Peaches's sister, comes in. She is a very pretty, attractively dressed and confident young woman. Turnbo assures her Youngblood won't be long and asks after their child, Jesse, who is now two going on three. Turnbo remembers Rena as a child, observing that her mother should be proud of the way she raised Rena. He goes on about the value of self-respect and respect for others, and about his own grandmother who taught him always to tell the truth.

TURNBO: Now I ain't trying to get in you business or nothing. Like I say, I just live and let live. But some things just come up on you wrong, and you have to say something about it, otherwise it throw your whole life off balance. I know you don't want to hear this . . . but you don't need no hot-headed young boy like Youngblood. What you need is somebody level-headed who know how to respect and appreciate a woman . . . I can see the kind of woman you is. You ain't the kind of woman for Youngblood, and he ain't the kind of man for you. You need a more mature . . . responsible man.

RENA: I don't think so.

TURNBO: You just wait awhile. You'll see that I'm right. I done seen many a young girl wake up when it's too late. Don't you be like that. You go on and find yourself a man that know how to treat you. You don't need nobody run the streets all hours of the day and night. You ain't that kind of woman.

RENA: Darnell don't run the streets. I don't know what you talking about.

TURNBO: Oh, I see him . . . running around with other women. I see him with your sister all the time.

The phone rings but Turnbo ignores it, telling her he's saying this for her own good. Rena leaves, and Turnbo answers the phone—it's Becker's wife Lucille, and Turnbo takes her message. Doub comes back and so does Youngblood, immediately followed by Rena. The phone rings again, and Doub insists it's Turnbo's turn to make a trip, so Turnbo goes off.

Doub exits too, leaving the young couple alone in the office. Youngblood doesn't seem pleased to see her—he doesn't like her "coming by his work." Rena in her turn complains that she's working very had to make a go of their relationship, to hold down a restaurant job and to take care of their little son Jesse.

RENA: Now, I come home from work I got to go to the store I go upstairs and look in the drawer and the food money is gone. Now you explain that to me. There was eighty dollars in the drawer that ain't in there now.

YOUNGBLOOD: I needed it. I'm gonna put it back.

RENA: What you need it for? You tell me. What's more important than me and Jesse eating?

YOUNGBLOOD: I had to pay a debt. I'm gonna put it back.

RENA: You know I don't touch the grocery money. Whatever happens, we got to eat. If I need clothes . . . I do without. My little personal stuff . . . I do without. If I ain't got no electricity . . . I do without . . . but I don't never touch the grocery money. Cause I'm not gonna be that irresponsible to my child. Cause he depend on me. I'm not going to be that irresponsible to my family. I ain't gonna be like that. Jesse gonna have a chance at life. He ain't going to school hungry cause I spent the grocery money on some nail polish or some Afro Sheen. He ain't gonna be laying up in the bed hungry and unable to sleep cause his daddy took the grocery money to pay a debt.

YOUNGBLOOD: Aw, woman, I try and do what's right and this is what I get.

RENA: You know what you be doing better than I, but whatever it is ain't enough.

He assures her he'll put the money back, but that isn't all that's bothering Rena. He's never home any more, he's out half the night. If the UPS says he's to work from 2 a.m. to 6 a.m., what can he do? Youngblood asks. He told her it would be that way. She hasn't seen any UPS money, though. He has debts to pay, and he pleads, "Hang with me a while."

And Rena wants him to know that she isn't a fool. She knows he's been with Peaches, "Doing whatever you be doing." Youngblood demands to know who told her such a thing. Rena insists she knows her sister well enough to know when Peaches is hiding something from her. "Ain't no need in you bothering to come home cause I just might not be there when you get there," Rena says as she exits. *"Youngblood starts to go after her, changes his mind and comes back . . . . . he takes his notebook from his pocket and throws it on the floor . . . . . regains his composure, picks up the book and exits."*

Becker comes in as the phone is ringing. It's someone asking for Shealy. He doesn't work here, Becker barks, slamming down the receiver. Doub comes in, upset that Clifford, next door, says his place is to be boarded up next month. Becker admits to knowing that, the "man from the city" came by two weeks ago. The whole block's going to be torn down. Doub is shocked that Becker hasn't told them. He's got rent to pay, and doctor bills. Everyone here counts on the station for their livelihood. What will they do in the two weeks they still have? Doub wonders.

BECKER: I don't know. I kinda figured we'd all just go in together somewhere else. Find another place. But I don't know now. I'm just tired, Doub. Can't hardly explain it none. You look up one day, and all you got left is what you ain't spent. Everyday cost you something, and you don't all the time realize it. I used to question God about everything. Why He hardened Pharaoh's heart? Why He let Jacob steal his brother's birthright? After Coreen died I told myself I wasn't gonna ask no more questions. Cause the answers didn't matter. They didn't matter right then. I thought that would change, but it never did. It still don't matter after all these years. It don't look like it's never gonna matter. I'm tired of waiting for God to decide whether he want to hold my hand. I been running cars out of here for eighteen years, and I think I'm just tired of driving.

DOUB: I been with you for twelve of them eighteen years, and I would have thought you would have told me we was gonna have to move cause they board up the station.

BECKER: I'm telling you now.

DOUB: That ain't what I mean. Becker. It's like you just a shadow of yourself. The station done gone downhill. Some people overcharge. Some people don't haul. Fielding stay drunk. I just watch you, and you don't do nothing.

BECKER: What's to be done? I try to keep cars running out of here and keep everybody happy. I post the rates up on the board. If somebody charge extra and people complain, I give them the difference and tell the driver about it. I ain't gonna put nobody out unless they totally irresponsible. As for Fielding, I don't let him drink in here, but I can't tell the man about his personal business unless people start to complain.

DOUB: Complain? Hell, they don't do no complaining. They just call somebody else. Somebody ask them for a number, they don't give them Court One-Nine-Eight-Oh-Two. They give them somebody else's number. Complain? You think they're gonna call you up and complain? Nigger, they don't even know you're alive.

BECKER: I just do the best I can do.

DOUB: Sometime your best ain't enough.

When Turnbo comes in, Doub tells him the station's going to be boarded up. Turnbo wonders if Becker is going to quit. He hasn't said he was quitting, Becker announces, he was only thinking about it. Doub suggests they all hold a meeting.

A phone call for Becker is from his wife Lucille telling him someone's called to inform him that his son, who was to have been released from the penitentiary next month, is being released sooner. Becker hangs up the receiver and tells Doub and Turnbo, "My boy's getting out tomorrow," as the scene's lights go down.

Scene 3

"*The lights come up on the jitney station early the following morning. It's obvious Youngblood has spent the night there. He is sitting on the couch figuring in his notebook,*" when Turnbo arrives and finds that Youngblood knows nothing of Becker's son, who today is getting out of the penitentiary down at Western State, where he's been for twenty years. Becker has never once gone to see his son, which Turnbo thinks is shameful. That's Becker's business, Youngblood opines. Turnbo goes on to explain that Becker's son was sentenced to die in the electric chair—a sentence later commuted—and it killed his mother, Becker's first wife. She came home, was put to bed and stayed there till she died a month later.

YOUNGBLOOD: What he do to get the electric chair?

TURNBBO: See, Becker's boy . . . Clarence is his name but everybody call him Booster . . . See now, Booster he liked that science. You know the science fair that they have over at the Buhel Planetarium every year where they have all them science experiments where they make the water run uphill and things like that? Booster won first place three years in a row. He the only one who ever did that. I can't even count how many times he had his picture in the paper. They let him in to the University of Pittsburgh. You know back then they didn't have too many colored out there, but they was trying to catch up to the Russians, and they didn't care if he was colored or not. Gave him a scholarship and everything. Becker was just as proud as he could be. Him and Booster was always close. Becker used to take him hunting down around Wheeling, West Virginia. They go hunting and fishing. Becker didn't have but the one boy. After he was born the doctor told his wife that if she had another one it was liable to kill her. Say she was lucky to have the one. Anyway, Booster goes out to Pitt there, and he meets this old white gal. Young gal . . . about eighteen, she was. Of course Booster wasn't about nineteen himself. Now, her old man was some kind of big shot down there at Gulf Oil. Had a lot of money and had done bought the gal a car for her birthday. Booster and that gal . . . they just go everywhere together. She ride him around like she was his chauffeur. Of course, she let him drive it too. I believe he drove it more than she did. That gal was crazy about Booster, and they was just sneaking around and sneaking around, you know. She didn't want her daddy to know she was fooling around with no colored boy. Well, one day, see, her father was up here in the neighborhood looking for one of them whores. He find one, and she tell him to drive up the dead end street there by the school, so she can turn the trick in the car. Don't you know they pulled right up in back of this gal's car where her and Booster done went to fool around! Her father recognizes the car, and he goes over and looks inside, and there's Booster just banging the hell out of his daughter! Well, that cracker went crazy. He just couldn't stand the sight of Booster screwing that gal and went to yanking open the car door. Booster didn't know who he was. All he knew was some crazy white man done opened the door and was screaming his head off. He proceeded to beat the man half to death. To get to the short of it . . . the police came, and the gal said that she was driving downtown on her way home from a movie, and when she stopped for a red light Booster jumped into her car and made her drive up there on the dead end street . . . where he raped her. They arrested Booster, and Becker got him out on bail cause he knew the gal was lying. The first day he was out . . . the first day! . . . he went over to that gal's house and shot her dead right on the front porch.

YOUNGBLOOD: Served the bitch right!

TURNBO: What you talking about! I knew you ain't had no sense. I don't know why I try and talk to you.

YOUNGBLOOD: Served her right for lying!

Turnbo argues that lying isn't any cause to kill someone. She lied, Youngblood reiterates. Then Youngblood's girl has a right to kill Youngblood (Turnbo scoffs) because he's been lying to her—everyone knows that Youngblood's business is "in the street" and how he treats Rena, tied up in the house with the baby while he runs around with her sister. *"Youngblood, enraged, rushes Turnbo and grabs him in the collar."* Words continue to fly, and Youngblood, unable to restrain himself, hits Turnbo in the mouth, knocking him to the floor and drawing blood.

Becker comes in, restrains Youngblood, sends Turnbo out and calms things down. But Turnbo soon returns with a pistol, which he points menacingly at Youngblood, telling him, "You don't believe that your business is in the street. I'll tell you something else. I done had that gal of yours." Youngblood, furious, knows that Turnbo is lying, and so does Becker. Turnbo cocks the pistol meaningfully, but Becker finally persuades him to put the gun back in his pocket and leave the room.

Becker warns Youngblood to stay away from Turnbo, he keeps that pistol in his car, and some day he'll use it. There's a call from somebody wanting to go to the bus station, but Youngblood doesn't want suitcases in his car. Fielding comes in and offers to make the trip, but Becker insists Youngblood go, and he does.

Turnbo comes back, still haranguing. Becker sees that Fielding is drunk and socks it to him: Fielding has done his last run from this station. Fielding argues that he's paid his monthly dues, and the month isn't up. Becker takes out some money to pay him off, but Fielding refuses to take it. Becker puts the money on the stove and leaves to take the trip to the bus station, warning Fielding to be gone when he returns. Fielding hollers after him that it's a free country, that he's a free man, and he takes another drink. *"The lights fade to black."*

Scene 4

In the jitney station half an hour later, Booster, 39, a handsome, clean-cut young man, has arrived, wearing his black prison-issued suit and a white shirt.

Fielding, still drinking, offers the bottle to Booster, who declines it. He assures Booster his father will be back shortly. Turnbo brings Booster up to date on the station: they're going to board it up, tear it down. The jitney service will have to move or split up.

Fielding launches into the details of a dream he had about the wife he has been separated from for 22 years. He climbed a ladder to heaven until he could see all the saints sitting around with his wife, in glory. He began to lose his hold on the ladder, and she was the only one who rose from her place and tried to keep him from falling. Fielding judges that this means she still loves him.

Fielding is having another drink when Becker comes on, glaring at him. Fielding somehow gets to his feet, announcing, "You win. I'm gone." But instead of taking his money, he begs to work the two weeks until the month is over. Becker relents and sends him home, warning him to come in sober the next day.

Becker than faces Booster, who greets him and extends his hand. *"Becker takes it awkwardly"* and returns the greeting, remarking that Booster looks well. Becker sends Turnbo next door to Clifford's for a fish sandwich, then asks his son if he's doing all right. He'll need time to accustom himself to all the commotion: "People going everywhere . . . . . Dogs and cats. Airplanes." Becker wonders what Booster will do with the remainder of his life, "Now that you done ruined it." He won't be able to get a job—nobody will hire him, he's got "a mark on him a foot wide." Booster doesn't want to hear this. He feels that he's paid his debt to society.

BECKER: You don't even know where your debt begins.

BOOSTER: I know where it ended. It ended after I did that twenty years. I don't owe nobody nothing. They tried to give me that parole five years ago, and I turned it down because I didn't want to owe nobody nothing. I didn't want nobody looking after me telling me what to do . . . asking me questions about my life. I walk in here to say hi, and you start telling me my life is ruined. How I'm gonna get a job . . . I don't want that, Pop. I'm a grown man, I'm thirty-nine years old. I'm young. I'm healthy. I ain't got no complaints . . . and I don't carry no grudges. Whatever was between us these twenty years I put aside, I don't hold no grudge.

BECKER: Who the hell care what you hold. I'm the one got to walk around here with people pointing at me. Talking about me behind my back. "There go his father. That's him." People trying to sneak a look at me out the corner of their eye. See if they can see something wrong with me. If they can see what kind of man would raise a boy to do something like that. You done marked me, and you walk in here talking about you ain't got no grudge!

BOOSTER: I'm just saying I don't have no hard feeling that you didn't come to see me, Pop. I been thinking about my life and all the things you did for me . . . all the things you gave me . . . all the things you taught me. All the things . . .

BECKER: Everything I give you . . . you threw away. You ain't got nothing now. You got less than the day you was born. Then you had some dignity. Some innocence. You ain't got nothing now . . . . .

Booster admits he might have lost some things, but that doesn't mean he doesn't have anything—and while they're on that subject, he asks his father what *he's* got. Becker sums up: he's a deacon at the church, boss of the jitney station, owns a house, has a pension for 27 years' work at the mill, and he's got respect. What he doesn't have is a son who does him honor, only a son that people point at, saying, "That's Becker's boy . . . the one that killed that gal . . . . . The one they gave the electric chair."

Booster declares he did what he had to do and has paid for it. Becker insists they could have fought the girl's lie—he'd already arranged for a lawyer. But a lawyer wouldn't have made any difference to Booster. He was not about to go to the penitentiary for nothing: "I wasn't gonna live a lie." And sometimes, he insists, two wrongs *do* make a right. "Sometime you got to add it up that way. Otherwise, it's just one wrong after another and you never get to what's right. I wasn't gonna hang no sign around my neck say 'rapist.' " Being called a murderer may be worse, but at least it's honest. Booster agrees that he learned from his father to respect life and hold it precious, but there were other things he learned on his own, such as the time the landlord, Mr. Rand, came around to collect the rent, which was two months behind because Becker had to help pay for Grandma Ada's funeral.

BOOSTER: I don't know if you knew it, Pop, but you were a big man. Everywhere you went people treated you like a big man. You used to take me to the barbershop with you. You'd walk in there and fill up the whole place. Everybody would stop cussing because Jim Becker had walked in. I would just look at you and wonder how you could be that big. I wanted to be like that. I would go to school and try to make myself feel big. But I never could. I told myself that's okay . . . when I get grown I'm gonna be big like that. Walk into the barbershop and have everybody stop and look at me. That day when Mr. Rand came to the house it was snowing. You came out on the porch, and he started shouting and cussing and threatening to put us out on the street where we belonged. I was waiting for you to tell him to shut up . . . to get off your porch. But you just looked at him and promised you would have the money next month. Mama came to the door, and Mr. Rand kept shouting and cussing. I looked at Mama . . . she was trying to get me to go in the house . . . and I looked at you . . . and you had got smaller. The longer he shouted, the smaller you got. When we went back to the barbershop you didn't seem so big no more. You was the same size as everybody else. You was just another man in the barbershop. That's when I told myself if I ever got big I wouldn't let nothing make me small. Then when I met Susan McKnight and found out her daddy was the vice president of Gulf Oil . . . that's when I got big. That made me a big man. I felt like I was somebody. I felt like I could walk in the barbershop and fill it up the way you did. Then when she told that lie on me, that's when I woke up. That's when I realized that I wasn't big from the inside. I wasn't big on my own. When she told that lie it made me small. I wanted to do something that said I wasn't just another nigger . . . that I was Clarence Becker. I wanted to make them remember my name. And I thought about you standing there and getting small and Mr. Rand shouting and Susan McKnight shouting out that lie, and I realized it was my chance to make the Beckers big again . . . my chance to show what I had learned on my own. I thought you would understand. I thought you would be proud of me.

BECKER: Proud of you for killing somebody!

BOOSTER: No, Pop. For being a warrior. For dealing with the world in ways that you didn't or couldn't or wouldn't.

Becker demands to know if it's his fault Booster pulled the trigger, for not knocking Mr. Rand on his ass. And did Booster's pulling the trigger knock Mr. Rand on his ass for him? No, Booster admits, he did it for himself, and he now realizes he was wrong. He and his father each made their own choices and now must accept the consequences of those choices, Booster says, starting to leave.

Before Booster goes, Becker wants him to know why he never visited him in prison. Becker kept seeing how Booster's face looked at his mother's funeral, how Booster never shed a tear. And he didn't go after Mr. Rand that day because he had to keep a roof over Booster's head as well as clothe him for school and supply lunch money. He did what he had to do, swallowing his pride but thinking to himself, "You bastards got it coming. Look out! Becker's boy's coming to straighten this shit out . . . . . Becker's taking this ass whipping so his boy can stride through this shit like Daniel in the lion's den. Watch out for Becker's boy!" And what did he get? Becker asks, nearly in tears. A murderer, a double murderer, because Booster caused his mother's death. She took to her bed after the sentencing and died 23 days later.

Booster in his turn accuses his father of letting his mother suffer through the courtroom procedings alone, without his "shoulder to cry on." Once, when she fainted, there was no one to help her because Booster was restrained by the deputies.

BOOSTER: You turned your back. Clinging to your rules . . .
BECKER: Don't you say nothing to me about turning my back!
BOOSTER: What you call it?
BECKER: I was there! I was holding her hand when she died. Where was you? Locked up in a cage like some animal. That's what killed her. To hear the judge say that the life she brought into the world was unfit to live. That you be "remanded to the custody of the Commissioner of Corrections at Western State Penitentiary and there to be executed in the electric chair. This order to be carried out thirty days from today." Ain't that what the judge said? Ain't that what she heard? "This order to be carried out thirty days from today." That's what killed her. She didn't want to live them thirty days. She didn't want to be alive to hear on the eleven o'clock news that they had killed you. So don't you say nothing to me about turning my back when I nursed that woman, talked to her, held her hand, prayed over her, and the last words to come out of her mouth was your name. I was there! Where were you, Mr. Murderer? Mr. Unfit to Live Amongst Society. Where were you when your mama was dying and calling your name? You are my son. I helped to bring you into this world. But from this moment on . . . I'm calling the deal off. You ain't nothing to me, boy. You just another nigger on the street. *"Becker exits. Booster stands looking down at the floor. The phone rings. The lights go down to black. Curtain."*

ACT II

Scene 1

In the jitney station the next day, Turnbo and Doub are discussing who is the prettier, Lena Horne or Sarah Vaughan. Fielding comes in, and soon they are all in agreement that women and money are the most dangerous things on earth: "Women and money will get a preacher killed," Doub observes.

Turnbo agrees and goes on, "The first thing a man do when he get a woman, he don't want nobody else to have her. He say this is mine. I'm gonna hold on to this. I'm gonna go over and see Betty Jean but I'm gonna hold on to this. If I catch anybody sneaking around her, sniffing . . . I'm gonna bust his nose and break both of his legs . . . if I don't shoot him with my 44. He say that, and then he go on over to Betty Jean. He don't know some fella done said the same thing about catching somebody around Betty Jean. That fellow . . . he go over to see Betty Sue while this other fellow sniffing around his Betty Jean. Sooner or later . . . somebody gonna get their wires crossed. Somebody gonna see Betty Sue when he should have been seeing Betty Jean, and that'll be all she wrote for him. The only thing left to do is write it on the tombstone: 'Here lie Bubba Boo. Was caught with Betty Jean instead of Betty Sue.' " Doub comments, "They got that on a whole lot of tombstones."

Turnbo and Fielding go out on calls. Youngblood comes in, upset about the station closing, complaining that white folks' sense of timing is bad, boarding up the station just when he's planning to buy a house. White folks don't know Youngblood is alive, Doub remarks, but Youngblood reminds him that they knew he was alive when they sent him to Vietnam. Doub joined the Army in 1950, hoping to make something of himself. He was sent to Korea, and three days later he was out on the front being told to stack the dead bodies six high. "Not five. Not seven. Six high." He did that for nine months, and it took him six of those to be able to keep his supper down. The Army never taught him to do anything else.

Doub thinks Youngblood should be doing something else besides driving a jitney. Youngblood agrees, but how else could he earn 50 tax-free dollars a day? Doub feels that Youngblood should get some schooling under the G.I. Bill and become anything he wants. The world isn't as limited now as it was when Doub was young. Menial jobs were all he could get. It's the present Youngblood is worrying about, getting some furniture and paying the mortgage, and Doub suggests that Becker might help him get a job at the mill. But Youngblood wants none of that. "It ain't all the time what you want," Doub counsels him. "Sometimes it's what you need. Black folks always get the two confused."

Fielding comes back and brings up the subject of the confrontation between Youngblood and Turnbo. Doub is distressed to hear this and warns them that Turnbo has pulled that gun on somebody four or five times before and is going to end up killing someone. Turnbo comes in and senses they've been talking about him. Doub admits it and advises him, "You gonna pull that gun on the wrong person one of these days." Doub leaves word for Becker that a man named Glucker from the steel mill called him, then exits.

Turnbo tells Fielding he has a job lined up when the station closes. He asks Youngblood what he's going to do, but Youngblood refuses to talk to him. Fielding goes out on a job. Shealy comes in expecting a call from some woman, and he is soon followed by Booster, who gives Shealy a bet on the numbers. Booster asks the others to tell his father he came by to see him, then exits. Youngblood goes to get a cup of coffee. Shealy gets his call from the woman and books Turnbo to take him to his rendezvous, promising, "This might be the one. If I don't see Rosie's face, I'll give you five dollars for the trip."

Youngblood comes back and is figuring in his book when Rena enters. They are very cool to each other, Rena wanting to know where he spent the night. He slept here, and why would be go home, since she told him she might not be there? He accuses her of jumping to conclusions, and she tells him she wants someone to share things with her, not hide them from her. If she wants to know what he was hiding from her, he'll tell her: He's been working day and night, not running the street, trying to earn money to buy a house so she and Jesse will have a decent place to live. He'd asked her sister Peaches to look at houses with him so he could surprise Rena. He wanted to pull a truck up in front of a house out in Penn Hills and say,

Russell Hornsby as Youngblood and Michole Briana White as Rena in *Jitney*

"This is yours. This is your house, baby." That's why Turnbo saw Peaches in his car. He found the house and was $150 short of closing the deal. That's why he took the $80.

Rena is utterly appalled that he bought a house without her, a house she hasn't even picked out! Youngblood describes it as "real nice. It's all on one floor . . . its got a basement . . . like a little den. We can put the TV down there."

She's sure to like it. He's bought a den for himself, to watch football, Rena decides, but what about closet space? windows? kitchen and bathroom? playing space for Jesse? washer-dryer hookup? and where is the school? He ought to know what's important to her—meanwhile, the food money is gone. If he had told her, they could have gotten $80 from her mother. He did a right thing, but he's done it all wrong. No matter what he does, Youngblood believes, she's going to jump to conclusions, and it will come out wrong to her.

YOUNGBLOOD: You can't look and see that I quit going to parties all the time . . . that I quit running with Ba Bra and Earl . . . that I quit chasing women. You just look at me and see the old Darnell. If you can't change the way you look at me . . . then I may as well surrender now. I can't beat your memory of who I was if you can't see I've changed. I go out here and work like a dog to try and do something nice for you, and no matter what I do, I can't never do it right cause all you see is the way I used to be. You don't see the new Darnell. You don't see I've changed.

RENA: I know people change . . . but I know they can slip back too.

YOUNGBLOOD: No, Rena . . . people believe what they want to believe . . . what they set up in their mind to believe. I know what it looked like when I was gone all the time and not bringing home any money. But you could have noticed that I was tired . . . you could have said Darnell ain't talking too much cause he's tired. You could have noticed that I didn't act like somebody running the streets . . . that I didn't come home smelling like alcohol and perfume . . . that I didn't dress like somebody running the streets. If you had thought it all the way through, you could have noticed how excited I was when I got the UPS job . . . how I asked you if I could take it . . . you would have noticed how I was planning things . . . that I wasn't sitting around drinking beer and playing cards . . . how I would get up early on Sunday and go out to the airport to try to make a few extra dollars before the jitney station opened. But you ain't seen all that. You ain't seen the new Darnell. You still working off your memory. But the past is over and done with. I'm thinking about the future. You not the only one who thinks about Jesse. That's why I'm trying to do something different. That's why I'm trying to buy a house. Maybe I should have told you about the house. Maybe I did do it wrong. But I done it. I tried to show you I loved you, but what I get for it?

RENA: Okay, Darnell . . . you right. I could have seen all that. But what you ain't looking at is, I changed too. We are both different people than we were . . . than when we first fell in love. I still love you, Darnell. But love can only go so far. When we were in high school that was enough. That was the world. That was everything. But it ain't everything no more. I don't have all the answers . . . sometimes I don't even have the right questions, but I do know it takes two to find them. All I know is we got somebody, a little two-year-old boy, counting on us.

YOUNGBLOOD: But I know when you place your hand in mine you got to say, "Darnell's not going to let me down . . . he loves me." I don't want to make no more mistakes in life. I don't want to do nothing to mess this up. I don't want to get old and be talking about I had me this little old gal one time . . . but I ain't seen her in twenty-two years.

RENA: If that's not what you want, then you got to let me know, Darnell. If we don't know what important to one another and learn to share that, then we can't make it. We can't make it with each other.

Youngblood assures her he wants her—she's his pride, and he wants her to be his joy. The only thing he did wrong, he allows, is stay away from her "one night too long." They kiss, and he tells her more about the house.

She's supposed to leave to go to accounting class (Jesse's at her mother's), but she might even have to miss class. They are kissing again as Becker comes into the station and remarks, "Hey . . . hey . . . You all got to take that home." They greet him, and Youngblood tells him he has bought a house in Penn Hills.

BECKER: Good! They got some nice houses out there. That's a smart move, Youngblood. I'm glad to see you do it. Ain't nothing like owning some property. They might even call you for jury duty. Most young men be on the other side of the law. How old is the baby now?

RENA: Two. He look like he's three. Big as he is.

BECKER: Ain't nothing left to do now but to get married. Come November it'll be seventeen years that me and Lucille been together. Seventeen years. I told her say work with me. She say okay. I wasn't sure what it meant myself. I thought it meant pull or push together. But she showed me one can push and the other can pull . . . as long as it's in the same direction. You know what I mean? It ain't all gonna flow together all the time. That's life. As long as it don't break apart. When you look around you'll see that all you got is each other. There ain't much more. Even when it look like there is . . . you come one day to find out there ain't much more worth having. Now, I ain't getting in your business or nothing, Youngblood, but the next time you feel like you want to spend the night apart . . . do like I do . . . go sleep on the couch in the living room. Don't put your business in the street. You put your business in the street, you'd be surprised how many people wanna have a hand in it.

YOUNGBLOOD: I found that out. Even if it ain't in the street, people wanna put it there.

BECKER: See, you're learning. Soon you gonna know as much as I do.

Becker wants Youngblood to pass the word to the others that there's a meeting tonight about the boarding-up. Before Rena and Youngblood go off, Youngblood gives Becker the message about the man from the mill. Becker calls Glucker, who wants a favor. Becker takes the opportunity to recommend Shealy's nephew for a job at the mill.

Booster comes in. Becker refuses to acknowledge him, pretending he's just another customer, telling him the station's closed. Booster tells his father, "I been thinking about what you said. So many things to think about . . . . . I went out and visited Mama's grave." Becker simply *"gathers up his papers and things and exits the station,"* leaving Booster stunned.

Fielding comes in and asks how Booster is doing.

BOOSTER: Fine. I'm doing fine. Just trying to figure out what to do.

FIELDING: If you in the treetop you can't do nothing but jump to the ground. But first you got to know how you got up there. Did you climb up to get some apples, or was you run up by a bear? You got to know that, cause you might have to start running when you hit the ground. If you trying to figure out what to do . . . you got to first figure out how you got in the situation you in. That's something simple. But you be surprised how many people can't figure that out.

Fielding comments on the poor quality of the suit the prison authorities gave Booster and on how he might be able to improve its looks. Fielding used to be a tailor, a master of the difficult double cross top stitch. He used to make all Billy Eckstine's clothes and once made a suit for for Count Basie, who tried unsuccessfully to lure him away from Eckstine. Pulling out a bottle and taking a drink from it, he admits that the bottle can tear many things apart and that his life didn't turn out the way he expected. Booster knows what he means: "I thought I was gonna be the heavyweight champion of the world. Be the next Albert Einstein. But I forgot you can't live in your dreams. I found that out when I was seven. I dreamt I had a bicycle. I went all over on the bicycle. I rode it around in circles. I rode it everywhere. I rode it to the store. I rode it to school. I went all over on the bicycle. Red bicycle. Had a coonskin tail hanging from the handlebars. Had a little bell on them handlebars. Anybody get in you way, you just ring that. Had real nice reflectors. Big old seat seem like it too big for you, but then again it seem like it was just big enough. Had fenders in the back . . . a little seat back there in case you want to give somebody a ride they could sit back there. That was one of the nicest bicycles anybody ever wanna see. I woke up and went looking for it. I had to go to school. Where the bike? Why don't I just hop on that? I looked all over for it. I looked in the back yard. The neighbor's yard. Where the bicycle? That when I decided right then, that dream didn't mean anything in this world. You could be the president or a bishop or something like that. You can dream you got more money than Rockefeller. See what happen when you wake up."

Fielding has another drink from the bottle, confessing he's not supposed to and mustn't let Becker catch him. It's against Becker's rules—and he supposes Booster knows something about Becker's rules. Booster claims Becker's rules are what got him into the penitentiary. Fielding drinks again, then hands the bottle to Booster, who takes a swig and hands it back before going off.

Philmore comes in with a duffle bag. His old lady put him out of their home, but he reckons she'll be missing him next week and begging him to come back. In the meantime, Philmore's mama will take him in. It costs three dollars to go to East Liberty, and Philmore only has two—but if Fielding will take him out there, he'll give him the other dollar next week. He works at the William Penn Hotel, been there six years and "Never missed a day." His mama might not like to see him coming, but she'll take him in. "You got to have somebody you can count on," Fielding agrees. "Now you take my wife. I ain't seen that woman in twenty-two years." The two men exit. "*The phone rings. Lights go down on the scene.*"

Scene 2

"*It is early evening. Turnbo, Fielding, Youngblood and Doub sit listening to Becker. The lights and postures of the men convey the idea of a clandestine meeting.*" They know why they're here, Becker tells them. The city plans to board up the building the first of the month. They will tear it down, tear the whole block down. The whole neighborhood, Youngblood adds.. They're supposed to be building housing, a hospital and another part of the settlement house. But Becker opines they'll never see anything built.

BECKER: All right. Since they boarding up the place we got to figure out what we gonna do. I talked to Tannehill about renting that place down on Centre what used to be Siegal's egg store. We can do that. Or we can try to get on with another station. We can go on and play by their rules like we have been. When I first came along I tried to do everything right. I figured that was the best thing to do. Even when it didn't look like they was playing fair I told myself they would come around. Time it look like you got a little something going for you, they would change the rules. Now you got to do something else. I told myself that's all right, my boy's coming. He's gonna straighten it out. I put it on somebody else. I took it off of me and put it on somebody else. I told myself as long as I could do that then I could just keep going along and making excuses for everybody. But I'm through making excuses for anybody . . . including myself. I ain't gonna pass it on. I say we stay here. We already here. The people know we here. We been here for eighteen years . . . and I don't see no reason to move. City or no city. I look around, and all I see is boarded-up buildings. Some of them been boarded up for more than ten years. If they want to build some houses, that's when they can tear it down. When they ready to build the houses. They board this place up the first of the month and let it sit boarded up for the next fifteen . . . twenty years.

TURNBO: That's just how they put Memphis Lee out of business.

BECKER: And if we don't do something they'll put Clifford out of business. Put Hester out of business. Put us out of business. Let Clifford go on and sell his fish sandwich till they get ready to build something. Let Hester go on and sell her milk and butter. Cause we gonna run jitneys out of here till the day before the bulldozer come. Ain't gonna be no boarding up around here. We gonna fight them on that. Let them go board up somewhere else.

The others agree, but Becker warns them they'll have to raise the dues to help pay a lawyer to do it legally. Becker sends Youngblood on an errand and then leaves to go to work at the mill—they're short-handed this week and need someone who can operate the machines. Turnbo, Doub and Fielding exit to talk things over with Clifford. *"The lights come down on the scene"*

Scene 3

The next day, Doub, Turnbo and Fielding are in the station, and *"Everyone is silent and in a solemn mood. The silence swells."* Fielding breaks it, asserting that Becker was all right by him. When the phone rings, he answers it—he has a trip and goes off. Turnbo wonders when the funeral is. It hasn't been set. He also wonders if Becker had any insurance. Irritated by Doub, he goes off. Youngblood comes in, claiming that no one could find a man nicer than Becker, always worrying about somebody else. Shealy follows him in.

SHEALY: I heard it on the news last night. Man work all them years down there and ain't nothing happened. Retire . . . and go back to work one day . . . and that's the day the bolt decide to break. I can't understand it. It don't make no sense to me. I went to see Lucille and take her some money. She hit for a quarter a couple of days ago.

DOUB: How's she taking it?

SHEALY: She's taking it pretty good. Considering how it happened. Sudden and all.

DOUB: I'll have to get by and see her.

Philmore enters. He is sober and somber.

SHEALY: Hey, Philmore.

PHILMORE: I'm sorry about Mr. Becker. I heard he got killed in an accident down at the mill. He was a nice man.

DOUB: Yeah. Thanks.

PHILMORE: You all need any pall bearers?

DOUB: As soon as the arrangements are made, I will let you know. Don't nobody know too much right now.

PHILMORE: If you do . . . let me know. I'll take off work.

Philmore leaves. Shealy contributes $10 toward flowers, and others kick in too. Shealy tells them that Becker's boy hit his number yesterday, but nobody has seen him, not even Lucille, and they wonder if he knows about what happened.

Booster turns up looking for his father—obviously he hasn't heard the bad news. Doub breaks it to him as gently as he can: "Boy, don't you know your daddy's dead?" Booster, in furious denial, turns violent and hits Doub in the face, as though "trying to shove the words back into his mouth." Youngblood, Shealy and Turnbo wrestle him to the floor, as Booster hollers, "What you talking about, nigger! Let me go! Let me go! That nigger tell me my daddy's dead!", and the lights go to black.

Scene 4

Three days later Doub, Youngblood, Turnbo, Fielding and Shealy are sitting around the station talking. Youngblood, who is moving to the Penn Hills house on Saturday, remarks that Reverend Flowers preached "a pretty funeral." Fielding wishes somebody would preach over him like that. Turnbo snorts that the only thing he'd say about Fielding is, he's an alcoholic. Doub suggests they stop bickering for the day.

Shealy wonders if Doub plans to fight the boarding up of the place. Doub isn't sure how he feels—"It just wouldn't be the same without Becker." Fielding agrees, but Youngblood is ready to fight the city if the others are. If not, he'll get a job somewhere, go to school, raise his family, whatever he has to do.

Booster comes in to thank them for everything they've done. He shakes Doub's hand and puts his arm around him.

DOUB: Ain't a man here wouldn't have done anything he could for Becker.

BOOSTER: Yeah, I know.

FIELDING: That's right. You can be proud of your daddy. He was all right by me. I ain't knowed him to have an enemy in the world. Ain't that right, Doub?

BOOSTER: I never knew him too much, you know. I never got to know him like you all did. I can't say nothing wrong by him. He took care of me when I was young.

He ain't run the streets and fuss and fight with my mama. The only thing I ever knew him to do was work hard. It didn't matter to me too much at the time cause I couldn't see it like I see it now. He had his ways. I guess everybody do. The only thing I feel sorry about . . . is he ain't got out of life what he put in. He deserved better than what life gave him. I can't help thinking that.

The phone rings.

But you are right . . . I'm proud of my old man. I'm proud of him. And I'm proud to be Becker's boy.

The phone rings. He stops and catches himself.

I didn't come here to preach no sermon.

He starts toward the door. He stops and turns around. The phone continues to ring. He crosses to it and picks up the receiver.

(Into phone.) Car service.

The lights go down to black. Curtain.

Special Citation

THE DESIGNATED MOURNER

A Play in Two Acts

BY WALLACE SHAWN

Cast and credits appear on page 308

WALLACE SHAWN was born November 12, 1943 in New York City, the son of The New Yorker *editor William Shawn. He attended the Dalton School, then continued his education at The Putney School, Harvard (B.A. 1965) and Oxford (M.A. 1967). It was during his Oxford years that he made his first serious attempt at playwriting (it was not produced) and has persisted in following this gleam while at the same time establishing himself in a stage and screen acting career in such films as* My Dinner With André *(which he co-authored with André Gregory),* Manhattan, The Hotel New Hampshire *and his own plays in New York and London.*

Shawn's first New York stage production of record, Our Late Night, *was developed off off Broadway at Gregory's Manhattan Project and formally presented January 9, 1975 for 38 performances by New York Shakespeare Festival Public Theater, winning an Obie Award for distinguished playwriting. In the 1977–78 season, the Public staged his translation of Niccolo Machiavelli's* The Mandrake. *On January 8, 1980 the Public produced his* Marie and Bruce *for 47 performances. Two seasons later, La Mama put on his* The Hotel Play.

Shawn's Aunt Dan and Lemon *was first produced by the Royal Court Theater in London in the summer of 1985. The Public produced it off Broadway October 1, 1985 for 191 performances, and it was named a Best Play of its season and won the George and Elisabeth Marton Award for playwriting. Shawn himself performed his next New York offering,* The Fever *at the Public November 17, 1990 for 12 performances, winning that season's Obie for best new play. It was repeated January 7, 1991 at the Royal Court Theater in London and again in New York at La Mama, the Public and Lincoln Center. The 1990–91* Best Plays *described* The Fever *as "a 105 minute monologue presented without intermission, with author-performer Wallace Shawn deploring the economic inequality and unfairness of modern society, in which he characterizes himself as comfortable while others are starving." Strong reverberations of this theme are to be found in* The Designated Mourner, *which made its first appearance at the Royal National Theater in London April 18, 1996 and then as a movie directed by David Hare. It made its New York stage debut off off Broadway May 13, 2000 under André Gregory's direction with Deborah Eisenberg as Judy, Larry Pine as Howard and Shawn himself as Jack.*

Shawn is also the author of A Thought in Three Parts *and appeared in* Vanya on 42nd Street, *directed by Louis Malle. He is a member of the Dramatists Guild and lives in New York City.*

In the off-off-Broadway section of this volume, Mel Gussow has selected The Designated Mourner *for one of his citations as an outstanding OOB production of 1999–2000, calling it "a darkly comic elegy about the end of civilization and civilized behavior."* Best Plays *echoes his critical admiration with this special citation for originality of concept and, in Gussow's words, as "a strange and mordant portrait of a culture consuming itself, as lowbrow rises and art declines." Each of the series of monologues which constitute most of this play is so richly endowed with ideas and emotions that the following synopsis is more of a sampling than an abridgement, with a selection of the play's body parts displayed on its skeleton of events.*

ACT I

JACK *(to the audience):* The designated mourner. I am the designated mourner. I have to tell you that a very special little world has died, and I am the designated mourner. Oh yes, you see, it's an important custom in many groups and tribes. Someone is assigned to grieve, to wail, and light the public ritual fire. Someone is assigned when there's no one else . . . . .

I remember saying to Judy, "I don't sort of understand this need you have to look for beauty in subtler things. Look at your own hand—look at your hand, the plate, the cake, the table . . . "

JUDY *(to the audience):* . . . . . I loved him so much, it was a kind of torture. Every morning, waiting, watching his face, in those squirming long moments of sleep and half-sleep as he turned and stretched—I sat there beside him, my hand beside him not touching him, and pain would fill up my body inch by inch, as if someone were pouring it out of a pitcher.

JACK *(to the audience):* You see, I think we ought to be precise about facts—I mean, very, very precise about historical facts. Or I mean, for God's sake, let's *try* to be. Or I mean, for God's sake, let's *pretend* to be. Or something, anyway. Well, at any rate . . . At any rate, there are those who believe that it was a columnist for a newspaper called The New York *Sun* who, in 1902, first coined that wonderful pair of neatly matching phrases, "highbrow" and "lowbrow" . . . . . A "highbrow" was a person who liked the finer things—you know, saving the Rembrandt from the burning building, rather than the baby or the fried chicken or whatever—while a "lowbrow" was someone who you might say liked to take the easy way in the cultural sphere—oh, the funny papers, pinups—you know, cheap entertainment.

JUDY: I love silence, the beauty of silence. The shadows of trees. Japanese monasteries buried in snow, surrounded by forest. Loneliness, death, in the dark forest. But my life was different, a different way: A city. People. Concerts. Poetry.

Jack confesses that he himself is not interesting: "A former student of English literature who—who—who went downhill from there." But he describes Howard, his father-in-law, as both interesting and a "remarkable man who responded so sensitively to the most obscure verses and also to the cries of the miserable and the downtrodden, sometimes virtually at the same instant." And Howard's most exceptional quality (Jack decides) was contempt.

Howard is telling Judy and Jack about a radio program he's just heard, ridiculing the manner in which the participants, Tom and Eddie, were discussing morality. Jack tells us more about his father-in-law: "Howard had really been frightfully mistreated in every possible way. Why, it was just outrageous! You know, a month after his very favorite little espresso bar in the park had been closed for good, they'd actually cut down his favorite grove of trees!" Jack says he often felt out of place because, around the house, Judy dressed very casually, sometimes even topless, and her father was usually in bedclothes, while Jack was the only one fully dressed.

Judy remembers a time when she was six years old, playing in the park, and the President, strolling by, left his entourage and came over to play with her for a moment, leaving with her his very best regards to her father. On the other hand, she also remembers a drunken party guest calling it a miracle that Howard was allowed to exist. She explains that they let him exist past the age of 30 because he stopped writing prose and devoted himself exclusively to poetry. "It meant that the charming little gang who led our country never read what he wrote, as the only members of the gang who could understand poetry at all were undoubtedly Father's own father and our playful President himself, who, out of respect for his old comrade-in-arms, my appalling grandfather, undoubtedly made the decision just to look the other way."

HOWARD *(to Judy and Jack):* Oh, I turned the volume on the radio to *loud.* I didn't want to miss a single word! Hee hee—did you know that morality was Eddie's favorite subject? Oh yes, he *loves* to talk about it. He finds it so enjoyable. You know, morality for Eddie is like—what?—like—what?—you know—it's like some terribly worthy old urn, some terribly worthy old urn that's wrapped up in some towels in his back closet. Well, it's got a few chips in it, one has to admit, and it is rather ugly, really, if you bother to look at it, and it's too heavy to lift, and in its style of course it's totally out of keeping with everything else in the house. So, well, you know, it can't be used, it has no function in his life at all—but ten times a day he has to exclaim, "Oh yes, that urn, it's my great possession, my greatest treasure."

Jack defends Tom relative to someone named Martin, whom Howard favors, but Howard believes that comparing one person to another is a waste of effort which would be better directed toward "the human suffering that is going on all around you." Howard concludes, "All the judging, all the condemning, who's superior, who's inferior, 'I was right,' and so on, are not terribly helpful to all the people who might actually be falling victim to every sort of horror while you're taking the time to debate these things."

Judy particularly liked an essay called *The Enemy* Howard once wrote about "the dirt-eaters," the hopelessly underprivileged, and "the ones, like this strange young woman, who rise up from the dirt to lead them." Howard met this woman in the park, brought her home and talked to her for hours in a life-changing conversation. Howard reads from his essay about her, "her hands nicked in a hundred places," describing the appalling conditions of her life in polite answers to Howard's questions. After her departure, he wept because he identified her as "the enemy" and yet yearned to help her.

Jack tells the audience that he and Judy were introduced to each other while shopping at the same store. They happened to meet again one night in the park, then she brought him to her home to meet Howard. Jack liked Howard but was never inclined to become one of his disciples, he says.

JACK: But of course I envied him. What are you talking about? I envied the whole gang of them—all the old unbearables—Bob, Arthur, the whole crowd. And Howard? Come on. The possibility of not envying Howard didn't even arise. It didn't even arise. Forget his writing—I envied him simply because of the way he could read. It was so easy, casual. The way I might have picked up an article about the latest approach to cooking string beans, he would pick up a book of poems by John Donne. I mean, I was clever enough to know that John Donne was offering something that was awfully enjoyable—I just wasn't clever enough to actually enjoy it. I'd devoted my life to it, I suppose you could say, but I couldn't get near to the great writers. Day after day and year after year, I read them and read them, but they always seemed remote. I didn't want them to. They just did. I was kept out of it all, kept away. Howard, on the other hand, was let right in. Come in, they said. Here we are. Come talk, come be with us. We're right here. Howard couldn't even comprehend what the problem was for the rest of us poor mortals. How could he, you see. But, do you know?—I always felt I was on the brink of understanding. I felt I could have learned. I was ready to learn. I would have humbled myself to any degree in order to learn, as a matter of fact. But he wouldn't teach me. None of them would. Howard, Judy, Bob, Arthur—the readers of poetry.

HOWARD: Jack wasn't actually a bad fellow, you know. I just found him a little bit vague at times. A little bit vague, a little bit lazy. You know, he *was* lazy. In fact, actually, he was so lazy that his favorite foods—I'm not making this up, because I observed it quite carefully—were soup, risotto, mashed potatoes, and ice cream. I'm not exaggerating!

At first, Howard was uncomfortable with Jack's courting of his daughter. "Of course the comical part was that I happened to know, and Howard didn't, that I wasn't actually a good lover at all," Jack admits. Judy wasn't experienced and didn't seem to mind and Jack never admitted to her his sexual inadequacy. At first they lived at Howard's, then finally got their own apartment—"It was a wonderful time"—but short, because Howard was chronically ill, and they had to move back to take care of him.

The explosive things her father wrote in his twenties didn't just go away, Judy observes, "Our beloved rulers were naturally reluctant to show any unfriendliness to the wayward son of one of their own, but that didn't mean they didn't all read that little volume of essays whose orange binding we knew so well, or that they ever forgot it. No one did. Everyone knew that the story wasn't over," so that people tended to be afraid to associate with Howard. Even Joan, who "was like a cloth you might use to polish silver" and to whom her father was very dear, finally went away and never came back.

The move back to Howard's marked the beginning of what Jack remembers as "that whole awful year." First, someone threw a rock through Howard's window. Then there came a time when Jack felt he had to get away from the house for a night, and he checked into a hotel in another town. He was lying in bed reading a book of poetry, when the couple in the next room interrupted his reading with the sounds of lovemaking.

JACK: After the couple had finished making love—and it took a long time—they went to bed, but I couldn't sleep. My hand reached out toward the book on the table, but then I thought, Wait—do I really want to go back to reading that book? Might I not actually in fact prefer to read the magazine that I'd bought in the lobby, the one with all the stories about healthy, well-exercised, rather young actresses? So I read for awhile in that very engaging magazine, but I still couldn't sleep, and so once again I started to reach for the book, but as I reached for the book my attention was drawn to the end of my bed, where a blank face looked expectantly into mine, a familiar framed screen which held inside it colors, songs, characters, drunkenness, love—beauty—And the faces that waited inside that blank face pulled me toward them, pulled my hand toward the knob to turn on the screen, and then toward my lamp to turn out the light. And as I sat in the darkness and watched the screen for hour after hour I thought to myself, Well, at some point we have to draw some distinctions—don't we? I mean, pardon me, but shouldn't there be some distinction drawn between the things we say, the lies, the "I like poetry," "I like Rembrandt" on the one hand—and I mean, of course it's important to say those things, because after all if you don't say them then you really become simply a zoo animal, you become an empty *thing,* you're nothing more then really than a large balloon with a mouth, genitals, paws and an asshole, a nice great big one—but still they're lies, they *are* lies—and then on the other hand things that are true, like "I'm watching this very nice screen right now, I'm watching it, and I'm enjoying it . . . . . "

JUDY: Suddenly, there were a group of rather quiet demonstrations on some rather quiet streets, leading people to ask, Well, were these demonstrations the usual fakes—or were they, could they be, real this time? Could we possibly be seeing the awakening of "the enemy" after all these years? Were "the dirt-eaters" somehow gently stirring? And were certain people whose hands were nicked in a hundred places suddenly making their presence felt? That would be funny, after we'd been told for so long that people of that sort no longer existed. And then, perhaps as a consequence of these developments, or maybe not—well, to use that perennially popular metaphor from cards—there were cabinet shuffles, over and over. And every time that the big governmental deck would be cut, more people we'd never heard of would rise to the top of it. Was it a card game or a card trick? The old officeholders, the filthy herd of swine whom we vaguely knew and would even vaguely nod to at cocktail parties, were quietly replaced by a new herd of swine whom we *didn't* know—the new generation, who dressed in new colors—those chalky colors, yellow and pink and various greens—and lived in new neighborhoods, and even ate in new restaurants with new styles of cooking.

Jack recalls a belief one of his uncles had, that people are like rats—they will do anything to thrive and survive. He sees both himself and Howard as that kind of rat. Yet folks such as Arthur and Bob, who "believed themselves to be tiny, beleagured, innocent creatures living in a world of rats," consider Howard a leader in their "war *against* the rats, the war against everything for which they held the rats responsible, from the unattractive figurines in the sculpture garden to the lamentable fact that there were no more free concerts." Jack sarcastically admits that Howard's group had never considered Jack officer material in that war. Jack turns his attention to those "snarling, snapping, unmuzzled dogs" who are the enemy.

JACK: If you look at the world, the world as a whole, actually most people in it are the ones we can only refer to, rather nervously and gingerly, by means of those terribly melodramatic and almost hysterical words like "wretched," "miserable," "unfortunate," "desperate," "powerless," "poor"—that's a very sympathetic one—or to put it a bit differently, God bless them, they're people who simply don't have any resources of any kind at all. And these particular people—and you know, God knows why—well, they just don't like us. They *don't like us.* They simply don't like us. So it's not hard to see what will happen one day. There's the majority, them, the minority, us, and the way they feel about us, great dislike, very very great dislike. So, in other words, "enemies" are not exactly imaginary beings. They're very, very real. But I'll tell you something interesting about enemies, you see. At least this is how I feel about it. I'm sure you know that rather nasty and not terribly thought-provoking old saying that "the enemy of my enemies is my friend." Well, what's really much more true to *my* sense of life is that the friend of my enemies is for sure

THE DESIGNATED MOURNER—Playwright and actor Wallace Shawn as Jack *(left)* in a scene from the off-off-Broadway production of his play, with Deborah Eisenberg as Judy and Larry Pine as Howard

my enemy, while in a funny way my enemies themselves don't bother me that much, and in an odd way I can even work up quite a bit of respect for them, looking at it all from a certain point of view.

It's that thing of people whom you actually know and with whom you actually live *deciding consciously* to be the friend of your enemies that can get you really terribly upset, because your enemies after all are actually trying very hard to kill you, no matter what you may happen to feel about them—and this is where things with Judy and Howard really became so difficult, because they'd worked themselves around to being so horribly appalled by the revolting rats that they saw encroaching everywhere on their perfect existence that they ultimately decided that the people whom they actually ought to *like* were, yes, that's right, precisely the ones who were sitting around making plans to slice our guts out, or in other words to perform that gesture cleverly referred to by one of our enemy-loving writers as "the disembow-eling of the overboweled." And that became ultimately rather revolting to me.

One night the group decided to see a play, a comedy in which, in Jack's opinion, "the writer's hatred of the human race—or for everyone not just exactly like him, one might say—kept oozing out of it, like blood oozing out from a closet full of bodies." Jack found the play to be very ugly, but after one particulary awful joke he looked at Howard to check his reaction and found that Howard was laughing up-roariously, and so were the rest of his group.

The following week, Judy gave Jack a large birthday party. A Danish student brought by one of the guests took a fancy to Jack, and he soon found himself alone with her in the garage. Howard, the cook at the party, came to get some more coal for the barbecue and saw Jack fondling her. The girl ran off, but Jack went into a tool shed and saw Howard through the window "wandering around on the lawn, not quite sure just how he should proceed, and I thought to myself, I can't stand this man, I can't stand this man, and I don't believe anything this man believes. Not a single thing."

JUDY: God, you know, it was so fitting in a way—everything started when I was at a concert! Emotional works for string orchestra. I'd decided to go off to spend an evening by myself, and I sat there watching, blissfully watching, watching the musicians under the bright lights. They were playing wonderfully, leaning forward, so committed, their heels digging into the stage—and then suddenly the lights seemed to flicker for a moment, but the players went on playing—and then all at once we were in total darkness. The audience made an odd little sound, like the hoarse sound of a broken bell, and started to run. I thought of a movie I'd seen of cows in a corral. Then a door opened at the back of the stage, and we could see through it into the street. Behind the scurrying musicians holding their instruments to their chests we saw flashes of light, and then—impossible—then we heard shots—not one or two pops, but shooting like you'd hear on the evening news, a sound that in spite of everything we never really thought we'd hear "live," so to speak. And so that was it. Everything started over from that moment.

A few days—a month—and all of a sudden ten thousand examples of "human remains," as the newspapers called them—"human remains"—or was it fifteen thousand?—had shown up in every sort of inappropriate spot, such as the carousel in the middle of the park, and at least that many people had been unceremoniously arrested by the police. There was a week when we went to three funerals of friends. Two had been sitting quietly in restaurants. Someone had come in, had said, "Don't get up," then walked behind them and shot a hole in the back of their heads, blood pouring out of them onto their plates.

Well—it hadn't happened for a long time, but now it was happening once again. Those who were suffering had whimpered a little, they'd made themselves known, and so of course it was inevitable that the serious individuals who led our country would begin to respond. As in all such periods, you could never predict the form of the response, just its filthiness.

Jack wanted to move away and leave Howard to his own devices. He found himself making impulsive comments to Judy on odd subjects. And to Judy, Jack's reactions to funerals, to an orphanage they'd visited—even to her kisses or her nakedness—seemed to be distorted, atrophied in some way. She tells him, "You can't imagine it, but yes—the many living under the heel of the few—one day it *will* end. I believe it will end. For you, that's a joke. You can't picture it. But I can."

Judy tells the audience that some men who looked perfectly ordinary came to the house to see her father. "Father put a robe on over his pajamas, put on his slippers, came downstairs. They said nothing, they smashed his face in with their hands and fists, left him bleeding, and ran away. The next day Jack moved out of the house."

Jack tells the audience that the afternoon of the day he left was very cold. He could hear sounds of Howard, battered, "coughing and choking." Judy was in bed, and Jack pulled up a chair beside her, to talk, but they soon grew silent: "I knew what she would say, I knew what I would say—so why say it? It was really as if she was tied to the bed, and as I sat beside her, a heavy silence kept hitting us repeatedly, like a wet towel, repeatedly hitting . . . . . Make love to her, I thought—or murder her, maybe." When Judy seemed to be drowsing, Jack went outside in search of some kind of a weapon. He picked up a croquet mallet, thinking, "Something had simply ended, that was all. As if all those years had been just a moment."

Jack returned to the bedroom and saw that Judy's sleep was troubled. He placed the mallet against the wall and stood watching her, thinking, "How could so much joy, so much happiness for me, have been contained in this one little package?" Then he got into bed with her and was soon dreaming of rockets being fired, of being wounded and cared for in a hospital, and then of Judy asking him, "Please, darling, would you just be very simple at the end of your life? Could you tell me you 'love' me? Say, 'I love you,' use those very words?—those very same words that have been used by everyone—by the poor, the ugly, the stupid, the weak?"

JACK *(to Judy):* For God's sake, don't you have any feelings at all? For the sake of Jesus—you're trying to kill me! *(To the audience.)* I was awakened by the sound of my own shouting. I ran out of the house, and I was out for good.

HOWARD: There was a fantasy I always used to have about Joan. Maybe I dreamt it too. I'm lying in bed with warm pillows and blankets, and there's a low fire sitting in the grate, and Joan comes into the room with a delicious sandwich on a white dish. And after I've eaten it, she sits beside me and we look out the window as she holds me very tightly.

Through the window, under a bright moon, we see horses playing on the grass, and birds playing in the sky above the house. And her very cold hand is stroking me slowly but purposefully with a delicate motion, up and down, and I'm thinking about this whole rather twisted question of death, and I say to myself, For God's sake, will you stop struggling? Lie back. Put your head on the pillow. Close your eyes. Don't you know how to enjoy *anything?* Just wait for the moment which you know will come. There. There. One, two—it's a certainty.

Curtain.

ACT II

Jack, having moved into a hotel, broods over the question of identity and the passage of time: he decides he'd be lying to himself if he pretended that he was the same person from one day to the next. He tells us of an affair with a girl named Peg he met in the park. One day on a beach she said to him, "Jack, I love you," but she was the one who left him when the affair finally ended.

Judy is confused about what is going on, with "the distant sound of violence—that vague, low roaring and groaning, the snapping of guns" starting at dawn each day. She has noticed at parties that half of the officials now in power are in their twenties.

Jack has finally decided that hope does not exist, neither his own hope for a life of happiness, nor hope for world peace. He will try to enjoy little things like "the quiet shade of a nice square of chocolate," one at a time.

One evening, the news on the radio was so bad that Howard and his friends instinctively clustered together—Mary, Herbert, Arthur, Bob and Sam gathering at Howard's for a cookout. After dinner, as it grew dark and the sounds of violence got louder, they retreated into the house.

JUDY: And then, with a crack, the rain was suddenly beating down on the garden, rattling wildly on the windows. And after a little time, through the roar of the rain, I heard the sound of breaking glass, as if bottles were being thrown and broken. And then the grinding gears of a truck pulling up, stopping in the driveway just where the milkman's truck always used to stop. Would they ring the bell like the milkman used to do, to give us the bill?

We drifted into the living room. Arthur sat in a chair—so did Bob, Mary—and their bodies slowly sort of curled up in the chairs. Their expressions, really, were just of waiting, a little bit puzzled, like patients sitting in their pajamas in hospitals. Then there were sounds of commotion in the garden, and at first no one even went to the window to find out what was happening. I finally did, though, and in the darkness and rain the light from the house picked out a few spots I could see on the lawn. A patch of flowers. Some dishes, food. I saw a blur of men moving quickly around. Then, by the table where we'd all had our meal, I saw a dead person lying—an old man—his skull had been crushed. He lay in the mud, face downward, the rain pouring over him, the inside of his head washing out onto the lawn ..... And then—it was almost funny, simply because it was so exactly like what one had always imagined—they knocked on the door.

So yes, we landed exactly where we knew we would land, like parachutists. Like the last pieces of a puzzle, we floated down into the space that had been waiting. And once it was happening, it seemed right, and all the times we'd prayed, God, don't let it happen, seemed far away.

I excused myself, went upstairs to the toilet, and vomited. Then I brushed my teeth, went back downstairs, and I was more or less fine. Shivering a bit as we went out into the rain, but still perfectly able to walk to the truck.

"Judy and Howard and their friends went to prison," Jack says, for five years. Arthur and Bob died in prison right away; Mary, Herbert and Sam lived a little longer. Howard, formerly ill, came out of prison in the best of health, but Judy came out with some sort of ailment.

Jack happened to meet Joan at a party, and they found that they both had had exactly the same problem with Howard—they hated him.

JACK: To be quite frank, one has to say those were not bad years for a lot of people. A lot of people were getting by, not doing that badly, or even doing a bit better than that. I myself had a pretty good job. I wrote a column on sex for *The Morning Urinal,* as everyone absolutely insisted on calling it. It wasn't really such a terrible paper, but everyone just loved to make fun of it, for some reason—it showed people's boldly independent spirits, I suppose.

After all he'd gone through, poor Howard didn't get to celebrate much after he got out of prison. Actually, it might seem to be, you know, a little absurd to lock somebody up for five years and *then* have someone come to his house and shoot him—all basically because of a couple of essays he'd written several decades before—but you have to understand that no one person plans these things: person A decides the first thing, person B decides the second, you know, I mean, that's just how it works.

Someone had a fetish about mealtime shootings, one is bound to conclude. He was in his bedroom, and Judy had just brought him a plate of cold meat and salad. Once again it was, "Don't get up," the guy walking behind him, the hole blasted into the back of his head, the blood pouring endlessly onto the plate.

When I heard about it, I went over, of course, to see Judy. A month later she sold the house, and I went over again to help her pack things up.

Oh my God, that whole thing of moving. So depressing. The sale of effects. The garage, cleaned. Even the oil stains partially removed by some new process. The books in boxes carried down the stairs—ever so gently, as if they were crates of eggs. I felt a sadness on the stairs as we took down the books as I hadn't really when we'd carried down the corpse.

Carrying the corpse down the stairs, I'd only thought, Well, he won't be going down *these* stairs again.

Judy and Jack left together to spend the night in a small seaside town. In the off season, their room was freezing cold. Jack felt his little flame of love for Judy die, as it "sputtered and spattered, bent its head and turned into a vague little plume of smoke . . . . . I didn't really want to, but I put my hand around Judy's waist and held her next to me. It was a small gesture which could lead to nothing. My dick lay limply inside my trousers, like a little lunch packed by Mother."

Judy in her turn felt that Jack was dead, and she had the urge to "bathe him, play with him, bring him back to life." But this did not occur, and the next day she moved into an apartment she'd found in a different town, where she enjoyed daily pre-dawn walks to the beach: "Darkness. The sea. The lighthouse. The gulls. The sand thick and wet like black ice cream."

As the months passed, Jack became obsessed with a contemplation of self. He decided that the self was just a pile of junk accumulated by chance, and he cast away his vision of self as an important something destined for achievement.

JACK: I guess I've always really been a lowbrow at heart. So I made a new life, and I was so happy, because it was so easy. I walked down the street with a different step, a sloppier one, I ate in different places, developed different tastes. I'd decided years before what foods I would always say that I didn't like, but I liked them now.

I found a new apartment, and some people might have said it wasn't really very nice. It was smelly, I suppose. But I enjoyed it. There was a window looking out on a courtyard filled with dirt, and children played there—kind of slummy kinds of games.

And you know how I'd always treated books with such respect? I would never even write in a book, or fold down a page, or toss a book casually onto a table. But one morning in my new apartment I did something funny—at least I thought it was funny. I put a book of poetry in the bathtub, and I urinated on it. An interesting experiment. Then I left it in the tub, and then, later, when I needed to shit—I hadn't *planned* this, it just came to me as an idea—instead of shitting into the toilet, I shat on the book. Just to see, you know, if it *could* be done. And apparently it was possible, despite what anyone might have told me. So, like a scientist, I noted in my diary that night, "Yes, the experiment has been a complete success."

Jack acquired a dog, but someone shot it. He found a plastic bag full of sex magazines lying in the street and brought them home. He enjoyed examining the group of people who appeared in them, at first; but finally, like his experience of everything else around him, they began shrinking and became as nothing to him.

Judy happened to meet Joan in her neighborhood and would see her occasionally. One night Judy went to a play she liked very much, but Joan's later criticism of it destroyed all Judy's enjoyment of remembering it: "Finally I emptied the whole evening out of my mind like trash."

JACK: It was one of those weeks when loose ends, apparently, were being tied up. You know, once the people who *do* cause trouble are gone, then it's time to get the ones who *might* cause trouble, or who might once possibly have been *able* to cause trouble twenty years ago—oh, you know the whole story. Eventually it's a matter of tying up loose ends. Tying up loose ends, or cutting them off, is just an inevitable part of the process, obviously. And so, of course, is the perennial parallel campaign for the betterment of humanity, or whatever you want to call it, in aid of which we were being treated now, every week or so, to demonstrations of a very new approach to executions, in which eight or ten people would be taken into a room, seated in these chairs that made their heads bend way back, and fitted up with brightly colored tubes in their mouths which supposedly did away with them with very little pain in this rather odd ceremony—somehow with music or God knows what. So, anyway, as I sat there in my apartment one morning, slowly reading in the paper about this latest attempt to elevate our moral and esthetic taste, I was looking at one of the photographs accompanying the article, and I happened to notice that among the bedraggled-looking people sitting in those chairs being fitted with tubes were those rather tiresome moralists whom Howard found so boring, Tom and

Eddie—I quickly scanned the row for their former friend Martin, until I somehow remembered that he'd recently been appointed Minister of Supplementary Tugboat Rewiring or something of the sort—and then I happened to notice that the woman sitting in the very last chair with her head at that rather odd angle was obviously Judy.

Well, I was lost. Where was I? Blinded, you know, like a caught fish jumping about on the floor of a boat. And the funny thing was that aside from sweating and sort of panting—well, more or less exactly as people say when they speak about such moments, I didn't know what to do. I mean, *literally,* what to do—stand up, remain seated, stay in, go out? I reached for my naked friends in the plastic bag, because there they were on the table right next to me. I looked at them all in the midst of their playing, and their hopeful smiles made me wonder if a more compassionate world might not perhaps come about one day. A tiny personal advertisement near one of the pictures asked the unknown reader a simple question: "Have you ever ridden on the train which carries the bodies of the dead?" it inquired disarmingly, and then it commented, "I have, and I was given a berth right next to theirs." There was a postal box number included, to which you could write to continue the discussion.

Jack finally went out for a stroll in the park. Sitting on a bench, it suddenly occurred to him that "everyone on earth who could read John Donne was now dead." In fact, Jack might be the only person who even knew that this special group had disappeared. He remembered reading about a tribal custom of designating a mourner to light a ceremonial fire and weep for people who had died with no one else to mourn for them. He moved toward a nearby cafe.

JACK: I went in, found a table, and ordered a cup of tea from an overworked waitress. Well, along with the tea, and of her own volition, apparently, or maybe it was the policy of the cafe's management, the waitress brought me a plate which held a small pastry, a sticky kind of cake whose bottom rested on a bit of paper. And as the waitress left me, I saw my opportunity. First, obviously, I ate the cake. And then I grabbed some matches which sat nearby me, and I glanced around, and I lit the bit of paper. "I am the designated mourner," I said.

The bit of paper wasn't very big, but it burned rather slowly, because of the cake crumbs. I thought I heard John Donne crying into a handkerchief as he fell through the floor—plummeting fast through the earth on his way to hell. His name, once said by so many to be "immortal," would not be remembered, it turned out. The rememberers were gone, except for me, and I was forgetting: forgetting his name, forgetting him, and forgetting all the ones who remembered him.

Already, Jack felt, it seemed to be more peaceful "without the presence on earth of our nerve-jangling friends." He was tired of "the search for perfection." Howard's favorite grove of trees had been cut down, yes, but much remained—the flowers, the air and the sky. "I sat on the bench for a very long time," Jack recalls, "lost—sunk deep—in the experience of unbelievable physical pleasure, maybe the greatest pleasure we can know on this earth—the sweet, ever-changing caress of an early evening breeze."

Curtain.

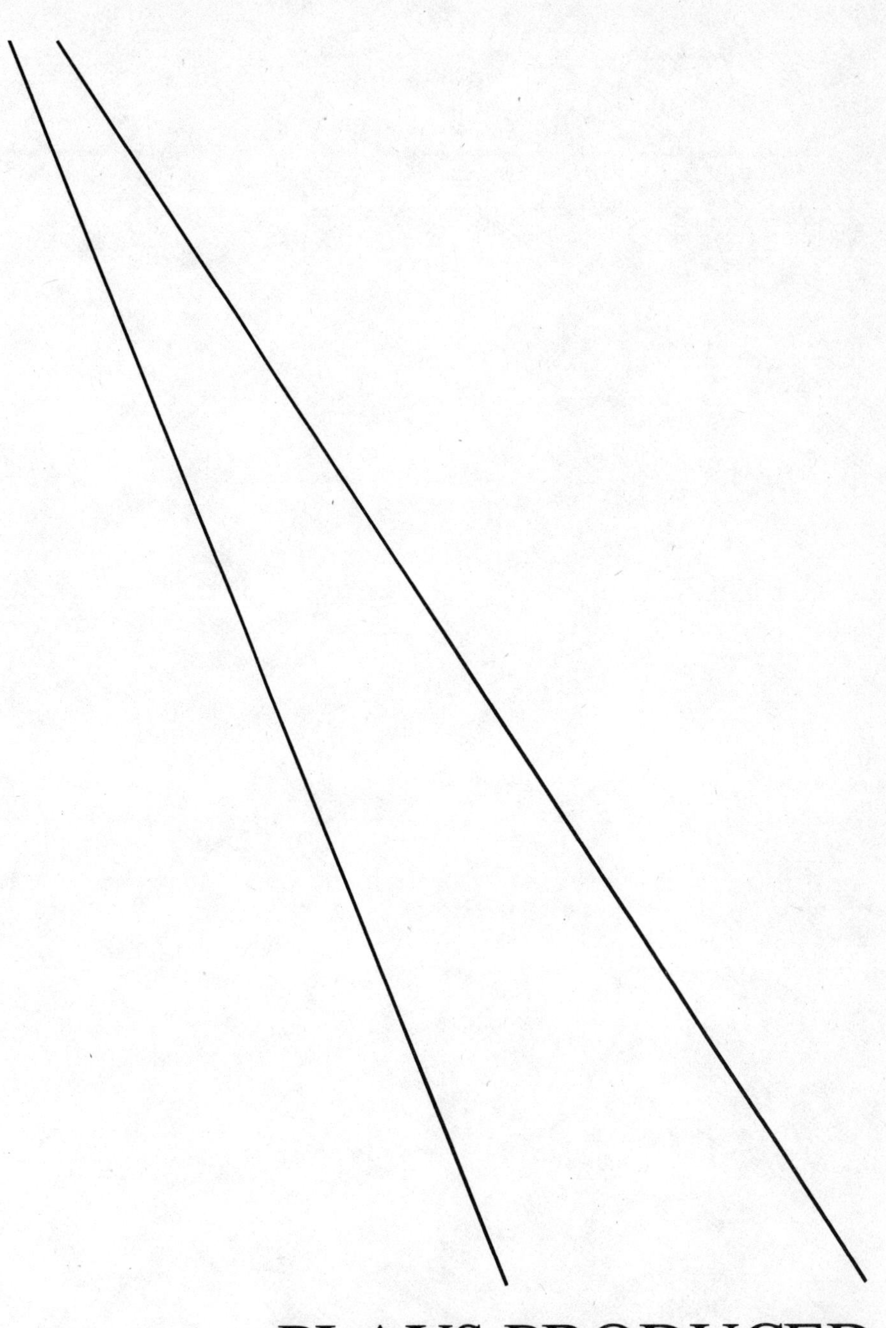

PLAYS PRODUCED IN NEW YORK

PLAYS PRODUCED ON BROADWAY

Figures in parentheses following a play's title give number of performances. These figures do not include previews or extra non-profit performances. In the case of a transfer, the off-Broadway run is noted but not added to the figure in parentheses.

Plays marked with an asterisk (*) were still in a projected run June 1, 2000. Their number of performances is figured through May 31, 2000.

In a listing of a show's numbers—dances, sketches, musical scenes, etc. —the titles of songs are identified wherever possible by their appearance in quotation marks (").

HOLDOVERS FROM PREVIOUS SEASONS

Broadway shows which were running on June 1, 1999 are listed below. More detailed information about them appears in previous Best Plays volumes of the years in which they opened. Important cast changes since opening night are recorded in the Cast Replacements section of this volume.

*__Cats__ (7,367; longest-running show in Broadway history). Musical based on *Old Possum's Book of Practical Cats* by T.S. Eliot; music by Andrew Lloyd Webber; additional lyrics by Trevor Nunn and Richard Stilgoe. Opened October 7, 1982.

*__Les Misérables__ (5,442). Musical based on the novel by Victor Hugo; book by Alain Boublil and Claude-Michel Schönberg; lyrics by Herbert Kretzmer; original French text by Alain Boublil and Jean-Marc Natel; additional material by James Fenton. Opened March 12, 1987.

*__The Phantom of the Opera__ (5,154). Musical adapted from the novel by Gaston Leroux; book by Richard Stilgoe and Andrew Lloyd Webber; music by Andrew Lloyd Webber; lyrics by Charles Hart; additional lyrics by Richard Stilgoe. Opened January 26, 1988.

*__Miss Saigon__ (3,820). Musical with book by Alain Boublil and Claude-Michel Schönberg; music by Claude-Michel Schönberg; lyrics by Richard Maltby Jr. and Alain Boublil; additional material by Richard Maltby Jr. Opened April 11, 1991.

*__Beauty and the Beast__ (2,483). Musical with book by Linda Woolverton; music by Alan Menken; lyrics by Howard Ashman and Tim Rice. Opened April 18, 1994.

Smokey Joe's Cafe (2,036; longest-running revue in Broadway history). Musical revue with words and music by Jerry Leiber and Mike Stoller. Opened March 2, 1995. (Closed January 16, 2000)

*__Rent__ (1,707). Transfer from off Broadway of the musical with book, music and lyrics by Jonathan Larson. Opened off off Broadway January 26, 1996 and off Broadway February 13, 1996 where it played 56 performances through March 31, 1996; transferred to Broadway April 29, 1996.

*__Chicago__ (1,476). Revival of the musical based on the play by Maurine Dallas Watkins; book by Fred Ebb and Bob Fosse; music by John Kander; lyrics by Fred Ebb; original production directed and choreographed by Bob Fosse. Opened November 14, 1996.

*__Jekyll & Hyde__ (1,290). Musical based on the novella *The Strange Case of Dr. Jekyll and Mr. Hyde* by Robert Louis Stevenson; conceived by Steve Cuden and Frank Wildhorn; book and lyrics by Leslie Bricusse; music by Frank Wildhorn. Opened April 28, 1997.

*__The Lion King__ (1,098). Musical adapted from the screen play by Irene Mecchi, Jonathan Roberts and Linda Woolverton; book by Roger Allers and Irene Mecchi; music by Elton John; lyrics by Tim Rice; additional music and lyrics by Lebo M, Mark Mancina, Jay Rifkin, Julie Taymor and Hans Zimmer. Opened November 13, 1997.

Ragtime (861). Musical based on the novel by E.L. Doctorow; book by Terrence McNally; music by Stephen Flaherty; lyrics by Lynn Ahrens. Opened January 18, 1998. (Closed January 16, 2000)

Art (600). By Yasmina Reza; translated by Christopher Hampton. Opened March 1, 1998. (Closed August 8, 1999)

The Sound of Music (540). Revival of the musical suggested by *The Trapp Family Singers* by Maria Augusta Trapp; book by Howard Lindsay and Russel Crouse; music by Richard Rodgers; lyrics by Oscar Hammerstein II. Opened March 12, 1998. (Closed June 27, 1999)

*__Cabaret__ (881). Revival of the musical based on the play by John Van Druten and stories by Christopher Isherwood; book by Joe Masteroff; music by John Kander; lyrics by Fred Ebb. Opened March 19, 1998.

Side Man (458). By Warren Leight. Opened June 25, 1998. (Closed October 31, 1999)

*__Footloose__ (670). Musical based on the original screen play by Dean Pitchford; adapted by Dean Pitchford and Walter Bobbie; music by Tom Snow; lyrics by Dean Pitchford. Opened October 22, 1998.

Peter Pan (214). Revival of the musical version of the play by J.M. Barrie; music by Moose Charlap; lyrics by Carolyn Leigh; additional lyrics by Betty Comden and Adolph Green; additional music by Jule Styne. Opened November 23, 1998. (Closed January 3, 1999 after 48 performances) Reopened April 7, 1999. (Closed August 29, 1999)

*__Fosse__ (584). Dance revue with choreography by Bob Fosse; conceived by Richard Maltby Jr., Chet Walker and Ann Reinking; artistic advisor, Gwen Verdon. Opened January 14, 1999.

You're a Good Man, Charlie Brown (150). Revival of the musical based on the comic strip "Peanuts" by Charles M. Schulz; book, music and lyrics by Clark Gesner. Opened February 4, 1999. (Closed June 13, 1999)

Death of a Salesman (274). Revival of the play by Arthur Miller. Opened February 10, 1999. (Closed November 7, 1999)

Not About Nightingales (125). By Tennessee Williams. Opened February 25, 1999. (Closed June 13, 1999)

***Annie Get Your Gun** (520), Revival of the musical with book by Herbert and Dorothy Fields as revised by Peter Stone; music and lyrics by Irving Berlin. Opened March 4, 1999.

Night Must Fall (120). Revival of the play by Emlyn Williams. Opened March 8, 1999. (Closed June 27, 1999)

Lincoln Center Theater. Via Dolorosa (99). Solo performance by David Hare; written by David Hare. Opened March 18, 1999. (Closed June 13, 1999)

Ring Round the Moon (70). Revival of the play by Jean Anouilh; adapted by Christopher Fry. Opened April 28, 1999. (Closed June 27, 1999)

Closer (172). By Patrick Marber. Opened March 25, 1999. (Closed August 22, 1999)

The Weir (276). By Conor McPherson. Opened April 1, 1999. (Closed November 28, 1999)

The Iceman Cometh (102). Revival of the play by Eugene O'Neill. Opened April 8, 1999. (Closed July 18, 1999)

Amy's View (103). By David Hare. Opened April 15, 1999. (Closed July 18, 1999)

The Civil War (61). Musical with book and lyrics by Frank Wildhorn, Gregory Boyd and Jack Murphy; music by Frank Wildhorn. Opened April 22, 1999. (Closed June 13, 1999)

It Ain't Nothin' But the Blues (276). Musical revue based on an original idea by Ron Taylor; written by Charles Bevel, Lita Gaithers, Randal Myler, Ron Taylor and Dan Wheetman. Opened April 26, 1999. (Closed January 9, 2000)

The Lonesome West (56). By Martin McDonagh. Opened April 27, 1999. (Closed June 13, 1999)

PLAYS PRODUCED JUNE 1, 1999–MAY 31, 2000

Voices in the Dark (68). By John Pielmeier. Produced by Ben Sprecher, William P. Miller, Neil Hirsch and Aaron Levy in association with Mindy Utay and Steven Rappaport at the Longacre Theater. Opened August 12, 1999. (Closed October 10, 1999)

Caller #1 .... Nicole Fonarow
Lil .... Judith Ivey
Hack .... Peter Bartlett
Bill .... Tom Stechschulte
Owen .... Ralph Sbarge
Red .... Lenny Blackburn
Blue .... John Ahlin
Egan .... Zach Grenier

Directed by Christopher Ashley; scenery, David Gallo, Lauren Helpern; costumes, David C. Woolard; lighting, Donald Holder; sound, T. Richard Fitzgerald; original music, Robert Waldman; fight staging, B.H. Barry; special effects, Gregory Meeh; casting, Pat McCorkle; production stage manager, John M. Galo; stage manager, Kate Broderick; press, Jeffrey Richards Associates, Caral Craig, Brett Kristofferson.

Place: A radio sound studio and a cabin in the Adirondacks over a November weekend. Act I, Scene 1: Friday, 10:45 P.M. Scene 2: Saturday, 3 P.M. Scene 3: Saturday, 7 P.M. Scene 4: Sunday, 5:15 P.M. Scene 5: Sunday, 9 P.M. Act II, Scene 6: Moments later.

A radio talk show host is menaced by a mysterious caller. Originally commissioned and produced by A Contemporary Theater, Seattle.

Kat and the Kings (157). Musical with book and lyrics by David Kramer; music by Taliep Petersen. Produced by Harriet Newman Leve and Judith & David Rosenbauer in association with Richard Frankel, Marc Routh, Willette Klausner, Kardana-Swinsky Productions, David Kramer, Taliep Petersen and Renaye Kramer, by special arrangement with Paul Elliott, Nick

Salmon and Lee Menzies, at the Cort Theater. Opened August 19, 1999. (Closed January 2, 2000)

Kat Diamond	Terry Hector	Bingo	Loukmaan Adams
Lucy Dixon	Kim Louis	Ballie	Junaid Booysen
Young Kat Diamond	Jody J. Abrahams	Magoo	Alistair Izobell

Orchestra: Jeff Lams conductor, keyboards; Francisco Centeno associate conductor, bass; Jerome Harris guitars; Warren Odze drums; Mark Gross sax, flute; Ravi Best trumpet.

Standbys: Mr. Hector—Rudy Roberson; Miss Louis—Pia Glenn; Messrs. Booysen, Izobell, Adams—E. Clayton Cornelious; Mr. Abrahams—Alistair Izobell.

Direction and musical staging by David Kramer; choreography, Jody J. Abrahams, Loukmaan Adams; musical direction, Jeff Lams; scenery and costumes, Saul Radomsky; lighting, Howard Harrison; sound, Orbital Sound/Sebastian Frost; music supervision, Gary Hind; music coordinator, John Miller; associate producer, Patrick Molony; U.S. casting, Jay Binder; production stage manager, Pat Sosnow; press, Helene Davis.

Act I: Cape Town, South Africa, 1999. District Six, 1957. Act II: Cape Town, South Africa, 1999/1959. Surban, South Africa, 1959.

The story of a mixed-race doo-wop harmony group, The Cavalla Kings led by Kat Diamond, and their struggle for recognition. A foreign play previously produced in South Africa and (in this production) at the Tricycle Theater and Vaudeville Theater, London.

ACT I

Overture	Orchestra
"Memory"	Lucy, The Kings
"American Thing"	Kat, Company
"Lucky Day"	Young Kat, Kat
"Mavis"	Kay, Bingo, Young Kat, Ballie, Magoo
"Boetie Guitar"	Kat, The Kings
"Cavalla Kings"	Lucy, The Kings
"If You Shoes Don't Shine"	Kat
"Dress to Kill"	Lucy, The Kings
"Shine"	Lucy, The Kings
"The Tafelberg Hotel"	Lucy, The Kings
"Lonely Girl"	Bingo, Magoo, Kat, Young Kat, Ballie
"Josephine"	Ballie, The Kings
"Wild Time"	Company

ACT II

"Happy To Be Nineteen"	Company
"Lonely Girl" (Reprise)	Bingo, The Kings
"Oo Wee Bay Bee"	Young Kat, The Kings
"Only If You Have a Dream"	Lucy, Magoo
"The Last Thing You Need"	Young Kat, Bingo, Magoo, Ballie
"Stupid Boy"	Kat
The Claridges Hotel Medley	
"Cavalla Kings" (Reprise)	The Kings
"The Singing Sensation"	Young Kat, Lucy, The Kings
"The Bell Hop"	Bingo, The Kings
"Blind Date"	Magoo
"Lonely Girl" (Reprise)	Lucy, The Kings
"The Invisible Dog"	Bingo, The Kings
"Hey Baby"	Young Kat, The Kings
"Cavalla Kings" (Reprise)	Lucy, The Kings
"Skeleton Dance"	The Kings
"Lagunya"	Bingo, Ballie, Young Kat, Magoo
"Lucky Day" (Reprise)	Young Kat, Kat
Finale	

"The Singing Sensation" (Reprise)	Young Kat, The Kings
"Hey Baby" (Reprise)	Magoo, The Kings
"We Were Rocking"	Kat, Company
"Lagunya" (Reprise)	Bingo, Company
"Wild Time"	Company

The Scarlet Pimpernel (129). Second revised version of the musical based on the novel by Baroness Orczy; book and lyrics by Nan Knighton; music by Frank Wildhorn. Produced by Radio City Entertainment and Ted Forstmann at the Neil Simon Theater. Informally dubbed "Scarlet Pimpernel 3.0." Opened September 10, 1999. (Closed January 2, 2000)

Marguerite	Carolee Carmello	Ozzy	Harvey Evans
Chauvelin	Marc Kudisch	Elton	Russell Garrett
Percy	Ron Bohmer	Dewhurst	Ken Land
Marie	Elizabeth Ward Land	Jessup	Charles West
Armand	Kirk McDonald	Ben	James Hindman
Tussaud	David Masenheimer	Farleigh	Matthew Shepard
Coupeau	Stephonne Smith	Hal	Danny Gurwin
Mercier	David St. Louis	Robespierre; Prince of Wales	David Cromwell

Opera Dancers, Soldiers, Prisoners, British Guests, Servants—Emily Hsu, Alicia Irving, David Masenheimer, Robb McKindles, Katie Nutt, Elizabeth O'Neill, Terry Richmond, Laura Schutter, Charles West, Debra Wiseman.

Orchestra: Ron Melrose conductor; Wendy Bobbitt Cavett associate conductor, keyboards; Andrew Wilder assistant conductor, keyboards; Laura Oatts concertmaster; Britt Swenson, Ashley Horne violin; Liuh-Wen Ting viola; Daniel D. Miller, Sarah Hewitt cello; Richard Sarpola bass; Steven Greenfield, James Roe woodwinds; Roger Lee trumpet; Mike Christianson trombone; Jill Williamson, Kelly Dent, French horn; Robert Gustafson keyboard; John Meyers, Benjamin Herman percussion.

Understudies: Mr. Bohmer—Peter Flynn, Matthew Shepard; Miss Carmello—Elizabeth Ward Land, Debra Wiseman; Mr. Kudisch—David Masenheimer, Matthew Shepard; Mr. McDonald—Danny Gurwin, Robb McKindles; Mr. Cromwell—David Masenheimer, James Van Treuren; Mr. Evans—James Hindman, James Van Treuren; Mr. Land—Peter Flynn, James Hindman, James Van Treuren; Miss Land—Terry Richmond, Debra Wiseman; Mr. Garrett—Peter Flynn, Drew Geraci; Messrs. Hindman, Gurwin—Drew Geraci, Robb McKindles. Swings: Peter Flynn, Drew Geraci, Cynthia Leigh Heim, Jennifer Smith, James Van Treuren.

Directed and choreographed by Robert Longbottom; musical direction and vocal arrangements, Ron Melrose; scenery, Andrew Jackness; costumes, Jane Greenwood; lighting, Natasha Katz; sound, Karl Richardson; fight direction, Rick Sordelet; special effects, Jim Steinmeyer; orchestrations, Kim Scharnberg; musical supervision, Jason Howland; music coordinator, John Miller; dance arrangements, David Chase; executive producer, Tim Hawkins; casting, Mark Simon; production stage manager, Bonnie L. Becker; stage manager, Kenneth J. Davis; press, Barlow-Hartman Public Relations, Michael Hartman, John Barlow.

A brave Englishman pretends to be a fop, as he leads a League of his countrymen rescuing French aristocrats from the guillotine, as in Baroness Orczy's novel and co-authored play produced on Broadway 10/24/10; in a musical version produced off Broadway 1/7/64 for 3 performances; in the movie starring Leslie Howard; and in this musical, which opened on Broadway 11/9/97 and played 373 performances through 10/3/98, reopened on Broadway in a revised version 11/4/98 for 239 performances through 5/30/99, and is re-presented in this second revision.

ACT I

"Storybook"	Marguerite, French Ensemble
"Madame Guillotine"	Chauvelin
"You Are My Home"	Percy, Marguerite
Wedding Dance	Ensemble
"Prayer"	Percy
"Into the Fire"	Percy, The League
The Rescue	Ensemble
"Falcon in the Dive"	Chauvelin

"When I Look at You" .... Marguerite
"Where's the Girl?" .... Chauvelin
"The Creation of Man" .... Percy, The League
"The Riddle" .... Chauvelin, Marguerite, Percy

ACT II

"The Scarlet Pimpernel" .... Percy, Marguerite, Ball Guests
"They Seek Him Here" .... Percy
The Gavotte .... Company
"She Was There" .... Percy
"I'll Forget You" .... Marguerite
The Duel .... Percy, Chauvelin, Marguerite
"Into the Fire" .... Company

Epic Proportions (92). By Larry Coen and David Crane. Produced by Philip & Patricia Barry Productions and Robert Dragotta at the Helen Hayes Theater. Opened September 30, 1999. (Closed December 19, 1999)

CAST: Narrator—Michael Carroll; Octavium, Slavemaster, Queen's Attendant, Cochette's Assistant—Tom Beckett; Louise Goldman—Kristin Chenoweth; Benny Bennet—Alan Tudyk; Phil Bennet—Jeremy Davidson; Jack, lst General, Brady—Richard Ziman; Shel, 2d General, Executioner—Ross Lehman; Extra Extra, Egyptian Dancing Girl, The Queen, Cochette—Ruth Williamson; D.W. DeWitt—Richard B. Shull. Conspirators—Richard Ziman, Ross Lehman, Ruth Williamson; Extras—Richard Ziman, Tom Beckett, Ross Lehman; Egyptians—Tom Beckett, Ross Lehman, Richard Ziman; Guards—Ross Lehman, Richard Ziman; Gladiators—Richard Ziman, Tom Beckett, Ross Lehman.

Standbys: Messrs. Beckett, Lehman, Shull, Ziman—Larry Cahn; Messrs. Davidson, Tudyk—Robert Petkoff; Misses Chenoweth, Williamson—Beverly Ward.

Directed by Jerry Zaks; scenery, David Gallo; costumes, William Ivey Long; lighting, Paul Gallo; sound, Aural Fixation; fight direction, Rick Sordelet; associate director, BT McNicholl; executive producer, Mark Schwartz; associate producer, William K. Ehrenfeld; casting, Stuart Howard, Amy Schecter; production stage manager, Rick Steiger; stage manager, Lisa Iacucci; press, The Pete Sanders Group, Pete Sanders, Bill Coyle.

Time: The early 1930s. Place; The Arizona desert. The play was presented in two parts.

Broad comedy version of the filming of an epic motion picture, previously produced off off Broadway at Manhattan Punch Line.

***Dame Edna: The Royal Tour** (260). Solo performance piece by Barry Humphries; devised and written by Barry Humphries; additional material by Ian Davidson. Produced by Leonard Soloway, Chase Mishkin, Steven M. Levy and Jonathan Reinis at the Booth Theater. Opened October 17, 1999.

CAST: Barry Humphries, Roxane Barlow, Andrew Ross, Tamlyn Brooke Shusterman.

Scenery, Kenneth Foy; costumes, Stephen Adnitt; lighting, Jason Kantrowitz; sound, Peter Fitzgerald; associate producers, Skylight Productions, Adam Friedson, David Friedson, Allen Spivak/Larry Magid, Richard Martini; production stage manager, James W. Gibbs; press, Kevin P. McAnarney.

Barry Humphries as Dame Edna Everage, a razor-edged comic persona disguised as a suburban housewife with opinions on all subjects aimed from a position of total self-satisfaction, in a British performance piece previously presented internationally. The play was presented in two parts.

***Saturday Night Fever** (256). Musical based on the Paramount/RSO picture based on a story by Nik Cohn, screen play by Norman Wexler; stage adaptation by Nan Knighton in collaboration with Arlene Phillips, Paul Nicholas and Robert Stigwood; songs by The Bee Gees (B., R. & M. Gibb). Produced by Robert Stigwood at the Minskoff Theater. Opened October 21, 1999.

Tony Manero .... James Carpinello
Stephanie Mangano .... Paige Price
Annette .... Orfeh
Bobby C .... Paul Castree

SATURDAY NIGHT FEVER—James Carpinello as Tony Manero with the company of the musical based on the movie

Joey	Sean Palmer
Double J	Andy Blankenbuehler
Gus	Richard H. Blake
Monty	Bryan Batt
Frank Manero	Casey Nicholaw
Flo Manero; Lucille	Suzanne Costallos
Frank Junior	Jerry Tellier
Fusci; Al	Frank Mastrone
Jay Langhart; Becker	David Coburn
Chester	Andre Ward
Cesar	Michael Balderrama
Vinnie	Chris Ghelfi
Sal	Danial Jerod Brown
Dino	Brian J. Marcum
Lou	Rick Spaans
Dom	Miles Alden
Roberto	Ottavio
Antonio	Drisco Fernandez
Ike	David Robertson
Shirley	Karine Plantadit-Bageot
Maria	Natalie Willes
Connie	Jeanine Meyers
Doreen	Angela Pupello
Linda Manero; Patti	Aliane Baquerot
Gina	Rebecca Sherman
Sophia	Paula Wise
Donna	Shannon Beach
Rosalie	Deanna Dys
Lola	Jennifer Newman
Inez	Danielle Jolie
Lorelle	Stacey Martin
Kenny	Kristoffer Cusick
Nick	Karl duHoffmann
Rocker	Roger Lee Israel
Natalie	Anne Nicole Biancofiore
Ann Marie	Marcia Urani
Angela	Gina Philistine

Orchestra: Martyn Axe conductor; Henry Aronson associate conductor, keyboard; Lawrence Feldman, William Meade reeds; David Stahl, Earl Gardner trumpet; Larry Farrell, Randall Andos trombone; Will Parker, French horn; Ian Stewart bass; Johan Nilson, Jeff Lee Campbell guitar; Philip Fortenberry, Eddie Rabin, John Samorian keyboard; Farah Alvin, Scott Beck, Julie Danao, Solomon, Alan Souza, Donna Vivino piano, vocals; Jon Berger, James Musto percussion; Chris Parker drums.

Understudies: Mr. Carpinello—Richard H. Blake, Sean Palmer; Miss Price—Jeanine Meyers, Angela Pupello; Orfeh—Jeanine Meyers, Gina Philistine; Mr. Castree—Miles Alden, Rick Spaans; Mr. Palmer—Chris Ghelfi, Rick Spaans; Mr. Blankenbuehler—Danial Jerod Brown, Chris Ghelfi; Mr. Blake—Miles Alden, Danial Jerod Brown, Kristoffer Cusick; Mr. Batt—David Coburn, Jerry Tellier; Mr. Nicholaw—David Coburn, Frank Mastrone; Miss Costallos—Deanna Dys, Angela Pupello; Mr. Tellier—Karl duHoffmann, Brian J. Marcum; Mr. Mastrone—David Coburn, David Eggers, Brian J. Marcum; Mr. Coburn—Karl duHoffmann, David Eggers. Swings: Anne Nicole Biancofiore, Kristoffer Cusick, Karl duHoffmann, David Eggers, Roger Lee Israel, Gina Philistine, Amanda Plesa, Marcia Urani. Dance captain: Marcia Rani. Fight captain: Ottavio.

Directed and choreographed by Arlene Phillips; musical direction, Martyn Axe; scenery, Robin Wagner; costumes, Andy Edwards; Broadway costumes, Suzy Benzinger; lighting, Andrew Bridge; sound, Mick Potter; orchestrations, Nigel Wright; dance and vocal arrangements, Phil Edwards; musical supervision, Phil Edwards; musical coordinator, William Meade; fight direction, J. Allen Suddeth; associate producers, Manny Kladitis, David Rocksavage; casting, Bernard Telsey; production stage manager, Perry Cline; stage manager, Maximo Torres; press, Bill Evans & Associates, Bill Evans, Jim Randolph, Terry Lilly, Jonathan Schwartz.

Time: 1976 . . . or whenever you were 19. Place: New York City (Brooklyn and Manhattan).

Stage version of the 1977 movie about a Brooklyn lad striving to make it in the Manhattan discos, with songs of the era. Originally produced in London by Robert Stigwood, Paul Nicholas and David Ian.

ACT I

Scene 1: The neighborhood—Bay Ridge, Brooklyn
"Stayin' Alive" .... Tony, Company
Scene 2: The Manero house
Scene 3: Outside 2001 Odyssey—Saturday night
"Boogie Shoes" .... Tony, The Faces
(by Harry Casey and Richard Finch)
Scene 4: Inside 2001 Odyssey—Saturday night
"Disco Inferno" .... Monty, Company
(by Leroy Green and Ron Kersey)
"Night Fever" .... Tony, Company
Scene 5: The neighborhood paint store
Scene 6: The Manero house
Scene 7: Dale Dance Studios
"Disco Duck" .... Monty
(by Rick Dees)
"More Than a Woman" .... Tony, Stephanie
Scene 8: The neighborhood
"If I Can't Have You" .... Annette
Scene 9: Inside 2001 Odyssey—Saturday night
"It's My Neighborhood" .... Company
"You Should Be Dancing" .... Tony, Company

ACT II

Scene 1: The Verrazano Narrows Bridge—Saturday night
"Jive Talkin'" .... Tony, Annette, The Faces, Company
Scene 2: Dale Dance Studios
"First & Last"/"Tragedy" .... Bobby C
Scene 3: The neighborhood
Scene 4: Stephanie's apartment, Manhattan
"What Kind of Fool" .... Stephanie
(by B. Gibb and A. Galuten)
Scene 5: Park bench near the bridge
Scene 6: The neighborhood
Scene 7: Inside 2001 Odyssey—Saturday night
"Nights on Broadway" .... Annette, Stephanie, Company

The Dance Competition:
"Night Fever" .... Company
"Open Sesame" .... Chester, Shirley
(by R. Bell/Kool and the Gang)
"More Than a Woman" .... Tony, Stephanie
"Salsation" .... Cesar, Maria
(by David Shire)
Scene 8: Exterior 2001 Odyssey—Saturday night
"Immortality" .... Tony
Scene 9: Verrazano Narrows Bridge—Saturday night
Scene 10: Park bench near the bridge
"How Deep Is Your Love" .... Tony, Stephanie

Other music credits: "A Fifth of Beethoven" by Walter Murphy, "Also Sprach Zarathustra" by Richard Strauss, "Night on Disco Mountain" by David Shire.

Radio City Entertainment. Schedule of two programs. **Radio City Christmas Spectacular** (210). Holiday spectacle including *The Living Nativity* pageant originally conceived by Robert F. Jani. Opened November 4, 1999. (Closed January 5, 2000). **A Christmas Carol** (72). Revival of the musical based on the story by Charles Dickens; book by Mike Ockrent and Lynn Ahrens; music by Alan Menken; lyrics by Lynn Ahrens. Opened November 26, 1999. (Closed December 30, 1999) *Radio City Christmas Spectacular* produced by Radio City Entertainment, Howard Kolins executive producer, at Radio City Music Hall; *A Christmas Carol* produced by American Express, Dodger Endemol Theatricals executive producer, at the Theater at Madison Square Garden.

RADIO CITY CHRISTMAS SPECTACULAR

Santa Claus .... Charles Edward Hall, Jeff Williams
Mrs. Claus .... Mary Stout, Beth McVey
Clara .... Tamara Allison, Jennifer Russell
Skaters .... Jennifer Bayer and Jeb Rand, Emmanuel Balmori and Andrew Naylor
Elves:
Tinker .... Michael Gilden
Tick-Tock .... Sammy Brullo
Beacon .... Adam Brown
Nifty .... Francesca Winston
Shifty .... Ethan Crough
Hoofer .... Lisa Blanchard
Inkwell .... Leslie Vanderpool
Mr. Spruce .... David Stienberg
Swings .... Marty Klebba, Emily Westhafer

Radio City Rockettes: Melanie Allen, Linda Baldwin, Kiki Bennett, Tara Bradley-Schweitzer, Amy Burnette, Elizabeth Charney-Sprei, Michelle Chase, Jacqueline Collins, Renee Collins, Lillian Colon-Jaramillo, Katherine Corp, Kimberly Corp, Jennifer Lee Crowl, Wendy DeRouen, Jocelyn Dowling, Rebecca Downing-Bartsch, Jenny Eakes, Ashlee J. Fife, Michelle Gaudette, Ida Gilliams, Heather Goetz, Michelle Hammar, Susan Heart, Cheryl Hebert-Cutlip (Rockette co-captain), Michele Imor, Jennifer Jones, Kimberly C. Jones, Pamela Jordan, Temple Kane, Donna Kapral, Natalie M. King, Debby Kole, Jenifer Krater, Amy N. Krawcek, Stephanie Lang, Melissa Rae Mahon, Jennifer Marquardt, Mindy Mason, Lisa J. Matsuoka, Patrice McConachie, Julie McDonald, Lori Mello, Cynthia M. Muller, Rachael Nelson, Michelle O'Steen-Vivona, Michelle Pampena, Wendy Pasquale, Heather Dee Perry, Cynthia Petrone, Mia Price, Erica A. Reed, Laureen Repp Russell, Allison Richy, Marisa Rozek, Jennifer Sagan, Kara Sandberg, Megan Schenck, Jennifer Leigh Schwerer, Maryellen Scilla-Greco, Cheryl Scott, Jane Silane, Leslie Simmons, Nicole Sistare, Amber Smith, Debra Denys Smith, Katherine Steers, Leslie Stroud, Christine Teixeira, Kristin Tudor (Rockette co-captain), Marilyn Westlake, Chryssie Whitehead, Jaime Windrow, Elaine Winslow-Redmond, Beth Woods, Eileen Woods, Courtney Young.

Ensemble: Alan Bennett, Barry Brown, Michelle Clowers, Gregory Daniels, Brad DeLima, Bill Disbennett, Caroline Doherty, Billy Fagen, Ramon Flowers, Cynthia Goerig, Jamie Harris, Selena Harris, Brittany Hastings, Peter Huck, Ashley Hull, Helen Hur, Susannah Israel, Ryan Jackson, Lesley Jennings, Lorin Latarro, Richard Lewis, Troy Magino, Melanie Malicote, Richie Mastascusa, Heather McFadden, Hannah Meadows, Halden Michaels, Carolyn Ockert, Steve Oltorik, Gary Plankell, Chelsey Powell, Keenah Reid, Jermaine Rembert, Alice Rietveld, Jim Ruttman, Tim Santos, Greg Schanuel, Joni Michelle Schenck, Megan Sikora, Matthew Sipress, Chris Snow, Jonathan Stahl, Michael Susko,

Erin Swanson, Kathleen Swanson, Susanne Trani, Andrew Turteltaub, Michelle Weber, Jacen Wilkerson.

Radio City Orchestra: David Chase conductor; Grant Sturiale associate conductor; Wayne Abravanel, Todd Ellison assistant conductors; Mary L. Rowell concertmaster; Andrea Andros, Eric De Gioia, Carmen DeLeo, Michael Gillette, Nannette Levi, Susan Lorentsen, Samuel Marder, Holly Ovenden violin; Richard Spencer, Barbara H. Vaccaro viola; Sarah Carter, Frank Levy cello; Dean Crandall bass; Kenneth Emery flute; Kenneth Arzberger, John M. Cippola, Gerard J. Niewood, Richard Oatts, Joshua Siegel reeds; Russ Rizner, Nancy Schallert, French horn; Hollis Burridge, Richard Raffio, Zachary Shnec trumpet; Mark Johanssen, Thomas B. Olcott, John D. Schnupp trombone; Andrew Rodgers tuba; Thomas J. Oldakowski drums; Mario DeCiutiis, Maya Gunji percussion; Anthony Cesarano guitar; Henry Aronson, Susanna Nason piano; Jeanne Maier harp; George Wesner, Fred Davies organ.

Directed and choreographed by Robert Longbottom; musical director, David Chase; associate musical director, Grant Sturiale; production design, Michael Hotopp, Charles Lisanby; scenery, Bill Hoffman, Mark Solan; costumes, Gregg Barnes; lighting, Ken Billington, Jason Kantrowitz; sound, Tom Clark; assistant director, Tom Kosis; assistant choreographers, Michael Clowers, John Dietrich, Tom Kosis, Lynn Sullivan, Darlene Wilson; vocal arrangements, David Chase, Don Pippin, Bryan Louiselle; original orchestrations, Elman Anderson, Douglas Besterman, Michael Gibson, Arthur Harris, Phillip J. Lang, Dick Lieb; dance music arrangements, David Chase, Peter Howard, Mark Hummel; "Silent Night" arrangement, Percy Faith; associate producer, Julie Oppermann-Knie; production stage manager, John Bonanni; lst assistant stage managers, Kathy Hoovler, Carey Lawless; stage managers, Tom Bouchard, Peggy Imbrie, Joseph Oronato, Beth Stiegel-Rohr, Nichola Taylor, Karl Thompson; press, Radio City Entertainment, Liz Bishko.

Original music: "Santa's Gonna Rock and Roll" and "I Can't Wait Till Christmas Day" music by Henry Krieger, lyrics by Bill Russell, arranged by Bryan Louiselle. Creative credits: Overture arrangement, Don Pippin; film score arrangement, Bryan Louiselle. Parade of the Wooden Soldiers choreography, Russell Markert; scenery, Charles Lisanby; costumes, Vincente Minnelli. Rag Dolls original choreography, Scott Salmon; original costumes, Pete Menefee. The Living Nativity Narrator, Charles Edward Hall; restaged by Linda Lemac; scenery, Charles Lisanby; costumes, Frank Spencer.

67th edition of Radio City Music Hall's Christmas show, starring the Rockettes and including the traditional Nativity pageant, presented without intermission.

SCENES: Overture—Radio City Orchestra. Scene 1: Santa's Gonna Rock and Roll. Scene 2: The Nutcracker. Scene 3: The Parade of the Wooden Soldiers. Scene 4: Here Comes Santa Claus. Scene 5: White Christmas in New York (Guest Forecasters: Al Roker, Sam Champion, Linda Church, Mark Danon, Bill Evans, Storm Field, Irv "Mr. G" Gokofsky, Janice Huff, Joe Moreno, Bonnie Schneider, Lisa Villasenor, Michelle White). Scene 6: Ice Skating in the Plaza. Scene 7: The North Pole. Scene 8: Santa's Toy Workshop. Scene 9: The Living Nativity with One Solitary Life ("Silent Night," "O Little Town of Bethlehem," "The First Noel," "We Three Kings," "O Come All Ye Faithful," "Hark, the Herald Angels Sing"). Jubilant: "Joy to the World"—Organ, Company.

A CHRISTMAS CAROL

Beadle .... Del-Bourree Bach
Mr. Smythe .... Chris Vasquez
Grace Smythe;
Want .... Brittany Alexander Campbell, Marissa Gould
Scrooge .... Tony Roberts
Cratchit .... Nick Corley
Old Joe; Mr. Hawkins .... Kenneth McMullen
Mrs. Cratchit .... Whitney Webster
Tiny Tim .... Dennis Michael Hall, Patrick Stogner
Poulterer; Judge .... Roland Rusinek
Sandwichboard Man; Ghost of
Christmas Present .... Reginald VelJohnson
Jonathon .... Matt Bowles, Marshall Pailet
Lamplighter;
Ghost of Christmas Past .... Didi Conn
Blind Hag; Scrooge's Mother ...... Joan Barber
Fred .... James Judy
Mrs. Mopps .... Marilyn Pasekoff
Ghost of Jacob Marley .... Paul Kandel
Scrooge at 8; Ignorance ...... Johnny Cennicola, Jimmy Walsh
Scrooge's Father;
Undertaker .... Wayne Schroder
Scrooge at 12 .... Andrew Keenan-Bolger, Kennedy Kanagawa
Fan .... Lexine Bondoc, Tristin Mays
Fezziwig .... Daniel Marcus
Scrooge at 18 .... Joe Cassidy
Young Marley; Undertaker .... Ken Barnett
Mrs. Fezziwig .... Debra Cardona

Emily .... Kristin Huxhold
Sally .... La Tanya Hall
Ghost of Christmas
Yet-To-Be .... Christine Dunham

Charity Men: Don Mayo, Roland Rusinek, Wayne Schroder.

Street Urchins: Andrew Keenan-Bolger, Johnny Cennicola, Lexine Bondoc, Kennedy Kanagawa, Tristin Mays, Jimmy Walsh.

Lights of Christmas Past: Leo Alvarez, Keith Fortner, Michael Lomeka, David Rosales.

The Cratchit Children: Andrew Keenan-Bolger, Lexine Bondoc, Kennedy Kanagawa, Tristin Mays.

Business Men, Gifts, Ghosts, People of London: Lori Alexander, Leo Alvarez, Del-Bourree Bach, Joan Barber, Ken Barnett, Hayes Bergman, Liam Burke, Debra Cardona, Joe Cassidy, Candy Cook, Juliet Fischer, Keith Fortner, La Tanya Hall, Kristin Huxhold, James Judy, Carrie Kenneally, Jessica Kostival, Michael Lomeka, Daniel Marcus, Don Mayo, Kenneth McMullen, Marilyn Pasekoff, Meredith Patterson, Gail Pennington, Josef Reiter, David Rosales, Wendy Rosoff, Roland Rusinek, Vikki Schnurr, Wayne Schroder, Erin Stoddard, Chris Vasquez, Whitney Webster. Swings: Ron Bagden, Jane Brockman, Jeffrey Hankinson, Ann Kittredge, Adam Pelty, Angela Piccinni, Rommy Sandhu, Cynthia Thole.

Angels: P.S. 390 and 330 La Petite Musicale; Park Middle School Broadway Chorus; South Side Middle School Chorale; YPC Jubilee Chorus. Red Children's Cast: Marissa Gould, Kennedy Kanagawa, Tristin Mays, Marshall Pailet, Patrick Stogner, Jimmy Walsh. Green Children's Cast: Andrew Keenan-Bolger, Lexine Bondoc, Matt Bowles, Brittany Alexander Campbell, Johnny Cennicola, Dennis Michael Hall. Swings: Patrick Dunn, Bret Fox, Molly Jobe.

Orchestra: Paul Gemignani conductor; Mark C. Mitchell assistant conductor; Aloysia Friedmann concertmaster; Karl Kawahara, Ann Labin, Sebu Serinian violin; Monica Gerard, Adria Benjamin viola; Clay Ruede cello; Charles Bergeron bass; David Weiss, Kenneth Dybisz, Alva Hunt, Daniel Wieloszynski, John Winder woodwinds; Ronald Sell, French horn; Bob Millikan, Phil Granger, Dominic Derasse trumpet; Bruce Eidem, Dean Plank trombone; Janet Aycock, Maggie Torre keyboard; Jennifer Hoult harp; Michael Berkowitz drums; Glenn Rhian percussion.

Directed by Mike Ockrent; choreography, Susan Stroman; musical direction, Paul Gemignani; scenery, Tony Walton; costumes, William Ivey Long; lighting, Jules Fisher, Peggy Eisenhauer; sound, Tony Meola; projections, Wendall K. Harrington; flying, Foy; orchestrations, Michael Starobin, Douglas Besterman; dance arrangements and incidental music, Glen Kelly; associate directors, Ray Roderick, Steven Zweigbaum; associate choreographer, Chris Peterson; producer, Tim Hawkins; casting, Julie Hughes, Barry Moss; production stage manager, Rolt Smith; stage manager, Gary Mickelson.

Time: 1880. Place: London.

This is the 6th annual production of this musical version of *A Christmas Carol*, which was presented without intermission.

SCENES AND MUSICAL NUMBERS

Scene 1: The Royal Exchange
"A Jolly Good Time" .... Charity Men, Smythe Family, Business Men, Wives, Children
"Nothing to Do With Me" .... Scrooge, Cratchit
Scene 2: The street
"You Mean More to Me" .... Cratchit, Tiny Tim
"Street Song (Nothing to Do With Me)" .... People of London, Scrooge, Fred, Jonathon, Sandwichboard Man, Lamplighter, Blind Hag, Grace Smythe
Scene 3: Scrooge's house
"Link by Link" .... Marley's Ghost, Scrooge, Ghosts
Scene 4: Scrooge's bedchamber
"The Lights of Long Ago" .... Ghost of Christmas Past
Scene 5: The law courts
"God Bless Us, Everyone" .... Scrooge's Mother
Scene 6: The factory
"A Place Called Home" .... Scrooge at 12, Fan, Scrooge
Scene 7: Fezziwig's Banking House
"Mr. Fezziwig's Annual Christmas Ball" .... Fezziwig, Mrs. Fezziwig, Guests
"A Place Called Home" (Reprise) .... Emily, Scrooge at 18, Scrooge
Scene 8: Scrooge and Marley's
"The Lights of Long Ago" (Part II) .... Scrooge at 18, Young Marley, Emily,

People From Scrooge's Past

Scene 9: A starry night
"Abundance and Charity" .... Ghost of Christmas Present, Scrooge, Christmas Gifts
Scene 10: All over London
"Christmas Together" .... Tiny Tim, The Cratchits, Ghost of Christmas Present, Fred, Sally, Scrooge, People of London
Scene 11: The graveyard
"Dancing on Your Grave" .... Ghost of Christmas Yet-To-Be, Monks, Business Men, Mrs. Mopps, Undertakers, Old Joe, Cratchit
"Yesterday, Tomorrow and Today" .... Scrooge, Angels, Children of London
Scene 12: Scrooge's bedchamber
"London Town Carol" .... Jonathon
Scene 13: The street, Christmas Day
"Nothing to Do With Me" (Reprise) .... Scrooge
"Christmas Together" (Reprise) .... People of London
"God Bless Us, Everyone" (Finale) .... Company

***Roundabout Theater Company.** Schedule of three programs. **The Rainmaker** (84). Revival of the play by N. Richard Nash. Opened November 11, 1999. (Closed January 23, 2000) ***Uncle Vanya** (36). Revival of the play by Anton Chekhov. Opened April 30, 2000. And *The Man Who Came to Dinner* by Moss Hart and George S. Kaufman scheduled to open 6/27/00. Produced by Roundabout Theater Company, Todd Haimes artistic director, Ellen Richard managing director, Julia C. Levy executive director of external affairs, at the Brooks Atkinson Theater.

ALL PLAYS: founding director, Gene Feist; associate artistic director, Scott Ellis; director of artistic development, Jim Carnahan; press, Boneau/Bryan-Brown, Adrian Bryan-Brown, Erin Dunn, Johnny Woodnal.

THE RAINMAKER

Lizzie Curry .... Jayne Atkinson
H.C. Curry .... Jerry Hardin
Noah Curry .... John Bedford Lloyd
Jim Curry .... David Aaron Baker
File .... Randle Mell
Sheriff Thomas .... Bernie McInerney
Bill Starbuck .... Woody Harrelson

Farmhands: Eric Axen, Scott McTyer Cowart, David Harbour, Brian Ibsen, Rey Lucas, Donovan McGrath, Dustin Tucker, Jason Winther.

Standbys: Mr. Harrelson—Stevie Ray Dallimore. Miss Atkinson—Angela Reed. Understudies: Mr. Hardin—Bernie McInerney; Mr. Lloyd—Mark Zimmerman, David Harbour; Mr. Baker—Scott McTyer Cowart; Messrs. Mell, McInerney—Mark Zimmerman.

Directed by Scott Ellis; scenery, James Noone; costumes, Jess Goldstein; lighting, Peter Kaczorowski; sound, Brian Ronan; sound effects design, Gregory Meeh; original music, Louis Rosen; fight choreographer, David Leong; casting, Jim Carnahan, Amy Christopher; production stage manager, Lori M. Doyle; stage manager, Michael Sisolak.

The Rainmaker was first produced on Broadway 10/28/54 for 125 performances. This is its first major New York revival of record, except in the form of the musical version *110 in the Shade* 10/24/63 for 330 performances and 7/18/92 for 12 performances.

UNCLE VANYA

Astrov .... Roger Rees
Marina .... Anne Pitoniak
Vanya .... Derek Jacobi
Telegin .... David Patrick Kelly
Serebryakov .... Brian Murray
Sonya .... Amy Ryan
Yelena .... Laura Linney
Maria Vasilyevna .... Rita Gam
Laborer .... Torben Brooks
Yefim .... James Coyle
Servants .... Jonah Bay, Greg Keller

Understudies: Messrs. Jacobi, Rees—Torben Brooks; Messrs. Murray, Kelly—James Coyle; Misses Gam, Pitoniak—Jane Cronin; Misses Linney, Ryan—Julia Gibson; Mr. Coyle—Jonah Bay; Mr. Brooks—Greg Keller.

Directed by Michael Mayer; scenery and costumes, Tony Walton; lighting, Kenneth Posner; original music and sound, David Van Tieghem; fight direction, J. Steven White; casting, Jim Carnahan; production stage manager, Lori M. Doyle; stage manager, Andrea J. Testani; press, Boneau/Bryan-Brown, Adrian Bryan-Brown, Erin Dunn, Johnny Woodnal.

Time: Mid-July through late September, 1899. Place: A Russian country estate. The play was presented in two parts. The last major New York production of *Uncle Vanya* was by Circle in the Square 2/24/95 for 29 performances.

The Price (128). Revival of the play by Arthur Miller. Produced by David Richenthal at the Royale Theater. Opened November 15, 1999. (Closed March 5, 2000)

Victor Franz .... Jeffrey DeMunn
Esther Franz .... Lizbeth Mackay
Gregory Solomon .... Bob Dishy
Walter Franz .... Harris Yulin

Directed by James Naughton; scenery, Michael Brown; costumes, Laurie A. Churba; lighting, Rui Rita; sound, Jerry M. Yager; executive producer, Robert Cole; casting, Amy Christopher; production stage manager, Grayson Meritt; stage manager, Kelly Kirkpatrick; press, Richard Kornberg & Associates, Richard Kornberg, Don Summa, Jim Byk, Tom D'Ambrosio, John Wimbs.

Time: Mid-afternoon on a Saturday in Winter, 1966. Act I: The attic of a brownstone on the West Side of Manhattan. Act II: Immediately following.

The last major New York revival of *The Price* was by Roundabout Theater Company on Broadway 6/10/92 for 47 performances.

Tango Argentino (63). Revival of the music and dance revue in the Spanish language conceived by Claudio Segovia and Hector Orezzoli; music by various authors (see listing below). Produced by DG Producciones at the Gershwin Theater. Opened November 17, 1999. (Closed January 9, 2000)

Dancers: Nelida and Nelson, Hector and Elsa Maria Mayoral, Carlos and Ines Borquez, Norma and Luis Pereyra, Carlos Copello and Alicia Monti, Roberto Herrera and Lorena Yacono, Guillermina Quiroga, Vanina Bilous, Antonio Cervila Jr., Johana Copes. Guest Artists: Juan Carlos Copes, Maria Nieves, Pablo Veron. Singers: Raul Lavie, Maria Grana, Jovita Luna, Alba Solis.

Musicians: Osvaldo Berlingieri, Christian Zarate piano; Roberto Pansera, Horacio Romo bandoneon; Ruben Oscar Gonzalez bandoneon, percussion, flute; Pablo Agri, Pablo Aznarez, Raul Di Renzo, Gustavo Roberto Mule, Walter Sebastian Prusac, Leonardo Suarez Paz violin; Dino Carlos Quarleri violincello; Enrique Guerra contrabass.

Directed by Claudio Segovia and Hector Orezzoli; choreographic conception, Claudio Segovia; choreography, the dancers; musical direction, Osvaldo Berlingieri, Julio Oscar Pane, Roberto Pansera; scenery, costumes and lighting conceived by Claudio Segovia and Hector Orezzoli; sound, Gaston Brisky; executive producers, Daniel Grinbank, Fernando Moya, Carlos Rivadella; associate producer, Phil Ernst; press, Boneau/Bryan-Brown, Chris Boneau, Brian Rubin.

A foreign production with the tango interpreted in song, story and dance by Argentinian artists, previously produced on Broadway 10/9/85 for 198 performances.

ACT I: "Quejas de Bandoneon" (by J. De Dios Filiberto)—Orchestra. El Apache Argentino (by M. Aroztegui and A. Mathon)—Antonio Cervila Jr., Pablo Veron, Luis Pereyra, Juan Carlos Lopes, Carlos Borquez, Carlos Copello. El Portenito (by A. Villaldo)—Guillermina Quiroga, Norma Pereyra, Alicia Monti, Johana Copes, Ines Borquez. El Esquinazo (by A. Villoldo)—Veron, Quiroga. "La Punalada" (by P. Castellanos and E.C. Flores) and "El Choclo" (by A. Villoldo and E.S. Discepolo)—Orchestra. La Cumparista (by G.M. Rodriguez)—Veron, Quiroga. "Mi Noche Triste"—Raul Lavie. El Entrerriano (by R. Mendizabal)—Norma and Luis Pereyra. "De Mi Barrio" (by R. Goyeneche)—Jovita Luna. Chique—Juan Carlos and Johana Lopes. Bandoneones—Roberto Pansera, Horacio Romo, Ruben Gonzalez, Alejandro Zarate.

Also Milonguita (by E. Delfino and S. Linning), Divina (by J. Mora and J. De la Calle), Melenita de Oro (by E. Delfino and S. Linning) and Re-Fa-Si (by E. Delfino)—Vanina Bilous, Nelson and Nelida,

Cervila, Elsa Maria, Norma and Luis Pereyra, Ines and Carlos Borquez, Monti, Quiroga, Johana Copes, Hector Mayoral, Veron, Copello.

Also "Nostalgias" (by J.C. Cobain and E. Cadicamo)—Orchestra. La Yumba (by O. Pugliese)—Ines and Carlos Borquez. "Cautivo"—Maria Grana. Recuerdo (by O. Pugliese)—Copello, Monti. "Canaro en Paris" (by A. Scarpino and J. Caldarella)—Orchestra. Nocturna (by J. Plaza)—Norma and Luis Pereyra, Ines and Carlos Borquez, Copello and Monti, Cervilla and Johana Copes, Roberto Herrera and Lorena Yacono.

ACT II: Milongueando en El '40—Herrera, Yacono. "Uno" (by E.S. Discepolo and M. Mores) and "La Ultima Curda"—Alba Solis. Milonguero Viejo—Hector and Elsa Maria Mayoral. Celos (by Gade)—Nelida and Nelson. "Naranjo en Flor" (by H.Y.V. Esposito)—Lavie. Tanguera (by M. Mores)—Veron, Quiroga. "La Mariposa"—Orchestra. Patetico—Juan Carlos Copes, Maria Nieves. "Cancion Desesperada"—Grana. Verano Porteno (by A. Piazzola)—Bilous, Cervila. "Balada Para Mi Muerte" (by H. Ferrer and A. Pizzola)—Orchestra.

Also Danzarin (by J. Plaza) and Quejas de Bandoneon (by J. De Dios Filiberto)—Juan Carlos Copes and Nieves, Nelida and Nelson, Hector and Elsa Maria Mayoral, Veron and Quiroga, Cervila, Inez and Carlos Borquez, Norma and Luis Pereyra, Copello and Monti, Herrera and Yacono.

***Kiss Me, Kate** (224). Revival of the musical with book by Sam and Bella Spewack, music and lyrics by Cole Porter. Produced by Roger Berlind and Roger Horchow at the Martin Beck Theater. Opened November 18, 1999.

Hattie .... Adriane Lenox
Paul .... Stanley Wayne Mathis
Stage Manager .... Eric Michael Gillett
Lois Lane; Bianca .... Amy Spanger
Bill Calhoun; Lucentio .... Michael Berresse
Lilli Vanessi; Katharine .... Marin Mazzie
Fred Graham; Petruchio ... Brian Stokes Mitchell
Harry Trevor; Batista .... John Horton
Stage Doorman .... Robert Ousley
Cab Driver; Nathaniel .... Jerome Vivona
1st Man; .... Lee Wilkof
2d Man .... Michael Mulheren
Harrison Howell .... Ron Holgate
Gremio .... Kevin Neil McCready
Hortensio .... Darren Lee
Gregory .... Vince Pesce
Philip .... Blake Hammond
Haberdasher .... Michael X. Martin

Ensemble: Eric Michael Gillett, Patty Goble, Blake Hammond, JoAnn M. Hunter, Nancy Lemenager, Darren Lee, Michael X. Martin, Kevin Neil McCready, Carol Lee Meadows, Elizabeth Mills, Linda Mugleston, Robert Ousley, Vince Pesce, Cynthia Sophiea, Jerome Vivona.

Orchestra: Paul Gemignani conductor; Mark Mitchell associate conductor, keyboard; Suzanne Ornstein concertmistress, violin; Xin Zhao violin; Richard Brice violin, viola; Igor Seedrov cello; Dennis Anderson woodwind #1; Eric Weidman woodwind #2; Charles Pillow woodwind #3; Don McGeen woodwind #4; Dominic Derasse trumpet #1; Larry Lunetta trumpet #2; Bruce Eidem trombone; Ronald Sell, French horn; Paul Pizzuti drums, percussion; John Beal bass.

Standby: Messrs. Mitchell, Holgate—Merwin Foard. Understudies: Mr. Mitchell—Michael X. Martin; Miss Mazzie—Patty Goble; Miss Spanger—JoAnn M. Hunter, Nancy Lemenager; Mr. Berresse—Kevin Neil McCready; Miss Lenox—Cynthia Sophiea; Mr. Horton—Robert Ousley; Mr. Mathis—T. Oliver Reid; Mr. Wilkof—Blake Hammond; Mr. Mulheren—Blake Hammond, Michael X. Martin; Mr. Holgate—Michael X. Martin; Mr. Lee—Vince Pesce, T. Oliver Reid; Mr. McCready—Jerome Vivona, T. Oliver Reid. Swings: Paula Leggett Chase, T. Oliver Reid.

Directed by Michael Blakemore; choreography, Kathleen Marshall; musical direction, Paul Gemignani; scenery, Robin Wagner; costumes, Martin Pakledinaz; lighting, Peter Kaczorowski; sound, Tony Meola; orchestrations, Don Sebesky; dance arrangements, David Chase; fight direction, B.H. Barry; associate choreographer, Rob Ashford; associate producers, Richard Godwin, Edwin H. Schloss; casting, Johnson-Liff Associates; production supervision, Steven Zweigbaum; production manager, Arthur Siccardi; stage manager, Ara Marx; press, Boneau/Bryan-Brown, Chris Boneau, Amy Jacob, Matt Polk.

Time: June 1948. Place, Act I: Ford's Theater, Baltimore. Act II: The same, immediately following.

The last major New York revival of *Kiss Me, Kate* was by New York City Center Light Opera Company 5/28/65 for 23 performances.

ACT I

Scene 1: The stage of Ford's Theater, Baltimore
"Another Op'nin' Another Show" .... Hattie, Company

KISS ME, KATE—Amy Spanger, Michael Berresse, Marin Mazzie and Brian Stokes Mitchell in a scene from the revival of the musical

Scene 2: The backstage corridor
"Why Can't You Behave" .... Lois, Bill
Scene 3: Fred and Lilli's dressing rooms
"Wunderbar" .... Fred, Lilli
"So in Love" Lilli
Scene 4: Padua
"We Open in Venice" .... Petruchio, Katharine, Bianca, Lucentio
Scene 5: A street in Padua (Piazza)
"Tom, Dick or Harry" .... Bianca, Lucentio, Gremio, Hortensio
"I've Come to Wive It Wealthily in Padua" .... Petruchio, Men
"I Hate Men" .... Katharine
"Were Thine That Special Face" .... Petruchio
Scene 6: The backstage corridor
Scene 7: Fred and Lilli's dressing rooms
Scene 8: A country road in Padua
"Cantiamo D'Amore" .... Ensemble
Scene 9: The church in Padua
"Kiss Me, Kate" .... Petruchio, Katharine, Ensemble

ACT II

Scene 1: The theater alley
"Too Darn Hot" .... Paul, Ensemble
Scene 2: Before the curtain
Scene 3: Petruchio's house

"Where Is the Life That Late I Led?" .... Petruchio
Scene 4: The backstage corridor
"Always True to You (In My Fashion)" .... Bianca
Scene 5: Fred and Lilli's dressing rooms
"From This Moment On" .... Harrison Howell, Lilli
Scene 6: The backstage corridor
"Bianca" .... Bill, Ensemble
"So in Love" (Reprise) .... Fred
Scene 7: Before the curtain
"Brush Up Your Shakespeare" .... 1st Man, 2d Man
Scene 8: Baptista's house, Padua
Pavane .... Bianca, Lucentio, Ensemble
"I Am Ashamed That Women Are So Simple" .... Katharine
"Kiss Me, Kate" (Finale) .... Company

Putting It Together (101). Revival of the musical revue with words and music by Stephen Sondheim. Produced by Cameron Mackintosh in association with the Mark Taper Forum, Gordon Davidson, artistic director, at the Ethel Barrymore Theater. Opened November 21, 1999. (Closed February 20, 2000)

Wife .... Carol Burnett
Husband .... George Hearn
Younger Man .... John Barrowman
Younger Woman .... Ruthie Henshall
Observer .... Bronson Pinchot
Wife, at certain performances .... Kathie Lee Gifford

Orchestra: Paul Raiman conductor, pianist; Nicholas Archer associate conductor, synthesizer; Matthew Sklar assistant conductor, keyboards; Louis Bruno bass; David Silliman drum, percussion; Elizabeth Kieronski oboe, English horn; Les Scott clarinet; John Campo bassoon; Stu Satalof trumpet.

Standbys: Misses Burnett, Gifford—Ronnie Farer; Mr. Hearn—John Jellison; Messrs. Barrowman, Pinchot—David Engel; Miss Henshall—Christina Marie Norrup.

Directed by Eric D. Schaeffer; musical staging, Bob Avian; musical direction, Paul Raiman; design, Bob Crowley; lighting, Howard Harrison; projections, Wendall K. Harrington; sound, Andrew Bruce/Mark Menard; orchestrations, Jonathan Tunick; Miss Burnett's costume, Bob Mackie; associate director–choreographer, Jodi Moccia; casting, Johnson-Liff Associates; executive producers, David Caddick, Martin McCallum; production stage manager, Peter von Mayrhauser; press, the Publicity Office, Marc Thibodeau, Bob Fennell, Michael S. Borowski, Brett Oberman.

Subtitled "a musical review" of Sondheim's work, *Putting It Together* was first produced in 1992 at the Old Fire Station, Oxford, England. Its New York premiere was presented by Manhattan Theater Club 4/1/93 for 59 performances.

ACT I

"Invocations and Instructions to the Audience" (*The Frogs*) .... Observer
"Putting It Together" (*Sunday in the Park with George*) .... Company
"Rich and Happy" (*Merrily We Roll Along*) .... Company
"Do You Hear a Waltz" (*Do I Hear a Waltz?*) .... Wife, Husband
"Merrily We Roll Along" #1 (*Merrily We Roll Along*) .... Observer
"Lovely" (*A Funny Thing Happened on the Way to the Forum*) .... Company
"Hello Little Girl" (*Into the Woods*) .... Husband, Younger Woman
"My Husband the Pig" (*A Little Night Music*) .... Wife
"Everyday a Little Death" (*A Little Night Music*) .... Wife, Younger Woman
"Everybody Ought to Have a Maid" (*A Funny Thing Happened on the Way to the Forum*) .... Observer
"Have I Got a Girl for You" (*Company*) .... Younger Man, Husband
"Pretty Women" (*Sweeney Todd*) .... Younger Man, Husband
"Sooner or Later" (*Dick Tracy*) .... Younger Woman
"Bang!" (*A Little Night Music*) .... Younger Man, Observer, Younger Woman
"Country House" (*Follies*) .... Wife, Husband
"Unworthy of Your Love" (*Assassins*) .... Younger Man, Younger Woman

"Merrily We Roll Along" #2 (*Merrily We Roll Along*) .... Observer
"Could I Leave You?" (*Follies*) .... Wife
"Rich and Happy" (Reprise) (*Merrily We Roll Along*) .... Company

ACT II

Entr'acte .... Orchestra
"Back in Business" (*Dick Tracy*) .... Company
"It's Hot Up Here" (*Sunday in the Park With George*) .... Company
"The Ladies Who Lunch" (*Company*) .... Wife
"The Road You Didn't Take" (*Follies*) .... Husband
"Live Alone and Like It" (*Dick Tracy*) .... Younger Man
"More" (*Dick Tracy*) .... Younger Woman
"There's Always a Woman" (*Anyone Can Whistle*) .... Wife, Younger Woman
"Buddy's Blues" (*Follies*) .... Observer
"Good Thing Going" (*Merrily We Roll Along*) .... Husband
"Marry Me a Little" (*Company*) .... Younger Man
"Not Getting Married Today" (*Company*) .... Wife
"Merrily We Roll Along" #3 (*Merrily We Roll Along*) .... Company
"Being Alive" (*Company*) .... Company
"Like It Was" (*Merrily We Roll Along*) .... Wife
Finale — "Old Friends" (*Merrily We Roll Along*) .... Company

***Lincoln Center Theater.** Schedule of three programs. **Marie Christine** (44). Musical with words and music by Michael John LaChiusa. Opened December 2, 1999. (Closed January 9, 2000) ***Contact** (72). Transfer from off Broadway of the dance play by Susan Stroman and John Weidman; written by John Weidman; directed and choreographed by Susan Stroman. Opened March 30, 2000. **Rose** (40). One-woman performance by Olympia Dukakis ; written by Martin Sherman; presented by arrangement with the Royal National Theater. Opened April 12, 2000. (Closed May 20, 2000) Produced by Lincoln Center Theater under the direction of Andre Bishop and Bernard Gersten, *Marie Christine* and *Contact* at the Vivian Beaumont Theater, *Rose* at the Lyceum Theater.

MARIE CHRISTINE

Prisoner #1 .... Jennifer Leigh Warren
Prisoner #2 .... Andrea Frierson-Toney
Prisoner #3 .... Mary Bond Davis
Marie Christine L'Adrese .... Audra McDonald
At Wednesday and Saturday
Matinees .... Sherry Boone
Marie Christine's Mother .... Vivian Reed
Serpent; Helena .... Donna Dunmire
Dante Keyes .... Anthony Crivello
Celeste .... Lovette George
Ozelia .... Rosena M. Hill
Jean L'Adrese .... Keith Lee Grant
Paris L'Adrese .... Darius de Haas
Lisette .... Kimberly JaJuan
Joachim; Monsieur
Archambeau .... Andre Garner
Osmond; Monsieur St. Vinson .... Jim Weaver
Beatrice .... Joy Lynn Matthews
Magdalena .... Mary Testa
Petal .... Janet Metz
Duchess .... Kim Huber
Gates .... Shawn Elliott
Bartender; Esau Parker .... Peter Samuel
Bar Patron .... Michael Babin
Leary .... Michael McCormick
McMahon .... Mark Lotito
Esau Parker .... Peter Samuel
Olivia Parker .... Janet Metz
Grace Parker .... Kim Huber
Chaka (drums) .... David Pleasant

Children: Powers Pleasant, Zachary Thornton, Joshua Walter. Ensemble: Franz C. Alderfer, Ana Maria Andricain, Michael Babin, Brent Black, Donna Dunmire, Andre Garner, Lovette George, Rosena M. Hill, Kim Huber, Mark Lotito, Joy Lynn Matthews, Michael McCormick, Janet Metz, Monique Midgette, Peter Samuel, Jim Weaver.

Orchestra: David Evans conductor; Lawrence Yurman associate conductor, keyboard; Seymour Red Press musical coordinator; Steven Kenyon, John Moses, Richard Heckman, John Winder woodwinds; Brian O'Flaherty, Kamau Adilifu trumpets; Peter Gordon, Janet Lantz, French horns; Robert Lawrence,

Maura Giannini violins; Kenneth Burward-Hoy viola; Scott Ballantyne cello; Raymond Kilday bass; Raymond Grappone, Lawrence Spivack percussion.

Understudies: Valets and Messrs. Weaver, Garner—Franz C. Alderfer; Miss Dunmire, Daughters—Ana Maria Andricain; Mr. Lotito—Michael Babin; Messrs. Crivello, Samuel—Brent Black; Mr. de Haas—Andre Garner; Miss Matthews—Lovette George; Miss JaJuan—Rosena M. Hill; Miss Reed—Joy Lynn Matthews; Mr. Elliott—Michael McCormick; Miss Testa—Janet Metz; Maids—Monique Midgette; Mr. McCormick—Peter Samuel; Mr. Grant—Jim Weaver; Misses Warren, Frierson-Toney, Davis—Lovette George, Joy Lynn Matthews, Monique Midgette.

Directed and choreographed by Graciela Daniele; musical direction, David Evans; scenery, Christopher Barreca; costumes, Toni-Leslie James; lighting, Jules Fisher, Peggy Eisenhauer; sound, Scott Stauffer; orchestrations, Jonathan Tunick; fight direction, Luis Perez; associate choreographer, Willie Rosario; associate producer, Ira Weitzman; casting, Alan Filderman; stage manager, Arturo E. Porazzi; press, Philip Rinaldi, Miller Wright.

Time: Moves from present to past, or to future. Place, Prelude: a Prison. Act I: 1894, A park on Lake Pontchartrain, Marie Christine's home on Mandolin Street in New Orleans and its interiors, as well as its garconniere and ballroom; a pier. Act II: 1899, A saloon in Chicago's First Ward, an alleyway, a small house and its interior.

Based on the Medea myth, this musical tracks the descent into madness and murder of an aristocratic black woman whose family is of Caribbean origins.

ACT I

"Before the Morning" .... Women
"Mamzell' Marie" .... Company
"Ton Grandpere est le Soleil" .... Marie Christine's Mother
"Beautiful" .... Marie Christine
"Way Back to Paradise" .... Marie Christine, Lisette
"Storm" .... Dante
"To Find a Lover" .... Marie Christine, Company
"Nothing Beats Chicago"/"Ocean Is Different"/"Danced With a Girl" .... Dante
"Tou Mi Mi" .... Lisette
"Miracles and Mysteries" .... Marie Christine's Mother, Prisoners
"I Don't Hear the Ocean" .... Dante, Marie Christine
"Bird Inside the House" .... Maids, Valets
"All Eyes Look Upon You" .... Jean
"A Month Ago" .... Maids
"Danced With a Girl" (Reprise) .... Dante
"We're Gonna Go to Chicago" .... Dante, Marie Christine
"Dansez Calinda" .... Lisette
"I Will Give" .... Marie Christine, Prisoners
Finale .... Paris, Company

ACT II

Opening/"I Will Love You" .... Prisoners, Dante, Marie Christine
"Cincinnati" .... Magdalena, Daughters
"You're Looking at the Man" .... Leary, McMahon, Dante, Company
"The Scorpion" .... Dante, Marie Christine
"Lover Bring Me Summer" .... Olivia, Grace Parker
"Tell Me" .... Marie Christine
"Paradise Is Burning Down" .... Magdalena
"Prison in a Prison" .... Marie Christine, Prisoners, Helena, Dante
"Better & Best" .... Leary, McMahon
"Good Looking Woman" .... Gates, Leary, McMahon
"No Turning Back" .... Paris, Mother, Jean, Lisette
"Beautiful" (Reprise) .... Marie Christine
"A Lovely Wedding" .... Magdalena
"I Will Love You" (Reprise) .... Marie Christine
"Your Name" .... Dante
Finale .... Women

CONTACT

Part I: Swinging
A Forest Glade, 1767. A Servant, an Aristocrat, a Girl on a Swing—Seán Martin Hingston, Stephanie Michels, Scott Taylor.
Part II: Did You Move?
An Italian Restaurant, Queens, 1954. A Wife, a Husband, a Headwaiter—Karen Ziemba, Jason Antoon, David MacGillivray, Rocker Verastique, Robert Wersinger, Tomé Cousin, Peter Gregus, Nina Goldman, Dana Stackpole, Scott Taylor, Seán Martin Hingston, Pascale Faye, Shannon Hammons.
Part III: Contact
New York City, 1999. An Advertising Executive, a Bartender, and a Girl in a Yellow Dress. Michael Wiley—Boyd Gaines. With Deborah Yates, Jason Antoon, Jack Hayes, Robert Wersinger, Nina Goldman, Scott Taylor, Shannon Hammons, Stephanie Michels, Seán Martin Hingston, Rocker Verastique, Pascale Faye, Mayumi Miguel, Tomé Cousin, Dana Stackpole, Peter Gregus.

Standbys: Michael Wiley—John Bolton; Girl in a Yellow Dress—Holly Cruikshank. Understudies: Frenchmen—John Bolton, Stacey Todd Holt, Robert Wersinger; Girl on a Swing— Holly Cruikshank, Shannon Hammons, Angelique Ilo, Joanne Manning; Husband—John Bolton, Peter Gregus, Stacey Todd Holt; Wife—Holly Cruikshank, Nina Goldman, Angelique Ilo; Head Waiter—Steve Geary, Rocker Verastique, Scott Taylor; Michael Wiley—Scott Taylor; Girl in a Yellow Dress—Joanne Manning; Bartender—John Bolton, Stacey Todd Holt

Scenery, Thomas Lynch; costumes, William Ivey Long; lighting, Peter Kaczorowski; sound, Scott Stauffer; associate choreographer, Chris Peterson; musical theater associate producer, Ira Weitzman; casting, Tara Rubin, Johnson-Liff Associates, Daniel Swee; production stage manager, Thom Widmann; press, Philip Rinaldi, Miller Wright.

Three dance episodes bring to life a variety of fantasies from the sexual to the comic to the despairing. The play was presented in two parts with the intermission following Part II. Winner of the 1999–2000 Tony Award for Best Musical; see its entry in the Prizewinning Plays section of this volume.

MUSIC: "My Heart Stood Still" by Richard Rodgers and Lorenz Hart; "Anitra's Dance" from *Peer Gynt Suite No. 1* by Grieg; "Waltz Eugene" from Eugene Onegin Op. 24; "La Farandole" from *L'Arlesienne Suite No. 2*; "O Mio Babbino Caro" by Puccini; "You're Nobody Till Somebody Loves You" by Russ Morgan, Larry Stock and James Cavanaugh; "Powerful Stuff" by Wally Wilson, Michael Henderson and Robert S. Field; "Put a Lid on It" by Tom Maxwell; "Sweet Lorraine" by Clifford Burwell and Maxwell Parish; "Runaround Sue" by Ernest Maresca and Dion DiMucci; "Beyond the Sea" by Charles Trenet and Jack Lawrence; "See What I Mean?" by J. Chapman; "Simply Irresistible" by Robert Palmer; "Do You Wanna Dance" by Bobby Freeman; "Topsy" by William Edgar Battle and Eddie Durham; "Sing Sing Sing" by Louis Prima; "Christopher Columbus" by Andy Razaf; "Moondance" by Van Morrison.

ROSE

Rose .... Olympia Dukakis

Directed by Nancy Meckler; written by Martin Sherman; designer, Stephen Brimson Lewis; lighting, Johanna Town; sound, Peter Salem, Scott Anderson; stage manager, Michael Brunner; press, Philip Rinaldi, Miller Wright, Barbara Carroll.

A Holocaust survivor spins her personal tale of horror, loss and love set against the backdrop of 20th century Europe, Israel and the United States.

Minnelli on Minnelli (19). Songs from the movies of Vincente Minnelli. Produced by Radio City Entertainment, Scott Nederlander, and Stewart F. Lane at the Palace Theater. Opened December 8, 1999. (Closed January 2, 2000)

With Liza Minnelli, Jeffrey Broadhurst, Stephen Campanella, Billy Hartung, Sebastian LaCause, Jim Newman, and Alec Timerman.

Orchestra: Bill LaVorgna musical director, conductor, drums; Russ Kassoff piano, keyboards; Lisa Brooke concertmaster; Ethel Abelson violin; John Dexter viola; Monica LaVorgna cello; Sean Smith bass; Mark Vinci lead alto sax, soprano sax, piccolo, flute, clarinet; Mike Migliore alto sax, piccolo, flute, clarinet; Frank Perowsky tenor sax, soprano sax, piccolo, flute, clarinet; Andrew Drelles tenor sax, piccolo, flute, clarinet, bass clarinet; Ed Xiques baritone sax, alto flute, bass clarinet; Dave Stahl lead trumpet; Ross Konikoff trumpet; Danny Cahn trumpet; Kaitilin Mahony, French horn; Clint Sharman, Dale Kirkland trombone; George Flynn bass trombone; Dom Cicchetti keyboards; Bill Washer guitars; Bill Hayes percussion.

Orchestrators: Michael Abene, William David Brohn, Jorge Calendrelli, Ned Ginsburg, Russell Kassoff, Peter Matz, Don Sebesky, Jonathan Tunick, Torrie Zito.

Written and directed by Fred Ebb; choreography, John DeLuca; musical direction, Bill LaVorgna; scenery, John Arnone; costumes, Bob Mackie; lighting, Howell Binkley; sound, Peter J. Fitzgerald; projections, Batwin + Robin; film sequence, Jack Haley Jr.; musical arrangements and supervision, Billy Stritch, Marvin Hamlisch; vocal arrangements, Billy Stritch; dance music arrangements, David Krane, Peter Howard; executive producers, Gary Labriola and Edward J. Micone Jr.; casting, Jay Binder; production stage manager, Karl Lengel; press, Barlow Hartman Public Relations, Michael Hartman, John Barlow.

***Swing!** (181). Musical revue by various authors (see listing below). Produced by Marc Routh, Richard Frankel, Steven Baruch, Tom Viertel, Jujamcyn Theaters and Lorie Cowen Levy/Stanley Shopkorn in assoication with BB Promotion, Dede Harris/Jeslo Productions, Pace Theatrical Group/SFX, Libby Adler Mages/Mari Glick, Douglas L. Meyer/James D. Stern at the St. James Theater. Opened December 9, 1999.

With Ann Hampton Callaway, Everett Bradley, Laura Benanti, Laureen Baldovi, Kristine Bendul, Carol Bentley, Caitlin Carter, Geralyn Del Corso, Desirée Duarte, Beverly Durand, Erin East, Scott Fowler, Ryan Francois, Kevin Michael Gaudin, Edgar Godineaux, Aldrin Gonzalez, Janine LaManna, Rod McCune, J.C. Montgomery, Arte Phillips, Robert Royston, Carlos Sierra-Lopez, Jenny Thomas, Keith Lamelle Thomas, Maria Torres, Casey MacGill and The Gotham City Gates, Michael Gruber.

The Gotham City Gates: Jonathan Smith conductor, piano, keyboard; Douglas Oberhamer associate conductor, trumpet; Dan Hovey guitar; Conrad Korsch bass; Scott Neumann drums, percussion; Matt Hong, Lance Bryant woodwinds; Steve Armour trombone.

Standbys: Misses Callaway, Benanti—Janine LaManna; Messrs. Bradley, Gruber, MacGill—J.C. Montgomery; Mr. Francois—Arte Phillips. Swings: Kristine Bendul, Desirée Duarte, Erin East, Kevin Michael Gaudin, Rod McCune.

Directed and choreographed by Lynne Taylor-Corbett; musical direction, Jonathan Smith; production supervised by Jerry Zaks; scenery, Thomas Lynch; costumes, William Ivey Long; lighting, Kenneth Posner; sound, Peter Fitzgerald; original concept, Paul Kelly; aerial flying, Antigravity, Inc.; orchestrations, Harold Wheeler; music supervisor, Michael Rafter; music coordinator, John Miller; associate choreographers, Scott Fowler and Rod McCune; associate choreographer and Lindy specialist, Ryan Francois; associate producers, TV Asahi/Hankyu, Mars Theatrical Productions, Judith Marinoff; casting, Carol Hanzel & Associates; production stage manager, Karen Armstrong; stage manager, Tripp Phillips; press representative, Helene Davis Publicity, Helene Davis, Ash Curtis.

A celebration of swing music and dance featuring classic songs, new numbers and choreography in a variety of regional styles.

MUSICAL NUMBERS, ACT I: "It Don't Mean a Thing" (by Duke Ellington, Irving Mills)—Casey MacGill, the Band. "Air Mail Special" (by Benny Goodman, James R. Mundy, Charles Christian), "Jersey Bounce" (by B. Plater, T. Bradshaw, E. Johnson, B. Feyhe, Duke Ellington), "Opus One" (by D. George, J. Hodges, H. James)—Company. "Jumpin' at the Woodside" (by William "Count" Basie; choreography, Ryan Francois, Jenny Thomas)—Ryan Francois, Jenny Thomas, Company. "Bounce Me Brother" (by Don Raye, Hughie Prince)—Ann Hampton Callaway, Douglas Oberhamer, Company. "Two and Four" (by Ann Hampton Callaway), "Hit Me With a Hot Note and Watch Me Bounce" (by Duke Ellington, Don George)—Laura Benanti, MacGill, Band. "Rhythm" (by Casey MacGill)—MacGill, Michael Gruber, Company. "Throw That Girl Around" (by Everett Bradley, Ilene Reid, Michael Heitzman), "Show Me What You Got" (by Everett Bradley, Jonathan Smith)—Everett Bradley, Company; West Coast Swing Couple, Beverly Durand, Aldrin Gonzalez; Latin Swing Couple, Carlos Sierra-Lopez, Maria Torres. "Bli-Blip" (by Duke Ellington, Sid Kuller; additional lyrics by Ann Hampton Callaway)—Callaway, Bradley. "Billy-A-Dick" (by Hoagy Carmichael, Paul Francis Webster; additional lyrics by Sean Martin Hingston)—Gruber, Company. "Harlem Nocturne" (by Earl H. Hagen)—

Caitlin Carter, Conrad Korsch. "Kitchen Mechanics' Night Out" (by Casey MacGill, Jonathan Smith, Lynne Taylor-Corbett, Paul Kelly)—MacGill, Francois, Jenny Thomas, Company. "Shout and Feel It" (by William "Count" Basie; choreography, Ryan Francois, Jenny Thomas)—Francois, Jenny Thomas. "Boogie Woogie Bugle Boy" (by Don Raye, Hughie Prince)—Bradley, Keith Lamelle Thomas, Edgar Godineaux with Oberhamer, Lance Bryant, Matt Hong.

The USO: "GI Jive" (by Johnny Mercer)—Benanti, Geralyn Del Corso, Carter. "A String of Pearls" (by Edgar DeLange, Jerry Gray), "I've Got a Gal in Kalamazoo" (by Mack Gordon, Harry Warren), "Candy" by (Mack David, Joan Whitney, Alex C. Kramer)—Aldrin Gonzalez, Keith Lamelle Thomas, Gruber, Company. "I'm Gonna Love You Tonight" (by Casey MacGill, Jack Murphy; additional lyrics by Lynne Taylor-Corbett)—Benanti, Gruber, Company. "I'll Be Seeing You" (by Sammy Fain, Irving Kahal)—Callaway, Scott Fowler, Carol Bentley. "In the Mood" (by Joe Garland), "Don't Sit Under the Apple Tree" (by Lew Brown, Sam H. Stept, Charlie Tobias)—Company.

ACT II: "Swing, Brother, Swing" (by Walter Bishop, Lewis Raymond, Clarence Williams; choreography Scott Fowler)—Scott Fowler, Callaway, Benanti, Bradley, Gruber, MacGill, Company. "Caravan" (by Duke Ellington, Juan Tizol)—The Gotham City Gates. "Dancers in Love" (by Duke Ellington)—Del Corso, Keith Lamelle Thomas. "Cry Me a River" (by Arthur Hamilton)—Benanti, Steve Armour. "Blues in the Night" (by Harold Arlen, Johnny Mercer)—Callaway, Carter, Godineaux. "Take Me Back to Tulsa" and "Stay a Little Longer" (by Bob Wills, Tommy Duncan)—Bradley, Gruber, MacGill, Company. "Boogie Woogie Country" (by Jack Murphy, Jonathan Smith; choreography, Robert Royston, Laureen Baldovi)—Robert Royston, Laureen Baldovi, Company. "All of Me" (by Seymour Simons, Gerald Marks), "I Won't Dance" (by Dorothy Fields, Otto A. Harbach, Jimmy McHugh, Jerome Kern, Oscar Hammerstein II; additional lyrics by Ann Hampton Callaway)—Bradley, Callaway. "Bill's Bounce" (by Bill Elliott)—Gonzalez, Scott Fowler, Durand, Bentley. "Stompin' at the Savoy" (by Benny Goodman, Edgar M. Sampson, Chick Webb, Andy Razaf; additional lyrics by Ann Hampton Callaway)—Callaway. "Swing, Brother, Swing" (by Walter Bishop, Lewis Raymond, Clarence Williams), "Sing, Sing, Sing" (by Louis Prima, Andy Razaf, L. Berry), "It Don't Mean a Thing" (Lindy choreography, Ryan Francois)—Company.

Amadeus (173). Revival of the play by Peter Shaffer. Produced by Kim Poster, PW Productions, Adam Epstein, SFX Theatrical Group, Center Theater Group/Ahmanson Theater, in association with Old Ivy Productions at the Music Box Theater. Opened December 15, 1999. (Closed May 7, 2000)

Antonio Salieri .... David Suchet
Wolfgang Amadeus Mozart ...... Michael Sheen
Constanze Weber .... Cindy Katz
Emperor Joseph II
of Austria .... David McCallum
Count Johann Kilian Von Strack .... J.P. Linton
Count Orsini-Rosenberg .... Terence Rigby
Baron Van Swieten .... Michael Keenan
The "Venticelli" ... Jake Broder, Charles Janasz
Major Domo .... John Rainer
Salieri's Valet .... William Ryall
Salieri's Cook .... Robert Machray
Kapellmeister Bonno .... John Towey
Teresa Salieri .... Glynis Bell
Katherina Cavalieri .... Kate Miller

Servants: Jeffrey Bean, Geoffrey Blaisdell, Dan Mason, Kevin Orton. Citizens of Vienna: Jeffrey Bean, Glynis Bell, Geoffrey Blaisdell, Robert Machray, Dan Mason, Kate Miller, Kevin Orton, John Rainer, William Ryall

Standby: Mr. Suchet—Rocco Sisto. Understudies: Mr. Suchet—Charles Janasz; Mr. Sheen—Jake Broder; Misses Katz, Bell—Kate Miller; Mr. Linton—William Ryall; Mr. Rigby—John Rainer; Mr. Keenan—Robert Machray; Messrs. Broder, Janasz—Dan Mason, Kevin Orton; Messrs. Rainer, Ryall—Geoffrey Blaisdell; Messrs. Machray, Towey—Jeffrey Bean; Miss Miller—Glynis Bell; Mr. McCallum—John Towey; Messrs. Bean, Blaisdell, Mason, Orton—Brian Rardin.

Directed by Peter Hall; design, William Dudley; lighting, Paule Constable; sound, Matt McKenzie; U.K. casting, Gillian Diamond; U.S. casting, Pat McCorkle, CSA; associate producers, Bradley R. Bernstein, Marc Epstein; production stage manager, Susie Cordon; stage manager, Allison Sommers; production manager, Peter Fulbright; press representative, Boneau/Bryan-Brown, Adrian Bryan-Brown, Jackie Green, Steven Padla.

Time: November, 1823 and 1781 to 1791. Place: Vienna.

Amadeus was first produced in New York 12/17/80 for 1,181 performances and was named a Best Play of its season and won the best-play Tony. This is its first major New York revival.

AMADEUS—Michael Sheen as Mozart, David McCallum as Joseph II and David Suchet as Salieri in a scene from the revival of Peter Shaffer's play

Waiting in the Wings (188). By Noel Coward; as revised by Jeremy Sams. Produced by Alexander H. Cohen, Chase Mishkin, Max Cooper, Leonard Soloway and Steven M. Levy at the Eugene O'Neill Theater. Opened December 16, 1999. (Closed May 28, 2000)

The Residents:
May Davenport .... Rosemary Harris
Cora Clarke .... Rosemary Murphy
Bonita Belgrave .... Elizabeth Wilson
Maudie Melrose .... Patricia Conolly
Deirdre O'Malley .... Helena Carroll
Almina Clare .... Bette Henritze
Sarita Myrtle .... Helen Stenborg
Lotta Bainbridge .... Lauren Bacall
Topsy Baskerville .... Victoria Boothby

Just Visiting:
Osgood Meeker .... Barnard Hughes
Dora, Lotta's dresser .... Sybil Lines
Zelda Fenwick .... Crista Moore
Alan Banfield .... Anthony Cummings

The Staff:
Sylvia Archibald .... Dana Ivey
Perry Lascoe .... Simon Jones
Doreen .... Amelia Campbell
Ted .... Geddeth Smith
St. John's Ambulance man ..... Collin Johnson

Standbys: Miss Harris—Isa Thomas; Misses Henritze, Wilson, Conolly, Lines, Boothby—Nancy C. Evers; Misses Carroll, Stenborg, Ivey—Sybil Lines; Mr. Hughes—Geddeth Smith; Messrs. Jones, Cummings—Collin Johnson; Misses Moore, Campbell—Stina Nielsen; Mr. Johnson—Scott Rollison.

Directed by Michael Langham; scenery, Ray Klausen; costumes, Alvin Colt; lighting, Ken Billington; sound, Peter Fitzgerald; production manager, Beverley Randolph; associate producer, Skylight Productions; casting, Johnson-Liff Associates; press, David Rothenberg Associates, David J. Gersten.

Time: The early 1960s. Place: "The Wings," a residential home for retired actresses.

Act I, Scene 1: Early fall. Scene 2: 3 a.m. on a Monday a month later. Scene 3: A Sunday afternoon in winter. Act II, Scene 1: A week later. Scene 2: New Year's Eve. Scene 3: A Sunday afternoon, a week later.

Waiting in the Wings, Noel Coward's play about the personal cross-currents among the inhabitants of a home for retired actresses, opened here on the 100th anniversary of its author's birth and has had no previous New York production of record.

*__Much Ado About Everything__ (132). Solo performance by Jackie Mason; written by Jackie Mason. Produced by Jyll Rosenfeld and Fred Krohn at the John Golden Theater. Opened December 30, 1999.

Directed by Jackie Mason; lighting, Stan Crocker; sound, Christopher Cronin; producers, Raoul Lionel Felder, Jon Stoll; associate producers, Howard Weiss, Henry Handler, JAM Theatricals; stage manager, Don Myers; press, Lawrence Weinberg Associates.

Fifth Broadway production of Jackie Mason's standup comedy, which comments on the social and political foibles of the day. The show was presented in two parts.

James Joyce's The Dead (112). Transfer from off Broadway of the musical version of the story by James Joyce; book by Richard Nelson; music by Shaun Davey; lyrics conceived and adapted by Richard Nelson and Shaun Davey. Produced by Gregory Mosher and Arielle Tepper at the Belasco Theater in the Playwrights Horizons production, Tim Sanford artistic director. Opened January 11, 2000. (Closed April 16, 2000)

The Hostesses:
Aunt Julia Morkan .... Sally Ann Howes
Aunt Kate Morkan .... Marni Nixon
Mary Jane Morkan .... Emily Skinner
The Family:
Gabriel Conroy .... Christopher Walken
Gretta Conroy .... Blair Brown
The Guests:
Mr. Browne .... Brian Davies
Freddy Malins .... Stephen Spinella
Mrs. Malins .... Paddy Croft
Miss Molly Ivors .... Alice Ripley
Bartell D'Arcy .... John Kelly
The Help:
Lily .... Brooke Sunny Moriber
Michael .... Dashiell Eaves
Rita .... Daisy Eagan
Cellist .... Daniel Barrett
Violinist .... Louise Owen
Ghost:
Young Julia Morkan .... Daisy Eagan

Musicians: Charles Prince conductor; Deborah Abramson associate musical director, piano; Daniel Barrett cello; Steve Benson guitar; Jaqui Leclair oboe, English horn; Louise Owen violin; Tom Partington percussion; Virginia Pike synthesizer, harmonium; Gen Shinkai flute.

Understudies: Misses Howes, Nixon, Croft—Patricia Kilgarriff; Misses Skinner, Ripley—Donna Lynne Champlin; Messrs. Walken, Spinella—Sean Cullen; Miss Brown—Anne Runolfsson; Messrs. Davies, Kelly—Gannon McHale; Misses Moriber, Eagan—Angela Christian; Mr. Eaves—Brandon Sean Wardell.

Directed by Richard Nelson; choreography, Seán Curran; musical direction, Charles Prince; scenery, David Jenkins; costumes, Jane Greenwood; lighting, Jennifer Tipton; sound, Scott Lehrer; orchestrations, Shaun Davey; casting, James Calleri, Mark Bennett; production stage manager, Matthew Silver; stage manager, Dan da Silva; press, The Publicity Office, Bob Fennell, Marc Thibodeau, Michael S. Borowski, Brett Oberman.

Time: Near the turn of the century. Place: Dublin, the Misses Morkans' annual Christmas-time party. The play was presented without intermission.

Adaptation of Joyce's *Dubliners* short story reflecting upon the personalities and relationships at a long-past, moderately festive gathering of family and friends. Winner of the 1999–2000 New York Drama Critics Circle and Lucille Lortel Award for best musical; see its entry in the Prizewinning Plays section of this volume.

MUSICAL NUMBERS

Scene 1: The drawing room of the Misses Morkans' flat.
Prologue .... Musicians
"Killarney's Lakes" .... Mary Jane, Aunt Kate, Rita
"Kate Kearney" .... Michael, Mary Jane, Company
"Parnell's Plight" .... Miss Ivors, Michael, Gabriel, Gretta, Company
"Adieu to Ballyshannon" .... Gabriel, Gretta

"When Lovely Lady" .... Aunt Julia, Aunt Kate
"Three Jolly Pigeons" .... Freddy, Browne, Company
"Goldenhair" .... Gretta, Gabriel

Scene 2: The drawing room arranged for dinner.

"Three Graces" .... Gabriel, Company
"Naughty Girls" .... Aunt Julia, Aunt Kate, Mary Jane, Company
"Wake the Dead" .... Freddy, Company

Scene 3: Aunt Julia's bedroom.

"D'Arcy's Aria" .... D'Arcy
"Queen of Our Hearts" .... Browne, Freddy, Gabriel, D'Arcy, Michael
"When Lovely Lady" (reprise) .... Young Julia, Aunt Julia

Scene 4: A room in the Gresham Hotel.

"Michael Furey" .... Gretta
"The Living and the Dead" .... Gabriel, Company

Authors' note: The lyrics to some of these songs have been adapted from or inspired by a number of 18th and 19th century Irish poems by Oliver Goldsmith, Lady Sydney Morgan, Michael William Balfe, William Allingham and an anonymous 19th century music hall song. Other lyrics are adapted from Joyce or are original.

Wrong Mountain (28). By David Hirson. Produced by Dodger Theatricals with American Conservatory Theater, Lauren Mitchell and the John F. Kennedy Center for the Performing Arts at the Eugene O'Neill Theater. Opened January 13, 2000. (Closed February 5, 2000)

Henry Dennett .... Ron Rifkin
Claire .... Beth Dixon
Jessica .... Ilana Levine
Adam .... Bruce Norris
Peter .... Reg Flowers
Guy Halperin .... Michael Winters
Maurice Montesor .... Daniel Davis
Festival Actors:
Duncan Hyde-Berk .... Tom Riis Farrell
Salome Blackwood .... Beth Dixon
Jason Elmore .... Reg Flowers
Miranda Cortland-Sparks .... Jody Gelb
Ariel .... Anne Dudek
Winifred Hill; Anne .... Mary Schmidtberger
Clifford Pike; Stevens .... Daniel Jenkins
Leibowitz .... Tom Riis Farrell
Bookstore Patrons .... Anne Dudek, Daniel Jenkins

Understudies: Mr. Rifkin—Ross Bickell, Tom Riis Farrell; Mr. Davis—Ross Bickell; Miss Dixon—Jacqueline Antaramian, Jody Gelb; Misses Levine, Schmidtberger—Jacqueline Antaramian, Mollie Stickney; Messrs. Norris, Jenkins—Bryan T. Donovan, Reg Flowers; Mr. Flowers—Bryan T. Donovan; Mr. Winters—Ross Bickell, Tom Riis Farrell; Mr. Farrell—Ross Bickell, Bryan T. Donovan; Miss Gelb—Jacqueline Antaramian; Miss Dudek—Mary Schmidtberger, Mollie Stickney.

Directed by Richard Jones; scenery and costumes, Giles Cadle; lighting, Jennifer Tipton; sound, John Gromada; casting, Jay Binder; executive producer, Dodger Management Group; production stage manager, James Harker; stage manager, Heather Cousins; press, Boneau/Bryan-Brown, Adrian Bryan-Brown, Susanne Tighe, Amy Jacobs.

Time: Now. Place: Here. The play was presented in two parts.

A bellicose poet of minor literary distinction finds satisfaction as an award-winning playwright at a second-rate regional theater.

Squonk (32). Transfer from off off Broadway of the musical revue created by Steve O'Hearn and Jackie Dempsey in collaboration with the New York Squonk Ensemble (Casi Pacilio, Kevin Kornicki, Jana Losey, T. Weldon Anderson); music by Jackie Dempsey with Squonk; lyrics by Jana Losey and Jackie Dempsey; images by Steve O'Hearn. Produced by William Repicci, Michael Minichiello, Lauren Doll, Cookie Centracco, C. Chris Groenewald, in association with Rare Gem Productions and Michael Stoller at the Helen Hayes Theater. Opened February 29, 2000. (Closed March 26, 2000)

Keyboard, Accordion .... Jackie Dempsey
Electronic & Acoustic Percussion, Sound Textures .... Kevin Kornicki
Flutes, Electronic Winds, Many-Belled Trumpet .... Steve O'Hearn

Double Bass	T. Weldon Anderson
Vocals	Jana Losey

Directed by Tom Diamond; musical direction, Jackie Dempsey; choreography and movement, Peter Kope, Michele de la Reza; scenery, puppets, costumes, Steve O'Hearn; lighting, Tim Saternow; sound, Bernard Fox; projections, Steve O'Hearn, Casi Pacilio, Nick Fox-Geig; additional casting, Stephanie Klapper; associate producers, Mastantuono/Palumbo, Eric Falkenstein; production stage manager, Casi Pacilio; press, Jeffrey Richards Associates, Caral Craig, Brett Kristofferson.

Whimsical multimedia assortment of images and music. The show was presented without intermission.

Porgy and Bess (10). Revival of the musical based on the play *Porgy* by Dorothy and DuBose Heyward; libretto by DuBose Heyward; music by George Gershwin; lyrics by DuBose Heyward and Ira Gershwin. Produced in repertory by New York City Opera, Paul Kellogg general and artistic director, Sherwin M. Goldman executive producer, at New York City Opera. Opened March 7, 2000. (Closed March 25, 2000)

Jasbo Brown	Gerald Steichen
Clara	Adina Aaron
Mingo	Robert Mack
Jake	Kenneth Floyd
Sportin' Life	Dwayne Clark
Robbins	Michael Austin
Serena	Angela Simpson
Jim	Edward Pleasant
Peter	Bert Lindsey
Lily	Shirley Russ
Maria	Sabrina Elayne Carten
Scipio	Nkosane Jackson
Porgy	Alvy Powell
Crown	Timothy Robert Blevins
Bess	Marquita Lister
Detective	Wynn Harmon
Policemen	Michael Hajek, Charles Mandracchia
Undertaker	Bryan Jackson
Annie	Jeanette Blakeney
Frazier	Marvin Lowe
Strawberry Woman	Devonne Douglas
Crab Man	Duane Martin Foster
Nelson	E. Mani Cadet
Coroner	John Henry Thomas

Ensemble: Adina Aaron, Jeanette Blakeney, Bert Boone, Elaugh Butler, E. Mani Cadet, Aixa Cruz-Falú, David Aron Damane, Jean Derricotte-Murphy, Devonne Douglas, Mia Douglas, Rochelle Ellis, Duane Martin Foster, Anne Fridal, Chinyelu Ingram, Clinton Ingram, Bryan Jackson, Nicola James, Quanda Johnson, Naomi Elizabeth Jones, Pamela E. Jones, Jason Phillip Knight, Bert Lindsey, Lisa Lockhart, Marvin Lowe, Robert Mack, Edward Pleasant, Dorian Gray Ross, Elizabeth Lyra Ross, Leonard Rowe, Shirley Russ, Martín Solá, Lucy Salome Sträuli, Marcelin Summers, Everett Suttle, Kellie Turner.

Children: Khalif Diouf, Ayanna Francis, Leilani Irvin, Nkosane Jackson, Kayla Leacock, Grace Price, Afrika Rhames, Khadijha Stewart, Lacey Thomas, Jamal Russ, Verne Watley.

Directed by Tazewell Thompson; conductor, John DeMain; choreography, Julie Arenal; scenery, Douglas W. Schmidt; costumes, Nancy Potts; lighting, Robert Wierzel; fight direction, Roddy Kinter; chorus master, Gary Thor Wedow; stage managers, Peggy Imbrie, Rachel Stern, John H. Finen III, Ruppert Hemmings; press, Susan Woelzl.

Time: Mid 1930s. Place: Charleston, South Carolina. The play was presented in two parts.

The last major revival of *Porgy and Bess* took place at Radio City Music Hall 4/7/1983 for 45 performances.

*__True West__ (96). Revival of the play by Sam Shepard. Produced by Ron Kastner at the Circle in the Square Theater. Opened March 9, 2000.

Austin; Lee	Philip Seymour Hoffman, John C. Reilly (alternating)
Saul Kimmer	Robert LuPone
Mom	Celia Weston

Standbys: Mr. LuPone—Philip LeStrange; Miss Weston—Lois Markle.

Directed by Matthew Warchus; scenery and costumes, Rob Howell; lighting, Brian MacDevitt; sound, Jim van Bergen; original music, Claire van Kampen; fight direction, Rick Sordelet; executive producer, Roy Gabay; associate producer, Sandi Johnson; casting, Jim Carnahan; production stage man-

TRUE WEST—Philip Seymour Hoffman and John C. Reilly in a scene from the revival of Sam Shepard's play

ager and associate director, William Joseph Barnes; stage manager, Jill Cordle; press representative, Boneau/Bryan-Brown, Adrian Bryan-Brown, Brian Rubin, Johnny Woodnal.

True West was first produced off Broadway by New York Shakespeare Festival 12/23/80 for 24 performances. It was revived off Broadway 10/17/82 for 258 performances.

***Riverdance on Broadway** (88). Return engagement of the dance and music revue with music and lyrics by Bill Whelan. Produced by Abhann Productions, Moya Doherty producer, Julian Erskine executive producer, at the Gershwin Theater. Opened March 16, 2000.

With Brian Kennedy, Eileen Martin, Tsidii Le Loka, Maria Pagés, Pat Roddy and the voice of Liam Neeson.

Riverdance Irish Dance Troupe: Dearbhail Bates (assistant dance captain), Natalie Biggs, Lorna Bradley, Martin Brennan, Zeph Caissie, Suzanne Cleary, Andrea Curley (dance captain), Marty Dowds, Lindsay Doyle, Shannon Doyle, Susan Ginnety, Paula Goulding, Connor Hayes, Gary Healy, Matt Martin, Tokiko Masuda, Sinéad McCafferty, Holly McGlinchy, Jonathan McMorrow, Joe Moriarty, Niall Mulligan, Catherine O'Brien, David O'Hanlon, Debbie O'Keeffe, Ursula Quigley, Kathleen Ryan, Anthony Savage, Rosemary Schade, Ryan Sheridan, Claire Usher, Leanda Ward, Margaret Williams.

Moscow Folk Ballet Company: Dennis Boroditski, Andrei Kisselev (dance captain), Yuri Koryagina, Olena Krutsenko, Svetlana Malinina, Ilia Streltsov, Vitaly Verterich, Yana Volkova.

Riverdance Singers: Sara Clancy (soloist), Patrick Connolly, Brian Dunphy, Joanna Higgins (choir leader), Darren Holden, Michael Londra, Tara O'Beirne, Sherry Steele, Ben Stubbs, Yvonne Woods.

Riverdance Drummers: Darren Andrews, Abe Doron, Eamon Ellams, Gary Grant.

Riverdance Tappers: Walter "Sundance" Freeman, Channing Cook Holmes, Karen Callaway Williams (dance captain).

Amanzi Singers: Ntombikhona Dlamini, Fana Kekana (choir leader), Ntombifuthi Pamella Mhlongo, Francina Moliehi Mokubetsi, Keneilwe Margaret Motsage, Isaac Mthethwa, Andile Selby Ndebele, Mbuso Dick Shange.

Special written verse: Theo Dorgan. Poetry excerpts: W.B. Yeats, Seamus Heaney, Arthur O'Shaughnessy.

Riverdance Orchestra: Cathal Synnott musical director, keyboards; Athena Tergis fiddle; Ivan Goff uilleann pipes, low whistles; Kenneth Edge soprano and alto saxophones; Nikola Parov gadulka, kaval, gaida, bazouki; Éilís Egan accordion; Des Moore electric and acoustic guitars; Noel Heraty percussion;

Desi Reynolds drums, percussion; Tony Steele bass guitar; Robbie Harris bodhrán, darrabukkas, dunbeg, ouda.

Directed by John McColgan; original principal Irish dance choreographer, Michael Flatley; original choreography, Mavis Ascott, Jean Butler, Colin Dunne, Carol Leavy Joyce, Andrei Kisselev; scenery, Robert Ballagh; costumes, Joan Bergin; lighting, Rupert Murray; sound, Michael O'Gorman; orchestrations, Bill Whelan, Nick Ingman, David Downes; production stage manager, Anne Layde; stage managers, Tariq Rifaat, Liz Nugent; press, Merle Frimark Associates.

Extravaganza featuring Irish step dancers as well as choral and solo songs and dances by European performers. A foreign show previously produced in Dublin and London and at the Radio City Music Hall, where its most recent return engagement took place 9/24/1998 for 23 performances.

ACT I

"Invocation: Hear My Cry" .... Brian Kennedy
Reel Around the Sun .... Pat Roddy, Irish Dance Troupe
"The Heart's Cry" .... Singers
The Countess Cathleen .... Eileen Martin, Irish Dance Troupe
"Caoineadh Chú Chulainn" (lament) .... Ivan Goff
Thunderstorm .... Roddy, Irish Dance Troupe
"Shivna" .... Moscow Folk Ballet, Singers
Firedance .... Maria Pagés, Irish Dance Troupe
"At the Edge of the World" .... Kennedy
Slip Into Spring–the Harvest .... Orchestra
"Riverdance" .... Roddy, Martin, Singers, Drummers, Irish Dance Troupe

ACT II

American Wake .... Company
"Life the Wings" .... Kennedy, Sara Clancy
Harbour of the New World: Trading Taps .... Walter "Sundance" Freeman, Channing Cook Holmes, Karen Callaway Williams
"I Will Set You Free" and "Let Freedom Ring" .... Tsidii Le Loka, Amanzi Singers
Morning in Macedonia .... Orchestra
The Russian Dervish .... Moscow Folk Ballet Company
Heartbeat of the World–Andalucia .... Pagés, Noel Heraty, Roddy
"Rí Rá" .... Martin, Irish Dance Troupe, Moscow Folk Ballet Company, Singers, Drummers
Homecoming .... Athena Tergis, Pagés, Robbie Harris
Anthem: "Endless Journey" .... Le Loka, Kennedy, Amanzi and Riverdance Singers, Irish Dance Troupe
Finale .... Company

*__A Moon for the Misbegotten__ (94). Revival of the play by Eugene O'Neill. Produced by Elliot Martin, Chase Mishkin, Max Cooper, Jujamcyn Theaters, in association with Anita Waxman, Elizabeth Williams and the Goodman Theater at the Walter Kerr Theater. Opened March 19, 2000.

Josie Hogan .... Cherry Jones
Mike Hogan .... Paul Hewitt
Phil Hogan .... Roy Dotrice
James Tyrone Jr. .... Gabriel Byrne
T. Stedman Harder .... Tuck Milligan

Standbys: Miss Jones—Effie Johnson; Mr. Byrne—Tuck Milligan; Mr. Dotrice—Jack Davidson.

Directed by Daniel Sullivan; scenery, Eugene Lee; costumes, Jane Greenwood; lighting, Pat Collins; original music and sound, Richard Woodbury; casting, Bernard Telsey Casting; production stage manager, Roy Harris; stage manager, Denise Yaney; press, Richard Kornberg & Associates, Richard Kornberg, Don Summa, Jim Byk, Tom D'Ambrosio, John Wimbs.

Time: Between the hours of noon on a day in early September 1923 and sunrise of the following day. Place: Connecticut, at the home of tenant farmer Phil Hogan. The play was presented in two parts.

The last major New York revival of *A Moon for the Misbegotten* took place on Broadway 5/2/84 for 40 performances.

***Aida** (80). Musical suggested by the Verdi opera; book by Linda Woolverton, Robert Falls and David Henry Hwang; music by Elton John; lyrics by Tim Rice. Produced by Hyperion Theatricals under the direction of Peter Schneider and Thomas Schumacher at the Palace Theater. Opened March 23, 2000.

Amneris	Sherie René Scott	Zoser	John Hickok
Radames	Adam Pascal	Pharaoh	Daniel Oreskes
Aida	Heather Headley	Nehebka	Schele Williams
Mereb	Damian Perkins	Amonasro	Tyrees Allen

Ensemble: Robert M. Armitage, Troy Allan Burgess, Franne Calma, Bob Gaynor, Kisha Howard, Tim Hunter, Youn Kim, Kyra Little, Kenya Unique Massey, Corinne McFadden, Phineas Newborn III, Jody Ripplinger, Raymond Rodriguez, Eric Sciotto, Samuel N. Thiam, Jerald Vincent, Schele Williams, Natalia Zisa.

Orchestra: Paul Bogaev conductor; Bob Gustafson associate conductor, keyboards; Jim Abbott, Rob Mikulski keyboards; Gary Seligson drums/percussion; Gary Bristol bass; Bruce Uchitel, Jon Herington acoustic/electric guitar; Dean Thomas percussion; Ron Oakland concertmaster; Amy Ralske cello; Carol Landon viola; Robin Zeh violin; Russ Rizner, French horn; Jim Roe oboe, English horn; Melanie Bradford flute, alto flute, piccolo.

Standbys: Miss Headley—Thursday Farrar; Messrs. Hickok, Oreskes—Neal Benari. Understudies: Miss Scott—Franne Calma, Kelli Fournier; Mr. Pascal—Bob Gaynor, Raymond Rodriguez, Eric Sciotto; Miss Headley—Schele Williams; Mr. Perkins—Tim Hunter, Phineas Newborn III; Mr. Hickok—Troy Allan Burgess; Mr. Oreskes—Robert M. Armitage; Miss Williams—Kyra Little, Endalyn Taylor-Shellman; Mr. Allen—Samuel N. Thiam, Jerald Vincent. Swings: Chris Payne Dupré, Kelli Fournier, Timothy Edward Smith, Endalyn Taylor-Shellman.

Directed by Robert Falls; choreography, Wayne Cilento; musical direction, Paul Bogaev; scenery and costumes, Bob Crowley; lighting, Natasha Katz; sound, Steve C. Kennedy; music arrangements, Guy Babylon, Paul Bogaev; orchestrations, Steve Margoshes, Guy Babylon, Paul Bogaev; music coordination, Michael Keller; dance arrangements, Bob Gustafson, Jim Abbott, Gary Seligson; fight direction, Rick Sordelet; asssociate producer, Marshall B. Purdy; casting, Bernard Telsey Casting; production stage manager, Clifford Schwartz; stage manager, Paul J. Smith; press, Boneau/Bryan-Brown, Chris Boneau, Jackie Green, Steven Padla.

Aida is the story of a politically star-crossed love affair between a Nubian princess and an Egyptian prince, finally entombed alive in punishment. Previously produced in regional theater at Alliance Theater Company, Atlanta.

ACT I

"Every Story Is a Love Story"	Amneris
"Fortune Favors the Brave"	Radames, Soldiers
"The Past is Another Land"	Aida
"Another Pyramid"	Zoser, Ministers
"How I Know You"	Mereb, Aida
"My Strongest Suit"	Amneris, Women of the Palace
"Enchantment Passing Through"	Radames, Aida
"My Strongest Suit" (Reprise)	Amneris, Aida
"The Dance of the Robe"	Aida, Nehebka, the Nubians
"Not Me"	Radames, Mereb, Aida, Amneris
"Elaborate Lives"	Radames, Aida
"The Gods Love Nubia"	Aida, Nehebka, the Nubians

ACT I I

"A Step Too Far"	Amneris, Radames, Aida
"Easy as Life"	Aida
"Like Father Like Son"	Zoser, Radames, the Ministers
"Radames' Letter"	Radames
"How I Know You" (Reprise)	Mereb
"Written in the Stars"	Aida, Radames
"I Know the Truth"	Amneris

"Elaborate Lives" (Reprise) .... Aida, Radames
"Every Story Is a Love Story" (Reprise) .... Amneris

***The Ride Down Mt. Morgan** (60). Revival of the play by Arthur Miller. Produced by the Shubert Organization, Scott Rudin, Roger Berlind, Spring Sirkin and ABC, Inc. at the Ambassador Theater. Opened April 9, 2000.

Lyman .... Patrick Stewart
Nurse Logan .... Oni Faida Lampley
Theo .... Frances Conroy
Bessie .... Shannon Burkett
Leah .... Katy Selverstone
Tom .... John C. Vennema
Pianist .... Glen Pearson

Hospital Staff, Dream Figures: Portia Johnson, Terry Layman, Jennifer Piech, Sherry Skinker.

Understudies: Misses Conroy, Selverstone—Sherry Skinker; Mr. Vennema—Terry Layman; Miss Burkett—Jennifer Piech; Miss Lampley—Portia Johnson; Hospital Staff, Dream Figures—Amy Ehrenberg.

Directed by David Esbjornson; scenery, John Arnone; costumes, Elizabeth Hope Clancy; lighting, Brian MacDevitt; original music and sound, Dan Moses Schreier; casting, Pat McCorkle, Jordan Thaler, Heidi Griffiths; production stage manager, Erica Schwartz; stage manager, Sally Jacobs; press, Barlow Hartman Public Relations, Michael Hartman, John Barlow, Andy Shearer.

Time: The Present. Place: Clearhaven Memorial Hospital, Elmira, New York.

The last major New York production of *The Ride Down Mt. Morgan* was its New York premiere off Broadway by New York Shakespeare Festival 10/27/98 for 40 performances, following its American premiere in regional theater at Williamstown, Mass. Theater Festival, Michael Ritchie producer, 6/26/96 and its world premiere presented by Robert Fox Ltd. at Wyndham's Theater in London in 1991.

***Copenhagen** (59). By Michael Frayn. Produced by James M. Nederlander, Roger Berlind, Scott Rudin, Elizabeth Ireland McCann, Ray Larsen, Jon B. Platt, Byron Goldman and Scott Nederlander by arrangement with Michael Codron, Lee Dean and the Royal National Theater, Trevor Nunn director, at the Royale Theater. Opened April 11, 2000.

Margrethe Bohr .... Blair Brown
Niels Bohr .... Philip Bosco
Werner Heisenberg .... Michael Cumpsty

Understudies: Mr. Bosco—Patrick Tovatt; Miss Brown—Laurie Kennedy; Mr. Cumpsty—Tony Carlin.

Directed by Michael Blakemore; design, Peter J. Davison; lighting, Mark Henderson, Michael Lincoln; costumes, Charlotte Bird; sound, Tony Meola; casting, Jim Carnahan; general manager, Joey Parnes; production stage manager, R. Wade Jackson; stage manager, Deirdre McCrane; press, Boneau/Bryan-Brown, Adrian Bryan-Brown, Dennis Crowley.

Two renowned physicists verbally spar over moral responsibility in a mysterious meeting, which is enacted again and again, during the World War II race for atomic weaponry. A foreign play previously produced in London. Winner of the 1999–2000 New York Drama Critics Circle Award for best foreign play and Tony Award for best play; see its entry in the Prizewinning Plays section of this volume.

***The Wild Party** (56). Musical based on the poem by Joseph Moncure March; book by Michael John LaChiusa and George C. Wolfe; music and lyrics by Michael John LaChiusa. Produced by the Joseph Papp Public Theater/New York Shakespeare Festival, George C. Wolfe producer, Scott Rudin/Paramount Pictures, Roger Berlind and Williams/Waxman at the Virginia Theater. Opened April 13, 2000.

Queenie .... Toni Collette
Burrs .... Mandy Patinkin
Jackie .... Marc Kudisch
Miss Madelaine True .... Jane Summerhays
Sally .... Sally Murphy
Eddie Mackrel .... Norm Lewis
Mae .... Leah Hocking
Nadine .... Brooke Sunny Moriber
Phil D'Armano .... Nathan Lee Graham
Oscar D'Armano .... Michael McElroy
Dolores .... Eartha Kitt
Gold .... Adam Grupper

Goldberg .... Stuart Zagnit
Black .... Yancey Arias
Kate .... Tonya Pinkins

Orchestra: Todd Ellison conductor; Linda Twine associate conductor, piano; William Easley, Jimmy Cozier, Steven Kenyon, Roger Rosenberg woodwinds; Brian O'Flaherty, Kamau Adilifu trumpet; Tim Sessions trombone; Lesa Terry, Ashley Horne, Julien Barber violin; Benjamin Brown bass; Brian Grice drums; Bruce Doctor percussion; Steve Bargonetti guitar.

Understudies: Miss Collette—Nicole Van Giesen, Dominique Plaisant; Mr. Patinkin—David Masenheimer, Jeff Gardner; Miss Pinkins—Dominique Plaisant, Jennifer Frankel; Miss Kitt—Ching Valdes-Aran; Messrs. Arias, Kudisch—René Millán; Misses Summerhays, Hocking—Jennifer Frankel; Messrs. Lewis, McElroy, Graham—Adrian Bailey; Messrs. Grupper, Zagnit—Jeff Gardner; Misses Moriber, Murphy—Jennifer Hall.

Directed by George C. Wolfe; choreography, Joey McKneely; music director, Todd Ellison; scenery, Robin Wagner; costumes, Toni-Leslie James; lighting, Jules Fisher, Peggy Eisenhauer; sound, Tony Meola; orchestrations, Bruce Coughlin; music coordinator, Seymour Red Press; casting, Jordan Thaler; production stage manager, Gwendolyn M. Gilliam; stage manager Rick Steiger; press, Barlow Hartman Public Relations, John Barlow, Michael Hartman.

Time: 1928. Place: New York, N.Y. No intermission.

The mad passions of the liquor-soaked Lost Generation lead to heartache and tragedy in an adaptation of the Joseph Moncure March epic poem.

The Vaudeville

"Queenie Was a Blonde"/"Marie Is Tricky"/"Wild Party" .... Queenie, Burrs, Company

Promenade of Guests

"Dry" .... Burrs, Jackie, Madelaine, Sally, Eddie, Mae, Nadine, Brothers D'Armano, Dolores
"Welcome to My Party" .... Queenie
"Like Sally" .... Madelaine
"Breezin' Through Another Day" .... Jackie
"Uptown" .... Brothers D'Armano
"Eddie and Mae" .... Eddie, Mae
"Gold and Goldberg" .... Gold, Goldberg
"Moving Uptown" .... Dolores

The Party

"Black Bottom" .... Queenie, Company
"Best Friend" .... Queenie, Kate
"A Little M-M-M" .... Brothers D'Armano
"Tabu"/"Taking Care of the Ladies" .... Oscar, Black, Company
"Wouldn't It Be Nice" .... Burrs
"Lowdown-Down" .... Queenie
"Gin" .... Burrs, Company
"Wild" .... Company
"Need" .... Madelaine, Company
"Black Is a Moocher" .... Kate
"People Like Us" .... Queenie, Black

After Midnight Dies

"After Midnight Dies" .... Sally
"Golden Boy" .... Eddie, Brothers D'Armano
"The Movin' Uptown Blues" .... Gold, Goldberg
"The Lights of Broadway" .... Nadine
"More" .... Jackie
"Love Ain't Nothin'"/"Welcome to Her Party"/"What I Need" .... Kate, Burrs, Queenie
"How Many Women in the World?" .... Burrs
"When It Ends" .... Dolores

Finale

"This Is What It Is" .... Queenie
Finale .... Queenie, Burrs, Company

***Jesus Christ Superstar** (52). Revival of the musical by Andrew Lloyd Webber, lyrics by Tim Rice. Produced by the Really Useful Superstar Company, Inc. and the Nederlander Producing Company of America Inc., in association with Terry Allen Kramer, at the Ford Center for the Performing Arts. Opened April 16, 2000.

Jesus of Nazareth	Glenn Carter	Caiaphas	Frederick B. Owens
Judas Iscariot	Tony Vincent	Annas	Ray Walker
Mary Magdalene	Maya Days	Simon Zealotes	Michael K. Lee
Pontius Pilate	Kevin Gray	Peter	Rodney Hicks
King Herod	Paul Kandel		

Apostles/Disciples: Christian Borle, Lisa Brescia, D'Monroe, Manoel Felciano, Somer Lee Graham, J. Todd Howell, Daniel C. Levine, Anthony Manough, Joseph Melendez, Eric Millegan, Michael Seelbach, Alexander Selma, David St. Louis, Shayna Steele, Max Von Essen, Joe Wilson Jr., Andrew Wright. Soul Girls/Disciples: Merle Dandridge, Deidre Goodwin, Lana Gordon. Priests/Guards: Hank Campbell, Devin Richards, Timothy Warmen. Swings: Bernard Dotson, Keenah Reid, Adam Simmons.

Orchestra: Patrick Vaccariello conductor; Jim Laev associate conductor, keyboard; Mark Berman, T. O. Sterrett keyboard; Gary Tillman drums; Joe Quigley bass; Doug Quinn, J. McGeehan guitar; Howard Joines percussion; Bob Millikan, Tino Gagliardi trumpet, piccolo trumpet; Lorraine Cohen-Moses trumpet, flugal horn; Larry DiBello, Theresa MacDonnell, French horns; Charles Gordon, Bob Suttmann trombone; John Hahn bass trombone, tuba; Gretchen Pusch flute, piccolo; Scott Shachter flute, clarinet, tenor sax.

Understudies: Mr. Carter—Max Von Essen; Mr. Vincent—Manoel Felciano; Miss Days—Merle Dandridge, Shayna Steele; Mr. Gray—Timothy Warren; Mr. Kandel—Adam Simmons, Ray Walker; Mr. Owens—Devin Richards, David St. Louis; Mr. Walker—Manoel Felciano, Adam Simmons; Mr. Lee—Anthony Manough; Mr. Hicks—Anthony Manough, Andrew Wright.

Directed by Gale Edwards; choreography, Anthony Van Laast; musical direction, Patrick Vaccariello; scenery, Peter J. Davison; costumes, Roger Kirk; lighting, Mark McCullough; musical supervisor, Simon Lee; sound, Richard Ryan; associate musical supervisor, Kristen Allen Blodgette; orchestrations, Andrew Lloyd Webber; musical coordinator, David Lai; casting, Johnson-Liff Associates, Tara Rubin; assistant choreographer, Denny Berry; production stage manager, Bonnie Panson; stage manager, Ira Mont; press, Boneau/Bryan-Brown, Adrian Bryan-Brown, Amy Jacobs, Matt Polk.

The last major revival of *Jesus Christ Superstar* took place on Broadway 1/17/95 for 16 performances.

ACT I

Overture	Ensemble
"Heaven on Their Minds"	Judas
"What's the Buzz"/"Strange Thing, Mystifying"	Jesus, Mary, Judas, Disciples
"Everything's Alright"	Mary, Judas, Jesus, Disciples
"This Jesus Must Die"	Caiaphas, Annas, Priests, Disciples
"Hosanna"	Caiaphas, Jesus, Disciples
"Simon Zealotes"/"Poor Jerusalem"	Simon, Jesus, Disciples, Roman Guards
"Pilate's Dream"	Pilate
"The Temple"	Jesus, Profiteers
"Everything's Alright" (Reprise)	Mary, Jesus
"I Don't Know How to Love Him"	Mary
"Damned for All Time"/"Blood Money"	Judas, Caiaphas, Annas, Priests, The Mob

ACT II

"The Last Supper"	Jesus, Judas, Apostles
"Gethsemane"	Jesus
"The Arrest"	Jesus, Judas, Peter, Apostles, Caiaphas, Annas, The Mob, Roman Guards
"Peter's Denial"	Peter, Mary, Apostles, The Mob
"Pilate and Christ"	Pilate, Jesus, Annas, Mary, Apostles, Roman Guards, the Mob
"King Herod's Song"	Herod, His Court
"Could We Start Again, Please?"	Mary, Peter, Simon, Disciples, Roman Guards
"Judas' Death"	Judas, Caiaphas, Annas, The Mob
"Trial by Pilate"	Pilate, Caiaphas, Annas, Jesus, The Mob

"Superstar"	Judas, Soul Girls, Angels, Paparazzi
"Crucifixion"	Jesus, Disciples
"John 19:41"	Jesus, Disciples

***The Real Thing** (51). Revival of the play by Tom Stoppard. Produced by Anita Waxman, Elizabeth Williams, Ron Kastner and Miramax Films in the Donmar Warehouse production at the Ethel Barrymore Theater. Opened April 17, 2000.

Max	Nigel Lindsay	Debbie	Charlotte Parry
Charlotte	Sarah Woodward	Billy	Oscar Pearce
Henry	Stephen Dillane	Brodie	Joshua Henderson
Annie	Jennifer Ehle		

Understudies: Messrs. Lindsay, Dillane—Ray Virta; Misses Ehle, Woodward—Tina Benko; Messrs. Pearce, Henderson—Matthew Greer; Miss Parry—Tina Jones.

Directed by David Leveaux; scenery and costumes, Vicki Mortimer; lighting, Mark Henderson, David Weiner; sound, John A. Leonard (for Aura Sound Design Ltd.); associate producers, ACT Productions, Randall L. Wreghitt; U.K. casting, Anne McNulty; production stage manager, Bonnie L. Becker; stage manager Kimberly Russell; press, Boneau/Bryan-Brown, Adrian Bryan-Brown, Jackie Green, Brian Rubin.

Time: Two years elapse between Acts I and II.

The first New york production of *The Real Thing* took place on Broadway 1/5/84 for 566 performances. It was named a Best Play of its season and won the New York Drama Critics Circle's best of bests and Tony Awards. This is its first major New York revival.

***The Green Bird** (51). Revival of the play by Carlo Gozzi;. translated by Albert Bermel and Ted Emery; original music, Elliot Goldenthal. Produced by Ostar Enterprises, Robert E. Wankel executive vice president, with Theater for a New Audience, Jeffrey Horowitz artistic director, and Nina Lannan at the Cort Theater. Opened April 18, 2000.

Brighella	Reg E. Cathey	Ninetta	Kristine Nielsen
Pantalone	Andrew Weems	Voice of Calmon; Beauticians; Pierrot	Andrew Weems
Smeraldina	Didi Conn	Tartaglia	Derek Smith
Truffaldino	Ned Eisenberg	Tartagliona	Edward Hibbert
Barbarina	Katie MacNichol	Pompea; Voice of Serpentina	Lee Lewis
Renzo	Sebastian Roché		
The Green Bird	Bruce Turk		

Singing Apples: Sophia Salguero (soloist), Meredith Patterson, Sarah Jane Nelson. Dancing Waters: Erico Villanueva (soloist), Ramon Flowers. Servants; Marching Band; Puppeteers: Ken Barnett, Ramon Flowers, Sarah Jane Nelson, Meredith Patterson, Sophia Salguero, Erico Villanueva.

Musicians: Bill Ruyle percussion; Antoine Silverman violin; Bruce Williamson woodwinds, keyboard.

Understudies: Messrs. Eisenberg, Weems; Servants—Bill Cohen; Misses Nielsen, Conn; Singing Apples, Servants—Jan Leslie Harding; Messrs. Cathey, Smith, Hibbert—Reggie Montgomery; Misses Lewis, MacNichol; Singing Apples, Servants—Tricia Paoluccio; Messrs. Roché, Turk—Ken Barnett; Misses Lewis, MacNichol—Meredith Patterson; Singing Apple (soloist)—Sarah Jane Nelson; Dancing Water (soloist)—Ramon Flowers.

Directed by Julie Taymor; musical staging, Daniel Ezralow; additional text, Eric Overmyer; music direction Rick Martinez; orchestrations, Elliot Goldenthal; scenery, Christine Jones; costumes, Constance Hoffman; lighting, Donald Holder; mask and puppet design, Julie Taymor; sound, Jon Weston; vocal direction, Joe Church; casting, Deborah Brown; "Oh, Foolish Heart" lyrics, David Suehsdorf; production stage manager, Kristen Harris; stage manager, Amanda W. Sloan; press, the Publicity Office, Bob Fennell, Marc Thibodeau, Michael S. Borowski, Brett Oberman.

Place: The imaginary city of Monterotondo, Serpentina's garden, the Ogre's mountain lair, and other suitably fabulous places.

The last major revival of *The Green Bird* was the Theater for a New Audience production off Broadway 3/7/96 for 15 Performances.

THE MUSIC MAN—Craig Bierko as Harold Hill leads the company through a number in the revival of Meredith Willson's musical

***Taller Than a Dwarf** (43). By Elaine May. Produced by Julian Schlossberg, Mark Golub, David Golub, Jon B. Platt, Ted Tulchin, Darren Bagert, and Hal Luftig at the Longacre Theater. Opened April 24, 2000.

Howard Miller .... Matthew Broderick
Selma Miller .... Parker Posey
Mrs. Miller .... Joyce Van Patten
Mrs. Shawl .... Marcia Jean Kurtz
Milton .... Marc John Jeffries, Dajon Matthews (alternating)
Mrs. Enright .... Cynthia Darlow
Policeman; Fireman .... Greg Stuhr
Mr. Enright .... Micheal McShane
Mr. Dupar .... Sam Groom

Standbys: Messrs. Broderick, Stuhr—Josh Alexander; Miss Posey—Valerie Geffner; Misses Van Patten, Kurtz, Darlow—Marilyn Pasekoff; Messrs. Adler, McShane, Groom—Joel Rooks.

Directed by Alan Arkin; scenery, Tony Walton; costumes, Martin Pakledinaz; lighting, Brian Nason; sound, Andrew Keister; special effects, Gregory Meeh; casting, Stuart Howard, Amy Schecter, Howard Meltzer; associate producer, Meyer Ackerman; production stage manager, Jane Grey; stage manager, William Gilinsky; press, Jeffrey Richards Associates, Matthew Brookshire, Brett Kristofferson.

Noisy desperation defines the lives of a young Jewish couple from Queens. The play was presented without intermission.

***Meredith Willson's The Music Man** (40). Revival of the musical with book, music and lyrics by Meredith Willson; story by Meredith Willson and Franklin Lacey. Produced by Dodger Theatricals, the John F. Kennedy Center for the Performing Arts, Elizabeth Williams/Anita Waxman, Kardana-Swinsky Productions and Lorie Cowen Levy/Dede Harris at the Neil Simon Theater. Opened April 27, 2000.

Train Conductor .... Andre Garner
Charlie Cowell .... Ralph Byers
Harold Hill .... Craig Bierko
Olin Britt .... Michael-Leon Wooley
Amaryllis .... Jordan Puryear
Maud Dunlop .... Martha Hawley
Ewart Dunlop .... Jack Doyle
Mayor Shinn .... Paul Benedict
Alma Hix .... Leslie Hendrix
Ethel Toffelmier .... Tracy Nicole Chapman
Oliver Hix .... John Sloman
Jacey Squires .... Blake Hammond
Marcellus Washburn .... Max Casella
Tommy Djilas .... Clyde Alves
Marian Paroo .... Rebecca Luker
Mrs. Paroo .... Katherine McGrath
Winthrop Paroo .... Michael Phelan
Eulalie Mackecknie Shinn .... Ruth Williamson
Zaneeta Shinn .... Kate Levering
Gracie Shinn .... Ann Whitlow Brown
Mrs. Squires .... Ann Brown
Constable Locke .... Kevin Bogue

Traveling Salesmen: Liam Burke, Kevin Bogue, E. Clayton Cornelious, Michael Duran, Blake Hammond, Michael McGurk, Dan Sharkey, John Sloman. Residents of River City: Cameron Adams, Kevin Bogue, Sara Brenner, Chase Brock, Liam Burke, E. Clayton Cornelious, Michael Duran, Andre Garner, Ellen Harvey, Mary Illes, Joy Lynn Matthews, Michael McGurk, Robbie Nicholson, Ipsita Paul, Pamela Remler, Dan Sharkey, Lauren Ullrich, Travis Wall.

Orchestra: David Chase conductor; Rob Berman associate conductor, piano; James Baker assistant conductor; Dick Clark, Kenneth Finn trombone; Matthew Ingman bass trombone, tuba; Danny Cahn, John Dent, Wayne J. du Maine trumpet; Chris Komer, French horn; Andrew Sterman, Tony Brackett, Chuck Wilson, Rick Heckman, Mark Thrasher woodwinds; Paul Woodiel violin; Sarah Carter cello; David Ratajczak drums; James Baker percussion; Richard Sarpola bass; Grace Paradise harp.

Standby: Messrs. Bierko, Casella, Byers—Jim Walton. Swings: Jennie Ford, Cynthia Leigh Heim, Jason Snow, Jeff Williams. Understudies: Mr. Bierko—John Sloman; Miss Luker—Mary Illes, Cynthia Leigh Heim; Mr. Casella—Kevin Bogue; Mr. Benedict—Ralph Byers, Jack Doyle; Miss Williamson—Leslie Hendrix, Ellen Harvey; Miss McGrath—Martha Hawley, Ellen Harvey; Mr. Phelan—Travis Wall, Lauren Ullrich; Miss Puryear—Lauren Ullrich, Sara Brenner; Mr. Byers—Jeff Williams; Mr. Alves—Chase Brock, Michael McGurk; Miss Levering—Sara Brenner, Jennie Ford; Miss Brown—Cameron Adams, Sara Brenner; Mr. Wooley—Dan Sharkey, Kevin Bogue; Mr. Doyle—Michael Duran, Jeff Williams; Mr. Sloman—Jeff Williams, Dan Sharkey; Mr. Hammond—Andre Garner, Michael Duran; Miss Hawley—Ellen Harvey, Joy Lynn Matthews; Miss Hendrix—Cynthia Leigh Heim, Ellen Harvey; Miss Brown—Cynthia Leigh Heim, Joy Lynn Matthews; Miss Chapman—Joy Lynn Matthews, Ipsita Paul.

Directed and choreographed by Susan Stroman; musical supervision and direction, David Chase; scenery, Thomas Lynch; costumes, William Ivey Long; lighting, Peter Kaczorowski; sound, Jonathan Deans; orchestrations, Doug Besterman; dance and incidental music arrangements, David Krane; music coordinator, John Miller; associate producers, Jack Cullen, Chase Mishkin; executive producer, Dodger Management Group; casting, Jay Binder; production stage manager, Steven Zweigbaum; stage manager, Rolt Smith; press, Boneau/Bryan-Brown, Adrian Bryan-Brown, Susanne Tighe, Matt Polk.

The last major revival of *The Music Man* took place on Broadway 6/5/80 for 21 performances with Dick Van Dyke as Harold Hill.

ACT I

Scene 1: A railway coach, morning, July 3, 1912
"Rock Island" .... Charlie Cowell, Traveling Salesmen
Scene 2: Train depot, River City, Iowa
Scene 3: The center of town
"Iowa Stubborn" .... Townspeople of River City
"Trouble" .... Harold, Townspeople
Scene 4: A street
Scene 5: The Paroos' House
"Piano Lesson" .... Marian, Mrs. Paroo, Amaryllis
"Goodnight, My Someone" .... Marian
Scene 6: Madison Gymnasium, July 4th
"Seventy Six Trombones" .... Harold, Townspeople
Scene 7: The center of town
"Sincere" .... Olin, Oliver, Ewart, Jacey
Scene 8: A street just off the center of town
"The Sadder-But-Wiser Girl" .... Harold, Marcellus

"Pickalittle" .... Alma, Ethel, Eulalie, Maud, Mrs. Squires, Ladies of River City
"Goodnight Ladies" .... Olin, Oliver, Ewart, Jacey

Scene 9: Madison library
"Marian the Librarian" .... Harold, Boys and Girls

Scene 10: A street, the following Saturday, late afternoon

Scene 11: The Paroos' porch, immediately following
"Gary, Indiana" .... Harold, Mrs. Paroo
"My White Knight" .... Marian

Scene 12: The edge of town, noon, the following Saturday
"The Wells Fargo Wagon " .... Winthrop, Townspeople

ACT II

Scene 1: Madison Gymnasium, the following Tuesday evening
"It's You" .... Olin, Oliver, Ewart, Jacey Harold, Townspeople
"Pickalittle" (Reprise) .... Eulalie, Maud, Ethel, Alma, Mrs. Squires, Ladies

Scene 2: The front of the hotel, the following Wednesday evening
"Lida Rose" .... Olin, Oliver, Ewart, Jacey
"Will I Ever Tell You?" .... Marian

Scene 3: The Paroos' Porch, immediately following
"Gary, Indiana" (Reprise) .... Winthrop, Mrs. Paroo, Marian

Scene 4: Madison Park
"Shipoopi" .... Marcellus, Harold, Townspeople

Scene 5: The footbridge
"Till There Was You" .... Marian
"Seventy Six Trombones," "Goodnight, My Someone" .... Harold, Marian
"Till There Was You" (Reprise) .... Harold

Scene 6: The center of town, immediately following
"Finale" .... The Company

*__Dirty Blonde__ (35). By Claudia Shear; conceived by Claudia Shear and James Lapine. Produced by the Shubert Organization, Chase Mishkin, Ostar Enterprises, ABC Inc., in association with the New York Theater Workshop, at the Helen Hayes Theater. Opened May 1, 2000.

Frank Wallace; Ed Hearn;
Others .... Bob Stillman
Jo; Mae .... Claudia Shear
Charlie; Others .... Kevin Chamberlin

Understudies: Miss Shear—Norma Mae Lyng; Mr. Chamberlin—Kevin Carolan; Mr. Stillman—Paul Amodeo.

Directed by James Lapine; musical staging, John Carrafa; scenery, Douglas Stein; costumes, Susan Hilferty; lighting, David Lander; sound, Dan Moses Schreier; arrangements, musical direction and song "Dirty Blonde," Bob Stillman; additional casting, Ilene Starger; production stage manager, Leila Knox; press, Richard Kornberg, Don Summa, Jim Byk, Tom D'Ambrosio, John Wimbs.

Two lonely people connect when they discover a mutual fascination with the life and career of Mae West. The play was presented without intermission.

PLAYS PRODUCED OFF BROADWAY

Some distinctions between off-Broadway and Broadway productions at one end of the scale and off-off-Broadway productions at the other end were blurred in the New York Theater of the 1990s. For the purposes of *Best Plays* listing, the term "off Broadway" signifies a show which opened for general audiences in a mid-Manhattan theater seating 499 or fewer and 1) employed an Equity cast, 2) planned a regular schedule of 8 performances a week in an open-ended run (7 a week for solo shows and some other exceptions) and 3) offered itself to public comment by critics after a designated opening performance.

Occasional exceptions of inclusion (never of exclusion) are made to take in visiting troupes, borderline "showcase" presentations and nonqualifying productions which readers might expect to find in this list because they appear under an off-Broadway heading in other major sources of record.

Figures in parentheses following a play's title give number of performances. These numbers do not include previews or extra non-profit performances.

Plays marked with an asterisk (*) were still in a projected run on June 1, 2000. Their number of performances is figured from opening night through May 31, 2000.

Certain programs of off-Broadway companies are exceptions to our rule of counting the number of performances from the date of the press coverage. When the official opening takes place late in the run of a play's regularly-priced public or subscription performances (after previews), we sometimes count the first performance of record, not the press date, as opening night—and in any such case in the listing we note the variance and give the press date.

In a listing of a show's numbers—dances, sketches, musical scenes, etc.—the titles of songs are identified wherever possible by their appearance in quotation marks (").

HOLDOVERS FROM PREVIOUS SEASONS

Off-Broadway shows which were running on June 1, 1999 are listed below. More detailed information about them appears in previous *Best Plays* volumes of appropriate date. Important cast changes since opening night are recorded in the Cast Replacements section of this volume.

***The Fantasticks**(16,594; longest continuous run of record in the American Theater). Musical suggested by the play *Les Romanesques* by Edmond Rostand; book and lyrics by Tom Jones; music by Harvey Schmidt. Opened May 3, 1960.

***Perfect Crime** (5,420). By Warren Manzi. Opened October 16, 1987.

***Tony 'n' Tina's Wedding** (4,109). By Artificial Intelligence. Opened February 6, 1988.

***Blue Man Group (Tubes)**(4,061). Performance piece by and with Blue Man Group. Opened November 17, 1991.

***Stomp** (2,633). Percussion performance piece created by Luke Cresswell and Steve McNicholas. Opened February 27, 1994.

***I Love You, You're Perfect, Now Change** (1,598). Musical revue with book and lyrics by Joe DiPietro; music by Jimmy Roberts. Opened August 1, 1996.

***Late Nite Catechism** (792). By Vicki Quade and Maripat Donovan. Opened October 3, 1996.

Secrets Every Smart Traveler Should Know (953). Musical revue with songs and sketches by Douglas Bernstein, Francesca Blumenthal, Michael Brown, Barry Creyton, Lesley Davison, Addy Fieger, Stan Freeman, Murray Grand, Glen Kelly, Barry Kleinbort, Jay Leonhart and Denis Markell. Opened October 30, 1997. (Closed February 21, 2000)

Hedwig and the Angry Inch (857). Musical with book by John Cameron Mitchell; music and lyrics by Stephen Trask. Opened February 14, 1998. (Closed April 9, 2000)

Symphonie Fantastique (425). Puppet show created by Basil Twist; music by Hector Berlioz. Opened June 5, 1998. (Closed August 15, 1999)

***De La Guarda** (794). Spectacle devised by De La Guarda (Pichon Baldinu, Diqui James, Gabriel Kerpel, Fabio D'Aquila, Tomas James, Alejandro Garcia, Gabriella Baldini). Opened June 16, 1998.

The Mystery of Irma Vep (335). Revival of the play by Charles Ludlam. Opened October 1, 1998. (Closed July 18, 1999)

***Over the River and Through the Woods** (691). By Joe DiPietro. Opened October 5, 1998.

Wit (545). By Margaret Edson. Opened October 6, 1998. (Closed April 9, 2000)

Killer Joe (283). By Tracy Letts. Opened October 18, 1998. (Closed June 27, 1999)

***Forbidden Broadway Cleans Up Its Act!** (218). Musical revue created and written by Gerard Alessandrini. Opened November 17, 1998.

A Couple of Blaguards (379). By Frank and Malachy McCourt. Opened January 13, 1999. (Closed August 29, 1999)

Beautiful Thing (152). By Jonathan Harvey. Opened February 14, 1999. (Closed June 27, 1999)

Jodie's Body (105). Solo performance by Aviva Jane Carlin; written by Aviva Jane Carlin. Opened February 18, 1999. (Closed June 27, 1999)

Snakebit (191). By David Marshall Grant. Opened March 1, 1999. (Closed August 1, 1999)

2.5 Minute Ride (100). Solo performance by Lisa Kron; written by Lisa Kron. Opened March 17, 1999. (Closed June 13, 1999).

Savion Glover: Downtown (72). Performance piece created by the cast. Opened April 10, 1999. (Closed June 19, 1999)

2 1/2 Jews (159). By Alan Brandt. Opened May 5, 1999. (Closed September 19, 1999)

Things You Shouldn't Say Past Midnight (174). By Peter Ackerman. Opened May 13, 1999. (Closed October 10, 1999)

East Is East (56). By Ayub Khan-Din. Opened May 25, 1999. (Closed July 11, 1999)

Goodnight Children Everywhere (29). By Richard Nelson. Opened May 26, 1999. (Closed June 20, 1999)

PLAYS PRODUCED JUNE 1, 1999–MAY 31, 2000

Brooklyn Academy of Music (BAM). 1998–99 schedule concluded with **The Image Makers** (4). By Per Olov Enquist. Produced by Brooklyn Academy of Music, Bruce C. Ratner chairman of the board, Harvey Lichtenstein president and executive producer, in the Royal Dramatic Theater of Sweden production, Ingrid Dahlberg artistic and managing director, in the Swedish language with simultaneous English translation, at the Majestic Theater. Opened June 2, 1999. (Closed June 6, 1999)

Selma Lagerlof .... Anita Bjork
Tora Teje .... Elin Klinga
Viktor Sjostrom .... Lennart Hjulstrom
Julius Jaenzon .... Carl-Magnus Dellow

Directed by Ingmar Bergman; scenery, Goran Wassberg; costumes, Mago; lighting, Pierre Leveau; sound, Jan Eric Piper; wigs and masks, Leif Quistrom; English translation by Charlotte Barslund and Kim Darnbaek, performed by Eva Engman, Paul Luskin and Tana Ross; producer, Sofi Lerstrom; stage manager, Tomas Wennerberg; press, Elena Park, Susan Yung.

Novelist shows her work to a filmmaker in the early days of the movies, in Stockholm, suggested by a real-life meeting between Selma Lagerlof and Viktor Sjostrom which took place in 1920. A foreign play first produced at the Royal Dramatic Theater of Sweden in February 1998.

Roundabout Theater Company. 1998–99 schedule concluded with **Hurrah at Last** (93). By Richard Greenberg. Produced by Roundabout Theater Company, Todd Haimes artistic director, Ellen Richard managing director, Julia C. Levy executive director, external affairs, at the Gramercy Theater. Opened June 3, 1999. (Closed August 22, 1999)

Laurie .... Peter Frechette
Thea .... Ileen Getz
Eamon .... Kevin O'Rourke
Oliver .... Paul Michael Valley
Thunder .... Dreyfus
Gia .... Judith Blazer
Sumner .... Larry Keith
Reva .... Dori Brenner

Standbys: Messrs. Frechette, O'Rourke—Neal Lerner; Misses Getz, Blazer—Janet Metz; Mr. Valley—Jonah Bay; Mr. Keith—Richard M. Davidson; Miss Brenner—Jana Robbins.

Directed by David Warren; scenery, Neil Patel; costumes, Candice Donnelly; lighting, Peter Maradudin; original music and sound, John Gromada; founding director, Gene Feist; associate artistic director, Scott Ellis; casting, Jim Carnahan, Amy Christopher; production stage manager, Jay Adler; stage manager, Nancy Elizabth Vest; press, Boneau/Bryan-Brown, Erin Dunn, Johnny Woodnal.

Time: The present. Place: New York City. The play was presented in two parts.

The baby-boomer generation's values and lifestyles satirized in the family relationships, career and character of a writer.

Thwak (206). Transfer from off off Broadway of the performance piece created by David Collins and Shane Dundas. Produced by John Bard Manulis & Liz Heller and Metropolitan Entertainment Group (John Scher & Jeff Rowland) at the Minetta Lane Theater. Opened June 6, 1999. (Closed January 2, 2000)

With David Collins, Shane Dundas (The Umbilical Brothers).

Directed by Philip Wm. McKinley; scenery, Bradley J. Mayer; lighting, Josh Monroe; sound, Raymond D. Schilke; co-producer, Arnold Engelman; press, Cromarty & Company, Peter Cromarty, Alice Cromarty, Sherri Jean Katz.

New Vaudeville clowning with acrobatics and audio presentations. The show was presented without intermission.

Manhattan Theater Club. 1998–99 schedule concluded with **La Terrasse** (48). By Jean-Claude Carrière; American version by Mark O'Donnell. Produced by Manhattan Theater Club, Lynne Meadow artistic director, Barry Grove executive producer, by special arrangement with Laura Pels Productions, at City Center Stage II. Opened June 8, 1999. (Closed July 18, 1999)

Madeleine .... Sarah Knowlton
Etienne .... Jeremy Davidson
Woman From the Agency .... Annie Golden
The General's Wife .... Margaret Hall
Mr. Astruc .... David Schramm
Maurice .... Bruce Norris
The General .... Tom Aldredge

Directed by Mike Ockrent; scenery, Santo Loquasto; costumes, William Ivey Long; lighting, Natasha Katz; sound, Fabian Obispo; fight direction, J. Allen Suddeth; associate artistic director, Michael Bush; general manager, Victoria Bailey; casting, Nancy Piccione; production stage manager, Ara Marx; press, Boneau/Bryan-Brown, Chris Boneau, Andy Shearer, Susanne Tighe, Jen Kelleher.

Time: Autumn. Place: Contemporary Paris. The play was presented without intermission.

Comic treatment of the flow of change in marriage, apartment-hunting, etc., in modern life. A foreign play previously produced in Paris.

If Love Were All (101). Musical revue devised by Sheridan Morley; adapted by Leigh Lawson from the works of Noel Coward. Produced by Julian Schlossberg, Mask Productions, Redbus, Mark S. Golub and Bill Haber, by special arrangement with the Lucille Lortel Theater Foundation, Inc., at the Lucille Lortel Theater. Opened June 10, 1999. (Closed September 5, 1999)

Gertrude Lawrence .... Twiggy
Noel Coward .... Harry Groener

Musicians: Tom Fay piano; William Meade reeds; Raymond Kilday bass; Raymond Grappone drums.

Standbys: Twiggy—Laurie Gamache; Mr. Groener—Jeffry Denman.

Directed by Leigh Lawson; musical direction and arrangements, Tom Fay; scenery and costumes, Tony Walton; lighting, Michael Lincoln; sound, Domonic Sack; wigs, Paul Huntley; assistant choreographer, Jeffry Denman; associate producer, Meyer Ackerman; casting, Stuart Howard/Amy Schecter; production stage manager, Denise Yaney; stage manager, Stacy P. Hughes; press, Jeffrey Richards Associates, Caral Craig, Brett Kristofferson.

Reflections, songs and scenes from the past offered by the performers playing the famous musical and comedy duo, Noel Coward and Gertrude Lawrence. The show was presented in two parts. Previously produced in regional theater at Bay Street Theater, Sag Harbor, N.Y.

ACT I

"Someday I'll Find You" .... Noel, Gertie
"A Room With a View" .... Noel, Gertie
"Mad About You" .... Noel, Gertie
"Don't Put Your Daughter on the Stage, Mrs. Worthington" .... Noel
"Parisian Pierrot" .... Gertie
"Mad Dogs and Englishmen" .... Noel
"Poor Little Rich Girl" .... Noel
"Twentieth Century Blues" .... Gertie
"You Were There" .... Noel, Gertie
"Has Anybody Seen Our Ship?" .... Noel, Gertie

ACT II

"Men About Town" .... Noel, Gertie

"Mad About the Boy"	Noel, Gertie
"I'll Follow My Secret Heart"	Gertie
"I Like America"	Gertie
"London Pride"	Noel, Gertie
"I'll See You Again"	Gertie
"Younger Generation"	Noel
"If Love Were All"	Noel, Gertie
"I'll Remember Her"/"I'll See You Again"	Noel, Gertie

Second Stage Theater. 1998–99 schedule concluded with **Gemini** (14). Revival of the play by Albert Innaurato. Opened June 16, 1999. (Closed June 27, 1999) And **Jar the Floor** (37). By Cheryl L. West. Opened August 11, 1999. (Closed September 12, 1999) Produced by Second Stage Theater, Carole Rothman artistic director, Carol Fishman managing director, Alexander Fraser executive director, at Second Stage Theater.

GEMINI

Francis Geminiani	Brian Mysliwy	Herschel Weinberger	Michael Kendrick
Bunny Weinberger	Linda Hart	Fran Geminiani	Joseph Siravo
Randy Hastings	Thomas Sadoski	Lucille Pompi	Julie Boyd
Judith Hastings	Sarah Rafferty		

Directed by Mark Brokaw; scenery, Riccardo Hernandez; costumes, Jess Goldstein; lighting, Mark McCullough; sound, Janet Kalas; wigs, Paul Huntley; dialects, Sarah Felder; casting, Johnson-Liff Associates; production stage managers, James FitzSimmons, Thea Bradshaw Gillies; press, Richard Kornberg, Don Summa, Rick Miramontez, Jim Byk.

Place: South Philadelphia, the Geminiani-Weinberger backyard. Act I, Scene 1: June 1, 1973, early morning. Scene 2: That evening. Act II, Scene 1: June 2, 1973, morning. Scene 2: That evening.

Gemini was first produced off Broadway by Circle Repertory Company 3/13/77 for 63 performances, then transferred to Broadway 5/21/77 for 1,788 performanmces. This is its first major New York revival.

JAR THE FLOOR

MaDear	Irma P. Hall	Vennie	Linda Powell
Maydee	Regina Taylor	Raisa	Welker White
Lola	Lynne Thigpen		

Directed by Marion McClinton; scenery, David Gallo; costumes, Michael Krass; lighting, Donald Holder; sound, Janet Kalas; casting, Johnson-Liff Associates; production stage manager, Diane DiVita; stage manager, Glynn David Turner.

Time: MaDear's 90th birthday. Place: Park Forest, Ill., a suburb of Chicago. The play was presented in two parts.

Mother-daughter relationships among four generations of women gathered for a family celebration.

The Joseph Papp Public Theater/New York Shakespeare Festival. Schedule of two outdoor programs. **The Taming of the Shrew** (21). Revival of the play by William Shakespeare. Opened June 17, 1999; see note. (Closed July 11, 1999) **Tartuffe** (23). Revival of the play by Molière; English verse translation by Richard Wilbur. Opened August 10, 1999; see note. (Closed September 5, 1999) Produced by The Joseph Papp Public Theater/New York Shakespeare Festival, George C. Wolfe producer, Rosemarie Tichler artistic producer, Mark Litvin managing director, at the Delacorte Theater in Central Park with the cooperation of the City of New York, Rudolph W. Giuliani mayor, Peter F. Vallone speaker of the City Council, Schuyler Chapin commissioner, Department of Cultural Affairs, Henry J. Stern commissioner, Department of Parks & Recreation.

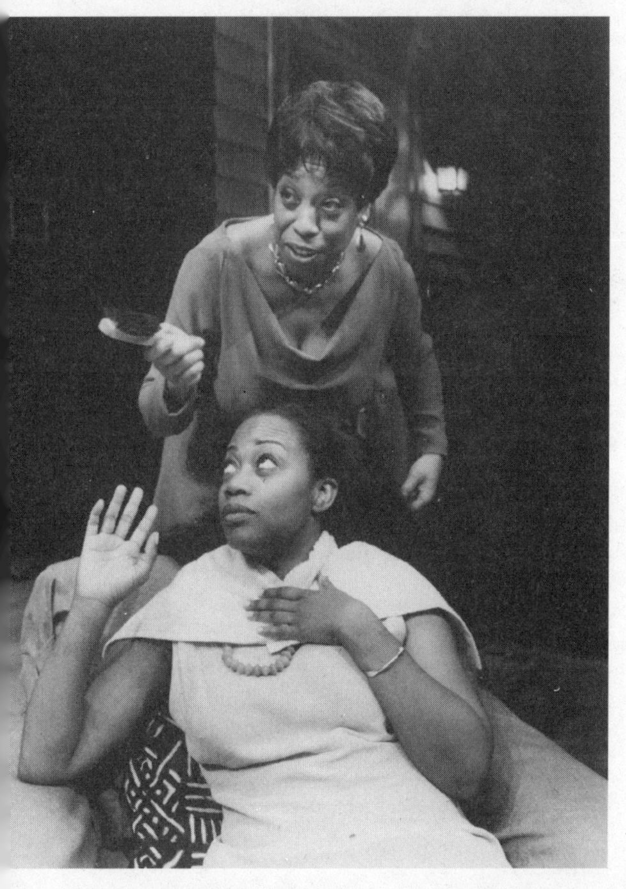

At Second Stage

In photo at left, Lynne Thigpen *(at top)* and Regina Taylor in a summer offering, Cheryl L. West's *Jar the Floor. Above,* in mid-season, Greg Zola, Rachel Ulanet, Clarke Thorell, Michael Benjamin Washington, Kirk McDonald, Joey Sorge *(seated)*, Christopher Fitzgerald and Natascia A. Diaz in a scene from the Stephen Sondheim-Julius J. Epstein musical *Saturday Night*

BOTH PLAYS: Margaret M. Lioi senior director of external affairs; Wiley Hausam, Bonnie Metzgar associate producers; Brian Kulick artistic associate; casting, Jordan Thaler, Heidi Griffiths; press, Carol R. Fineman, Thomas V. Naro, Nefertiti Nguvu.

THE TAMING OF THE SHREW

Lady; Haberdasher; Widow .... Olga Merediz
Christopher Sly .... Max Wright
Hostess .... Magaly Colimon
Bartholomew; Officer .... Ramon Deocampo
Lucentio .... Scott Denny
Tranio .... Peter Jacobson
Baptista Minola .... Tom Mardirosian
Gremio .... MacIntyre Dixon
Katherina .... Allison Janney
Hortensio .... Reg E. Cathey
Bianca .... Erika Alexander
Biondello .... Danyon Davis
Petruchio .... Jay O. Sanders
Grumio .... Mario Cantone
Servants to Petruchio:
Nathaniel .... Chad Smith
Philip .... Jesse Pennington
Joseph .... Ramon Deocampo
Gregory .... Rio Puertollano
Peter .... Dion Flynn
Tailor .... Stephen Mo Hanan
Vincentio .... Don Mayo

Servants to Lady—Evan Robertson, Dion Flynn, Jesse Pennington, Chad Smith. Players—Erika Alexander, Stephen Mo Hanan, Rio Puertollano. Monks—Stephen Mo Hanan, Don Mayo, Rio Puertollano, Chad Smith. Servants to Baptista—Magaly Colimon, Olga Merediz, Jesse Pennington, Evan Robertson.

Directed by Mel Shapiro; scenery, Karl Eigsti; costumes, Marina Draghici; lighting, Brian MacDevitt; sound, Tom Morse; composer, Mark Bennett; chorcography, Naomi Goldberg; fight direction, J. Steven White; production stage manager, James Latus; stage manager, Erica Schwartz.

Place: A lady's garden, used by the players to represent Padua, Verona and the road in between. The play was presented in two parts.

The last major New York revival of *The Taming of the Shrew* was in the New York Shakespeare Festival Shakespeare Marathon 6/22/90 for 27 performances.

TARTUFFE

Mme. Pernelle .... Dana Ivey
Elmire .... J. Smith-Cameron
Dorine .... Mary Testa
Damis .... Curtis McClarin
Mariane .... Danielle Ferland
Cleante .... Wendell Pierce
Flipote .... Michi Barall
Orgon .... Charles Kimbrough
Valere .... Christopher Duva
Tartuffe .... Dylan Baker
Laurent .... Justin Hagan
M. Loyal .... Bill Buell
Officer .... Patrick Garner
Policemen .... Tim McGeever, Matthew Montelongo

Directed by Mark Brokaw; scenery, Riccardo Hernandez; costumes, Jess Goldstein; lighting, Mark McCullough; sound, Tom Morse; original music, John Gromada; wigs, Paul Huntley; production stage manager, Roy Harris; stage manager, Janet Takami.

Place: Orgon's house in Paris. The play was presented in two parts.

The last major New York revival of *Tartuffe* was by the Acting Company last season 5/20/99 for 11 performances.

Note: Press date for *The Taming of the Shrew* was 6/27/99, for *Tartuffe* was 8/22/99.

New York Theater Workshop. 1998–99 season concluded with **The Trestle at Pope Lick Creek** (20). By Naomi Wallace. Produced by New York Theater Workshop, James C. Nicola artistic director, Jo Beddoe managing director, at New York Theater Workshop. Opened June 30, 1999. (Closed July 17, 1999)

Dalton .... Michael Pitt
Pace .... Alicia Goranson
Chas .... Philip Goodwin
Gin .... Nancy Robinette
Dray .... David Chandler

Directed by Lisa Peterson; scenery, Riccardo Hernandez; costumes, Katherine Roth; lighting, Scott Zielinski; music and sound, David Van Tieghem; fight direction, Rick Sordelet; production stage manager, Katie J. Garton; press, Richard Kornberg, Don Summa.

Pair of Depression-era small-town teenagers trying to find love and opportunity in their struggling lives. The play was presented in two parts. Previously produced in regional theater at the Actors Theater of Louisville Humana Festival in 1998.

Lincoln Center Festival 99. Schedule of three plays by Brian Friel. **Uncle Vanya** (14). Newly adapted from the play by Anton Chekhov; presented in the Gate Theater production, Michael Colgan director. Opened July 7, 1999. (Closed July 18, 1999) **The Freedom of the City** (14). Revival presented in the Abbey Theater production, Patrick Mason artistic director, Richard Wakely managing director. Opened July 8, 1999. (Closed July 18, 1999). **Aristocrats** (6). Revival presented in the Gate Theater production. Opened July 20, 1999. (Closed July 25, 1999) Produced by Lincoln Center Festival 99, Nigel Redden director, Carmen Kovens producer, *Uncle Vanya* and *Aristocrats* at the La Guardia Drama Theater, *The Freedom of the City* at John Jay College Theater.

UNCLE VANYA

Marina .... Daphne Carroll
Astrov .... John Kavanagh
Vanya .... Niall Buggy
Serebryakov .... T.P. McKenna
Telegin .... Eamon Morrissey
Sonya .... Donna Dent
Elena .... Susannah Harker
Maria .... Ann Rowan
Laborer .... Ciaran Reilly

Directed by Ben Barnes; scenery, David Gaucher; costumes, Jacqueline Kobler; lighting, Rupert Murray; production manager, Liam Pawley; press, Eileen McMahon.

Time: The late 19th century. Place: A provincial estate in Russia. Act I: The garden on the Serebryakov estate, late summer afternoon. Act II: The dining room, some days later. Act III: The gallery, early afternoon in September. Act IV: Vanya's study, late evening the same day.

The last major New York revival of *Uncle Vanya* was by Circle in the Square on Broadway 2/24/95 for 29 performances.

THE FREEDOM OF THE CITY

Michael Hegerty .... Gerard Crossan
Lily Doherty .... Sorcha Cusack
Skinner;
Adrian Casimir Fitzgerald .... Michael Colgan
Dr. Dodds .... Bosco Hogan
Brigadier Johnson-Hanbury .... Brian de Salvo
Liam O'Kelly;
RTE Commentator .... Barry Barnes
Father Brosnan .... Lalor Roddy
Police Constable .... Vincent Higgins
Judge .... Ian Price
Dr. Winbourne; Forensic Expert .... Pat Laffan
Prof. Cuppley; Pathologist .... Niall O'Brien
Army Press Officer .... Miche Doherty
Press Photographer .... Alan Smyth
Ballad Singer .... Dennis Conway

Various roles: Nora Mullan. Soldiers and various roles: Gerry McCann, Seamus Fox, Enda Kilroy.

Directed by Conall Morrison; scenery, Francis O'Connor; costumes, Joan O'Clery; lighting, Ben Ormerod; sound, Dave Nolan; stage director, Colette Morris.

Time: 1970. Place: Derry City. The play was presented in two parts.

The Freedom of the City was first produced on Broadway 2/17/74 for 9 performances. This is its first major New York revival.

ARISTOCRATS

Tom Huffnung .... William Roberts
Willie Diver .... Joe Gallagher
Uncle George .... Eamon Kelly
Casimir .... Mark Lambert
Alice .... Donna Dent
Eamon .... Frank McCusker
Claire .... Alison McKenna

Directed by Ben Barnes; scenery, Christopher Oram; costumes, Joan Bergin; lighting, Rupert Murray.

Aristocrats was first produced off Broadway by Manhattan Theater Club 4/25/89 for 186 performances. This is its first major New York revival. The play was presented in two parts.

Summer 69 (105). Musical with book by Bill Van Horn, Leer Paul Leary and Ellen Michelmore; music by various authors (see listing below). Produced by Ira Shapiro, Robert E. Schneider, Stuart A. Ditsky, in association with Stephen Rose, at the Douglas Fairbanks Theater. Opened July 15, 1999. (Closed October 10, 1999)

E. Alyssa Claar
Jamie Hurley
Brian Maillard
Ron McClary
Kirk McGee
Anne Moore
Rik Sansone
Rachel Stern
Christine M. Williamson

Summer 69 Band: Faser Hardin director, keyboard; Lou Gentile, Mark McCarron guitar; Hugh Mason bass; Ray Grappone drums.

Understudies: Male Roles— Jeremy Webb; Female Roles—Casey Daniel.

Directed by Bruce Lumpkin; scenery and projections, John Farrell; costumes, Colleen McMillan; lighting, Jeffrey S. Koger; sound, James Tomaselli; music arrangements and transcriptions, Faser Hardin; production stage manager, Patrick O'Leary; stage manager, Scott H. Schneider; press, Publicity Outfitters, Timothy Haskell, Christopher Joy.

A selection of the music and events of the title summer revisited.

MUSICAL NUMBERS, ACT I: "Woodstock" (by Joni Mitchell)—Christine M. Williamson, Jamie Hurley, Brian Maillard, Ron McClary, Kirk McGee, Anne Moore, Rik Sansone. "Summer in the City" (by John Sebastian, Mark Sebastian and Steve Boone)—Rachel Stern, E. Alyssa Claar, Company. "Goin' Up the Country" (by Alan Wilson)—Sansone, Maillard; "Mercedes Benz" (by Janis Joplin, Michael McClure and Bob Neuwirth)—Claar; "The Times They Are A'Changin' " (by Bob Dylan)—Maillard, Hurley, McGee, Moore, Sansone, Williamson, McClary. "Black Magic Woman" (by Peter Alen Green)—Claar, Maillard. "Somebody to Love" (by Darby Slick)—Claar. "Teach Your Children Well" (by Graham Nash)—Stern, Claar, Hurley, Maillard, McClary, McGee, Moore, Sansone, Williamson. "I Feel Like I'm Fixin' to Die Rag" (by Joe McDonald)—McClary, Hurley, Moore, McGee, Maillard, Sansone, Williamson. "Find the Cost of Freedom" (by Stephen Stills)—Sansone, Maillard, McClary, McGee, Moore, Hurley, Williamson.

ACT II: "For What It's Worth" (by Stephen Stills)—Stern, Company. "White Rabbit" (by Grace Slick)—Claar. "With a Little Help From My Friends" (by John Lennon and Paul McCartney)—McClary, Claar, Stern, Company. "The Weight" (by JR Robinson)—Stern, Company. "Piece of My Heart" (by Bert Berns and Jerry Ragovoy)—Claar. "Let's Get Together" (by Chet Powers)—Stern, Claar. "The Star Spangled Banner" (by Francis Scott Key)—Band. "Turn, Turn, Turn (To Everything There Is a Season)" (by Pete Seeger)—Hurley, Maillard, McClary, McGee, Moore, Sansone, Williamson, Stern, Claar. "Woodstock"—Company. "Dance to the Music" (by Sylvester Stewart)—Company.

The York Theater Company. 1998–99 schedule concluded with **After the Fair** (30). Musical based on a story by Thomas Hardy; book and lyrics by Stephen Cole; music by Matthew Ward. Opened July 15, 1999. (Closed August 8, 1999) Produced by The York Theater Company, James Morgan artistic director, Robert A. Buckley managing director, at the Theater at St. Peter's.

Edith Harnham .... Michele Pawk
Anna .... Jennifer Piech
Charles Bradford .... James Ludwig
Arthur Harnham .... David Staller

Musicians: Georgia Stitt keyboard 1; Deborah Abramson keyboard 2; Audrey Terry cello; Dan Willis reed.

Understudies: Misses Pawk, Piech—Erica Schroeder; Messrs. Ludwig, Staller—Michael Mendiola.

Directed by Travis L. Stockley; musical direction, Georgia Stitt; scenery, James Morgan; costumes, Michael Bottari, Ronald Case; lighting, Michael Lincoln; orchestrations, David Siegel; additional orchestrations, Georgia Stitt; founding artistic director, Janet Hayes Walker; produced by arrangement with Ballantrae, Ltd., Raymond Wright artistic director; casting, Joseph McConnell; production stage manager, Michael J. Chudinski; press, Keith Sherman & Associates.

Time : 1897. Place: Melchester, England (100 miles from London) and London.

Adapted from Hardy's short story *On the Western Circuit,* about tangled emotions and ill-fated love in the 19th century English provinces. Originally produced by Lyric Stage, Irving, Tex.

The Gathering (99). Transfer from off off Broadway of the play by Arje Shaw. Produced by The Jewish Repertory Theater, Ran Avni artistic director, Kathleen Germann managing director, in association with The 92d Street Y and Diaspora Productions, Robert N. Ruffin, Esther Shaw and Mary Wadkins, at Playhouse 91. Opened July 20, 1999. (Closed October 10, 1999)

Gabe .... Theodore Bikel
Michael .... Jesse Adam Eisenberg
Diane .... Susan Warrick Hasho
Stuart .... Robert Fass
Egon .... Peter Hermann

Directed by Rebecca Taylor; scenery, Robert Joel Schwartz; costumes, Susan L. Soetaert; lighting, Scott Clyve; music, Andy Stein; sound, Jeremy M. Posner; casting, Laurie Smith; production stage manager, D.C. Rosenberg; stage manager, Adam Grosswirth; press, Keith Sherman & Associates, Tom Chiodo.

Time: Spring 1985. Act I, Scene 1: Gabe's studio in New York City. Scene 2: Later that day, Stuart and Diane's dining room. Act II: One week later, Bitburg, West Germany.

Dachau survivor's family in conflict over the significance of Reagan's visit to the German cemetery at Bitburg. Produced 6/10/99 by Jewish Repertory Theater and raised to off-Broadway status 7/20/99.

*__Naked Boys Singing!__ (366). Musical revue conceived by Robert Schrock; written by various authors (see listing below). Produced by Jamie Cesa, Carl D. White, Hugh Hayes, Tom Smedes and Jennifer Dumas at the Actors' Playhouse. Opened July 22, 1999.

ACT I

"Gratuitous Nudity" .... Company
Music and lyrics by Stephen Bates; additional lyrics by Robert Schrock and Mark Winkler; additional music by Shelly Markham
"The Naked Maid" .... Sean McNally
Music and lyrics by David Pevsner
"Bliss" .... Daniel C. Levine, Company
Music and lyrics by Marie Cain
"Window to Window" .... Adam Michaels
Music and lyrics by Rayme Sciaroni
"Fight the Urge" .... Sean McNally, Daniel C. Levine, Tim Burke, Company
Music by David Pevsner and Rayme Sciaroni; lyrics by David Pevsner
"Robert Mitchum" .... Tom Gualtieri, Company
Music by Shelly Markham; lyrics by Mark Winkler
"Jack's Song" .... Company
Music by Ben Schaechter, lyrics by Jim Morgan

ACT II

"Members Only" .... Trance Thompson, Glenn Seven Allen, Jonathan Brody, Company
Music by Stephen Bates; lyrics by Stephen Bates and Robert Schrock
"Perky Little Porn Star" .... Daniel C. Levine
Music and lyrics by David Pevsner
"Nothin' But the Radio On" .... Glenn Seven Allen, Company
Music by Shelly Markham; lyrics by Mark Winkler
"Kris, Look What You've Missed" .... Jonathan Brody
Music by Stephen Bates; lyrics by Robert Schrock
"Muscle Addiction" .... Tim Burke, Company
Music and lyrics by Mark Savage; mix produced by Trance Thompson

"The Entertainer" .... Trance Thompson, Company
Music and lyrics by Trance Thompson and Perry Hart
"Window to Window" (Reprise) .... Sean McNally
"Window to the Soul" .... Sean McNally, Adam Michaels, Trance Thompson, Jonathan Brody
Music and lyrics by Stephen Bates.
"Finale/Naked Boys Singing" .... Company
Music and lyrics by Stephen Bates

Pianist: Stephen Bates.
Understudy: Patrick Herwood.
Directed by Robert Schrock; choreography, Jeffry Denman; musical direction and arrangements, Stephen Bates; scenery and costumes, Carl D. White; lighting, Aaron Copp; casting, Alan Filderman; production stage manager, Christine Catti; press, Cromarty & Company, Peter Cromarty.
Musical spectacle of male nudity. Originally presented by the Celebration Theater, Los Angeles.

A Good Swift Kick (13). Musical revue with words and music by John Forster. Produced by Sandy Faison, Chase Mishkin, Steven M. Levy and Leonard Soloway at the Variety Arts Theater. Opened July 29, 1999. (Closed August 8, 1999)

D'Monroe
Wanda Houston
David Naughton
Jim Newman
Elisa Surmont

Musicians: John DiPinto conductor, keyboards; Robert C. Kelly drums, percussion, additional keyboards; Gillian Berkowitz keyboards.
Directed by Paul Kreppel; choreography, Murphy Cross; musical direction, John DiPinto; scenery, Kenneth Foy; costumes, Marian Hale; lighting, Jason Kantrowitz; sound, Peter Fitzgerald; orchestrations, Steve Orich, John Forster; musical supervision, Steve Orich; casting, Jay Binder; production stage manager, Robert V. Thurber; stage manager, Jason Brouillard; press, Boneau/Bryan-Brown, Chris Boneau, Jackie Green.
Collection of satirical songs on a pot pourri of subjects from sex to politics, previously produced in regional theater at Goodspeed Opera House. The show was presented without intermission.

MUSICAL NUMBERS: "In the Closet," Tone Deaf," "The PAC Man," "Helium," "Legacy," "One Billion Litttle Emperors," "Whole," "The Ballad of Robert Moses," "Fusion," "Way Down Deep," "A Mismatch Made in Hell," "Spores," "Bye Bye Future," "The Big Mac Tree," "The Tragique Kingdom," "Entering Marion," "Nothing Ventured, Nothing Lost," "Virtual Vivian" "Codependent With You," "Passing."

Y2K, You're OK (169). Comedy revue with sketches by Joe DeGise II, Denny Siegel and Paul Zuckerman, plus improvisations by Chicago City Limits. Produced by Chicago City Limits, Paul Zuckerman executive producer, at the Chicago City Limits Theater. Opened August 6, 1999. (Closed December 31, 1999)

Joe DeGise II
Carol Kissin
Denny Siegel
Victor Varnado

Directed by Paul Zuckerman; musical direction, Frank Spitznagel; producers, Linda Gelman, Jay Stern; production stage managers, Jay Stern, Steven Bostwick; press, Keith Sherman & Associates.
The Chicago-born troupe, renowned for its improvisational skills, in its 20th year in New York with scripted satirical reflections on the millennium from the Crusades to the current Mideast frictions.

The Exact Center of the Universe (142). By Joan Vail Thorne. Produced by Elsa Daspin Haft, Martin Markinson, Judith Resnick, Sheilah Goldman, Jerome Rosenfeld and Allen M. Shore at the Century Theater. Opened September 8, 1999. (Closed January 9, 2000)

Vada Love Powell .... Frances Sternhagen
Appleton Powell .... Reed Birney
Mary Ann .... Tracy Thorne
Enid .... Sloane Shelton
Marybell .... Marge Redmond

Directed by John Tillinger; scenery, Michael Brown; costumes, Carrie Robbins; lighting, Brian MacDevitt; sound, Laura Grace Brown; associate director, Jules Ochoa; casting, Deborah Brown; production stage manager, Christine Catti; stage manager, Christina Massie; press, Springer/Chicoine Public Relations, Gary Springer, Susan Chicoine.

Time: Act I, the 1950s. Act II, the 1960s. Place: A small town in the Deep South.

About a Southern doyenne, her son and the woman who dares come between them. Previously produced off off Broadway by the Women's Project and Productions.

New York Theater Workshop. Schedule of five programs. **A Streetcar Named Desire** (40). Revival of the play by Tennessee Williams. Opened September 12, 1999. (Closed October 16, 1999) **Dirty Blonde** (40). By Claudia Shear; conceived by Claudia Shear and James Lapine. Opened January 10, 2000. (Closed February 13, 2000 and transferred to Broadway; see its entry in the Plays Produced on Broadway section of this volume). **What You Get and What You Expect** (16). By Jean-Marie Besset; translated by Hal J. Witt. Opened March 28, 2000. (Closed April 9, 2000) **Lydie Breeze, Part I: Bullfinch's Mythology** (26), opened May 4, 2000, and **Lydie Breeze, Part II: The Sacredness of the Next Task** (26), opened May 5, 2000. Revival of the two-play cycle by John Guare presented in rotating repertory. (Repertory closed May 28, 2000) Produced by New York Theater Workshop, James C. Nicola artistic director, Jo Beddoe managing director, at New York Theater Workshop.

A STREETCAR NAMED DESIRE

Blanche DuBois .... Elizabeth Marvel
Stella Kowalski .... Jenny Bacon
Stanley Kowalski .... Bruce McKenzie
Harold Mitchell .... Christopher Evan Welch
Eunice Hubbell .... Saidah Arrika Ekulona
Steve Hubbell .... Erik LaRay Harvey
Pablo Gonzales .... Johnny Garcia
Young Collector .... Justin Klosky
Nurse .... Voice of Joan MacIntosh
Doctor .... Voice of Johnny Garcia

Directed by Ivo van Hove; production design, Jan Versweyveld; original music and sound, Harry de Wit; production stage manager, Martha Donaldson; press, Richard Kornberg & Associates, Richard Kornberg, Don Summa.

The last major New York revival of *A Streetcar Named Desire* took place on Broadway 5/12/92 for 137 performances.

DIRTY BLONDE

Frank Wallace;
Ed Hearn; Others .... Bob Stillman
Jo; Mae .... Claudia Shear
Charlie; Others .... Kevin Chamberlin

Directed by James Lapine; musical staging, John Carrafa; musical direction and arrangements, Bob Stillman; scenery, Douglas Stein; costumes, Susan Hilferty; lighting, David Lander; sound, Dan Moses Schreier; production stage manager, Leila Knox.

Homage to Mae West, as two of her ardent fans meet at her gravesite and share their memories and enthusiasm. The play was presented without intermission.

MUSICAL NUMBERS: "Dirty Blonde" music and lyrics by Bob Stillman. From the movie *I'm No Angel:* "I Want You, I Need You" lyrics by Ben Ellison, music by Harvey Brooks; "I'm No Angel" and "I Found a New Way to Go to Town" lyrics by Gladys Dubois and Ben Ellison, music by Harvey Brooks.

WHAT YOU GET AND WHAT YOU EXPECT

Phillipe Derrien .... Stephen Caffrey
Robert Lebret .... Peter Jacobson
Guard .... Adam Greer
Louise Erkanter .... Pamela Payton-Wright
Nathalie Derrien .... Kathryn Meisle
Pericles Feyder .... T. Scott Cunningham
Neil Abbot .... Daniel Gerroll

Directed by Christopher Ashley; scenery, Klara Sieglerova; costumes, Amela Baksic; lighting, Frances Aronson; sound, Kurt B. Kellenberger; production stage manager, Lee J. Kahrs.

LYDIE BREEZE—Bill Camp, Elizabeth Marvel, Matt Servitto, Scott Schmidt, Joanna P. Adler and Boris McGiver in New York Theater Workshop's revival of John Guare's two-play cycle

Competition between two architects to design a monument on the moon is complicated by political and sexual rivalry. A French play previously produced in France and England. The play was presented without intermission.

LYDIE BREEZE, PARTS I & II

Repertory Cast:

Lydie Breeze .... Elizabeth Marvel
Amos Mason .... Boris McGiver
Joshua Hickman .... Bill Camp
Dan Grady .... Matt Servitto
Beaty .... Joanna P. Adler
Young Jeremiah Grady .... Scott Schmidt
O'Malley;
Lucian Rock .... Christopher McCann
Lydie Breeze Hickman .... Alicia Goranson
Gussie Hickman .... Alexandra Oliver
Jude Emerson .... Thomas Shaw
Jeremiah Grady .... Jefferson Mays

Repertory Credits: Directed by Itamar Kubovy; scenery, Neil Patel; costumes, Gabriel Berry; lighting, Brian MacDevitt; sound, Kurt B. Kellenberger; original music, Adam Guettel; production stage manager, Marci A. Glotzer.

Part I: Bullfinch's Mythology—Act I, 1875, Nantucket. Act II, 1884, Charlestown Prison, Boston.

Part II: The Sacredness of the Next Task—Act I, 1895, Nantucket. Act II, 1895, Nantucket.

These plays were first produced off Broadway in the 1981–82 season as *Gardenia* (4/13/82 for 48 performances) and *Lydie Breeze* (2/25/82) for 29 performances). This is their first major New York revival of record.

*__The Countess__ (391). By Gregory Murphy. Produced by The Villar-Hauser Theater Development Fund at the Samuel Beckett Theater. Opened September 28, 1999.

John Ruskin .... James Riordan
Mr. Ruskin .... Frederick Neumann
Mrs. Ruskin .... Honora Fergusson
Crawley .... John Quilty
Lady Eastlake .... Kristin Griffith
Millais .... Jy Murphy
Effie .... Jennifer Woodward

Directed by Ludovica Villar-Hauser; scenery, Mark Symszak; costumes, Christopher Lione; lighting, Carrie Sophia Hash; sound, Randy Morrison; composer, Dewey Dellay; casting, Marcia Turner; production stage manager, Shan Bryant; press, L.S. Public Relations, Les Schecter.

Prologue. Act I, Scene l: London, The Royal Academy. Scene 2: The drawing room at Denmark Hill, the South London home of John James Ruskin, June 21, 1853. Scene 3: Brig O'Turk, Scotland, schoolmaster Alex Stewart 's cottage, 1853. Scene 4: July 10, 1853. Scene 5: Mid-August. Scene 6: Mid-September. Scene 7: Late October, afternoon. Scene 8: Late October, evening. Entr'acte. Act II, Scene 1: Edinburgh, The Philosophical Institution, November 1853. Scene 2: London, the drawing room at Denmark Hill, late December 1853. Scene 3: Early January, 1854. Scene 4: April 13. Scene 5: Afternoon, April 14. Scene 6: Morning, April 25. Scene 7: Evening, April 25. Epilogue.

Based on real Victorian events, the marriage of John and Effie Ruskin, wracked with cruelty and pain. Previously produced off off Broadway in this production, which moved to this theater 6/8/99 and to full off-Broadway status 9/28/99.

*__The Vagina Monologues__ (269). Solo performance by Eve Ensler; written by Eve Ensler. Produced by David Stone, Willa Shalit, Nina Essman, Dan Markley/Mike Skipper and The Araca Group at the Westside Theater. Opened October 3, 1999.

Production supervised by Joe Mantello; scenery, Loy Arcenas; lighting, Beverly Emmons; associate producer, Sally Fisher; production stage manager, Barnaby Harris; press, The Publicity Office, Marc Thibodeau, Bob Fennell.

Feminist message in a series of humorous and dramatic monologues portraying aspects of sexuality. The play was presented without intermission. Previously produced off off Broadway at Home for Contemporary Theater and Art.

Roundabout Theater Company. Schedule of three programs. **Give Me Your Answer, Do!** (104). By Brian Friel. Opened October 5, 1999. (Closed January 2, 2000) **Arms and the Man** (93). Revival of the play by George Bernard Shaw. Opened February 10, 2000. (Closed April 30, 2000). And *Hotel Suite* by Neil Simon scheduled to open 6/15/00. Produced by Roundabout Theater Company, Todd Haimes artistic director, Ellen Richard managing director, Julia C. Levy executive director of external affairs, at the Gramercy Theater.

ALL PLAYS: Founding director, Gene Feist; associate artistic director, Scott Ellis; director of artistic development, Jim Carnahan; press, Boneau/Bryan-Brown, Adrian Bryan-Brown, Erin Dunn, Johnny Woodnal.

GIVE ME YOUR ANSWER, DO!

Bridget Connolly .... Woodwyn Koons
Tom Connolly .... John Glover
Nurse .... Nancy Robinette
Daisy Connolly .... Kate Burton
David Knight .... Michael Emerson
Jack Donovan .... Joel Grey
Maggie Donovan .... Lois Smith
Garret Fitzmaurice .... Gawn Grainger
Grainne Fitzmaurice .... Helen Carey

Standbys and understudies: Messrs. Glover, Emerson—Martin LaPlatney; Messrs. Grey, Grainger—John Seidman; Misses Smith, Carey—Nancy Robinette; Misses Burton, Robinette—Caitlin O'Connell; Miss Koons—Lanie MacEwan.

Directed by Kyle Donnelly; scenery, Thomas Lynch; costumes, Martin Pakledinaz; lighting, Kenneth Posner; music and sound, Donald DiNicola; casting, Jim Carnahan, Amy Christopher; production stage manager, Jay Adler; stage manager, Bradley McCormick.

Time: The present. Place: The old manse, Ballybeg, County Donegal. The play was presented in two parts.

Novelist suffering from writer's block and sundry financial difficulties and family sorrows. A foreign play previously produced in Dublin and London.

ARMS AND THE MAN

Raina Petkoff	Katie Finneran	Russian Officer	Mark Deklin
Catherine Petkoff	Sandra Shipley	Nicola	Michael Potts
Louka	Robin Weigert	Maj. Paul Petkoff	Tom Bloom
Capt. Bluntschli	Henry Czerny	Maj. Sergius Saranoff	Paul Michael Valley

Standbys and Understudies: Messrs. Czerny, Valley—Mark Deklin; Misses Finneran, Weigert—Julie Lund; Mr. Bloom—Doug Stender; Miss Shipley—Barbara Sims; Messrs. Potts, Deklin—Matthew Montelongo.

Directed by Roger Rees; scenery, Neil Patel; costumes, Kaye Voyce; lighting, Frances Aronson; sound and original music, Donald DiNicola; casting, Amy Christopher; production stage manager, Jay Adler; stage manager, Julie Baldauff.

Time: Act I, late November 1885; Acts II and III, spring 1886. Place: A small town near the Dragoman Pass, Bulgaria. The play was presented in two parts.

The last major New York revival of record of *Arms and the Man* was also by the Roundabout off Broadway 5/17/89.

Lincoln Center Theater. Schedule of three programs. **Contact** (101). A dance play by Susan Stroman and John Weidman; written by John Weidman; directed and choreographed by Susan Stroman. Opened October 7, 1999. (Closed January 2, 2000 and moved to the Vivian Beaumont Theater 3/9/00; see its entry in the Plays Produced on Broadway section of this volume) **The Time of the Cuckoo** (88). Revival of the play by Arthur Laurents. Opened February 21, 2000. (Closed May 7, 2000) And *Spinning Into Butter* by Rebecca Gilman scheduled to open 6/29/00. (Also see note.) Produced by Lincoln Center Theater under the direction of Andre Bishop and Bernard Gersten at the Mitzi E. Newhouse Theater.

CONTACT

Part I: Swinging
A forest glade, 1767. A Servant, an Aristocrat, a Girl on a Swing—Seán Martin Hingston, Stephanie Michels, Scott Taylor.

Part II: Did You Move?
An Italian restaurant, Queens, 1954. A Wife, a Husband, a Headwaiter—Karen Ziemba, Jason Antoon, David MacGillivray, Rocker Verastique, Robert Wersinger, Tomé Cousin, Peter Gregus, Nina Goldman, Dana Stackpole, Scott Taylor, Seán Martin Hingston, Pascale Faye, Shannon Hammons, Stacey Todd Holt.

Part III: Contact
New York City, 1999. Michael Wiley—Boyd Gaines. An Advertising Executive, a Bartender, a Girl in a Yellow Dress.—Deborah Yates, Jason Antoon, Jack Hayes, Robert Wersinger, Nina Goldman, Scott Taylor, Shannon Hammons, Stephanie Michels, Seán Martin Hingston, Rocker Verastique, Pascale Faye, Mayumi Miguel, Tomé Cousin, Dana Stackpole, Peter Gregus, Stacey Todd Holt.

Understudies: Frenchmen—John Bolton, Robert Wersinger; Girl on the Swing—Shannon Hammons; Husband, Uncle Vinnie, Bartender—John Bolton; Wife—Nina Goldman; Head Waiter—Rocker Verastique, Scott Taylor; Busboy, Waiter, Restaurant Patrons—Jack Hayes; Waiter—Mayumi Miguel; Michael Wiley—John Bolton, Scott Taylor; Girl in the Yellow Dress—Stephanie Michels. Swings—Danny Herman, Angelique Ilo, David MacGillivray, Joanne Manning.

Scenery, Thomas Lynch; costumes, William Ivey Long; lighting, Peter Kaczorowski; sound, Scott Stauffer; associate choreographer, Chris Peterson; musical theater associate producer, Ira Weitzman; casting, Tara Rubin, Johnson-Liff Associates, Daniel Swee; stage manager, Thom Widmann; press, Philip Rinaldi.

Three dance episodes bringing to life a variety of fantasies from the comic to the sexual to the despairing. The play was presented in two parts with the intermission following Part II. Winner of the 1999–2000 Tony Award for best musical following its transfer to Broadway; see its entry in the Prize-winning Plays section of this volume.

MUSIC: "My Heart Stood Still" by Richard Rodgers and Lorenz Hart; "Anitra's Dance" from *Peer Gynt Suite No. 1* by Grieg; "Waltz Eugene" from Eugene Onegin Op. 24; "La Farandole" from *L'Arlesienne Suite No. 2*; "O Mio Babbino Caro" by Puccini; "You're Nobody Till Somebody Loves

You" by Russ Morgan, Larry Stock and James Cavanaugh; "Powerful Stuff" by Wally Wilson, Michael Henderson and Robert S. Field; "Put a Lid on It" by Tom Maxwell; "Sweet Lorraine" by Clifford Burwell and Maxwell Parish; "Runaround Sue" by Ernest Maresca and Dion DiMucci; "Beyond the Sea" by Charles Trenet and Jack Lawrence; "See What I Mean?" by J. Chapman; "Simply Irresistible" by Robert Palmer; "Do You Wanna Dance?" by Bobby Freeman; "Topsy" by William Edgar Battle and Eddie Durham; "Sing Sing Sing" by Louis Prima; "Christopher Columbus" by Andy Razaf; "Moondance" by Van Morrison.

THE TIME OF THE CUCKOO

Signora Fioria .... Cigdem Onat
Eddie Yaeger .... Adam Trese
Jane Yaeger .... Ana Reeder
Giovanna .... Chiara Mangiameli
Leona Samish .... Debra Monk
Mrs. Edith McIlhenny .... Polly Holliday
Mr. Lloyd McIlhenny .... Tom Aldredge
Mauro .... Sebastian Uriarte
Renato Di Rossi .... Olek Krupa
Vito .... Paolo Pagliacolo

Understudies: Miss Monk—Kathryn Rosseter; Mr. Uriarte—Nicholas Cutro; Messrs. Trese, Pagliacolo—David Harbour; Misses Reeder, Mangiameli—Mireille Enos; Messrs. Krupa, Aldredge—Peter Samuel; Misses Onat, Holliday—Maria Cellario.

Directed by Nicholas Martin; scenery, James Noone; costumes, Theoni V. Aldredge; lighting, Brian MacDevitt; original music and sound, Mark Bennett; casting, Daniel Swee; stage manager, Kelly Kirkpatrick.

Time: Summer, 1950s. Place: Venice, the garden of the Pensione Fioria. Act I, Scene 1: Late afternoon. Scene 2: The next day, early afternoon. Scene 3: Later that evening. Act II, Scene 1: The next day, late afternoon. Scene 2: Later that evening. Scene 3: The next morning.

The Time of the Cuckoo was first produced on Broadway 10/15/52 for 263 peformances and was named a Best Play of its season. Its only previous New York revival of record took place off Broadway in the 1958–59 season, and it was adapted by its author for the book of the Richard Rodgers-Stephen Sondheim musical *Do I Hear a Waltz?* on Broadway 3/18/65 for 220 performances.

NOTE: 47 readings of *Ancestral Voices* by A.R. Gurney took place at the Mitzi Newhouse Theater on Sunday and Monday evenings, 20 of them 10/17/99–12/20/99 and 27 of them 2/6/00–5/8/00. They were directed by Daniel Sullivan, with lighting by Rui Rita. It is a full-length one-acter about a Buffalo family of the 1930s and 1940s upset by the breaking up of the grandparents' marriage. The first cast (Eddie—David Aaron Baker, Harvey—Edward Herrmann, Jane—Blythe Danner, Eddie's Grandmother—Elizabeth Wilson and Eddie's Grandfather—Philip Bosco) gave the first two performances, after which a revolving cast included Mason Adams, Maureen Anderman, Frank Converse, Mariette Hartley, Robert Sean Leonard, Anne Pitoniak, James Rebhorn, Fritz Weaver, Irene Worth and others.

Chesapeake (38). Solo performance by Mark Linn-Baker; written by Lee Blessing; produced by James B. Freydberg, William P. Suter and Susann Brinkley in association with Second Stage Theater. Opened October 14, 1999. (Closed November 14, 1999)

Directed by Max Mayer; scenery, Adrianne Lobel; costumes, Susan Hilferty; lighting, James F. Ingalls; sound, Darron L. West; associate producers, Steven Chaikelson, Gary R. Marano; production stage manager, Laura Brown MacKinnon; press, Barlow-Hartman Public Relations, John Barlow, Michael Hartman, Andy Shearer.

Mark Linn-Baker as a performer who believes he's a dog named Kerr belonging to a Senator who wants to cut off government support of the arts. The play was presented in two parts.

Shockheaded Peter (15). Musical inspired by Heinrich Hoffmann's *The Struwwelpeter;* created by Julian Bleach, Anthony Cairns, Graeme Gilmour, Tamzin Griffin, Jo Pocock; music by The Tiger Lillies—Adrian Huge, Martyn Jacques, Adrian Stout; lyrics adapted from Heinrich Hoffmann by Martyn Jacques; a Cultural Industry Project, Michael Morris director, produced in collaboration with West Yorkshire Playhouse, Jude Kelly artistic director, and Lyric Theater Hammersmith, Sue Storr chief executive, Neil Bartlett artistic director. Produced by The New 42nd Street Inc., Cora Cahan president, at the New Victory Theater. Opened October 14, 1999. (Closed October 31, 1999)

CAST: Julian Bleach, Anthony Cairns, Graeme Gilmour, Tamzin Griffin, Jo Pocock.

Directed by Phelim McDermott and Julian Crouch; musical direction, Martyn Jacques; scenery, Julian Crouch, Graeme Gilmour; costumes, Kevin Pollard; lighting, Jon Linstrum; sound, Mic Pool, Andy Brooks; associate producer, Rachel Feuchtwang; stage manager, Graeme Nixon; press, Lauren Daniluk.

Subtitled *A Junk Opera,* a version of the *Slovenly Peter* horrible example of a very bad boy who comes to a very bad end, portrayed by actors and puppetry. A foreign play previously produced in England.

Stars in Your Eyes (41). Musical with book, music and lyrics by Chip Meyrelles. Produced by Tom Wirtshafter/Planetearth Partners, Inc. at the Cherry Lane Theater. Opened October 24, 1999. (Closed November 28, 1999)

Man in the Moon;
Taylor St. Joseph .... James Stovall
Reginald Barclay .... David M. Lutken
Charles Swanson .... John Braden
Jo Jensen .... Christy Carlson Romano
Annie Patterson .... Barbara Walsh
Helen Stevens .... Heather Mac Rae
Leigh Hunt-Smith .... Crista Moore

Stars in Your Eyes Ensemble: Georgia Stitt piano; Audrey Terry Bass, cello.

Understudy: Misses Walsh, Mac Rae, Moore—Donna Lynne Champlin.

Directed by Gabriel Barre; choreography, Jennifer Paulson Lee; musical direction and arrangements, Georgia Stitt; scenery, James Youmans; costumes, Pamela Scofield; lighting, Tim Hunter; sound, Brian Ronan; casting, Stuart Howard, Amy Schecter; production stage manager, Daniel Zittel; press, Barlow-Hartman Public Relations, John Barlow, Michael Hartman.

Time: 1862. Place: Milford and Bloomfield.

The Man in the Moon plays Cupid for the romantically inclined inhabitants of a small town.

ACT I

Scene 1: A June evening in Milford—an observatory, a park, Milford Dance Studio
"Endless Possibilities" .... Company
Scene 2: The park, a few days later
"Somebody (More or Less) Like Me" .... Annie, Helen
"Can't Say for Sure" .... Man in the Moon
Scene 3: Reginald's classroom, a few days later
"That's What They Said" .... Reginald, Jo, Charles
"I'm Leigh Hunt-Smith" .... Leigh
Scene 4: Charles's office at Milford High School, a few days later
"Another Day" .... Charles
Scene 5: Milford Dance Studio, the following Saturday
"Dance by Numbers" .... Annie, Reginald
Scene 6: The park, Fourth of July
"Must Be Something" .... Company
"Saturn Rising" .... Company
Scene 7: The park, a few weeks later
"Stars in Your Eyes" .... Annie, Reginald

ACT II

Entr'acte
"I've Got a Light on You" .... Man in the Moon
Scene 1: The park, an October evening
Scene 2: Milford Dance Studio, the same evening
"Men!" .... Annie, Helen
Scene 3: The park, a few nights later
"Thinking the Impossible" .... Company
Scene 4: Jo's room at Bloomfield Academy/Milford Dance Studio, the next Saturday morning
"Ordinary Jo" .... Jo
Scene 5: The Hunt-Smith mansion in Bloomfield
"The Best of Everything" .... Taylor, Leigh

Scene 6: Milford Dance Studio
"Why Do We Dance?" .... Helen, Reginald
Scene 7: A Bloomfield Academy classroom, later that morning
"Conventional Wisdom" .... Man in the Moon
Scene 8: Jo's room in Milford, that evening
"Can't Say for Sure" (Reprise) .... Man in the Moon
Scene 9: The park, a few nights later
"Take Me to Heart" .... Reginald, Annie
"Saturn Rising" (Reprise) .... Company

Playwrights Horizons. Schedule of four programs. **James Joyce's The Dead** (38). Musical version of the story by James Joyce; book by Richard Nelson; music by Shaun Davey; lyrics conceived and adapted by Richard Nelson and Shaun Davey; produced by special arrangement with Gregory Mosher and Arielle Tepper. Opened October 28, 1999. (Closed November 28, 1999 and transferred to Broadway 1/11/00; see its entry in the Plays Produced on Broadway section of this volume) **Lobster Alice** (17). By Kira Obolensky. Opened January 9, 2000. (Closed January 23, 2000) **The Moment When** (8). By James Lapine. Opened March 21, 2000. (Closed March 26, 2000) And *The Bubbly Black Girl Sheds Her Chameleon Skin* by Kirsten Childs scheduled to open 6/20/00. Produced by Playwrights Horizons, Tim Sanford artistic director, Leslie Marcus managing director, Lynn Landis general manager, at Playwrights Horizons.

JAMES JOYCE'S THE DEAD

The Hostesses:
Aunt Julia Morkan .... Sally Ann Howes
Aunt Kate Morkan .... Marni Nixon
Mary Jane Morkan .... Emily Skinner
The Family:
Gabriel Conroy .... Christopher Walken
Gretta Conroy .... Blair Brown
The Guests:
Mr. Browne .... Brian Davies
Freddy Malins .... Stephen Spinella
Mrs. Malins .... Paddy Croft
Miss Molly Ivors .... Alice Ripley
Bartell D'Arcy .... John Kelly
The Help:
Lily .... Brooke Sunny Moriber
Michael .... Dashiell Eaves
Rita .... Daisy Eagan
Cellist .... Daniel Barrett
Violinist .... Louise Owen
Ghost:
Young Julia Morkan .... Daisy Eagan

Musicians: Charles Prince conductor; Deborah Abramson piano; Daniel Barrett cello; Steve Benson guitar; Jaqui Leclair oboe, English horn; Louise Owen violin; Tom Partington percussion; Virginia Pike synthesizer, harmonium; Gen Shinkai flute.

Directed by Jack Hofsiss and Richard Nelson; choreography, Seán Curran; musical direction, Charles Prince; scenery, David Jenkins; costumes, Jane Greenwood; lighting, Jennifer Tipton; sound, Scott Lehrer; orchestrations, Shaun Davey; casting, James Calleri, Mark Bennett; production stage manager, Kelly Kirkpatrick; stage manager, Matthew Silver; press, The Publicity Office, Bob Fennell, Marc Thibodeau, Michael S. Borowski, Brett Oberman.

Time: Near the turn of the century. Place: Dublin, the Misses Morkans' annual Christmas-time party. The play was presented without intermission.

Adaptation of Joyce's *Dubliners* short story reflecting upon the personalities and relationships at a long-past, moderately festive gathering of family and friends. Winner of the 1999–2000 New York Drama Critics Circle and Lucille Lortel Awards for best musical; see its entry in the Prizewinning Plays section of this volume.

MUSICAL NUMBERS

Scene 1: The drawing room of the Misses Morkans' flat
Prologue .... Musicians
"Killarney's Lakes" .... Mary Jane, Aunt Kate, Rita

LOBSTER ALICE—Jessica Hecht and Reg Rogers in the play by Kira Obolensky at Playwrights Horizons

"Kate Kearney" .... Michael, Mary Jane, Company
"Parnell's Plight" .... Miss Ivors, Michael, Gabriel, Gretta, Company
"Adieu to Ballyshannon" .... Gabriel, Gretta
"When Lovely Lady" .... Aunt Julia, Aunt Kate
"Three Jolly Pigeons" .... Freddy, Browne, Company
"Goldenhair" .... Gretta, Gabriel

Scene 2: The drawing room arranged for dinner

"Three Graces" .... Gabriel, Company
"Naughty Girls" .... Aunt Julia, Aunt Kate, Mary Jane, Company
"Wake the Dead" .... Freddy, Company

Scene 3: Aunt Julia's bedroom

"D'Arcy's Aria." .... D'Arcy
"Queen of Our Hearts" .... Browne, Freddy, Gabriel, D'Arcy, Michael
"When Lovely Lady" (Reprise) .... Young Julia, Aunt Julia

Scene 4: A room in the Gresham Hotel

"Michael Furey" .... Gretta
"The Living and the Dead" .... Gabriel, Company

Authors' note: The lyrics to some of these songs have been adapted from or inspired by a number of 18th and 19th century Irish poems by Oliver Goldsmith, Lady Sydney Morgan, Michael William Balfe, William Allingham and an anonymous 19th century music hall song. Other lyrics are adapted from Joyce or are original.

LOBSTER ALICE

Alice Horowitz .... Jessica Hecht
John Finch .... Reg Rogers
Salvador Dali .... David Patrick Kelly
Thorton .... Derek Richardson

Directed by Maria Mileaf; scenery, Neil Patel; costumes, Ann Hould-Ward; lighting, Frances Aronson; music and sound, David Van Tieghem; projections, Jan Hartley; production stage manager, William Joseph Barnes.

In Hollywood in 1946, a movie studio secretary meets a champion of surrealist art. The play was presented without intermission.

THE MOMENT WHEN

Alice	Illeana Douglas	Dana	Arija Bareikis
Steven	Mark Ruffalo	Wilson	Kieran Culkin
Paula	Phyllis Newman	Nurse; Waitress	Ann Harada

Directed by Michael Lindsay-Hogg; scenery, Eugene Lee; costumes, Ann Roth; lighting, Yael Lubetzky; music and sound, David Van Tieghem; casting, James Calleri; production stage manager, Renee Lutz.

Act I— 1984, Scene 1: Paula's apartment. Scene 2: Steven's loft, later that evening. 1986, Scene 3: A hospital waiting room. Scene 4: A hospital room and the nursery, three days later. Scene 5: Steven's loft. Scene 6: The Russian Tea Room. Act II— 1993, Scene 1: Central Park playground. 1995, Scene 2: Michael's Restaurant. 2000, Scene 3: Royalton Hotel.

Comic and dramatic turning points in the lives of a couple who meet at a cocktail party and proceed through marriage, parenthood and divorce.

***Manhattan Theater Club**. Schedule of seven programs. **An Experiment With an Air Pump** (49). By Shelagh Stephenson. Opened October 31, 1999. (Closed December 12, 1999) **Fuddy Meers** (166). By David Lindsay-Abaire. Opened November 2, 1999. (Closed April 16, 2000; see note) **Y2K** (46). By Arthur Kopit. Opened December 7, 1999. (Closed January 22, 2000) **The Wild Party** (54). Musical based on the poem by Joseph Moncure March; book, music and lyrics by Andrew Lippa. Opened February 24, 2000. (Closed April 9, 2000) **The Tale of the Allergist's Wife** (56). By Charles Busch. Opened February 29, 2000. (Closed April 16, 2000) ***Proof** (10). By David Auburn. Opened May 23, 2000. And *Current Events* by David Marshall Grant scheduled to open 6/13/00. Produced by Manhattan Theater Club, Lynne Meadow artistic director, Barry Grove executive producer, *An Experiment With an Air Pump, The Wild Party* and *Proof* at City Center Stage 1, *Fuddy Meers, The Tale of the Allergist's Wife* and *Current Events* at City Center Stage 2, *Y2K* by special arrangement with the Lucille Lortel Theater Foundation at the Lucille Lortel Theater.

ALL PLAYS: Associate artistic director, Michael Bush; general manager, Victoria Bailey; director of musical theater program, Clifford Lee Johnson III; press, Boneau/Bryan-Brown, Chris Boneau, Amy Jacobs, Brian Rubin.

AN EXPERIMENT WITH AN AIR PUMP

Susannah Fenwick; Ellen	Linda Emond	Harriet Fenwick; Kate	Ana Reeder
Maria Fenwick	Clea Lewis	Peter Mark Roget	Christopher Duva
Joseph Fenwick; Tom	Daniel Gerroll	Isobel Bridie	Seana Kofoed
Thomas Armstrong; Phil	Jason Butler Harner		

Understudy: Misses Lewis, Kofoed, Reeder—Laura Marie Duncan.

Directed by Doug Hughes; scenery, John Lee Beatty; costumes, Catherine Zuber; lighting, Brian MacDevitt; original music and sound, David Van Tieghem; fight direction, Rick Sordelet; casting, Nancy Piccione; production stage manager, Charles Means.

Time: 1799/1999. Place: Newcastle Upon Tyne, same house. The play was presented in two parts.

Values and morals of science at the end of two centuries examined and compared. A foreign play previously produced in England in Manchester and London.

FUDDY MEERS

Richard	Robert Stanton	Gertie	Marylouise Burke
Claire	J. Smith-Cameron	Millet	Mark McKinney
Kenny	Keith Nobbs	Heidi	Lisa Gorlitsky
Limping Man	Patrick Breen		

Directed by David Petrarca; scenery and costumes, Santo Loquasto; lighting, Brian MacDevitt; sound, Bruce Ellman; original music, Jason Robert Brown; fight direction, Rick Sordelet; casting, Nancy Piccione, David Caparelliotis; production stage manager, Thea Bradshaw Gillies.

Woman tries to recover from a form of amnesia which wipes out her memory each night. Previously produced in 1998 in MTC's "Writers in Performance" series. Note: *Fuddy Meers* closed at Manhattan Theater Club 1/2/00 and reopened at the Minetta Lane Theater 1/27/00 in the same production, with Jean Doumanian as co-producer and John Christopher Jones replacing Mark McKinney and Clea Lewis replacing Lisa Gorlitsky in the cast.

Y2K

Costa Astrakhan .... Eric Jensen
Orin Slake .... Armand Schultz
Dennis McAlvane .... David Brown Jr.
Joseph Elliot .... James Naughton
Joanne Summerhays Elliot .... Patricia Kalember

Directed by Bob Balaban; scenery, Loy Arcenas; costumes, Tom Broecker; lighting, Kevin Adams; sound, Darron L. West; production stage manager, James Fitzsimmons.

A malevolent hacker invades the computer and with it takes control of the lives of a couple whom he victimizes. The play was presented without intermission. Previously presented in regional theater at the Actors Theater of Louisville's Humana Festival.

THE WILD PARTY

Queenie .... Julia Murney
Burrs .... Brian d'Arcy James
Reno .... Todd Anderson
Kegs .... Ron J. Todorowski
Madelaine True .... Alix Korey
Eddie .... Raymond Jaramillo McLeod
Peggy .... Megan Sikora
Max .... James Delisco Beeks
Rose Himmelsteen .... Felicia Finley
Sam Himmelsteen .... Peter Kapetan
Ellie .... Amanda Watkins
Jackie .... Lawrence Keigwin
Oscar d'Armano .... Charles Dillon
Phil d'Armano .... Kevin Cahoon
Dolores .... Kena Tangi Dorsey
Mae .... Jennifer Cody
Nadine .... Kristin McDonald
Kate .... Idina Menzel
Black .... Taye Diggs
The Neighbor .... Charlie Marcus
Cop .... Steven Pasquale

Orchestra: Stephen Oremus conductor, keyboard; Paul Loesel associate conductor, keyboard; Vincent Della-Rocca reed 1; Edward Salkin reed 2; Frank Santagata reed 3; Bob Millikan trumpet, flugelhorn; Konrad Adderley bass; Matt Beck guitar; Steve Bartosik drums, percussion.

Understudies: Miss Murney—Felicia Finley, Amanda Watkins; Mr. James—Steven Pasquale, Charlie Marcus; Mr. Diggs—James Delisco Beeks; Miss Menzel—Felicia Finley; Swings—Joyce Chittick, Collen Hawks, Steven Ochoa, Steven Pasquale.

Directed by Gabriel Barre; choreography, Mark Dendy; musical direction, Stephen Oremus; scenery, David Gallo; costumes, Martin Pakledinaz; lighting, Kenneth Posner; sound, Brian Ronan; orchestrations, Michael Gibson; music coordinator, Michael Keller; fight direction, Rick Sordelet; casting, Bernard Telsey; production stage manager, Ed Fitzgerald.

A love affair takes a tragic turn at a 1920s party of vaudeville performers. Previously presented in readings at the 1997 Eugene O'Neill Theater Conference in Waterford, Conn.

ACT I

"Queenie Was a Blonde" .... Queenie, Burrs, Company
"The Apartment (Sunday Noon)" .... Queenie, Burrs, Company
"Out of the Blue" .... Queenie
"What a Party" .... Company
"Raise the Roof" .... Company
"Look at Me Now" .... Kate
"Poor Child" .... Kate, Black, Queenie, Burrs
"An Old-Fashioned Love Story" .... Madelaine True
"The Juggernaut" .... Queenie, Black, Kate, Burrs, Company
"A Wild, Wild Party" .... Oscar, Phil, Queenie, Burrs, Company

"Two of a Kind" .... Eddie, Mae
"Maybe I Like It This Way" .... Queenie
"What Is It About Her?" .... Burrs, Queenie

ACT II

"The Life of the Party" .... Kate
"Who Is This Man?" .... Queenie
"I'll Be Here" .... Black
"Listen to Me" .... Black, Burrs, Kate, Queenie
"Let Me Drown" .... Burrs, Kate, Company
"The Fight" .... Company
"Mary Jane" .... Sam, Max, Reno, Kegs
"Come With Me" .... Queenie, Black, Company
"Jackie's Last Dance" .... Jackie
"Make Me Happy" .... Burrs, Black, Queenie
"How Did We Come to This?" .... Queenie

THE TALE OF THE ALLERGIST'S WIFE

Mohammad .... Anil Kumar
Marjorie .... Linda Lavin
Ira .... Tony Roberts
Frieda .... Shirl Bernheim
Lee .... Michele Lee

Understudy: Miss Bernheim—Sylvia Kauders.

Directed by Lynne Meadow; scenery, Santo Loquasto; costumes, Ann Roth; lighting, Christopher Akerlind; sound, Bruce Ellman; production stage manager, Bradley McCormick.

Emotional disturbances and cultural longings of an Upper West Side matron. The play was presented in two parts.

PROOF

Robert .... Larry Bryggman
Catherine .... Mary-Louise Parker
Hal .... Ben Shenkman
Claire .... Johanna Day

Understudies: Miss Parker—Catherine Bootle; Mr. Shenkman—Adam Danheisser; Mr. Bryggman— Richard M. Hughes.

Directed by Daniel Sullivan; scenery, John Lee Beatty; costumes, Jess Goldstein; lighting, Pat Collins; sound, John Gromada; casting, Nancy Piccione/David Caarelliotis; production stage manager, James Harker.

Place: The back porch of a house in Chicago. The play was presented in two parts.

A daughter copes, emotionlly and intellectually, with mathematical genius and eccentric personality inherited from her father.

Sail Away (10). Limited concert engagement of the musical with book, music and lyrics by Noel Coward. Produced by Carnegie Hall at Joan and Sanford J. Weill Recital Hall. Opened November 3, 1999. (Closed November 13, 1999)

Joe .... Jonathan Freeman
Mimi Paragon .... Elaine Stritch
Elmer Candijack .... Bill Nolte
Maimie Candijack .... Anne Allgood
Alvin Lush .... Paul Iacono
Mrs. Lush .... Alison Fraser
Sir Gerard Nutfield .... Herb Foster
Lady Nutfield .... Gina Ferrall
Johnny Van Mier .... Jerry Lanning
Mrs. Van Mier .... Jane White
Barnaby Slade .... James Patterson
Mrs. Sweeney .... Jane Connell
Mr. Sweeney .... Gordon Connell
Elinor Spencer Bollard .... Marian Seldes
Nancy Foyle .... Andrea Burns
Adlai .... Phyllis Gutierrez

Passengers, Stewards, etc.—Danny Burstein, Tony Capone, Dale Hensley, Jennifer Kathryn Marshall, Bill Nolte. The Little Ones: Tanya Desko, Paul Iacono, Alexandra Jumper.

Carnegie Hall Theater Orchestra: Ben Whiteley music director; Joel Fram associate music director;

FUDDY MEERS—Lisa Gorlitsky, Marylouise Burke, Keith Nobbs *(on floor)*, Patrick Breen, Mark McKinney, J. Smith-Cameron and Robert Stanton in the play by David Lindsay-Abaire at Manhattan Theater Club

Belinda Whitney-Barratt concertmistress; Mineko Yajima, Rebekah Johnson, Lisa Matricardia, Ashley Horne, Katherine Livolsi-Stern violin; Clay Ruede, Maxine Neuman cello; Richard Sarpola bass; Harvey Estrin flute, piccolo, alto flute, clarinet, saxophone; Albert Regni flute, piccolo, clarinet, E-flat clarinet, bass clarinet, alto saxophone; Ed Zuhlke flute, oboe, English horn, clarinet, tenor saxophone; Mark Thrasher flute, clarinet, bassoon, tenor saxophone; Roger Rosenberg flute, clarinet, bass clarinet, baritone saxophone; Roger Wendt horn; Glen Drewes, Hollis Burridge, Daryll Shaw trumpet; Jack Gale, Jack Schatz trombone; Tony Geralis piano, celeste; Susan Jolles harp; David Nyberg percussion; Lee Appleman drums; Scott Kuney guitar.

Directed by Gerald Gutierrez; orchestrations, Irwin Kostal; dance arrangements, Peter Matz; vocal arrangements, Fred Werner; casting, Johnson-Liff Associates; production coordinator, Michael Brunner.

Sail Away's first New York production took place on Broadway 10/3/61 for 167 performances, with Elaine Stritch as Mimi Paragon. This is its first major New York revival of record.

ACT I

Scene 1: The dockside, New York Harbor
"Come to Me" .... Mimi, Stewards
Scene 2: The Sundeck at night aboard the U.S.S. Coronia
"Sail Away" .... Johnny
"Come to Me" (Reprise) .... Mimi
"Sail Away" (Reprise) .... Johnny, Company
Scene 3: Elinor Spencer Bollard's cabin
"Where Shall I Find Him?" .... Nancy
Scene 4: The Sundeck, day

"Beatnik Love Affair" .... Barnaby
"Later Than Spring" .... Johnny
"The Passenger's Always Right" .... Joe, Stewards

Scene 5: Mimi's cabin
"Useful Phrases" .... Mimi

Scene 6:The Sundeck at night
"Where Shall I Find Her?" (Reprise) .... Barnaby

Scene 7:The Promenade Deck
"Go Slow Johnny" .... Johnny

Scene 8:The ship's nursery
"The Little Ones' ABC" .... Mimi, Little Ones

Scene 9: The Sundeck (night of the Ship's Ball)
"You're a Long, Long Way From America" .... Mimi, Company

ACT II

Scene 1: Tangier
"The Customer's Always Right" .... Ali, Arabs
"Something Very Strange" .... Mimi

Scene 2: An Italian Interlude: Ballet

Scene 3: The Sundeck at night, Bay of Naples
"Don't Turn Away From Love" .... Johnny

Scene 4: The Promenade Deck at night
"Bronxville Darby & Joan" .... Mr. and Mrs. Sweeney
Restored by Stewart Nicholls, orchestrated by Rowland Lee

Scene 5: Athens, the Parthenon
"When You Want Me" .... Nancy, Barnaby

Scene 6: The Sundeck at night
"Later Than Spring" (Reprise) .... Mimi

Scene 7: The Sundeck, New York Harbor
"When You Want Me" (Reprise) .... Company
"Why Do the Wrong People Travel" .... Mimi

***Dinner With Friends** (240). By Donald Margulies. Produced by Mitchell Maxwell, Mark Balsam, Ted Tulchin, Victoria Maxwell, Mari Nakachi and Steven Tulchin at the Variety Arts Theater. Opened November 4, 1999.

Gabe .... Matthew Arkin
Karen .... Lisa Emery
Beth .... Julie White
Tom .... Kevin Kilner

Directed by Daniel Sullivan; scenery, Neil Patel; costumes, Jess Goldstein; lighting, Rui Rita; sound, Peter Fitzgerald; music and sound score, Michael Roth; associate producers, Fred H. Krones, Bob Cuillo; casting, Stephanie Klapper; production stage manager, R. Wade Jackson; stage manager, Deirdre McCrane; press, Barlow-Hartman Public Relations, Michael Hartman, John Barlow, Andy Shearer.

Act I, Scene 1: Karen and Gabe's kitchen in Connecticut, evening, winter. Scene 2: Tom and Beth's bedroom, later that night. Scene 3: Karen and Gabe's living room, later still. Act II, Scene 1: A house on Martha's Vineyard, summer, 12 1/2 years earlier. Scene 2: Karen and Gabe's patio, five months after the events in Act I. Scene 3: A bar in Manhattan, the same afternoon. Scene 4: Karen and Gabe's bedroom, that night.

The disintegration of a marriage over time. Previously produced in regional theater at Actors Theater of Louisville and South Coast Repertory. Winner of the 1999–2000 Pulitzer Prize and Lucille Lortel Award for best play; see its entry in the Prizewinning Plays section of this volume.

Jonathan Walker replaced Kevin Kilner and Carolyn McCormick replaced Julie White 3/00; Dana Delany replaced Lisa Emery 6/00.

Maybe Baby, It's You (67). By Charlie Shanian and Shari Simpson; performed by Charlie Shanian and Shari Simpson. Produced by Madeline Austin, Roger Alan Gindi, Bruce Lazarus, Dana Matthow, Scott Benedict, Libby Anne Russler and Allan Sandler at the Soho Playhouse. Opened November 9, 1999. (Closed January 2, 2000)

Directed by Jeremy Dobrish; scenery, Eric L. Renschler; costumes, Bernard Grenier; lighting, Michael Gottlieb; sound, Chris Todd; production stage manager, Joe McGuire; press, Origlio Public Relations, Tony Origlio, Phil Geoffrey Bond.

Comedy sketches about the pitfalls of romance, presented without intermission. Previously produced off off Broadway at the Currican Theater.

Last Train to Nibroc (33). By Arlene Hutton. Produced by Leonard Soloway, Chase Mishkin and Steven M. Levy at the Douglas Fairbanks Theater. Opened November 21, 1999. (Closed December 19, 1999)

Raleigh .... Benim Foster
May .... Alexandra Geis

Directed by Michael Montel; scenery, Si Joong Yoon; costumes, Shelley Norton; lighting, Christopher Gorzelnik; sound, Peter J. Fitzgerald; production stage manager, Tamara K. Heeschen; press, Bill Evans & Associates, Jim Randolph, Jonathan Schwartz, Terry Lilly.

Scene 1: December 28, 1940, a train somewhere west of Chicago. Scene 2: Summer 1942, a park bench near a woods. Scene 3: Spring 1943, May's front porch. The play was presented without intermission.

A couple find each other on a train and fall in love. The play was presented without intermission. Previously co-produced off off Broadway by the Journey Company and the 78th Street Theater Lab.

The Joseph Papp Public Theater/New York Shakespeare Festival. Schedule of five programs. **In the Blood** (32). By Suzan-Lori Parks. Opened November 22, 1999. (Closed December 19, 1999) **Space** (17). By Tina Landau. Opened December 5, 1999. (Closed December 19, 1999) **Hamlet** (25). Revival of the play by William Shakespeare. Opened December 19, 1999. (Closed January 9, 2000) **Two Sisters and a Piano** (32). By Nilo Cruz. Opened February 15, 2000. (Closed March 12, 2000) **House Arrest** (24). Solo performance by Anna Deavere Smith; conceived and written by Anna Deavere Smith. Opened March 27, 2000. (Closed April 16, 2000)

Produced by The Joseph Papp Public Theater/New York Shakespeare Festival, George C. Wolfe producer, Rosemarie Tichler artistic producer, Mark Litvin managing director, at the Joseph Papp Public Theater (see note).

ALL PLAYS: Senior director of external affairs, Margaret M. Lioi; associate producers, Wiley Hausam, Brian Kulick, Bonnie Metzgar; casting, Jordan Thaler/Heidi Griffiths; press, Carol R. Fineman, Thomas V. Naro.

IN THE BLOOD

Hester; La Negrita .... Charlayne Woodard
Jabber; Chilli .... Rob Campbell
Baby; Reverend D .... Reggie Montgomery
Bully; Welfare Lady .... Gail Grate
Trouble; Doctor .... Bruce MacVittie
Beauty; The Amiga Gringa ... Deirdre O'Connell

Directed by David Esbjornson; scenery, Narelle Sissons; costumes, Elizabeth Hope Clancy; lighting, Jane Cox; sound and original music, Donald DiNicola; production stage manager, Kristen Harris.

Time: Now. Place: Here. Act I, Scene 1: Under the bridge. Scene 2: Street practice. lst Confession: The Doctor—Times Are Tough: What Can We Do? Scene 3: The Reverend on his soapbox. Scene 4: With the Welfare. 2d Confession: The Welfare—I Walk the Line. Scene 5: Small change and sandwiches. 3d Confession: Amiga Gringa—In My Head I Got it Going On. Scene 6: The Reverend on the rock. 4th Confession: The Reverend—Suffering Is an Enormous Turn-On. Scene 7: My song in the street. 5th Confession: Chilli—We Was Young. Scene 8: The hand of fate. 6th Confession: Hester, La Negrita—I Shoulda Had a Hundred-Thousand. Scene 9. The prison door. The play was presented in two parts with the intermission following 2d Confession.

An unmarried mother struggles to raise her children, a la Hawthorne's *The Scarlet Letter.*

SPACE

Dr. Allan Saunders .... Tom Irwin
The Singer .... Theresa McCarthy
Dr. Bernadette Jump Cannon .... Amy Morton
Dr. Jim Lacey .... Larry Keith

Devin McFallen .... Andersen Gabrych
Joan Bailey .... Kristine Nielsen
Taj Mahal .... Teagle F. Bougere
Carl Himayo .... Daniel Lee Smith

Directed by Tina Landau; scenery, James Schuette; costumes, Melina Root; lighting, Scott Zielinski; original music and sound, Rob Milburn, Michael Bodeen; projection, Jan Hartley; production stage manager, James Latus.

Time: December, the present. Place: A university and its surroundings. The play was presented in two parts.

A doctor probes the claims of his patients that they have encountered creatures from outer space. Previously produced in regional theater by Chicago's Steppenwolf Theater Company.

HAMLET

Francisco .... David Wilson Barnes
Barnardo .... Andrew Garman
Marcellus .... Adam Greer
Horatio .... Christian Camargo
Claudius;
Ghost of the Late King .... Colm Feore
Laertes .... Hamish Linklater
Polonius .... Richard Libertini
Hamlet .... Liev Schreiber
Gertrude .... Diane Venora
Ophelia .... Lynn Collins
Rosencrantz .... Jeremy Shamos
Guildenstern .... Jonathan Fried
Player King; Gravedigger .... George Morfogen
Player Queen; Osric .... Francis Jue
Lucianus; Fortinbras Captain .... Dion Flynn
Gentlewoman .... Robin Weigert
Sailor .... Marc Gwinn
Priest .... Robert Alexander Owens
Fortinbras .... Justin Campbell, Wendy Rich Stetson

Musician: Ameenah Kaplan.

Directed by Andrei Serban; scenery, John Coyne; costumes, Marina Draghici; lighting, Michael Chybowski; sound, Donald DiNicola, Obadiah Eaves; original music, Elizabeth Swados; screen art design, Mariella Bancou; production stage manager, Abbie H. Katz.

The last major New York revival of *Hamlet* took place off Broadway in Royal Shakespeare Company repertory 5/21/98 for 10 performances.

TWO SISTERS AND A PIANO

Militia Guard #1; Victor Manual ... Gary Perez
Militia Guard #2;
Lt. Portuondo .... Paul Calderon
Maria Celia .... Adriana Sevan
Sofia .... Daphne Rubin-Vega

Directed by Loretta Greco; scenery, Robert Brill; costumes, Alex Jaeger; lighting, James Vermeulen; sound, Fabian Obispo; production stage manager, Buzz Cohen.

Time: 1991. Place: A spacious colonial house in Havana. The play was presented in two parts.

Sisters under house arrest in Castro's Cuba, like Chekhov's sisters yearning to change the boredom of their lives.

HOUSE ARREST

Directorial consultant, Jo Bonney; scenery, Richard Hoover; costumes, Ann Hould-Ward; lighting, Kevin Adams; sound, Ken Travis; projection design, Batwin + Robin Productions; composer, Julia Wolfe; production stage manager, James Latus.

Anna Deavere Smith monologue portrayal of a number of characters (see below) in her exploration of the Presidency of the United States down through history.

ACT I

Clowns—Studs Terkel

The Deal—George Stephanopoulos

A Visit to Jefferson's Home at Monticello: Pantops—Cinder Stanton, historian; Justice Is in One Scale—Penny Kiser, tour guide. The Sally Hemings Story: James Callender—Ken Burns; The Man Whom It Delighteth the People—James Callender, 1803 journalist.

A Constructed Dialogue, These People Said These Words, But Not in Each Other's Presence: Unconsummated Affections/Deep Denial—Roger Kennedy, Jefferson scholar; Unconsummated Affections/Deep Denial—Annette Gordon-Reed, legal scholar; Interview Between Cinder Stanton and Anna Deavere Smith—Cinder Stanton.

Scientific Evidence, 1781–1998: From *Notes on the State of Virginia*—Thomas Jefferson; Could Have Not Had Our Mess as Bad—Roger Kennedy; Probability—Dr. Eugene Foster, author of the 1998 report on the DNA of Jefferson; "Tea Cup"—Ken Burns.

The Roosevelt White House, A Family: An Easier Time—Walter Trohan, press corps; A Canary Bird—Bernard Asbell, historian; A Canary Bird—Lizzie McDuffie, White House cook; Bowling—Michael K. Frisby, journalist; How Could I Say—Walter Trohan.

Exposures: Hot Water Bottle/Peeved—Lizzie McDuffie; Look in Windows—Gary Hart; Asylum—Peggy Noonan, speechwriter.

The Lincoln White House: Only as a Loan—Elizabeth Keckley, former slave, dressmaker to Mary Todd Lincoln; An Actual Dream Related by Abraham Lincoln—Abraham Lincoln; Body Watch—Brian Palmer, photographer; Human Jackstraws—Walt Whitman. Performers—Ben Bradlee; The Figure Booth—Walt Whitman; Political Theater—Brian Palmer; Little Bubbles on theLips—Walt Whitman; Three Murders—Gloria Steinem; Birds That Were Loose—Ann Richards.

ACT II

Bit by Bit, Drop by Drop: Presidential Peach—Alice Waters, chef.

Party Politics: Well, She Was Just Great—Graydon Carter, editor; Lambs to Dinner—Anonymous Man; Didn't Bother Me—Graydon Carter; A Scream—Judith Butler, professor of rhetoric; Way Too Academic—Anonymous Man; That Arc—Graydon Carter.

Sending the Canaries Into the Mines: Slick, Dirty—Anita Hill; Lie Detecting—Maggie Williams, former chief of staff to First Lady; Washington Political Insider Alexis Herman, Secretary of Labor; Making a Kind of Political Point—Maggie Williams; House Arrest—Anita Hill.

Darkness at Noon: Captives— Ed Bradley; A Troubling Time—Mike McCurry, former press secretary; Sex and Death—Christopher Hitchens, journalist; Are You Now or Have You Ever Been?—Walter Shapiro, columnist; Is Is—David Kendall, counsel; Persistence—Michael Isikoff, journalist; The Blue Dress—Chris Vlasto, ABC News producer.

Political Theater: Grand Jury Testimony of President Clinton 8/17/98—Prosecutor, Office of the Independent Counsel; Baby Huey Dolls—Bill Clinton.

Shadow Side: Shaman—Anonymous Woman; A Baby Face Down in the Water—Cheryl Mills, former desputy White House counsel; Mirror to Her Mouth—Paulette Jenkins, inmate; Getting Beaten Up in an Alley—Brian Palmer.

One Card at a Time: Right by the Rope—Blese Canty, church member; Communication—Studs Terkel.

Note: In The Joseph Papp Public Theater there are many auditoria. *In the Blood* and *Two Sisters and a Piano* played the Susan Stein Shiva Theater, *Space* played Martinson Hall, *Hamlet* and *House Arrest* played the Estelle R. Newman Theater.

Inappropriate (112). Musical based on original material from the graduation books of DiSisto School alumni; book co-conceived by A. Michael DeSisto and Lonnie McNeil; music and lyrics by Michael Sottile. Produced by A. Michael DeSisto and Butterfly Productions at Theater Row Theater. Opened November 23, 1999. (Closed February 27, 2000)

Mia Benenate
Averie Boyer
Josh Geyer
Elizabeth Irwin
Jamie Ourisman
Diane Schwartz
Sarah Seckinger
Adam Shiffman

Musicians: Ben Butler, Richard Hammond, Steve Hass, Ann Marie Milazzo, Sasi Shalom.

Directed by Ray Leeper and Michael Sottile; choreography, Ray Leeper; original choreography and direction, Lonnie McNeil; musical direction and arrangements, Michael Sottile; scenery and costumes, Shane Ballard; lighting, S. Ryan Schmidt; sound, David A. Arnold; production stage manager, Richard Costabile; press, Origlio Public Relations.

The theater company of the DeSisto School in Stockbridge, Mass. portraying teenagers troubled in their parental and other relationships. The play was presented without intermission. Previously produced off off Broadway 12/1/99.

JOLSON & CO.—Nancy Anderson as Ruby Keeler and Stephen Mo Hanan as Al Jolson in the musical play at York Theater Company

MUSICAL NUMBERS: "Our World Within" Part I and Part II—Company; "Let Me Be the One"—Averie Boyer, Elizabeth Irwin, Company; "Dear Dad"—Diane Schwartz, Irwin, Sarah Seckinger, Mia Benenate; "Feels Good (Drugs)"—Company; "Real"—Schwartz, Company; "A Good Boy"—Josh Geyer, Company; "I Wonder"—Boyer, Irwin, Company; "The Dream"—Adam Schiffman, Company; "Mexico"—Schwartz, Jamie Ourisman; "Kaleidoscope"—Company; "Lost"—Boyer,

Irwin, Company; "Found—The Discovery"—Company; "Everything That You Are"—Irwin, Company.

The York Theater Company. Schedule of five programs. **Jolson & Co.** (38). Musical play by Stephen Mo Hanan and Jay Berkow. Opened December 9, 1999. (Closed January 2, 2000) **Taking a Chance on Love** (29). Musical revue devised by Erik Haagensen; music by Leonard Bernstein, Vernon Duke, Duke Ellington, Donald Fuller, Fritz Kreisler, John Latouche, Richard Lewine, Douglas Moore, Jerome Moross, Wolfgang Mozart, James Mundy, Earl Robinson and John Strauss. Opened March 2, 2000. (Closed March 26, 2000) Also **Musicals in Mufti,** concert performances of three musical revivals. **Kean** (5). Book by Peter Stone, music and lyrics by Robert Wright and George Forrest, based on the play by Jean-Paul Sartre and the play by Alexandre Dumas. Opened January 14, 2000. (Closed January 16, 2000) **Wish You Were Here** (5). Book by Joshua Logan and Arthur Kober, music and lyrics by Harold Rome, based on the play *Having Wonderful Time* by Arthur Kober. Opened January 21, 2000. (Closed January 23, 2000) **70, Girls, 70** (5). Book by David Thompson and Norman L. Martin, music by John Kander, lyrics by Fred Ebb, based on the play *Breath of Spring* by Peter Coke, adaptation by Joe Masteroff. Opened January 28, 2000. (Closed January 30, 2000) Produced by York Theater Company, James Morgan artistic director, Robert A. Buckley managing director, at the Theater at St. Peter's.

JOLSON & CO.

CAST: Al Jolson—Stephen Mo Hanan. Barry Gray, Hirsch (later Harry), Poppa, Dockstader, Lloyd, Chuck, Col. Webster, Harry Cohn, Morris—Robert Ari. Naomi Yoelson, Mae, Ethel, Josephine, Ruby Keeler, Martha, Erle—Nancy Anderson.

Musicians: Peter Larson keyboard 1, piano; Joe Brent violin, banjo; Randall Klitz bass.

Standby: Messrs. Hanan, Ari—David Edwards; Miss Anderson—Abby Lindsay.

Directed by Jay Berkow; musical direction, Peter Larson; scenery, James Morgan; costumes, Gail Baldoni; lighting, Annmarie Duggan; casting, Joseph McConnell; production stage manager, Jack Gianino; press, Keith Sherman & Associates, Tom Chiodo.

Time: December 1949. Place: The stage of the Winter Garden Theater and various locales from Jolson's past. The play was presented in two parts.

Episodes from the career and personal life of Al Jolson in flashbacks from a Jolson performance in a radio talk show.

MUSICAL NUMBERS: "Swanee" by Irving Caesar and George Gershwin, "A Bird in a Gilded Cage" by Arthur J. Lamb and Harry von Tilzer, "I'm Sitting on Top of the World" by Ray Henderson, Joe Young and Sam Lewis, "The Little Victrola" by Billy Murray and Norbert Roscoe, "You Made Me Love You" by James Monaco and Joseph McCarthy, "Where Did Robinson Crusoe Go With Friday on Saturday Night?" by George Meyer, Joe Young and Sam Lewis, "California Here I Come" by Joseph Meyer, B.G. DeSylva and Al Jolson, "Sonny Boy" by Ray Henderson, Lew Brown and B.G. DeSylva, "When the Red, Red Robin Comes Bob-Bob-Bobbin' Along" by Harry M. Woods, "My Mammy" by Walter Donaldson, Joe Young and Sam Lewis, "Toot Toot Tootsie Goodbye" by Gus Kahn, Ernie Erdman and Dan Russo, "Hello Central Give Me No Man's Land" by Jean Schwartz, Joe Young and Sam Lewis, "Rock a Bye Your Baby With a Dixie Melody" by Jean Schwartz, Joe Young and Sam Lewis, "You Made Me Love You" (Reprise), "April Showers" by B.G. DeSylva and Louis Silvers, "You Made Me Love You" (Reprise).

TAKING A CHANCE ON LOVE

Terry Burrell
Jerry Dixon
Donna English
Eddie Korbich

Pianists: Jeffrey R. Smith, David Harris.

Standbys: Kevin R. Free, Patti Butler.

Directed by James Morgan; musical direction and arrangements, Jeffrey R. Smith; musical staging, Janet Watson; scenery, James Morgan; costumes, Suzy Benzinger; lighting, S. Ryan Schmidt; casting,

Joseph McConnell; production stage manager, Jack Gianino; stage manager, Hugh P. Klitzke; press, Keith Sherman & Associates.

Subtitled "The Lyrics and Life of John Latouche," celebrating his work in 20 musicals between 1936 and 1956, including *The Golden Apple, Cabin in the Sky, The Ballad of Baby Doe* and contributions to *Candide.*

Musicals in Mufti

KEAN

Lady Delmore; Winnifred Wallington Sparrow .... Jennifer E. Brown
Christie; Narrator .... Jesse Tyler Ferguson
Lady Amy Goswell; Caroline Rosa St. Albans .... Diane J. Findlay
Barnaby .... Hans Friedrichs
Solomon .... Douglas Holmes
Anna Danby .... Christiane Noll
Lord Neville .... Eric Riley
Francis; Count de Koeberg .... Arthur Rubin
Prince of Wales .... Robert Sella
Mrs. Polly Pott .... Trudy Wallace
Countess Elena de Koeberg ..... Susan Watson
Edmund Kean .... Walter Willison

Directed by Richard Sabellico; musical direction, Fred Barton; lighting, Ryan Schmidt; production stage manager, Jack Gianino.

Time: Early 19th Century. Place: London.

The musical *Kean* was first produced on Broadway 11/2/61 for 92 performances. This is its first New York revival of record.

ACT I

"Penny Plain, Twopence Colored" .... Christie, Ensemble
"Man and Shadow" .... Kean
"Mayfair Affair" .... Elena, Amy, Ensemble
"Sweet Danger" .... Elena, Kean
"To Look Upon My Love" .... Kean, Solomon
"Let's Improvise" .... Kean, Anna
"Elena" .... Kean, Francis, Ensemble
"The Fog and the Grog" .... Barnaby, Christie, Francis, Kean, Ensemble
Finale .... Kean, Ensemble

ACT II

"Inevitable" .... Anna
"Civilized People" .... Kean, Anna, Elena
"Service for Service" .... Elena, Kean
"Willow, Willow, Willow" .... Anna
"Chime In!" .... Christie, Barnaby, Francis, Ensemble
"Swept Away" .... Elena, Kean
"Apology" .... Kean

WISH YOU WERE HERE

Fay Fromkin .... Melissa Rain Anderson
Herman Fabricant .... Robert Ari
Pinky Harris .... Matt Bogart
Eli .... Miguel Cervantes
Lou Kandel .... David Green
Muscles, etc. .... Michael Colby Jones
Chick Miller .... Perry Laylon Ojeda
Miriam .... Sunita Param
Itchy Flexner .... Ward Saxton
Teddy Stern .... Sara Schmidt
Henrietta .... Carla Woods
Gussie .... Kirsten Wyatt

Directed by Michael Montel; musical direction, Kevin Wallace; lighting, Ryan Schmidt; stage manager, Jack Gianino.

Time: Summer, early 1950s. Place: Camp Karefree, a summer camp for adults, "where friendships are formed to last a whole lifetime through," located in the heart of the Catskills.

Wish You Were Here was first produced on Broadway 6/25/52 for 598 performances. This is its first major New York revival of record.

ACT I

Scene 1: Outside Teddy's cabin
"Camp Karefree" .... Kandel, Waiters, Ensemble
"There's Nothing Nicer Than People" .... Teddy, Fay, Girls
"Social Director" .... Itchy, Ensemble
"Shopping Around" .... Fay
Scene 2: Locker room
"Bright College Days" .... Waiters
"Mix and Mingle" .... Chick, Waiters
Scene 3: Porch of the Social Hall
"Could Be" .... Girls, Teddy
Scene 4: Social Hall
"Tripping the Light Fantastic" .... Ensemble
Scene 5: A path through the woods
"Wish You Were Here" .... Chick, Teddy
"Where Did the Night Go?" .... Chick, Teddy, Ensemble
Scene 6: Athletic field
"Certain Individuals" .... Fay, Ensemble
Scene 7: A path through the woods
Scene 8: They won't know me
"They Won't Know Me" .... Chick
Scene 9: The boat house
"Summer Afternoon" .... Pinky, Ensemble
Scene 10: The lake front

ACT II

Scene 1: The Campfire
"Where Did the Night Go?" (Reprise) .... Ensemble
"Don Jose" .... Itchy, Ensemble
"Everybody Love Everybody" .... Fay, Ensemble
"Wish You Were Here" .... Chick, Waiters
Scene 2: A path through the woods
Scene 3: Pinky's cabin
"Relax" .... Pinky,Teddy
Scene 4: Porch of the Social Hall
"Where Did the Night Go?" (be-bop version) .... Fay, Ensemble
"Flattery" .... Teddy, Itchy
Scene 5: Basketball court
Finale .... Company

70, GIRLS, 70

Lorraine .... Janet Aycock
Pete; Callahan; Priest; Guard .... Danny Carroll
Eunice .... Jane Connell
Sadie .... Marilyn Cooper, Chevi Colton
Harry .... Robert Fitch
Gert .... Helen Gallagher
Fritzi .... Mimi Hines
Walter .... George S. Irving
Eddie .... Christopher Morgan
Joe; Lubliner; Guard .... Don Percassi
Ida .... Jane Powell
Melba .... Charlotte Rae

Directed by Michael Leeds; musical diretion, Patrick Vaccariello; lighting, Ryan Schmidt; casting, Joseph McConnell; production stage manager, Jack Gianino.

Time: Now. Place: The Sussex Arms.

70, Girls, 70 was first produced on Broadway 4/15/71 for 36 performances. This is its first major New York revival of record.

ACT I

Scene 1: Limbo
"Old Folks" .... Ida, Eunice, Walter, Harry, Gert, Melba, Fritzi

Scene 2: The Sussex Arms
"Home" .... Ida, Eunice, Walter, Harry, Gert, Melba Fritzi
Scene 3: Ida's Room
"The Caper" .... Harry
Scene 4: Sadie's Fur Salon
Scene 5: Limbo
"Coffee in a Cardboard Cup" .... Melba, Fritzi
Scene 6: The Sussex Arms
"Hit It Lorraine" .... Ida, Eunice, Gert, Harry, Lorraine
"Do We?" .... Walter, Eunice
Scene 7: Bloomingdale's
"Emma Finch" .... Gert, Pete, Joe
Scene 8: The Sussex Arms
"Broadway, My Street" .... Fritzi, Melba, Ida, Eunice, Walter, Harry, Gert

ACT II

Scene 1: Cold Storage Vault
"Believe" .... Fritzi, Melba, Ida, Eunice, Walter, Harry, Gert
Scene 2: Limbo
"Go Visit Your Grandmother" .... Eddie, Sadie
Scene 3: The Sussex Arms
"I Can't Do That Anymore" .... Harry, Walter
Scene 4: Limbo
"Where Does an Elephant Go?" .... Ida, Company
Scene 5: Fur Show
"70, Girls, 70" .... Ida, Eunice, Gert, Harry, Walter, Melba, Fritzi
Scene 6: The Sussex Arms
"Yes" .... Company

*__The Bomb-itty of Errors__ (216). By Jordan Allen-Dutton, Jason Catalano, G.Q. and Erik Weiner; music by J.A.Q. Produced by Daryl Roth, Michael Lynne, Q Brothers and Hal Luftig at 45 Bleeker. Opened December 12, 1999.

CAST: Antipholus of Ephesus, Adriana, Bike Messenger, Others—Jordan Allen-Dutton; Dromio of Syracuse, Desi, Dr. Pinch, Others—Gruff; Antipholus of Syracuse, Hendelberg, Abbess, Others—G.Q.; Dromio of Ephesus, Luciana, Policeman, Stranger, Others—Red Dragon; DJ—J.A.Q.

Understudy: Charles Anthony Burks.

Directed and developed by Andy Goldberg; scenery, Scott Pask; costumes, David C. Woolard; lighting, James Vermeulen; sound, One Dream Sound, Sunil Rajan; associate producer, Andrew Kato; production stage manager, Kate Broderick; press, The Karpel Group, Craig Karpel, Bridget Klapinski.

Self-described as "an add-RAP-tation" of Shakespeare's *The Comedy of Errors,* broadly conceived and performed in rhymed hip-hop verses to music presented by a disc jockey.

If Memory Serves (17). By Jonathan Tolins. Produced by Charles H. Duggan, Ostar Enterprises, Jennifer Manocherian in association with Richard Frankel and Marc Routh at the Promenade Theater. Opened December 12, 1999. (Closed December 26, 1999)

Linda Simmons; Helen Menken .... Marilyn Sokol
Diane Barrow .... Elizabeth Ashley
Pam Goldman; Michelle .... Melanie Vesey
Russell Burke; Adam Burke .... Sam Trammell
Paul Michael .... Jeff Whitty
Taylor McDonald; Tim .... Ron Mathews
Dr. Margaret Thurm;
Mrs. Kennedy .... Lynda Gravatt
Stan Burke; Mr. Wilcox .... Tony Campisi

Directed by Leonard Foglia; scenery, Michael McGarty; costumes, Ilona Somogyi; lighting, Russell H. Champa; sound, Laura Grace Brown; music, Peter Matz; casting, Bruce H. Newberg, James Calleri; production stage manager, Patrick Ballard; stage manager, Linda Barnes; press, Helene Davis Publicity, Helene Davis, Beth Stevens, Barbara Carroll.

Time: 1995. Place: New York and Los Angeles. The play was presented in two parts.

Dark comedy, an actress's attempt to revive her career is complicated by intimations of former child abuse of her now-grownup son.

***Fully Committed** (192). Transfer from off off Broadway of the Vineyard Theater production of the solo performance by Mark Setlock; written by Becky Mode; based on characters created by Becky Mode and Mark Setlock. Produced by David Stone, Jesse L. Martin, Adam Pascal and Susan Quint Gallin at the Cherry Lane Theater. Opened December 14, 1999.

Directed by Nicholas Martin; scenery, James Noone; lighting, Frances Aronson; sound, Bruce Ellman; associate producers, Nancy Nagel Gibbs/David Turner, Mary Lu Rubnitz Roffe; production stage manager, Bess Marie Glorioso; press, Sam Rudy/Shirley Herz Associates.

Place: The basement of a four star restaurant on the Upper East Side of Manhattan. The play was presented without intermission.

An actor between engagements has a job in a posh restaurant at which he can observe—and characterize—its motley patrons. Previously presented off off Broadway 9/30/99 by the Vineyard Theater, Barbara Zinn Krieger executive director, Douglas Aibel artistic director, Jeffrey Solis managing director.

Elsa Edgar (38). Solo performance by Bob Kingdom; written by Bob Kingdom and Neil Bartlett. Produced by Primary Stages, Casey Childs artistic director, at Primary Stages. Opened December 15, 1999. (Closed January 16, 2000).

Directed by Casey Childs; scenery, Gary N. Hygom; lighting, Deborah Costantine; sound, Fabian Obispo; associate producer, Seth Gordon; stage manager, Renee Lutz; press, Origlio Public Relations, Karen Greco.

Elsa Maxwell meets J. Edgar Hoover. The play was presented without an intermission.

***Our Sinatra** (188). Musical revue conceived by Eric Comstock, Christopher Gines and Hilary Kole; music and lyrics by various authors (see listing below). Produced by Jack Lewin and Scott Perrin at the Blue Angel Theater. Opened December 19, 1999.

Eric Comstock
Christopher Gines
Hilary Kole

Entire production supervised by Richard Maltby Jr.; directed by Kurt Stamm; scenery, Troy Hourie; lighting, Jeff Nellis; sound, Matt Berman; bassist, Dean Johnson; production stage manager, Marian DeWitt; press, Origlio Public Relations, David Lotz.

Sinatra's outstanding singing career celebrated with a selection of his song numbers.

ACT I: "These Foolish Things Remind Me of You" by Holt Marvell and Jack Strachey—Company. "Where or When" by Lorenz Hart and Richard Rodgers—Christopher Gines. "Come Rain or Come Shine" by Johnny Mercer and Harold Arlen—Hilary Kole. "I Like to Lead When I Dance" by Sammy Cahn and Jimmy Van Heusen—Eric Comstock. "A Lovely Way to Spend an Evening" by Harold Adamson and Jimmy McHugh—Company. "I Fall in Love too Easily" by Sammy Cahn and Jule Styne—Gines. "Time After Time" by Sammy Cahn and Jule Styne—Kole. "All the Way" by Sammy Cahn and Jimmy Van Heusen—Comstock. "The Tender Trap" by Sammy Cahn and Jimmy Van Heusen—Kole. "From Here to Eternity" by Bob Wells and Fred Karger— Gines. "You're Sensational" by Cole Porter— Comstock. "Well, Did You Evah?" by Cole Porter—Company. "My Kind of Town" by Sammy Cahn and Jimmy Van Heusen—Company. "As Long as There's Music" by Sammy Cahn and Jule Styne—Company. "Nice 'n Easy" by Alan & Marilyn Bergman and Lew Spence—Gines, Kole. "I'm a Fool to Want You" by Jack Wolf, Joel Herron and Frank Sinatra—Kole. "Everything Happens to Me" by Tom Adair and Matt Dennis—Comstock. "Day In–Day Out" by Johnny Mercer and Rube Bloom—Comstock, Kole. "Ol' Man River" by Oscar Hammerstein II and Jerome Kern—Gines. "Without a Song" by Billy Rose, Edward Eliscu and Vincent Youmans—Company.

ACT II: "One for My Baby (And One More for the Road)" by Johnny Mercer and Harold Arlen—Comstock. "Angel Eyes" by Earl K. Brent and Matt Dennis—Kole. "In the Wee Small Hours of the Morning" by Dave Mann and Bob Hilliard—Comstock. "It Never Entered My Mind" by Richard Rodgers and Lorenz Hart—Kole. "Last Night When We Were Young" by E.Y. Harburg and Harold Arlen—

OUR SINATRA—Eric Comstock, Hilary Kole and Christopher Gines in a program of songs that Frank Sinatra sang

Gines. "At Long Last Love" by Cole Porter—Company. "How Do You Keep the Music Playing?" by Alan and Marilyn Bergman and Michel Legrand—Gines. "I've Got the World on a String" by Ted Koehler and Harold Arlen—Kole. "To Love and Be Loved" by Sammy Cahn and Jimmy Van Heusen—Comstock. "The One I Love Belongs to Somebody Else" by Gus Kahn and Isham Jones—Comstock, Gines. "I Have Dreamed" by Richard Rodgers and Oscar Hammerstein II—Kole. "If You Are But a Dream" by Moe Jaffe, Jack Fulton and Nat Bonx—Gines. "The Song Is You" by Oscar Hammerstein II and Jerome Kern—Company. "Day by Day" by Sammy Cahn & Alex Stordahl and Paul Weston—Gines. "Night and Day" by Cole Porter—Kole."The Way You Look Tonight" by Dorothy Fields and Jerome Kern—Comstock. "They Can't Take That Away From Me" by Ira & George Gershwin—Kole. "Guess I'll Hang My Tears Out to Dry" by Sammy Cahn and Jule Styne—Gines. "I'll Never Smile Again" by Ruth Lowe—Company. "Come Fly With Me" by Sammy Cahn and Jimmy Van Heusen—Comstock. "East of the Sun and West of the Moon" by Brooks Bowman—Gines, Kole. "Fly Me to the Moon (In Other Words)" by Bart Howard—Kole. "The Lady Is a Tramp" by Lorenz Hart and Richard Rodgers—Gines. "Luck, Be a Lady" by Frank Loesser—Comstock. "Here's That Rainy Day" by Johnny Burke and Jimmy Van Heusen—Kole. "All or Nothing at All" by Jack Lawrence and Arthur Altman—Gines. "I've Got You Under My Skin" by Cole Porter—Comstock. "High Hopes" by Sammy Cahn and Jimmy Van Heusen—Comstock, Kole. "The Best Is Yet to Come" by Carolyn Leigh and Cy Coleman—Gines. "I've Got a Crush on You" by Ira & George Gershwin—Kole. "All My Tomorrows" by Sammy Cahn and Jimmy Van Heusen—Comstock. "How Little We Know" by Carolyn Leigh and Phil Springer—Gines, Cole. "Witchcraft" by Carolyn Leigh and Cy Coleman—Gines, Kole. "I Get a Kick Out of You" by Cole Porter—Comstock. "Saturday Night (Is the Loneliest Night in the Week" by Sammy Cahn and Jule Styne—Comstock. "Strangers in the Night" by Charles Singleton and Eddie Snyder & Bert Kaempfert—Gines, Comstock. "Come Dance With Me" by Sammy Cahn and Jimmy Van Heusen—Comstock, Kole. "I Won't Dance" by Otto Harbach and Oscar Hammerstein II & Jerome Kern—Comstock, Kole. "Summer Wind" by Johnny Mercer and Henry Mayer—Gines. "The Second Time Around" by Sammy Cahn and Jimmy Van Heusen—Kole. "Young at Heart" by Carolyn Leigh and Johnny Richards—Company. "You Make Me Feel So Young" by Mack Gordon and Josef Myrow—Company. "My Way" by Paul Anka and Jacques Revaux—Company. "The Song Is You" by Oscar Hammerstein II and Jerome Kern—Company. "Put Your Dreams Away (For Another Day)"—Company.

Brooklyn Academy of Music. Schedule of four programs. **Jane Eyre** (6). By Polly Teale; adapted from the novel by Charlotte Bronte; presented in the Shared Experience production, Nancy Meckler and Polly Teale artistic directors. Opened February 8, 2000. (Closed February 13, 2000) **The Family Reunion** (4). Revival of the play by T.S. Eliot. Opened May 10, 2000. (Closed May 13, 2000). **Don Carlos** (5). Revival of the play by Friedrich Schiller; translated by Robert David MacDonald. Opened May 16, 2000. (Closed May 20, 2000) **A Midsummer Night's Dream** (6). Revival of the play by William Shakespeare. Opened May 21, 2000. (Closed May 27, 2000). Produced by Brooklyn Academy of Music, Bruce C. Ratner chairman of the board, Karen Brooks Hopkins president, Joseph V. Melillo executive producer, at the BAM Harvey Theater, *The Family Reunion, Don Carlos* and *A Midsummer Night's Dream* in Royal Shakespeare Company productions, Adrian Noble artistic director.

JANE EYRE

Bertha .... Harriette Ashcroft
Mrs. Reed; Mrs. Fairfax .... Joan Blackham
Jane Eyre .... Penny Layden
Brocklehurst; Pilot; Lord Ingram;
St. John Rivers .... Michael Matus
Bessie; Blanche Ingram;
Grace Poole; Diana Rivers;
Old Woman in the Ruins ...... Hannah Miles
Rochester .... Sean Murray
Richard Mason; Cellist .... Philip Rham
Abigail; Helen Burns; Adele;
Mary Rivers .... Octavia Walters

Others—Company.

Directed by Polly Teale; design, Neil Warmington; company movement, Liz Ranken; lighting, Chris Davey; music, Peter Salem; assistant director, Sue Nash.

Bronte's melodramatic romance staged to emphasize the contrast between the characters and personalities of Jane and Grace Poole. A foreign play previously produced in London. The play was presented in two parts.

Royal Shakespeare Company Productions

THE FAMILY REUNION

Amy .... Margaret Tyzack
Agatha .... Lynn Farleigh
Ivy .... Cherry Morris
Violet .... Bridget Turner
Charles .... Christopher Good
Gerald .... Nicholas Jones
Mary .... Zoë Waites
Denman .... Alison Reid
Harry .... Greg Hicks
Downing .... Derek Hutchinson
Dr. Warburton .... Richard Cordery
Sgt. Winchell .... Rod Arthur

Eumenides: James Auden, Mary Duddy, Susan Dury, Graeme Eton, Jennifer McEvoy.

Understudies: Mr. Jones—Rod Arthur; Mr. Hicks—James Auden; Misses Farleigh, Reid—Mary Duddy; Miss Tyzack—Susan Dury; Messrs. Good, Cordery, Arthur—Graeme Eton; Misses Morris, Turner—Jennifer McEvoy; Miss Waites—Alison Reid.

Directed by Adrian Noble; design, Rob Howell; lighting, Mark Henderson; sound, Matt McKenzie for Autograph; assistant director, Helen Raynor; company stage manager, Eric Lumsden; American stage manager, R. Michael Blanco.

Time: A day in late March 1939. Place: Wishwood, a country house in the North of England, home of the Monchensey family. Part I: After tea. Part II: After dinner.

The last New York revival of record of *The Family Reunion* was off Broadway by Equity Theater 11/20/67 for 3 performances.

DON CARLOS

Domingo .... Geoffrey Whitehead
Don Carlos .... Rupert Penry-Jones
Marquis of Posa .... Ray Fearon
Elizabeth of Valois .... Josette Simon
Princess Eboli .... Claire Price
Marchioness of Mondecar ...... Michele Moran
Duchess of Olivarez .... Jo Martin
Page; Taxis .... Joseph England
King Philip II of Spain .... John Woodvine
Duke of Alba .... Ewen Cummins
Count Lerma .... David Collings
Grand Inquisitor .... John Rogan

Others—Members of the company.

Musicians: Ben Grove guitar; Janet Crouch cello; Tony McVey timpani, percussion; Tony Stenson keyboard.

Directed by Gale Edwards; scenery, Peter J. Davison; costumes, Sue Wilmington; lighting, Mark McCullough; music, Gary Yershon; sound, Charles Horne; fight direction, Malcolm Ransom; music direction, Tony Stenson.

Time: The spring of 1568. Place: Spain, the Queen's court in Aranjuez and the Royal Palace, Madrid.

The last major New York revival of *Don Carlos* was by the Schiller Theater of West Berlin, in German, on Broadway 11/24/64 for 8 performances.

A MIDSUMMER NIGHT'S DREAM

Athens
Duke of Athens .... Nicholas Jones
Hippolyta .... Josette Simon
Egeus .... Geoffrey Whitehead
Hermia .... Catherine Kanter
Lysander .... Fergus O'Donnell
Demetrius .... Henry Ian Cusick
Helena .... Hermione Gulliford
Philostrate .... Aidan McArdle
Men and Women of Athens .... Company
The Players
Peter Quince .... Peter Kelly
Nick Bottom .... Daniel Ryan
Francis Flute .... Orlando Wells
Tom Snout .... Rod Arthur
Snug .... Andrew Dennis
Robin Starveling .... David Hobbs
The Woods
Oberon .... Nicholas Jones
Titania .... Josette Simon
Puck .... Aidan McArdle
Peaseblossom .... Sirine Saba
Cobweb .... Kemi Baruwa
Moth .... Rebecca Lenkiewicz
Mustardseed .... Mary Duddy
Fairies .... Ben Elliot, Farimang Singhateh

Musicians: Ben Grove guitar, percussion; John Francis violin; Janet Crouch cello; Christopher Lacey flutes; Brian Newman, Philip Thorne horn; David Hissey trombone; Tony McVey percussion; Richard Brown keyboards.

Understudies: Mr. Ryan—Rod Arthur; Miss Saba—Kemi Baruwa; Mr.Jones—Andrew Dennis; Mr. Hobbs—Mary Duddy; Messrs. Wells, McArdle—Ben Elliot; Messrs. Kelly, Whitehead—David Hobbs; Misses Gulliford, Simon—Rebecca Lenkiewicz; Miss Kanter—Sirine Saba; Messrs. O'Donnell, Dennis—Farimang Singhateh; Messrs. Cusick, Arthur—Orlando Wells.

Directed by Michael Boyd; design, Tom Piper; lighting, Chris Davey; music, John Woolf; sound, Mic Pool; movement, Liz Ranken; fight direction, Terry King; musical direction, Richard Brown; company stage manager, Gabrielle Sanders; American stage manager, R. Michael Blanco.

The last major New York revival of *A Midsummer Night's Dream* took place on Broadway 3/31/96 for 65 performances.

Encores! Great American Musicals in Concert. Schedule of three musical revivals presented in limited concert engagements. **On a Clear Day You Can See Forever** (5). Musical with book and lyrics by Alan Jay Lerner; music by Burton Lane. Opened February 10, 2000. (Closed February 13, 2000) **Tenderloin** (5). Musical based on the novel by Samuel Hopkins Adams; book by George Abbott and Jerome Weidman; music by Jerry Bock; lyrics by Sheldon Harnick. Opened March 24, 2000. (Closed March 27, 2000) **Wonderful Town** (5). Musical based on the play *My Sister Eileen* by Joseph Fields and Jerome Chodorov and the stories by Ruth McKenney; book by Joseph Fields and Jerome Chodorov; music by Leonard Bernstein; lyrics by Betty Comden and Adolph Green; sketches for "What a Waste" by Betty Comden and Adolph Green. Opened May 4, 2000. (Closed May 8, 2000) Produced by City Center, Kathleen Marshall artistic director, Rob Fisher musical director, Judith E. Daykin president and executive director, at the City Center.

ON A CLEAR DAY YOU CAN SEE FOREVER

Dr. Mark Bruckner .... Peter Friedman
Preston .... Brooks Ashmanskas
Mrs. Hatch .... Nancy Opel
Daisy Gamble .... Kristin Chenoweth

Muriel .... Darcie Roberts
Millard .... Jim Newman
Mr. Welles .... Dale Hensley
Mrs. Welles .... Beth McVey
Sir Hubert Insdale .... Ed Dixon
Edward Moncrief .... Brent Barrett
Warren Smith .... Roger Bart
Flora .... Rachel Coloff
Dr. Conrad Bruckner .... Gerry Bamman
Bolagard .... Bryan T. Donovan
Themistocles Kriakos .... Louis Zorich
Airline Official .... Timothy Breese
Melinda (Perhaps) .... Kristin Chenoweth

Singing Ensemble: Anne Allgood, Timothy Breese, Rachel Coloff, Susan Derry, Bryan T. Donovan, Colm Fitzmaurice, Dale Hensley, Damon Kirsche, Ann Kittredge, Beth McVey, Joseph Webster, Laurie Williamson.

Dancing Ensemble: Stephen Campanella, Celina Carvajal, Kim Craven, Derric Harris, Tina Ou, Shonn Wiley.

The Coffee Club Orchestra: Rob Fisher conductor; Seymour Red Press flute, piccolo, clarinet; Albert Regni clarinet; David Tofani clarinet, bass clarinet; Rob Ingliss oboe, English horn; John Campo bassoon; Russ Riszner, Roger Wendt, French horn; John Frosk, Glen Drewes, Kamau Adilifu trumpet; Jack Gale, Jack Schatz trombone; Jeffrey Harris piano, celeste, harpsichord; John Redsecker drums; Eric Kivnick percussion; Grace Paradise harp; Suzanne Ornstein concert mistress; Belinda Whitney-Barratt, Mineko Yajima, Maura Giannini, Christoph Franzgrote, Rebekah Johnson, Martin Agee, Ronald Oakland, Xin Zhao violin; Jill Jaffe, Kenneth Burward-Hoy, David Blinn viola; Clay Ruede, Lanny Paykin cello; Richard Sarpola acoustic bass.

Directed by Mark Brokaw; concert adaptation, David Ives; choreography, John Carrafa; scenic consultant, John Lee Beatty; costume consultant, Wallace G. Lane Jr.; lighting, Donald Holder; sound, Scott Lehrer; original orchestrations, Robert Russell Bennett; musical coordinator, Seymour Red Press; casting, Jay Binder; associate choreographer, Robert Ashford; casting, Jay Binder; production stage manager, Gary Mickelson; press, Philip Rinaldi.

On a Clear Day You Can See Forever was first produced on Broadway 10/17/65 for 272 performances. This is its first major New York revival of record.

ACT I

Overture .... Orchestra & Ensemble
The Office of Dr. Mark Bruckner
"Hurry! It's Lovely Up Here" .... Kristin Chenoweth
"Ring Out the Bells" .... Ensemble
"Tosy and Cosh" .... Chenoweth
"On a Clear Day You Can See Forever" .... Peter Friedman
The Rooftop of Daisy's Apartment, later that night
"On the S.S. Bernard Cohn" .... Chenoweth, Newman,
Darcie Roberts & Brooks Ashmanskas, Derric Harris, Celina Carvajal
The office of Dr. Mark Bruckner, the next day
At the Hellrakers' .... Dancers
"Don't Tamper With My Sister" .... Brent Barrett, Ed Dixon, Ensemble
"She Wasn't You" .... Barrett
The office of Dr. Mark Bruckner, a few evenings later
"Melinda" .... Friedman

ACT II

Entr'acte .... Orchestra
The solarium of the Bruckner Clinic, a week later
"When I'm Being Born Again" .... Louis Zorich
The office of Dr. Mark Bruckner, immediately following
"What Did I Have That I Don't Have" .... Chenoweth
The rooftop of Daisy's apartment, later that day
"Wait 'Til We're Sixty-Five" .... Roger Bart, Chenoweth, Ashmanskas, Newman, Roberts
The office of Dr. Mark Bruckner, a few days later
"Come Back to Me" .... Friedman
The airport, later that day
"On a Clear Day You Can See Forever" (Reprise) .... Friedman, Ensemble

TENDERLOIN

Tommy .... Patrick Wilson
Rev. Brock .... David Ogden Stiers
Gertie .... Yvette Cason
Nita .... Debbie Gravitte
Margie .... Jessica Stone
Liz .... Sara Gettelfinger
Purdy .... Guy Paul
Joe .... Tom Alan Robbins
Martin .... Stanley Bojarski
Jessica .... Melissa Rain Anderson
Laura .... Sarah Uriarte Berry
Frye .... Bruce MacVittie
Lt. Schmidt .... Kevin Conway

The Women: Julie Connors, Mindy Cooper, Margaret Ann Gates, Sara Gettelfinger, Ann Kittredge, Shannon Lewis, Tina Ou, Angie L. Schworer.

The Men: David Eggers, Angelo Fraboni, Gregg W. Goodbrod, Sean Grant, Derric Harris, Dale Hensley, Denis Jones, Mark Price, Gregory Emanuel Rahming, Timothy Shew.

The Coffee Club Orchestra: Rob Fisher conductor; Seymour Red Press flute, piccolo, alto flute, clarinet; Albert Regni clarinet, bass clarinet, flute, alto flute, piccolo; Dennis Anderson oboe, English horn, tenor sax, flute, clarinet; John Campo bassoon, baritone sax, bass clarinet, clarinet, flute; Roger Wendt, Kaitilin Mahony, French horn; John Frosk, Lowell Hershey trumpet; Jack Gale, Jack Schatz trombone; Jeffrey Harris piano, celeste, harpsichord; John Redsecker drums; Erik Charlston percussion; Jay Berliner guitar, mandolin, banjo; Victoria Drake harp; Suzanne Ornstein, Maura Giannini, Christoph Franzgrote, Rebekah Johnson, Eric De Gioia, Katherine Livolsi-Stern, Mia Wu, Lisa Matricardia, Robert Lawrence violin; Jill Jaffe, David Blinn, Crystal Garner viola; Clay Ruede, Lanny Paykin cello; John Beal acoustic bass.

Directed by Walter Bobbie; concert adaptation, John Weidman, Walter Bobbie; choreography, Rob Ashford; scenery consultant, John Lee Beatty; costume consultant, Jonathan Bixby; lighting, Mike Baldassari; sound, Scott Lehrer; original orchestrations, Irwin Kostal; musical coordinator, Seymour Red Press; casting, Jay Binder; production stage manager, Maximo Torres.

Tenderloin was first produced on Broadway 10/17/60 for 216 performances. This is its first major New York revival of record.

ACT I

Overture .... Orchestra
Prologue
"Bless This Land" .... Ensemble
"Little Old New York" .... Debbie Gravitte, Yvette Cason, Jessica Stone, Ensemble
A Parish House
"Dr. Brock" .... David Ogden Stiers
"Artificial Flowers" .... Patrick Wilson, Melissa Rain Anderson, Ensemble
"What's in It for You?" .... Wilson, Stiers
19th Police Precinct stationhouse
A street
"Reform" .... Cason, Stone, Sara Gettelfinger, Shannon Lewis, Angie L. Schworer
Living room in Purdy's Fifth Avenue house
"Tommy, Tommy" .... Sarah Uriarte Berry, Wilson
Clark's in the Tenderloin
"The Picture of Happiness" .... Wilson, Stone, Ensemble
Coney Island
"Dear Friend" .... Stiers, Ensemble
"The Army of the Just" .... Stiers, Stanley Bojarski, Dale Hensley, Gregory Emanuel Rahming, Timothy Shew
Clark's
"How the Money Changes Hands" .... Gravitte, Gettelfinger, Cason, Stone, Stiers, Bruce MacVittie, Ensemble

ACT II

Entr'acte .... Orchestra
Central Park
"Good Clean Fun" .... Stiers, Ensemble
"My Miss Mary" .... Wilson, Berry, Ensemble

Clark's
"My Gentle Young Johnny" .... Gravitte, Ensemble
"The Picture of Happiness" (Reprise) .... Cason, Stone, Ensemble
The trial
"The Trial" .... Anderson, Berry, Guy Paul, Tom Alan Robbins, Ensemble
A street
"Reform" (Reprise) .... Cason, Stone, Gettelfinger, Lewis, Schworer, Kevin Conway
The Parish House
"Tommy, Tommy" (Reprise) .... Berry, Wilson
Epilogue
"Little Old New York" (Reprise) .... Company

WONDERFUL TOWN

Guide; Associate Editor .... Patrick Quinn
Appopolous .... Lewis J. Stadlen
Lonigan .... Steve Ryan
Wreck .... Raymond Jaramillo McLeod
Helen .... Jenny Hill
Violet .... Alix Korey
Speedy Valenti .... Stephen DeRosa
Eileen .... Laura Benanti
Ruth .... Donna Murphy
Strange Man; Associate Editor; Ruth's Escort .... Ray Wills
Frank Lippencott .... David Aaron Baker
Robert Baker .... Richard Muenz
Mrs. Wade .... Becky Ann Baker
Chick Clark .... Gregory Jbara

Singers: Christopher Eaton Bailey, Carson Church, Rachel Coloff, Susan Derry, David Engel, Colm Fitzmaurice, John Halmi, Ann Kittredge, Ian Knauer, Laurie Williamson.

Dancers: Michael Arnold, Joyce Chittick, Jeffrey Hankinson, Michelle Kittrell, Cynthia Onrubia, Tina Ou, Vince Pesce, Alex Sanchez.

The Coffee Club Orchestra: Rob Fisher conductor; Lawrence Feldman alto sax, flute, clarinet, E flat clarinet; Roger Rosenberg clarinet, bass clarinet, alto/baritone/bass sax; Dennis Anderson oboe, English horn, tenor sax, clarinet; Seymour Red Press tenor sax, clarinet, flute, piccolo; John Winder bassoon, alto/bass sax, clarinet; John Frosk, Stu Satalof, David Gale, Christian Jaudes trumpet; Jack Gale, Jason Jackson, Jack Schatz trombone; Leslie Stifelman piano; John Redsecker drums; Erik Charlston percussion; Ronald Oakland concertmaster; Belinda Whitney-Barratt, Maura Giannini, Christoph Franzgrote, Mineko Yajima, Martin Agee, Rebekah Johnson, Lisa Matricardia, Marilyn Reynolds violin; Jill Jaffe, Kenneth Burward-Hoy, Crystal Garer viola; Jeanne LeBlanc, Lanny Paykin cello; Louis Bruno acoustic bass.

Directed and choreographed by Kathleen Marshall; concert adaptation, David Ives; scenery consultant, John Lee Beatty; costume consultant, William Ivey Long; lighting, Peter Kaczorowski; sound, Scott Lehrer; original orchestration, Don Walker; musical coordinator, Seymour Red Press; associate choreographer, Joey Pizzi; production stage manager, Karen Moore.

The last major New York revival of *Wonderful Town* was by New York City Opera 11/8/94 for 14 performances.

ACT I

Overture .... Orchestra
Christopher Street
"Christopher Street" .... Patrick Quinn, Ensemble
The Studio
"Ohio" .... Donna Murphy, Laura Benanti
All around New York
"Conquering New York" .... Murphy, Benanti, David Aaron Baker, Ensemble
Christopher Street
"One Hundred Easy Ways" .... Murphy
Baker's office
"What a Waste" .... Richard Muenz, Quinn, Ray Wills
Ruth's Story Vignettes .... Muenz, Murphy, Quinn, Wills
(by Betty Comden and Adolph Green)
Christopher Street
"A Little Bit in Love" .... Benanti

The studio
- "Pass the Football" .... Raymond Jaramillo McLeod, Dancers
- "Conversation Piece" .... Baker, Benanti, Murphy, Gregory Jbara, Muenz
- "A Quiet Girl" .... Muenz
- "A Quiet Girl" (Reprise) .... Murphy

The Navy Yard
- "Conga!" .... Murphy, Men

Christopher Street
- "Conga!" (Reprise) .... Company

ACT II

Entr'acte .... Orchestra

The Jail
- "My Darlin' Eileen" .... Colm Fitzmaurice, Benanti, Men

Christopher Street
- "Swing!" .... Murphy, Ensemble

The studio
- "Ohio" (Reprise) .... Murphy, Benanti

The street in front of the Vortex
- "It's Love" .... Benanti, Muenz, Singers

The Vortex
- Ballet at the Village Vortex .... Dancers
- "Wrong Note Rag" .... Murphy, Benanti, Company
- "It's Love" (Reprise) .... Company

Panache (126). By Don Gordon. Produced by David A. Cox, Edmund Gaynes and Michael Taylor at the Players Theater. Opened February 10, 2000. (Closed May 28, 2000)

Harry Baldwin .... Eric Pierpoint
Kathleen Trafalger .... Lisa Pelikan
Irwin Alcott .... James Benjamin Cooper
Laura Baldwin .... Jillian McWhirter
Jumbo Dombroski .... Wesley Thompson

Directed by David A. Cox; scenery and lighting, Mark Bloom; original music written and performed by Charlie Golden; associate producer, Pamela Hall; stage manager, Duff Dugan; press, David Rothenberg Associates.

Act I, Scene 1: Harry Baldwin's apartment, Brooklyn, N.Y. Scene 2: The same, two hours later. Act II, Scene 1: Harry Baldwin's apartment, a week later. Scene 2: In the mountains, three days later. Scene 3: Harry Baldwin's apartment, three weeks later. Scene 4: The same, four weeks later.

Comedy, socialite meets artist in a quarrel over the word "panache" for their license plates and ultimately change each other's lives for the better.

Joyful Noise (44). Play with music by Tim Slover. Produced by Lamb's Players Theater, Robert Smyth artistic director, at the Lamb's Theater. Opened February 17, 2000. (Closed March 25, 2000)

Susannah Cibber .... Mary Miller
Charles Jennens .... Paul Eggington
George Frederick Handel .... Tom Stephenson
John Christopher Smith .... Doren Elias
Kitty Clive .... Deborah Gilmour Smyth
Mary Pendarves .... Linda Bush
George II .... Robert Smyth
Bishop Henry Egerton .... David Cochran Heath

In Service—Jason Makiaris, Ted McCann, KB Mercer.

Directed by Robert Smyth; scenery and lighting, David Thayer; costumes, Jeanne Reith; sound supervision, Greg Campbell; stage manager, Kerrie McCann; press, Keith Sherman & Associates.

Time: 1741–1743. Places: The Town of London, Jennens' study at Gopsal in Leicestershire, the salon of Handel's house on Brook Street, backstage at the Drury Lane Theater, the salon of Mary Pendarves, St. James Palace, Covent Garden Theater. The play was presented in two parts.

Events leading to the first London production of Handel's *Messiah.* Previously produced in San Diego.

***Second Stage Theater.** Schedule of two programs (see note). **Saturday Night** (45). Musical based on the play *Front Porch in Flatbush* by Julius J. Epstein and Philip G. Epstein; book by Julius J. Epstein; music and lyrics by Stephen Sondheim. Opened February 17, 2000. (Closed March 26, 2000) ***Jitney** (43). By August Wilson; co-produced by Center Theater Group/Mark Taper Forum in association with Sageworks—Benjamin Mordecai producer. Opened April 25, 2000. Produced by Second Stage Theater, Carole Rothman artistic director, Carol Fishman managing director, Alexander Fraser executive director, at Second Stage Theater.

SATURDAY NIGHT

Ted .... Michael Benjamin Washington
Artie .... Kirk McDonald
Ray .... Greg Zola
Dino .... Joey Sorge
Bobby .... Christopher Fitzgerald
Celeste .... Andrea Burns
Hank .... Clarke Thorell
Gene .... David Campbell
Pinhead .... Frank Vlastnik
Mildred .... Rachel Ulanet
Vocalist; Mr. Fletcher .... Donald Corren
Plaza Attendant; Clune .... Michael Pemberton
Helen .... Lauren Ward
Mr. Fisher; Waiter;
Lieutenant .... David A. White
Florence; Dakota Doran ...... Natascia A. Diaz

Orchestra: Steven Freeman conductor, piano; Stephen Marzullo associate conductor, keyboards; Steve Kenyon, Richard Heckman, John Winder woodwinds; Brian O'Flaherty, Tino Gagliardi trumpet; Clint Sharman trombone; Raymond Kilday bass; Raymond Grappone drums, percussion.

Understudies: Messrs. Vlastnik, Washington, Thorell, Zola—Andy Karl; Mr. Fitzgerald—Kirk McDonald; Messrs. Campbell, McDonald, Sorge—Jim Stanek; Mr.Corren—David A. White; Misses Burns, Ulanet, Ward, Diaz—Lisa Datz.

Directed and choreographed by Kathleen Marshall; musical direction, Rob Fisher; scenery, Derek McLane; costumes, Catherine Zuber; lighting, Donald Holder; sound, Scott Lehrer; orchestrations, Jonathan Tunick; music coordinator, Seymour Red Press; casting, Johnson-Liff Associates, Tara Rubin; production stage manager, Karen Moore; stage manager, Karen Evansouskas; press, Richard Kornberg & Associates.

In pre-Depression 1929, Brooklyn youths dream of fame and fortune across the river but find happiness at home; a 40-year old Sondheim-Epstein work unproduced until now.

ACT I

Overture .... Orchestra
The front porch of Gene Gorman's house in Flatbush, Brooklyn, Saturday Night, spring 1929
"Saturday Night" .... Ted, Artie, Kay, Dino
"Class" .... Gene, Hank, Celeste, Bobby, Ted, Artie, Dino
"Delighted I'm Sure" .... Celeste, Mildred, Hank, Bobby, Ted, Artie, Ray, Dino
An anteroom outside of the Grand Ballroom at the Plaza Hotel, later that evening
"Love's a Bond" .... Vocalist
"Isn't It?" .... Helen
A movie house in Flatbush, a little later
"In the Movies" .... Ted, Artie, Ray, Dino, Hank, Celeste, Mildred
The front porch, later
"Exhibit A" .... Bobby
"A Moment With You" .... Vocalist, Gene, Helen
The street outside the porch, immediately after
"Saturday Night" (Reprise) .... Ted, Artie, Ray, Dino
The empty interior of a Sutton Place apartment, the next afternoon
Gracious Living Fantasy .... Gene & The Gang
The street outside the porch, Monday through Friday of the following week
"Montana Chem" .... Ted, Artie, Ray, Dino, Hank, Celeste
The front porch, the next night
"So Many People" .... Helen, Gene
"One Wonderful Day" .... Celeste, Hank, Bobby, Mildred, Florence, Ted, Artie, Ray, Dino

ACT II

Entr'acte .... Orchestra
The front porch, 7 o'clock Saturday night, a week later
"Saturday Night" (Reprise) .... Ted, Arte, Ray, Dino
"I Remember That" .... Hank, Celeste
Dakota Doran's nightclub, 3 o'clock the following morning
"'Love's a Bond' Blues" .... Dakota Doran
"All for You" .... Helen
Outside a police station, later that night
"That Kind of Neighborhood" .. Hank, Celeste, Mildred, Florence, Bobby, Ted, Artie, Ray, Dino
Inside the police station, immediately after
"What More Do I Need?" .... Gene, Helen, Hank, Celeste, Mildred, Florence, Bobby, Ted, Artie, Ray, Dino, Clune, Lieutenant
"One Wonderful Day" (finale) .... Company

JITNEY

Youngblood .... Russell Hornsby
Turnbo .... Stephen McKinley Henderson
Fielding .... Anthony Chisholm
Doub .... Barry Shabaka Henley
Shealy .... Willis Burks II
Philmore .... Leo V. Finnie III
Becker .... Paul Butler
Rena .... Michole Briana White
Booster .... Carl Lumbly

Directed by Marion McClinton; scenery, David Gallo; costumes, Susan Hilferty; lighting, Donald Holder; sound, Rob Milburn; fight direction, David S. Leong; associate artistic director, Christopher Burney; production stage manager, Narda Alcorn; stage manager, Mike Schleifer; press, Richard Kornberg & Associates, Richard Kornberg, Don Summa.

Time: 1977. Place: Pittsburgh's Hill District.

The uphill struggle of black members of a taxi service to make a living and a life. Winner of the 1999–2000 New York Drama Critics Circle Award for best play; see its entry in the Prizewinning Plays section of this volume.

Note: This season, Second Stage Theater was also the associate producer of *Chesapeake,* a solo performance by Mark Linn-Baker written by Lee Blessing, opened 10/14/99, and *The Waverly Gallery* by Kenneth Lonergan, opened 3/22/00; see their entries elsewhere in this section of this volume.

The Big Bang (55). Musical with book and lyrics by Boyd Graham; music by Jed Feuer. Produced by Eric Krebs and Nancy Nagel Gibbs in association with Pam Klappas-Pariseau at the Douglas Fairbanks Theater. Opened March 1, 2000. (Closed April 16, 2000)

With Jed Feuer, Boyd Graham.

The Big Bang Band: Albert Ahronheim keyboard.

Standbys: Mr. Graham—Kevin Del Aguila; Mr. Feuer—David Benoit.

Directed by Boyd Graham; musical direction, additional arrangements and orchestrations, Albert Ahronheim; scenery, Edward T. Gianfrancesco; costumes, Basil Du Maurier; lighting, James Vermeulen; sound, Raymond D. Schilke; musical and vocal arrangements, Jed Feuer; assistant director, Christopher Scott; production stage manager, Doug Hosney; press, David Rothenberg Associates, David J. Gersten.

The two authors and stars appear as producers in a borrowed Park Avenue apartment playing all the roles in an audition, for prosepctive backers, of their new musical about the history of civilization. The play was presented without intermission.

MUSICAL NUMBERS

"The Big Bang" .... Jed Feuer, Boyd Graham
"Free Food and Frontal Nudity" .... Adam and Eve
"Pyramid" .... Slaves
"Viva La Diva" .... Nefertiti
"Pyramid" (Reprise) .... Slaves

AMERICAN BUFFALO—Philip Baker Hall and William H. Macy in the Atlantic Theater Company revival of the play by David Mamet

"Wake Up, Caesar"	Caesar, Soothsayer
"Hell of a Job"	The Blessed Virgin Mary, Mrs. Gandhi
"Coliseum"	Leo
"Emperor Man"	Constantine the Great
"Number One"	Attila the Hun
"Cantata"	Sisters of the Sacre Bleu
"A New World"	Columbus, Queen Isabella
"Cooking for Henry"	Chefs
"The True Tale of Pocahontas"	Pocahontas, Minihaha
"Today's Just Yesterday's Tomorrow"	Napoleon, Josephine
"Freedom"	Inertia, Phlegm
"Potato"	Paddy O'Gratin
"Two Asian Ladies"	Shanghai Lil, Tokyo Rose
"We're Gonna Fly"	The Wright Brothers
"Loving Him"	Eva Braun
"The Twentieth Century"	Feuer, Graham
"The Big Bang" (Finale)	Feuer, Graham

American Buffalo (78). Revival of the play by David Mamet. Produced by Atlantic Theater Company, Neil Pepe artistic director, Hilary Hinckle managing director, at Atlantic Theater Company. Opened March 16, 2000. (Closed May 21, 2000)

Don	Philip Baker Hall	Teach	William H. Macy
Bobby	Mark Webber		

Directed by Neil Pepe; scenery, Kevin Rigdon; costumes, Laura Bauer; lighting, Howard Werner; fight director, Rick Sordelet; casting, Marcia DeBonis; production stage manager, Darcy Stephens; press, Boneau/Bryan-Brown.

Time and Place: Don's resale shop, a junk shop, one Friday. Act I: Morning. Act II: Around 11 p.m. that night.

The last major New York revival of *American Buffalo* took place on Broadway in the Long Wharf Theater production 10/27/83 for 102 performances.

The Waverly Gallery (70). By Kenneth Lonergan. Produced by Anita Waxman, Elizabeth Williams and Randall L. Wreghitt in association with Second Stage Theater at the Promenade Theater. Opened March 22, 2000. (Closed May 21, 2000)

Gladys Green .... Eileen Heckart, Scotty Bloch (Wed. & Sat. matinees)
Ellen Fine .... Maureen Anderman
Daniel Reed .... Josh Hamilton
Howard Fine .... Mark Blum
Don Bowman .... Anthony Arkin

Standby: Mr. Blum—Martin LaPlatney. Understudies: Messrs. Hamilton, Arkin—Sean Arbuckle; Miss Anderman—Rebecca Nelson.

Directed by Scott Ellis; scenery, Derek McLane; costumes, Michael Krass; lighting, Kenneth Posner; sound, Bruce Ellman; original music, Jason Robert Brown; casting, Amy Christopher; production stage manager, Lloyd Davis Jr.; stage manager, Bethany Ford; press, Barlow-Hartman Public Relations, Michael Hartman, John Barlow, Wayne Wolfe, Bridget Klapinski.

Time: 1989–1991. Place: New York City—Greenwich Village and the Upper West Side. The play was presented in two parts.

A stage portrait of encroaching senility, previously produced at the Williamstown Theater Festival.

Family Week (8). By Beth Henley. Produced by Jean Doumanian and Ron Kastner at the Century Center for the Performing Arts. Opened April 10, 2000. (Closed April 16, 2000)

Claire; Sandra .... Angelina Phillips
Ricky; Sandra; Sally .... Carol Kane
Kay; Sandra .... Julia Weldon
Lena; Sandra .... Rose Gregorio

Directed by Ulu Grosbard; scenery, John Arnone; costumes, Clifford Capone; lighting, Paul Gallo; sound, T. Richard Fitzgerald; production stage manager, Alex Volckhausen; press, Richard Kornberg & Associates.

Family members visit a woman suffering from an emotional breakdown and under treatment in a Recovery Center.

Suite in 2 Keys (8). Program of two one-act plays by Noel Coward: *Shadows of the Evening* and *A Song at Twilight*. Produced by Mirage Theater Company, Miranda d'Ancona and Doris Kaufman artistic directors; StageWrite Entertainment Inc. (Todd Alan Price), Jonathan Reinis Productions, the RJO Group (Robert O'Leary), by special arrangement with the Lucille Lortel Theater Foundation, at the Lucille Lortel Theater. Opened April 10, 2000. (Closed April 16, 2000)

Shadows of the Evening
Linda Savignac .... Judith Ivey
Anne Hilgay .... Hayley Mills
Felix .... Christian Maelen
George Hilgay .... Paxton Whitehead

Time: The 1960s. Place: The sitting room of a private suite in a luxurious hotel, Lausanne, Switzerland. Scene 1: Late afternoon on a day in autumn. Scene 2: One hour later.

A Song at Twilight
Hilde Latymer .... Hayley Mills
Sir Hugo Latymer .... Paxton Whitehead
Felix .... Christian Maelen
Carlotta Gray .... Judith Ivey

Time: The 1960s. Place: The same hotel suite. Scene 1: Early evening. Scene 2: A few minutes later.

Standbys: Misses Ivey, Mills—Lucy Martin; Mr. Whitehead—Ian Stuart. Understudy: Mr. Maelen—Paulo Andino.

Directed by John Tillinger; scenery, James Noone; costumes, David Loveless; lighting, Dennis Parichy; sound, Jim van Bergen; original music, Jonathan Faiman; associate producers, Thomas Barbour,

Electric Factory Concerts, Richard Martini, Adam Friedson, David Friedson; production stage manager, Scott Pegg; press, Origlio Public Relations, Tony Origlio, David Lotz.

Foreign plays originally produced in London in 1966 on a program entitled *Noel Coward's Suite in 3 Keys. Shadows of the Evening* is in its American premiere in this production and is about a publisher suffering from a terminal illness accompanied by both wife and mistress in a Swiss luxury hotel; *A Song at Twilight* is a revival previously presented on the Broadway program *Noel Coward in Two Keys* 2/28/74 for 140 performances.

The Acting Company. Schedule of two revivals. **The Rivals** (9). By Richard Brinsley Sheridan. Opened May 2, 2000. (Closed May 9, 2000) **Macbeth** (5). By William Shakespeare. Opened May 11, 2000. (Closed May 13, 2000) Produced by The Acting Company, Margot Harley producing director, Richard Corley associate producting director, at The Theater at St . Clements.

Performer	*The Rivals*	*Macbeth*
Matt Anderson	Capt. Absolute	Donalbain
Mia Barron	Julia	Weird Sister
Christopher Jean	Drudge	Macbeth
John Kinsherf	Thomas	Banquo
Andrew McGinn	Sir Anthony Absolute	Macduff
Royden Mills	David	Lenox; Doctor
Angela Pierce	Lydia Languish	Lady Macduff; Seyton
Heather Raffo	Errand Boy	Lady Macbeth
Erik Steele	Faulkland	Malcolm
Jeff Swarthout	Sir Lucius O'Trigger	Duncan; Old Man; Siward
Michele Tauber	Mrs. Malaprop	Weird Sister
April Yvette Thompson	Lucy	Weird Sister
Jonathan Uffelman	Bob Acres	Rosse; Porter

THE RIVALS: Directed by Nicholas Martin; scenery, Alexander Dodge; costumes, Michael Krass; lighting, Dennis Parichy; sound, Jerry M. Yager; fight direction and movement, Felix Ivanov; production stage manager, Leslie Leutwiler; press, Springer/Chicoine Public Relations, Susan Chicoine, Joe Trentacosta.

Place: In and around the city of Bath, England. The play was presented in two parts.

The last major New York revival of *The Rivals* was by Roundabout Theater Company off Broadway 12/3/74 for 79 performances.

MACBETH: Lords, Officers, Murderers, Messengers—Company.

Directed by Anne Justine D'Zmura; scenery, Nephelie Andonyadis; costumes, Anna Oliver; lighting, Dennis Parichy; original music and sound, Lewis Flinn; fight direction, Felix Ivanov; production stage manager, Leslie Leutwiler.

The last major New York revival of *Macbeth* was by New York Shakespeare Festival off Broadway 3/15/98 for 17 performances. The play was presented without intermission.

Sweeney Todd, the Demon Barber of Fleet Street (3). Concert version of the musical with book by Hugh Wheeler; music and lyrics by Stephen Sondheim; from an adaptation by Christopher Bond. Produced by New York Philharmonic, Kurt Masur music director, at Avery Fisher Hall. Opened May 4, 2000. (Closed May 6, 2000)

Anthony Hope .... Davis Gaines
Sweeney Todd .... George Hearn
Beggar Woman .... Audra McDonald
Mrs. Lovett .... Patti LuPone
Judge Turpin .... Paul Plishka
The Beadle .... John Aler
Johanna .... Heidi Grant Murphy
Tobias Ragg .... Neil Patrick Harris
Pirelli .... Stanford Olsen

Company: New York Choral Artists, Joseph Flummerfelt music director, Grant Gershon guest conductor.

Conductor, Andrew Litton; director, Lonny Price; consulting producer, Andre Bishop; executive producer, Welz Kauffman; design, James Noone; costumes, Gail Brassard; lighting, Phil Monat; sound, Tom Clark; production stage manager, Heather Fields; stage manager, Charles M. Turner.

Time: The 19th century. Place: London—Fleet Street and environs.

The last major New York revival of this musical was as *Sweeney Todd* by Circle in the Square on Broadway 9/14/89 for 189 performances.

MUSICAL NUMBERS, ACT I: "The Ballad of Sweeney Todd," "No Place Like London," "The Worst Pies in London," "Poor Thing," "My Friends," "Green Finch and Linnet Bird," "Ah, Miss," "Johanna" (Anthony), "Pirelli's Miracle Elixir," "The Contest," "Wait," "Johanna" (Judge Turpin),"Kiss Me" (Part I), "Ladies in Their Sensitivities," "Kiss Me" (Part II), "Pretty Women," "Epiphany," "A Little Priest."

ACT II: "God, That's Good!", "Johanna" (Todd), "By the Sea," "The Letter," "Not While I'm Around," "Parlor Songs," "City on Fire!", "Searching," "The Judge's Return," "Final Scene," "The Ballad of Sweeney Todd."

*__Wake Up and Smell the Coffee__ (32). Solo performance by Eric Bogosian; written by Eric Bogosian. Produced by Frederick Zollo, Nicholas Paleologos and Robert Birmingham at the Jane Street Theater. Opened May 4, 2000.

Directed by Jo Bonney; scenery, John Arnone; lighting, Kevin Adams; original music and sound, Donald DiNicola; production stage manager, Arabella Powell; press, Philip Rinaldi.

The actor-writer focuses his abrasive comedy on various conspicuous aspects of modern life including air travel, celebrity and himself. The performance was presented without intermssion.

Hansen's Cab (24). By Mark R. Giesser. produced by Alces Productions at the Jose Quintero Theater. Opened May 9, 2000. (Closed May 28, 2000)

Arthur Gateman	Avrom Berel	Jennifer Talavera	Heather Randall
Florence Gateman	Melissa Hart	Clay Mitchell	John Wayne Shafer

Directed by Mark R. Giesser; scenery, John C. Scheffler; costumes, Melanie Ann Schmidt; lighting, Aaron Meadow; choreography, Sharon Halley; stage manager, Marcos Dinnerstein; press, Cromarty & Co.

Time: October 1958. Place: In an around the ruins of a stagecoach station in the Guadalupe Mountains of northwest Texas.

Conflicts between a woman suffering from leprosy and the couple whose job it is to take her from her home to a U.S. military hospital.

*__The Laramie Project__ (14). By Moisés Kaufman and members of the Tectonic Theater Project. Produced by Roy Gabay and the Tectonic Theater Project in association with Gayle Francis and the Araca Group at the Union Square Theater. Opened May 18, 2000.

CAST: Himself, Doc O'Connor, Matt Galloway, Andrew Gomez—Stephen Belber. Herself, Trish Steger, Marge Murray, Baptist Minister—Amanda Gronich. Reggie Fluty, Rebecca Hilliker—Mercedes Herrero. Moisés Kaufman, Stephen Mead Johnson, Jon Peacock, Harry Woods—John McAdams. Himself, Jedediah Schultz, Matt Mickelson, Doug Laws—Andy Paris. Himself, Sgt. Hing, Rob DeBree, Father Roger, Rulon Stacey—Greg Pierotti. Herself, Catherine Connolly, Zubaida Ula, Lucy Thompson—Barbara Pitts. Leigh Fondakowski, Romaine Patterson, Aaron Kreifels, Zackie Salmon—Kelli Simpkins.

Directed by Moisés Kaufman; head writer and assistant director, Leigh Fondakowski; associate writers. Stephen Belber, Greg Pierotti, Stephen Wangh; scenery, Robert Brill; costumes, Moe Schell; lighting, Betsy Adams; composer, Peter Golub; video and slide design, Martha Swetzoff; associate producers, Mara Isaacs, Hart Sharp Entertainment; production stage manager, Charles Means; press, KPM Associates, Kevin McAnarney.

Dramatization of the events which took place around the brutal murder of a gay student, Matthew Shepard, in 1998. The play was presented in three parts. Previously produced in regional theater at Denver Theater Center, Donovan Marley artistic director, in February.

CAST REPLACEMENTS AND TOURING COMPANIES

Compiled by Jeffrey Finn Productions

The following is a list of the major cast replacements of record in productions which opened in previous years, but were still playing in New York during a substantial part of the 1999–2000 season; and other New York shows which were on a first-class tour in 1999–2000.

The name of each major role is listed in *italics* beneath the title of the play in the first column. In the second column directly opposite appears the name of the actor who created the role in the original New York production (whose opening date appears in *italics* at the top of the column). In shows of the past five years, indented immediately beneath the original actor's name are the names of subsequent New York replacements, together with the date of replacement when available. In shows that have run longer than five years, only this season's or the most recent cast replacements are listed under the names of the original cast members.

The third column gives information about first-class touring companies. When there is more than one roadshow company, #1, #2, etc., appear before the name of the performer who created the role in each company (and the city and date of each company's first performance appears in *italics* at the top of the column). Their subsequent replacements are also listed beneath their names in the same manner as the New York companies, with dates when available.

ANNIE GET YOUR GUN

	New York 3/4/99
Buffalo Bill	Ron Holgate Christopher Councill 9/99 Dennis Kelly 1/00
Frank Butler	Tom Wopat
Dolly Tate	Valerie Wright Michelle Blakely
Tommy Keeler	Andrew Palermo
Winnie Tate	Nicole Ruth Snelson
Charlie Davenport	Peter Marx
Annie Oakley	Bernadette Peters

ART

	New York 3/1/98	*San Francisco 9/14/99*
Marc	Alan Alda Brian Cox 9/1/98 Judd Hirsch 12/22/98 Buck Henry 5/11/99	Judd Hirsch

Serge	Victor Garber Henry Goodman 9/1/98 Joe Morton 12/22/98 George Segal 5/11/99	Cotter Smith
Yvan	Alfred Molina David Haig 9/1/98 George Wendt 12/22/98 Wayne Knight 5/11/99	Jack Willis

BEAUTY AND THE BEAST

	New York 4/18/94	*#1 Minneapolis 11/7/95* *#2 Tulsa 9/7/99*
Beast	Terrence Mann Jeff McCarthy Chuck Wagner James Barbour Steve Blanchard	#1 Frederick C. Inkley Roger Befeler #2 Grant Norman
Belle	Susan Egan Sarah Uriarte Christianne Tisdale Kerry Butler Deborah Gibson Kim Huber Toni Braxton Andrea McArdle	#1 Kim Huber Erin Dilly 2/11/98 #2 Susan Owen
Lefou	Kenny Raskin Harrison Beal Jamie Torcellini Jeffrey Howard Schecter Jay Brian Winnick 11/12/99	#1 Dan Sklar Jeffrey Schecter Aldrin Gonzalez #2 Michael Raine
Gaston	Burke Moses Marc Kudisch Steve Blanchard Patrick Ryan Sullivan	#1 Tony Lawson #2 Chris Hoch
Maurice	Tom Bosley MacIntyre Dixon Tom Bosley Kurt Knudson Tim Jerome J.B. Adams 11/12/99	#1 Grant Cowan #2 Ron Lee Savin
Cogsworth	Heath Lamberts Peter Bartlett Gibby Brand John Christopher Jones Jeff Brooks 11/12/99	#1 Jeff Brooks #2 John Alban Coughlan
Lumiere	Gary Beach Lee Roy Reams Patrick Quinn Gary Beach Meschach Taylor Patrick Page	#1 Patrick Page David DeVries Gary Beach David DeVries #2 Ron Wisniski

Babette	Stacey Logan Pamela Winslow Leslie Castay Pam Klinger	#1 Leslie Castay Mindy Paige Davis 2/15/97 Heather Lee #2 Jennifer Shrader
Mrs. Potts	Beth Fowler Cass Morgan Beth Fowler Barbara Marineu 11/12/99	#1 Betsy Joslyn Barbara Marineu 7/2/97 #2 Janet MacEwen

CABARET

	New York 3/19/98	*Los Angeles 2/99*
Emcee	Alan Cumming Robert Sella 9/17/98 Alan Cumming 12/1/98 Michael Hall 6/8/99	Norbert Leo Butz Jon Peterson 1/2/00
Sally Bowles	Natasha Richardson Jennifer Jason Leigh 8/4/98 Mary McCormack 3/2/99 Susan Eagan 6/17/99	Teri Hatcher Joely Fisher 9/4/99 Lea Thompson 3/19/00
Clifford Bradshaw	John Benjamin Hickey Boyd Gaines 3/2/99 Michael Hayden 8/3/99	Rick Holmes Jay Goede 10/16/99
Ernst Ludwig	Denis O'Hare Michael Stuhlbarg 5/4/99 Martin Moran 11/9/99	Andy Taylor Drew McVety 10/16/99
Fraulein Schneider	Mary Louise Wilson Blair Brown 8/20/98 Carole Shelley 5/4/99	Barbara Andres Alma Cuervo 9/4/99
Fraulein Kost	Michele Pawk Victoria Clark 5/4/99	Jeanine Morick Lenora Nemetz 2/20/00
Herr Schultz	Ron Rifkin Laurence Luckinbill 5/4/99 Dick Latessa 11/9/99	Dick Latessa Hal Robinson 9/4/99

CATS

	New York 10/7/82	*National tour 1/94*
Alonzo	Hector Jaime Mercado Lenny Daniel 11/1/99	William Patrick Dunne Matt Rivera 3/23/99
Bustopher	Stephen Hanan Michael Brian 6/8/98 John Dewar 8/21/99	Richard Poole Kelly Briggs 3/16/99
Bombalurina	Donna King Marlene Danielle 1/9/84	Helen Frank Parisa Ross 9/1/98
Cassandra	Rene Ceballos Lynn Calamis 7/5/99 Melissa Rae Mahon 3/10/00	Laura Quinn Naomi Kakuk 4/6/99
Demeter	Wendy Edmead Celina Carvajal 5/17/99	N. Elaine Wiggins Carol Shuberg 10/26/99
Grizabella	Betty Buckley Linda Balgord	Mary Gutzi Renee Venaziale 8/10/99

Andrea McArdle as Belle in *Beauty and the Best*

Jellylorum	Bonnie Simmons Jean Arbeiter	Patty Goble Robin Boudreau Alice C. DeChant
Jennyanydots	Anna McNeely Sharon Wheatley 6/21/99	Alice C. DeChant
Mistoffeles	Timothy Scott Jacob Brent 9/27/99 Julius Sermonia 12/28/99	Christopher Gattelli Julius Sermonia 2/1/99
Mungojerrie	Rene Clemente Roger Kachel 5/11/92	Gavan Palmer David Petro 4/19/99

Munkustrap	Harry Groener Michael Gruber 5/10/99 Jeffry Denman 9/13/99	Robert Amirante Paul Clausen 2/1/99
Old Deuteronomy	Ken Page Jimmy Lockett	John Treacy Egan Stephen Carter-Hicks 11/16/99
Plato/Macavity	Kenneth Ard Keith Wilson 5/17/99	Steve Bertles Chadwick T. Adams 2/23/99
Pouncival	Herman W. Sebek Jon-Erik Goldenberg 1/17/00	Joey Gyondla Jon-Erik Goldenberg 3/16/99
Rum Tum Tugger	Terrence Mann Stephen Bienskie	Ron Seykell Kevin Loreque 4/27/99
Rumpleteazer	Christine Langner Tesha Buss	Jennifer Cody Dina Lynn Margotin 10/18/99
Sillabub	Whitney Kershaw Maria Jo Ralabate	Lanene Charters Claci Miller 3/23/99
Skimbleshanks	Reed Jones Jon Paul Christensen 6/28/99 James Hadley 3/27/00	Carmen Yurich Shaun Parry 9/6/99
Tumblebrutus	Robert Hoshour Patrick Mullaney	Joseph Favolora Angelo Rivera 1/6/98
Victoria	Cynthia Onrubia Missy Lay Zimmer	Tricia Mitchell Jessica Dillan 1/12/99

Note: Only this season's or the most recent cast replacements are listed above under the names of the original cast members. For previous replacements, see previous volumes of *Best Plays*.

CHICAGO

	New York 11/14/96	*#1 Cincinatti 3/25/97* *#2 Ft. Myers, Fla. 12/12/97*
Roxie Hart	Ann Reinking Marilu Henner Karen Ziemba Belle Calaway Charlotte d'Amboise Sandy Duncan 8/12/99 Belle Calaway 1/18/00 Charlotte d'Amboise 3/24/00	#1 Charlotte d'Amboise Belle Calaway Ann Reinking 4/22/99 Belle Calaway 5/18/99 Sandy Duncan 4/22/99 Ann Reinking 5/1/99 Belle Calaway 6/1/99 Sandy Duncan 7/13/99 Belle Calaway 8/3/99 Nana Visitor 11/16/99 Tracy Shane 1/4/00 #2 Karen Ziemba Nancy Hess Charlotte d'Amboise Amy Spranger 11/10/98 Charlotte d'Amboise 11/24/98 Amy Spranger 12/1/98 Chita Rivera 2/2/99 Marilu Henner 7/6/99 Charlotte d'Amboise 8/24/99 Marilu Henner 12/22/99 Nana Visitor 1/3/00

Velma Kelly	Bebe Neuwirth Nancy Hess Ute Lemper Bebe Neuwirth Ruthie Henshall 5/25/99 Mamie Duncan-Gibbs 10/26/99 Bebe Neuwirth 1/18/00 Donna Marie Asbury 3/23/00 Sharon Lawrence 4/11/00	#1 Jasmine Guy Janine LaManna Jasmine Guy Donna Marie Asbury Stephanie Pope Jasmine Guy 7/7/98 Stephanie Pope 7/14/98 Mamie Duncan-Gibbs 1/12/99 Deidre Goodwin 2/16/99 Ruthie Henshall 4/22/99 Deidre Goodwin 5/18/99 Ruthie Henshall 4/22/99 Deidre Goodwin 6/1/99 Donna Marie Asbury 10/12/99 Vicki Lewis 11/16/99 Roxanne Carrasco 1/4/00 Vicki Lewis 3/14/00 Roxanne Carrasco 3/21/00 #2 Stephanie Pope Jasmine Guy Stephanie Pope Khandi Alexander 8/4/98 Donna Marie Asbury 9/29/98 Stephanie Pope 2/2/98 Ute Lemper 2/19/99 Stephanie Pope 4/5/99 Mamie Duncan-Gibbs 8/3/99 Jasmine Guy 8/24/99 Marianne McCord 12/22/99 Vicki Lewis 1/3/00
Billy Flynn	James Naughton Gregory Jbara Hinton Battle Alan Thicke Michael Berresse Brent Barrett Robert Urich 1/11/00 Clarke Peters 2/1/00 Brent Barrett 2/15/00	#1 Obba Babatunde Alan Thicke Michael Berresse 8/18/98 Alan Thicke 8/25/98 Destin Owens 10/13/98 Alan Thicke 10/27/98 Destin Owens 1/26/99 Adrian Zmed 2/16/99 Hal Linden 8/6/99 Gregory Jbara 8/17/99 Robert Urich 10/19/99 Lloyd Culbreath 1/4/00 Alan Thicke 1/18/00 Lloyd Culbreath 2/29/00 Alan Thicke 3/14/00 Clarke Peters 3/21/00 #2 Brent Barrett Michael Berresse 11/3/98 Brent Barrett 11/24/98 Michael Berresse 12/1/98 Ben Vereen 2/19/99 Hal Linden 8/31/99 Gregory Jbara 1/3/00 Clarke Peters

Amos Hart	Joel Grey Ernie Sabella Tom McGowan P.J. Benjamin Ernie Sabella 11/23/99	#1 Ron Orbach Michael Tucci Bruce Winant 12/22/98 Ray Bokhour 10/19/99 P.J. Benjamin 4/4/00 #2 Ernie Sabella Tom McGowan Ron Orbach Tom McGowan Ron Orbach P.J. Benjamin 11/10/98 Joel Grey 12/1/98 P.J. Benjamin 12/29/98 Ernie Sabella 2/2/99 Michael Tucci 8/24/99 P.J. Benjamin 1/3/00
Matron "Mama" Morton	Marcia Lewis Roz Ryan Marcia Lewis	#1 Carol Woods Lea DeLaria Carol Woods 8/4/98 #2 Avery Sommers Marcia Lewis 2/2/99 Roz Ryan 7/27/99
Mary Sunshine	D. Sabella J. Loeffenholz R. Bean A. Saunders J. Maldonado	#1 M.E. Spencer D.C. Levine M.E. Spencer 7/7/98 R. Bean 7/28/98 A. Saunders 10/13/98 R. Bean 10/20/98 J. Maldonado 10/27/98 J. Roberson 2/9/99 M. Von Essen 5/12/99 J. Maldonado 10/12/99 M. Agnes 1/4/00 #2 D.C. Levine M.E. Spencer D. Sabella 9/7/99

THE FANTASTICKS

	New York 5/3/60
El Gallo	Jerry Orbach Paul Blankenship 2/99
Luisa	Rita Gardner Natasha Harper 1/25/00
Matt	Kenneth Nelson Charles Hagerty 11/99

Note: Only this season's or the most recent replacements are listed above under the names of the original cast members. For previous replacements, see previous volumes of *Best Plays*.

FOOTLOOSE

	New York 10/22/98	*Cleveland 12/15/98*
Reverend Shaw Moore	Stephen Lee Anderson	Daren Kelly

Wendy Jo	Rosalind Brown Katie Harvey	Katie Harvey
Lulu Warnicker	Catherine Campbell	Tina Johnson
Ethel McCormack	Catherine Cox (Evans)	Marsha Waterbury Eileen Barnett 8/6/99
Urleen	Kathy Deitch Jennifer Gambatese	Andrea McCormack
Chuck Cranston	Billy Hartung	Richard H. Blake Matthew Morrison 6/21/99
Vi Moore	Dee Hoty	Mary Gordon Murray Jana Robbins 9/21/99
Ren McCormack	Jeremy Kushnier	Joe Machota
Wes Warnicker	Adam LeFevre	Steve Luker
Willard Hewitt	Tom Plotkin	Christian Borle Luther Creek 12/14/99
Ariel Moore	Jennifer Laura Thompson	Niki Scalera Teresa Marie Sanchez 12/14/99

FOSSE

New York 1/14/99

Juliu Agustin
Brad Anderson
Andy Blankenbuehler
Bill Burns
Marc Calamia
Holly Cruikshank
Eugene Fleming
Lisa Gajda
Kim Morgan Greene
Scott Jovovich
Christopher R. Kirby
Dede LaBarre
Mary Ann Lamb
Susan LaMontagne
Jane Lanier
Deborah Leamy
Shannon Lewis
Mary MacLeod
Dana Moore
Brad Musgrove
Sean Palmer
Elizabeth Parkinson
Michael Paternostro
Varlerie Pettiford
  Stephanie Pope 8/99
Rachelle Rak
Josh Rhodes
Desmond Richardson
  Keith Richard 12/99
  Julia Bocca 2/00
Lainie Sakakura
Alex Sanchez
Sergio Trujillo
J. Kathleen Watkins
Scott Wise

Chicago 9/22/99

Ken Alan
  Mark Swanhart 4/12/99
Ashley Bachner
Linda Bowen
Andrew Boyle
John Carroll
Christine Colby Jacques
Dylis Croman
Janice Cronkhite
Rick Delancy
Anika Ellis
Rick Faugno
Sara Gelletfinger
  LaMae Caparas 2/1/00
Darren Gibson
Meg Gillentine
Amy Hall
Sara Henry
Terace Jones
Shawn Ku
  Janes Kinney 12/20/99
Gelan Lambert, Jr.
Matt Loehr
Krisha Marcano
Cassel Miles
Julio Monge
April Nixon
Greg Reuter
Reva Rice
Vincent Sandoval
Jennifer Savelli

HEDWIG AND THE ANGRY INCH

	New York 7/14/98
Hedwig Schmidt	John Cameron Mitchell Michael Cerveris 1/4/99 Ally Sheedy 12/13/99 Matt McGrath 1/6/00

I LOVE YOU, YOU'RE PERFECT, NOW CHANGE

New York 8/1/96

Jordan Leeds
Danny Burstein 10/1/96
Adam Grupper 8/22/97
Gary Imhoff 2/9/98
Adam Grupper 4/1/98
Jordan Leeds 3/17/99

Robert Roznowski
Kevin Pariseau 5/25/98

Jennifer Simard
Erin Leigh Peck 5/25/98
Kelly Anne Clark 1/10/00
Andrea Chamberlain 3/13/00

Melissa Weil
Cheryl Stern 2/16/98

JEKYLL & HYDE

	New York 4/28/97	*Wallingford, Conn. 4/13/99*
Sir Danvers Carew	Barrie Ingham	Dennis Kelly Jamie Ross
Dr. Henry Jekyll; Edward Hyde	Robert Cuccioli Robert Evan (alt.) Robert Evan 1/5/99 Joseph Mahowald (alt.) Jack Wagner 1/25/00 Sebastian Bach 6/13/00	Chuck Wagner Brian Noonan (alt.)
Emma Carew	Christiane Noll Anastasia Barzee Andrea Rivette 1/25/00	Andrea Rivette Kelli O'Hara
Lucy	Linda Eder Luba Mason Coleen Sexton 1/25/00	Sharon Brown Deb Lyons Becca Ayers

LES MISERABLES

	New York 3/12/87	*Tampa 11/18/88*
Jean Valjean	Colm Wilkinson Tim Shaw 9/7/99 J. Mark McVey 3/7/00	Gary Barker Ivan Rutherford 1/19/99
Javert	Terrence Mann Greg Edelman 9/7/99	Peter Samuel Stephen Bishop 8/3/99
Fantine	Randy Graff Jane Bodle 9/7/99	Hollis Resnik Joan Almedilla 3/2/99
Enjolras	Michael Maguire Christopher Mark Peterson 6/21/99	Greg Zerkle Stephen Tewksbury 2/15/00
Marius	David Bryant Peter Lockyer 3/12/97	Matthew Porretta Tim Howar
Cosette	Judy Kuhn Tobi Foster 11/6/98	Jacquelyn Piro Regan Thiel
Eponine	Frances Ruffelle Rona Figueroa 6/3/99 Megan Lawrence 6/24/99 Jessica-Snow Wilson 8/31/99 Rona Figueroa 9/14/99 Jessica Bovers 12/7/00	Michele Maika Diana Kaarina 3/21/00

Note: Only this season's or the most recent cast replacements are listed above under the names of the original cast members. For previous replacements, see previous volumes of *Best Plays.*

THE LION KING

	New York 11/13/97
Rafiki	Tsidii LeLoka Thuli Dumakude 11/11/98
Mufasa	Samuel E. Wright
Sarabi	Gina Breedlove Meena T. Jahi 8/4/98
Zazu	Geoff Hoyle Bill Bowers 10/21/98 Robert Dorfman
Scar	John Vickery Tom Hewitt 10/21/98
Banzai	Stanley Wayne Mathis Keith Bennett 9/30/98
Shenzi	Tracy Nicole Chapman Vanessa S. Jones
Ed	Kevin Cahoon Jeff Skowron 10/21/98 Jeff Gurner

Timon	Max Casella Danny Rutigliano 6/16/98
Pumba	Tom Alan Robbins
Simba	Jason Raize
Nala	Heather Headley Mary Randle 7/7/98 Heather Headley 12/8/98 Bashirrah Creswell

MISS SAIGON

	New York 4/11/91	*Seattle 3/16/95*
The Engineer	Jonathan Pryce Luoyong Wang 10/2/95	Thom Sesma Joseph Anthony Foronda 4/22/97
Kim	Lea Salonga Deedee Lynn Magno	Deedee Lynn Magno Mika Nishida 7/21/99
Chris	Willy Falk Will Chase 7/20/98	Matt Bogart Will Swenson 12/22/99

Note: Only this season's or the most recent cast replacements are listed above under the names of the original cast members. For previous replacements, see previous volumes of *Best Plays.*

OVER THE RIVER AND THROUGH THE WOODS

	New York 10/5/98
Nick Cristano	Jim Bracchitta Paul Urcioli 3/29/99 Ken Garito 10/12/99
Frank Gianelli	Val Avery Ralph Lucarelli 3/23/99 John LaGioia 7/5/99
Aida Gianelli	Joan Copeland Kaye Ballard 4/6/99 Vera Lockwood 7/5/99
Nunzio Cristano	Dick Latessa Allen Swift 2/8/99
Emma Cristano	Marie Lillo
Caitlin O'Hare	Marsha Dietlein Heather Raffo 12/18/98 Geneva Carr 11/2/99

THE PHANTOM OF THE OPERA

	New York 1/26/88	*#1 Los Angeles 5/31/90* *#2 Chicago 5/24/90* *#3 Seattle 12/13/92*
The Phantom	Michael Crawford Howard McGillin 8/23/99	#1 Michael Crawford Frank D'Ambrosio 3/28/94 #2 Mark Jacoby Davis Gaines 8/98 #3 Frank D'Ambrosio Ted Keegan 2/28/00

Christine Daae	Sarah Brightman Sarah Pfisterer (alt.) Sarah Pfisterer 1/17/00 Adrienne McEwan (alt.)	#1 Dale Kristien Karen Culliver (alt.) 6/3/97 #2 Karen Culliver Marie Danvers 6/98 Susan Facer (alt.) 6/98 #3 Tracy Shane Megan Starr-Levitt (alt.) 1/21/98 Rebecca Pitcher 3/31/99
Raoul	Steve Barton Gary Mauer 4/19/99	#1 Reece Holland Christopher Carl 7/2/96 #2 Keith Buterbaugh Lawrence Anderson 7/98 #3 Ciaran Sheehan Jim Weitzer 1/12/00

Note: Only this season's or the most recent cast replacements are listed above under the names of the original cast members. For previous replacements, see previous volumes of *Best Plays.*

RAGTIME

	New York 1/18/98	*Washington, D.C. 4/29/98*
Father	Mark Jacoby John Dossett 4/99 Joseph Delgar 9/99	Chris Groenendaal Stephen Zinnato 7/31/99
Mother	Marin Mazzie Donna Bullock 1/99	Rebecca Eichenberger Cathy Wydner 7/31/99
Mother's Younger Bro.	Steven Sutcliffe Scott Carollo	Aloysius Gigl Adam Hunter 2/14/00 John Frenzer 2/8/00
Coalhouse Walker, Jr.	Brian Stokes Mitchell Alton Fitzgerald White 1/99	Alton Fitzgerald White Lawrence Hamilton 12/28/98
Sarah	Audra McDonald LaChanze 1/99 Darlesia Cearcy 9/99	Darlesia Cearcy Lovena Fox 7/31/99
Tateh	Peter Friedman John Rubinstein 1/99 Michael Rupert 7/99	Michael Rupert Jim Corti 7/31/99
Harry Houdini	Jim Corti Bernie Yvon	Bernie Yvon Eric Olson 7/31/99
Henry Ford	Larry Daggett David Masenheimer 9/98 Larry Daggett 3/99	Larry Cahn Jay Bodin 7/31/99
Emma Goldman	Judy Kaye	Theresa Tova Cyndi Neal 7/31/99
Evelyn Nesbit	Lynette Perry Janine LaManna 8/98	Melissa Dye Michele Ragusa 7/31/99 Jacqueline Bayne

Cast replacements in the two long-run off-Broadway hits by Joe DiPietro have included, *above,* Allen Swift, Marie Lillo, Ken Garito, Vera Lockwood and John LaGioia in a scene from the comedy *Over the River and Through the Woods; below,* Kevin Pariseau, Cheryl Stern, Andrea Chamberlain and Jordan Leeds in the musical *I Love You, You're Perfect, Now Change,* with book and lyrics by DiPietro and music by Jimmy Roberts

RENT

	New York 4/29/96	#1 Boston 11/18/96 #2 La Jolla 7/1/97
Roger Davis	Adam Pascal Manley Pope	#1 Sean Keller Dean Balkwill #2 Christian Mena Cary Shields 11/30/99
Mark Cohen	Anthony Rapp Jim Poulos	#1 Luther Creek Trey Ellet #2 Neil Patrick Harris Matt Caplan
Tom Collins	Jesse L. Martin Rufus Bonds Jr. 9/7/99 Alan Mingo Jr. 4/10/00	#1 C.C. Brown Mark Leroy Jackson #2 Mark Leroy Jackson Horace V. Rogers Mark Ford 6/13/99
Benjamin Coffin III	Taye Diggs Stu James 3/13/00	#1 James Rich Brian Love #2 D'Monroe Stu James 8/31/99 Brian Love 2/29/00
Joanne Jefferson	Fredi Walker Danielle Lee Greaves 10/4/99	#1 Sylvia MacCalla Kamilah Martin #2 Kenna J. Ramsey Jacqueline B. Arnold
Angel Schunard	Wilson Jermaine Heredia Andy Senor 1/31/00	#1 Stephan Alexander Shaun Earl #2 Wilson Cruz Shaun Earl 11/23/99
Mimi Marquez	Daphne Rubin-Vega Maya Days Loraine Velez 2/28/00	#1 Simone Sharon Leal #2 Julia Santana Saycon Sengbloh 11/30/99
Maureen Johnson	Idina Menzel Cristina Fadale 10/4/99	#1 Carrie Hamilton Erin Keaney #2 Leigh Hetherington Michelle Joan Smith 9/28/99 Erin Keaney 4/7/00

THE SCARLET PIMPERNEL

	New York 11/9/97
Percy Blakeney	Douglas Sills Ron Bohmer
Chauvelin	Terrence Mann Rex Smith Marc Kudisch
Marguerite St. Just	Christine Andreas Rachel York Carolee Carmello

SIDE MAN

	New York 6/25/99
Clifford	Robert Sella Christian Slater 10/20/99 Robert Sella 3/2/99 Scott Wolff 5/28/99 Andrew McCarthy 7/19/99
Terry	Wenda Makkena Edie Falco 1/8/99 Angelica Torn
Patsy	Angelica Torn Marissa Matrone
Gene	Frank Wood Michael O'Keefe
Al	Joseph Lyle Taylor
Ziggy	Michael Mastro
Jonesy	Kevin Geer

TITANIC

	New York 4/23/97	*Los Angeles 1/5/99*
Capt. E.J. Smith	John Cunningham	William Parry
1st Officer William Murdoch	David Costabile Danny Burstein	David Pittu Joe Farrell
Frederick Barrett	Brian d'Arcy James Clarke Thorell Stephen R. Buntrock	Marcus Chait
Harold Bride	Martin Moran Don Stephenson	Dale Sandish
Henry Etches	Allan Corduner Henry Stram	Edward Conery
Thomas Andrews	Michael Cerveris Matthew Bennett Joseph Kolinski	Kevin Gray Thom Sesma
Isidor Straus	Larry Keith	S. Marc Jordan
Ida Straus	Alma Cuervo	Taina Elg Kay Walbye
Edgar Beane	Bill Buell	David Beditz
Alice Beane	Victoria Clark	Liz McConahay Sarah Solie Shannon
Kate McGowen	Jennifer Piech	Melissa Bell
Jim Farrell	Clarke Thorell Christopher Wells	Richard Roland

WIT

	New York 10/6/98
Vivian Bearing	Kathleen Chalfant Judith Light 8/10/99 Lisa Harrow 1/20/00

OTHER NEW YORK SHOWS ON FIRST CLASS TOURS IN 1999–2000

CHESS

	Wilmington 1/28/00
Freddie	Brad Drummer
Florence	Kim Lindsay
Anatoly	Philip Hernandez
Svetlana	Kirsti Carnahan
Molokov	David Brummel
Walter	Mark McGrath
Arbiter	David Masenheimer

COMPANY

	Raleigh 9/99
Robert	Tom Galantich
Sarah	Lunne Wintersteller
Harry	Mark McGrath
Susan	Patricia Ben Peterson
Peter	Peter Reardon
Jenny	Karen Culp
David	Michael Licata
Amy	Shauna Hicks
Paul	David Lowenstein
Joanne	Emily Zacharias
Larry	David Brummel
Marta	Andrea Burns Denise Summerford
Kathy	Rachel Warren
April	Dana Lynn Mauro

FAME

	Toronto 11/17/98
Serena Katz	Jennifer Gambatese Erika Shannon Sheri Sanders Erika Weber Maria Eblerline
Miss Greta Bell	Kim Cea Christia Leigh Mantzke Jennifer Simser
Iris Kelly	Nadine Isenegger Jennifer Cohen

THE SOUND OF MUSIC

	Minneapolis 8/30/99
Maria	Meg Tolin
Captain Von Trapp	Richard Chamberlain Robert Stoeckle
Max	Drew Eshelman
Mother Abess	Jeanne Lehman
Rolf	Ben Sheaffer
Liesel	Megan McGinnis

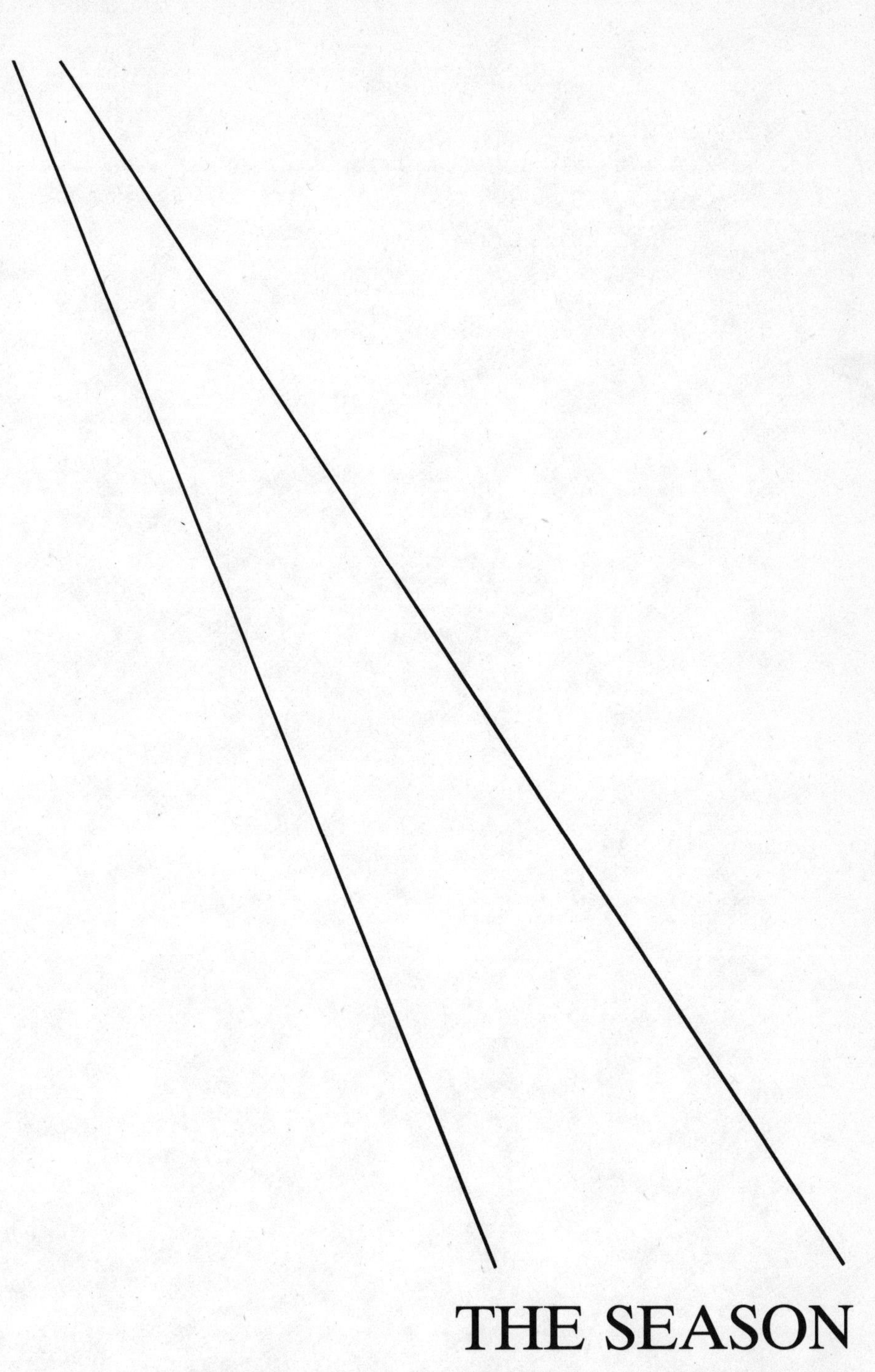

THE SEASON OFF OFF BROADWAY

○
○
○

OFF OFF BROADWAY

○ *By Mel Gussow*
○
○

ON South William Street in Manhattan's financial district, there is a derelict building that was formerly the home of a men's club. Several flights up, in a makeshift room, some 30 unmatched chairs are arranged before a bed and several other pieces of furniture. A play is about to take place, but before it does, the director Andre Gregory and the author and star Wallace Shawn greet theatergoers as they enter. In this unlikely setting, the play, *The Designated Mourner,* was a vintage off-off-Broadway event, redolent of earlier, intrepid days in the experimental theater, when the watchword was risk and when it was often difficult for audiences to find the theater itself. It was also a reminder of the theatrical contributions of the two principal artists. They span several decades of innovative creativity: Gregory with his iconoclastic version of *Alice in Wonderland,* as well as his work with Shawn, including *Our Late Night* and *Vanya on 42nd Street*; Shawn with those plays and also *Aunt Dan and Lemon, The Fever* and *The Hotel Play* (his mini-extravaganza at La Mama).

With fanfare, *The Designated Mourner* had first been staged at London's Royal National Theater, with a cast starring Mike Nichols and Miranda Richardson directed by David Hare. Hare subsequently filmed it with those two actors. Appropriately, the play eventually opened May 13 in New York in these far more unusual circumstances. Shawn, who is an actor as well as a playwright, assumed the title role. His companion, the prizewinning short story writer Deborah Eisenberg, played his wife, and Larry Pine played her father.

An outstanding OOB production, *The Designated Mourner* is a strange and mordant portrait of a culture consuming itself, as lowbrow rises and art declines. In common with the fascistic Aunt Dan in the author's earlier play, Jack (Shawn's character) is insidious. Yet, as played by the author, he becomes oddly ingratiating. *The Designated Mourner* is a darkly comic elegy about the end of civilization and civilized behavior. The play is proof of the continuing vitality—and popularity—of experimental theater. The size of the audience was intentionally limited, which added to the exclusivity and also the intimacy of the performance. The play sold out its brief run and deservedly became one of the more talked-about cultural events in

Mel Gussow
Citations

Pictured here are scenes from sh
cited by Mel Gussow as outstanc
1999–2000 OOB productions.
photo above, Jeff Webster in *Jet*
at The Kitchen; *at left,* Gary Wil
and company in Richard Forem
Bad Boy Nietzsche! at Ontologi
Hysteric Theater; *on opposite p*
Linda Chapman as Alice B. To
and Lola Pashalinski as Gertr
Stein in *Gertrude and Alice: A L*
ness to Loving at The Foundry. A
cited but covered elsewhere in
volume is Wallace Shawn's *The I*
ignated Mourner.

New York this season, earning a special *Best Plays* citation (see its entry and synopsis in the Prizewinning Plays section of this volume).

Off off Broadway continues to be a place of development. Plays begin here and sometimes are transferred to commercial runs on or off Broadway. The Vineyard Theater, which in past seasons presented the New York premieres of two Pulitzer Prizewinners, Edward Albee's *Three Tall Women* and Paula Vogel's *How I Learned to Drive,* this year turned to Becky Mode's *Fully Committed,* a very amusing one-man play about dining out and the snobbism of New York restaurants. Mark Setlock manned the reservation line with elan and arrogance. Deservedly, *Fully Committed* moved into a long off-Broadway run.

So much of the most original OOB work (like *The Designated Mourner)* is of and by itself, plays performed in tiny spaces for a knowing and faithful audience. No pipeline here, and if a theatergoer does not move swiftly, a play will complete a brief engagement and then exist largely in the memory of those fortunate enough to have been there at the time. Such was the case with another oustanding OOB production, *Jet Lag,* at that avant garde center, The Kitchen. The combined handiwork of the MacArthur prizewinning architectural team of Diller + Scofidio (Elizabeth Diller and Ricardo Scofidio) and the Builders Association (a troupe of highly skilled theatrical experimentalists), *Jet Lag* was an adventurous, double-edged journey about time, space and travel. Technologically, it was top of the line, using ad-

vanced methods of video and computer techniques for two stories inspired by actual events. The first half, *Roger Dearborn,* was about a sailor whose solo trip around the world proved to be a fake and who ended as a suicide. The fantasized voyage was witnessed with three-dimensional effects, as the sailor videotaped his progress (or lack of it). The audience was at sea with him, and also back in the studio. With full media manipulation, the adventure became seismic and semiotic.

In the second half, *Doris Schwartz,* a woman responds to a custody battle by taking her grandson on a record-breaking 160 flights between Paris and New York. Helpless travelers, the two live in a no man's land in the air and in airports, brought to stage life (by director Marianne Weems) with stunning visual imagery. The two parts are linked by time travel, in a play that asks, what is time, what is travel? The child, a vagabond incessantly transported, wears two watches on each wrist. The sailor in the first half moves in an incessant whirlpool of doubt and indirection. Who are the pilots of our lives, and what do they know of the passengers? *Jet Lag* was a feast for the eye as well as a stimulant for the mind, a linking of architecture and performance art.

Richard Foreman is the grandmaster of off off Broadway. Unfailingly, he is represented by at least one new play each season, opening his cameo Ontological Hysteric showshop at St. Mark's in the Bowerie and delighting his admiriers with idiosyncratic excursions into his own mind and memory. This season, with *Bad Boy Nietzsche!,* an outstanding OOB production, he tackled a biographical subject. This was a play about Nietzsche, man and philosophy, and also about Foreman's place in that story. It was more nightmare than dream, more vaudeville than dissertation.

As always, Foreman was at the controls as director, designer and author, orchestrating the elements of the play as we watched it, but this time he seemed to allow for more performance invention. In his intense interpretation of the title role, Gary Wilmes was a cross between Gene Wilder and the Flying Karamazovs. For this portrait, Foreman drew from Nietszche and also from himself, lining the stage with ghoulish heads, a flying fish, dead horses and pop-up people. Is this the real Nietszche—or the mock? As the philosopher sat stonefaced and watched the performance, the audience laughed and wondered: Was he actually frightened by watching the beating of a dray horse, and, if so, did that drive him insane? With this piece, Foreman opened the window on a fascinating and apparently maligned figure.

Other celebrated experimentalists appeared with new work, including Martha Clarke with a brief visit of *Vers la Flamme,* her cross-cultural dance-theater interpretation of stories by Anton Chekhov and music by Alexander Scriabin. Curiously, only one word was spoken in this choreographic piece, but the spirit—or, rather, a spirit—of Chekhov emanated, and Christopher O'Riley's piano accompaniment added passionate highlighting. Chekhov and Scriabin were an odd couple, synthesized by the art of Clarke. That venturesome British company Théâtre de Complicité was represented by a dark (and dimly lit) biographical docudrama about Dmitri Shostakovich, as part of a festival of the composer's work. Dramatically, this was a step down from previous Complicité pieces. The music by the Emerson Quartet, which dominated the second half with a Shostakovian dirge, was the most memorable part of the evening.

Robert Wilson was featured in the Lincoln Center festival with *The Days Before: Death, Destruction and Detroit III* inspired by Umberto Eco's novel *The Island of the Day Before.* In many ways the Wilson piece was as difficult and as inapproachable as the original Eco, but the play (more like a skein of Wilson "knee plays") had its striking moments: a chorus of headless men, images on a triptych screen and with excerpts from the novel spoken by the eloquent Fiona Shaw. The annual Mac Wellman season (usually two or three plays a year) was highlighted by *Infrared,* a tantalizing frou-frou about a search for identity; or, as stated, a search for one's "inner theater." Three actresses playing different aspects of a single woman descended a rabbit hole and emerged with surprises. With *Pojagi: Korea,* Ping Chong studied Korea, in the fourth part of his East-West series of historical explorations. Eugenio Barba and his venturesome Odin Teatret returned to La Mama with *Mythos* and other works.

Over the years, the plays of Gertrude Stein have often been a subject of off-off-Broadway productions. With *Gertrude and Alice: A Likeness to Loving,* Lola Pashalinski and Linda Chapman dipped into the lives as well as the works of Stein and Alice B. Toklas, with artful results. Pashalinski, for many years a valuable member of Charles Ludlam's Ridiculous Theatrical Company, had the look and feel of Stein. Her lines rang with rhythmic timbre, as the play alternately revealed the strengths of each character, and as their loyalty to each other eventually overcame waves of envy and jealousy. This was a somewhat rarefied experience, but as superbly directed by Anne Bogart, it was an outstanding OOB production. Credit also to the exquisite design by Myung Hee Cho (and lighting by Mimi Jordan Sherin) which placed the pair in a starkly modern Mondrianesque environment.

Maria Irene Fornes, who through her plays, her directing and her teaching has become an icon of off off Broadway, was the subject of this season's series at the Signature Theater Company, with a sequence of revivals and new plays, including *Mud, Drowning* and *Enter the Night.* Taking a cue from Signature, the Atlantic Theater Company devoted an entire season to one playwright, in this case David Mamet, one of the company's founders. Mamet was represented by revivals of *Sexual Perversity in Chicago, The Duck Variations, The Water Engine, Mr. Happiness* and, most notably, *American Buffalo.* In that last play, presented at the off-Broadway level, William H. Macy rose to the role of Teach, adding his imprint to a character previously played by such eminent actors as Robert Duvall, Al Pacino and Dustin Hoffman.

Under the leadership of Charlotte Moore, the Irish Repertory Theater has become a formidable member of the New York theater, presenting homegrown as well as imported productions, this year with *Our Lady of Sligo* by Sebastian Barry. Justifiably acclaimed in London, especially for the performance of Sinead Cusack in the title role, the play found itself at this small off-off house, intimate enough to enhance Cusack's portrayal of a woman (based on the author's grandmother) trapped in a dreary life partly of her own creation. Although the play is beautifully written, it is not overly dramatic, more of a monologue than a work of conflict, but one that gives additional certification to Barry as a gifted chronicler of his family and its place in Irish times and Irish history. At the Irish Arts Center there was a revival of J.P. Dunleavy's *The Ginger Man* presented by the Dublin Theater Company. English companies visited other stages. A pair of postmodern clowns who call themselves The Right Size (Sean Foley and Hamish McColl) arrived in *Do You Come Here Often?,* a neoBeckettian romp about two men trapped forever in a bathroom. There were a few laughs, but the play was far too long and very silly.

Several talented new American playwrights were represented. Jessica Goldberg's *Refuge,* winner of the 1999 Susan Smith Blackburn Award, was staged upstairs at Playwrights Horizons New Theater Wing. A disturbing look at a desperate situation, the play offered a low-key view of a differently dysfunctional family unit. Despite the various problems besetting the characters, the home becomes a kind of refuge, a sanctuary for siblings abandoned by their parents. Unfortunately, the production was somewhat underdone. The opposite was true of another Goldberg play, *The Hologram Theory,* presented later in the season by the Blue Light Theater Company. In this case, the subject was a drug subculture. A brutal, intriguing story, it was broadly enacted, raucous rather than resonant. Earlier in the season Blue Light offered *The Clearing,* Helen Edmundson's impassioned study of conflict in Ireland in the 1650s.

Daniel Goldfarb, a classmate of Miss Goldberg's in the playwriting program at the Juilliard School, made his debut with *Adam Baum and the Jew Movie,* which was an imaginary trek through problem movies and anti-Semitism in Hollywood in the 1950s. The first act, with a battle between Ron Leibman as a movie mogul and his WASP screen writer, had a few amusing moments, but in the second act the play became irresolute. The film director Neil LaBute moved to the stage with *Bash,* three short plays about violent episodes in American life. They were sharply acted by Calista Flockhart, Paul Rudd and Ron Eldard: cynical slices of life, with a tinge of Mormonism (La Bute is a convert to that religion). Bryan Goluboff's *Shyster* was a touching play about fathers and sons. The father, recently dead, was apparently small minded, but his wife (Phyllis Newman) had a resilient charm, as did Fisher Stevens as her crafty loser of a son.

The MCC, which last season presented the New York premiere of Margaret Edson's prizewinning *Wit,* offered Marsha Norman's *Trudy Blue,* a sympathetic study of illness and marriage on the rocks; and *Yard Gal,* a Rebecca Prichard play about girl gangs in London. In addition to its annual marathon of one-act plays, the Ensemble Studio Theater presented Frank D. Gilroy's *Contact With the Enemy,* a look back with two veterans of World War II, and Arthur Giron's *Moving Bodies,* a biographical play about the Nobel Prizewinning physicist Richard Feynman.

In its 15th season, Primary Stages offered *Barefoot Boy With Shoes On* by Edwin Sanchez; *Elsa Edgar,* a double-edged look at J. Edgar Hoover and gossip columnist Elsa Maxwell (written by Bob Kingdom with Neil Bartlett and starring Kingdom in both roles) presented at the off-Broadway level; and Michael Hollinger's *An Empty Plate in the Cafe du Grand Boeuf,* one of several food-centered works on stage this season. Primary Stages closed the year with a Foote family celebration: *When They Speak of Rita* written by Daisy B. Foote, directed by her father Horton Foote and starring her sister Hallie Foote. This was a tender, evocative play about sad, unfulfilled lives among working class people in a small town in New Hampshire. The play was threaded through with the flavor of Foote: understated and with high drama studiously kept offstage. Under Horton Foote's knowing direction, Hallie Foote created a portrait of a woman confined by her own dreams and unable to take charge of her life.

At New York's repertory companies, the CSC, Jean Cocteau Rep and the Pearl, there was a full measure of classic revivals. One of the more interesting was Harley Granville-Barker's *Waste* at Theater for a New Audience, following a recent London revival. In the smaller scaled American version, the cast was uneven, with the best work coming from Byron Jennings in the central role as a rising politician defeated by a moral outrage from his constituents. Richard Easton and Henry Stram were also noteworthy. Granville-Barker was also represented by *The Voysey Inheritance* at the Mint Theater. The CSC gave center stage to a revival of *Look Back in Anger* and to Mira Sorvino in Pirandello's *Naked.* The Pan Asian Repertory took a second look at John Patrick's *The Teahouse of the August Moon,* casting the Broadway comedy with Asian American actors.

The Drama Dept. unearthed *The Torch-Bearers* by George Kelly. A chestnut about a woeful community theater, it was turned into a delightful backstage comedy, largely through the efforts of Marian Seldes. With great panache and wit, she played Mrs. Pampanelli, the director of the artless company. With her, every flamboyant gesture was a laugh line, and strong support was given by Joan Copeland. Earlier in the season, Miss Seldes joined Donal Donnelly in a revival of *Dear Liar* at the Irish Rep. As always, monologuists abounded: David Cale with *Betwixt,* Holly Hughes with *Preaching to the Perverted,* Bruce Vilanch with *Almost Famous.*

For decades, Joseph Papp was the godfather of off Broadway, introducing new plays as well as producing Shakespeare in and out of Central Park. One of his occasional house favorites was Michael Weller. In *The Heart of Art,* Weller wrote a spoof of Papp, here called Anthony Dick and played with full megalomania by Allan Corduner. The character was whimsical, ferocious and sentimental—and highly theatrical—just like his role model. Unfortunately, the rest of the meandering play and others in the cast were not on this level. When Dick-Papp was on, however, there were self-mocking pronouncements like "Theater will die when I die." The fact is, post-Papp, theater continues to thrive, especially off off Broadway with work like *The Designated Mourner.*

PLAYS PRODUCED OFF OFF BROADWAY

AND ADDITIONAL N.Y.C. PRODUCTIONS

Compiled by Camille Dee

Here is a comprehensive sampling of off-off-Broadway and other experimental or peripheral 1999–2000 productions in New York. There is no definitive "off-off-Broadway" area or qualification. To try to define or regiment it would be untrue to its fluid, exploratory purpose. The listing below of hundreds of works produced by more than 140 OOB groups and others is as inclusive as reliable sources will allow, however, and takes in all leading Manhattan-based, new-play producing, English-language organizations.

The more active and established producing groups are identified in **bold face type**, in alphabetical order, with artistic policies and the names of the managing directors given whenever these are a matter of record. Each group's 1999–2000 schedule, with emphasis on new plays and with revivals of classics usually omitted, is listed with play titles in CAPITAL LETTERS. Often these are works-in-progress with changing scripts, casts and directors, sometimes without an engagement of record (but an opening or early performance date is included when available).

Many of these off-off-Broadway groups have long since outgrown a merely experimental status and are offering programs which are the equal in professionalism and quality (and in some cases the superior) of anything in the New York theater, with special contractual arrangements like the showcase code, letters of agreement (allowing for longer runs and higher admission prices than usual) and, closer to the edge of the commercial theater, a so-called "mini-contract." In the list below, all available data on opening dates, performance numbers and major production and acting credits (almost all for Equity members) is included in the entries of these special-arrangement offerings.

A large selection of lesser-known groups and other shows that made appearances off off Broadway during the season appears under the "Miscellaneous" heading at the end of this listing.

Amas Musical Theater. Dedicated to bringing people of all races, creeds, colors, religious and national origins together through the performing arts. Rosetta LeNoire founder, Donna Trinkoff producing director.

FOUR GUYS NAMED JOSÉ ... AND UNA MUJER NAMED MARIA (16). Conceived by Dolores Prida and David Coffman; written by Dolores Prida. April 21, 2000. Director, Lisa Portes; choreography, Maria Torres; scenery, Mary Houston; lighting, Aaron Spivey; costumes, Tania Bass; musical direction, Steve Sandberg. With Ana Maria Andricain, Henry Gainza, Allen Hidalgo, Ricardo Puente, Caesar Samayoa.

Workshop production:

A VIRTUAL WOMAN (6). Book, Donna Trinkoff and Marsha Sheiness; music, Rick Cummings; lyrics, Luis Santeiro, June Siegal and Greer Woodward. December 14, 1999. Director, Nancy Rhodes.

American Place Theater. Issue-oriented and community-focused plays in their world premieres. Wynn Handman artistic director, Carl Jaynes general manager.

WONDERLAND (57). Written and directed by Julia Dahl. June 14, 1999. Scenery and costumes, Beowulf Boritt; lighting, Ryan E. McMahon. With Kate Jennings Grant, Paul Fitzgerald, Henry Strozier, Christine Marie Burke, James Patrick Stuart, Brad Beyer.

SURFACE TRANSIT (one-woman show) (18). By and with Sarah Jones. November 11, 1999. Director, Gloria Feliciano.

MANCHILD IN THE PROMISED LAND (56+). Adapted from Claude Brown's autobiography by Joseph Edward and Wynn Handman. April 17, 2000. Director, Wynn Handman; scenery and costumes, Beowulf Boritt; lighting, Chad McArver; sound, David D. Wright. With Joseph Edward.

American Theater of Actors. Dedicated to providing a creative atmosphere for new American playwrights, actors and directors. James Jennings artistic director.

Schedule included:

SAY WHEN. By Donald Dewey. June 2, 1999. Director, Christopher Williams. With Jane Brown, Joe Corey, Shanton Granger, Jon Panczyk, Brownwyn Ryan.

A PUBLIC FIGURE. By Alex Menza. June 2, 1999. Director, Barbara Pitcher. With Janine Aloisi, Pete Barker, Andrey Galvani, Kevin Carlsten, John Koprowski, Nick Sakellarios.

BILLY WOULD HAVE BEEN THIRTY TODAY. By Robert Leland Taylor. July 21, 1999. Director, Karen Millard. With Clyde Baldo, Stacee Mandeville, Deborah Moore.

THE RENTAL. By Mark Levine. July 28, 1999. Director, Jeff Catanese. With Pancho Gustein, Jennifer Barnhart.

A QUESTION OF WATER. By Steven Schutzman. August 4, 1999. Director, Jessica Ammirati. With James Crafford, Mark Evans, Stephen Kasprzak, Pete Barker, James McAllister, Leah Owen, Joshua Polenberg, Berkley Priest, Alex Sapot.

COUNTRY BOY BLUES. Written and directed by James Jennings. August 11, 1999. With Jill Alexander, Ken Coughlin, Rick Mowat, Christina Parker.

THAT'S THE WAY IT IS. By Gene Ruffini. October 6, 1999. Director, Matthew B. Baker. With Jan Gelberman, Pete Barker, Bill Greville, Peter Thewes, Lisa Valdez.

EVERYBODY DOES. By Alex Echevarria. October 13, 1999. Director, Rich Cook. With Jill Alexander, Joanne Cregg, Amy Conant, Michael Fegley.

HAPPY TRAILS. Written and directed by James Jennings. October 14, 1999. With Peter Meade, Rachael Lyerla, James McAllister, Karen Trella.

SHAKESPEARE'S WORDS AND SWORDS. Conceived and directed by James Jennings. November 10, 1999. With James Amler, Samantha Coughlin, Daniel Dale, Jenny Deller, Antoinette Doherty, Joseph T. King, Stephen Karver, Rachel Lundgren, Timothy Rowe.

POPPA'S WILL. By Marilyn vos Savant. November 17, 1999. Director, Barbara Pitcher. With Janine Aloisi, Rachel Davey, Stephen De Cordova, Bill Greville, Bobby Gritz, S. Lue McWilliams, Nick Sakellarios.

THE TRIALS OF MARTIN GUERRE. By Frank Cossa. December 1, 1999. Director, Mark Bloom. With Jeff Berry, Gene Burke, Ken Coughlin, Eric Hansen, H. Clark Kee, Ned Levine, Rachael Lyerla, Selma Oshen.

CHRISTMAS AT SANDY'S. Written and directed by Vincent A. Apollo. December 5, 1999. With Wanda O'Connell, Alex Keomurjian, Al Choy, Brian Hyman, Peter Vita, Michael Cohen, Anne Leachman, Seth Greenleaf.

AMAS MUSICAL THEATER—Henry Gainza, Ricardo Puente, Allen Hidalgo and Caesar Samayoa holding AnaMaria Andricain in *Four Guys Named José . . . and Una Mujer Named Maria*

TOGETHER AGAIN. Written and directed by James Jennings. January 12, 2000. With Rachel Lundgren, Timothy Rowe.

THE PRODIGALS. By Stephen Gnojewski. January 12, 2000. Director, Todd Lepre. With Carolyn Seiff, Danielle Stilli, Reginald Veneziano.

THE OUTER-LOPER. Written and directed by James Jennings. January 20, 2000. With James Amler, Jenny Deller, Michael G. Johnson.

SHAKESPEARE IN CONCERT. Conceived and directed by James Jennings. January 26, 2000. With Martin Carey, Bill Greville, Courtney Everett, James Hazard, Jessica Jennings, Rachael Lyerla, Gregory Pekar, Melanie McCarthy, Marie Thomas.

BURIED IN THE STARS. Written and directed by James Jennings. February 9, 2000. With Bill Greville, Tony Lamm Peter Meade, Rebecca Pelletier, Brian Townes.

THE GOD-SEND. By Erik Slagle. March 1, 2000. Director, Joe Pellegrino. With Tony Lamm, Korey J. Knecht, Rebakah Scoffin, Fred Pellegrino.

SAINTS IN RETROGRADE. By Alan Arnold. March 29, 2000. Director, Christopher L. Bellis. With Rachael Lyerla, Sean Patterson, Brian Townes.

JUDITH'S STORY. By Betty Jane Isquith. April 7, 2000. Director, Barbara Pitcher. With Michael Dale, Jacqueline Bowman, Jennifer Anderson, Epiphany Alexander, Jill Alexander, Samantha Coughlin, Bill Greville, Karen Landis, Rachel Lundgren, Deborah Moore, Christopher Sutherland, Julie Wallach.

ASHES TO ASHES. Written and directed by James Jennings. April 12, 2000. With John Snyder, Scott Tatman.

BEWITCHED. By Colleen Neuman. April 26, 2000. Director, Matthew B. Baker. With Jerry Berk, Florence Cohen, Selma Oshen.

ALONG QUEENS BOULEVARD. By Meny Beriro. May 3, 2000. Director, Gregory Pekar. With Pete Barker, Lyndi Prettyman, John Snyder, Wendell Ward.

Atlantic Theater Company. Produces new plays or reinterpretations of classics that speak to audiences in a contemporary voice on issues reflecting today's society. Neil Pepe artistic director, Hilary Hinckle managing director.

THE WATER ENGINE and MR. HAPPINESS (one-act plays) (33). By David Mamet. October 20, 1999. Director, Karen Kohlhaas; scenery, Walt Spangler; lighting, Robert Perry; costumes, Rick Gradone; sound, Andrew Keister. With Bob Balaban, Steven Goldstein, Mary McCann, Peter Jacobson, Jordan Lage, Maryann Urbano, Peter Maloney, Carl J. Matusovich, Josh Stamberg, Kelly Maurer, Maggie Kiley, Jody Lambert.

SEXUAL PERVERSITY IN CHICAGO and THE DUCK VARIATIONS (26). By David Mamet. January 12, 2000. Director, Hilary Hinckle; scenery, Alexander Dodge; lighting, Robert Perry; costumes, Rick Gradone. With John Tormey, Peter Maloney, Josh Hamilton, Clark Gregg, Kate Blumberg, Kristin Reddick.

AMERICAN BUFFALO (78). By David Mamet. March 16, 2000. See its entry in the Plays Produced off Broadway section of this volume.

Blue Light Theater Company. Produces a wide range of plays and strives to give young working actors the opportunity to grow by working with established theater artists. Greg Naughton actor-manager, Mandy Greenfield producing manager, Peter Manning artistic director.

THE CLEARING (44). By Helen Edmundson. October 7, 1999. Director, Tracy Brigden; scenery, Jeff Cowie; lighting, Howell Binkley; costumes, Susan Hilferty; music and sound, John Gromada. With Patricia Dunnock, Simon Brooking, Joseph Costa, Michael Countryman, Alyssa Bresnahan, Sam Catlin, Steve Juergens.

ADAM BAUM AND THE JEW MOVIE (29). By Daniel Goldfarb. December 12, 1999. Director, Brian Kulick; scenery, Walt Spangler; lighting, Kevin Adams; costumes, Elizabeth Hope Clancy; sound, Aural Fixation. With Ron Leibman, Adam Lamberg, Christopher Evan Welch.

THE HOLOGRAM THEORY (25). By Jessica Goldberg. March 27, 2000. Director, Ruben Polendo; scenery, Scott Spahr, Ryan M. Mueller; lighting, Ryan M. Mueller; costumes, Carol Bailey; music and sound, Ray Sweeten. With Daniel Bess, T.R. Knight, Joie Susannah Lee, Chris Messina, Kellie Overbey, Michael Alexis Palmer, Jennifer Rau, Elizabeth Reaser, Corey Stoll, Bill Torres.

HOTEL UNIVERSE (20). By Philip Barry. April 27, 2000. Director, Darko Tresnjak; scenery, David P. Gordon; lighting, Christopher J. Landy; costumes, Linda Cho; sound, David A. Gilman. With Arija Bareikis, Cheryl Lynn Bowers, Liam Craig, Richard Easton, Keira Naughton, Gregor Paslawski, Kali Rocha, Armand Schultz, Adam Stein.

Brooklyn Academy of Music Next Wave Festival. Since 1981, this annual three-month festival has presented over 200 events, including more than 50 world premieres. Featuring leading international artists, it is one of the world's largest festivals of contemporary performing arts. Joseph V. Melillo executive producer.

Schedule included:

THE WHITEHEADED BOY (5). By Lennox Robinson, adapted by Barabbas . . . the Company. October 6, 1999. Director, Gerard Stembridge; production design, Sean Hillen; lighting, Paul Keogan; costumes, Kathy Kavanagh. With Raymond Keane, Mikel Murfi, Veronica Coburn, Louis Lovett.

LIFE IS A DREAM (6). By Pedro Calderon de la Barca, translated by John Clifford. October 12, 1999. Director, Calixto Bieito; choreography, Malcolm Shields; scenery, Calixto Bieito and Carles Pujol; lighting, Xavier Clot; costumes, Merce Paloma; music, Miguel Poveda and José Miguel Cerro. With Olwen Fouere, Sylvester McCoy, George Anton, Sylvester Morand, Nicholas Bailey, Hilary Maclean, Jeffrey Kissoon, Joseph Greig, Simon Turner, José Miguel Cerro, Manuel Goméz (Royal Lyceum Theater Company). Co-produced by the Edinburgh International Festival and the Barbican Center.

GEOMETRY OF MIRACLES (6). Written and directed by Robert Lepage. November 30, 1999. Scenery, Carl Fillion; lighting, Eric Fauque; costumes, Marie-Chantale Vaillancourt; image design, Jacques Collin and Carl Fillion. With Ex Machina (Tea Alagic, Daniuel Bélanger, Jean-Francois Blanchard, Marie Brassard, Denis Gaudreault, Tony Guilfoyle, Catherine Martin, Kevin McCoy, Rick Miller, Thaddeus Phillips, Rodrigue Proteau).

LOVE SONGS (4). Conceived, written and choreographed by David Rousséve/REALITY. December 8, 1999. Scenery and puppets, Debby Lee Cohen; lighting, Beverly Emmons; costumes, Carol Ann Pelletier; sound, David Meshter. With REALITY (David Rousséve, Ilaan Egeland, Terry Hollis, Kyle Sheldon, Charmaine Warren, Steven Washington, Julie Tolentino Wood).

Classic Stage Company. Reinventing and revitalizing the classics for contemporary audiences. Barry Edelstein artistic director, Beth Emelson producing director.

LOOK BACK IN ANGER (42). By John Osborne. October 17, 1999. Director, Jo Bonney; scenery, Narelle Sissons; lighting, James Vermeulen; costumes, Kaye Voyce; sound, Ken Travis. With Reg Rogers, James Joseph O'Neill, Enid Graham, Angelina Phillips, Michael Lombard.

HURRICANE (16). By Erin Cressida Wilson. December 11, 1999. Director, Barry Edelstein; scenery, Rachel Nemec; lighting, Russell H. Champa; costumes, Linda Cho; sound, Robert Kaplowitz. With Vivienne Benesch, Ralph Buckley, Marissa Chibas, Marissa Copeland, Paula Garces, Erica Leerhsen, John Ortiz, Adina Porter, Phyllis Somerville, Jenna Stern. Co-produced by Naked Angels.

THE ALCHEMIST (39). By Ben Jonson. February 17, 2000. Director, Barry Edelstein; scenery, Adrianne Lobel; lighting, Stephen Strawbridge; costumes, Michael Krass; sound, Robert Kaplowitz. With Dan Castellaneta, Jeremy Shamos, Johann Carlo, Michael Showalter, Hillel Meltzer, Lee Sellars, Matthew Saldívar, Umit Celebi, Steve Rattazzi, Reuben Jackson, Yaani King, Buzz Bovshow.

NAKED (34). By Luigi Pirandello, adapted by Nicholas Wright. April 9, 2000. Director, John Rando; scenery, Derek McLane; lighting, Russell H. Champa; costumes, Ilona Somogyi; sound, David Van Tieghem. With Mira Sorvino, Daniel Benzali, Rebecca Schull, Bray Poor, Peter Rini, Tina Bruno, Michel R. Gill.

Drama Dept. A collective of actors, directors, designers, stage managers, writers and producers who collaborate to create new works and revive neglected classics. Douglas Carter Beane artistic director, Michael S. Rosenberg managing director.

THE COUNTRY CLUB (92). By Douglas Carter Beane. September 29, 1999. Director, Christopher Ashley; scenery, James M. Youmans; lighting, Frances Aronson; costumes, Jonathan Bixby, Gregory A. Gale; sound, Laura Grace Brown. With Cynthia Nixon, Amy Hohn, Amy Sedaris, Peter Benson, Tom Everett Scott, Frederick Weller, Callie Thorne.

THE TORCH-BEARERS (26). By George Kelly. February 23, 2000. Director, Dylan Baker; scenery, Michael Vaughn Sims; lighting, Mark Stanley; costumes, Jonathan Bixby, Gregory A. Gale; sound, Robert Murphy. With David Garrison, Faith Prince, Marian Seldes, Judith Blazer, Joan Copeland, Paul Mullins, Don Mayo, Albert Macklin.

Ensemble Studio Theater. Membership organization of playwrights, actors, directors and designers dedicated to supporting individual theater artists and developing new works for the stage. Over 200 projects each season, ranging from readings to fully-mounted productions. Curt Dempster artistic director.

OCTOBERFEST 1999. Festival of over 80 new works by members. October 1–31, 1999.

CONTACT WITH THE ENEMY (16). By Frank D. Gilroy. November 15, 1999. Director, Chris Smith; scenery, Kert Lundell; lighting, Michael Lincoln; costumes, Julie Doyle; sound, Beatrice Terry. With Paul Bartholomew, Nesbitt Blaisdell, Kathryn Gayner, Cynthia Hayden, Christopher Murney.

THICKER THAN WATER: HEIGHTS by Amy Fox, directed by Jimmy Bohr; BABY BLUE by S. Vasanti Saxena, directed by Rebecca VerNooy; TOOTH by Crystal Skillman, directed by Abigail Zealey Bess; HEARTBREAK OF THE LAST HANDWRITING by Jeremy Soule, directed by Tomi Tsunoda (one-act plays) (13). January 23, 2000. Scenery, Michael Allen; lighting, Shawn Gallagher; costumes, Kimberly Matela; sound, Dean Gray. With Peter Rini, Sally Wheeler, Andersen Gabrych, Anne Newhall, Amy Staats, Marc Romeo, Michael Ryan Segal, Frank Whaley, Francie Swift, Amy Love, Jason O'Leary.

GOING TO THE RIVER (second annual festival of plays by African-American women): THE SHANEEQUA CHRONICLES by Stephanie Berry; LOST CREEK TOWNSHIP by Charlotte A.

Gibson; NOTES OF NEGRO NEUROTIC by Nancy Giles; TALKING BONES by Shay Youngblood; FIVE ROOMS OF FURNITURE by Dhana-Marie Branton. February 12–20, 2000.

DISTRICT OF COLUMBIA (16). By Michael Louis Wells. March 6, 2000. Director, Jamie Richards; scenery, Bruce Goodrich; lighting, Greg MacPherson; costumes, Julie Doyle; sound, Robert Gould. With Joseph Lyle Taylor, Thomas Lyons, Miranda Black, Brad Bellamy, Chris Wight, Geneva Carr, Janet Zarish.

MOVING BODIES (17). By Arthur Giron. April 10, 2000. Director, Chris Smith; scenery, Kert Lundell; lighting, Greg MacPherson; costumes, Chris Peterson; sound, Robert Gould. With Chris Ceraso, William Wise, Polly Adams, Amy Love, Kurt Sinnamon, Julie Leeds, Peter Hermann, Tracy Sallows, Robert Boardman, David Teschendorf. (Part of the First Light Festival of new dramatic works exploring the worlds of science and technology.)

MARATHON 2000 (festival of new one-act plays). LITTLE AIRPLANES OF THE HEART by Steve Feffer, directed by Eliza Beckwith; LIGHT YEARS by Billy Aronson, directed by Jamie Richards; TWENTY-FOUR YEARS by Leslie Ayvazian, directed by Curt Dempster; MADMEN by Romulus Linney, directed by Eileen Myers; LIVES OF THE SAINTS by David Ives, directed by John Rando; THE 17TH OF JUNE by Edward Allan Baker, directed by Jamie Richards; ACCIDENT by Peter Maloney, directed by Beatrice Terry; THE ROTHKO ROOM by Stuart Spencer, directed by John Ruocco; BIRTH MARKS by Leslie Caputo, directed by Abigail Zealey Bess; CANNIBALS by Heather Dundas, directed by India Cooper; THE FINAL INTERROGATION OF CEAUSESCU'S DOG by Warren Leight, directed by Jack Hofsiss; PROOF by Jeff Reich, directed by Kevin Confoy; ALIEN BOY by Will Scheffer, directed by Mark Roberts. May 3-June 11, 2000.

INTAR. Mission is to identify, develop and present the talents of gifted Hispanic American theater artists and multicultural visual artists. Max Ferra artistic director.

NUYORICAN STORIES: CULTURE CLASH IN THE CITY (25). By and with Culture Clash (Richard Montoya, Ric Salinas, Herbert Siguenza). September 22, 1999. Direction, Max Ferra and Culture Clash; scenery, Van Santvoord; lighting, Philip Widmer; costumes, Donna Zakowska; sound, Johnna Doty.

NewWorks Lab Series 2000, 3 performances each

I NEVER EVEN SEEN MY FATHER and ZORAIDA by Nicholasa Mohr, directed by José Garcia; FOOL'S JOURNEY by Mariana Carreno, directed by Angel David; PILGRIM'S PASSION by Henry Guzman, directed by Marissa Bejar; SEBASTIAN by Alejandro Morales, directed by Eduardo Vega. March 10-April 2, 2000.

NIGHT OF THE ASSASSINS (24). By Jose Triana. June 7, 2000. Directed by Max Ferra; scenery, Van Santvoord; lighting, Chris Dallos; costumes, Mimi O'Donnell; sound, Johnna Doty. With Vanessa Aspillaga, Michael John Garces, Sol Miranda.

Irish Repertory Theater. Aims to bring works by Irish and Irish American masters and contemporary playwrights to a wider audience and to develop new works focusing on a wide range of cultural experiences. Charlotte Moore artistic director, Ciaran O'Reilly producing director.

DEAR LIAR (46). By Jerome Kilty. July 22, 1999. Director, Charlotte Moore; scenery, David Raphel; lighting, Gregory Cohen; costumes, David Toser; sound, Murmod, Inc. With Marian Seldes, Donal Donnelly.

INVASIONS AND LEGACIES (20). By Tommy Makem. September 27, 1999. Director, Charlotte Moore; scenery, Klara Zieglerova; lighting, Jason A. Cina. With Tommy Makem, Ron D'Addario, Bob Mastro.

ECLIPSED (56). By Patricia Burke Brogan. November 7, 1999. Director, Charlotte Moore; scenery, Klara Zieglerova; lighting, Kirk Bookman; costumes, Linda Fisher. With Terry Donnelly, Rosemary Fine, Jacqueline Kealy, Aedin Moloney, Heather O'Neill, Amy Redmond, Erika Rolfsrud, Fiona Walsh.

THE IRISH . . . AND HOW THEY GOT THAT WAY. By Frank McCourt. Reopened December 28, 1999 for 28 performances.

THE COUNTRY BOY (42). By John Murphy. March 1, 2000. Director, Charlotte Moore; scenery, David Raphel; lighting, Gregory Cohen; costumes, David Toser. With Dara Coleman, Valorie Hubbard, Aideen O'Kelly, Heather O'Neill, Ciaran O'Reilly, James A. Stephens.

OUR LADY OF SLIGO (83). By Sebastian Barry. April 20, 2000. Director, Max Stafford-Clark; scenery and costumes, Julian McGowan; lighting, Johanna Town; sound, Paul Arditti; music, Corin Buckeridge. With Sinead Cusack, Andrea Irvine, Jarlath Conroy, Melinda Page Hamilton, Sinead Colreavy, Tom Lacy.

Jewish Repertory Theater. Presents plays in English relating to the Jewish experience. Ran Avni artistic director.

THE JAZZ SINGER (31). Adapted and directed by Richard Sabellico, based on Samson Raphaelson's play. October 31, 1999. Choreography, Kirby Ward; scenery, Thomas M. Beall; lighting, Richard Latta; costumes, John Russell; sound, Nevin D. Steinberg; musical direction, Christopher McGovern. With Ric Ryder, Evalyn Baron, Beth Leavel, James Murtaugh, Jimmy Peters, Reuben Schafer, Seth Swoboda, Raymond Thorne.

HOME OF THE BRAVE (24). By Arthur Laurents. December 12, 1999. Director, Richard Sabellico; scenery, Richard Ellis; lighting, Richard Latta; costumes, Gail Baldoni; sound, Joshua Bender. With Jeff Talbott, Mark Deklin, C.J. Wilson, Robert Sella, Stephen Kunken, Dylan Chalfy.

LOVE IN A THIRSTY LAND (24). By Alan Glass. February 27, 2000. Director, Robert Kalfin; scenery, Mark Nayden; lighting, Chris Dallos; costumes, Gail Cooper-Hecht; music and sound, Margaret Pine. With David Hess, Lee Beltzer, David Julian Hirsh, Susan May Pratt, Suzanne Toren.

ABIE'S ISLAND ROSE (22). Book, Ron Sproat; music and direction, Doug Katsaros; lyrics, Richard Engquist and Frank Evans. May 7, 2000. Choreography, Haila Strauss; scenery, James Morgan; lighting, Mary Jo Dondlinger; costumes, Daryl Stone; sound, Randy Hansen. With Heather Mac Rae, Keith Lee Grant, Steven Rosen, Carla Woods.

The Joseph Papp Public Theater/New York Shakespeare Festival. Schedule of special projects, in addition to its regular off-Broadway productions. George C. Wolfe producer, Rosemarie Tichler artistic producer, Mark Litvin managing director, Michael Hurst general manager, Margaret M. Lioi senior director of external affairs.

Joe's Pub. Schedule included:

UTE LEMPER (cabaret) (4). June 3, 1999. Reopened October 4, 1999.

ANN MAGNUSON (performance art) (4). June 18, 1999.

FAITH PRINCE (cabaret) (2). July 15, 1999.

HAZELLE: TO THE TOP, TOP, TOP! (one-woman show) (6). By and with Hazelle Goodman. August 18, 1999.

LEAP OF FAITH (cabaret) (3). September 13, 1999. With Faith Prince. Reopened January 7, 2000.

PATTI LuPONE (cabaret) (1). September 26, 1999.

BOOGIE-RICAN (one-woman show) (1). By and with Caridad de la Luz. October 2, 1999.

WHAT EVER: AN AMERICAN ODYSSEY IN EIGHT ACTS (one-woman show) (4). By and with Heather Woodbury. October 21, 1999.

DAUGHTER OF HORROR (one-woman show) (5). By and with Ann Magnuson. October 28, 1999.

WHO YOU CALLIN' A HO, HO, HO—A VERY LEA CHRISTMAS (9). By Lea Delaria. December 3, 1999. With Lea Delaria, Jesse Tyler Ferguson, Justynn Daniels.

ALL GIRL BAND: THE SONGS OF DAVID ZIPPEL (3). January 17, 2000. With Randy Graff, Debbie Gravitte, Adriane Lenox.

I REMEMBER MAPA (one-man show) (1). By and with Alec Mapa. January 13, 2000.

CLASSIC STAGE COMPANY—Daniel Benzali and Mira Sorvino in a new version of Pirandello's *Naked* by Nicholas Wright

BEYOND THE CRADLE: THE MUSIC OF MARC BLITZSTEIN (3). Conceived by Ted Sperling. February 7, 2000. With Brooks Ashmanskas, Victoria Clark, Lauren Flanigan, Malcolm Gets.

A TRIBUTE TO JEROME MOROSS (3). February 28, 2000. Musical director, Eric Stern. With Philip Chaffin, Jenny Giering, Jessica Molasky, Richard Muenz, Alice Ripley.

THE REAL EMOTIONAL GIRL: MELISSA ERRICO SINGS RANDY NEWMAN (3). May 8, 2000. Musical director, Jason Robert Brown.

AIRING LAUNDRY: PAMELA SNEED (performance art). May 31, 2000.

NEW WORK NOW! (festival of staged readings): ISAAC by David Schulner; A.M. SUNDAY by Jerome Hairston; STRANGE GRACE by Jane Shepard; THE DOLL PLAYS by Alva Rogers; BREATH, BOOM by Kia Corthron; MY TIRED ASS PONTIFICATING SLAPSTICK FUNK by Euijoon Kim; 36 VIEWS by Naomi Iizuka; ST. PETERSBURG by Edward Bok Lee; WAVE by Sung Rno; RICE BOY by Sunil Kuruvilla; FORBIDDEN CITY BLUES by Alexander Woo; HIT by Alice Tuan; I DON'T KNOW WHY THAT CAGED BIRD WON'T SHUT UP by Tracey Scott Wilson; WHEN IT'S COCKTAIL TIME IN CUBA by Rogelio Martinez; CYCLONE by Ron Fitzgerald; SUMMERTIME by Charles L. Mee; HORTENSIA AND THE MUSEUM OF DREAMS by Nilo Cruz; FURIOUS BLOOD by Kelly Stuart. April 10–30, 2000.

PERFORMANCE NOW! (performance art festival). Schedule included: STAR LUST by and with Joey Arias and Sherry Vine; MAKING TRACKS book and lyrics by Welly Yang and Brian Yorkey, music by Woody Pak; HEADING EAST book, music and lyrics by Leon Ko; NIGHT VISION (opera) by Fred Ho and Ruth Margraff; QUEEN ESTHER: UNEMPLOYED SUPERSTAR by and with Queen Esther, directed by Jeff Cohen. April 14–30, 2000.

La Mama (a.k.a. LaMama) Experimental Theater Club (ETC). A busy workshop for experimental theater of all kinds. Ellen Stewart founder and director.

Schedule included:

TALES FROM A TRAVELER. By and with Erwin Kokkelkoren. June 17, 1999. Director, Bert Oele; scenery and costumes, Les Enfants Terribles; lighting, Bas Standaar.

END OF THE ROPE. By George R. Lupu. September 23, 1999. Director, Steve Pearson; choreography, Robert Davidson. With Thea Mercouffer, Michael Lopez, Mika Burns, Ebbe Ebbesen (The Seattle Company).

ROMAN RUINS. By Philippe Minyana, translated and directed by Philomena Nowlin. September 23, 1999.

MYTHOS text based on poems by Henrik Nordbrandt; ODE TO PROGRESS; DONA MUSICA'S BUTTERFLIES text, Julia Varley; ITSI BITSI text, Iben Nagel Rasmussen and Eugenio Barba; JUDITH text, Roberta Carreri and Eugenio Barba; WHITE AS JASMINE; THE ECHO OF SILENCE; TRACES IN THE SNOW, THE DEAD BROTHER, THE PATHS OF THOUGHTS; THE CASTLE OF HOLSTEBRO II (in repertory) by and with Odin Teatret of Denmark. October 14–31, 1999. Director, Eugenio Barba. With Kai Bredholt, Roberta Carreri, Jan Ferslev, Tage Larsen, Else Marie Laukvik, Iben Nagel Rasmussen, Julia Varley, Torgeir Wethal, Frans Winther.

UNDERCURRENT INCORPORATED (12). By Jim Neu. October 28, 1999. Director, Keith McDermott; scenery, David Fritz; lighting, Carol Mullins; costumes, Gabriel Berry; music, Harry Mann. With Black-Eyed Susan, Bill Rice, Mary Shultz, Clio Young, Jim Neu, Harry Mann.

PLAGUES FOR OUR TIME (opera). Text, Eve Merriam; music, lyrics and direction, Tom O'Horgan. November 6, 1999.

THE BEARD. By Michael McClure. November 18, 1999. Director, Lawrence Sacharow.

MURDER IN MIND. By Xavier Durringer. December 2, 1999. See its entry under Ubu Repertory Theater in this section.

THE FILAMENT CYCLE. By Tea Alagic and Thaddeus Phillips. December 9, 1999.

SKY PLOTS: A CHAOS OF RITUALS (3). Conceived and directed by The Ransom Corp. (Geoff and Taylor Kaye, Kathi von Koerber, Victor Attar and Geula Attar). December 17, 1999.

DARIO D'AMBROSI'S PATHOLOGIC THEATER FESTIVAL. (Retrospective of Dario D'Ambrosi's works, including TUTTI NON CI SONNO, FRUSTRA-AZIONI, THE PRINCE OF MADNESS, DAYS OF ANTONIO, BESTIALITY, CAFÉ LA MAMA and TO FLY.) December 28, 1999-January 16, 2000.

OPERA BURLESQUE (festival of opera parodies). By Desi Vasquez and John Kolody. January 20–23, 2000.

THE MEMOIRS OF GLÜCKEL OF HAMELN. Conceived by Jenny Romaine, Adrienne Cooper and Frank London; written by Jenny Romaine, Adrienne Cooper and Deborah Artman. January 20, 2000. Director, Jenny Romaine; scenery, Jenny Romaine, Alessandra Nichols, Clare Dolan, Mark Sussman; lighting, Mark Sussman; puppets, Clare Dolan, Meredith Holch; music and lyrics, Frank London, Adrienne Cooper; musical direction, Frank London. With Trudi Cohen, Adrienne Cooper, Ralph Denzer, Clare Dolan, Frank London, Roberto Rossi, Jenny Romaine. Co-produced by Great Small Works.

THE SADNESS OF OTHERS. By Mike Taylor. January 27, 2000.

THE FLAME AT THE BOTTOM OF THE SEA by Dah Teatar of Belgrade, Serbia; THE PASSION ACCORDING TO G.H. by North American Cultural Laboratory. February 7, 2000.

MR. BALDWIN GOES TO HEAVEN. By Damon Wright. February 17, 2000. Director, Terrell Robinson; scenery, Mark Tambella; lighting, Daniel Ordower; costumes, John McKinnon; sound, Jacob Burckhardt. With Kenyon Farrow, Spencer Aste.

POJAGI: KOREA (Part 4 of the East/West Quartet). Written and directed by Ping Chong. February 24, 2000. Scenery, Watoku Ueno; lighting, Darren McCroom; costumes, Stefani Mar; sound, Brian Hallas. With Esther K. Chae, Shin Young Lee.

ROOMS. Written and directed by Elia Schneider. March 10, 2000. Scenery and costumes, Maitena de Elguezábal; lighting, Jose Novoa; music, Juan Carlos Nunez. With Dad Dáger, Ricarda Klingenhöfer, Bettina Grand.

BONEJESTERS. By Nicholas Trotter and David Leicht. March 9, 2000.

CIRCLE. By and with Yara Arts Group. March 24, 2000. Director, Virlana Tkacz.

JOHANNES DOKCHTOR FAUST (A PETRIFYING PUPPET KOMEDYE). March 23, 2000. Director, Vit Horejs. With James Bowen, Michael Greenlake, Vit Horejs, Theresa Linnihan, Molly Parker. Co-produced by Czechoslovak-American Marionette Theater and GOH Productions.

ULTRA-LIGHT. By and with the Fabulous Giggin' Brothers. April 13, 2000.

THE VALLEY OF IAO (performance art). By and with Lee Nagrin. April 28, 2000.

WHAT HAPPENED TO ME. By Harold Dean James. May 4, 2000.

LOUISE BOURGEOIS: I DO, I UNDO, I REDO. By and with Denise Stoklos, based on Louise Bourgeois writings and life. May 18, 2000. Scenery, Louise Bourgeois.

DREAMBOATS AND SLEEPYHEADS. By Charles Allcroft. May 25, 2000. Scenery, Mark Tambella. With Bill Rice, Jim Neu, Clio Young, Agosto Machado, Lavinia Coop, Ron Jones, Black-Eyed Susan, Nicky Paraiso, Little Annie, Glenn Santiago, Chris Maresca, Terrell Robinson, Joe Munley, Jenneth Webster.

HIGH. By and with Slant (Richard Ebihara, Wayland Quintero, Perry Yung). June 8, 2000.

The Club

I-SELF. By and with Anthony Bellov. October 14, 1999.

ONE MUST DO WHAT ONE MUST DO. By Christopher Tanner and Lance Cruce. November 4, 1999. With Christopher Tanner.

SIN, AN ORIGINAL MUSICAL. Book and lyrics, Ami Goodheart; music Richard Applegate. December 9, 1999.

LADY/SPEAK/EASY. Written and directed by Sean Power. January 27, 2000. Scenery, Douglas Davis; lighting, Matthew O'Neill; costumes, Al Ribaya; musical direction, Michael Johnson. With Bemshi Shearer, Abiola Wendy Abrams, Patrick Michael Buckley, Ron L. Cox, Michael Johnson, Kwana Martinez, Scott McNeil, Alex Parisien, Charles Parnell, David Peterson, Shawn Seymour, Malcolm Smith.

SALAD OF THE BAD CAFÉ. Adapted from Carson McCullers's novel *Ballad of the Sad Café* and performed by Split Britches (Lois Weaver, Peggy Shaw) and Stacy Mikishi. February 17, 2000. Choreography, Stormy Brandenberger.

SHIKU HAKKU: THE EIGHT SUFFERINGS. By Shikeko Suga and Indalo Artists. March 9, 2000.

METAMORPHOSIS. Adapted from Franz Kafka's story, *The Metamorphosis,* by George Bennett and Cati Blanche. March 23, 2000. Director, Jorji Knickrem. With H.R. Britton, Stacy Chbosky, Marie Bridget Dundon, Jim Hazzard, Reyna Kahan.

BRACE YOURSELF. By Ray Dobbins. April 13, 2000. Director, Brenda Bergman. With Chris Kapp, Mark Baker, Nate Mooney, Michael Arian.

THE DROWNING PAGES. By Edgar Oliver. May 4, 2000. Director, Michael Laurence. With Rebecca Wisocky, Mary Lou Wittmer, Marc Palmeri.

THE WOUND. Adapted from Paul Willems's novel and directed by David Willinger. May 18, 2000. Scenery and costumes, Mary Myers; lighting, Aaron Meadow.

DOO WOP DRACULA. Book, lyrics, music and direction by William Electric Black. June 8, 2000. Choreography, Sandra Kaufmann; scenery, Shana Lahr; lighting, Daniel Ordower; costumes, David Brockman.

Lincoln Center Festival. An annual international summer arts festival offering classic and contemporary works. Nigel Redden festival director.

Schedule included:

BRIAN FRIEL FESTIVAL. *Uncle Vanya* by Anton Chekhov, adapted by Brian Friel; *The Freedom of the City* by Brian Friel; *Aristocrats* by Brian Friel; see their entries in the Plays Produced off Broadway section of this volume.

THE PEONY PAVILION (opera in six episodes). By Tan Xianzu; music notation, Ye Tang; Pingtan adaptation, Rao Yichen. July 7, 1999. Director, Chen Shi-Zheng; scenery, Huang Hai Wei; lighting, Yi Li Ming; costumes, Cheng Shu Yi; musical direction, Zhou Ming. With Qian Yi, Wen Yu Hang, Wen Fu Lin, Lin Sen, Shan Jing, Song Yang, Yu Qing Wang, Jia Yong Hong, Liu Ming.

THE DAYS BEFORE: DEATH, DESTRUCTION AND DETROIT III (5). Conceived, designed and directed by Robert Wilson; text from *The Island of the Day Before* by Umberto Eco and *Tone Poems* by Christopher Knowles; music, Ryuichi Sakamoto July 7, 1999. Choreography, Suzushi Hanayagi; scenery and images, Peter Bottazzi; lighting, A.J. Weissbard; costumes, Jacques Reynaud; sound, Peter Cerone. With Fiona Shaw, Jeremy Geidt, Tony Randall, Isabella Rossellini, Semiha Berksoy, Dadon Dawadolma, Arthur Beatty, Elettra Bottazzi, Francis Bouc, Fritzi Haberlandt, Meg Harper, Makram Handan, Marianna Kavalieratos, Christopher Knowles, Restu Kusumaningrum, Keith McDermott, Brian Nishii, Fernando Nogueira, Maria Pessino, Arco Renz, Elisabetta Rosso, Ines Somellera, Carlos Soto, Tassy Thompson.

Mabou Mines. Theater collective whose work is a synthesis of motivational acting, narrative acting and mixed-media performance. Collective artistic leadership. Frederick Neumann, Terry O'Reilly, Ruth Maleczech, Lee Breuer artistic directors.

LAS HORAS DE BELEN – A BOOK OF HOURS. Poems and lyrics by Catherine Sasanov, translated by Luz Aurora Pimentel and Alberto Blanco. Reopened March 9, 2000 for 16 performances.

ANIMAL MAGNETISM (12). By Terry O'Reilly. March 29, 2000. Director, Lee Breuer; production design, Manuel Lutgenhorst; lighting, Manuel Lutgenhorst and David Overcamp; animal costumes, Susan Tsu; animation, Judson Wright; music, Eve Beglarian; lyrics, Robin Lorentz, Terry O'Reilly, J. Daniel Stanley, Lee Breuer. With Clove Galilee, Sean Runette, Robin Lorentz, Bohdan Hilash, Jay Peck.

MCC Theater. Dedicated to the promotion of emerging writers, actors, directors and theatrical designers. Robert LuPone and Bernard Telsey artistic directors, William Cantler associate artistic director.

TRUDY BLUE (27). By Marsha Norman. December 2, 1999. Director, Michael Sexton; scenery, Mark Wendland; lighting, James Vermeulen; costumes, David Zinn; music and sound, David Van Tieghem. With Polly Draper, Sarah Knowlton, John Dossett, Aasif Mandvi, Julia McIlvaine, Pamela Isaacs, Judith Roberts.

SUEÑO (18). By José Rivera. March 1, 2000. Director, Lisa Peterson; scenery, Riccardo Hernandez; lighting, Christopher Akerlind; costumes, Anita Yavich; original music, Aaron Gilmartin; music and sound, Fabian Obispo. With Geno Silva, Yusef Bulos, Ken Parker, Michi Barall, David Greenspan, John Ortiz, James Urbaniak, Rebecca Wisocky, Sam Wellington, Lorenzo Gregorio.

YARD GAL (26). By Rebecca Prichard. April 26, 2000. Director, Gemma Bodinetz; scenery and costumes, Es Devlin; lighting, Frances Aronson; sound, Bruce Ellman. With Sharon Duncan-Brewster, Amelia Lowdell.

Medicine Show. Dedicated to offering creative alternatives to conventional theater by creating and presenting works that experiment with language, music, movement, form and ideas and meld the strengths of theatrical tradition with innovation. Barbara Vann, James Barbosa artistic directors.

UBU TAKES MANHATTAN (16). Text, Alfred Jarry, translated and directed by Barbara Vann; additional texts, Howard Pflanzer and Ben Miller. October 21, 1999. Choreography, Nicole Colbert; scenery, Knox Martin; lighting, Doug Filomena; costumes, Aimee Grubel; music, Sandra Sprecher. With Ken Scudder, Diane Dunbar, Mark Gering, Ethan Aronoff, Kevin Clayborn, Joy E. Styles, Claudia Choi, James Barbosa.

AN ORDINARY MIRACLE (20). By Yevgeny Schwartz, translated by Arnold Bratov. January 7, 2000. Director, Barbara Vann; choreography, Tim Harling; scenery, Paul Gugliotta, Knox Martin; lighting, Izzy Einsidler; costumes, Erin Hunt. With Kurt Edwards, Sheba Riley, Ethan Aronoff, Kenyon Gordon, Kari Nielsen, James Barbosa, Barbara Vann, Cheri Mims, Vivian G. Kalinov, David H. Kramer, Ramon Rodriguez, Jeremy Johnson, Tony Eaton, Kevin Clayborn.

THE LYNCHING OF LEO FRANK (16). By Robert Myers. April 13, 2000. Director, Barbara Vann; choreography, Margot Colbert; scenery, Knox Martin; lighting, Doug Filomena; costumes, Melanie Wehrmacher; music, Sandra Sprecher. With Izzy Einsidler, Evelyn Adler, James Barbosa, Christopher Gasti, Monrico T. Ward, Brad Russell.

THE NEW YORKERS (15). Book, Herbert Fields; music and lyrics, Cole Porter. June 8, 2000. Director, Barbara Vann; choreography, Nicole Colbert, Tim Harling, Ali Gangi; scenery, Knox Martin; lighting, Sebastian Trainor; costumes, Manuela Mendieta. With Monrico T. Ward, Melanie Whermacher, Morton Banks, James Barbosa, Jennifer Pace, Benita Charles, Dieter Riesle, Sylvie Jensen, Barbara Vann, Jon Laskin, Paul Cosentino, Nick Sakellarios, Danny Gil.

Melting Pot Theater. Presents multicultural theater in an effort to reflect the ethnic diversity of the city. Larry Hirschhorn artistic director.

ICE ISLAND: THE WAIT FOR SHACKLETON (42). By Marjorie Duffield. November 14, 1999. Director, Lori Steinberg; scenery, Anna Louizos; lighting, Debra Dumas; costumes, Sue Gandy; music, Greg Pliska. With Lou Sumrall, Ramón de Ocampo, Bostin Christopher, Charles McIver, Michael Medeiros, Christopher Burns, Godfrey L. Simmons Jr.

COBB (54). By Lee Blessing. April 17, 2000. Director, Joe Brancato; scenery, Matt Maraffi; lighting, Jeff Nellis; costumes, Daryl A. Stone; sound, Faith Drewry. With Michael Cullen, Matthew Mabe, Michael Sabatino, Clark Jackson.

Mint Theater Company. Committed to bringing new vitality to worthy but neglected plays. Jonathan Bank artistic director.

THE VOYSEY INHERITANCE (20). By Harley Granville-Barker. June 14, 1999. Director, Gus Kaikkonen; scenery, Vicki R. Davis; lighting, William Armstrong; costumes, Henry Shaffer; music, Ellen Mandel. With George Morfogen, Kurt Everhart, Kraig Swartz, Jack Koenig, Chet Carlin, Christa Scott-Reed, Sioux Madden, Arleigh Richards, Lisa Bostnar, Sally Kemp, Robert Boardman. Reopened January 18, 2000 for 63 performances.

ALISON'S HOUSE (20). By Susan Glaspell. September 26, 1999. Director, Linda Ames Key; scenery, K Maynard; lighting, Mark T. Simpson; costumes, Moe Schell. With Sharron Bower, Sarah Brockus, David Fitzgerald, Ann Hillary, Ruth Kulerman, Karla Mason, Lee Moore, Gerard O'Brien, Matt Opatrny.

MISS LULU BETT (34). By Zona Gale. March 26, 2000. Director, James C. Nicola; scenery, Vicki R. Davis; lighting, Michael Gottlieb; costumes, Marianne Powell-Parker. With Nick Dantos, Peter Davies, Katharine Leonard, Valerie Leonard, Melissa O'Malley, Angela Reed, Ed Sala, John Sloan, Billie Lou Watt.

Negro Ensemble Company. Provides quality productions of material written, performed by, and relevant to the needs and interests of black people around the world. Susan Watson Turner producing director.

THE ABSOLUTION OF WILLIE MAE (38). By Joseph A. Walker. November 23, 1999. Director, Susan Watson Turner; scenery, Gmerice Carter; lighting, Alan Baron; costumes, Anne Skeete; sound, Richard V. Turner. With O.L. Duke, Meka Lawrence, Gabrielle Lee, Gregory Marlow, Sean Allen Rector, Joyce Sylvester, Michael Wright.

New Dramatists. An organization devoted to playwrights; member writers may use the facilities for anything from private cold readings of their material to public script-in-hand readings. Todd London artistic director, Joel Ruark director of administration and finance, Paul A. Slee executive director.

Readings:

MUD, RIVER, STONE written and directed by Lynn Nottage; ANNA BELLA EEMA by Lisa D'Amour, directed by Anna Kaufman; EASTWEST written and directed by Mark Bazzone; ALICE: TALES OF A CURIOUS GIRL by Karen Hartman, directed by Jonathan Mascone; CHINA CALLS by Lonnie Carter, directed by Andre DeShields; THE BODY OF BOURNE by John Belluso, directed by Jaye Austin Williams; DOTTING AND DASHING written and directed by David Lindsay-Abaire. September 13, 1999.

BLACK FOREST. By Jens Christian Grondahl. September 24, 1999. Director, David Wheeler.

MOONS. By Mark Bazzone. September 27, 1999. Director, Abigail Deser.

CHIMPS. By Simon Block. October 1, 1999. Director, Sabrina Peck.

THE BREAKING LIGHT. By Sander Hicks. October 4, 1999. Director, Lane Savadove.

BEACH. By Ann Marie Healy. October 6, 1999. Director, Shawn Fagan.

MOTHERHOUSE. By Victor Lodato. October 7, 1999. Director, Daniel Banks.

ELOISE AND RAY. By Stephanie Fleischmann. October 8, 1999. Director, Ian Belton.

THE AMERICAN BULLFIGHTER. By Roger Darling. October 18, 1999. Director, Lou Jacob.

MEDEAD. By Fiona Templeton. October 20, 1999. Director, Rachel Dinkstein.

WILDER. By Erin Cressida Wilson. October 21, 1999. Director, Lisa Portes.

INTO THE FIRE. By Deborah Baley Brevoort. October 28, 1999. Director, Roberta Levitow.

CHINA CALLS. By Lonnie Carter. November 1, 1999. Director, Loy Arcenas.

STAR MESSENGERS. By Paul Zimet; music, Ellen Maddow. November 5, 1999.

ST. JOAN AND THE DANCING SICKNESS. By Julie Hebert. November 9, 1999. Director, Ron Daniels.

SEBASTIAN. Written and directed by Alejandro Morales. November 10, 1999.

A BEAUTIFUL WHITE ROOM. By Barry Jay Kaplan. November 15, 1999. Director, Ethan McSweeney.

ARABIAN NIGHTS. Written and directed by Carlyle Brown. November 22, 1999.

THE BREAKING MANAGER. By Sander Hicks. December 2, 1999. Director, Richard Eion Nash.

SICK AGAIN. Written and directed by Gordon Dahlquist. December 4, 1999.

LANDSCAPE OF DESIRE. By Barry Jay Kaplan. December 6, 1999. Director, Greg Leaming.

MRS. FEUERSTEIN. By Murray Mednick. December 7, 1999. Director, Andy Robinson.

ELEGY FOR LONELY GUYS. By Itamar Moses. December 9, 1999. Director, Garrett Eisler.

BANANAS AND WATER. By Barry Jay Kaplan. January 8, 2000. Director, Jean Randich.

WORLD SPEED CARNIVAL. By Stephanie Fleischmann. January 10, 2000. Director, Rachel Dickstein.

RAW DEALS AND SOME SATISFACTION. By Silvia Gonzalez S. January 12, 2000. Director, Eleanor Holdridge.

DUSK. By Lenora Champagne. January 21, 2000. Director, Rachel Dickstein.

SAILING WITH MAGELLAN. By Herbert Appelman. January 24, 2000.

JUMP/CUT. By Neena Beber. January 28, 2000. Director, Maria Mileaf.

CHINATOWN. By Catherine Filloux. February 3, 2000. Director, Jean Randich.

RULES OF CHARITY. By John Belluso. February 10, 2000. Director, David Herskovits.

LOVE MINUS. By Mary Gallagher. February 28, 2000. Director, Garrett Eisler.

NOTORIOUS, FOR MEN by Brian Robinson, directed by Casey Childs; BAGGING GROCERIES by Mark Novum, directed by K. Elizabeth Stevens; HUGGERMUGGER by Betty Shamieh, directed by Eleanor Holdridge. March 3, 2000.

NICK'S WIFE. Written and directed by Mark Druck. March 14, 2000.

BABY GLO. By Lonnie Carter. March 20, 2000.

THE UNWRITTEN LAW by Lynne Alvarez, directed by Jim Simpson; HISTORIC TIMES by Andrew Case, directed by Ivan Taliancic; HOTEL TRAUMBAD by Andrea Stolowitz, directed by Daisy Walker. March 28, 2000.

SPARROW ON THE ROOF. By Adam Rapp. March 31, 2000. Director, Brad Rouse.

INTERIOR LANDSCAPE. By Harding Lemay. April 4, 2000. Director, Sarala Dee.

A SHOE IS NOT A QUESTION. By Kelly Stuart. April 7, 2000. Director, Jeff Teare.

ANNA BELLA EEMA. By Lisa D'Amour. April 14, 2000. Director, Katie Pearl.

MOONS. By Mark Bazzone. May 5, 2000.

LOVE IN THE ENTR'ACTE. By Clifford Mason. May 9, 2000.

THREE CONTINENTS. By Catherine Filloux. May 24, 2000.

THE BREAKING LIGHT by Sander Hicks; MARY AND MYRA by Catherine Filloux. May 25, 2000.

DELIRIUM PALACE. By Gordon Dahlquist. June 6, 2000.

New Federal Theater. Dedicated to integrating minorities and women into the mainstream of American theater by training artists and by presenting plays by minorities and women to integrated, multicultural audiences. Woodie King Jr. producing director.

THE TRIAL OF ONE SHORT-SIGHTED BLACK WOMAN VS. MAMMY LOUISE AND SAFREETA MAE. By Marcia L. Leslie. Reopened October 27, 1999 for 39 performances.

SPERMEGGA (42). By and with Clarice Taylor. January 12, 2000. Director, Walter Dallas; scenery, Nick Embree; lighting, Peter J. Jakubowski; costumes, Andre Harrington; sound, Peter Ryberg.

DEFENDING THE LIGHT (29). By Ron Milner, adapted from Earl Conrad's novel, *Seward for the Defense.* February 3, 2000. Director, Jay Broad; scenery, Robert Joel Schwartz; lighting, David Segal; costumes, Michael Alan Stein; sound, Jarious Parker. With Ned Coulter, James Kiberd, Victoria G. Platt, Eddie Robinson, Lex Monson, Kathleen Turco-Lyon.

OUR PLACE IN TIME. By Clare Coss. February 6, 2000. Co-produced by Women's Project and Productions; see its entry under Women's Project and Productions in this section.

JAMES BALDWIN: A SOUL ON FIRE (30). By Howard Simon. April 6, 2000. Director, Chuck Patterson; scenery, Terry Chandler; lighting, Antoinette Tynes; costumes, Anita D. Ellis; video and sound, Sean O'Halloran. With Forrest McClendon, Charles Reese.

THE BROTHERS BERG (25). By Richard Abrons. April 21, 2000. Director, Jay Broad; scenery, Robert Joel Schwartz; lighting, David Segal; costumes, Susan Soetaert; sound, Jarious Parker. With Davis Hall, Doug Olear, Lisa Bostnar, Len Stanger, Carolyn Vujcec.

THE DANCE ON WIDOWS' ROW (27). Written and directed by Samm-Art Williams. June 22, 2000. Scenery, Felix Cochren; lighting, Shirley Prendergast; costumes, Evelyn Nelson. With Elain Graham, Jack Landron, Barbara Montgomery, Marie Thomas, Elizabeth Van Dyke, Ed Wheeler, Adam Wade.

The New Group. Provides an artistic home for artists by launching fresh acting, writing and design talent. Committed to cultivating a young and diverse theater-going audience by providing accessible ticket prices. Scott Elliott artistic director, Liz Timperman managing director.

CRANES (39). By Dmitry Lipkin. October 20, 1999. Director, Scott Elliott; scenery, Derek McLane; lighting, Jeff Croiter; costumes, Mattie Ullrich; sound, Red Ramona. With Laura Esterman, Mira Furlan, David Margulies, Josh Mostel, Amy Whitehouse.

ANOTHER AMERICAN: ASKING AND TELLING (52). By and with Marc Wolf. December 16, 1999. Director, Joe Mantello; scenery, Robert Brill; lighting, Brian MacDevitt; sound, David Van Tieghem.

BETWIXT (27). By David Cale. March 30, 2000. Direction, Scott Elliott, Andy Goldberg; scenery, Zaniz Jakubowski, Kevin Price; lighting, James Vermeulen; costumes, Eric Becker; sound, David A. Arnold; music, Jonathan Kreisberg. With Cara Seymour, David Cale.

The New Victory Theater. Purpose is to introduce young people and families, reflective of New York City's diverse communities, to live performances. Cora Cahan president.

Schedule included:

SHOCKHEADED PETER: A JUNK OPERA (15). Inspired by Heinrich Hoffmann's *The Struwwelpeter.* October 14, 1999; see its entry in the Plays Produced off Broadway section of this volume.

TOMAS KUBINEK: THE MAESTRO RETURNS (one-man show) (6). By and with Tomas Kubinek. November 5, 1999.

THE FLYING FRUIT FLY CIRCUS (21). December 3, 1999.

TIR NA N'OG (6). By the Traveling Light Theater Company, based on Jim Sheridan's film, *Into the West.* February 4, 2000. Director, Greg Banks; scenery and costumes, Katie Sykes; lighting, Andy Shewan; music and musical direction, Thomas Johnson. With Craig Edwards, David Anen, Cerianne Roberts, Fiona Barrow, Thomas Johnson.

THE FLAMING IDIOTS (8). By and with Jon O'Connor, Rob Williams and Kevin Hunt. February 18, 2000. Scenery, Heyd Fontenot; lighting, Mack D. Guinn; music, Thomas A. Nuendel, Allen Robertson and Arnie Yanez; musical direction, Allen Robertson.

THE RED BALLOON (6). By the Visible Fictions Theater Company, adapted from Albert Lamorisse's novel. March 3, 2000. Director, Annie Wood; scenery, Karen Tennent; lighting, Stuart Jenkins; musical direction, Yngvil Vatn Guttu. With Veronica Leer, Douglas Irvine, Kate Brailsford, Yngvil Vatn Guttu.

FROGS, LIZARDS, ORBS AND SLINKYS (6). By Carol Triffle and Jerry Mouawad. March 31, 2000. Lighting, Jeff Forbes; music, Katie Griesar. With the Imago Theater Mask Ensemble (Graydon Kouri, Kimberly Dahle, Michael Vertlieb, Quinn Casey, Ryan Custer).

DO JUMP! (11). Conceived, directed and choreographed by Robin Lane. April 14, 2000. Lighting, Tad Shannon; costumes, Annie Warnock, Daniela Steiner, Katharine Salzmann, Poppy Pos, Heather Pearl; music, Joan Szymko, Mike Van Liew, Courtney Von Drehle. With Wendy Cohen, Heather Pearl, Daniela Steiner, Aaron Wheeler-Kay, Kelli Wilson, Robin Woolman, David Brittain.

RUNT (9). By Ro Theater Company, based on Daniel Pennac's story, *Cabot Caboche*, translated by Adrienne Altenhous, text edited by Jules Noyons. May 5, 2000. Direction, Mark Rietman, Rieks Swarte; scenery, Rieks Swarte; lighting, Henk Van Der Geest; costumes, Carly Everaert; music, Fay Lovsky; puppets, Beatrijs Persijn. With Rogier in 't Hout , Feike Looyen, Siem van Leeuwen, Marian Luif, Hans Thissen, Ferdi Jansen, Cornell van Vuuren, Joost Belinfante.

Ontological-Hysteric Theater. Avant garde productions designed by Richard Foreman. Richard Foreman artistic director, Judson Kniffen associate artistic director.

Schedule included:

CHOSEN SPEED (11). Written and directed by Nathan Parker. July 1, 1999. With Zack Bonnie, Kristin Dispaltro, Joel Garland, Gail Neil, Chris Rocco Morro, Carlo Vogel.

FINALLY (12). By Julian Clark. July 20, 1999. Director, Tom Nelis; scenery and costumes, Merope Vachliotis; lighting, Kara Herzog. With Tom Nelis, Stephanie Cannon, Salvatore Interlandi.

THE BLUEPRINT SERIES (10). Works directed by Natalie de Campos, Owen Hughes, Kevin Oakes, Shilarna Stokes. August 11, 1999.

Granville-Barker OOB

In photo at left, Byron Jennings and Kristin Flanders in the American premiere of British actor-director-playwright Harley Granville-Barker's 1906 play *Waste,* presented by Theater for a New Audience; *above,* George Morfogen and Kraig Swartz in *The Voysey Inheritance,* a Granville-Barker turn of the 19th century hit, produced by Mint Theater

SUNDAYS OUT OF COUNTRY (20). Written and directed by Judy Elkan. September 23, 1999. Scenery, Moussie Chalfant, Judy Elkan; lighting, Michael O'Connor. With Arthur Nelson Capone, Matthew Courtney, Emily Donahue, Timothy Jenkins, Susan Tierney.

BAD BOY NIETZSCHE! (63). Written, directed and designed by Richard Foreman. January 27, 2000. Costumes, Sarah Beadle. With Gary Wilmes, Sarah Louise Lilley, Kevin Hurley, Juliana Francis.

YIELD BURNING (14). By Jill Szuchmacher. May 25, 2000. Director, Heidi R. Miller; choreography, Barbara Allen; scenery, Kevin Cunningham; lighting, Susan Hamburger; costumes, Michael Oberle; sound Shane Rettig. With Rory Kelsch, Jason Maher, Lee Means, Eric Dean Scott, Gregory VanderPyl.

Pan Asian Repertory Theater. Celebrates and provides opportunities for Asian American artists to perform under the highest professional standards and to create and promote plays by and about Asians and Asian Americans. Tisa Chang artistic/producing director.

THE JOY LUCK CLUB. By Susan Kim, based on Amy Tan's novel. Reopened July 7, 1999 for 80 performances.

THE TEAHOUSE OF THE AUGUST MOON (35). By John Patrick, adapted from Vern Sneider's novel. February 11, 2000. Director, Ron Nakahara; scenery, Robert Klingelhoefer; lighting, Jeffrey Cady; costumes, Terry Leong; sound, Peter Griggs. With Ernest Abuba, Kevin Bergen, Peter Von Berg, Scott Klavan, Carol Honda, Ako, Tran T. Thuc Hanh, Tom Matsusaka, John Baray, David Kimo Ige, Paul Keoni Chun, J.B. Barricklo, John Daggett.

THE POET OF COLUMBUS AVENUE (35). By Dennis Escobedo. June 28, 2000. Director, Ron Nakahara; scenery, Peter Cabuay; lighting, Victor En Yu Tan; costumes, Kenneth Chu; sound, Peter Griggs. With Charlee Chiv, Marcus Ho, Donna Leichenko, Les J.N. Mau, Andrew Pang.

Performance Space 122. Exists to give artists of a wide range of experience a chance to develop their work and find an audience. Mark Russell executive/artistic director.

Schedule included:

SQUONK: BIGSMORGASBORDWUNDERWERK (61). Book, music, machinery and decoration by Squonk. June 11, 1999. Director, Tom Diamond; movement director, Jana Losey; lighting, Tim Saternow. With Squonk (Jackie Dempsey, Jana Losey, Steve O'Hearn, Kevin Kornicki, T. Weldon Anderson). Transferred to off Broadway; see its entry in the Plays Produced off Broadway section of this volume.

BRAVE SMILES: ANOTHER LESBIAN TRAGEDY (14). By and with the Five Lesbian Brothers (Maureen Angelos, Babs Davy, Dominique Dibbell, Peg Healey, Lisa Kron). June 18, 1999. Director, Kate Stafford; scenery, Jamie Leo; lighting, Lori E. Seid; costumes, Susan Young.

NAKED WILL (16). Written and directed by Blair Fell. August 4, 1999. Scenery and costumes, David Ripp; lighting, Frank Den Danto III. With Christopher Baker, Eric Brooks, Greg Felden, Marc Geller, Effie Johnson.

MONSTER (12). By Daniel MacIvor and Daniel Brooks. September 9, 1999. Lighting, Daniel Brooks, Andy Moro; music and sound, Richard Feren. With Daniel MacIvor.

DO YOU COME HERE OFTEN? (33). By Sean Foley, Hamish McColl and Jozef Houben. September 16, 1999. Director, Jozef Houben; choreography, Ryan Francois; scenery and costumes, Alice Power; lighting, Tom Albu; music, Chris Lamer. With The Right Size (Sean Foley, Hamish McColl).

SHOWY LADY SLIPPER (20). Written, directed and composed by Richard Maxwell. October 14, 1999. Scenery, Joseph Silovsky; costumes, Jane Cox. With Ashley Turba, Sibyl Kempson, Jean Ann Garrish, Jim Fletcher.

VELVETVILLE (one-man show) (14). By and with Paul Zaloom. January 5, 2000.

PREACHING TO THE PERVERTED (one-woman show). By and with Holly Hughes. April 27, 2000. Director, Lois Weaver; lighting, Frank Den Danto III; sound, Vivian Stoll.

Playwrights Horizons New Theater Wing. Full productions of new works, in addition to the regular off-Broadway productions. Tim Sanford artistic director.

REFUGE (29). By Jessica Goldberg. December 1, 1999. Director, Neil Pepe; scenery, based on a concept by Scott Pask; lighting, Tyler Micoleau; costumes, Sarah Edwards; sound, David Carbonara. With Chris Messina, Chris Bauer, Catherine Kellner, Mandy Siegfried.

Primary Stages. Dedicated to new American plays by new American playwrights. Casey Childs artistic director, Margaret Chandler managing director, Janet Reed associate artistic director.

BAREFOOT BOY WITH SHOES ON (13). By Edwin Sanchez. October 20, 1999. Director, Casey Childs; scenery, Walt Spangler; lighting, Deborah Constantine; costumes, Debra Stein; music and sound, Fabian Obispo. With Dennis Parlato, Lazaro Perez, Keith Reddin, Jamie Sanchez, Nelson Vasquez.

ELSA EDGAR (39). By Bob Kingdom and Neil Bartlett. December 15, 1999; see its entry in the Plays Produced off Broadway section of this volume.

AN EMPTY PLATE IN THE CAFÉ DU GRAND BOEUF (19). By Michael Hollinger. March 8, 2000. Director, John Rando; scenery, Rob Odorisio; lighting, Brian Nason; costumes, David C. Woolard; sound, Jim van Bergen. With George Wendt, Matt Stinton, Jonathan Freeman, Michael McCormick, Annie Golden, Nance Williamson.

WHEN THEY SPEAK OF RITA (41+). By Daisy B. Foote. May 17, 2000. Director, Horton Foote; scenery, Jeff Cowie; lighting, Deborah Constantine; costumes, Debra Stein; music and sound, Fabian Obispo. With Hallie Foote, Ken Marks, Jamie Bennett, Ebon Moss-Bachrach, Margot White. Co-produced by the Herrick Theater Foundation.

FIRST RUN (works-in-progress): DULCE DE LECHE by Daniel Goldfarb, directed by David Warren; JANUARY by Janis Astor del Valle, directed by Cliff Goodwin; LOS ANGELES by Julian Sheppard, directed by Seth Gordon; TRUST by Janet Reed Ahearn, directed by Julie Boyd; RHYTHM, I WAS SAYIN' by Bruce Faulk, directed by Dion Graham; TRASHED by Jessica Goldberg, directed by Seth Gordon. April 10–23, 2000.

Puerto Rican Traveling Theater. Professional company presenting bilingual productions of Puerto Rican and Hispanic playwrights, emphasizing subjects of relevance today. Miriam Colon Valle founder and producer.

Schedule included:

TIENE LA MUERTE ATADA (THEY'VE GOT DEATH BOUND UP). By Hugo Bardallo. August 11, 1999. Director, Nelson Landrieu; music and musical direction, Pablo Zinger. With Bill Blechinberg, Ana Campos, Pietro Gonzalez, Alicia Kaplan, Francisco Martinez, Gladys Perez, Juan Villarreal.

KING WITHOUT A CASTLE (REY SIN CASTILLO). By Candido Tirado, Spanish translation, Manuel Martin. March 16, 2000. Director, Michael John Garcés; scenery, Troy Hourie; lighting, Shawn K. Kaufman; costumes, Mimi O'Donnell. With Francisco Lorite, Anilu Pardo, Selenis Leyva.

BLIND ALLEY (CALLEJON SIN SALIDA). By Nancy Nevárez. May 11, 2000. Director, Alex Furth; scenery, David Barber; lighting, Frank DenDanto; costumes, Karen Flood; sound, Joao Vincent Lewis, Melinda Davila. With Annie Henk, Joselin Reyes, Mariana Carreno, Milena Davila, Monica Read, Nancy Rodriguez.

Signature Theater Company. Dedicated to the exploration of a playwright's body of work. James Houghton founding artistic director, Bruce E. Whitacre managing director.

MUD and DROWNING (one-act plays) (28). By Maria Irene Fornes. September 26, 1999. Director, David Esbjornson; scenery, Christine Jones; lighting, Scott Zielinski; costumes, Teresa Snider-Stein; sound, John Kilgore. With Deirdre O'Connell, Paul Lazar, John Seitz, Marc Damon Johnson, Philip Goodwin, Jed Diamond.

ENTER THE NIGHT (27). By Maria Irene Fornes. December 5, 1999. Director, Sonja Moser; scenery, Christine Jones; lighting, Jane Cox; costumes, Gabriel Berry; sound, Glen Tarachow. With Barbara Tarbuck, Dallas Roberts, Rebecca Harris.

LETTERS FROM CUBA (35). Written and directed by Maria Irene Fornes. February 20, 2000. Scenery, Donald Eastman; lighting, Matthew Frey; costumes, Teresa Snider-Stein; sound, Kurt B. Kellenberger. With Chris De Oni, Tai Jimenez, Matthew Floyd Miller, Peter Starrett, Peter Van Wagner, Rick Wasserman.

Soho Rep. Dedicated to new and avant-garde American playwrights. Daniel Aukin artistic director, Alexandra Conley executive director.

SUMMER CAMP 5: Schedule included A PHAEDRA PLAY by Judy Elkan, directed by Daniel Aukin; [SIC] by Melissa Gibson, directed by Melissa Kievman; SPACE written and directed by Jonathan Jacobs; EATING DIRT by Aya Agawa, directed by Ron Russell; BE AGGRESSIVE by Annie Weisman, directed by Lisa Portes; THE MASTER OF THINGS by Scott Blumenthal; SOUL MONSTERS by Allison Zell. July 6-August 7, 1999.

R & D FESTIVAL: Schedule included CHRISTINA by Marina Shron, directed by Amy Boyce; CAT'S PAW by Mac Wellman, directed by Daniel Aukin; 5 written and directed by Yehuda Duenyas; A 12 LB. DISCOURSE written and directed by Matt Schneck and Pete Simpson. December 1, 1999 – January 22, 2000.

THE YEAR OF THE BABY (21). By Quincy Long. March 30, 2000. Director, Daniel Aukin; scenery, Louisa Thompson; lighting, Michael O'Connor; costumes, Maiko Matsushima; music, Maury Loeb. With Annette Hunt, Joseph Jamrog, Rebecca Soler, Tina Stafford, Trevor A. Williams, Jonathan Mark Woodward, Greg Hirte, Christopher Kirkman.

HYPATIA (16). By Mac Wellman. May 13, 2000. Director, Bob McGrath; scenery, Molly Hughes; lighting, Jane Cox; costumes, Laurie Olinder; music and sound, J. Hagenbuckle. With Aysan Celik, Sophia Fox-Long, Jonathan Hova, Leopold Lowe, Jeremy Proctor, Fred Tietz, Daniel Zippi. Co-produced by Ridge Theater.

Theater for the New City. Developmental theater and new American experimental works. Crystal Field executive director.

Schedule included:

SURVIVAL NEW YORK (13). Music, Joel Diamond; lyrics and direction, Crystal Field. August 7, 1999. Scenery, Walter Gurbo; costumes, Alessandra Nichols, Gail Strum; sound, Paul Garrity. With Stephen DeLorenzo, Crystal Field, Michael-David Gordon, Jerry Jaffe, Terry Lee King, Mark Marcante, Craig Meade, Michael Vasquez, Anna Zastrow.

TIME IT IS. Written and directed by Lissa Moira. Reopened November 11, 1999.

SAVANNAH BAY. By Marguerite Duras, translated by Barbara Bray. November 22, 1999. Director, Andrew Wolkoff; scenery, Beowulf Boritt; lighting, Jeff Croiter; sound, Jim van Bergen. With Peg Small, India Blake.

RATS IN THE TUNNEL. Written and directed by Bina Sharif. December 2, 1999. Scenery, Kyle Kasakaitas; lighting, Jon D. Andreadakis. With Terry Lee King, Kevin Mitchell Martin, Bina Sharif.

THE IDIOT. Adapted and directed by Anatole Fourmantchouk from Fyodor Dostoyevsky's novel. January 6, 2000. Scenery, costumes and lighting, Natalie Rudyuk. With Stass Klassen, Christopher Cartmill, Bill Green, David Greenwood, Ruth Kulerman, Michael Graves, Alexis Raben, James Rutigliano, Marcus Powell, Sandra Trullinger, Cory Walter. Co-produced by New York Art Theater.

DESERT WIND: A TEXAS FABLE. Written and directed by Ian L. Gordon. January 6, 2000. Scenery, Mark Marcante; lighting, Kyle Kasakaitas. With John Bravo, Susanne Bruno, Stephen DeLorenzo, Robert Madden, Craig Meade, Caroline Mica, Joanna Rhyns, Rookie Tiwari, Michael Thompson, Juan Villegas.

JEWS AND CHRISTIANS IN THE END ZONE. By Arthur Sainer. January 20, 2000. Directed by Tanya Kane-Parry; scenery, Rona Taylor; lighting, Ben Kato. With Bruce Barton, Bostin Christopher, Karen Grenke, Andrew Hurley, Greg Petroff, Liat Ron, David Vining, Seana Lee Wyman, Aaron Pierce, Nina Zavarin.

LONG DISTANCE. Book, music and lyrics, Todd Tagliaferro. January 27, 2000. Musical direction, Bill Wolf. With Joshua Vink, Todd Tagliaferro.

THE BABY BOOMER. Book, music and lyrics, Joel Diamond. January 27, 2000. Director, Jill Wisoff; lighting, Jon D. Andreadakis; costumes, Nina Simich; sound, James Bauer. With Anthony Pick, Marion Markham, Donna Smythe, Glenn Wein, Marrielle Monte, Richard Herron.

TO KISS THE CHEEK OF THE MOON. By Yolanda Rodriguez. February 12, 2000. Director, Crystal Field; scenery, Donald L. Brooks; lighting, Jon D. Andreadakis; costumes, Marisa Timperman; sound, Kyle Kasakaitas; music, Joel Diamond. With Michael Vasquez, Mira Rivera, Desteny Cruz, Sol Echeverria, Sergio Garcia Aguilar.

THE GOSPEL OF CYRUS ACCORDING TO CYRUS. By Chris Talbott. February 17, 2000. Director, Laramie Dennis; scenery, Clayton Binkley; lighting, Shawn P. Gallagher; costumes, Matt Bedell. With Jessejames Locorriere, Rowland Stebbins.

BOHEMIA ON WRY: BEAUTY AND THE BEAT and LIFESTYLES OF THE POOR AND BOHEMIAN (one-act plays). By Richard West. March 9, 2000. Director, Lissa Moira; lighting and sound, Debbie Thame. With Danny Ashkenasi, Colleen Carroll, Frank Craven, Susan Mitchell, Eric

R. Moreland, Jack Tynan, Joshua Koehn, Martina Lotun, Robert Madden, Lissa Moira, Jill M. Simon, Daniel Passaro, Cynthia Savage, Crystal Scott, Richard West.

THREE BY GRACE: A CONVERSATION WITH MY FATHER, THE IMMIGRANT STORY and GOODBYE AND GOOD LUCK (one-act plays). By Grace Paley. March 9, 2000. Director, Marjorie Melnick Heymann; scenery, Ze'ev Willy Neumann; lighting, Dana Sterling; costumes, Kirby Wendland; sound, Scott Armstrong; music, Dawn Buckholz. With Margo Lee Sherman.

BENNY'S BARBERSHOP. Book and lyrics, T. Scott Lilly and Mark Marcante; music, Joel Diamond, T. Scott Lilly. Reopened March 16, 2000.

HOW TO COOK A MAN (9). By and with Evert Eden. March 23, 2000. Director, Aviva Jane Carlin.

GET DOWN OFF THE CEILING, JOANNA (12). By Barbara Kahn. March 30, 2000. Direction, Barbara Kahn and Marjorie Barnes; choreography, Sansan Fibri; lighting, Christopher Weston; costumes, Andy Wallach. With Debbie Marchese, Jennifer De Martino, Sansan Fibri, Camille Torres, Kathleen Carthy, Katy Hawley, Stacy Deemar, Vita Dennis, Barbara Kahn.

AMERICAN HIEROGLYPHICS: FISHNET & SECONDARY SMOKE and THE CHRISTIAN CAT CLUB (one-act plays). By Larry Myers. March 30, 2000. Director, Monte Zanca; scenery, Mark Marcante; lighting, Jon D. Andreadakis. With Joshua Bresette, Jessica Merritt, Noelle Teagno, Alexandra Cremer, Monte Zanca, Jordan Dyck, Scott Stevens, P.J. Marshall, Joseph Napoli, Jeff Broitman, Kevin White.

SPAIN. By Ralph Pezzullo. April 20, 2000. Director, Yuji Takematsu; scenery, Mark Marcante; lighting, Yoshikazu Tatsuno. With Julie Kay Swift, Kevin Mitchell Martin.

A MIDWINTER'S NIGHTMARE by Walter Corwin, directed by Ian L. Gordon; REPORT TO THE HOUSE by Walter Corwin, directed by Marian Sarach. May 4, 2000. With Stephen DeLorenzo, Rookie Tawari, John Hutton, Ron Leir.

NELSON 'N' SIMONE: OUT OF THE SENSES. By Laurence Holder. May 6, 2000. Director, Murray Changar; lighting, Jon D. Andreadakis; music, Ken Lauber. With Kathryn Chilson, Theo Polites.

THE POPE AND THE WITCH. By Dario Fo, translated by Ed Emery. May 3, 2000. Director, Jim Niesen; scenery, Ken Rothchild; lighting, Herrick Goldman; costumes, Christianne Myers; music, Walter Thompson. With Terry Greiss, Heidi K. Eklund, Christian Brandjes, Damen Scranton, Sven Miller, Michael-David Gordon, Patrena Murray. Co-produced by the Irondale Ensemble Project.

Ubu Repertory Theater. Committed to acquainting American audiences with new works by contemporary French-speaking playwrights from around the world in English translations, as well as modern classics in the original French. Francoise Kourilsky artistic director.

Schedule included:

MURDER IN MIND (10). By Xavier Durringer, translated by Timothy Johns. December 2, 1999. Director, David Géry; scenery, Watoku Oeno; lighting, Greg MacPherson; costumes, Carol Ann Pelletier; sound, Robert Gould. With Jacinto Taras Riddick, Willie C. Carpenter, Chris Edwards, Zabryna Guevara, Heather Robbins, Michael Medico. Co-produced by La Mama Experimental Theater Club.

ANTIGONE (5). By Jean Anouilh. February 17, 2000. Director, Francoise Kourilsky; lighting, Greg MacPherson; costumes, Carol Ann Pelletier. With Carlos Arévalo, Myriam Cyr, Jacqueline Bertrand, Isabelle Cyr, Dominick Aries, Jean Leclerc, Byron Walker, Simon Fortin, Morgan Dowsett, Michael Bradley Griffith.

The Vineyard Theater. Multi-art chamber theater dedicated to the development of new plays and musicals, music-theater collaborations and innovative revivals. Douglas Aibel artistic director, Barbara Zinn Krieger executive director, Jeffrey Solis managing director.

FULLY COMMITTED (45). By Becky Mode, based on characters developed by Becky Mode and Mark Setlock. September 30, 1999. Director, Nicholas Martin; scenery, James Noone; lighting,

Frances Aronson; sound, Bruce Ellman. With Mark Setlock. Transferred to off Broadway; see its entry in the Plays Produced off Broadway section of this volume.

TRUE HISTORY AND REAL ADVENTURES (40). By Sybille Pearson. December 13, 1999. Director, Michael Mayer; scenery and costumes, G.W. Mercier; lighting, Kevin Adams; sound, Bruce Ellman; music, Mel Marvin. With Kathleen Chalfant, Angela Goethals, Donovan Patton, Daniel Bess, Adrienne Carter, Damon Gupton, Wally Dunn, John Michael Gilbert, Aleta Mitchell, David Alan Bunn.

THE ALTRUISTS (46). By Nicky Silver. March 6, 2000. Director, David Warren; scenery, Neil Patel; lighting, Kenneth Posner; costumes, Teresa Snider-Stein; sound, John Gromada. With Joey Slotnick, Veanne Cox, Eddie Cahill, Kali Rocha, Sam Robards, Monica Plank.

The Women's Project and Productions. Nurtures, develops and produces plays written and directed by women. Julia Miles artistic director, Patricia Taylor managing director.

27 performances each

GUM. By Karen Hartman. October 17, 1999. Director, Loretta Greco; scenery, Myung Hee Cho; lighting, Frances Aronson; costumes, Elizabeth Hope Clancy; sound, Obadiah Eaves; songs, Kim D. Sherman. With Firdous Bamji, Angel Desai, Lizan Mitchell, Juan Rivera-Lebron, Daphne Rubin-Vega.

OUR PLACE IN TIME. By Clare Coss. February 6, 2000. Director, Bryna Wortman; scenery, Narelle Sissons; lighting, Jane Cox; costumes, Gail Cooper-Hecht; sound, Stefan Jacobs. With Gena Bardwell, Elizabeth Hess, Jacqueline Knapp, Norman Maxwell, Daniel McDonald, Keith Randolph Smith. Co-produced by New Federal Theater.

TWO-HEADED. By Julie Jensen. May 11, 2000. Director, Joan Vail Thorne; scenery, David P. Gordon; lighting, Michael Lincoln; costumes, Carrie Robbins; music and sound, Scott Killian. With Deirdre O'Connell, Lizbeth Mackay.

WPA Theater. Produces new American plays and neglected American classics in the realistic idiom. Kyle Renick artistic director, Ellen Mittenthal producing director, Roger T. Danforth associate producer.

BLOOD ON THE DINING ROOM FLOOR (25). Libretto and music, Jonathan Sheffer, based on Gertrude Stein's novella. April 16, 2000. Director, Jeremy Dobrish; choreography, Erica Murkofsky; scenery, Steven Capone; lighting, Michael Gottlieb; costumes, Markas Henry; musical direction, Steven Osgood. With Carolann Page, Wendy Hill, Sandra Joseph, Anna Bergman, Mary Ann Stewart, Patrick Porter, Michael Zegarski, Keith Howard.

Miscellaneous

In the additional listing of 1999–2000 off-off-Broadway productions below, the names of the producing groups or theaters appear in CAPITAL LETTERS and the titles of the works in *italics*. This list consists largely of new or reconstituted works. It includes a few productions staged by groups which rented space from the more established organizations listed previously.

ABINGDON THEATER COMPANY. *Cannibal's Waltz* written and directed by Lanie Robertson. October 10, 1999. With David Mazzeo, T. Cat Ford, Kevin Hogan, Diane Ciesla, John FitzGibbon, Craig Fols. *Nuclear Family* written and directed by Bernice Rohret. December 1, 1999. With Steve Parris, Dolores Kenan, David Marantz, Natily Blair, Stephanie Barton-Farcas. *Zona the Ghost of Greenbriar* by Jan Buttram. March 19, 2000. Directed by James F. Wolk.

ACCESS THEATER. *Chekhov Now* (festival of Anton Chekhov's work). Schedule included *Anton Himself* by Karen Sunde; *At Sea* (puppet show) by David Gochfeld, adapted from Chekhov's short story; *The Cherry Orchard*, directed by Hyoung-Taek Limb; *The Jubilee*, directed by Adam Melnick; *Screeching Chalk* adapted from Chekhov's *A Wedding* and *Smoking Is Bad for You,* directed by Francesca Viscardi. September 22-October 10, 1999.

NAKED ANGELS—Annabella Sciorra and Fisher Stevens in a scene from *Shyster* by Bryan Goluboff

ACTORS PLAYHOUSE. *Naked Boys Singing* (musical revue) conceived and directed by Robert Schrock, written by Stephen Bates, Marie Cain, Perry Hart, Shelly Markham, Jim Morgan, David Pevsner, Rayme Sciaroni, Mark Savage, Ben Schaechter, Robert Schrock, Trance Thompson, Bruce Vilanch and Mark Winkler. July 22, 1999. With Glenn Allen, Jonathan Brody, Tim Burke, Tom Gualtieri, Patrick Herwood, Daniel C. Levine, Sean McNally, Adam Michaels, Trance Thompson. Transferred to off Broadway; see its entry in the Plays Produced Off Broadway section of this volume.

ACTORS STUDIO FREE THEATER. *Lemonade* by Eve Ensler. January 19, 2000. Directed by David Wheeler; with Sherri Parker Lee, Lisa Richards, Stephen Mendillo.

ADOBE THEATER COMPANY. *Down the Drain* by Stanton Wood. March 22, 2000. Directed by Paul Zablocki; with Arthur Aulisi, Tami Dixon, Giuseppe Jones, Janice O'Rourke, Nick Phelps, Molly Renfroe, Zach Shaffer.

AMERICAN PLACE THEATER SPACE. *The Winds of God* written, directed and performed by Masayuki Imai. Reopened September 16, 1999.

AQUILA THEATER COMPANY. *The Iliad: Book I* by Homer, translated by Stanley Lombardo; music by Anthony Cochrane. November 24, 1999. Directed by Robert Richmond; with Louis Butelli, Anthony Cochrane, Lisa Carter, Grant Goodman, Jens Martin Krummel, Tracey Mitchell. *King Lear* by William Shakespeare. November 28, 1999.

ARCLIGHT THEATER. *It's My Party(And I'll Die If I Want To)* by Elizabeth Coleman. August 19, 1999. Directed by Jeannie Berlin; with F. Murray Abraham, Joyce Van Patten, Rene Augesen, John Cariani, Andrea Gabriel, Adam Grupper. *The Passion of Frida Kahlo* by Dolores C. Sendler. October 25, 1999. Directed by Michael John Garcés; with Priscilla Lopez, Anilú Pardo, David Anzuelo, Claudia J. Arenas, Bill Torres. *The Director* by Nancy Hasty. February 15, 2000. Directed by Evan Bergman; with John Shea, Tasha Lawrence, Tanya Clarke, Warren Press, Todd Simmons, Shula Van Buren.

ATLANTIC THEATER SPACE. *The Brave* by Sharman Macdonald. July 22, 1999. Directed by Dave Mowers; with Kimberly Anne Ryan, John August Baker, Alice Barden, Randy Scott, Aasif Mandvi, David Marantz.

BANK STREET THEATER. *The Beauty Part* by S.J. Perelman. September 18, 1999. Directed by Dan Wackerman; with Lisa Altomare, Dale Carman, Nicole S. Eaton, Ruth Jaffe, Philip Levy, Jeff Patterson, Nicole Ravenna. *Camelot's Ruby* by Erwin Pally. February 14, 2000. Directed by Sylvia Boyd; with Steven David, Marit DeLozier, John Joseph Gallagher, Deann Halper, Richard Kelly, Joseph Pallister,

Jerome Richards, James Sweeney, Gene Terinoni. *My Blackie* by Arne Sierens. April 29, 2000. Directed by Victoria Pero; with Bart Vanlaere, Foutain Yount, Tom Epstein, Jef Awada, Nick Gomez, Bret Mosley, Stelio Savante, Louise Seyffert.

THE BARROW GROUP. *Desperate Territory* by J.S. Staniloff; *Cat's Paw* by William Mastrosimone; *The Little Black Dress* by Cary Fagan; *The Straight and Narrow* by Ken Prestininvi; *Marcus is Walking* by Joan Ackerman; *Practically Cousins* by Chris Van Groningen (staged readings). October 23-November 18, 1999.

BAT THEATER COMPANY. *Noses Off* by the New York Goofs and the Bat Theater Company. February 3, 2000. With Dick Monday. *Carnival Knowledge* by and with Paola Styron and Rob Faust. February 23, 2000. Directed by Rob Faust.

BLUE HERON THEATER. *Black Russian* by Tom Gibbons. June 5, 1999. *Steam* (one-act plays): *Some Bodies* written and directed by Gail Noppe-Brandon and *The Door* by Susan Kim, directed by Gail Noppe-Brandon. October 21, 1999. With Kelly Ebsary, Susan Gordon-Clark, Eunice Wong. *Bedside Manners* by Lisa Stephenson. October 29, 1999. Directed by Tom Franco; with Lucia Puccia Ruvolo. *Steam, Too* (one-act plays): *Laura & Wendy* by Lucy Thurber and *In and Out* by Shawn Hirabayshi. May 18, 2000. Directed by Gail Noppe-Brandon; with Susan Gordon-Clark, Elizabeth Fairfax Brown, Steven F. Blye, Eunice Wong. *The Penis Responds* (twelve short plays) written and directed by Ernest Thompson. May 25, 2000. With Ernest Thompson, Richard Gilliland.

CENTER STAGE. *In Arabia We'd All Be Kings* by Stephen Adly Guirgis. June 23, 1999. Directed by Philip Seymour Hoffman; with Russell G. Jones, Trevor Long, David Zayas, Liza Zayas, Ana Ortiz, Tiprin Mandalay, Sal Inzerillo, Richard Petrocelli, Mark Hammer, Begonya Plaza. *The Tailor-Made Man* written and directed by Claudio Macor. October 3, 1999. With Matt Walton, Dennis Matthews, Roger Rathburn, J.M. McDonough, Kelly Corvese, Sarah Burns, Helen Buck, Rick Meese, Franca Barchiesi.

CENTURY CENTER THEATER. *Ghosts* by Henrik Ibsen. November 21, 1999. Directed by J.C. Compton; with Kathleen Garrett, Mark Elliot Wilson. *The Wild Duck* by Henrik Ibsen. May 4, 2000. Directed by J.C. Compton; with Patricia Chilsen, John August Baker, Tom Morrissey, D. Michael Berkowitz, Riley Wood, Duncan Rogers, Karla Nielson, Kameron Steele, Lexie Kahanovitz.

CHAIN LIGHTNING THEATER. *Minstrel Show or The Lynching of William Brown* by Max Sparber. October 21, 1999. Directed by Rob Urbinati; with Spencer Scott Barros, Tim Cain. *Balloon* by Karen Sunde. March 23, 2000. Directed by Lisa Brailoff; with Jean Brassard, Matt Bray, Fred Burrell, Peter Lewis, Virginia Roncetti, Michael Shelle.

CHELSEA PLAYHOUSE. *Splendora* book by Peter Webb, based on Edward Swift's novel; music by Stephen Hoffman; lyrics by Mark Campbell. February 8, 2000. Directed by Donna Drake; with Teri Dale Hansen, Kristine Zbornik, Susan Roberts, Carol Tammen, Culver Casson, Shannon Carson, Mark Cortale, Tod Mason. *Enough About Me: An Unauthorized Biography* by Jeffery Roberson; conceived by Jeffery Roberson and Michael Schiralli; additional material by Jeffery Roberson, Michael Schiralli and Joe Pirolli. February 18, 2000. Directed by Michael Schiralli; with Jeffery Roberson.

CHERRY LANE ALTERNATIVE MENTOR PROJECT. Schedule included *Crocker Land* by Peter Buchman, directed by Susann Brinkley (Michael Weller, mentor); *Notes From the Confederacy* by Heather Hill, directed by Eduardo Machado (A.R. Gurney, mentor); *Saint Lucy's Eyes* by Bridgette Wimberly (Wendy Wasserstein, mentor); *Razing Houses* by Lizzie Olesker (Tony Kushner, mentor); *Four* by Christopher Shinn (Charles Fuller, mentor). September 14-October 23, 1999. *Gun Club* by Hunt Holman, directed by Amy Feinberg (Michael Weller, mentor); *Refreshment of the Spirit* by Anne Washburn, directed by Anne Kauffman (Craig Lucas, mentor); *Aunt Pieces* by Rosemary Moore, directed by Michael Sexton (A.R. Gurney, mentor); *Golem* by Gary Winter, directed by Hayley Finn (Alfred Uhry, mentor); *Lowell Limpett* by Ward Just, directed by Bob Gasper (Wendy Wasserstein, mentor). April 5-June 16, 2000.

CLUB EL FLAMINGO. *The Donkey Show: A Midsummer Night's Disco* created and directed by Diane Paulus and Randy Weiner; conceived by Randy Weiner. August 18, 1999. With Emily Hellstrom, Rachel Benbow Murdy, Jordin Ruderman, Anna Wilson, Dan Cryer, Oscar Estevez, Luke Miller, Roman Pietrs, Quinn, Barbara Rellstab, Orlando Santana, Kevin Shand (Project 400 Theater Group).

COLLECTIVE UNCONSCIOUS. *Charlie Victor Romeo* by Bob Berger, Patrick Daniels and Irving Gregory. January 13, 2000. Directed by Bob Berger, Patrick Daniels, Irving Gregory, Michael Bruno, and Stuart Rudin; with Audrey Crabtree, Oliver Wyman, Michael Bruno, Stuart Rudin, Bob Berger, Julia Berger, Patrick Daniels, Justin Davila, Irving Gregory, Dan Krumm, Darby Thompson.

CURRICAN THEATER. *Maybe Baby, It's You* by and with Charlie Shanian and Shari Simpson. July 28, 1999. Directed by Jeremy Dobrish. Transferred to off Broadway; see its entry in the Plays Produced off Broadway section of this volume. *Extreme Girl* (one-woman show) by and with Barbara Blackburn. December 10, 1999. Directed by Courtney Munch. *Waiting* by Frank Basloe. April 28, 2000. Directed by Daniella Topol; with Todd Davis, Joe Feuer, Meg Howrey, Robert Douglas Marko. *Common Things About 16 Dicks From Philadelphia* (one-act plays): *The Philadelphia* and *Sure Thing* by David Ives; *The Dicks* by Jules Feiler; *16E* by Alexander Dawson; *Common Ground* by Richard Harlan Smith. May 24, 2000. Directed by Charles Gale; with Jennifer Barrett, Peter Bisgaier, Jeff Dorau, James Lee, Justin Barrett, Steven Dominguez, Sidney Williams, Colleen Cosgrove.

DANCE THEATER WORKSHOP. *Live Sax Acts* by and with David Dorfman and Dan Froot. August 24, 1999. *Infrared* by Mac Wellman. December 10, 1999.

THE DIRECTORS COMPANY. *Goodbye, My Friduchita* by Dolores C. Sendler. July 12, 1999. Directed by Michael John Garcés; with Priscilla Lopez, Anilú Pardo, David Anzuelo, Claudia J. Arenas, Bill Torres. Reopened as *The Passion of Frida Kahlo* at ArcLight Theater October 25, 1999.

DIXON PLACE. *The Child* by Sarah Schulman. September 9, 1999. Directed by Craig Lucas; with Fiona Gallagher, Daniel Eric Gold, Angie Phillips, David Rakoff, Bobby Rivers. *Necromance: A Night of Conjuration* (performance-magic) by and with Derek Hughes. October 4, 1999. Directed by Chris Bayes. *Armchair America: The Recline of Western Civilization* by and with Tom Bondi and Mark Holt. March 11, 2000.

DOMINION THEATER. *Simply Barbra* (cabaret) by and with Steven Brinberg. November 5, 1999.

DOUGLAS FAIRBANKS THEATER. *Bash* (one-act plays): *Medea Redux, Iphigenia in Orem* and *A Gaggle of Saints* by Neil LaBute. June 24, 1999. Directed by Joe Mantello; with Calista Flockhart, Ron Eldard, Paul Rudd.

DUPLEX CABARET THEATER. *Sheridan Square* conceived and written by Phil Geoffrey Bond; songs by Irving Berlin, David Evans, Winnie Holzman, Micki Grant, John Kander, Fred Ebb, Richard Maltby Jr., David Shire, Alan Menken, Amanda McBroom, Stephen Sondheim and Brett Kristofferson. June 5, 1999. Directed by Joseph Verlezza; with Tim Cahill, AJ Centauri. *This Love* words and music by Brett Kristofferson; conceived and directed by Dawn M.J. Bates. November 4, 1999. With Jesse Tyler Ferguson. *No Minimum* by Roy Leake Jr., April Winchell and James May. March 3, 2000. Directed by Mark Cannistraro; with Sandy Rosenberg, Ben Lipitz.

EAST COAST ARTISTS. *Hamlet* by William Shakespeare. June 10, 1999. Directed by Richard Schechner; with George Hannah, Gerry Bamman, Omar Shapli, Marissa Copeland, Paula Cole, Michele Minnick, Debora Cahn, David Anzuelo, Lars Hanson.

EXPANDED ARTS. *Richard III* by William Shakespeare. July 7, 1999. Directed by David Levine; with Tonya Canada, Colleen DeSalvo, Adam Feldman, Dawn Fuller, Eben Klemm, John McClure, Jason Pugatch. *The Citadel* by Phil Geoffrey Bond. October 23, 1999. Directed by Jerry McAllister; with Kelly McAllister, Phil Geoffrey Bond.

FLORENCE GOULD HALL. *Paul and Virginie* by Jean Cocteau and Raymond Radiguet; music by Charles Kalman. March 31, 2000.

FLATIRON THEATER. *Northanger Abbey* adapted from Jane Austen's novel by Lynn Marie Macy. February 5, 2000. Directed by David Scott; with Kevin Connell, Sterling Coyne, Madeline Gomez-Bianchi, Shirl Guest, Annalisa Hill, Lynn Marie Macy, Lynn McNutt, Dan O'Driscoll, Andrew Oswald, Mark Rimer, Greaton Sellers, Laura Standley, Amy Stoller, Ellen Turkelson, David Winton.

FLEA THEATER. *Theater of Light* by Rudi Stern. December 12, 1999.

FOUNDRY THEATER. *Gertrude and Alice: A Likeness to Loving* by and with Lola Pashalinski and Linda Chapman. June 9, 1999. Directed by Anne Bogart.

FREESTYLE REPERTORY THEATER (improvisation). *Olde & News*. October 28, 1999. *The News*. April 20, 2000. With Paula Boyajian, Trevor Davis, Mike Durkin, Laura Livingston, Kelly McCaffery, Adam Nowak, Anthony Veneziale.

THE FRYING PAN. *Daniel Pelican* by Chris Van Strander. November 4, 1999. Directed by Tor Ekeland; with Natalie Burgess, Chris Van Strander.

GREENWICH STREET THEATER. *The Song of Songs* book, lyrics and direction by Daniel Goldstein, adapted from Sholom Alecheim's story, translated by Curt Levant; music by Michael Friedman. May 9, 2000. With Rebecca Borash, Vivien Weiss, Sandy Rustin, Patrick Mellen, Rachel Jacobs, Cormac Bluestone, Jordan Matthew Smith, Eliza Ladd, Kathryn Blume, Jesse Hawks, Paul Siemens.

GROVE STREET PLAYHOUSE. *Missionary Position* (one-woman show) by and with Tara Greenway. September 16, 1999. Directed by Ariane Brandt. *B.J: The Trail of a Transgender Country Singing Star* (one-man show) by and with Scott Hess. April 6, 2000. Directed by David Drake.

HAROLD CLURMAN THEATER. *Tiger Tail* by Tennessee Williams. July 7, 1999. Directed by Henry Mastrogeorge; with Shae D'lyn, Matthew Burnett, Jane Cecil, Glenn J. Cohen, Silas Weir Mitchell, Jay Veduccio, Sybyl Walker, Joseph Whipp. *Hundreds of Sisters and One Big Brother* by and with Deborah Swisher. January 31, 2000. Directed by Elyse Singer.

HENRY STREET SETTLEMENT. *Sky Woman Festival.* Schedule included *Sara & Susie* by and with Sharon Shorty and Jackie Bear; *Moonlodge* (one-woman show) by and with Margo Kane; *Ragged Dog* (performance art) by Laura Ortman; *The Lesser Wars* by Diane Glancy. November 3–21, 1999. *Voices From the Holy and Not So Holy Land* (one-man show) by and with Steve Greenstein. February 10, 2000.

HERE. *Queer @ HERE* (new works' festival by gay and Lesbian writers and performers). Schedule included *Romeo and Medea and Beauty* by Blair Fell; *Agamemnon vs. Liberace* by Aaron Mack Schloff; *Rough Trade* by Dennis Davis; *B.J: The Trail of a Transgender Country Singing Star* by and with Scott Hess, directed by Craig Rhyne; *About Bernard Carlton* by David Gaard. June 15–27, 1999. *American Living Room Festival* (works by emerging and established theater artists). July 3-August 29, 1999. *My Last Year with the Nuns* by Matt Smith. September 9, 1999. Directed by Brad Fetzer. *Caught in the Act Festival* (one-act plays in translation): *Still Life* by Ferenc Molnar, translated by Eugene Brogyanyi; *The Orphan's Dowry* by Pierre-Henri Cami, translated by Daniel C. Gerould; *Fair Kirsten* by Kaj Nissen, translated by Julian Garner; *Bacchanalia* by Arthur Schnitzler, translated by Eugene Brogyanyi; *The Mute Canary* by Georges Ribemont-Dessaignes, translated by Lili Scheiber; *Ladies at Play* by Julio Matas, translated by Francesca Colecchia and Julio Matas; *European Cabaret: Several Pieces*, translated by Lawrence Senelick; *The Open Couple* by Dario Fo and Franca Rame, translated by Stuart Hood. September 11-October 3, 1999. *Night Vision: A New Third to First World Vampyre Opera* libretto and lyrics by Ruth Margraff; music and concept by Fred Ho. February 2, 2000. Directed by Tim Maner; with Ron Brice, Daphne Gaines, Kimberly Gambino, Peter McCabe, Greg Purnhagen, Kaipo Schwab, Asa Somers. *Hamlet* by William Shakespeare. March 19, 2000. Directed by Ellen Beckerman; with James M. Saidy, Margot Ebling, Josh Conklin, Shawn Fagan, Sheri Graubert. *Nosferatu* adapted from F.W. Murnau's film and Bram Stoker's *Dracula,* and directed by Renés Migliaccio. May 27, 2000. With Nikolai Kinski, Annie Alquist, Suzan Beraza, James E. Berrier, Bunzy Bunworth, Lori Vincent.

HOURGLASS GROUP. *Sex* by Mae West. December 9, 1999. Directed by Elyse Singer; with Carolyn Baeumler, T Ryder Smith, Nina Hellman, Cynthia Darlow, Andrew Elvis Miller, Bruce Kronenberg, Dominic Hamilton-Little, Chuck Montgomery, Pedro Serrazino, Fred Velde.

HYPOTHETICAL THEATER COMPANY. *The Heart of Art* by Michael Weller. October 31, 1999. Directed by Amy Feinberg; with Allan Corduner, Stewart Clarke, David Logan Rankin, David Fitzgerald, Stefanie Zadravec, Robert Bowen Jr., Dannah Chaifetz, Mark Zeisler, Melinda Wade. *The Garden of Hannah List* by Michael McKeever. February 2, 2000. Directed by Henry Fonte; with Christine Jones, Antony Hagopian, Kimberly Kay, Kendra Bahneman, David Fitzgerald, Callum Keith King, Ryan Hillyard, Joe MacDougal, Patrick Buonaiuto.

IRISH ARTS CENTER. *The Urn* by Peter Ackerman. July 8, 1999. Directed by Robert Davenport; with Pat Buckley, Schuyler Grant, Matt Lawler, Scott Prendergast, Barbara Rubenstein, Greta Storace, Frank Bogt, John Wylie. *The Ginger Man* by J.P. Dunleavy. May 25, 2000. Directed by Ronan Wilmot; with David Murray, Julie Hale, Mary McEvoy, Karl Hayden.

JEAN COCTEAU REPERTORY. *On the Razzle* by Tom Stoppard. August 21, 1999. Directed by Scott Shattuck; with Craig Smith, Tim Deak, Harris Berlinsky, Jolie Garrett, Jason Crowl, Jennifer Lee Dudek, Angela Madden, Elise Stone. *The Balcony* by Jean Genet, translated by Bernard Frechtman. October 10, 1999. Directed by Eve Adamson; with Elise Stone, Harris Berlinsky, Christopher Black, Tim Deak, Angela Madden, Craig Smith, Jason Crowl. *The Servant of Two Masters* by Carlo Goldoni, translated and adapted by James Duncan. December 5, 1999. Directed by Jonathan R. Polgar; with Craig Smith, Tim Deak, Jason Crowl, Angela Madden, Elise Stone. *Edward II* by Bertolt Brecht, translated by Eric Bentley. January 23, 2000. Directed by Karen Lordi; with Harris Berlinsky, Elise Stone, Craig Smith, Jason Crowl. *Medea* by Euripides, translated by Philip Vellacott. April 9, 2000. Directed by Eve Adamson; with Elise Stone, Jolie Garrett, Craig Smith, Harris Berlinsky, Angela Madden.

JEWEL BOX THEATER. *It's Impossible to Sing and Play the Bass* by and with Jay Leonhart. February 21, 2000.

JOHN HOUSEMAN THEATER. *The True Confessions of a Dog Eater* (one-man show) by and with Jonathan Lopez. August 18, 1999. Directed by Bill Primavera. *Heads Up* by Kevin Hammonds and Eric Hunt. September 17, 1999. Directed by Kent Paul; with Eric Hanson, Glenn Howard, Roxanne Racitano, Ethie Stempler, Payton Thomas, Diane Vilardi, Michelle Wood. *When Words Fail . . .* by David Dannenfelser. October 10, 1999. Directed by Kevin Kittle; with Marco Jo Clate, Jackie Kamm, Danielle Liccardo, Christy Marie Moore, Michael Puzzo, Rhett Rossi, Mala Santouri, Mike Sears. *Sun Flower: The Life and Loves of Elizabeth Cady Stanton* (one-woman show) by and with Elizabeth Perry. October 30, 1999. Directed by Anita Khanzadian. *The Wound of Love* by Kathryn Grant. October 30, 1999. Directed by Ed Setrakian; with Evan Pappas, Brett Somers. (*Sun Flower* and *The Wound of Love* ran in repertory.) *Actor Found Dead* written and directed by Charles Messina. October 31, 1999. With Paul Goncalves, Andrew I. Mones, David B. Martin. *=celebration* (one-man show) by Ethan Sandler and Josie Dickson. January 25, 2000. Directed by Daniel Goldstein; with Ethan Sandler. *Small Potatoes* by Bob Rogers. January 27, 2000. Directed by Martha Pinson; with Bob Adrian, Dan Anderson, Carla Bianchi, Christopher Benson Reed, Michael Fegley, Jinn S. Kim, Lee Moore, Genevieve Schartner, Anthony Spina, Eric Taylor.

JOHN JAY COLLEGE THEATER. *The Noise of Time* conceived and directed by Simon McBurney; creative collaborator Gerard McBurney; created by Théâtre de Complicité with Charlotte Medcalf, Jan Knightley; music by Dmitri Shostakovich. March 2, 2000. With Antonio Gil Martinez, Richard Katz, Tim McMullan, Toby Sedgwich, Emerson String Quartet (Philip Setzer, Eugene Drucker, Lawrence Dutton, David Finckel).

JUDY'S CHELSEA CABARET. *Black Market Marlene: A Dietrich Cabaret* by and with James Beaman. October 1, 1999.

KEY THEATER. *Eastern Standard* by Richard Greenberg. February 18, 2000. Directed by Nathan Halvorson; with Matt Mulin, Brent Smith, Braden Joy Pospisil, Angie Den Adel, Angie Toomsen, Nathan Halvorson.

THE KITCHEN. *Jet Lag* conceived by Elizabeth Diller and Ricardo Scofidio; created by Elizabeth Diller, Ricardo Scofidio and the Builders Association. January 6, 2000. Directed by Marianne Weems; with Ann Carlson, Tim Cummings, Dominique Dibbell, Kevin Hurley, Heaven Phillips, Jeff Webster.

KRAINE THEATER. *Cheap Talk With . . .* (one-woman show) by Donna Linderman and Yosi Wanunu. August 3, 1999. Directed by Yosi Wanunu; with Donna Linderman. *The Word* written and directed by Ian McCulloch. February 5, 2000. With David Cote, Jack Fitzpatrick, Eleanor Hutchins, Gloria Falzer, William Peden.

LAMBS THEATER. *Nellie* book, music and lyrics by Bernice Lee. June 5, 1999. Directed by Patricia Heuermann and Bernice Lee; with Becky Lillie, Len West, John Kelly, Jill Corey. *The Great Debate* by Mona Johnian. July 24, 1999. Directed by Patti Freeman; with Elizabeth Chiang, Chaundra Cameron, Jamie Collins, Jim Gardner, Danny Gilroy, Paul-Anthony Giglio, Jessica Lynn Isner, Joel Liestman, Mary Mossberg, Tom Schmid, Benjamin Spierman. *Now Hear This!* (one-woman show) by and with Kathy Buckley. October 12, 1999. Directed by Sue Wolf.

LARK THEATER COMPANY. *A Hole in the Dark* by Hilly Hicks Jr. February 10, 2000. With Mary Testa.

LAURIE BEECHMAN THEATER. *Take It Like Amanda!* (cabaret) by and with Amanda Green. September 23, 1999. *Finishing the Act: Act One Finales From Broadway* (cabaret) by and with Craig Rubano. February 25, 2000. Directed by Scott Barnes.

MA-YI THEATER ENSEMBLE. *Mother Courage and Her Children* by Bertolt Brecht, adapted by Rodolfo Vera. August 13, 1999. Directed by Tazewell Thompson; with Ching Valdes-Aran. *Li'l Brown*

Brothers/Nikimalika written and directed by Chris B. Millado. May 7, 2000. With Art Acuna, Miguel Braganza, Paul Buckner, Tom Fenaughty, Lydia Gaston, JoJo Gonzales, Yvonne Jung, Eileen Rivera.

MARTIN R. KAUFMAN THEATER. *Monster* by Frank Hertle. February 20, 2000. Directed by David Copeland; with Silverio Avellino, Jessica Faith, Haley Graham, Joe Hoover, Joanna McNeilly, David Copeland.

MCGINN/CAZALE THEATER. *Anonymous* by Glen Merzer. May 31, 2000. Directed by Pamela Berlin; with Chip Zien, Rosemarie DeWitt, David Arrow, Kevin O'Rourke, Betsy Aidem, Peter Appel, Elizabeth Franz.

MEDICINE SHOW THEATER SPACE. *Exact Change* by David Epstein. June 5, 1999. Directed by Jacques Levy; with Charles Stransky, Ken Ryan, Geoff Pierson.

MEFISTO THEATER COMPANY. *Vampire Dreams* by Suzy McKee Charnas. December 1, 1999. Directed by Matthew von Waaden; with Mark Nichols, Kate Lunsford, Damien Midkiff, Carrie Wilshusen.

MINT THEATER SPACE. *Wuthering Heights: A Romantic Musical* adapted from Emily Brontë's novel; book, music and lyrics by Paul Dick. October 23, 1999. Directed by David Leidholdt; with William Thomas Evans, Jennifer Featherston, Christian Stuck.

MIRANDA THEATER COMPANY. *Landlocked* by Cusi Cram. November 14, 1999. Directed by Jim Gaylord; with Helen Wassell, Matt Servitto, Peter Hirsch, Kate Mailer, Amy Wilson, Michael Port. *Handshake* by Julie Gilbert and Robert A. Brodner. January 15, 2000. Directed by Yanna Kroyt-Brandt; with Dan Pinto, Brian Delate, M.J. Karmi, Ariane Brandt, Oliver Vaquer, Donald Symington.

NADA SHOW WORLD. *Us* by Karen Malpede. May 10, 2000. Directed by Mahayana Landowne; with Veronica Cruz, Anthony Giangrande.

NAKED ANGELS. *Shyster* by Bryan Goluboff. November 30, 1999. Directed by Dante Albertie; with Phyllis Newman, Fisher Stevens, Saundra McClain, Annabella Sciorra, Charles Malik Whitfield. *Hurricane* by Erin Cressida Wilson. December 11, 1999. See its entry under Classic Stage Company in this section.

NATIONAL ASIAN AMERICAN THEATER COMPANY. *Othello* by William Shakespeare. February 16, 2000. Directed by Jonathan Bank; with Joshua Spafford, Joel de la Fuente, Tina Horii, Tess Lina, Andrew Pang, James Saito, Jennifer Kato, John Roque, Joel Carino. *The Harmfulness of Tobacco* by Anton Chekhov and *A Phoenix Too Frequent* by Christopher Fry (one-act plays). May 31, 2000. Directed by Stephen Stout; with James Saito, Michi Barall, Joel Carino, Mia Katigbak.

NEIGHBORHOOD PLAYHOUSE. *Angels Don't Dance* by Richard Brockman. September 29, 1999. Directed by Mirra Bank; with Jeff Sugarman, Eliza Foss, Dreya Weber, Holly Hawkins, Brad Calcaterra, Fidelma Murphy.

NEW 42ND STREET THEATER. *On the Middle Watch: The Titanic Inquest* by Nicholas van Hoogstraten, adapted from government transcripts; with Culleen Wheeler, Larry Swansen, Fred Burrell, Lynne Otis. July 22, 1999. Directed by Reagan Fletcher. *Someone's Comin' Hungry* by Neil R. Selden. February 20, 2000. Directed by Sandy Harper; with Kathryn Smith McGlynn, Anselm Richardson, Elena Katzap, Randy Frazier. *Bridges: Reach Out and Touch Someone* and *You and the Night and the Music* (one-act plays) written and directed by Lionel Kranitz. April 7, 2000. With Miriam Babin, Ross Haines, Joseph Riccobene, Richard Springle.

NEW YORK GILBERT AND SULLIVAN PLAYERS. *The Pirates of Penzance.* December 29, 1999. *Princess Ida.* January 6, 2000. Directed by Albert Bergeret and Jan Holland; with Frank Gorshin, Lynn Vardaman, Philip Reilly, Keith Jameson, Lara Wilson, Maariana Vikse, Patrick Gallagher, Edward Prostak, Noah Sferra, Walter DuMelle, Larry Picard, Valerie Stadler. *H.M.S. Pinafore.* April 13, 2000.

NEW VICTORY THEATER SPACE. *Vers la Flamme (Toward the Flame)* (dance theater piece) by Martha Clarke, adapted from Anton Chekhov's stories *Enemies, The Lady With The Lap Dog, The Darling, The Grasshopper* and *A Nervous Breakdown*; music by Alexander Scriabin. September 15, 1999. With Paola Styron, Margie Gillis, Felix Blaska, George de la Pena. (Presented as part of Lincoln Center's Great Performers series.)

NEW YORK INTERNATIONAL FRINGE FESTIVAL. Schedule included *Admissions* by Tony Vellela, directed by Austin Pendleton; *Alien Intercourses* by and with Gary Hernandez, Eric Hunt and Jim

Swimm; *Audience* by Vaclav Havel; *The Black Rider* (opera) by Tom Waits, Robert Wilson and William S. Burroughs; *Cathleen's Carnage* by and with Fools Company; *Clowning the Bible* by and with Six Figures Theater Company; *Flight to Freedom: Eastville on the Underground Railroad* by E.M. Lewis, directed by Erma Duricko; *Jaywalker* (one-woman show) by and with Marga Gomez; *Jinkies! The Totally Unauthorized, Partially Improvised Scooby Doo Mysteries Live on Stage* by and with Fun and Games Stage Company; *Last Tango in Transylvania* by John Taylor; *Margaret Atwood's Good Bones and Simple Murders* adapted by Eileen Glenn and Vincent P. Mahler, directed by Vincent P. Mahler; *Messages for Gary* by Patrick Horrigan; *The Phoenix* by Morgan Spurlock; *Time/Bomb* by Collision Theory Explosive Physical Theater; *Tough Choices for the New Century* by Jane Anderson, directed by Alex Lippard; *United States: A Day in the Life of Clark Chipman* by Jon Schumacher. August 18–29, 1999.

NEW YORK PERFORMANCE WORKS. *Taxicab Chronicles* by Gary Gere. September 23, 1999. Directed by Abigail Zealey Bass; with Denny Dale Bess, Laura Bell Bundy, Gary Gere, Marlene Hodgdon, Bill Lewis, Mary Jane Wells, Karen Young. *Imperfect Love* written and directed by Brandon Cole. March 1, 2000. With Leslie Lyles, Christopher McCann, Ed Hodson, Peter Dinklage, John Gould Rubin. *Closet Land* by Radha Bharadwaj. May 25, 2000. Directed by Jeremy B. Cohen.

NEW YORK THEATER WORKSHOP. *The Trestle at Pope Lick Creek* by Naomi Wallace. June 30, 1999. Directed by Lisa Peterson; with Michael Pitt, Alicia Goranson, David Chandler, Nancy Robinette, Philip Goodwin. Transferred to off Broadway; see its entry in the Plays Produced Off Broadway section of this volume.

NUYORICAN POETS CAFÉ. *Monk* by Laurence Holder. February 3, 2000. Directed by Rome Neal and Laurence Holder; with Rome Neal.

PANTHEON THEATER. *The Persecution of Arnold Petch* by David Hauptschein. June 16, 1999. Directed by Jennifer Markowitz; with Carl Tarcangeli, Dawn McGee, Wesley Walker, Roger Del Pozo, Vincent LoRusso, Maite Wokoeck. *The Odd Couple* by Neil Simon. April 5, 2000. Directed by David M. Pincus; with Kristina Latour, Jodie Bentley.

PEARL THEATER COMPANY. *Mirandolina* by Carlo Goldoni, translated by Michael Feingold. September 27, 1999. Directed by Lou Jacob. *John Gabriel Borkman* by Henrik Ibsen. November 22, 1999. *The Merry Wives of Windsor* by William Shakespeare. January 17, 2000. Directed by James Alexander Bond; with Dan Daily, Shona Tucker, Carol Schultz, Ray Virta, Jay Russell, Robin Leslie Brown, Dominic Cuskern; *The Way of the World* by William Congreve. March 19, 2000. Directed by Ray Virta. *The Oresteia: Agamemnon, The Libation Bearers* and *The Furies* by Aeschylus, translated by Peter Meineck. April 17, 2000. Directed by Shepard Sobel; with Robert Hock, Mikel Sarah Lambert, John Wylie, Joanne Camp, Katherine Leask, Dan Daily, Rachel Botchan, Jay Russell, Christopher Moore.

PLAYERS THEATER. *Keep Bangin'* by Jared Crawford. September 23, 1999. Directed by Savion Glover; with Darrell Dove Jr., David Dove, Dennis J. Dove, Marc Durham, Raymond King, Christopher Little, Darryl Warner.

PRODUCERS' CLUB II. *The Lady in the Jukebox* book, music and lyrics by Sheila Geer. November 11, 1999. Directed by Beau Decker.

PULSE THEATER ENSEMBLE. *Solo Flight* (one-person shows). Schedule included *The Serpent's Sermon* by and with Ron Stroman; *In the Shadow of the Third Rail* by and with Michael Schwartz; *Songs My Father Taught Me* by and with Alan Aymie; *Comedy Isn't Pretty, Tragedy Isn't Ugly* by and with Eren T. Gibson; *Off the Wall* by and with Robin Brenner; *An Hour of Hell in Harmony* by and with Melissa Dodd. July 27-August 10, 1999. *Living with Dragons* by Kevin Brofsky. September 14, 1999. Directed by Craig Rhyne; with Julie Hera DeStephano, Alice Gold, Laura Leopard, Sam Stewart, Jim Wisniewski, Mark Wesley Freedman.

RIVERSIDE STAGE COMPANY. *Ampersand* by David L. Williams. October 13, 1999. *Watching My Hair Grow* by and with Jeff Shade. November 14, 1999. Directed by Brian Feehan. *Carrin Beginning* by W. August Schulenberg. December 1, 1999. Directed by Brian Feehan; with Norman Allen, Dawn Denvir, Katrina Ferguson, Stephen Guarino, Mary Jo McConnell, Liam Christopher O'Brien, G.W. Reed, Cara Stoner.

ST. LUKE'S CHURCH. *Finnegan's Farewell* (interactive theater piece) by Kevin Alexander. September 22, 1999. Directed by Chuck Santoro; with Tommy Carroll, Norma Crawford, Bart Shatto, Erin Pender, Tade Reen, Christine Siracusa, Mark Aldrich, Elizabeth Nagengast.

ST. MARK'S THEATER. *Simone De Beauvoir on Sex, Art and Feminism* (one-woman show) by and with Emily Blake. March 24, 2000. Directed by John Murnin.

ST. PETER'S CHURCH. *Mt. Asagi* written and directed by Yuko Hamada. June 22, 1999. With Ben Wang, Katie Takahashi, Ken Park, Emi Kikuchi, Yuko Hamada.

THE SALON. *A Tale of Two Cities* adapted from Charles Dickens's novel and directed by Will Pomerantz. September 24, 1999. With Yusef Bulos, Gary Brownlee, Tertia Lynch, Greg McFadden, Michael Pemberton, Juliet Pritner, Mark Rimer, Rebecca Wisocky.

SANFORD MEISNER THEATER. *This Is a Test* (one-man multimedia piece) by and with Michael D. Conway. January 17, 2000. Directed by Melinda McGraw and Charlie Otte.

SARGENT THEATER. *Brotherly LoveS* by Kyaw Tha Hla and Jeff Clinkenbeard. September 14, 1999. Directed by Elysabeth Kleinhans; with Jeanne L. Austin, Nick Bosco, Jeff Clinkenbeard, Dave Dwyer, Jezabel Montero, Tom Morrissey, Patricia Naggiar, Duncan M. Rogers. *Meet George Orwell* by Mark Weston. January 18, 2000. Directed by Michael Alexander; with Michael Allinson.

78TH STREET THEATER LAB. *Lick* by Catherine Celesia Allen. June 13, 1999. Directed by Eva Saks; with Florencia Lozano, Peter McCabe, Quentin Maré. *Guinevere* by Pam Gems. May 19, 2000. Directed by Eric Nightengale; with Alan Nebelthau, Jeanne Ruskin.

SOHO PLAYHOUSE. *Dressing Room* book and lyrics by Mimi Scott; music by Matthew Gandolfo. April 11, 2000. Directed by Dennis Edenfield; with Paula Newman, Jaid Barrymore, Nina Fine, Lorraine Fogliano, Melissa Marlin, Christine Nardone, Sidney Myer, Tommy Femia, James Daguanno.

STORM THEATER COMPANY. *Arrah-na-Pogue* by Dion Boucicault. January 14, 2000. Directed by Peter Dobbins; with Kate Brennan, Conn Horgan, Marian Thomas Griffin, Laurence Drozd, Bernard Smith, J.J. Reap, Dan Berkey. *Eurydice: Legend of Lovers* by Jean Anouilh. May 12, 2000. Directed by John Regis; with Tiffany Weigel, Christian Conn, Jimmy Flannery.

THE TALKING BAND. *Black Milk Quartet* (one-act musicals) librettos and direction by Paul Zimet: *Actaeon* by Gina Leishman; *Black Milk* by Ellen Maddow; *Price Slasher* by Harry Mann; *Colored Glasses* by Dan Froot. January 23, 2000. With Robert Aronson, William Badgett, David Duffield, Dina Emerson, Cecilia Engelhart Lopez, Jack Ferver, Marcy Jellison, Ellen Maddow.

TARGET MARGIN THEATER. *Tulpa* by Todd Alcott, directed by David Herskovits. October 19, 1999. With Melody Cooper, Chuck Montgomery, Mary Neufeld, Lenore Pemberton, Kavitha Ramachandran, Yuri Skujins. *Some Assembly Required* (laboratory festival of readings and productions). Schedule included *Zulu Pet* written and directed by Kent Alexander; *Dick in London* by Cahir O'Doherty, directed by Elizabeth Stevens; *Innocent* by Nicholas Ridout, directed by Steven Rattazzi; *Rook* by Kathy Hemingway Jones, directed by Yuri Skujins; *The Anti-Muse* by Michael Brodsky, directed by Mary Neufeld; *Trueblinka* by Adam Rapp, directed by James Hannaham; *The Insomniac* written and directed by Teddy Jefferson. January 12–30, 2000. *The Five Hysterical Girls Theorem* by Rinne Groff. April 26, 2000. Directed by David Herskovits; with Purva Bedi, Angela Bullock, Tonya Canada, Joyce Lee, Charles Parnell, Steven Rattazzi, Abigail Savage.

THEATER AT ST. CLEMENT'S. *O! Freedom!* book, music and lyrics by Ted Reinert. February 18, 2000. Directed by Jack Waddell.

THEATER FOR A NEW AUDIENCE. *King John* by William Shakespeare. January 30, 2000. Directed by Karin Coonrod; with Ned Eisenberg, Michael Rogers, Myra Carter, Derek Smith, Pamela Nyberg, Nicholas Kepros, Bruce Turk, Michael Ray Escamilla. *Waste* by Harley Granville-Barker. March 12, 2000. Directed by Bartlett Sher; with Byron Jennings, Brenda Wehle, Kristin Flanders, Richard Easton, Ross Bickell, Graeme Malcolm, Pamela Nyberg, Jordan Charney, Henry Stram.

THEATER FOUR. *After the Rain* by Sergi Belbel, translated by David George. June 2, 1999. Directed by Daniel Kadin; with Jennifer Chambers, Joel Rooks, Diana Henry, James Tupper, Laura Wickens, Kristen Lee Kelly, Mari-Esther Magaloni, Laura Wickens, Greg Sims.

THEATER OFF PARK. *Vick's Boy* by Ben Bettenbender. October 3, 1999. Directed by Bob Balaban; with Johanna Day, Andrew Polk, Rob Sedgwick, Jim Bruchitta, Justin Hagan. *The Messenger* by David Van Asselt. March 19, 2000. Directed by Stephen Di Menna.

THEATER ROW THEATER. *Inappropriate* by A. Michael DeSisto and Lonnie McNeil; music and lyrics by Michael Sottile. November 23, 1999. Directed by Ray Leeper and Michael Sottile; with Mia

NEW 42ND STREET THEATER—Culleen Wheeler and Larry Swansen in a scene from the Theater Outrageous production of *On the Middle Watch—The Titanic Inquest*

Benenate, Averie Boyer, Josh Geyer, Liz Irwin, Jamie Ourisman, Diane Schwartz, Sarah Seckinger, Adam Schiffman.

THIRTEENTH STREET THEATER. *Tricycle* by Carson Coulon. May 11, 2000. Directed by Russ Valvo.

TRIAD THEATER. *Miami Beach Monsters* conceived by Helen Butleroff, Georgia Bogardus Holof, Robert Leahy, George Robert Minkoff, Ellen M. Schwartz and Carol Spero; book by Dan Berkowitz, Georgia Bogardus Holof and Ellen M. Schwartz; music by Michael Brown, Dick Gallagher, David Mettee, Steven Silverstein and David Strickland; lyrics by Michael Brown, Stephen Cole, Georgia Bogardus Holof and Ellen M. Schwartz. October 31, 1999. Directed by Helen Butleroff; with Steve Elmore, Diane J. Findlay, Laurie Gamache, Craig Mason, Richard Rowan, Jimmy Spadola. *yConfidentially Cole* music by Cole Porter, Steve Ross and Ann Hampton Callaway. February 10, 2000. Directed by Lina Koutrakos; with Sean Hayden.

TRIBECA PLAYHOUSE. *Night Blooming Jasmine* by Israela Margolit. February 16, 2000. Directed by Jeremy Dobrish; with Melissa Gabriel, Thom Christopher, Pierre Epstein, Joshua Annex, Dean

Strober, Ian Kahn, Frances Anderson, Tricia Paoluccio. *Sure of This One* by and with Michael McCauley. March 10, 2000. Directed by Charles Gale.

29TH STREET REP. *Avenue A* by David Steen. September 16, 1999. Directed by Jim Holmes; with Patrick Burchill, Moira McDonald, David Mogentale, Thomas Wehrle. *South of No North: Stories of the Buried Life* by Charles Bukowski, adapted and directed by Leo Farley and Jonathan Powers. March 3, 2000. With Tim Corcoran, Elizabeth Elkins, Pamela Ericson, Paula Ewin, Stephen Payne, Thomas Wehrle, Charles Willey.

21 SOUTH WILLIAM STREET. *The Designated Mourner* by Wallace Shawn. May 13, 2000. Directed by Andre Gregory; with Deborah Eisenberg, Larry Pine, Wallace Shawn.

URBAN STAGES. *The Queen Bee's Last Stand or Why Your Mail Is Sometimes Late* by Rob Santana. September 8, 1999. Directed by T.L. Reilly; with Valorie Hubbard, Idi Janko, Carlo D'Amore, K.C. Ramsey, Michael Alexis Palmer. *Coyote on a Fence* by Bruce Graham. March 26, 2000. Directed by Lou Jacob; with Tom Stechschulte, Paul Sparks, Pam Hart, David Letwin.

WEISSBERGER THEATER GROUP. *Enter the Guardsman* book by Scott Wentworth, based on Ferenc Molnar's *The Guardsman*; music by Craig Bohmler; lyrics by Marion Adler. May 21, 2000. Directed by Scott Wentworth; with Robert Cuccioli, Marla Schaffel, Mark Jacoby, Kate Dawson, Rusty Ferracane, Buddy Crutchfield.

WEST END THEATER. *Flyer* by Kate Aspengren. November 1, 1999. Directed by Linda Ames Key; with Tandy Cronyn, Sara Berg, Nick Dantos, Monique Gramby, Gay Isaacs, Michael Latshaw, Shayne Mishler, Joseph O'Brien, Clea Rivera, Susan P. Vaughn. *Exhibit #9* by Tracey Wilson. February 28, 2000. Directed by Lenora Pace; with Jeanine T. Abraham, Christopher Kirk Allen, Regge Allan Bruce, Tracey A. Leigh, Karim Sekou, L. Trey Wilson.

WESTBETH THEATER CENTER. *I'm the One That I Want* (one-woman show) by and with Margaret Cho. July 8, 1999. Directed by Karen Taussig. *Circles* by and with Eddie Izzard. *Shut Up and Love Me* by and with Karen Finley. April 14, 2000. *Almost Famous* (one-man show) by and with Bruce Vilanch. May 11, 2000. Directed by Scott Wittman.

WILLIAMS LAFAYETTE THEATER. *Gospel Is* book and lyrics by Vy Higginsen and Ken Wydro; music by Wesley Naylor. October 9, 1999. Directed by Ken Wydro; with Richard Hartley, Doris Troy, Darryl Copeland, Knoelle Higginsen-Wydro, Tonya Lewis, Kelvin Lowery, Darren Page, Sissy Peoples, Melanie Price, Dejahnee Richardson, Melvin Thomas, Anita Wells.

WILLOW CABIN THEATER. *Nighthawks* by Lynn Rosen. February 14, 2000. Directed by Miriam Weiner; with Angela Nevard, Cynthia Bestman, Ken Forman, John Billeci, Larry Gleason, Kathryn Langwell, Joel Van Liew, Christina Kirk. *Lucrece* adapted by Thornton Wilder, from André Obey's play *Le Viol de Lucréce*. May 15, 2000. Directed by Edward Berkeley; with Linda Powell, David Paluck, John Bolger, Terry Schappert, Robert Harte, Maria Radman, Larry Gleason.

WINDSOR REPERTORY THEATER. *Dewpoint* by Vincent Sessa. May 13, 2000. Directed by Elfin Frederick Vogel; with Mark Shelton, Charlene Tosca Rees, Carey Woodworth, Rachel Sledd, Alan Jestice, Sam Kitchin, Roslyne Hahn.

WOMEN'S SHAKESPEARE COMPANY. *Measure for Measure* by William Shakespeare. April 2, 2000. Directed by R.J. Tolan; with Ellen Lee, AnneMarie Falvey, Natalie Zea, Kate Sandberg, Lisa Raymond, Kelli Lynn Harrison, Kate Hess.

THE WOOSTER GROUP. *North Atlantic* (multimedia piece) text by James Strahs. October 14, 1999. Directed by Elizabeth LeCompte; with Willem Dafoe, Kate Valk, Steve Buscemi, Chad Coleman, Steve Cuiffo, Ari Fliakos, Koosil-ja Hwang, Emily McDonnell, Helen Eve Pickett, Scott Shepherd, Michelle Stern. Reopened January 11, 2000.

WORTH STREET THEATER COMPANY. *Small Craft Warnings* by Tennessee Williams. June 28, 1999. Directed by Jeff Cohen; with Michael Cannis, Stewart Steinberg, Eliza Pryor Nagel, Anthony Mangano, Cristine McMurdo-Wallis, John DiBenedetto, David Greenspan, Liam Christopher O'Brien. Reopened May 8, 2000. *Uncle Jack* written and directed by Jeff Cohen, based on Anton Chekhov's *Uncle Vanya*. November 8, 1999. With Leila Danette, Bernard K. Addison, Gerald Anthony, Paul Whitthorne, Ronald Guttman, Keira Naughton, Francesca Faridany, Betty Low.

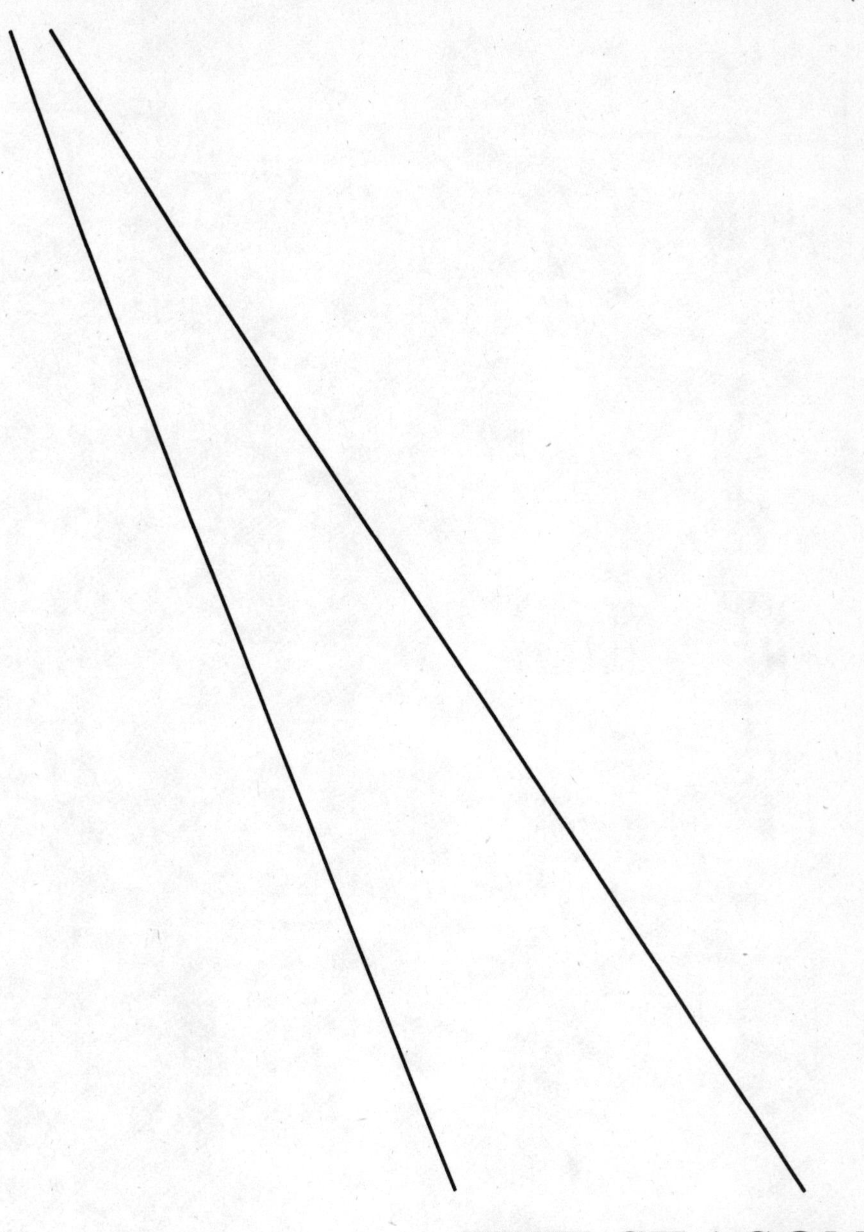

THE SEASON AROUND THE UNITED STATES

OUTSTANDING NEW PLAYS CITED BY AMERICAN THEATER CRITICS ASSOCIATION and A DIRECTORY OF NEW-PLAY PRODUCTIONS

THE American Theater Critics Association (ATCA) is the organization of drama critics in all media in all sections of the United States. One of this group's stated purposes is "To increase public awareness of the theater as a *national* resource" (italics ours). To this end, beginning in 1977 ATCA has annually cited outstanding new plays produced around the U.S., to be represented in our coverage by excerpts from each of their scripts demonstrating literary style and quality. This year, one of these—*Oo-Bla-Dee* by Regina Taylor, produced by the Goodman Theater in Chicago—has been designated ATCA's 24th annual principal citation and its 15th annual New Play Award, this year renamed the American Theater Critics Association/Steinberg New Play Award carrying with it an annual cash prize of $15,000, thanks to a grant from the Harold and Mimi Steinberg Charitable Trust. To celebrate the onset of this new arrangement, we have augmented our coverage of *Oo-Bla-Dee* hereinunder.

Two 1999–2000 American Theater Critics Association/Steinberg New Play Citations went to *Compleat Female Stage Beauty* by Jeffrey Hatcher, which premiered at Pittsburgh's City Theater, and *Syncopation* by Allan Knee, co-produced by the Long Wharf Theater in New Haven, Conn. and the George Street Playhouse in New Brunswick, N.J. Thanks to the generosity of the Steinberg Charitable Trust, each of these citations carries with it a cash prize of $5,000.

ATCA's sixth annual Elizabeth Osborn Award for an emerging playwright was voted to Coby Goss for *Marked Tree,* produced by Seanachai Theater in Chicago.

Of the new scripts nominated by ATCA members for the ATCA/Steinberg prizes, six were selected as finalists by the 1999–2000 ATCA New Plays Committee before making their final citations. A second play by Jeffrey Hatcher, *Sockdology* at Alabama Shakespeare Festival in Montgomery, made it to the finals, which also included Kira Obolensky's *The Adventures of Herculina* at the Next Theater in Evanston, Ill., and Chay Yew's *Wonderland* at the La Jolla, Calif. Playhouse.

The process of selection of these outstanding plays is as follows: any American Theater Critics Association member may nominate the first full professional production of a finished play (not a reading or an airing as a play-in-progress) during the calendar year under consideration. Nominated 1999 scripts were studied and discussed by the New Plays Committee chaired by Lawrence Bommer (Chicago *Tribune* and Chicago *Reader)* and comprising assistant chairman Alec Harvey (Birmingham *News),* Jackie Demaline (Cincinnati *Enquirer),* Marianne Evett (Cleveland *Plain Dealer),* Ellen Foreman *(Theater News London),* Barbara Gross (freelance, Washington *Post),* Robert Hurwitt (San Francisco *Examiner),* Elizabeth Maupin (Orlando *Sentinel)* and Herb Simpson (Rochester, N.Y. *City Newspaper).* These committee members made their choices on the basis of script rather than production. If the timing of nominations and openings prevents some works from being considered in any given year, they will be eligible for consideration the following year if they haven't since moved to New York. We offer our sincerest thanks and admiration to the ATCA members and their committee for the valuable insights into the 1999 theater year around the United States which their selections provide for this *Best Plays* record, in the form of excerpts from the outstanding scripts, and most particularly in the introductory reviews by Richard Christiansen *(Oo-Bla-Dee),* Alice T. Carter *(Compleat Female Stage Beauty)* and Rosalind Friedman *(Syncopation).*

To celebrate the turn of the millennium and ATCA's own 25th anniversary, the several hundred members of the Association made their selections of 25 American plays and 25 American musicals which, in the words of the organization's chairman, Jeffrey Eric Jenkins, "have had a significant and lasting impact on American theater and culture." 422 plays and musicals were mentioned among lists submitted. Here are the composite top-25 results, with ties for any position listed in alphabetical order.

25 Significant American Musicals of the 20th Century

1. Oklahoma!
2. West Side Story
3. Guys and Dolls
   Show Boat
5. A Chorus Line
6. Cabaret
7. My Fair Lady
8. Porgy and Bess
9. Fiddler on the Roof
10. Gypsy
    Hair
    South Pacific
13. Carousel
14. Company
    Sweeney Todd
16. The Fantasticks
17. Kiss Me, Kate
18. Pal Joey
19. Follies
    The King and I
21. Hello, Dolly!
22. Chicago
23. The Music Man
24. Anything Goes
    A Little Night Music

25 Significant American Plays of the 20th Century

1. A Streetcar Named Desire
2. Death of a Salesman
3. Long Day's Journey Into Night
4. Our Town
5. The Glass Menagerie
6. Who's Afraid of Virginia Woolf?
7. Angels in America
   A Raisin in the Sun
9. You Can't Take It With You
10. The Crucible
11. The Little Foxes
12. Fences
    The Iceman Cometh
14. The Odd Couple
15. Cat on a Hot Tin Roof
16. Waiting for Lefty
17. American Buffalo
    Inherit the Wind
19. The Skin of Our Teeth
20. Glengarry Glen Ross
21. The Front Page
    Picnic
23. The Boys in the Band
24. Buried Child
    The Zoo Story

ATCA/Steinberg New Play Award

OOO
OOO
OOO
OOO
OOO
OOO

OO-BLA-DEE

A Play in Three Acts

BY REGINA TAYLOR

Cast and credits appear on page 406 of *The Best Plays of 1998–99*

REGINA TAYLOR is an actress with a long list of credits on Broadway (Romeo and Juliet, As You Like It, Macbeth), *off Broadway* (Machinal, Map of the World, The Illusion, Dr. Faustus, The Tempest), *in the movies and on TV. Her acting has won her a Dramalogue Award, a Golden Globe Award for best leading dramatic actress and an Emmy nomination, and now the 1999–2000 ATCA/Steinberg New Play Award-winning* Oo-Bla-Dee *proves that she is the theater's version of a triple threat, flourishing also as a playwright and a director.*

Taylor is an Artistic Associate of Chicago's Goodman Theater, which commissioned and produced Oo-Bla-Dee *(co-directed by its author) and has housed her* The Ties That Bind *(1994, the one-acts* Watermelon Rinds *and* Inside the Belly of the Beast) *and* Escape From Paradise *(1995–96, a solo show she adapted from one of her own plays,* Jenine's Diary). *Her New York writing credits have included* Escape From Paradise *at Circle Repertory,* Mudtracks *at Ensemble Studio Theater and* Ghost Train *and* Sty Farm, *both adapted from Franz Xavier Kroetz one-acts for New York Shakespeare Festival. In cross-country theater, Alliance Theater commissioned Taylor to write the book for* Jubilee, *about the Fisk Jubilee Singers; and this very season the Actors Theater of Louisville offered* Beside Every Good Man, *written and directed by Taylor, on its schedule of Phone Plays, and Alabama Shakespeare Festival premiered her* A Night in Tunisia, *also under her direction.*

INTRODUCTION: The inspiration for *Oo-Bla-Dee* came to Regina Taylor when she met and visited with a Chicago friend's great aunt, a former jazz musician who had played with various bands in the 1940s and 1950s. "She had great stories about those days," Taylor recalls, "and I took notes."

Her interest sparked by that initial conversation, Taylor began research on the period, gathering information through newspapers and journals and conducting further interviews with women musicians who were survivors of the World War II era. Already isolated as jazz artists and by their skin color, they bore the additional onus of being females who were intruding on what had been considered male turf.

Using these memories, and picking up bits of dialogue she had written but had yet to pin down in a play, Taylor fashioned *Oo-Bla-Dee.* The core strory concerns Gin Del Sol, a gifted young saxophonist who joins the hard-living, hard-driving musicians of a group called Evelyn Waters and the Diviners.

Taylor's script, however, does not proceed in strict linear style. It moves back and forth in time and place, and one of its chief characters is Luna, a chameleon-like presence who is witness to and master of ceremonies, setting the scene and commenting on the story. Along with the flavorful shop talk and small talk of the musicians, Taylor spins out her own jazz riffs of language, her women soaring off into rhapsodic arias of syncopated speech.

You get an idea of the color and pace of her imagery in the play's second act, which takes place in memory and as the musicians—Gil and Evelyn, Lulu and Ruby—are driving with the band manager, Shorty, to a Chicago gig in 1946. As Gin remembers, and as the women talk, Taylor inserts a letter from overseas from Evelyn's man Leroi, and she caps off the scene with a marvelous monologue from Shorty on the meaning of "C.P. Time."

—RICHARD CHRISTIANSEN

Editor's Note: In honor of the first annual ATCA/Steinberg New Play Award, we are celebrating its winner with a fuller representation of the script than is customary in this section. Much of Oo-Bla-Dee *is expressed in stagecraft and musical effects that cannot be adequately reproduced on the printed page, but we have synopsized the adventures of Regina Taylor's young saxophonist Gin Del Sol as comprehensively as possible in the following series of verbally dramatized selections from the play, including the one cited above in Mr. Christiansen's introduction.*

As in the synopses in the Prizewinning Plays section, an abridgement within a scene is indicated by five dots (. . . . .). The appearance of three dots (. . .) is the script's own punctuation, usually to denote the timing of a spoken line.

ACT I

Scene 1

LUNA C: The year is 1946. It is after another war before Vietnam, after Jesse Owens. There is the Women's Baseball League, the Negro Baseball League, Frank Sinatra, Coloreds Only. Leroi Jones would become—but not yet. Recently Mussolini was killed—Hitler—suicide—FDR died this past year—this is before JFK, LBJ or Clinton—before MLK or Malcolm X were even thought about.. Today Reagan is in Hollywood making picture shows. The atom bomb has dropped. Rosie's riveting has stopped—waiting for her man to march home.

Sound of train is constant underneath this scene.

GIN: Soon as I got this telegram to join Evelyn Waters and the Diviners—I grabbed my ax—bought a one-way ticket—left everything behind and took to the road ..... Tomorrow I'll be in St. Louis ..... Now nothing can hold me back—box me in.

Train whistle blows. . . . .

My name—Del Sol—of the sun. Gin Del Sol. My mother a Creole from New Orleans. My father—Jose from Cuba by way of Spain.

She sees light change to morning.

My father taught me to play from the age of six. Gave me my first horn and said—"These here are your wings."

One day I'm going to find that sound
like Satchmo
like Valaida Snow
You know their name
by that first breath
—soon as they blow

Horn riff.

One day I'm going to find that sound—
That lays me bare.
Catch a ride on the rhythms of Evelyn Waters—
She'll take me there—
To my beginning and my end—
I'll leave this black skin—
White bones
I'll dare.
Lines and barriers
Will all fall away.
And I'll fly—
on the air—

Scene 2

Gin arrives backstage at Jake's Club in St. Louis, wearing *"a simple sweater, skirt and high-heeled shoes"* and carrying both saxophone and trumpet cases. Luanne ("Lu") comes in with her drum set and offers Gin a drink, which she refuses. Lu feels that Gin needs to improve her wardrobe and hairdo, because Evelyn ("Eve"), the boss of this combo, believes that "You better look like a woman if you're sitting in her band trying to play like a man."

Gin explains to Lu she has come up here from Memphis in response to a telegram from Alexander ("Shorty") Styles, manager of Evelyn Waters and the Diviners, who had heard her play in Texas with another group and liked what he heard. Lu wonders where other members of the band can be—they're supposed to go on in about half an hour. She inquires about Gin's love life and learns that there was a man Gin wanted to marry, but (Gin says) he left her to go up north and better himself.

Ruby enters, introduces herself to Gin and informs them that Eve has arranged for the band to perform later than they had expected tonight.

LU: We been out on the road with Evelyn a year now.

RUBY: Eight months. Since Lu joined.

LU: Eight months, three weeks and two days, now. Ruby started a week before me.

RUBY: Lu and I are the only survivors. Been with this group since the beginning.

LU: Been through four horn players. Evil-lean may have wanted to get rid of us too. But she couldn't find nobody better along the way.

GIN: I've heard all her records. She did arrangements for Benny Goodman. Played with Ellington, Basie, Armstrong—I'm a great admirer—

LU: She ain't made a record in the last three years—cause of her reputation—

RUBY: She's a perfectionist—that's all.

LU: She's evil is all. Downright mean.

RUBY: She just wants it done right.

LU: Yeah, it's done right but you know she wrong sometimes the way she do things. You sign on into this group and you're signing away your soul—just so you know. She needs us as much as we need her. She needs a record deal. That's why we're headed to Chicago.

RUBY: The sound will be right once we get to Chicago.

GIN *(wanting to be included; off the beat):* Chicago.

RUBY: Maybe we get some added attention because we're ladies—but you have to have something to back it up.

Gin is almost afraid to ask what happened to the girl she's replacing—she was a wild one, it seems, and was fired after she became pregnant and vomited on the bandstand during one of Eve's piano solos. Eve, Lu observes, "plays like she's possessed. It starts to feelin good to her, and she starts playing with her knuckles, her elbows, her knees." Gin comments, "You have to follow wherever the music leads. Otherwise you can't breathe. First time I split my lip—I put the horn to my mouth—It felt like a sin. My Aunt Selene said I was going to hell for sure, playing the devil's music. I told her—As sure a as God created heaven and earth he must have known what he was doing when he uttered the first sound that became jazz."

Ruby remembers that she had to choose between her marriage and her music. At first, her husband indulged her with music lessons for different instruments, but when she began to concentrate on the bass fiddle and play with jazz combos, he drew the line. Ruby chose music.

GIN: Do you ever regret?

RUBY: I never looked back—he never followed.

GIN: And your child?

RUBY: A mother—a woman leaving behind her child—the way you look at me as if—

GIN: No need to explain to me. My father said to begin with C. That's what I played the first four years. C. He said, "If you master the C it will unlock the door, take you whatever direction you want to go." C.

Studying the music: "In the Land of Oo-Bla-Dee." She practices a bar.

RUBY: B flat at the bridge.

Gin plays more.

You read pretty good. Played with a band where nobody could read. I said what key? He said—don't worry your head—when I knock three times, just play.

GIN: The sound has to be right when we get to Chicago.

The manager, Shorty, comes in and introduces himself. Soon he and Gin are arguing over whether the telegram which led Gin to leave a paying gig and come to St. Louis is a binding contract. Eve enters throwing what Ruby calls "a hissy"—she is angry at Shorty for bringing in a new girl without having consulted her. She, Evelyn, is the star, she reminds him, and Shorty is only a temporary substitute for their real manager, his brother Leroi, who is in the army. Shorty argues that they need three Diviners in addition to Evelyn, that's what the contract with the club calls for.

Ruby interrupts with the information that she's heard Gin practice, implying that Gin's playing was satisfactory. Eve asks Gin who she is.

GIN: Gin Del Sol—my mother owned a cafe in New Orleans—my father—a band leader from Cuba, taught me to play early on. Joined International Sweethearts of Rhythm when I was seventeen and then struck out on my own. I've followed your career for years, Miss Evelyn Waters. First time I saw you, you were conducting a band with one hand, composing with the other and all the while playing the piano—you didn't miss a beat. That was back in Thirty-five when I first saw you.

Pause.

EVE: Gin?

GIN: Gin Del Sol.

EVE: Never heard of you—See, this is what I'm up against. Starting a woman's band—amateurs. Leroi's idea. Evelyn Waters doing a novelty act. Get people in the business interested again. Hell, where are we gonna find some chicks that can play—I've played with men all my life. Fronted all-men bands. I told them what to do.

SHORTY: Everybody knows you're a genius, Eve.

EVE: Get me a drink, Shorty. A woman piano player is feminine— She's square in anybody's book. While the rest of it—bass, drums, sax—is for the boys, always has been, always will be—you're all freaks, Tell her, Ruby.

Shorty pours her a drink from a flask.

RUBY: First time I played in a dive they threw eggs at me—

EVE: Like she had snakes hissing out of her head. A woman plucking strings between her legs.

RUBY: Later they threw coins—

EVE: A passing fad. That's what this is. Sweethearts of Rhythm. Swinging Rays of Rhythm . . .

SHORTY *(overlap):* With Earl Fatha Hines . . .

EVE: . . . The Darlings of Rhythm.

SHORTY *(overlap):* Then Harlem Playgirls.

EVE: That Ina Ray Hutton hussy . . .

SHORTY *(overlap):* The Blond Bombshell.

EVE: . . . and her Melodears . . . All of them circus acts. They sing—they tap—they tell some jokes—they twirl batons—but the music—sometimes fair—sometimes good—like Lulu—like Ruby here—Most just inexperienced. Don't get the chance to sit in where they want to. When they can—Inexperience don't cut it—not with me. I have a reputation to uphold. Evelyn Waters a side show act—that's not me—maybe for some little Podunk town, but not in the metropolis, not where I'm known—

SHORTY: You're a star, Duchess.

EVE: I started out playing piano for a carny show out on my own by the time I was thirteen years old. I ain't going back to that . . .

Shorty reassures Eve that she has developed her sound to the point that the band is ready for Chicago and all that it promises: "Your name in lights. Sparkling bright as before." Eve decides that Gin can play with the group tonight: "I'll see if you got the balls or whatever." With this opportunity, Gin finds herself face to face with the tomorrow she thought might never come. As the women exit, Moms Mabley's voice is heard—that act is just winding up. Then an Announcer's voice is heard.

ANNOUNCER: And now, ladies and gentlemen, we have an act for you tonight. You may see and not believe. But feast your eyes on this most novel attraction.

SHORTY: A whistling woman and crowing hen often come to no good end.

Lights out on Shorty. Lights up on women on the stage in front of mikes. Song cue. The women "play" "In the Land of Oo-Bla-Dee," an ensemble effort. Toward the end of the song Gin takes over the lead—haltingly at first . . . . . Gin courageously blows. The women grow silent as she flies solo. She's really good. Pause.

EVE *(half bitter, half admiring):* Damn.

Eve leads the rest of the group back in for ensemble finish, as recorded music comes up. Lights out. Curtain.

ACT II

Scene 1

LUNA C: By the time you get the words out to talk about what is now going on/Now has already been done gone/Try to hold it in your hands/And all that's left is memory and myth/The fall of 1946.

Gin in a square of light as if in a radio booth or window of a hotel room, with Eve, Shorty, Ruby and Lu.

GIN: How long—

EVE: How long since—

RUBY: I remember—

SHORTY: That time we were in St. Louis—

LU: —and took on that new girl.

EVE: I remember—

SHORTY: Trying to make it

RUBY: Up to Chicago

GIN: How long

LU: How long since—

EVE: Been ages since I played now.

RUBY: I lasted off and on through the Seventies.

LU: I had hungry mouths to feed—never sleep with a musician child. Finally had to get a real job—

RUBY: Play my grandchildren some of my records—the few that I can find and say—That's your grandma child.

LU: Seventy-six working in a canning plant lost three fingers on this hand —my thumb on my right.

EVE: Played up through the Seventies.

RUBY: Listen child—your grandma was a hot potato back then.

EVE: Revivals—

SHORTY: Jazz festivals—women don't get invited much—

LU: Talk about Lu the Deuce—she was swell.

SHORTY: People remember men—what's they name, whoever and you know who . . .

EVE: I could hang with the best of them.

SHORTY: Legends—

LU: Legends you remember—female bands you don't remember.

EVE: Don't care.

RUBY: Like we never existed sometimes.

EVE : Like we were some made-up fiction for some play.

EVE, RUBY, LU *(overlap):* But I was there.

GIN *(overlap):* How long till I get to tomorrow?

In her St. Louis hotel room, Gin is controlling her impatience, practicing in the key of C, telling herself, "I wonder why I lie so much to myself and everyone around. Can't lie to the music. Maybe why Eve says—I haven't gotten to my own sound. Making it up as I go along. Piecing it together till it fits. That's what jazz is, isn't it?"

Scene 2

In the blackout we hear "Besame Mucho" as from a car radio. Against a scrim we see projected suggested movement of passing landscape. We are in a car speeding up a highway, Eve reading aloud to the group the letter from Leroi. Shadow play of soldier—he reads along with Eve.

OO-BLA-DEE—En route to Chicago in the Goodman Theater production of Regina Taylor's play are *(in front seat)* Jacqueline Williams as Evelyn and Ernest Perry Jr. as Shorty and *(in back seat)* Margo Moorer as Lulu, Caroline Clay as Gin and Cheryl Lynn Bruce as Ruby

LEROI: Walking along the left bank . . . among the bombed buildings wading through the debris of wasted civilization. A tow-headed boy runs along beside me—pointing and smiling—American he says to me—American—I pat his head and give him chocolate. He grabs my hand and examines it palm down—in awe he says—

EVE & LEROI: "Oooh . . . American."

LEROI: He gives me a big laugh. His head thrown back—I have to laugh too—at circumstances.

EVE & LEROI: —Circumstances, distance and time.

LEROI: I'm thinking of you in America—here so far from home. My home is America. The black skin is shining armor of the liberator. Doors are open—the booze is free— I speak fluent French with a touch of . . .

EVE & LEROI: . . . Alabama *au jus.* I'm dreaming of you so far away.

The music ends and static comes from the radio. Shorty turns off the radio and hums "Careless Love."

EVE *(continues reading):* Yet when I close my eyes I swear you're standing next to me. We continue our love making like it was just a breath between a caress—-

There's no meaning to yesterday today and tomorrow. In between closed eyelids—Thinking of you—time stands still.

Shadow play out. We hear a car rush past. Everyone watches—paranoid, as it passes.

GIN: How long till we get to Chicago?

LU: Can't you drive any faster?

SHORTY: Maybe you want somebody to sprout wings.

LU: I could get out and walk and been done there, having had T-bones and oysters on the half shell, a bath and some good, slow, deep conversation before you'd creep into Chicago.

SHORTY: I'm not going too slow not going too fast. That way we're sure to get there on time—As long as we get there we're on time. That's all I got to say.

LU: And what time you figured that'd be?—

SHORTY: Soon enough.

LU: Soon ain't good enough for me. Cause soon's we get there is the sooner I get from being a gap legged colored drummer gal to being a recognized artist. We'll play at all the best clubs—make that record and hit—travel around Europe—go to Paris, France—Them white folks 'preciate Negroes playing over in Paris, France, ain't that what Leroi said in his letters—

EVE: They call him Le Royal—over there. *L'Americain.*

LU: See soon's we get to Chicago—the sooner I get to wear a shiny crown on my head.

GIN: The fastest running car I ever saw—I believe it was my Uncle Jebediah's. It ran over Monday, killed Tuesday—sent Wednesday to the hospital, crippled Thursday and told Friday to tell Saturday to be at the funeral Sunday by four o'clock.

LU: Swear your type Rastus-ass driving is killing progress.

SHORTY: Don't you worry—I know how to steer this thing—I know which way we going—how to get there and how soon.

LU: As long as soon ain't too late. Cause I been waiting too long.

GIN: Junebug has a golden wing. Lightbug has a flame. Bedbug has no wings at all, but he gets there just the same.

RUBY: Well you know how C.P. Time is.

SHORTY: Don't you be riding my back about my driving too.

RUBY: Your driving just fine—We'll get to Chicago plenty of time—unless it's grown legs it'll still be there—whatever time we get there. Just that an understanding of C.P. Time gives one patience. Late and too slow. Late to work, late for rent. That's C.P. Time.

SHORTY: Who want to hurry to get to back-breaking work that pays fifty cents a day—which is why we always late for rent—cause we always broke—

LU: Too slow—and always the last in line to get our share—last ones at the table cause of C.P. Time.

RUBY: Aunt Delilah invited her wedding guests to arrive at the stroke of 3 so the ceremony could begin promptly at 8—

GIN: Fifty miles an hour times twenty-four hours equals twelve hundred miles to . . . *(With Luna C.)* tomorrow.

SHORTY: Sure colored folks is on a different time—ain't about early or late. C.P. Time is our own time—come from the attitude of being free. See. When we were slaves—nobody had no clock—But you start work at sunup when you could see—finish work at sundown when you couldn't see—when the sun was directly above beatin' down the hardest—scorching the tops of them woolly heads—that's when you stopped—figured out some shade—took out the big black pot, cut up some onions—and potatoes—some field greens—see when the sun said stop—that's when you sat down to eat. And that's how it went every day of the week—sun said get up Negroes. Sun said eat—later on it said go on home and sleep till I tell you to get up and start over again. That's how it went every day except Sunday, and don't you know Negroes be shouting come Sunday meeting cause that was the onliest day the sun had no hold on them—They come to Sunday service singing about the day of Jubilee—cause on that day they gonna pull the sun down from the sky—yolk it and have it do their bidding. That was what freedom day was . . .

GIN: Freedom!

SHORTY: . . . Seemed like on Sunday the sun rose and fell the fastest just for spite—and sure enough—when slaves were set free, all of a sudden they got all this time on their hands—time to do what they want to do when they want to do it. Some tried lassoing old yellow, course they got burnt up in the trying—and that old laughing sun ran on its own course as it should be—at its own pace, but we was emancipated from its orbit to go every which way we pleased. Everyone didn't agree on which way that was—but those different ways of thinking and owning our time is called . . .

EVERYONE: *Colored People Time.*

SHORTY: . . . Ain't early ain't late just our own to do with to shape and form as we damn well please.

Shorty is taking it easy because he doesn't want to be stopped by some white police officer. Shorty remembers a time when he was stopped very late at night on a Georgia road and was forced to entertain the police, singing and dancing. Lu comments that if that had happened to Leroi, he would have used his .45 on them. "Then they wouldn't rest till they found who did it," Shorty tells her, "And if they couldn't find him would've hanged the first twenty-five colored men they found—at least."

Ruby brings up a recent incident in Detroit where they lynched a homecoming black soldier because he was wearing his uniform. More and more of them are coming home now, Lu observes, and Eve reminds them that Leroi will be coming home soon, and "Things will be set right. When the men come home."

Shorty notices that another car has been riding his tail. They hear its horn honking, and Shorty pulls over, promising the women that he'll take care of the situation, they have nothing to fear. When he gets out of the car, the women plan a fierce resistance if they are threatened. But Shorty soon comes back to the car. He *"looks disheveled"* and *"tries to cover his anger"* and informs the women that the people in the other car only wanted directions to Cleveland. Soon they are again on their way.

LUNA C *(dances):*

Doing a time step down this road—
Shuffle fullap ball change
one and two and three and fo'
you still got a ways to Chicago
what comes after that—only I know—

Luna C taps faster and faster.

EVERYONE: Chicago.

El train passes overhead, as Arthur appears . . . . . Curtain.

ACT III

Scene 1

Gin is in her Chicago hotel room, practicing in the key of C as usual but still unable to find her own sound. Eve comes in, and Gin tells her, "Been trying to find that jumping-off point." Eve has brought her a piece of music.

EVE: Some people think we just making it up as we go along. Wave our hands in the air, make some wild nappy-headed sounds and that's jazz. Music can't go nowhere without its history pushing it from behind. Its course is concentric. Turns upon itself. Can't go nowhere without its tail which is its beginning.

GIN: In the beginning was the sound.

EVE:

Got to walk before you can fly.
Or did we fly then crawl.

GIN:

What was the first sound.

EVE:

Ma Rainey knew it
All she had to do is moan
and you felt it
by the tone in her voice.
You know she had met up with the devil
and given him a good wrestling with.
That sound was passed
down to Bessie—
who passed it down
to Billie—

Lady Day, say she charmed death
with her sound
For you to raise the spirits up
To pass the stories down
For you to find
a voice that can
turn time whichever way around—

You and time
have gotta come to an
understanding.

Eve hands Gin the music and exits. As Gin practices, she *"steps into tomorrow,"* and the scene shifts to the club where the Diviners are going to perform.

Scene 2

At the club, Shorty tells Ruby that his brother Leroi isn't coming back to America, they are treating him like a hero in Paris. He's opening his own jazz club. He's going to tell Eve later tonight.

Eve comes in, angry because she's found out that the contract calls for her to dance with the customers.

RUBY: The understanding is just us girls will be fulfilling that obligation. You're the head of the band—Evelyn—no one expected you to—

EVE: I just spoke to the owner. That's not what he said.

SHORTY: A misunderstanding—Shorty will take care of it—no problem—Let me show you to your dressing room—I'll straighten out the owner—and by the way—a lettter—

Eve takes the letter ..... Arthur (in his Air Force uniform) enters the club.

EVE: Leroi? . . . No . . . for a moment I thought you were . . . Who are you?

ARTHUR: Coleman—Arthur Coleman—I'm looking for Virginia. A woman by the name of Virginia August.

EVE: Never heard of her—You just get back—

ARTHUR: Eight months ago.

EVE: You know a Leroi Burns—Army—over in Paris France—

SHORTY: Now Eve—Paris is a big place—I'm sure—

ARTHUR: No Ma'am, never ran into him—

EVE *(to Shorty):* My room better have fresh towels. Shorty, I need fresh *pink* towels—and some violets for the table.

SHORTY: I'm always here by your side to fulfill your every wish—Eve—you can count on Shorty.

Shorty and Eve exit.

ARTHUR: Been looking for Virginia since I got back—eight months now—heard she may have joined some kind of band—been traveling through Florida—up the coast—looking in every club along the way—Told her I was coming back—and when I did—I was going to marry her—That's the last words I said to her. It was a promise I intend to keep, once I find her. Went back home. She's been gone three years. Nobody knew where she went. She just took to the road one day—didn't take nothing with her—left everything behind—didn't take a dress or a comb or a picture or a piece of linen—most of a pineapple upside down cake was left sitting on the table—full pot of greens on the stove—I wrote her every day—Letters come to an empty home—Don't know where she gone—but when I find her—I'm going to marry her—start a business—buy a nice sized house—start a family—Give her everything she could dream of—I can do that now—Got the GI Bill—I got plans for that money—things are gonna be different now—the war is over—I made it back.

RUBY: You remind me of someone I once knew.

ARTHUR: I keep searching till I find her—

The others come in, gathering for the performance. When Gin enters, Arthur immediately recognizes her as his Virginia from Tallahassee, Florida, daughter of a seamstress and a blacksmith—"He conducted the marching band in which you played tuba down Main Street every second Saturday of the month." At first, Gin pretends she doesn't know Arthur but soon realizes that the jig is up as far as Gin Del Sol's phony identity is concerned. The truth is, however, that she's no longer the person Arthur knew and promised to marry.

GIN:

The music renamed me
It 's not Virginia August you see—

ARTHUR:

What these eyes have seen
I don't recognize these hands—
These hands that have killed so many men—
I come back to touch my Virginia August.

GIN:

It's the music that held me—rocked me—
wailed my name—shaking the walls—
made me feel

ARTHUR:

Give me back my hands—
the way I used to touch you.
Need to see myself in your eyes—
Hear you speak my name—like before—

GIN:

I can't go back now—Not tonight.

ARTHUR:
I'm not asking you to—
Take my hands—go forward with me
Take my hand—I'm offering you my name.

GIN: Don't want you to give me a name. Want to make one of my own. I'm Gin Del Sol. I'm a musician now.

ARTHUR: A musician's life. That just isn't you.

GIN: You don't know me . . . . .
I can't turn back now.
Tonight is almost here.
Tonight I'm going to push myself
through my horn
blow a hole in the sky.
Tonight I'm going to earn my wings

Eve is so disgusted with all Gin's lies, she doesn't want her to play with the group. Shorty insists, and Eve gives in, but just for tonight. Arthur exits. *"The light shifts to Luna C."*

Scene 3

Luna C remarks, "Twenty years later—1966," and Ruby and Lu are reminiscing about the Diviners. They don't know what became of that sax player, but they remember that "Evil-lean" finally got around to marrying Shorty.

Lights up on Eve and Shorty, out on Ruby and Lu.

EVE: The Diviners was a good group—one of the best I've had the privilege to play with—male or female—before or since—Ruby played bass—Lu the Deuce—

SHORTY: And Gin Del Sol—that's what she called herself—

EVE: We all called ourselves something or was called something or other—Hell, in them times we was making it up as we went along—

SHORTY: —Breaking the rules—that was what it was about—

EVE: —Bebop.

Lights out on Eve and Shorty . . . . . Lights up on Ruby and Lu.

RUBY: They say that night all the clocks stopped—a minute lost somewhere—just at that bridge she held a note for an eternity—Grown men wept remembering things forgotten—

LU: The note twisted and turned finding its way—

RUBY: —The voice of her instrument—Was she riding time—

LU: Or was time riding her?

RUBY: Never heard of her again.

LU: —But I hear her sometimes in the sound of musicians—I'll be in the audience and say—yeah—her spirit's in her—and her—maybe that's what happened to her—she keeps skipping into different generations escaping time—

RUBY: —But she made a sound that night that will live on forever.

The lights shift to Eve and Shorty, who are remembering what happened later that night, after the arrival of the record people for the Diviners' second set. "It is the fall of 1946. Saturday night," Luna C announces, and a white woman comes in to the Chicago club, *"bruised and disheveled,"* telling how her husband arrived home from the war the previous night and found her absent. When she came back to the house, she defended herself by claiming she had a right to some sort of life while he was absent those three and a half years. As Arthur appears, the Woman tells how her husband was furious, beat her, and with his buddies took her to "dump me off in darkie town."

WOMAN: They got twelve Negroes unlucky enough to cross their path—they really went crazy when they saw this Negro man in uniform—started cursing—tearing at his medals—his shirt—his shoes—dragged him into the car—I tried to stop them.

GIN *(bitter remorse):*

If I could find that sound to turn the clock around—
turn the moon to green—
and step in between
then you and I—

WOMAN/LUNA C *(to Gin):* —Think—If he had not been out there at all—or had walked a little faster or passed a little late . . .

GIN: No.

WOMAN/LUNA C: Then time would tell of a different fate.

GIN: NO. . . . .

We hear a siren like a screaming woman . . . . . Gin approaches Arthur, when she reaches him, touches him—(Light change.)—We see him illuminated . . . . . lynched. The sirens are joined by a screaming sax . . . . . After a few moments the sax is cut off by a sound hit, and the lights come back up in the club.

SHORTY: The record people are getting restless—ladies . . . . .

RUBY *(decisively taking her place on the stage):* Come too far to stop now.

She begins the music. Lu joins her, then Eve. Light change. Sirens stop. Gin . . . . . takes her place with the women—halting at first . . . Spotlight on Gin as she tries to find her voice—The tune . . . . . is searing Bebop—a calling to the sun and moon. Gin is inside the music—snipping away the layers. The stage shifts—Gin continues . . . alone on the bare stage. The stage is filled with sky—space—as Gin ascends. Blackout. Curtain.

Oo-Bla-Dee *premiered March 15, 1999 at the Goodman Theater in Chicago under the direction of Regina Taylor and Susan V. Booth.*

ATCA/Steinberg New Play Citation

OOO
OOO
OOO
OOO
OOO
OOO

COMPLEAT FEMALE STAGE BEAUTY

A Play in Two Acts

BY JEFFREY HATCHER

Cast and credits appear on pages 375–376

JEFFREY HATCHER was born in Steubenville, Ohio in 1957. He earned a B.F.A. in theater and film from Denison University in Granville, Ohio and did postgraduate work at New York University. He is a four-time participant in the Eugene O'Neill Theater Center's National Playwrights Conference and a two-time recipient of the Minnesota State Arts Board grant. In 1995 he was a Lila Wallace Readers Digest Fund Artist Fellow at the American Antiquarian Society and a Dayton-Hudson Visiting Artist Fellow at Carleton College in Northfield, Minn. In 1997 he was a Jonathan Reynolds Playwright-in-Residence at Denison. Hatcher's plays seen in New York include Three Viewings *(Manhattan Theater Club),* Scotland Road *and an adaptation of Henry James's* The Turn of the Screw *(Primary Stages) and* Fellow Travelers *(Manhattan Punchline and Actors Outlet). His other adaptations include Herman Melville's* Pierre, Smash *based on George Bernard Shaw's novel* An Unsocial Socialist *and* Sail Away *from Noel Coward's* Bon Voyage.

INTRODUCTION: At once delightfully amusing and deeply thoughtful, Jeffrey Hatcher's *Compleat Female Stage Beauty* uses the dilemma of a Restoration stage actor to examine some very modern issues.

Edward Kynaston (circa 1640–1706) was one of the last and most celebrated men to play women's roles on the English stage before King Charles II forbade that practice. In this play about him, barred from doing what he does best, stripped of occupation, friends and social ties, Kynaston searches for his identity. "It's not a question of acting like a man," he tells the King. "I can act like a man. There's no artistry in that. But there are things I can be as a woman I cannot be as a man."

In the play as in his real life, Kynaston eventually adjusted to a new identity and went on to have an equally successful career with male roles including Othello. "What I like was that he didn't end tragically. The fact that he went on seems more realistic," says Hatcher. "It doesn't have a fake tragic ending. In this case you have a man who made accommodations to survive." Hatcher says what captured his creative imagination was that this was a man who played women but had to learn to be something else both offstage and in life— "A lot of people understand what it means to stifle yourself and to try to find some way to let those passions out."

Hatcher's fiction is rooted solidly in historic fact. It weaves its story around real events of the Restoration and enlivens it with people who actually existed in the middle of the 17th century—diarist Samuel Pepys, Nell Gwynn (who was an actress as well as one of King Charles's mistresses), playwright Sir Charles Sedley and actor-manager Thomas Betterton.

But don't mistake this play for a docudrama that accurately depicts the period in which it's set. It's more of a costume piece dressed in the powdered wigs and heavily brocaded costumes of the Restoration while exploring and expanding on such contemporary themes and issues as sexual orientation and definition, women's rights, homophobia, gay-bashing, class prejudice, loyalty and professional identity.

Compleat Female Stage Beauty begins as a quick-witted backstage comedy filled with some very up-to-date rivalries and intrigues of life upon the stage. After a first act that entices you into this engaging and interesting world, the play turns darker and more serious, yet retains your interest and sympathies throughout.

Hatcher's play contains some 24 characters and nine separate locations that require rapid scene and costume changes and some doubling of roles. The design team at City Theater Company surmounted most of these challenges with style, imagination and inventiveness that created a complete and seamless world embroidered with sly comic touches and a feel for the period.

The role of Kynaston requires an actor capable of moving credibly and instantaneously from attractive female coquette to assertive male without a hint of self-parody. Actor David Hornsby achieved this as neatly as did the man he was portraying. He was, in the words of Samuel Pepys, "clearly the prettiest woman in the whole house . . . and then likewise did appear the handsomest man in the house."

—Alice T. Carter

Excerpt from *Compleat Female Stage Beauty*

The Green Room. Backstage at the Duke's Theater. Betterton plops into a chair and starts to remove his dark makeup. Pepys perches on a stool next to Betterton, jotting in his diary. Villiers stands a bit upstage. Kynaston sits at his makeup table, removing makeup. The pillow sets on the table.

BETTERTON *(deep in his point):* This is what I don't grasp. King comes to the play last week—

PEPYS *(jotting):* This is Othello?

BETTERTON: This's Othello—and he says, King says, "Bravo, Betterton, good show, thrills and chills; see it again Saturday next. Question, though: Could it be a bit . . . cheerier?" "Cheerier?" say I. "Yes," says Charlie, "something more jolly." And I say, all bowed and unctuous, "Would His Majesty prefer a comedy?" And he says, "Oh, no, Othello again, by all means, but make it jolly." And I say, "Well, Your Majesty, Mr. Shakespeare does end his play with Desdemona strangled, Emilia stabbed, Iago arrested, and Othello disemboweling himself. Do you suggest we do away with that?" And he says, "Heavens no, kill 'em all; just make it jollier." I mean, really, what is one to do with such criticism?

KYNASTON: I think it shows great theatrical sense. The King knows a good death scene when he sees it, and he knows the audience wants to go out on an "up." It's a math problem.

BETTERTON: And how do I solve it?

KYNASTON: What do I care, long as I die beautifully.

PEPYS: You could rewrite it . . . Othello smothers Desdemona, Iago confesses. Othello forgives him.

BETTERTON: What about Ned's death scene?

KYNASTON *(mock groan):* I start to groan. "Oh—Oh— Oh-thello . . . "

BETTERTON *(Othello voice):* "What? Desdemona not dead?"

KYNASTON: "Not quite."

Betterton cradles Kynaston in his arms.

BETTERTON: "I did not mean to smother you. Forgive me?"

KYNASTON: "C'mon, give us a kiss!"

Betterton and Kynaston break from their embrace. Kynaston removes his wig.

BETTERTON: They'll laugh us out of town. *(He slumps in his chair and drinks.)* Have to figure something before he shows; we play Othello again day after tomorrow. *(He sighs.)* Maybe we'll get lucky.

KYNASTON: Maybe there'll be an interregnum.

PEPYS *(picking up pen):* Ooh!

KYNASTON: Don't write that down, Pepys.

VILLIERS: What none of you glean is that in his preferences, the King is expressing a particularly salient stage view.

BETTERTON: And what is that, your grace?

VILLIERS: He wants surprises. He's been away—and the theaters have been closed—for eighteen years. Now he's back and the theaters are open—what does he find? The same old stuff. Poetry, he approves; ideas he approves; love, death, tragedy, comedy, yes! But *surprise* him!

KYNASTON: What about sex?

VILLIERS: Mr. Kynaston?

KYNASTON: Vis-à-vis the stage. You claim the King approves love, the idea, but what about sex, the expression?

PEPYS: Poetry can express sex.

KYNASTON: And so can sex. Fit the action to the word, the word to the action.

VILLIERS: Mr. Kynaston, if you insist on something more graphic, show a tit; the King won't complain.

KYNASTON *(looking down his bust):* And how would you suggest I do that?

VILLIERS *(deadpan):* Surprise me .....

KYNASTON *(putting wig back on):* Got to put my face back on. They want the illusion, not some Green Room hermaphrodite. *This*, Tommy, is why I deserve a share.

BETTERTON *(burying his head in his hands):* Oh, no.

PEPYS: What are you two talking about?

BETTERTON: Mr. Kynaston's contract is up and he's putting the screws to me.

KYNASTON: All I want is what is fair.

BETTERTON: You have the best deal in London. Five pounds a week, forty-two weeks a year, choice of roles, and I provide the handkerchiefs. You won't get that over at Mr. Killigrew's theater.

KYNASTON: I want a share. You make me a shareholder, I won't argue salary; I won't argue clothes; I won't even insist you wash the pillow you shove in my nose—

BETTERTON: Yes, you will.

KYNASTON: I want to own something. I'm as much a draw as you. More so.

BETTERTON: Prove it.

KYNASTON *(holds up letter):* Where's your love note? Where're your ladies?

BETTERTON: A share in the company is out of the question. Tell you what. As a gesture of good faith, as proof that I am seeking to find a way, in the interim, from this day forth you have casting approval. For your co-stars.

KYNASTON *(to the others):* You are my witnesses.

Kynaston agrees to go riding in the park with two society ladies while dressed as a woman. He returns to the theater where Villiers, the Duke of Buckingham, is waiting for him. Villiers has just seen Margaret Hughes playing Desdemona, though it's against the law for women to appear on stage. Kynaston and Villiers are lovers and begin to make love. Villiers asks Kynaston to wear his blonde Desdemona wig. Kynaston's dresser, Maria, observes their lovemaking from the wings.

After King Charles prohibits men from appearing onstage as women, Kynaston is unable to play women's parts. Rejected by his friends, he descends to drunken performances as a woman in a bawdy and humiliating tavern show. Maria takes him to an inn and announces she will spend the night with him. Kynaston admits he has never slept with a woman.

She takes off her Desdemona gown. She wears a shift ..... She sits next to Kynaston on the bed.

MARIA: Tell me what men do.

KYNASTON: With women?

MARIA: With men.

KYNASTON: They . . . we . . . Well, it depends.

MARIA: On?

KYNASTON: Who's the man and who's the woman.

MARIA: I said men with men.

KYNASTON: Yes, I know, but . . . with men and women, there's a "man," and there's a "woman." Well, it's the same with men and men.

MARIA: Were you the man or the woman?

KYNASTON: . . . I was the woman.

MARIA: That means?

KYNASTON: Would you like me to show you?

Maria nods. Kynaston rises. He indicates that Maria stand. She does. Kynaston lies down on the bed, face down. He looks up at her. He indicates that she "mount" him from behind.

KYNASTON: Right, in the saddle.

Tentatively, Maria does so. She "rides" his haunches.

MARIA: I see. And am I the man now or the woman?

KYNASTON: You're the man.

MARIA: And you're the woman.

KYNASTON: Yes.

MARIA: Isn't much to do.

KYNASTON: Not with what we're given.

MARIA: What's it like the other way?

Kynaston indicates that Maria hop off. She does. Kynaston indicates that she lie down, face forward. Maria does so. Then, Kynaston comes behind her and lies gently on top of her.

MARIA: So . . . who am I now?

KYNASTON: You're the woman.

MARIA: And you're—?

KYNASTON: I'm the man. Or so I assume. I've never been up here before. Quite a view.

MARIA: But I'm the man-woman.

KYNASTON: Yes, you're the man-woman. Or the woman-woman. It works both ways.

Maria turns over, so that she is now on her back looking up at Kynaston above her.

MARIA: And what am I now?

KYNASTON: The woman.

MARIA: Still?

KYNASTON: Yes.

Maria puts one leg around his back and slowly, slowly revolves him until he's lying with his back on the bed and she is above him.

MARIA: And now what am I?

KYNASTON: The woman.

Maria undoes Kynaston's garment and removes her shift.

MARIA: And now?

KYNASTON: The woman.

MARIA: And you are—

KYNASTON: The man.

Maria rises and pulls Kynaston up, so that's he's kneeling on the bed, facing her.

MARIA: And now? Who are you now?

KYNASTON: I don't know.

Silence. Maria comes forward to kiss Kynaston on his chest, where the bruises and scars are.

MARIA *(kissing):* Can you feel that?

KYNASTON: No.

MARIA *(kissing):* That?

KYNASTON *(closes his eyes):* No

MARIA *(kissing):* That?

KYNASTON *(eyes closed):* . . . Yes. It hurts . . .

Maria stops kissing him. She puts her arms around his torso. She looks up at him. He looks at her. He may kiss her. Finally:

KYNASTON: Wait. Before we do . . . Tell me something.

MARIA *(eyes closed):* Anything.

KYNASTON: How do you die?

MARIA: Die?

KYNASTON: As Desdemona. How do you die?

Maria opens her eyes and stares at him. Then she pulls her shift back up. She sits on the side of the bed, away from him. She starts to cry.

KYNASTON: I'm sorry. I should not have asked, I—I'm—I really shouldn't—

MARIA *(bitter, through tears):* I fight him!

KYNASTON: Excuse me?

MARIA: I fight him off; I fight for my life! I won't let him kill me! But he still kills me! I always hated you as Desdemona! You never fought! You just died "beautifully!" No woman would die like that, no matter how much she loved him! A woman would fight! She'd fight and leave her love, if that were it! Only a man would act it any other way!

Maria gathers her things, her cloak, etc. and rushes to the "door." She stops, her hand on the knob. She does not turn to Kynaston.

You can stay here the week. I've paid.

She exits. Door slam. The candle near the bed goes out. Lights go out.

When the King makes it legal for women to appear onstage, Nell Gwynn begs Kynaston to coach Margaret to play Desdemona opposite Betterton, and Betterton promises to make Kynaston a partner if he can make Margaret passable as Desdemona. Margaret enters and they begin to work on Desdemona's death scene.

COMPLEAT FEMALE STAGE BEAUTY—Michelle Federer, David Hornsby (as Edward Kynaston) and Douglas Rees in Jeffrey Hatcher's play at Pittsburgh City Theater

KYNASTON: Strip down to your shift. NOW!

MARGARET *(after a beat):* I am told to do as you will tell me.

Margaret shimmies out of her gown.

KYNASTON: Muss the hair before the scene. Not like that. That's puffing to make it look attractive when it's merely arranged. Roll on a sheet, make it real. Flat on one side would be good. And no blush on your cheeks. No lip paint. White cheeks, pale lips. Blood drains down at sleep, not up to the face.

MARGARET: I know you consider this "your" part—

KYNASTON: No. It's your part. And frankly, it's not that "good" a part. Most of Shakespeare's women aren't very good parts, except the crazy ones. Couple of scenes, then off they go. Even their death scenes aren't very good. No great speeches for the girls. What's Desdemona's last line? "Farewell." What's that?

MARGARET: *You* played that line with a whisper and a cough.

KYNASTON: Shit with sugar on it. The way Betterton does the last scene, there are thirty-two lines, cutting seventeen. You start on the bed. Go.

Margaret drapes herself on the bed.

KYNASTON: Not like that. That's like me.

MARGARET *(sits up):* Well, then, how should I do it?

KYNASTON: How do you get into *bed*? C'mon, woman, how'd you get this *part*?

Margaret fumes. She flops down on the bed and pulls the duvet cover over her.

It's Cyprus in summer.

Margaret flings off the duvet. She flips over on her back.

Is that how you sleep?

MARGARET *(sits up again):* How am I supposed to know how I sleep? I'm *sleeping* while I sleep!

KYNASTON: What do your lovers tell you?

Beat. Margaret turns over on her stomach and curls up in a fetal position.

Good, curled up in ball, spread snoring over both sides of the bed, sounds right to me.

MARGARET *(head up):* Snoring? Who says I snore?

KYNASTON: *Do* you snore?

MARGARET: *YOU* never snored.

KYNASTON: I never *thought* to.

MARGARET *(after a beat):* . . . You want them to laugh at me.

KYNASTON *(quickly, honestly):* Maybe. For a moment. A woman is snoring. Normal. Humorous, in contrast to her demeanor. And then she's murdered. When you're dead, they'll think back on that snore. Nice. Not *too* loud, though, just a whistle and a rumble . . . liquid sound. Suck the white of an egg before you go onstage. It'll make the first few lines sound sleepful.

MARGARET *(flops down again):* Suck an egg.

KYNASTON: Right! First line!

MARGARET *(sits up):* "Who's there? Othello?

KYNASTON: Why's she say that? "Who's there? Othello?" She think it's not really him? No. She knows it's him, she's just not AWAKE yet.

MARGARET: Yes, I see.

KYNASTON: So, lie back down. Stay down for four lines. She won't really be awake until she says: "Alas, my lord, what do you mean by that?" Onward.

MARGARET *(lies down; sleep sound):* "Will you come to bed, my lord?"

KYNASTON: "Have you pray'd tonight, Desdemona?

MARGARET *(yawns):* "Ay, my lord."

KYNASTON:

"If you bethink yourself of any crime
Unreconciled as yet to heaven and grace,
Solicit for it straight."

MARGARET *(sits up; alert):* "Alas, my lord, what may you mean by that?"

KYNASTON:

"Well, do it, and be brief; I will walk by:
I would not kill thy unprepared spirit;
No; heaven forfend! I would not kill thy soul.
There'll be thunder there."

MARGARET *(rises to stand; smiles uncertainly):* "Talk you of killing?

KYNASTON: Why are you smiling?

MARGARET: *You* always—I think he's joking.

KYNASTON: Othello's funny? Plays jokes on you a lot, does he?

MARGARET: No, but—

KYNASTON: Then don't act with what isn't there! The man's been a festering boil for three fucking hours, hasn't he?

MARGARET: Yes.

KYNASTON: And now he's come to your bedroom, woke you up, and told you pray before you die!

MARGARET: Yes.

KYNASTON: So, what's the line?

MARGARET *(shocked, stands):* "Talk you of killing?"

KYNASTON: Keep going. *(Othello voice.)* "Ay, I do."

MARGARET *(crosses herself):* "Then heaven have mercy on me."

KYNASTON: Good, keep that. "Think on thy sins."

MARGARET: "They are loves I bear to you."

KYNASTON: "Ay, and for that thou diest."

As the rehearsal continues, the audience can be heard offstage, entering the theater. Margaret is anxious to put the finishing touches on the scene.

MARGARET: Now do it.

KYNASTON: What.

MARGARET: Throw me on the bed. Kill me.

KYNASTON: No.

MARGARET: We start the play in fifteen minutes. We've got to finish this off.

KYNASTON: Save something for the moment. Always do something different than you planned. Good to throw yourself off a bit. Recall what we've done to this point in the scene. Then when you die . . . surprise me. Tommy!

MARGARET: But how do I know Mr. Betterton will do as you have done?

KYNASTON: You don't. Because he won't.

Betterton and Sedley enter.

BETTERTON: All ready to go?

KYNASTON: Yes. I'm playing the Moor.

BETTERTON: Pardon?

KYNASTON: Mrs. Hughes insists.

Pause. Betterton and Sedley turn to her.

BETTERTON: Mrs. Hughes—

MARGARET: I do.

SEDLEY: Does he even know the part?

BETTERTON *(glowers at Kynaston):* Oh, yes. He knows it.

SEDLEY: This is an outrage!

KYNASTON: Wait'll you see us do *Macbeth*!

BETTERTON *(staggers back):* AHHH!

KYNASTON: Right, now, clear off.

SEDLEY: Wait! He'll need boot black!

KYNASTON: Why?

SEDLEY: WHY? OTHELLO'S A MOOR!

KYNASTON: Audience knows that. Think I'm going to fool them? Let them use their imaginations.

SEDLEY: You wore dresses and wigs when you played women!

KYNASTON: I'd never do it now. Off my stage.

Sedley and Betterton exit. Audience noise louder now.

MARGARET: Mr. Kynaston. My thanks.

KYNASTON: It's not a good role, Desdemona. Go for Lavinia. Or Cleopatra.

MARGARET: Why they?

KYNASTON: Because when Lavinia loses her tongue and hands . . . she still must assert herself.

MARGARET: And Cleopatra?

KYNASTON: She kills herself with the sting of an asp. A snake to her breast, that men had kissed and a child would suckle. "Those who do die, Do never recover."

Kynaston holds the pillow and fixes her with a dead stare.

I blame you for my death.

MARGARET: What's that from?

KYNASTON: Nothing. *(Beat.)* See you onstage.

Loud thunder.

Kynaston and Margaret play *Othello* vigorously and realistically, leaving the audience to wonder whether he has actually killed her or merely acted it. The lights narrow to Kynaston, who ends the play with a verse epilogue that explains he went on to play men's roles but never again Othello—"He found himself upon a shore/ Where he could act/And asked no more."

Compleat Female Stage Beauty *was first staged in the summer of 1999 by Contemporary American Theater Festival in Shepherdstown, W.Va., under the direction of Ed Herendeen. A revised version premiered on October 27, 1999 under the direction of Marc Masterson at City Theater Company in Pittsburgh.*

ATCA/Steinberg New Play Citation

SYNCOPATION

A Play in Two Acts

BY ALLAN KNEE

Cast and credits appear on page 372

ALLAN KNEE, a graduate of Yale School of Drama, has written seven other produced plays and musicals for the stage: The Man Who Was Peter Pan, Sholom Aleichem Lives, St. Valentine's Day Massacre, Shmulnik's Waltz, Late Nite Comic, Second Avenue Rag *and* Santa Anita 42. *These works have been produced at the Jewish Repertory Theater, American Repertory Theater, Manhattan Punchline, Theaterworks/USA. Theater Four (in Richmond, Va.), the Ritz Theater and the Brooklyn Academy of Music. For TV and film he has written* The Scarlet Letter *(PBS) and* Journey *(American Film Institute). He received the Richard Rodgers Musical Theater Award for a book of* Little Women *in 1998 and the Cine Eagle Award from the Washington Film Festival.*

INTRODUCTION: In the seamless and passionate script of *Syncopation* by Allan Knee, the playwright follows the dictum, "Write what you know." He has set his offbeat fairy tale on the Lower East Side of New York City where his grandparents, great aunts and great uncles lived. Knee paints a world "full of turmoil and change, a world in which people were trying to break new ground, find a new expression for the self, expand their boundaries."

The romantic comedy is set in one of the author's favorite historical periods—the 1910s—an era often known for "a revolution of expression." At the age of five, Knee was thrilled when his aunt took him to see the Harvest Moon Ball finalists. He loved watching the way dancers partnered with each other, and he dreamt of being one of them.

Using two disparate characters who are factory workers, Knee recreates both the excitement and the discontent that simmered below the surface of everyday life at that time. Henry Ribalow, a 42-year-old Jewish meat packer who lives with his hypochondriac mother, burns with an unquenchable fire to become a ballroom dancer. Intent on performing and competing—and bursting with hope—he rents a dusty, ghost-filled room and places a series of newspaper advertisements looking for a partner. Anna Bianchi. a 25-year-old Catholic "beader," lives with her father and is engaged to be married. Inspired by Henry's creative ads, and after waiting seven weeks, she climbs 176 urine-stained stairs to a spare studio where they begin lessons and rehearsals.

Over the next year, accompanied by Jeffrey Lunden's lilting and spirited original music, they practice the steps that they hope will set them free from their oppressive day jobs. While Henry is sure of success, Anna is terribly uncertain and fearful of Henry, whom she is afraid to touch at first. Knee's play is given authentiucity by the charming awkwardness of his characters.

As Anna postpones her marriage, her rocky relationship with Henry waxes and wanes. All the while, the unlikely pair learn to communicate with each other through dance and conversation. They pursue a dream not only of emulating the greatest dancers of their time, Vernon and Irene Castle, but aspiring to be even better. Through language and movement, the playwright captures elements of a unique courtship and the essence of a time when all things, even those most unlikely, seemed possible. *Syncopation* is truly an American story.

—ROSALIND FRIEDMAN

Excerpt From *Syncopation*

Henry has been teaching Anna dance steps. "*After a practice session, he turns to her.*"

HENRY: You ever want—you ever want to break a rule? Do something unacceptable?

ANNA: Like what?

HENRY: I don't know. Make a spectacle of yourself.

ANNA: No. Why, do you?

HENRY: Sometimes. Sometimes I wanna do something—really outrageous. I wanna shock even myself. When I was a boy, I always wanted to go places that were forbidden. I wanted to read books that were outlawed. I'd search bookstalls for stuff that'd say—"Not for children . . . " The radicals, you know—for all their talk of freedom—all they really want to do is replace one set of rules with another. Sometimes I think nobody truly wants you to be free.

ANNA: . . . It's very warm in here.

HENRY: I'll open a window . . . It was a stupid thing to bring up. I'm sorry.

ANNA: No—

HENRY: It's all make-believe. Nonsense.

ANNA: At the factory we're required to follow rules. The workers don't talk about it—but we all know. Dress codes. Behavior codes. If you're late, you lose pay.

If you fall asleep on the job, you're fired. And as far as design is concerned, you must follow what they give you to the letter. No deviations. "Every bead has its place." Sometimes I want to design something—exotic. Wild, even.

HENRY: Wild?

ANNA: Untraditional. Bright, with brilliant colors.

HENRY: Do it!

ANNA: I will. One day.

HENRY: Do it tomorrow! I danced with one of the ghosts yesterday. I looked up—and there she was.

ANNA: Who?

HENRY: Anna Pavlova. A Russian dancer. I danced a waltz with her. We twirled about nearly two hours. We should go *out* dancing some time.

ANNA: Go out dancing?

HENRY: Go to a dance hall. Or a club. Or even Tony Pastor's.

ANNA *(after a beat):* . . . I'll see you next Tuesday.

HENRY: July Third. I hate Sundays. Sundays and holidays. Days of escape. Days when people have the excuse to do nothing. To be lazy. To sleep. Take walks. Read newspapers. On such days I feel—"the world has died."

ANNA: July Sixth. I ask my superior if I can change the design—and he looks at me as if I were crazy. "A simple change," I say. I bring out a set of beads. "What about these," I say. He gives a hard look of disapproval. I shouldn't have brought it up . . . I eat lunch at the railway station and talk with one of the "odd women." Her name is Roslyn. She's been to Texas and once shot a man.

HENRY *(front, dancing):* July Fifteenth. We dance every Tuesday. She always arrives at the same time. 7:15. And leaves at 8:30. From one week to another, she seems to remember very little. It feels like we're always at the starting gate. It's time we touched, Miss Bianchi. It's time we came together . . .

He puts music on and goes to her.

Are you ready?

ANNA: No.

HENRY: I put my hand on you here . . . What's the matter?

ANNA: It tickles.

HENRY: Sorry. I'll try again.

ANNA *(laughing):* Sorry. It still tickles.

HENRY: Is there any place on your body I might touch you without evoking laughter?

ANNA *(she points to her elbow):* You might try here.

HENRY: Here?

ANNA: Or a little lower. (*He touches her cautiously.)* That's good.

They begin to move.

HENRY: Try not to be so stiff.

ANNA: Yes.

HENRY: Am I holding you too tight?

ANNA: No.

HENRY: You don't believe I'm going to ravish you?

ANNA: No.

HENRY: Well, I am!

He makes a sound. She screams. Then she realizes quickly he was joking.

ANNA: That wasn't funny, Mr. Ribolow.

HENRY: I'm sorry. I don't know what made me do that. I never make jokes. Please, forgive me. Come—let's try again.

He takes hold of her.

We'll start slowly. Like we're just waking up. The sun hasn't even risen yet. Our eyes are half closed. We sway gently, side to side, back and forth—trying to clear away the sleep. Listen to the music.

ANNA: I am.

HENRY: Hear its heartbeat. Feel the music touching you. Feel it talking to you.

HENRY: August Fourth. We dance two hours. Maybe longer. We repeat the same step. Miss Bianchi, it's a simple step. A simple movement.

ANNA: I know.

HENRY: Let's do it again. We'll get it right eventually.

ANNA: Why don't you just give up on me?

HENRY: Because I don't want to. And stop counting out loud.

ANNA: I'm not.

HENRY: I can see your lips moving.

ANNA: Mr. Parva is pressing me to set a wedding date.

HENRY: I know.

He stops the music.

I watch you.

ANNA: You watch me where?

HENRY: Lots of places.

ANNA: While I'm changing clothes?

HENRY: Outside.

ANNA: You watch me outside?

HENRY: I follow you.

ANNA: You follow me?

HENRY: I thought you knew. I could have sworn you saw me.

ANNA: You follow me when I leave here?

HENRY: Sometimes.

ANNA: You follow me from work?

HENRY: Yes.

ANNA: I don't understand. This is very disturbing, Mr. Ribolow. You follow me from home?

HENRY: I have—on occasion.

ANNA: And you know where I live?

HENRY: Why—is it a secret?

ANNA: You could be arrested for such behavior.

HENRY: So have me arrested.

ANNA: ... Why do you follow me?

HENRY: Isn't it obvious? I wanna know you better.

ANNA: Don't you know me well enough?

HENRY: I want to know your soul.

ANNA: My soul?

HENRY: The way you have of doing things. The way you walk and talk—how you use your hands—the expressions on your face when you think no one is looking ... I've discovered some surprising things about you. You follow the same path to work every day. I could draw a line mapping out the streets you cross—the shop windows you stop to look in. The way you sometimes just abruptly turn about.

ANNA: As if someone were following me.

HENRY: ... And your smile.

ANNA: My smile?

HENRY: How you use it to invite people in—but at the same time, to keep them out. It's like you open a door to see who's there, and when you do, you smile—and close it again.

ANNA: I want you to stop following me.

HENRY: I don't believe you would ever break a rule, Miss Bianchi.

ANNA: What do you think my coming here is? There are rules and there are rules. You break yours—I'll break mine.

ANNA: September Twelfth. I've decided on a date. I shall become Mrs. Anthony Parva the last Sunday in October. I myself am beginning to feel more relaxed.

HENRY: September Fifteenth. She doesn't come ... September Twenty-second. I wait all night for her ... September Twenty-eighth. I put another advertisement in the paper. I wait for an answer ... October First. A woman comes. She is actually quite lively. Better looking than Miss Bianchi. More interesting.

He turns to a woman; we do not see her.

So, can we try it again? It's a step and a glide. Yes. The glide is quite simple. Like this. No, no, no. More like this. I wouldn't wave the arms about so. It's a good gesture, but it could cause accidents. Keep the arms close to the body. Like this.

Front.

Her name is Shirley. From Romania. Works in a tin factory. Has metal filings under her nails. Says she can't get rid of them. *(To the woman.)* Thank you for coming. The pleasure was all mine. *(Front.)* I miss Miss Bianchi. I don't know why. What is there to miss? She's unreliable. She can't remember a step from one week to the next. The worst part is—she's not in the least enthusiastic. It's just a hobby with her. Like a sewing club. Something she'll tell her grandchildren about. "He was a peculiar man. Not the sort you'd ever take for a dancer."

He dances a few steps.

HENRY: October Seventh. I decide to give myself a deadline. If nothing happens in six months—I quit. I leave the city. Go live somewhere else. Albany. Schenectady. Some place people learn to live their lives in quiet desperation.

HENRY: October Tenth. Another woman responds to my advertisement. She is twice my size and yet I find her very fascinating. *(To the woman.)* You're good. *(Front.)* She'll never stay. *(To the woman.)* You've got spark. *(Front.)* She looks angry. *(To the woman.)* You're very light on your feet. *(Front.)* She's hardly moving. *(To the woman.)* I like your style. *(Front.)* She stands there like a colossus. *(To the woman.)* I've got several offers for dance engagements. *(Front.)* I lie. *(To the woman.)* You have a wonderful smell. *(Front.)* She works in a cigar factory. Brings me an imported smoke. *(To the woman.)* Thank you. *(Front.)* Unfortunately, she develops a fungus on her feet— *(To the woman.)* I am sorry. *(Front.)* And never returns.

HENRY: October Twenty-first. You'd think in this great city of hungry people, there'd be someone—some *one* person—some kindred soul who feels like you do—one person who has the same dreams—the same passion.

He gets up and dances alone.

ANNA: October Twenty-eighth. Walk with father last Sunday. He is quite proud of me. Proud I've settled on a date. I take him to the railway station. Point out the "odd women." He ridicules them.

Weeks later, Anna suddenly reappears at Henry's dance studio.

ANNA: Am I late?

Henry stops dancing, turns and looks at her. Turns off the music. He speaks to her in an amazed, ironic tone.

HENRY: Are you late? Are you really asking me if you're late? Am I—am I an idiot or something? You're standing there calmly and asking me if you're late? (*He shouts.)* You're six or seven weeks late! *(More calmly.)* And close the door, please!

ANNA: Has it been that long—six weeks?

HENRY: Seven! I believe it's seven!

ANNA: I am sorry.

HENRY: Sorry, yes—sorry, of course. What? You lose track of the time?

ANNA: I just didn't—

HENRY: What? What didn't you? Didn't remember? Didn't think? What, Miss Bianchi? Losing an hour here or there is understandable. But—*(Shouting.) seven weeks*!

ANNA: I got new shoes. You like them?

HENRY: I don't understand you. Did you come to show me your shoes?

ANNA: Are you going to be disagreeable?

SYNCOPATION—Lorca Simons as Anna and David Chandler as Henry in the Long Wharf Theater production of Allan Knee's play

HENRY: Excuse me, but you come marching in here—

ANNA: I didn't march, Mr. Ribolow—I climbed. I climbed six flights of stairs. Six flights of creaky stairs with broken banisters and the stench of urine! I'm exhausted. I'm sorry about the absence. I've been occupied.

HENRY: Occupied?

ANNA: With family matters?

HENRY: Family matters?

ANNA: Yes.

HENRY: Entire generations are strangled by family matters! Like an—umbilical cord wrapped around the neck—family matters pull, jerk, squeeze—until finally—aaggh!—finished! That's what I call family matters!

ANNA: . . . So, how is your mother?

HENRY: Thank you. Thank you very much for reminding me. She's dead.

ANNA: Your mother died?

HENRY: Almost. Twice. Since I last saw you. She's hanging on by a thread. Or a rope—maybe. I don't know. Yesterday I walked in the house and she was holding a thirty-five pound box. Said she was rearranging. We live like monks. We got nothing. And she's rearranging.

ANNA: I can't stay too long.

HENRY: Well, of course not. Family matters—right?

ANNA: Stop it, Mr. Ribolow. Whatever it is you're doing—stop it, please! I came back. I'm here. Is that not enough?

HENRY: No! What is it—one of your boyfriends—I forgot, your fiance—What's his name?—Parva? Mr. Parva?—of dry goods fame?— what?—was he busy?—couldn't make it tonight?—so you thought maybe you'd look in on Mr. Ribolow? "Well, I'm fine, thank you. I'm glad you asked."

ANNA: I saw your advertisement in today's paper. It touched me. You worded it differently—but the word "royalty" was still there. It was so open and direct. Henrietta—one of the girls I work with—she thinks you're very clever.

HENRY: Clever?

ANNA: You're getting quite a reputation at Marx & Shapiro.

HENRY: Maybe they could use a ballroom dancer?

ANNA: . . . I like your shirt. You bought it?

HENRY: I found it.

ANNA: You stole it?

HENRY: I *took* it—from the loading dock of Wanamaker's. It's a reject.

ANNA: It looks good . . . I'm sorry for the absence.

HENRY: What do you want, Miss Bianchi?

ANNA: Have you found someone to dance with?

HENRY: Several extraordinary women have come. Very refreshing women.

ANNA: You don't think I'm refreshing?

HENRY: I see girls like you every day, Miss Bianchi. Hundreds of them. I know you. You read magazines. You daydream. But you have no adventure in you. No spark.

ANNA: I have adventure in me.

HENRY: I want you to go.

ANNA: Are you sure?

HENRY: Positive.

ANNA: . . . We could make believe. That we just met. That I just read your advertisement. We could start from the beginning. Like strangers. Make believe—

HENRY: I'm tired of making believe! I continually make believe that this is happening and that is happening—

ANNA: Try me. See if I've got the stuff of a dancer, Mr. Ribolow. Tell me if I'm cut out for this sort of thing.

HENRY: You come at a bad time. Perhaps in another lifetime. I got things to do.

ANNA: I made you a handkerchief.

HENRY: A handkerchief?

ANNA: It's beaded.

HENRY: What for?

ANNA: To dress up in.

HENRY: I need dressing up?

ANNA: I think you look all right. A little somber sometimes. You need some color, that's all. You need—

HENRY: What?

ANNA: A beaded hankie. It could be your thing. People would say, "There goes the man with the beaded handkerchief."

HENRY: You made that for me?

ANNA: It'll look good against your shirt. Go on—Put it in your pocket. Go on, Mr. Ribolow. Go on. Take it!

HENRY: No.

ANNA: Take it!

HENRY: I don't want it! Don't come in here thinking you owe me anything!

ANNA: That's not what I think.

HENRY: You owe me nothing!

ANNA: You have scruples about everything, don't you. It's all got to be by your rules.

HENRY: Seven weeks I don't see you! Seven weeks I don't get word from you! I put ten—twelve advertisements in the paper. Nothing! . . . I think of you a lot. I stand outside Marx & Shapiro—sometimes in the pouring rain. I walk down Mulberry Street. I almost knocked on your door. Go! Go—marry—marry Mr.—what's his name? Go—please!

ANNA *(after a beat):* . . . At the factory—during lunch—the girls and me—we've been dancing the fox trot.

HENRY: I've seen you.

ANNA: You've seen us dancing?

HENRY: And you don't dance the fox trot at all. You move around like idiots. What you do has nothing to do with fox trot. The real fox trot has grace and design. You girls are clumsy and careless. You have no style. You make a joke of everything. You have absolutely no sense of beauty!

ANNA: I'm sorry, Mr. Ribolow! I'm sorry I'm such a disappointment! I'm sorry I'm not the woman of your dreams! I'm sorry I'm not lighter on my feet! I'm sorry it takes me so long to learn the steps! I'm sorry I'm just an awkward little shop girl! I'm sorry you think so little of me!

HENRY *(after a beat):* . . . I like to begin the fox trot in this position. *(Music starts.)* I call up the fox in me. I wag my tail and show my teeth—and then I'm ready.

They begin to move in time to the music.

ANNA: Under my bench—where I bead—my feet move. Nobody can see them. But it gives me immense pleasure.

They dance.

Syncopation *was first produced at the Long Wharf Theater, New Haven, Conn. November 23, 1999 (co-produced by the George Street Theater, New Brunswick, N.J.) under the direction of Greg Leaming.*

A DIRECTORY OF NEW-PLAY PRODUCTIONS

Professional productions June 1, 1999–May 31, 2000 (plus a very few that opened too late in the spring of 1999 to be included in last year's *Best Plays* volume) of new plays by leading resident companies around the United States, who supplied information on casts and credits at Camille Dee's request, are listed here in alphabetical order of the locations of 67 producing organizations. Date given is opening date. Most League of Resident Theaters (LORT) and other regularly-producing Equity groups were queried for this comprehensive Directory. Active cross-country theater companies not included in this list either did not offer new or newly-revised scripts during the year under review or had not responded to our query by press time. Most productions listed below are world premieres; a few are American premieres, new revisions, noteworthy second looks or scripts not previously reported in *Best Plays.*

Abingdon, Va.: Barter Theater

(Richard Rose artistic director)

WUTHERING HEIGHTS. Adapted by Richard Rose from the novel by Emily Brontë. October 7, 1999. Director, Richard Rose; scenery, Lynn Pecktal; costumes, Amanda Aldridge; lighting, Kevin Shaw; sound, Bobby Beck.

Mr. Lockwood .... John Hedges
Heathcliff .... Michael Ostroski
Joseph .... Tom Celli
Zillah .... Quinn Hawkesworth
Candy Linton Heathcliff .... Laura Morton
Hareton Earnshaw .... Will Bigham
Ellen Dean .... Debra Gillingham
Catherine Earnshaw
Age 8–10 .... Stephanie Demaree
Hindley Earnshaw Age 14–16 .... Doug Presley
Mrs. Earnshaw .... Katy Brown
Mr. Earnshaw .... Robert Anglin
Heathcliff Age 8–10;
Hareton Age 7 .... Davis Sweatt
Catherine Earnshaw .... Susan Haefner
Hindley Earnshaw .... John Hardy
Edgar Linton .... Jim Van Valen
Isabella Linton .... Catherine Gray
Linton Heathcliff .... Andreas Lopez

Servants of Thrushcross Grange—Robert Anglin, Will Bigham, Doug Presley.

Time: 1780–1814. Place: Interior of Wuthering Heights; outside of Thrushcroft Grange; the moors; outside of Wuthering Heights; outside of Thrushcroft Grange; a bedroom in Thrushcroft Grange. One intermission.

Arlington, Va.: Signature Theater

(Eric Schaeffer artistic director; Paul Gamble managing director; Ronnie Gunderson producing director)

Staged Readings

FALLEN FROM PROUST. By Norman Allen. January 17, 2000.

IN THE GARDEN. By Norman Allen. January 24, 2000.

Ashland, Ore.: Oregon Shakespeare Festival

(Libby Appel artistic director)

THE THREE MUSKETEERS. Adapted from Alexandre Dumas by Linda Alper, Douglas Langworthy and Penny Metropoulos. June 20, 1999. Director, Penny Metropoulos; scenery, William Bloodgood; costumes, Deborah M. Dryden; lighting, Robert Peterson; composer and music director, Todd Barton; associate director and fight choreographer, John Sipes.

Soldiers and Civilians:
De Treville .... Ken Albers
Athos .... Richard Howard
Porthos .... David Kelly
Aramis .... U. Jonathan Toppo
D'Artagnan .... John Hansen
Planchet .... Tyrone Wilson
Bonancieux .... Dennis Robertson
Mme. Constance Bonancieux ..... Jodi Somers
Mme. de Coquenard;
Abbess .... Elizabeth Norment
Jussac .... James J. Peck
Biscarrat .... Thom Rivera
Grimaud .... Brad Whitmore
Bazin .... James Oliver

Musketeers and Cardinal's Guards: Leith Burke, Christopher Duval, Charlie Kimball, James Oliver, James J. Peck, Jeff A. Pierce, Thom Rivera, Timothy Rush, Brad Whitmore, Tyrone Wilson.

The Court in France:
King Louis XIII .... Dan Donohue
Queen Anne .... Vilma Silva
Cardinal Richelieu .... James Edmondson
Mme. d'Astree .... Carolyn Hitt
Mme. de Chevreuse .... Christine Williams
Attendants .... James Oliver, Jeff A. Pierce
The Court in England:
Duke of Buckingham .... Jonathan Adams
Patrick .... Brad Whitmore
John Felton .... Leith Burke
Reilly .... Christopher Duval
Parisian Society:
Count de Rochefort .... John Pribyl
Milady de Winter .... Linda Alper
Kitty .... Catherine Lynn Davis
Count de Wardes .... Charlie Kimball
Lubin .... Jeff A. Pierce

French Citizenry—Christopher Duval, Carolyn Hitt, Elizabeth Norment, Timothy Rush, Brad Whitmore.

Time: 1625. Place: France and England.

Atlanta: Alliance Theater Company

(Kenny Leon artistic director; Gus Stuhlreyer managing director)

HE LOOKS GREAT IN A HAT. By Janece Shaffer. September 22, 1999. Director, Lawrence Keller; scenery, Rochelle Barker; costumes, Stephanie Kaskel Bogle; lighting, Ann G. Wrightson; sound, Brian Kettler.
Gwenn Layson .... Michelle Beamer
Max Knight .... Jason Max Feldman
Alan Solomon .... Al Hamacher
Rachel Solomon .... Diana Henry
Charles Knight .... Curt Hostetter
Aunt Edna .... Lois Markle
Sylvia Solomon .... Marilyn Sokol

Time: Late 1990s. Place: Atlanta, Ga. One intermission.

Berkeley, Calif.: Berkeley Repertory Theater

(Tony Taccone artistic director; Susan Medak managing director)

THE ALCHEMIST. By Ben Jonson; new adaptation by Joan Holden. February 18, 2000. Director, Tony Taccone; scenery, Kent Dorsey; costumes, Gabriel Berry; lighting, Peter Maradudin; sound, Matthew Spiro.
Makepeace .... Ron Evans
Dapper .... David Paul Francis
Drugger .... Gerald Hiken
Face .... Geoff Hoyle
Dame Pliant .... S.J. LeMay
Subtle .... Sharon Lockwood
Tribulation .... Jack Powell
Sir Epicure Mammon .... Ken Ruta
Surly .... Robert Sicular
Dol Common .... Audrey Ann Smith
Lovewit .... W. Francis Walters

One intermission.

THE FIRST HUNDRED YEARS. By Geoff Hoyle; developed by Geoff Hoyle and Tony Taccone. April 14, 2000. Director, Tony Taccone. Produced in association with Arizona Theater Company, Tucson; see its entry in that section of this listing.

Boca Raton, Fla.: Caldwell Theater Company

(Michael Hall artistic and managing director)

DON'T TELL THE TSAR. By Michael McKeever. December 31, 1999. Director, Kenneth Kay; scenery, Tim Bennett; lighting, Ginny Adams; costumes, Penny Koleos Williams; original music and sound, Steve Shapiro.

ATLANTA—Jason Max Feldman and Curt Hostetter in a scene from *He Looks Great in a Hat* at Alliance Theater Company

Rasputin	George Kapetan
Prince	Michael McKeever
Grand Duke	Tom Wahl
Deputy	Steve Wise
Doctor	John Felix

Time: December 16, 1917. Place: A great palace in St. Petersburg. No intermission; presented on a program with *Black Comedy* by Peter Shaffer.

Playsearch: Staged Readings

THE OTHER BED. By T.M.B. Hirsch. December 6, 1999.

ROSCOE. By Eileen Lottman. January 17, 2000.

HERE WE GO AGAIN! Musical with book and lyrics by Richard Wolf; music by Jerry Goldberg. March 6, 2000.

SUMMER FEVER. By Catherine Burns and Jake Shire. May 15, 2000.

Buffalo, N.Y.: Studio Arena Theater

(Gavin Cameron-Webb artistic director)

THINGS WE DO FOR LOVE. By Alan Ayckbourn. September 11, 1999 (American premiere). Director, Gavin Cameron-Webb; scenery, Ann Sheffield; costumes, Gail Brassard; lighting, Tom Hase; sound, Chester Popiolkowski; fight choreography, Dale Anthony Girard.

Barbara	Henny Russell
Gilbert	Robin Chadwick

Nikki .... Allison Briner
Hamish .... Julian Gamble

Act I, Scene 1: Monday, 6 p.m. Scene 2: Tuesday, 5 p.m. Scene 3: Friday, 8:30 p.m. Scene 4: Saturday, 9:30 p.m. Act II, Scene 1: Monday, 6 p.m. Scene 2: Thursday, 7 p.m. Scene 3: Friday, 7 a.m. Scene 4: Friday, 6:30 p.m.

Burlington, Vt.: Vermont Stage Company

(Blake Robison artistic director)

THE LAST STATION. By Blake Robison and Connan Morrissey; based on the novel by Jay Parini. June 30, 1999. Director, Blake Robison; scenery, Jeff Modereger; costumes, Jennifer Noe Adkins; lighting, Kenton Yeager; co-produced by Green Mountain Theater Festival.

Tolstoy .... Jerome Kilty
Sofya Andreyevna .... Sybil Lines
Chertkov .... Ray Dooley
Bulgakov .... Kevin Cristaldi
Makovitzky .... Bill Gorman
Masha .... Jenny Langsam

No intermission.

Cambridge, Mass.: American Repertory Theater

(Robert Brustein artistic director; Robert J. Orchard managing director)

BOSTON MARRIAGE. By David Mamet. June 4, 1999. Directed by David Mamet; scenery, Sharon Kaitz, J. Michael Griggs; costumes, Harriet Voyt; lighting, John Ambrosone.

Claire .... Rebecca Pidgeon
Anna .... Felicity Huffman
Catherine .... Mary McCann

Two intermissions.

Cedar City, Utah: Utah Shakespearean Festival

(Fred C. Adams founder and executive producer)

New Plays-in-Progress Readings

AUTUMN IN THE VALLEY. By John D. and James A. Bell. August 5, 1999. Director, George Judy.

THE LAMENTABLE TRAGEDY OF SIR THOMAS MORE. By Ann Chamberlin. August 12, 1999. Director, George Judy.

E PLURIBUS ANARCHY. By Paavo Hall. August 19, 1999. Director, Bruce Sevy.

DISPUTED BONES. By Jonathan Graham. August 26, 1999. Director, Davey Marlin-Jones.

Chester, Conn.: Goodspeed at Chester

(Michael Price executive director; Sue Frost associate producer; Michael O'Flaherty music director)

FANNY HILL. Musical by Ed Dixon; based on the novel by John Cleland. August 5, 1999. Director and choreographer, Gabriel Barre; musical direction and orchestrations, Constantine Kitsopoulos; scenery, James Youmans; costumes, Pamela Scofield; lighting, Timothy Hunter; sound, J.W. Hilton Jr.

Fanny .... Nancy Anderson
Phoebe .... Teri Dale Hansen
Mrs. Brown .... Barbara Tirrell
Martha .... Becky Barta
Esther; Count Brodski .... Lynn Eldredge
Rev. Fallwell .... Ken Jennings
Charles .... Will Gartshore
Mr. Sneed; Mr. Barville .... Michael Cone
Lord Hereford; Father Norbert .. David Pursley
Will .... Bryan T. Donovan

Peasants, Londoners, Sailors, Clientele—Company.

MUSICAL NUMBERS, ACT I: Opening, "Mrs. Brown's House," "Fallwell," "Welcome to London," "Sailor Song," "I Have Never Been So Happy," "I Have Never Been So Happy" (Duet), "Marriage," "I Wish Her All the Best," "The Weeping Song."

ACT II: Opening, "Tea Service," "Honor Lost," "My Only Love," "Every Man in London," "Back Home," "I Came to London," "Pleasure Dance," "Goodbye," "Storm," "My Only Love" (Finale).

GLIMMERGLASS. Musical suggested by James Fenimore Cooper's *Leatherstocking Tales*; book by Jonathan Bolt; music by Douglas J. Cohen; lyrics by Ted Drachman. November 11, 1999. Director, Tony Phelan; musical staging, Janet Bogardus; musical direction, Michael O'Flaherty; scenery, William Barclay; costumes, Martha Bromelmeier; lighting, Phil Monat; sound, J.W. Hilton Jr.; fight direction, Paul Kiernan.

A frontier town in Upstate New York, 1809:

Leatherstocking .... Casper Roos
Chingachgook .... David Aron Demane
Elizabeth .... Jennifer Piech
Squire Doolittle .... John Little
Judge Temple .... Dan Sharkey
Mrs. Hollister .... Catherine Anne Gale
Mayor March .... Richard M. Davidson
Preacher Bone .... Henry Gainza
Kirby .... James Fall
Hiram .... Jeff Gardner

Townspeople: Erin Browne, Stephanie Kurtzuba, Kalani Queypo, Brandon Sean Wardell.

In the past, 1767 & 1779:

Natty Bumppo .... Jay Douglas
Chingachgook .... David Aron Damane
Harry March .... Tom Zemon
Judith .... Marla Schaffel

Also in the wilderness, 1767:

Tom Hutter .... Dan Sharkey
Rivenoak .... Jeff Gardner
Shebear .... Catherine Anne Gale
Catamount .... James Fall
Shaman .... John Little
Mingo Indians .... Kalani Queypo, Brandon Sean Wardell

Also in the war, 1779:

Pvt. Cobb .... James Fall
Sgt. Dunham .... John Little
Butler .... Dan Sharkey
Maj. Clayton .... Jeff Gardner
Capt. Muir .... Henry Gainza
Molly Campbell .... Stephanie Kurtzuba
Pioneer Women .... Erin Browne, Catherine Anne Gale
Iroqouis Indians .... Kalani Queypo, Brandon Sean Wardell

Continental Army Soldiers: Henry Gainza, Jeff Gardner, Kalani Queypo, Dan Sharkey, Brandon Sean Wardell.

One intermission following Part I.

MUSICAL NUMBERS, PART I: "Chingachgook's Song," "Why Are They Here?", "Glimmerglass," "Read the Ground," "Skin!", "Stick to Your Gifts," "Run Away With Me," "Hawkeye," "Things I Need to Know."

PART II: "A War in My Heart," "Soft Things;" "Why Can't I Speak?", "Money Grows on Trees," "So Brief a Happiness," "Far Away."

PART III: "Oh, That I Had Wings Like a Dove," "Dark Cloud on the Horizon," "Hero," "Setting Sun," Glimmerglass Finale.

Chicago: Court Theater

(Charles Newell artistic director; Diane Claussen managing director)

FAIR LADIES AT A GAME OF POEM CARDS. By Peter Oswald; based on an 18th century work by Chikamatsu Monzaemon. March 17, 2000 (American premiere). Director, Charles Newell; scenery, Dan Ostling; costumes, Joyce Kim Lee; lighting, John Culbert; sound, Andre Pluess, Ben Sussman.

Moon; Empress .... Lisa Dodson
Titmouse .... Kurt Brocker
Lord Shigemori .... Thomas Joseph Carroll
Takiguchi .... Steven Rishard
Yoshitsugu .... Guy Adkins
Moritsugu .... Matthew Fahey
Lady Tonase .... Hollis Resnik
Kojiju .... Jen Dede
Kohagi .... Arie Thompson
Karumo .... Kate Fry
Yokobue .... Carey Peters
Lord Morotaka .... John Reeger
Katsuyori .... Bradley Mott
Genjo; Muzo .... Matthew Krause
Peasant Girl .... Tanera Marshall
Servant .... David Baca
Boy .... Kurt Brocker
Genkuro .... Kristin Goodman

One intermission.

Chicago: Goodman Theater

(Robert Falls artistic director; Roche Schulfer executive director)

SPINNING INTO BUTTER. By Rebecca Gilman. May 16, 1999. Director, Les Waters; scenery, Linda Buchanan; costumes, Birgit Rattenborg Wise; lighting, Robert Christen; composer and sound, Rob Milburn, Larry Schanker.

Dean Sarah Daniels .... Mary Beth Fisher
Patrick Chibas .... Andrew Navarro
Ross Collins .... Jim Leaming
Dean Burton Strauss .... Robert Breuler

Dean Catherine Kenney ..... Mary Ann Thebus
Mr. Meyers .... Matt DeCaro
Greg Sullivan .... Bruch Reed

Time: The present. Place: Belmont College, Belmont, Vermont. One intermission.

THE ODYSSEY. New adaptation from the Robert Fitzgerald translation of Homer's *The Odyssey* by Mary Zimmerman. September 27, 1999. Director, Mary Zimmerman; scenery, Daniel Ostling; costumes, Mara Blumenfeld; lighting, T.J. Gerckens; sound, Michael Bodeen; original music, Michael Bodeen, Willie Schwarz.

CAST: Helen, Melantho, Others—Anjali Bhimani; Phemious, Arete, Eurylochus, Others—Antoinette Broderick; Laertes—Nathan Davis; Zeus, Cyclops, Demodokos—Ed Dixon; Odysseus—Christopher Donahue; Hermes, Others—Kyle Hall; Telemachus, Others—Doug Hara; Penelope, Others—Felicity Jones; Eteoneus, Leodes, Others—Chris Kipiniak; Denizen of Heaven, Circe, Others—Louise Lamson; Athena—Mariann Mayberry; Neoman, Ladonis, Elpenor, Others—Andrew Navarro; Antinous, Others—David New; Poseidon, Others—Jonathan Partington; Menelaus, Mentor, Others—Yasen Peyankov; Nausica, Others—Geryll Robinson; Muse, Calypso, Argos, Aiolos, Others—Heidi Stillman; Aiolos, Others—Paul Oakley Stovall; Eurycleia, Odysseus's Mother, Others—Lisa Tejero; Eumaeus—Gary Wingert; Alcinous, Others—Dexter Zollicoffer.

The Sailor's Dance, Lotus Eaters Dance, Nausica Laundry Dance, Poseidon and Odysseus sea fight by Kirsten Showalter Hara.

BOY GETS GIRL. By Rebecca Gilman. March 13, 2000. Director, Michael Maggio; scenery, Michael Philippi; costumes, Nan Cibula-Jenkins; lighting, John Culbert; sound and original music, Rob Milburn, Michael Bodeen.

Theresa Bedell .... Mary Beth Fisher
Tony .... Ian Lithgow
Howard Siegel .... Matt DeCaro
Mercer Stevens .... David Adkins
Harriet .... Shayna Ferm
Les Kennkat .... Howard Witt
Madeleine Beck .... Ora Jones

Time: The present. Place: Various locales in New York City. One intermission.

Chicago: Steppenwolf

(Martha Lavey artistic director; Michael Gennaro executive director)

ORSON'S SHADOW. By Austin Pendleton; conceived by Judith Auberjonois. January 16, 2000. Director, David Cromer; scenery, Mark Loman; costumes, Jennifer Keller; lighting, J.R. Lederle; sound, Chris Johnson.

Ken .... David Warren
Sean .... Dominic Conti
Orson .... Jeff Still
Larry .... John Judd
Joan .... Sarah Wellington
Vivien .... Lee Roy Rogers

Time: Spring of 1960. Place, Act I: The stage of the Gaiety Theater, Dublin. Acts II, III and IV: The stage of the Royal Court Theater London. One intermission between Acts II and III.

THE INFIDEL. By Bruce Norris. March 5, 2000. Director, Anna D. Shapiro; scenery, Mark Netherland; costumes, Janice Pytel; lighting, Heather Gilbert; sound, Lindsay Jones; video design, Logan Kibens.

Garvey .... Mike Nussbaum
Moss .... Robert Breuler
Guard .... Dale Rivera
Helen .... Maureen Gallagher
Casper .... Will Zahrn
Alma .... Charin Alvarez
Cop 1 .... Brendan Grant Phillips
Cop 2 .... Michael Simons
Cop 3 .... Jonathan Singer
Cop 4 .... M. Steven Schwarz

Time: The present. Place: A room in a federal building.

Chicago: Victory Gardens Theater

(Dennis Zacek artistic director; Marcelle McVay managing director)

WINTER. By Claudia Allen. June 4, 1999. Director, Sandy Shinner; scenery, Jeff Bauer; costumes, Karin Kopischke; lighting, Rita Pietraszek; sound, Andre Pluess, Ben Sussman.

Dotha .... Julie Harris
Miriam .... Nancy Lollar
Mark .... Mike Nussbaum
Ora .... Meg Thalken

Time: The present, winter. Place: Smalltown Michigan. No intermission.

On Chicago Stages

In the photo at right, Dexter Zolicoffer as W.E.B. Du Bois with Yvonne Huff as his daughter and Delane Jason as Countee Cullen in *Knock Me a Kiss* at Victory Gardens; *below,* Christopher Donahue as Odysseus and Mariann Mayberry as Athena in Mary Zimmerman's adaptation of *The Odyssey* at the Goodman Theater

BLUFF. By Jeffrey Sweet. September 17, 1999. Director, Sandy Shinner; scenery, Jack K. Magaw; costumes, Judith Lundberg; lighting, Rita Pietraszek; sound, Andre Pluess, Ben Sussman.

Neal .... Jon Cryer
Gene .... Tim Grimm
Bonnie; Marta .... Beth Lacke
Loring; Fred .... Jeff Parker
Georgia .... Kristine Thatcher
Emily .... Sarah Trigger

Time: The present. Place: New York City. No intermission.

DOOR TO DOOR. By James Sherman. November 12, 1999. Director, Dennis Zacek; scenery, Timothy Morrison; costumes, Karin Kopischke; lighting, Geoffrey Bushor; sound, Andre Pluess, Ben Sussman.

Bessie .... Roslyn Alexander
Mary .... Cheryl Ross Mitchell
Deborah .... Kim Wade

Time: 1936 to 1999. Place: A number of locations in and around Chicago.

KNOCK ME A KISS. By Charles Smith. January 21, 2000. Director, Chuck Smith; scenery, Mary Griswold; costumes, Birgit Rattenborg Wise; lighting, Todd Hensley; sound, Benjamin T. Getting, Benjamin Recht.

Countee Cullen .... Jason Delane
Yolande Du Bois .... Yvonne Huff
Jimmy Lunceford .... Morocco Omari
Lenora .... LeShay Tomlinson
Nina Du Bois .... Celeste Williams
W.E.B. Du Bois .... Dexter Zollicoffer

Time: 1927 and 1928. Place: Locations in and around Harlem, New York. One intermission.

VOICE OF GOOD HOPE. By Kristine Thatcher. March 17, 2000. Director, Dennis Zacek; scenery, Jeff Bauer; costumes, Karen Kopischke; lighting, Joel Moritz; sound, Andre Pluess, Ben Sussman.

Heart .... Karla L. Beard
Barbara Jordan .... Cheryl Lynn Bruce
John Ed Patten .... Kenn E. Head
Julie Dunn .... Yvonne Huff
Robert Strauss .... Daniel Mooney
Nancy Earl .... Meg Thalken
Karen Woodruff .... Kim Wade

Act I, Scene 1: August 1994, a private room in Brackenridge Hospital, Austin, Texas. Scene 2: The summer of 1948, the backyard of John Ed Patten, Houston, Texas. Scene 3: Winter 1975, Barbara Jordan's congressional office, Washington, D.C. Act II, Scene 1: February 1990, Barbara Jordan's home at Onion Creek, Austin, Texas. Scene 2: August 1994, the hospital room (bits of August 1994 are interwoven).

CAHOOTS. By Claudia Allen. May 12, 2000. Director, Sandy Shinner; scenery, Mary Griswold; costumes, Judith Lundberg; lighting, Todd Hensley; sound, Andre Pluess, Ben Sussman.

Gwendoline .... Deanna Dunagan
Madeleine Ballantine .... Sharon Gless
Ray O'Keefe .... Sean Grennan
Jerry; Harry; Director;
Undertaker .... Brad Harbaugh
Lee Barry .... Brighid O'Shaughnessy
Roland Jameson .... Rob Riley
Chester Chesterton .... Jordan Teplitz
Lola Lorraine .... Meg Thalken

Time: 1934–1963. Place: A hotel room, rehearsal and opening night party, 1934; the same hotel, 1938; Ray's penthouse, 1941 (intermission). An off-Broadway rehearsal, 1953; a funeral, 1953.

Cincinnati: Playhouse in the Park

(Edward Stern producing artistic director; Buzz Ward executive director)

THE DEAD EYE BOY. By Angus MacLachlan. March 18, 2000. Director, Charles Towers; scenery, Karen TenEyck; costumes, David Zinn; lighting, Nancy Schertler; fight director, Drew Fracher.

Billy .... Kyle Fabel
Shirley-Diane .... Raye Lankford
Soren .... Dan McCabe

Time: The present. Place: North Carolina. One intermission.

Cleveland: The Cleveland Play House

(Peter Hackett artistic director; Dean R. Gladden managing director)

UNDER THE FLESH: THE FINAL DESCENT OF EDGAR ALLEN POE. By Eric Coble in collaboration with Scott Kanoff. October 26, 1999. Director, Scott Kanoff; scenery and lighting, Michael Roesch; costumes, Michelle Sampson; sound, Richard Ingraham; choreography, Marla Kanoff.

Edgar Allen Poe .... Ron Bagden
William Wilson .... Daniel Pearce
Helen Whitman .... Laura Perrotta

Time: 5 a.m., Sunday, October 7, 1849. Place: Baltimore. No intermission.

A DREAM PLAY. New translation by Gerry Bamman and Irene S. Berman of the play by August Strindberg. January 11, 2000. Director, Pavel Dobrusky; design, Pavel Dobrusky; sound, Richard Ingraham; choreography, Doug Elkins; composer, Lee Stametz.

Ensemble Cast: Arthur T. Acuña, Lesley Blumenthal, Nora Cole, Evangelia Costantakos, Carl J. Danielsen, Ron Domingo, Tyrone Mitchell Henderson, Ken Jennings, Andrew May, Kola Ogundiran, Derdriu Ring, Christa Scott-Reed.

Extras: Jovana Batkovic, Joy Daniels, Liz DuChez, Arthur Grothe, Neela Haverstick, Bob Keefe, Jay Kim, Mariah Sage Leeds, Jennifer Mates, Christine McBurney, Shannon McNamara, Mike Sestili, Bradley Speck, Cheri Walters, Jonathan D. Wray.

No intermission.

THE EMANCIPATION OF VALET DE CHAMBRE. Adapted by Murphy Guyer from *The Tragedy of Pudd'nhead Wilson* by Mark Twain. April 11, 2000. Director Murphy Guyer; scenery, Vicki Smith; costumes, David Kay Mickelsen; lighting, Don Darnutzer; sound, Robin Heath; composer, Larry Delinger.

Youth Griffin .... Ernest Perry Jr.
David Pudd'nhead Wilson .... Keith Reddin
Patsy Cooper .... Suzanna Hay
Percy Barclay Driscoll;
York Leicester Driscoll .... Kevin Hogan
Jim Blake;
John Buckstone ...... Richard Russell Ramos
Roxy .... Siobhan Juanita Brown
Thomas a Beckett Driscoll .... James Ludwig
Valet de Chambre .... Myk Watford
Rowena Cooper .... Mary Hammett
Angelo Tocci .... Mark Giordano
Luigi Tocci .... Matte Osian
Pembroke Howard .... Christopher Wynkoop

Time: 1894. Place: Hadley's Landing, Missouri. One intermission.

TOUCH THE NAMES: LETTERS TO THE VIETNAM VETERANS MEMORIAL. Conceived by Randal Myler and Chic Street Man; music, Chic Street Man. May 9, 2000. Director, Randal Myler; musical direction, Chic Street Man; scenery and costumes, G. W. Mercier; lighting, Don Darnutzer; sound, Richard Ingraham.

Ensemble: Christopher Collet, Ann Guilbert, Gwen Harris, Mike Hartman, Keith Hatten, Adale O'Brien, Mike Regan, Chic Street Man, Rachel Kae Taylor, Charles Weldon.

No intermission.

THE INFINITE REGRESS OF HUMAN VANITY. By Murphy Guyer. May 16, 2000. Director, David Colacci; scenery and lighting, Michael Roesch; costumes, Mary Schilling-Martin; sound, Michael Benson.

Greg Lug .... Mark Giordano
Christie Butter .... Mary Hammett
Liz Hazel .... Suzanna Hay
Barry Cob .... Kevin Hogan
Kirk Chest; Nat Wall .... Matte Osian
Andrei Zag .... Myk Watford
Cyril Filbert; Max Beer .... Steve McCue
Dylan Gall; Gabe Leechy ..... Anthony Peeples
Nathan Pine .... Andrew May
Jonathan .... Ron Wilson
Ben .... James Ludwig

Next Stage Festival
Of New Play Readings

NO NIGGERS, NO JEWS, NO DOGS. By John Henry Redwood. January 15, 2000.

GERMANY SURRENDERS. By Michele Lowe. January 22, 2000.

JERUSALEM. By Seth Greeenland. January 29, 2000.

Cleveland: Great Lakes Theater Festival

(James Bundy artistic director)

THE WILD DUCK. New adaptation by Anthony Clarvoe of the play by Henrik Ibsen. January 27, 2000. Director, Bill Rauch; scenery, Alec Hammond; costumes, Nephelie Andonyadis; lighting, Scott Zielinski; sound, Joe Romano.

Peterson; Relling ..... Raphael Nash-Thompson
Jensen; Groberg; Molvik ...... Matthew Schneck
Mrs. Southern .... Emily Yancy
Party Guest Who Ate Too Much .... Dana Hart
Blindfolded Party Guest .... John Buck Jr.
Party Guest Who Gossips .... Laura Perrotta
Henry Worley .... Mike Hartman
Gregory Worley .... Michael Ornstein
Harold Akers .... Billy Jones
Lt. Akers .... William Jay Marshall
Gina Akers .... Katherine Heasley
Hallie Akers .... Sarah Lord

Time: Friday night through Sunday morning. Place: Henry Worley's study in a Cleveland suburb and the Akers' studio loft in the Warehouse District. One intermission.

Costa Mesa, Calif.: South Coast Repertory

(David Emmes producing artistic director; Martin Benson artistic director)

THE HOLLOW LANDS. By Howard Korder. January 7, 2000. Director, David Chambers; scenery, Ming Cho Lee; costumes, Shigeru Yagi; lighting, Chris Parry; sound, Jon Gottlieb; original music, Dennis McCarthy; fight choreographer, Randy Kovitz

James Newman .... Michael Stuhlbarg
Mercy .... Rene Augesen
Tommy; Crowd .... Simon Billig
Daniel; Drummer; Crowd .... Graham Shiels
Samuel Markham Hayes .... Mark Harelik
Roscius; Crowd .... Doug Spearman
Spivey; Besmahal; Crowd .... Rob King
Devoy; Stanwick; Blount;
Ephryheram; Crowd .... Richard Doyle
Elias Chase; Proskauer; Kashtenk;
Crowd .... Hal Landon Jr.
Itinerant; Weeks; Lauderbeck;
Tresguerras .... Armando Duran
Marshall; Carson; Sheriff;
Col. Leland .... Don Took
Woodsman; Bonte; Congregationalist;
Mulcahy; Sergeant .... Art Koustik
Sauk Indian; Arikara Boy; Crowd .. Sol Castillo
Sauk Indian; Congregationalist;
Crowd .... Mark Coyan
Mrs. Rogers; Congregationalist;
Crowd .... Marika Becz
Boy .... Alex Mehra, Steven Morse

Time: Act I, 1815–1818. Act II, 1818. Act III, 1838–1857. Place: America during the first half of the 19th century.

REFERENCES TO SALVADOR DALI MAKE ME HOT. By Jose Rivera. January 25, 2000. Director, Juliette Carrillo; scenery, Monica Raya; costumes, Meg Neville; lighting, Geoff Korf; composer and sound design, Mitch Greenhill.

Coyote .... Victor Mack
Cat .... Svetlana Efremova
Martin .... Wells Rosales
Gabriela .... Ana Ortiz
Benito .... Robert Montano

Place: Barstow, California. One intermission

THE BEGINNING OF AUGUST. By Tom Donaghy. April 25, 2000. Director, Neil Pepe; scenery, Scott Pask; costumes, Shigeru Yagi; lighting, Chris Akerlind; sound, B.C. Keller.

Jackie .... Geoffrey Nauffts
Ben .... Todd Lowe
Joyce .... Barbara Tarbuck
Ted .... Jeff Allin
Pam .... Mary B. McCann

Place: A backyard. One intermission.

THE EDUCATION OF RANDY NEWMAN. Musical with music and lyrics by Randy Newman; conceived by Michael Roth, Jerry Patch and Randy Newman. May 26, 2000. Director and choreographer, Myron Johnson; musical direction, vocal arrangements and orchestrations, Michael Roth; scenery, Ralph Funicello; costumes, Judith Dolan; lighting, Donald Holder; sound, François Bergeron; projection design, John Boesche.

Dad; Others .... Jordan Bennett
A Kingfish; Others .... Gregg Henry
Mom; Others .... Sherry Hursey
Dr. Tap (Ph.D.); Others .... John Lathan
First Love; Others .... Allison Smith
Songwriter .... Scott Waara
Teacher; Others .... Jennifer Leigh Warren

Place: Louisiana and Los Angeles. One intermission.

MUSICAL NUMBERS, Prologue: "The Great Nation of Europe," "Sail Away." ACT I, La.: "My Country" (Part I), "Dixie Flyer," "New Orleans Wins the War," "Jolly Coppers on Parade," "Four Eyes," "Louisiana 1927," "Kingfish," "Birmingham," "Rednecks," "Lullaby," "Roll With the Punches," "My Country" (Part II), "Follow the Flag," "Falling in Love"/"Maybe I'm Doing It Wrong," "Davy the Fat Boy," "There's a Party at My House," "Shame," "Bad Boy," "Mama Told Me Not to Come," "New Orleans Wins the War" (Reprise), "I Love L.A."

Entr'acte: "It's Money That I Love," "Short People." ACT II, L.A.: "It's Money That Matters," "Vine Street"/"They Tell Me It's Summer"/"Lucinda," "I Think It's Going to Rain Today," "Love Story," "Better Off Dead," "Love Story" (Reprise), "Song for the Dead," "My Life Is Good," "Miami," "Real Emotional Girl," "You Can Leave Your Hat On," "When He Loved Me," "Take Me Back," "I Want You to Hurt Like I Do," "Marie," "Political Science," "Texas Girl at the Funeral of Her Father," "Old Man," "Texas Girl at the Funeral of Her Father" (Reprise), "Days of Heaven," "Feels Like Home," "Days of Heaven" (Reprise), "The World Isn't Fair," "Days of Heaven" (Finale).

2d Annual Pacific Playwrights Festival

(Jerry Patch director)

Staged Readings

LUPE NOW! By Jonathan Ceniceroz. June 12, 1999. Director, Luis Alfaro.

CUCHIFRITO. By Eduardo Andino. June 13, 1999. Director, Octavio Solis.

EVERETT BEEKIN. By Richard Greenberg. June 18, 1999. Director, Mark Rucker.

COSTA MESA—Ana Ortiz and Robert Montano in the South Coast Repertory production of Jose Rivera's *References to Salvador Dali Make Me Hot*

THE MYSTERY OF ATTRACTION. By Marlane Mayer. June 18, 1999. Director, Jody McAuliffe.

GOD OF VENGEANCE. By Donald Margulies, adapted from Sholem Asch. June 19, 1999. Director, Gordon Edelstein.

THE BEGINNING OF AUGUST. By Tom Donaghy. June 20, 1999.

Workshop Productions

ILLUMINATING VERONICA. By Rogelio Martinez. June 16, 1999. Director, Lisa Portes.

REFERENCES TO SALVADOR DALI MADE ME HOT. By Jose Rivera. June 17, 1999. Director, Juliette Carillo.

Dallas: Dallas Theater Center

(Richard Hamburger artistic director; Edith H. Love managing director)

A CHRISTMAS CAROL. New adaptation by Preston Lane and Jonathan Moscone of the story by Charles Dickens; music, Kim D. Sherman. November 26, 1999. Director, Jonathan Moscone; musical direction, Raymond Allen; choreography, David Shimotakahara; scenery, Narelle Sissons; costumes, Giva R. Taylor; lighting, Frances Aronson; sound, Kim D. Sherman, Bruce Richardson; additional music, Bruce Richardson.

Scrooge .... Laurence O'Dwyer

Bob Cratchit;
Joe the Keeper .... Chamblee Ferguson
Fred; Ali Baba; Young Scrooge ... Chris Carlos
Charitable Gentleman; Rich Gentleman;
Debtor .... James Crawford
Charitable Gentlewoman; Cynthia;
Debtor's Wife .... Liz Piazza Davey
Marley's Ghost; Mr. Fezziwig;
Rich Gentleman .... Akin Babatunde
Spirit of Christmas Past;
Peter Cratchit .... Hunter Tharp
Child Scrooge; Tiny Tim;
Ignorance .... Alexander Ferguson
Adolescent Scrooge;
James Cratchit .... Tony Delgado
Fan; Martha Cratchit .... Melanie R. Nelson
Dick Wilkins; Rich Gentleman
Topper .... David Novinski
Mrs. Fezziwig; Spirit of Christmas Present;
Laundress .... Liz Mikel
Belle; Lily .... Joanna Schellenberg
Mrs. Cratchit; Mrs. Dilber .... Dolores Godinez
Ensemble .... Cristina Dominique McAlister
Belinda Cratchit; Turkey Girl .... Jordan Rhyner
Sarah Cratchit; Want ...... Mackenzie Ferguson
One intermisson.

INEXPRESSIBLE ISLAND. By David Young. February 16, 2000 (American premiere). Director, Preston Lane; scenery, Walt Spangler; costumes, Claudia Stephens; lighting, Robert Perry; sound, Shane Rettig.

Preistly .... Adrian La Tourelle
Campbell .... Rufus Collins
Dickason .... James Crawford
Levick .... Mark Boyett
Abbott .... Kelly E. Cole
Browning .... Russell Pickering
Time: 1912. Place: Antarctica. Two intermissions.

DREAMLANDIA. By Octavio Solis. May 13, 2000. Director, Richard Hamburger; scenery, Russell Parkman; costumes, Claudia Stephens; lighting, Steve Woods; sound, Martin Desjardins; fight direction, Bill Lengfelder.

Blanca (Alfonso) .... Zabryna Guevara
Lazaro .... Carlo Alban
Pepin .... Felix Solis
Celestino .... Geno Silva
Sonia .... Maggie Palomo
Frank .... Bernie Sheredy
Dolores .... Dolores Godinez
Seth .... Scott Phillips
Carl .... T.A. Taylor
Place: El Paso, Juarez and the border. One intermission.

Denver: Denver Center Theater Company

(Donovan Marley artistic director)

A HOTEL ON MARVIN GARDENS. By Nagle Jackson. September 23, 1999. Director, Nagle Jackson; scenery and costumes, Michael Ganio; lighting, Don Darnutzer; sound, Matthew C. Swartz.

KC .... Nance Williamson
Bo .... John Hutton
Erna .... Annette Helde
Henry .... Sam Gregory
Rose .... Lauren Berst
Time: The present. Place: One of the Thimble Islands off the coast of Connecticut in Long Island Sound. One intermission.

BARRIO BABIES. Musical with book and lyrics by Luis Santeiro; music by Fernando Rivas. November 10, 1999. Director, Susana Tubert; choreography, A.C. Ciulla; musical direction, Douglas Coates; scenery, James Youmans; costumes, David Kay Mickelsen; lighting, Howell Binkley; sound, David R. White; musical arrangements and orchestrations, Fernando Rivas.

Ray Reyes .... Philip Anthony
Josie Lopez .... Sara Ramirez
Madelin Menendez .... Annie Kozuch
Oscar Garces .... Edgar Garcia
Lola Roldan .... April Ortiz
Various Agents & Producers ... Steve Routman
One intermission.

MUSICAL NUMBERS, ACT I: Overture, "LA Is Calling," "Time to See Me," "The Line Up," "When I Was Exotic," "The Hollywood Cha Cha," "Made for Each Other," "The Audition," "Court Room Tango," "Make Love to Me in Spanish," "Duel Duet," "Barrio Babies."

ACT II: Entr'acte, "The Problem With Hispanics," "Love Among the Lepers," "A Night at the Oscars," "Close Your Eyes to See," "The Big Banana," "Puerto Rico," "The Face on the Cutting Room Floor," "Ends of the Earth," "Bring Back the Love," "Barrio Babies" Finale.

WAITING TO BE INVITED. By S.M. Shephard-Massat. January 13, 2000. Director, Israel Hicks; scenery, Bill Curley; costumes, David Kay Mickelsen; lighting, Charles R. MacLeod; sound, Matthew C. Swartz.

Miss Louise .... Lynette Du Pre
Miss Delores .... Candy Brown Houston

Miss Odessa .... Ebony Jo-Ann
Palmeroy Bateman .... Keith L. Hatten
Miss Grayson .... Jane Welch
Miss Ruth .... Michele Shay
Musicians .... Sam Gill, Warren Smith

Time: Summer 1961. Place: Atlanta, Ga. One intermission.

THE LARAMIE PROJECT. By Moisés Kaufman and members of the Tectonic Theater Project: Leigh Fondakowski head writer; Stephen Belber, Greg Pierotti, Stephen Wangh associate writers; Amanda Gronich, Sarah Lambert, John McAdams, Maude Mitchell, Andy Paris, Barbara Pitts, Kelli Simpkins contributing writers. February 26, 2000. Director, Moisés Kaufman; scenery, Robert Brill; costumes, Moe Schell; lighting, Betsy Adams; sound, Craig Breitenbach; video and slides, Martha Swetzoff; assistant director, Leigh Fondakowski; project advisor, Stephen Wangh; produced in association with the Tectonic Theater Project, Moisés Kaufman artistic director, Jeffrey LaHoste managing director.

With Stephen Belber, Amanda Gronich, Mercedes Herrero, John McAdams, Andy Paris, Greg Pierotti, Barbara Pitts, Kelli Simpkins.

GIVE 'EM A BIT OF MYSTERY: SHAKESPEARE AND THE OLD TRADITION. Solo performance by Tony Church; conceived and written by Tony Church. May 4, 2000. Director, Bruce K. Sevy; scenery and costumes, Andrew V. Yelusich; lighting, Charles MacLeod; sound, David R. White.

THE MISER. By Molière; new translation and adaptation by Nagle Jackson. May 11, 2000. Director, Nagle Jackson; scenery, Vicki Smith; costumes, Kevin Copenhaver; lighting, Dawn Chiang; sound, Matthew C. Swartz.

Harpagon .... Randy Moore
Cleante .... Douglas Harmsen
Elise .... Stephanie Cozart
Valere .... Jared Reed
Mariane .... Gloria Biegler
Anselme .... William Denis
Frosine .... Kathleen M. Brady
Master Simon .... Mark Rubald
Master Jacques .... Richard Risso
La Fleche .... Robert Westenberg
Dame Claude .... Gabriella Cavallero
Magistrate .... Jamie Horton
Magistrate's Clerk .... Archie Smith

East Farmingdale, N.Y.: Arena Players Company of Long Island

(Frederic DeFeis producer/director)

OBIT. (period is part of title). By Todd Lepre. February 10, 2000. Director, Joseph Yoga; scenery, Fred Sprauer; costumes, Lois Lockwood; lighting, Al Davis.

Dennis Preston .... Martin Edmond
Curtis Gladding .... Michael Lang
Larry Ferguson .... Vito Pipitone
Roger Dosman .... Frank McGeeney
Michael Momuson .... Stephen Chan

Time: The present. Place: Manhattan. One intermission.

Evanston, Ill.: The Next Theater

(Kate Buckley artistic director; Allison Sciplin managing director)

THE BOARDING HOUSE. By Ann Noble Massey. November 21, 1999. Director, Sarah Tucker; choreography, Mark Rector; scenery, Jack K. Magaw; costumes, Vicky J. Strei; lighting, Charles W. Jolls; sound, Teff Uchima.

Mr. John .... John Judd
Lilah .... Laura Jones Macknin
Sylvia .... Natasha Lowe
Imogen .... Molly Glynn Hammond
Paul .... Guy Massey
Dell .... Coby Goss

Time: November 1945. Place: A boarding house in Boston.

AMONG THE THUGS. By Bill Buford; adapted by Tom Szentgyorgyi, April 28, 2000. Director Kate Buckley; scenery, Rick Paul; costumes, Vicky J. Strei; lighting, Jack Magaw; sound, Lindsay Jones; fight choreography, Robin McFarquhar.

CAST: Supporters—Aaron Christensen, Dominic Conti, Scott Cummins, Eric Fraisher Hayes, Brad C. Light, Andrew Micheli, Mark Vanasse. Roy, Supporter—R.J. Jones. Bill—Christian Kohn. Mick, Supporter—John Sierros.

One intermission.

Hartford, Conn: Hartford Stage

(Michael Wilson artistic director)

THE DEATH OF PAPA. By Horton Foote. May 27, 1999. Director, Michael Wilson; scenery, Jeff Cowie; costumes, McKay Coble; lighting, Michael Lincoln; original music and sound, Johnna Doty.

Horace Robedaux Jr. .... Frankie Muniz
Eliza .... Beatrice Winde
Gertrude .... Preslaysa Edwards
Elizabeth Robedaux .... Hallie Foote
Mary Vaughn .... Dana Ivey
Brother Vaughn .... Andrew McCarthy
Corella Davenport .... Jean Stapleton
Inez Kirby .... Julie Fishell
Horace Robedaux Sr. .... Devon Abner
Will Borden .... Frank Girardeau
Walter .... Ed Wheeler

Time: 1928. Place: Harrison, Texas. One intermission.

ENCHANTED APRIL. By Matthew Barber; adapted from the novel *The Enchanted April* by Elizabeth von Arnim. February 24, 2000. Director, Michael Wilson; scenery, Tony Straiges; costumes, Jess Goldstein; lighting, Rui Rita; original music and sound, John Gromada.

Frederick Arnott .... Christopher Donahue
Wilding .... Christopher Duva
Rose Arnott .... Enid Graham
Mellersh Wilton .... John Hines
Lotty Wilton .... Isabel Keating
Lady Caroline .... Stephanie March
Costanza .... Irma S. Paule
Mrs. Graves .... Jill Tanner

1st Brand: NEW Festival
Of Works for the Theater
Readings and Workshops, June 11–13

THE BEGINNING OF AUGUST. By Tom Donaghy. Director, Neil Pepe.

THE HUNGER EDUCATION. By Jessica Goldberg. Director, Diane Rodriguez.

FIRE EATER. By Brighde Mullins. Director, Mark Wing-Davey.

THE TWO ORPHANS. Musical with book by Theresa Rebeck; lyrics by Theresa Rebeck and John Sheehy; music by Kim D. Sherman. Director, Tracy Brigden.

SINCE YOU BEEN GONE. By Walter Mosley. Director, Oz Scott.

2d Brand:NEW Festival
Of Works for the Theater
Readings and Workshops, March 17–19

THE MEASURE OF MY DAYS. By Keith Bunin. Director, Tracy Brigden.

HOMEBODY/KABUL. By Tony Kushner. Director, Tony Kushner.

NO NIGGERS, NO JEWS, NO DOGS. By John Henry Redwood. Director, Jonathan Wilson.

TOPOGRAPHICAL EDEN. By Brighde Mullins.

NECESSARY TARGETS. By Eve Ensler. Director, Michael Wilson.

Houston: Alley Theater

(Gregory Boyd artistic director; Paul R. Tetreault managing director)

LEMONADE. By Eve Ensler. October 13, 1999. Director, David Wheeler; scenery, Richard Hoover; costumes, Karyl Newman; lighting, Kevin Rigdon; sound and original music, Malcolm Nicholls.

Bernard .... Stephen Mendillo
Alice .... Lisa Richards
Jane .... Sherri Parker Lee
Policeman .... Jason Douglas

One Intermission.

A CHRISTMAS CAROL, A GHOST STORY OF CHRISTMAS. Adapted by Stephen Rayne from the story by Charles Dickens. December 1, 1999. Director, Stephen Rayne; musical direction, Deborah Lewis; scenery, Douglas W. Schmidt; costumes, Esther Marquis; lighting, Rui Rita; sound, Malcolm Nicholls; original music and arrangements, Steven Edis; musical staging and movement, Karen Stokes.

Ebenezer Scrooge .... James Black
Miss Goodleigh;
Mrs. Dilber .... Bettye Fitzpatrick
Bob Cratchit; Topper .... John Tyson
Coutts; Fezziwig .... Paul Hope
Priest; Marley; Old Joe .... Charles Krohn
Boz .... John Feltch
Phizz .... James Belcher
Blindman; Present .... Darrin Lamont Byrd
Past; Mrs. O'Malley .... Elizabeth Heflin
Moll; Miss; Fred's Sister .... Danica Dawn
Deedles .... Kevin Waldron
Turkey Boy; Young Scrooge;
Guest .... Joshua Pohja
Miss Bumble; Miss;
Mrs. Fred .... Nathalie Cunningham
Fred .... Jason Curtis
Belle; Martha .... Luci Christian

HOUSTON—The distinguished author of *The Play About the Baby* at the Alley Theater: Edward Albee

Mrs. Cratchit;
Mrs. Fezziwig .... Shelley Calene Black
Undertaker; Man; Guest; Pall Bearer;
Vendor .... David Born
Caroler; Man; Guest; Pall Bearer;
Vendor .... Christopher Patton
Future; Laborer; Guest; Man;
Pall Bearer .... Jason Douglas
Doll; Miss; Guest .... Kara Greenberg
Caroler; Vendor; Guest .... Mia Fisher
Caroler; Vendor; Guest .... Marion Wood
Girl; Fan; Caroler; Guest .... Megan Kane, Alyssia Thomas
Boy; Child Scrooge; Caroler ...... Will Rimmer, Scott Braddock
Older Boy; Dick Wilkins; Peter; Young Man;
Caroler .... Chris Tow, Adam Wiggins
Ignorance; Boy; Albert; Caroler ... Aaron Harp, Mark Jackson
Girl; Victoria; Caroler .... Auden Thornton, Elizabeth Turner
Tiny Tim; Child ...... Alex Dugan, Kevin Corn
Want; Young Girl; Caroler .. Leydon Thornton, Deanna Orozco
Belinda; Teenage Girl .... Courtney Roche, Natalie Arnold
Teenage Boy; Caroler .... Cameron Bautsch, Ross Bautsch

THE PLAY ABOUT THE BABY. By Edward Albee. April 12, 2000 (American premiere). Director, Edward Albee; scenery, E. David Cosier; costumes, Teresa Snider-Stein; lighting, Jeffrey S. Koger; sound, Malcolm Nicholls.

Girl .... Rebecca Harris
Boy .... David Burtka
Man .... Earle Hyman
Woman .... Marian Seldes

Houston Young Playwrights Exchange Of One-Acts, August 6 & 7

MOMENT BEFORE THE TRUTH. By Hwan-Joon Choi. Director, Travis Mader.

SO THIS WAS LOVE. By Andrea Davulis. Director, Travis Mader.

STRIKE ZONE. By Jason Price. Director, Rene Wells.

BEATING A DEAD HORSE: A COMPLETE DELUSION IN ONE ACT. By Travis Johns. Director, Dennis Draper.

Indianapolis: Indiana Repertory Theater

(Janet Allen artistic director; Brian Payne managing director)

AMBER WAVES. By James Still. February 11, 2000. Director, James Still; scenery, Russell Metheny; costumes, Joyce Kim Lee; lighting, Michelle Habeck; sound, Andrew Hopson; video, Mark Williams; original songs and music, Tim Grimm, Jason Wilbur.

Deb .... Courtney Bolin
Penny .... Jan Lucas
Mike .... Tim Grimm
Scott .... Mat Hostetler
Julie .... Kristen Cooler
Voice of the Umpire;
Johnny .... John Henry Redwood

Place: The Olson farm and other places in and around their Indiana town. Act I: Summer & fall. Act II: Winter & spring.

Key West: Key West Theater Festival

(Charles Munroe executive producer; Joan McGillis artistic director; Katie Tierney general manager)

BIG HEARTS. By Gary Bonasorte. October 7, 1999. Director, Tom Caruso; scenery and lighting, Gary MacDonald.

Ross .... Tom Sardinia
David .... Charlie Schroeder
Trudy .... Tasha Lawrence
Tony .... Richard Rosario-Velazquez
Bumble Beena .... John Evans

DOMESIC TRANQUILITY. By Rich Orloff. October 7, 1999. Director, Barry Steinman; scenery and lighting, Matt Crowder; costumes, Ellis Tillman.

Herbert Miller .... Tom Wahl
Ethel Miller .... Angie Radosh
Cindy Miller .... Kathy Kay Kurtz
Tony .... Michael McKeever
Lou Calendo .... Steve Wise
Spot .... Jim Doyle

THE LEMON COOKIE. By Jack Heifner. October 8, 1999. Director, Joan McGillis; scenery and lighting, Matt Crowder; costumes, Joy Delgado.

Eric .... Lawrence Cohen
Lee Ann .... Michele Leavy
Marta .... Diana Bellar
Matt .... Scott Gilmore
Candy .... Jennifer Jacques Naugler
Sybil .... Diana Haegelin
Larry .... Richard Grusin

PRODIGAL KISS. Play with songs by Caridad Svich. October 8, 1999. Director, Ellen Davis; scenery and lighting, Gary Macdonald; costumes, Ellis Tillman.

Marcela .... Delma Miranda
Ignacio; Rafael; Paco .... Steve Wise
Coral; Woman on the Road;
Miriam Mocha .... Judith Delgado
Rider; Carlo; Half Dressed Man .... Oscar Isaac

Readings

IN THE VALLEY OF THE SUN. By Richard Warren. October 11, 1999.

VELVETEEN UNDERTOW. By Michael McKeever. October 12, 1999.

BIZET'S LOCKET. By Stuart Warmflash. October 13, 1999.

HEART OF A WOMAN. By Robert E. Williams. October 14, 1999.

THE PASSION OF CLAIRE. By Cheryl Royce. October 15, 1999.

La Jolla, Calif: La Jolla Playhouse

(Michael Greif artistic director; Terrence Dwyer managing director)

JANE EYRE. Musical based on the novel by Charlotte Brontë; book and additional lyrics by John Caird; music and lyrics by Paul Gordon. July 13, 1999. Directors, John Caird, Scott Schwartz; music direction, Steven Tyler; scenery, John Napier; costumes, Andreane Neofitou; lighting, Chris Parry; sound, Tom Clark, Mark Menard; orchestrations, Larry Hochman; incidental music and vocal arrangements, Steven Tyler.

Mrs. Reed; Lady Ingram .... Anne Allgood
Grace Poole; Amy Eshton .... Nell Balaban
Edward Rochester .... James Barbour
Schoolgirl .... Lauren Campbell
Blanche Ingram .... Elizabeth DeGrazia
Robert .... Bruce Dow
Helen Burns .... Megan Drew
Schoolgirl .... Kelly Felthous
Miss Satcherd; Mrs. Dent;
Bertha .... Marguerite MacIntyre
Richard Mason .... Bill Nolte
Jane's Mother; Mary Ingram .... Jayne Paterson
Brocklehurst; Col. Dent; Vicar .... Don Richard
Young Jane Eyre .... Tiffany Scarritt
Jane Eyre .... Marla Schaffel
Adele .... Joelle Shapiro
Mrs. Fairfax .... Mary Stout
Louisa Eshton .... Rachel Ulanet
Jane's Father; Mr. Eshton;
St. John Rivers .... Christopher Yates
John Reed; Young Lord Ingram .... Lee Zarrett

MUSICAL NUMBERS, ACT I: "Secrets of the House," "Let Me Be Brave," "Children of God," "Forgiveness," "The Fever," "The Farewell," "Sweet Liberty," "Perfectly Nice," "The Icy Lane," "The Master Returns," "The Governess," "As Good As You," "Sirens," "Society's Best," "Finer Things," "Enchanté," "The Pledge," "Secret Soul."

ACT II: "Secrets of the House" (Reprise), "Sirens" (Reprise), "Painting Her Portrait," "In the Light of the Virgin Morning," "Oh Sister," "Second Self," "The Chestnut Tree," "Slip of a Girl," "The Wedding," "Wild Boy," "Farewell, Good Angel," "The Fever" (Reprise), "Child in the Attic," "Forgiveness" (Reprise), "The Voice Across the Moors," "Oh Sister" (Reprise), "Second Self" (Reprise), "Brave Enough for Love."

WONDERLAND. By Chay Yew. September 14, 1999. Director, Lisa Peterson; scenery, Rachel Hauck; costumes, Joyce Kim Lee; lighting, Geoff Korf; original music and sound, Mark Bennett.

Woman .... Tsai Chin
Young Man .... Joel de la Fuente
Son .... Alec Mapa
Man .... Sab Shimono

One intermission.

Los Angeles: Mark Taper Forum

(Gordon Davidson artistic director and producer; Charles Dillingham managing director; Robert Egan producing director)

THE FIRST PICTURE SHOW. Play with music with book and lyrics by Ain Gordon and David Gordon; music by Jeanine Tesori. August 12, 1999. Director and choreographer, David Gordon; music direction, Kimberly Grigsby; scenery, Robert Brill; costumes, Judith Dolan; lighting, Jennifer Tipton; sound, Jon Gottlieb, Philip G. Allen; associate director, Ain Gordon; co-produced by American Conservatory Theater, Carey Perloff artistic director, in association with AT&T: OnStage and in association with the Pick Up Performance Company.

CAST: Anne First (age 99)—Estelle Parsons. Censor, Customs Official, Train Announcer, Movie Crew, Pianist—Christian Nova. Louie's Mother, Louie's Friend, Movie Crew, Newsman—Chuck Rosen. Lois Weber, Thelma March—Kathleen Conry. Anne First (ages 15–38), Jane Furstmann—Ellen Greene. May Furstmann, Connie Gardner, Gene Gauntier—Norma Fire. Censor, Percy Waters, Movie Crew, Cleo Madison, Rep. Hughes—Harry Waters Jr. Louis Furstmann, Henry Hooks, Monty Latour, Margery Wilson—Steven Skybell. Nurse Tina, Cindy Su, Justice McKenna, Marion E. Wong—Jeanne Sakata. Louie's Friend, Jane's Assistant, Billy's Assistant, Nell Shipman—Karen Graham. Carl Laemmle, Ad-Man, Billy Friend, Ida May Park, Pianist—Ken Marks. Rev. Wilbur F. Crafts, Alice Guy Blaché, Movie Crew, Awards Host—Valda Setterfield. TV Newscaster, Movie Crew—Kerry K. Carnahan. Naomi the Piano Player—Kimberly Grigsby.

Time: The years 1893–1995. Place: The United States. One intermission.

THE DINNER PARTY. By Neil Simon. November 21, 1999. Director, John Rando; scenery, John Lee Beatty; costumes, Jane Greenwood; lighting, Brian MacDevitt; sound, Jon Gottlieb.

Claude Pichon .... John Ritter
Albert Donay .... Henry Winkler
Andre Bouville .... Edward Herrmann
Mariette Levieux ...... Anette Michelle Sanders
Yvonne Fouchet .... Veanne Cox
Gabrielle Buonocelli .... Frances Conroy

Time: The present. Place: A private dining room in a first rate restaurant in Paris. No intermission.

New Work Festival '99

(Anthony Byrnes associate producer; Sharon Morrissette festival coordinator; presented in association with A.S.F. Theater Projects)

Workshops

BE AGGRESSIVE. By Annie Weisman. November 10, 1999.

FALL. By Bridget Carpenter. November 13, 1999.

WHAT DIDN'T HAPPEN. By Christopher Shinn. November 17, 1999.

CONJUNTO. By Oliver Mayer. November 20, 1999.

THE BODY OF BOURNE. By John Belluso. December 1, 1999.

THE BLACK WHITE MAN. By OyamO (Charles Gordon). December 4, 1999.

A SHOE IS NOT A QUESTION. By Kelly Stuart. December 8, 1999.

MIDONS. By Lillian Garrett-Groag. December 14, 1999.

Readings

SWING, OR THE IDENTICAL SAME TEMPTATION. By Robert Glaudini. November 5, 1999.

MRS. FEUERSTEIN. By Murray Mednick. November 6, 1999.

HOBSON'S CHOICE. By Steven Drukman. November 6, 1999.

RICE BOY. By Sunil Kuruvilla. November 7, 1999.

DRIVE MY COCHE. By Roy Conboy. December 11, 1999.

HORTENSIA AND THE MUSEUM OF DREAMS. By Nilo Cruz. December 12, 1999.

THE SONG OF ORFEO. By Octavio Solis. December 12, 1999.

THE CIRCLE. By Shem Bitterman. December 12, 1999.

Louisville, Ky.: Actors Theater of Louisville

(Jon Jory producing director; Alexander Speer executive director)

24th Annual Festival
Of New American Plays
February 29-April 8

TAPE. By Stephen Belber. February 29, 2000. Director, Brian Jucha; scenery, Paul Owen; costumes, Suttirat Larlarb; lighting, Greg Sullivan; sound, Martin R. Desjardins; fight director, Drew Fracher.

Vince .... Dominic Fumusa
Jon .... Stephen Kunken
Amy .... Erica Yoder

Time: The Present. Place: A motel room in Lansing, Michigan. One intermission.

NO. 11 (BLUE AND WHITE). By Alexandra Cunningham. March 4, 2000. Director, Brian Mertes; scenery, Paul Owen; costumes, Suttirat Larlarb; lighting, Greg Sullivan; sound, Martin R. Desjardins; fight director, Drew Fracher.

Alex .... Savannah Haske
Suzanne Callahan .... Lauren Klein
Reid Callahan .... Blair Singer
Danny .... Patrick J. Dall'Occhio
Brian .... Patrick Darragh
Paige .... Jessica Wortham
Tammy .... Christy Collier
Coach Coyle; Dad;
Lt. Cleary .... William McNulty
Jenny; Voice of Kristin .. Shawna Joy Anderson
Lindsay .... Woodwyn Koons

Time: Right now. Place: In Connecticut. No intermission.

WAR OF THE WORLDS. Conceived by Anne Bogart; created by The SITI Company; written by Naomi Iizuka. March 9, 2000. Director, Anne Bogart; scenery, Neil Patel; costumes, James Schuette; lighting, Mimi Jordan Sherin; sound, Darron L. West.

Beatrice Nelson .... Akiko Aizawa
Thompson .... J. Ed Araiza
Bernstein .... Will Bond
Stratten .... Tom Nelis
Leni Tamiroff .... Ellen Lauren
Stephen Webber .... Barney O'Hanlon
Orson Welles .... Stephen Webber

Entourage: Phil Bolin, Carey Calebs, Cabe McCarty, Mark Watson.

Time: Now. Place: Here. No intermission.

ANTON IN SHOW BUSINESS. By Jane Martin. March 11, 2000. Director, Jon Jory; scenery, Paul Owen; costumes, Marcia Dixcy Jory; lighting, Greg Sullivan; sound, Martin R. Desjardins.

T-Anne; Andwyneth; Don Blount;
Editor .... Saidah Arrika Ekulona
Lisabette .... Monica Koskey
Casey .... Gretchen Lee Krich
Kate; Ben; Jackey;
Gate Manager .... Annette Helde
Ralph; Wikewitch; Lola; Joe Bob .... Chick Reid

LOUISVILLE—Annette Helde and Saidah Arrika Ekulona in *Anton in Show Business* by Jane Martin in the 2000 Humana Festival

Holly .... Caitlin Miller
Joby .... Stacey Swift

Time: The present. Place: Various locations in New York and San Antonio. One intermission.

TOUCH. By Toni Press-Coffman; conceived by Toni Press-Coffman and Jonathan Ingbretson. March 16, 2000. Director, Mladen Kiselov; scenery, Paul Owen; costumes, James Schuette; lighting, Mimi Jordan Sherin; sound, Martin R. Desjardins.

Kyle Kalke .... Stephen Kunken
Bennie Locasto .... Dominic Fumusa
Serena .... Kaili Vernoff
Kathleen .... Joanna Glushak

Place: Kyle's mind and the places he conjures there. One intermisssion.

BIG LOVE. By Charles L. Mee. March 23, 2000. Director, Les Waters; scenery, Paul Owen; costumes, Marcia Dixcy Jory; lighting, Greg Sullivan; sound, Malcolm Nicholls.

Lydia .... Carolyn Baeumler
Guiliano .... Tony Speciale
Olympia .... Aimee Guillot
Thyona .... Karenjune Sanchez
Bella; Eleanor .... Lauren Klein
Piero; Leo .... Fred Major
Nikos .... T Ryder Smith
Constantine .... Mark Zeisler
Third Cousin .... Jeff Jenkins

Time: The present. Place: A villa on the coast of Italy. No intermission.

BACK STORY. Anthology based on characters created by Joan Ackermann. March 25, 2000. Scenery, Paul Owen; costumes, Kevin McLeod; lighting, Greg Sullivan; sound, Martin R. Dejardins.

Time to Think by Joan Ackermann—Rachel Burttram.

Good Morning to the Horse by Craig Lucas—Heather Springsteen, Tom Johnson.

What Became of the Polar Bear? by Mayo Simon—Patrick Dall'Occhio.

The Reluctant Instrument by Neena Beber—Christy Collier.

Ethan's Got Get by Edwin Sanchez—Jeff Jenkins.

Trying to Get There by Eduardo Machado—Samantha Desz.

Maid of Athens by David Rambo—Molly Binder.

Moby Ethan at the Sculptor's Museum by Constance Congdon—Travis York.

Turn Down by Shirley Lauro—Jessica Wortham.

Misadventure by Donald Margulies—Kimberly Megna, Carey Calebs.

Something to Do With Bolivia by Jon Klein—Zach Welsheimer.

Or Maybe Not by Adele Edling Shank—Melody Fenster.

Dead Men Make No Dollars by Val Smith—Tom Moglia.

The Deal by Jane Martin—Holly Sims.

Blackfish by Courtney Baron—Stephen Sisen.

Star Skating by John Olive—Cabe McCarty.

Barbra Live at Canyon Ranch by Tanya Palmer—Shawna Joy Anderson.

Introducing Dad by Susan Miller—Mark Watson

Norman Rockwell's Thanksgiving in the Year 2000 by Joan Ackermann—Aimee Kleisner, Phil Bolin.

Directors: *Trying to Get There, Moby Ethan at the Sculptor's Museum*—Pascaline Bellegarde. *Ethan's Got Get, Or Maybe Not*—Aimee Hayes. *What Became of the Polar Bear, Maid of Athens*—Dano Madden. *Time to Think, Good Morning to the Horse, Misadventure, Something to Do With Bolivia, The Deal, Barbra Live at Canyon Ranch*—Meredith McDonough. *The Reluctant Instrument, Turn Down, Dead Men Make No Dollars, Blackfish, Introducing Dad, Star Skating, Norman Rockwell's Thanksgiving in the Year 2000*—Sullivan Canaday White.

No intermission.

Ten-Minute Plays
April 2, 2000

THE DIVINE FALLACY. By Tina Howe. Director, Jon Jory.
Victor .... Tom Nelis
Dorothy .... Woodwyn Koons

Time: The present. Place: Victor Hugo's studio in downtown Manhattan.

ARABIAN NIGHTS. By David Ives. Director, Jon Jory.
Interpreter .... Gretchen Lee Krich
Flora .... Ellen Lauren
Norman .... Will Bond

Time: The Present. Place: Flora's shop.

STANDARD TIME. By Naomi Wallace. Director, Michael Bigelow Dixon.
Young Man .... James Cornwell

Time: The present. Place: A cell.

Designers: Scenery, Paul Owen; costumes, Kevin McLeod; lighting, Paul Werner; sound, Martin R. Desjardins.

Phone Plays

THE REPRIMAND. By Jane Anderson
Rhona .... Adale O'Brien
Mim .... Katie Blackerby

SHOW BUSINESS. By Jeffrey Hatcher.
Voice .... Molly Binder
Barry .... William McNulty
Howard .... Brad Bellamy

TRESSPASSION. By Mark O'Donnell
Gina .... Suzanna Hay
George .... Brad Bellamy

LOVERS OF LONG RED HAIR. By Jose Rivera.
Adriana .... Roxanne Raja
Mario .... Bryan Taylor

BESIDE EVERY GOOD MAN. By Regina Taylor
Winnie Mandela .... Linda Sithole
Coretta Scott King .... Opal Alladin

Director, Jon Jory.

Madison, N.J.: New Jersey Shakespeare Festival

(Bonnie J. Monte artistic director; Michael Stotts managing director)

ENTER THE GUARDSMAN. Musical based on *The Guardsman* by Ferenc Molnar; book by Scott Wentworth; music by Craig Bohmler; lyrics by Marion Adler. September 7, 1999 (American premiere). Director, Scott Wentworth; musical direction, Craig Bohmler; scenery and costumes, Molly Reynolds; lighting, Bruce Auerbach; orchestrations, Craig Bohmler.
Actor .... Robert Cuccioli
Actress .... Dana Reeve
Playwright .... Mark Jacoby
Dresser .... Derin Altay
Wardrobe Mistress .... Kate Dawson
Wigs Master .... Russell Ferracane
Assistant Stage Manager ..... Buddy Crutchfield

Place: Onstage, backstage and in the wings of a theater.

MUSICAL NUMBERS ACT I: "Tonight Was Like the First Night," "Chopin," "My One Great Love," "The Language of Flowers," "Drama," "The Actor's Fantasy," "You Have the Ring," "Enter the Guardsman," "True to Me."

ACT II: "She's a Little Off," "I Can't Go On," "Waiting in the Wings," "My One Great Love" (Reprise), "They Die," "The Long Run," "The First Night" (Reprise), "Art Imitating Life."

Madison, N.J.: Playwrights Theater of New Jersey

(John Pietrowski executive director; Joseph Megel artistic director; Buzz McLaughlin founding director)

Workshop Productions

A SOUTHERN CHRISTMAS. By Guillermo Reyes. December 12, 1999. Director, Joseph Megel; scenery, Yong-Seok Choi; costumes, Scott Masters; lighting, Chuck Cameron; sound, Dean Gray.

Fernando .... George Castillo
Ignacio .... Nick Forgione
Natalia .... Danielle Delgado
Octavio .... Steven Blye
Rosalia .... Neda Tavassoli

Time: December through January. Place: Mulchen, a small town in Southern Chile (Aunt Natalia's house). One intermission.

FATHERS & SONS. By J. Rufus Caleb. February 3, 2000. Director, Susan Fenichell; scenery and costumes, Louisa Thompson; lighting, Mark Barton; sound, Susan Fenichell, John Pietrowski.

John Lomax .... Richard Kintner
Huddie "Leadbelly" Ledbetter Charles Turner

Time: 1933–34 during the Great Depression.

RADIUM GIRLS. By Dolores Whiskeyman. May 11, 2000. Director, Joseph Megel; scenery, John Bazewicz; costumes, Valerie Holland Hughes; lighting, Ted Mather; sound, Dean Gray, Jonathan Taylor.

The Women of the Factory:
Grace Farley .... Mary Bacon
Katharine Schmidt .... Sarah Winkler
Irene Rudolph .... Elizabeth Baron
Mrs. Alma McNeil .... T. Cat Ford
Louise Conlon .... Jennifer Ginsberg
Other Girls .... Michael Perilstein, Karl Kenzler

The Company Men:
Arthur Roeder .... Daren Kelly
Edward Markley; Dr. Von Sochocky .... Jim Ligon
C.B. Lee .... Michael Perilstein
Board Members .... Sarah Winkler, Karl Kenzler, Elizabeth Baron

Their Family and Friends:
Tom Kreider .... Karl Kenzler
Diane Roeder .... T. Cat Ford

The Advocates:
Katharine Wiley .... Elizabeth Baron
Raymond Berry .... Karl Kenzler

The Scientists:
Dr. Cecil Drinker .... Michael Perilstein
Dr. Harrison Martland; Dr. Marie Curie .... Jim Ligon
Dr. Joseph Knef .... T. Cat Ford

The Press:
Jack Youngwood .... Karl Kenzler
Nancy Jane Harlan .... T. Cat Ford
Other Reporters .... Jennifer Ginsberg

The Regulators:
Young .... Elizabeth Baron
Roach .... Michael Perilstein

Witnesses:
William J. A. Bailey .... Michael Perilstein
Mrs. Michaels .... Sarah Winkler

Members of the Public .... Company

Time: The 1920s. Place: Orange, New Jersey. One intermission.

Concert Readings

OUROBOROS. By Tom Jacobson. October 15, 1999. Director, Joseph Megel.

BART THE TEMP. By Steve Feffer. January 7, 2000. Director, Joseph Megel.

YEARNINGS. By Sachi Oyama. February 11, 2000. Director, Joseph Megel.

CHEAT. By Julie Jensen. February 25, 2000. Director, Joseph Megel.

CRIMINAL ACTS. By Kim Merrill. March 10, 2000. Director Joseph Megel.

HUMAN INTEREST. By Jeanmarie Williams. June 2, 2000.

Miami: Coconut Grove Playhouse

(Arnold Mittelman producing artistic director)

PRAYING WITH THE ENEMY. By Luis Santeiro. April 28, 2000. Director, Michael John Garces; scenery, Troy Hourie; costumes, Ellis Tillman; lighting, Kirk Bookman; sound, Steve Shapiro.

Arturo .... Gilbert Cruz
Adriana .... Josie De Guzman
Cuqui .... Eileen Galindo
Lenny .... Oscar Isaac
Omar .... Gonzalo Madurga
Cynthia .... Kim Ostrenko

One intermission.

Mill Valley, Calif: Marin Theater Company

(Lee Sankowich artistic director; James A. Kleinmann managing director)

SPRING STORM. By Tennessee Williams. November 11, 1999. Director, Lee Sankowich; scenery Kate Edmunds; costumes, Meg Neville; lighting, Kurt Landisman; sound, Don Seaver.

Heavenly Critchfield .... Allison McDonell
Dick Miles .... Jamie Gannon
Agnes Peabody;
Mrs. Adams .... Terry Amara Boero
Rev. Hooker; Oliver Critchfield .. Charles Dean
Mrs. Asbury; Mrs. Buford .... Karen Hall
Susan Lamphrey; Mabel .... Lizzie Calogero
Mrs. Lamphrey;
Birdie Schlagmann .... Suzanne Voss
Arthur Shannon .... Richard Robichaux
Hertha Nielson .... Stacy Ross
Aunt Lila .... Linda Hoy
Esmeralda Critchfield .... Sharon Lockwood
Jackson .... Brian Yates
Mrs. Dowd; Mrs. Kramer .... Gwyneth Richards
Henry; Ralph .... Jeffrey Draper

Time: Spring 1937. Place: Port Tyler, Miss. Act I: A high bluff overlooking the Mississippi River. Act II, Scene 1: The Critchfield home, afternoon of the next day. Scene 2: The same, that evening. Scene 3: The same, 2 in the morning. Act III, Scene 1: Lawn of the Lamphrey residence, the next evening., Scene 2: The Port Tyler Carnegie Public Library, the same evening. Scene 3: The Critchfield home, toward evening of the next day.

Milwaukee: Milwaukee Repertory Theater

(Joseph Hanreddy artistic director; Timothy J. Shields managing director)

PARAGON SPRINGS. By Steven Dietz; based on Henrik Ibsen's *An Enemy of the People.* April 4, 2000. Director, Joseph Hanreddy; scenery and lighting, Kent Dorsey; costumes, Helen Q. Huang; original music and sound, Lindsay Jones; choreography, Ed Burgess.

Dr. Thomas Stockman .... James Pickering
Katrina Stockman .... Laurie Birmingham
Lorna Stockman .... Kirsten Potter
Peter Stockman .... Ron Frazier
Erik Hovstad .... Lee E. Ernst
Lars Hovstad .... Brian Vaughn
Odegaard .... Torrey Hanson
The Widow Kroger .... Rose Pickering
Hollis Lindgren .... Jonathan Gillard Daly
Rose Lindgren .... Deborah Staples

Time: April 1926. Place: Paragon Springs. One intermission.

Montgomery, Ala.: Alabama Shakespeare Festival

(Kent Thompson artistic director; Kevin K. Maifeld managing director)

SOCKDOLOGY. By Jeffrey Hatcher. June 4, 1999. Director, Terence Lamude; scenery, Richard Isackes; costumes, Kristine Kearney; lighting, Rachel Budin; sound, Bethany Tucker; composer, Jim Conely; fight direction, Colleen Kelly.

John Mathews .... Sam Gregory
Mrs. Muzzy .... Sonja Lanzener
Harry Hawk .... Rodney Clark
T.C. Gourley .... Barry Boys
Jeannie Gourley .... Stephanie Cozart
Soldier; Stagehand .... Charlton David James
Army Captain; Stagehand ...... Zachary Fischer
Edwin M. Stanton .... Philip Pleasants
Laura Keene .... Greta Lambert
Billy Ferguson .... Noel Etienne Velez
John Wilkes Booth .... Charlton David James
Mr. Ford .... Traber Burns

Time: 1865. Place: Ford's Theater, Washington, D.C. Prologue: 8:22 AM, Saturday, April 15—onstage. Act I, Scene 1: 11:45 AM, Friday, April 14—onstage. Scene 2: 8:30 PM, Friday, April 14—backstage. Act II: 9 AM, Saturday, April 15—onstage. Epilogue.

A LESSON BEFORE DYING. Adapted by Romulus Linney from the novel by Ernest Gaines. January 21, 2000. Director, Kent Thompson; scenery, Vicki Smith; costumes, Alvin Perry; lighting, Terry Cermak; sound, Don Tindall; composer, Chic Street Man.

MILWAUKEE—Laurie Birmingham and James Pickering in *Paragon Springs* by Steven Dietz at Milwaukee Repertory Theater

Emma Glenn .... Barbara Meek
Paul Bonin .... Aaron Harpold
Grant Wiggins .... Isiah Whitlock Jr.
Sam Guidry .... Stephen Bradbury
Jefferson .... Jamahl Marsh
Vivan Baptiste .... Melissa Maxwell
Rev. Moses Ambrose .... Robert Colston
Time: 1948. Place: Bayonne Parish, Louisiana.

A NIGHT IN TUNISIA. By Regina Taylor; music by Bob Telson; lyrics by Regina Taylor. May 26, 2000. Director, Regina Taylor; scenery, Edward E. Haynes Jr.; costumes, Karen Perry; lighting, Liz Lee; sound, Bethany Tucker; co-musical directors, Leroy Clouden, Melvin Crispell.

Simone .... Tina Fabrique
Amanda .... Yvette Jones-Smedley
Ma Dear .... Lynda Gravatt
M&M .... Shona Tucker
Gin xyz .... Quincy Tyler Bernstine
The Man .... Carl J. Cofield
No intermission

Mountain View, Calif.: TheaterWorks

(Robert Kelley artistic director)

EVERYTHING'S DUCKY. Musical with book by Bill Russell and Jeffrey Hatcher; music by Henry Krieger; lyrics by Bill Russell. January 22, 2000. Director, Gip Hoppe; choreography, Linda Goodrich; musical direction and additional vocal arrangements, Shawn Gough; scenery, Robert

Bissinger; costumes, Beaver Bauer; lighting, Christopher Guptill; sound, Christopher Neumeyer; orchestrations, Harold Wheeler; vocal arrangemenrs, David Chase.

Mrs Bovine; Galinda .... Gina Ferrall
Mr. Lambkins; Wolf .... David McDonald
Mayor Mule; King; Armand Dillo;
Giorgio Grouse .... Danny Burstein
Rooster Bob; Drake .... Michael McEachran
Mrs. Mallard; Aunt Leda;
Queen .... Karen Murphy
Mildred Mallard; Others .. Andrea Chamberlain
Serena .... Angela Robinson
Carl Coyote; Runway Model ...... Bobby Daye
Clem Coyote; Runway Model ...... Josh Prince

One intermission.

MUSICAL NUMBERS: "That's One Ugly Duck," "Fit In"/"Stand Out," "I Could Be Good for You," "A Helping Paw," "Glad I'm Not Related to You," "Juicy and Tender and Young," "Glide Like a Swan," "I Eat Meat," "You've Got the Wings to Fly," "Good Times Are Here at Last," "Wipe the Egg off Your Face," "I'd Love to Sing a Love Song," "Let's Play," "Beauty Inside," "You Look Good Enough to Eat," "Don't Start Playing My Swan Song," "Everything's Ducky."

New Brunswick, N.J.: Crossroads Theater Company

(Ricardo Khan artistic director; Andre Robinson Jr. executive producer; Deborah L Stapleton general manager)

YELLOW EYES. By Migdalia Cruz. January 27, 2000. Director, Talvin Wilks; scenery, Evan Alexander; costumes, Elizabeth Hope Clancy; lighting, Darren W. McCroom; original score and sound, David Molina; associate artist, Harold Scott.

Sharon McNair .... Pascale Armand
Dolores Lulu Tirado .... Elisa Bocanegra
Joselito; Ian Durant .... Dyron Holmes
Don Jose .... Jack Landron
Isabel Nieves .... Amarelys Perez
Doña Ana Cecilia Sandoval
de Sotillo .... Virginia Rambal

Time: One unusually snowy fall in 1971 and flashbacks from 1859–1971. Place: Present—a rundown apartment in the Soundview section of the Bronx, New York. Past—Various locations such as a plaza in the northeast corner of Puerto Rico, near Aguadilla, and on a ship in San Juan Harbor. One intermission.

VENICE. By Kathleen McGhee-Anderson. March 9, 2000. Director, Timothy Douglas; scenery, Michael Schweikart; costumes, Tracy Dorman; lighting, Victor En Yu Tan; sound, Perchik Miller.

LaBrea Mobley .... Kim Brockington
Carrie Poe .... Tarah Flanagan
Leon Mobley .... Keith Josef Adkins
Roland Mobley .... Ray Anthony Thomas
Tank Poe; Willard Poe .... Noel Johansen
Clerk; Police Officer;
Judge; Deputy .... Brian J. Coffey

Time: In the present and in recall. In the Seventies and Eighties. Place: In Venice, California and in Vietnam. One intermission.

Genesis Festival 2000
Rehearsed Readings

5 MOJO SECRETS. By Kathleen McGhee-Anderson. April 28, 2000.

LAS MENINAS. By Lynn Nottage. April 29, 2000.

DANCING WITH DEMONS. By Don Evans. May 5, 2000.

A.M. SUNDAY. By Jerome Hairston. May 6, 2000.

MANDELA. Musical based on Fatima Meer's biography of Nelson Mandela; book, music and lyrics by Steven Fisher. May 7, 2000.

New Brunswick, N.J.: George Street Playhouse

(David Saint artistic director; Michael Stotts managing director)

DOWN THE GARDEN PATHS. By Anne Meara. November 23, 1999. Director, David Saint; scenery, James Youmans; costumes, David Murin; lighting, Michael Lincoln; sound, Chris Bailey; presented in association with the Long Wharf Theater, New Haven, Conn.

Prof. Cramer .... Angela Pietropinto
Herschel Strange .... Jerry Stiller
Arthur Garden .... David Wohl
Stella Dempsey Garden .... Anne Jackson
Sid Garden .... Eli Wallach
Liz Garden .... Ann McDonough
Max Garden .... Michael Countryman
Sharon Garden; Jodie Garden ...... Amy Stiller
Claire Shayne; Garden .... Roberta Wallach

Place: At the Herschel Strange Awards ceremony and in Arthur Garden's apartment. No intermission.

SYNCOPATION. By Allan Knee. January 12, 2000. Produced in association with the Long Wharf Theater, New Haven, Conn., Doug Hughes artistic director (see its entry below). Winner of a 1999–2000 ATCA/Steinberg New Play Citation; see introduction to this section.

New Haven, Conn: Long Wharf Theater

(Doug Hughes artistic director; Michael Ross managing director)

SYNCOPATION. By Allan Knee. November 23, 1999. Director, Greg Leaming; choreography, Willie Rosario; music, Jeffrey Lunden; scenery, Judy Gailen; costumes, Jess Goldstein; lighting, Dan Kotlowitz; sound, Fabian Obispo; produced in association with the George Street Playhouse, New Brunswick, N.J., David Saint artistic director.

Henry .... David Chandler
Anna .... Lorca Simons

Time: 1911–12. Place: The Lower East Side of New York City. One intermission.

Winner of a 1999–2000 ATCA/Steinberg New Play Citation; see introduction to this section.

DOWN THE GARDEN PATHS. By Anne Meara. January 26, 2000. Produced in association with George Street Playhouse, New Brunswick, N.J., David Saint artistic director (see its entry above).

THE DOG PROBLEM. By David Rabe. February 16, 2000. Director, Scott Ellis; scenery, Allen Moyer; costumes, Michael Krass; lighting, Brian Nason; sound, Eileen Tague; fight direction, David Leong.

Ronnie .... Joe Pacheco
Ray .... Larry Clarke
Joey .... David Wike
Uncle Malvolio .... Victor Argo
Tommy Stones .... Tony Cucci
Teresa .... Andrea Gabriel
Priest .... Michael Kell

Time and place: Urban nighttime. One intermission.

BLACK FOREST. By Anthony Giardina. March 15, 2000. Director, Doug Hughes; original music, Paul Sullivan; scenery, Hugh Landwehr; costumes, Jess Goldstein; lighting, Michael Chybowski; sound, Matthew Mezick.

Jacob Freundlich .... Reed Birney
Wendy Cunningham .... Kim Awon
Margaret Olin .... Sharon Scruggs
Frank Leech .... Jack Ryland
Chris Macaden .... Dave Simonds
Homer Boykin .... Ron Parady
Aaron Goldman .... Tom Tammi
Heidi Leech .... Jennifer Harmon
Leah Freundlich .... Laura Hughes
Nicole Goldman .... Patricia Hodges

Time: The present. Place: In and around one of the last surviving women's colleges. One intermission.

THE GOOD PERSON OF NEW HAVEN. Adapted by Alison Carey from Bertolt Brecht's *The Good Person of Szechuan* as translated by Ralph Manheim. May 10, 2000. Director, Bill Rauch; choreographer, Sabrina Peck; musical director, Richard Hill; scenery, Lynn Jeffries; costumes, David Zinn; lighting, Tyler Micoleau; sound, Paul James; composer, Shishir Kurup; arrangements, Richard Hill, Shishir Kurup.

Quinn .... Christopher Liam Moore
Angel 1 .... Peter Howard
Angel 2 .... Bill Kux
Angel 3 .... Chris Wells
Tyesha Shore;
Taiwo Highwater .... Patrice Johnson
Prostitute; Waitress; Student ...... Gracy Brown
Prostitute; Waitress; Student ... Adelaida Nunez
Prostitute; Waitress;
Student .... Jennifer Ayres Weyburn
Mrs. Shin .... Carol A. Honda
Wife .... Gloria J. Richardson
Nephew .... Joshua Harper
Husband .... Brian Nicholas Olivieri
Unemployed Man .... Daniel John Kelly
Carpenter .... Aaron Jafferis
Carpenter's Kid .... Joel Teron, Eva Simone Wilson
Brother .... Rodney Moore
Sister-in-Law .... Maritza Cordero
Ms. Cash .... Michele Massa
Grandfather .... Horace Little
Junior .... Mike Gaetano, Rosa Miller Polan
Step-Daughter .... Leididiana Castro Ortega
Woman in White .... Dana Elizabeth Fripp
Police Officer .... Armando Molina
Pipsqueak .... Christopher Dickerson, Danny Diaz
Pat .... William Graustein, Edi Jackson
Eddie .... Raul E. Esparza
Henry .... Milton R. Cohen
Mama .... Maritza Rosa

On
New England
Stages

In photo above, Ari Graynor and Ronobir Lahiri in a scene from *Fall* by Bridget Carpenter at Trinity Repertory Company in Providence, R.I.; *at left,* Larry Clarke with Ed in David Rabe's *The Dog Problem* at the Long Wharf Theater in New Haven, Conn.; *below,* a scene from *Glimmerglass,* a musical by Jonathan Bolt, Douglas J. Cohen and Ted Drachman at Goodspeed at Chester, Conn., suggested by James Fenimore Cooper's *Leatherstocking Tales,* with Jay Douglas as Natty Bumppo, Tom Zemon as Harry March and David Aron Damane as Chingachgook

Rev. Marsh .... Jeffery V. Thompson
Priest .... Stephen J. Papa

Place: Various locations around New Haven. One intermission.

New Haven, Conn.: Yale Repertory Theater

(Stan Wojewodski Jr. artistic director; Victoria Nolan managing director)

THE IMAGINARY INVALID. By Molière; new adaptation and translation by James Magruder. September 16, 1999. Director, Mark Rucker; original music and arrangements, Gina Leishman; musical direction, Dmitri Novgorodsky; scenery, Luke Cantarella; costumes, Miguel Angel Huidor; lighting, Marcus Doshi; sound, Fitz Patton.

Shepherdess .... Susan Spencer
Argan .... Raye Birk
Toinette .... Veanne Cox
Angelique .... Jennifer Brooke Riker
Beline .... Susan Marie Brecht
Bonnefoi; Dr. Diafoirus;
Dr. Purgon .... Paul Mullins
Polichinelle; Louise; Fleurant ..... Danny Scheie
Zerbinetta .... Maria Francesconi
Cleante .... Jay Snyder
Thomas Diafoirus;
The President .... Brennan Brown
Beralde .... John Wojda

Satyrs, A Norwegian, Night Watchmen, Harem Women, Ganeshes, Doctors, Apothecaries, Showgirls—Company.

Place: A private chamber in the home of Argan, Paris. One intermission.

Nyack, N.Y.: Helen Hayes Performing Arts Center

(Tony Stimac executive producer; Rod Kaats artistic director; Marilyn Stimac associate producer)

HONK! Musical based on *The Ugly Duckling* by Hans Christian Andersen; book and lyrics by Anthony Drewe; music by George Stiles. February 12, 2000. Director, Gordon Greenberg; choreography, Scott Wise, John MacInnis; music direction, Kimberly Grigsby; scenery, James Youmans, Dawn Robyn Petrlik; costumes, Dawn Robyn Petrlik; lighting, Jeff Croiter; sound, Peter Fitzgerald; orchestrations, John Cameron; co-produced by *The Journal News.*

Drake .... Darin De Paul
Ida .... Alison Fraser
Maureen; Snowy; Queenie; Swan .... Jill Geddes
Billy; Swan .... Gerard Salvador
Beaky; Swan .... Brian Swasey
Downy; Swan .... Adriene Daigneault
Fluff; Swan .... Melissa Rain Anderson
Ugly .... Gavin Creel
Turkey; Barnacles; Bullfrog ... Michael Mandell
Maggie Pie; Henrietta; Pinkfoot;
Penny .... Nancy Anderson
Cat .... Stephen DeRosa
Grace; Dot; Lowbutt .... Evalyn Baron
Greylag .... Darin De Paul

SCENES AND MUSICAL NUMBERS, ACT I, Scene 1: Various locations around the duckyard, spring—"A Poultry Tale of Folk Down on the Farm," "The Joy of Motherhood," "Different," "Hold Your Head Up High," "Look at Him," "Different" (Reprise). Scene 2: The Cat's lair, inside one of the farm buildings—"Play With Your Food." Scene 3: The duckyard, later that evening—"The Elegy," "Every Tear a Mother Cries." Scene 4: The marsh, late summer—"The Wild Goose Chase," "Hold Your Head Up High" (Reprise).

ACT II, Scene 1: The Old Woman's cottage, late summer—"It Takes All Sorts," "Hold Your Head Up High" (Reprise), "Together." Scene 2: Back in the duckyard—"The Collage." Scene 3: Collage, various locations, late autumn. Scene 4: A ditch on the moors, late autumn—"Now I've Seen It All," "Warts and All," "The Blizzard." Scene 5: The open countryside, late winter—"Transformation," "Different" (Reprise). Scene 6: The duckyard, early spring—"Look at Him" (Reprise).

KING LEVINE. By Richard Krevolin. April 1, 2000. Director, Joseph Bologna; scenery, Tom Buderwitz; costumes, Monica Lisa Sabedra; lighting, Marianne Schneller; sound, Peter Stenschoel.

King Levine .... Sammy Shore
Rikki; Bobbi; Jami ... Melonie Mazman Hayden

Act I, Scene 1: Morning. Scene 2: One day later. Scene 3: Two months later. Act II, Scene 1: One week later. Scene 2: Three hours later. Scene 3: Early the next morning.

Philadelphia: Philadelphia Theater Company

(Sara Garonzik producing artistic director; Ada Coppock general manager)

WHITE PEOPLE. By J.T. Rogers. January 21, 2000. Director, Gus Reyes; scenery, Michael McGarty; costumes, Tom Broecker; lighting, Phil Monat; sound, Eileen Tague.

Alan Harris .... Robert Sean Leonard
Mara Lynn Doddson .... Carole Healey
Martin Bahmueller .... Philip Anglim

Time: Now, Sunday. Place: Alan's favorite bench in Stuyvesant Square, New York City; Mara Lynn's kitchen in Fayetteville, N.C.; Martin's office on the waterfront in downtown St. Louis. No intermission.

Philadelphia: Walnut Street Theater

(Bernard Havard producing artistic director; Mark D. Sylvester managing director)

EDWIN FORREST. By Will Stutts. February 1, 2000. Director, Will Stutts; scenery, Conrad Maust; costumes, Courtney Bambrick; lighting, Michael Lyons; sound, Scott Smith.

Edwin Forrest .... Curt Karibalis
Thomas Ball .... Michael P. Toner

Time: Three successive afternoons in March 1863. Place: A third-floor storage loft on the Philadelphia waterfront. No intermission.

EVERY *OTHER* INCH A LADY. By Susan Borofsky and Steven Bloom; music and lyrics by various authors. February 29, 2000. Director, Steven Bloom; scenery, Conrad Maust; costumes, Courtney Bambrick; lighting, Graham Kindred; sound, Scott Smith; orchestrations, Christopher Drobney.

Bea Lillie .... Susan Borofsky
Music Director; Accompanist ... Mark Yurkanin

Place: Bea Lillie's hotel, New York City.

MUSICAL NUMBERS, ACT I: "Marvelous Party," "The Fan," "Michigan," "Three White Feathers," "Please Be Kind," "Mad About the Boy," "Maud," "Wind Round My Heart."

ACT II: "Paree," "Limehouse Blues," "I've Always Been Keen to Entertain the Troops," "There Are Times," "There Are Fairies in the Bottom of My Garden," "Manhattan," "Rhythm," "The Party's Over Now."

Pittsburgh: Pittsburgh Public Theater

(Edward Gilbert artistic director; Stephen Klein managing director)

KING HEDLEY II. By August Wilson. December 15, 1999. Director, Marion Isaac McClinton; scenery, David Gallo; costumes, Toni-Leslie James; lighting, Donald Holder; sound, Rob Milburn; presented in association with the Seattle Repertory Theater, Sharon Ott artistic director.

King Hedley II .... Tony Todd
Ruby .... Marlene Warfield
Mister .... Russell Andrews
Tonya .... Ella Joyce
Stool Pigeon .... Mel Winkler
Elmore .... Charles Brown

Time: The mid-1980s. Place: Ruby's back yard. One intermission.

Pittsburgh: City Theater

(Thomas Hollander president)

COMPLEAT FEMALE STAGE BEAUTY. By Jeffrey Hatcher. October 22, 1999. Director, Marc Masterson; scenery, Tony Ferrieri; costumes, Lorraine Venberg; lighting, Andrew David Ostrowski; sound, Elizabeth Atkinson; co-commissioned by City Theater and Contemporary American Theater Festival.

Samuel Pepys; Edward Hyde .. Don Wadsworth
Edward (Ned) Kynaston .... David Hornsby
Thomas Betterton;
King Charles II .... Douglas Rees
George Villiers, Duke of Buckingham;
Ruffian; Drunk .... Michael Tisdale
Maria; Ruffian .... Robin Rundquist
Lady Meresvale; Emelia Two;
Lely .... Kellee Van Aken
Miss Frayne; Emilia One; Thug;
Bouncer .... Brian Czarniecki
Sir Charles Sedley; Mistress Revels;
Ruffian .... Doug Mertz

Nell Gwynn; Justice .... Michelle Federer
Margaret Hughes; Page .... Laurie Klatscher

Time: 1600s. Place: Restoration London. One intermission.

Winner of a 1999 ATCA/Steinberg New Play Citation; see introduction to this section.

Princeton: McCarter Theater

(Emily Mann artistic director; Jeffrey Woodward managing director)

NOT SUITABLE FOR CHILDREN. Program of three one-act plays by Doug Wright: *Lot 13: The Bone Violin, Wildwood Park* and *Baby Talk*. January 16, 2000. Director, Doug Wright; scenery, Klara Zieglerova; costumes, Linda Fisher; lighting, Blake Burba; sound, Laura Brown.

Lot 13: The Bone Violin

Doctor .... Joanna P. Adler
Father .... Tom Nelis
Mother .... Olivia Birkelund
Professor .... Jefferson Mays
Auctioneer .... Jonathan Walker

Wildwood Park

Haviland .... Olivia Birkelund
Simian .... Jonathan Walker

Baby Talk

Psychiatrist .... Jefferson Mays
Husband .... Jonathan Walker
Alice .... Joanna P. Adler
Baby .... Tom Nelis

No intermission.

THE CHERRY ORCHARD. New adaptation by Emily Mann of the play by Anton Chekhov. March 31, 2000. Director, Emily Mann; scenery, Adrianne Lobel; costumes, Jennifer von Mayrhauser; lighting, James F. Ingalls; composer, Mel Marvin; sound, David Budries; choreography, Peter Pucci.

Lyubov Andreyevna
Ranevskaya .... Jane Alexander
Anya .... Anne Dudek
Varya .... Caroline Stefanie Clay
Gayev .... John Glover
Lopakhin .... Avery Brooks
Trofimov .... Rob Campbell
Semeonov-Pishchik .... Allen Swift
Charlotta .... Barbara Sukowa
Yepikhodov .... Glenn Fleshler
Dunyasha .... Kate Goehring
Firs .... Roger Robinson
Yasha .... Jefferson Mays
Grisha .... Benjamin Neumann
Vagrant; Postmaster .... Hamilton Oliveira
Stationmaster .... Nicholas Kohn
Party Guest .... Michael Connolly
Violinist .... Marcus Lampert

Musicians—Connor Barrett, Adam Gertler, Brian Kuchta, Robert A. Pinter.

Place: Ranevskaya's estate. One intermission.

THE NIGHT GOVERNESS. Musical by Polly Pen; based on *Behind a Mask* by Louisa May Alcott. May 5, 2000. Director, Lisa Peterson; choreography, Doug Varone; musical direction, Alan Johnson; scenery, Riccardo Hernandez; costumes, Anita Yavich; lighting, Mimi Jordan Sherin; sound, Jeffrey S. Carlson; orchestrations, Bruce Coughlin.

The Family:
Mrs. Coventry .... Mary Stout
Gerald .... Robert Sella
Ned .... Danny Gurwin
Nellie .... Danielle Ferland
Chloe .... Erin Hill
Sir John Coventry .... John Jellison

The Other Ones:
Dean .... Alma Cuervo
Chaos .... John Jellison
Jean Muir .... Judith Blazer

Time: Spring 1857. Place: A fine home outside of Philadelphia. One intermission.

Providence, R.I.: Trinity Repertory Company

(Oskar Eustis artistic director; William P. Wingate managing director)

FALL. By Bridget Carpenter. May 12, 2000. Director, Neil Baron; scenery, Eugene Lee; costumes, Marilyn Salvatore; lighting, Yael Lubetzky; original music and sound, David Van Tieghem; choreography, Sharon Jenkins; flying, Foy.

Lead and Follow .... Jones & Boyce
Jill .... Anne Scurria
Dog .... Dan Welch
Lydia .... Ari Graynor
Gopal .... Ronobir Lahiri
Mr. Gonzales .... Mauro Hantman

One intermission.

Staged Readings

TWO SEPTEMBER. By Mac Wellman. January 21, 2000.

GUINEVERE. By Gina Gionfriddo. January 28, 2000.

THE NEW ENGLAND SONATA. By Eliza Anderson. February 4, 2000.

THE BODY OF BOURNE. By John Belluso. March 3, 2000.

Richmond: TheatreVirginia

(George Black producing artistic director; Barbara S. Wells managing director)

SANDALS. Musical revue conceived by Ralph Allen and Danny Daniels; sketches by Ralph Allen; songs by Hal Hackady, Brad Ross, Terry Waldo, Michael Valenti and others. November 17, 1999. Director and choreographer, Danny Daniels; musical direction, Terry Waldo; scenery and lighting, Harry Feiner; costumes, George Sarofeen; sound, Nathan H. Kahler; associate director, Ralph Allen; music and dance arrangements, Peter Howard.

With Darrin Baker, Kimberly Breault, Jennifer Clippinger, Maria Davidson, Bill Davis, Robert Fitch, Melissa Giattino, Jerold Goldstein, Mylinda Hull, Nadine Isenegger, Heather Morris, Kristi Rau, Richard Ruiz, Dick Van Patten.

One intermission.

Sag Harbor, N.Y.: Bay Street Theater

(Sybil Christopher and Emma Walton artistic directors; Stephen Hamilton executive director; Murphy Davis producer; Norman Kline general manager)

SOMETHING IN THE AIR. By Richard Dresser. June 16, 1999. Director, Melia Bensussen; scenery, Christine Jones; costumes, David Zinn; lighting, Dan Kotlowitz; sound, Randall Freed.

Neville .... Jude Ciccolella
Walker .... Steven Weber
Cram .... Mark Blum
Sloane .... Janet Zarish
Holloway .... Anne O'Sullivan

Time: The present, except more so. Place: Various locations in a large city. One intermission.

FACTORY GIRLS. By Frank McGuinness. July 14, 1999 (American premiere). Director, Nye Heron; scenery, Michael Brown; costumes, Melissa Schlachtmeyer; lighting, Jeff Nellis; sound, Jerry Yager; produced in association with Williamstown Theater Festival, Michael Ritchie artistic director.

Ellen .... Celia Weston
Vera .... Kate Burton
Rebecca .... Bernadette Quigley
Una .... Rebecca Schull
Rosemary .... Gretchen Cleevely
Bonner .... Christopher McHale
Rohan .... Malcolm Adams

Time: Spring 1982. Place: County Donegal, Ireland. One intermission.

FIT TO PRINT. Program of eight one-acts by various authors (see listing below). August 11, 1999. Director, Marcia Milgrom Dodge; scenery, Gary N. Hygom; costumes, Nan Young; lighting, Eric Schlobohm; sound, Randall Freed.

In Media Res by Constance Congdon

Branch Saunders .... Dennis Ryan
Gee .... Randy Graff
Bop .... Roger Bart
Haw .... Robert Sella
Alyssa Stein .... Joanna Glushak

Place: A small television studio near LaGuardia Airport.

Tina at the Times by Wendy MacLeod

Tina .... Randy Graff
Tim .... Roger Bart
Melissa .... Joanna Glushak
Darren .... Dennis Ryan
Jeremy .... Robert Sella

Place: A large newspaper's conference room.

R.C.A. by Marsha Norman

Anchor .... Joanna Glushak
Station Manager .... Dennis Ryan
Controller .... Robert Sella
Baro Indarsis .... Roger Bart

Place: A television news studio.

The Entertainment Report by Christopher Durang

Alicia Goober .... Randy Graff
Felicia Ferrante .... Roger Bart
Jimbo Dunfee .... Robert Sella
Sarah Gazelle Beller .... Joanna Glushak

Place: A television studio.

Unmemorable by Craig Lucas

Earl .... Dennis Ryan
Lois .... Randy Graff
Enoch .... Robert Sella
Roz .... Joanna Glushak

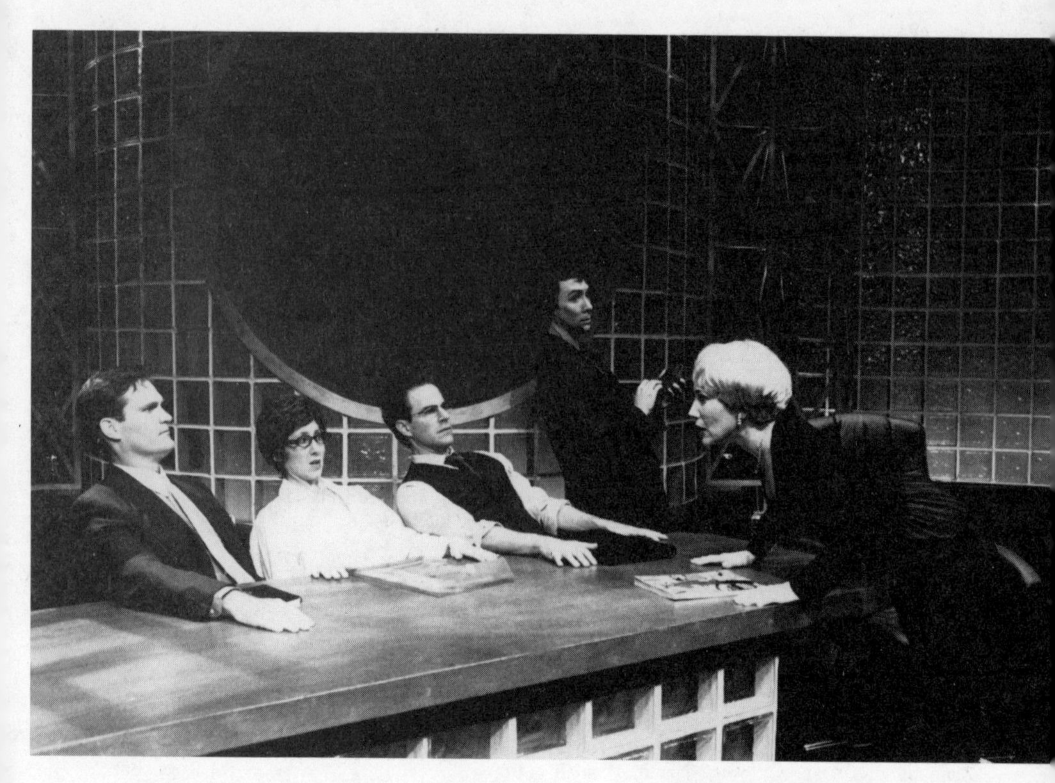

SAG HARBOR—Dennis Ryan, Joanna Glushak, Roger Bart, Robert Sella and Randy Graff in *Fit to Print* at Bay Street Theater

Theo .... Roger Bart
Place: A bedroom, a bathroom and a street corner.

A Tooth for a Tooth by Terry George
Ali .... Dennis Ryan
Peter .... Robert Sella
Jack .... Roger Bart
Jimmi .... Joanna Glushak
Place: Somewhere in Saaghabistan.

This Town by Sidney Blumenthal
Frank Langley .... Robert Sella
Loretta Hall .... Randy Graff
Burton Bird .... Dennis Ryan
Alberta Whitney .... Joanna Glushak
Bobby Rochester .... Roger Bart
Place: The White House Press Briefing Room.

Captive Audience by David Ives
Television Man .... Roger Bart
Television Woman .... Randy Graff
Rob .... Robert Sella
Laura .... Joanna Glushak
Place: A living room.
One intermission following *The Entertainment Report.*

Fall Play Readings

MARRIED MOMENTS. By B.H. Friedman. October 23, 1999.

THE MEN FROM THE BOYS. By Mart Crowley. October 23, 1999.

KARMA BOOMERANG. By Joe Pintauro. October 24, 1999.

Spring Play Readings

SCHOOLGIRL FIGURE. By Wendy MacLeod. April 10, 2000.

THIS TOWN. By Sidney Blumenthal. April 10, 2000.

SIGHT SEEING. By Margaret Dulaney. April 11, 2000.

St. Paul, Minn.: Ordway Center for the Performing Arts

(Kevin McCollum president and CEO)

ROMEO AND JULIET. Musical version of the play by William Shakespeare; adapted by Terrence Mann; music by Jerome Korman and Terrence Mann. August 18, 1999. Director, Terrence Mann; choreography, Christopher d'Amboise; music direction, Christopher Jahnke; music supervision, Jerome Korman; scenery, Kenneth Foy; costumes, Ann Hould-Ward; lighting, Mark Stanley; sound, Tony Meola; orchestrations, Kim Scharnberg; vocal arrangements, Yaron Gershovsky; dance music arrangements, Joseph Baker.

Prince of Verona .... Joe Thomas
Paris .... Abe Sylvia
Lord Montague .... T. Mychael Rambo
Lady Montague .... Rebecca Fay
Lord Capulet .... Thom Sesma
Lady Capulet .... Therese Walden
Romeo .... Patrick Wilson
Juliet .... Irene Molloy
Mercutio .... Joe Wilson Jr.
Benvolio .... Joshua Wade
Tybalt .... Mark Deklin
Friar Laurence .... Matthew Bennett
Nurse .... Candy Buckley

Ensemble: Jennifer Gambatese, Bryan S. Haynes, Patricia Kenny, David Kent, Joe Langworth, Michael Lomeka, Aixa M. Rosario Medina, Joni Michelle, Jill Nicklaus, T. Oliver Reid, J. Robert Spencer, Jenny-Lynn Suckling.

SCENES AND MUSICAL NUMBERS, ACT I, Scene 1: Opening, "Where's Romeo," "O Brawling Love." Scene 2, the Capulet home: "Capulet Woman's Trio." Scene 3, a street where Romeo, Benvolio and Mercutio congregate: "Queen Mab." Scene 4, the Capulet home: "Ball." Scene 5, Juliet's balcony and garden: "Balcony." Scene 6, Friar Laurence's cell: "Friar's Song." Scene 7, Juliet's balcony and garden: "Shall I Compare Thee?". Scene 8, square/Juliet's room/Friar's cell/cathedral: "Wedding," "Amen."

ACT II, Scene 1, the square: Opening, "Mercutio's Death Dance," "Juliet's Prayer." Scene 2, the square/Friar's cell/Juliet 's room: "Back Foolish Tears." Scene 3, Juliet's chamber: Shadow Pas de Deux, "Mistress Minion," "Nurse's Counsel." Scene 4, Friar Laurence's cell. Scene 5: "Come Vial," "Passacaglia." Scene 6, Capulet family tomb: "Romeo in the Tomb," "Juliet Awakens," "Glooming Peace."

ADVENTURES IN LOVE. Musical with book by Shari Simpson and Charlie Shanian; music by Zina Goldrich; lyrics by Marcy Heisler. April 11, 2000. Director and choreographer, Mark Waldrop; musical direction, David Lohman; scenery, Rick Polenek; costumes, Sonya Berlovitz; lighting, William P. Healey; sound, Chris Heagle; orchestrations, Robert Elhai; co-produced by The Ruth Easton Fund.

Ensemble: Kevin R. Free, Ellie Grosso, Timothy Gulan, Kendra Kassebaum, Jennifer Prescott, Bernie Yvon.

SCENES AND MUSICAL NUMBERS, ACT I: "Everything There Is to Know About Love." The Adventure Begins— "I Could Say Hello." Merry Christmas!—"There's Nothing I Wouldn't Do," "Taylor." Chapter l: In Touch With Your Feminine Side—"Susanna," "Apathetic Man." Blah, Blah Blah—"Beautiful You." Happy Valentine's Day. Chapter 2: In Touch With Your Masculine Side—"Be a Man." Moving Day—"Out of Love." "Son of Aphrodite." ACT II: Love Is Calling—"Revenge," "Funny How the Love Gets in the Way," "The Morning After." Chapter 3: Touch and Go—"The Last Song." Happy Birthday! Great Expectations—"Over the Moon." Chapter 4: Stay in Touch—"What if We Lose?" Happy Anniversary!—"Baby, Baby, Baby." A Wedding Toast—"We Remember Love," "Adventure in Love."

San Diego: Old Globe Theater

(Jack O'Brien artistic director)

THE FULL MONTY. Musical with book by Terrence McNally; music and lyrics by David Yazbek. May 23, 2000. Director, Jack O'Brien; choreography, Jerry Mitchell; musical direction, Ted Sperling; scenery, John Arnone; costumes, Robert Morgan; lighting, Howell Binkley; sound, Jeff Ladman; orchestrations, Harold Wheeler; vocal arrangements, Ted Sperling; dance arrangements, Zane Mark.

Georgie Bukatinsky .... Annie Golden
Buddy "Keno" Walsh .... Denis Jones
Carroll Crosby .... Todd Weeks
Jerry Lukowski .... Patrick Wilson
Dave Bukatinsky .... John Ellison Conlee
Harold Nichols .... Marcus Neville
Vicki Nichols .... Emily Skinner
Malcolm MacGregor .... Jason Danieley
Ethan Girard .... Romain Frugé

On California Stages

In photo above, Henry Winkler and Veanne Cox in Neil Simon's *The Dinner Party* at the Mark Taper Forum, Los Angeles. *At left,* Amy Tung and Lorri Holt in *Hillary & Soon-Yi Shop for Ties* by Michelle Carter at the Magic Theater, San Francisco. *On opposite page,* John Ellison Conlee, Marcus Neville, Romain Frugé *(seated),* Jason Danieley and Andre De Shields in a scene from the Terrence McNally-David Yazbek musical *The Full Monty* at the Old Globe Theater, San Diego

Nathan Lukowski .... Adam Covalt, Thomas Michael Fiss (alternating)
Pam Lukowski .... Lisa Datz
Joanie Lish .... Jannie Jones
Susan Hershey .... Laura Marie Duncan
Teddy Slaughter .... Angelo Fraboni
Molly MacGregor .... Patti Perkins
Jeanette Burmeister .... Kathleen Freeman
Noah "Horse" T. Simmons .. Andre De Shields
Estelle Genovese .... Liz McConahay
Police Sergeant .... C.E. Smith
Tony Giordano .... Jimmy Smagula

Time: The present. Place: Buffalo, New York.

San Francisco: American Conservatory Theater

(Carey Perloff artistic director; Heather Kitchen managing director; Melissa Smith concervatory director)

THE FIRST PICTURE SHOW. Play with music with book and lyrics by Ain Gordon and David Gordon; music by Jeanine Tesori. August 12, 1999. Director, David Gordon. Co-produced by Mark Taper Forum, Gordon Davidson artistic director; see its entry in the Los Angeles section of this listing.

WRONG MOUNTAIN. By David Hirson. October 27, 1999. Director, Richard Jones; scenery and costumes, Giles Cadle; lighting, Jennifer Tipton; sound, John Gromada; creature designs and prosthetics, Stephen Dupuis; co-produced by Dodger Theatrical Holdings.

Henry Dennett .... Ron Rifkin
Claire .... Beth Dixon
Jessica .... Ilana Levine
Adam .... Bruce Norris
Peter .... Reg Flowers
Guy Halperin .... Larry Pine
Maurice Montesor; Stevens .... Daniel Davis
Festival Actors:
Duncan Hyde-Berk .... Tom Riis Farrell
Salome Blackwood .... Beth Dixon
Jason Elmore .... Reg Flowers
Miranda Cortland-Sparks .... Jody Gelb
Ariel .... Anne Dudek
Winifred Hill; Anne .... Mary Schmidtberger
Clifford Peak .... Daniel Jenkins
Leibowitz .... Tom Riis Farrell
Woman in Bookshop .... Jody Gelb

Place and Time: Here and Now. One intermission.

THE INVENTION OF LOVE. By Tom Stoppard. January 14, 2000 (American premiere). Director, Carey Perloff; scenery, Loy Arcenas; costumes, Deborah Dryden; lighting, James F. Ingalls; music, Michael Roth; sound, Garth Hemphill.

A.E. Houseman at 77 .... James Cromwell
Charon .... Steven Anthony Jones
A.E. Houseman at 18–26 .... Jason Butler Harner
Alfred William Pollard .... Gord Rand
Moses John Jackson .... Garret Dillahunt
John Ruskin .... Ken Ruta
Oscar Wilde .... Marco Barricelli

One intermission

THE HOUSE OF MIRTH. By Edith Wharton; newly adapted by Giles Havergal. April 10, 2000. Director, Giles Havergal; scenery, Kate Edmunds; costumes, Anna Oliver; lighting, Peter Maradudin; original music and sound, Garth Hemphill, James Winquist.

Lily Bart .... Roxanne Raja
Lawrence Selden .... J. Paul Boehmer
Gerty Farish .... Lorri Holt
Simon Rosedale .... Troy West

The Furies: Judy Trenor, Mrs. Peniston—Domenique Lozano; Carry Fisher, Mrs. Haffen—Maureen McVerry; Bertha Dorset, Grace Stepney—Julie Eccles; George Dorset, Percy Gryce—Charles Dean; Gus Trenor, Lawyer—Charles Lanyer.

The Servants: Linda Jones Nicholson, Susan Papa, Michael Burke, Damon K. Sperber.

One intermission.

San Francisco: Magic Theater

(Larry Eilenberg artistic dirctor; Dianne M. Terp managing director)

STONES IN HIS POCKETS. By Marie Jones. June 2, 1999. Director, Kent Nicholson; scenery, Melpomene Katakalos; costumes, Jane Sayer; lighting, Robert T. Anderson; sound, Drew Yerys.

Charlie, et al. .... Kurt Reinhart
Jake, et al. .... Mark Phillips

One imtermission.

HILLARY & SOON-YI SHOP FOR TIES. "Vaudeville for the new millennium" by Michelle Carter; music by Randy Craig; lyrics and additional music by Michelle Carter. October 29, 1999. Director, Joan Mankin; scenery, Richard Olmsted; costumes, Jane Sayer; lighting, Scott Cannon.

Hillary; Demeter; Marilyn; Maureen O'Sullivan; Blessed Virgin .... Lorri Holt
Soon-Yi, Persephone, Monica .... Amy Tung

ACT I: Tempus Fugit, Tarzan, Father's Day, Pizza Delivery, Music School, Special Prosecution, Cookies, Photo Shoot, The Game, The Game Revisited, Awards Night, Catwalk.

ACT II: Feminist Studies 201, Feminist Studies Revisited, Ishtar, Teiresias, Prayers, the BVM, Prometheus, Crosstown Party.

BRONTE. By John O'Keefe. February 11, 2000. Director, Barbara Damashek; scenery, Mikiko

Uesagi; costumes, Todd Roeherman; lighting, Steven B. Mannshardt; sound, Michael Woody; composer, Barbara Damashek.

Patrick; Tom Spring;
Mr. Williams .... Robert Parnell
Charlotte .... N. Alexander Storm
Branwell .... Andrew Hurteau
Emily; Mrs. Wooler .... Natasha Kelly
Anne; Schoolgirl .... Sarah Overman
William Weightman; Arthur Bell Nicholls;
Mr. Smith .... Michael Eliopoulos
Mother Maria .... Elizabeth Fighera
John Brown .... David Morris

One intermission.

WYOMING. By Barry Gifford. April 7, 2000. Director, Amy Glazer; scenery, Lauren Elder; costumes, Fumiko Bielefeldt; lighting, Jim Cave; composer and sound, David Molina.

Kitty .... Anne Darragh
Roy .... Alex Brightman

No intermission.

Festival of Lesbian Playwrights

CATASTROPHE OF PEACE. By Bernadette Flagler. January 13, 2000. Director, Amy Glazer; lighting, Robert T. Anderson.

Martha .... Maria Candelaria
Vicki .... Amanda Duarte
Joe .... Michael Keys Hall
Esther .... Margaret Schenck
Christopher .... Liam Vincent

Raw Play: Script in Hand Series

KNOCK OFF BALANCE. By Cherylene Lee. September 21, 1999. Director, Karen Amano.

TRACY PETUNIA. By Susan Bernfield. October 18, 1999. Director, Kent Nicholson.

THE AMERICAN IN ME. By Rebecca Gilman. November 15, 1999. Director, Amy Glazer.

THE WIVES OF THE MAGI. By Adele Edling and Theodore Shank. Decemnber 20, 1999. Director, Frank Coppola.

ILIAD VARIATIONS (special workshop production). By and with John O'Keefe. March 13, 2000.

San Jose, Calif.: San Jose Repertory Theater

(Timothy Near artistic director; Alexandra Urbanowski managing director)

LOVE IN THE TITLE. By Hugh Leonard. March 11, 2000. Director, Patrick Mason; scenery and costumes, Joe Vanek; lighting, Mick Hughes; music, Conor Linehan; Abbey sound, Dave O'Brien; San Jose sound, Jeff Mockus; produced in association with the National Theater of Ireland in the Abbey Theater production, Ben Barnes artistic director, Richard Wakely managing director, Tony Wakefield technical director.

Cat .... Karen Ardiff
Triona .... Catherine Walsh
Katie .... Ingrid Craigie

Time: 1932/1964/1999. Place Meadow at Corcamore. One intermission.

4th Annual New Playwrights Festival
Workshop Productions, May 20–21

LOST VEGAS ACTS. Musical with book and lyrics by Cherylene Lee; music by Donald Eldon Wescoat. Director, Margaret Booker; music supervisor, Donald Eldon Wescoat.

Luellen; Ensemble .... Bonnie Akimoto
Ben; Golden; Square Dance Caller;
Ensemble .... Teli Cardaci
Father; Reporter; Guard; Announcer;
Ensemble .... Michael Ching
Adult Amy Lee .... Linda S.L. Chuan
Adult Alice .... Kimiko Gelman
Bob; MC; Ensemble .... David E. Kazanjian
Adult Annie .... Mimosa
Young Amy .... Sophie Tamiko Oda
Young Annie .... Kaila O'Neill
Reporter; Tutor;
Ensemble .... Sheila O'Neill Ellis
Young Alice .... Hollis Audrey Wear

THE DARKEST HOUR IS JUST BEFORE DAY. By John Henry Redwood. Director, Amy Gonzalez.

Aeneas Jappa .... Steven Anthony Jones
Yesenia .... Valerie de Jose
Agnes Riley .... Rashida "Cocoa" Bryant
Irene Riley .... Janis Bergmann
Marva Scott .... Olivia Michele Groves
Choy Lu Chin .... Rhoda Gravador

IS LIFE A DREAM? Adaptation of Pedro Calderon de la Barca's *Life Is a Dream* by Tommy Shepherd and Dan Wolf. Director, John McCluggage.

Segismundo .... Carlos Aguirre
Clarion .... Gendell Hernandez
Esterella .... Anna Marie Luera
Basilio .... Robert Sicular
Astolfo .... Keith Pinto
Rosaria .... Joy Osmanski
Clotaldo .... B. Chico Purdiman

Sarasota, Fla.: Asolo Theater Festival

(Howard J. Millman artistic director)

THE COUNT OF MONTE CRISTO. Adapted by Barbara Redmond and Eberle Thomas from the novel by Alexandre Dumas. January 21, 2000. Directors, Barbara Redmond, Eberle Thomas; scenery, Robert Barnett; costumes, Vicki S. Holden; lighting, James D. Sale; sound and original music, Matthew Parker; music direction and original music, E. Suzan Ott.

CAST: Edmond Dantes—Patrick James Clark. Gringole, M. de Baville, Carlo Bertuccio, Albert—Erik R. Uppling. Corot, Valet, Benedetto Bertuccio—Keith Edie. Harbor Inspector, 1st Gendarme, Giovanni Bertuccio, Lucien Debray, Barrois—David Baecker. Captain of Gendarmes, Customs Official, 2d Jailer, Gustave, Maximilien Morel—Scott Johnson. Pierre Morel, Maj. Timoteo Cavalcanti—Walter Rhodes. Eugene Danglars—Douglas Jones. Dantes the Elder, Gaetano Bertuccio—Bradford Wallace. LaCarconte—Sharon Spelman. Gaspard Caderousse—Allen Gilmore. Stranger (Noirtier), Jacopo Bertuccio, Ali, Dr. d'Avrigny—Jefferson Slinkard. Mercedes—Devora Millman. Fernand Mondego—Steve Wilson. Pamphile, Abbe Faria, Baptistin, President of the House of Peers—David S. Howard. Waitress, Mme. d'Istel, Nurse—Gretchen Meyerhoefer. Waitress, Mme. de Valgenceuse, Usher—Amanda Eaglen. Friend of Mercedes, Haydee—Aubrey Caldwell. Friend of Mercedes, Chambermaid, Valentine de Villefort—Sarah Anderson. 2d Gendarme, Germain, Governor of the Prison, Emile Beauchamp, Notary, Seurat—Bill Martin. Gerard de Villefort—David Breitbarth. Renee de St. Meran, Mme. Grignon—Stephanie Burden. 1st Jailer, Marquis Chateaubrun, Firing Range Attendant, Luigi Vampa—Vic Browder. Mme. Danglars—Tessie Hogan. Mme de Villefort—Carolyn Michel. Edouard—Michael DeSantis, Daniel Thorenson.

Act I, Scene 1–5: Feb. 28, 1815—In and around Marseilles. Scenes 6–9: Sept. 30, 1819—The prison of the Chateau d'If, the Morcerfs in Paris, Auteuil. Scene 10–11: March, 1834—The Chateau d'If; the Isle of Monte Cristo. Act II, Scene 12: July 1834—The Pont du Gard Inn near Nimes. Scenes 13–31: June-August 1839—Paris and Auteuil; Scene 32: Late August, 1839—the Catacombs, Rome. Scene 33: Early September, 1839—The Isle of Monte Cristo.

Seattle: A Contemporary Theater

(Gordon Edelstein artistic director; Susan Bond Trapnell managing director; Vito Zingarelli producing director)

TEMPORARY HELP. By David Wiltse. August 19, 1999. Director, Gordon Edelstein; scenery, Hugh Landwehr; costumes, Rose Pederson; lighting, Peter Maradudin; composer, Bill Frisell; sound, Stephen LeGrand; fight direction, Geoffrey Alm.

Karl Streber .... Thomas Kopache
Faye Streber .... Stephanie Faracy
Ron Stucker .... John Proccacino
Vincent Castelnuovo-Tedesco ...... Chad Allen

Time: The present. Act I, Scene 1: The Streber farmhouse, Cascade, Nebraska. Scene 2: Six weeks later. Scene 3: Two weeks later. Scene 4: The following day, evening. Act II, Scene 1: Two hours later, night. Scene 2: One week later. Scene 3: Later that day. One intermission.

GOD OF VENGEANCE. Newly adapted by Donald Margulies from the play by Sholem Asch; based on a literal translation by Joachim Neugroschel. April 13, 2000. Director, Gordon Edelstein; scenery, Hugh Landwehr; costumes, Anna Oliver; lighting, Robert Wierzel; composer and sound, John Gromada; fight director, Jeffrey Alm.

Jack Chapman aka Yankel
Tshaptshovitsh .... Matthew Boston
Sara .... Nike Doukas
Rivkele .... Rachel Miner
Manke .... Naama Potok
Hindl .... Johanna Melamed
Shloyme .... Mikael Salazar
Reyzl .... Betsy Schwartz
Basha .... Tricia Rodley
Reb Eli .... Larry Block
The Scribe (Reb Aaron) .... Sol Frieder
Orthodox Man .... Andrew Traister
Lower East Side Kids .... Ian Nelson-Roehl, Scott Ross
Prospective In-Law .... Wauchor Stephens
Indigents .... Frank Krasnowsky, Jay A. Hurwitz
Poor Women .... Ilene Fins, Hinda Kipnis

Partygoers, Minyan: Mike Christensen, Matt Purvis, Joe Shapiro, Mary Unruh.

Time: 1923. Place: The Lower East Side, New York City. One intermission.

First ACT 1999, November 18–21

THE HAIRY BABY. By Ki Gottberg. Director, Rosa Joshi; scenery, Peggy McDonald.
Claire .... Sarah Gunnell
Michael .... Andrew Heffernan
Doctor; Monster; Voice .... Tom Spiller
Mary; Z .... Annette Toutonghi
Thezda .... Peggy Poage
Delpha; Xeena .... Mary Machala
Bevo; Head; Goon .... Bill terKuile
Bill; Clown; Deek .... Burton Curtis

POINT DECEPTION. By Allison Gregory. Director, Steven Dietz; scenery, Peggy McDonald.
Claire .... Laura Ann Worthen
Corrinne .... Carol Roscoe
Sheryl .... Laurel Green-Fisher
Jean .... Katie Forgette
Earl .... Laura Kenny

THE ROBESON TAPE. By Vincent Delaney. Director, Leslie Swackhamer. scenery, Peggy McDonald
Tanja .... Demene E. Hall
Nate Calley .... Bill terKuile
Bernard Calley .... Andrew Heffernan
Vera Calley .... Mary Kae Irvin
Marian Wicker .... Stephanie Shine
Sam Wicker .... Mark Chamberlin
Paul Robeson .... Timothy McCuen Piggee

THE FETCH. By Dawson Nichols. Director, Robert Sindelar; scenery, Peggy McDonald.
Fetch .... Timothy Hyland
Mary .... Karen Kay Cody
Terry .... Jose J. Gonzales
Kerry .... Carol Roscoe
Alan; Others .... Peter Anthony Jacobs
Spencer; Others .... Chad Kelderman
Phil .... Michael Whistler
Robert; Others .... David Scully
Lucy; Others .... Kate Wisniewski

Women Playwrights Festival

LAS MENINAS. By Lynn Nottage. May 12, 2000.

AJAX. By Alice Tuan. May 13, 2000.

RAIN EXPECTED. By Michele Lowe. May 14, 2000.

HELEN. By Ellen McLaughlin. May 14, 2000.

Seattle: Seattle Repertory Theater

(Sharon Ott artistic director)

KING HEDLEY II. By August Wilson. December 15, 1999. Director, Marion Isaac McClinton. Produced in association with Pittsburgh Public Theater, Edward Gilbert artistic director; see its entry in the Pittsburgh listing in this section.

Stockbridge, Mass.: Berkshire Theater Festival

(Kate Maguire producing director)

SHOOT THE PIANO PLAYER. By Richard Corley; after the novel by David Goodis. July 22, 1999. Director, Richard Corley; scenery, Carol Bailey; costumes, Rachel Carr; lighting, Brian Aldous; sound, Robert Kaplowitz; music, David Sherman.
Turley Lynn .... John Cooper
Eddie Lynn .... Lance Williams
Lena; Teresa .... Maggie Lacey
Harriet .... Leslie Bandle
Wally Plyne .... Jay Duckworth
Feather; Woodling .... Erik Steele
Morris .... Deron Bayer

Chorus: Anthony Luciano, Troy Miller, Joni Weisfeld, Nora Zimmett.

Time and Place: 1956, late November and early December in and around Philadelphia, and some years before that in New York. One intermission.

CONVICTION. By Eve Ensler. August 12, 1999. Director, Eve Ensler; scenery, Myung Hee Cho; costumes, Jane Greenwood; lighting, Michael Chybowski; sound, Darron L. West; fight direction, Rick Sordelet. Produced by Music-Theater Group, Lyn Austin producing director, Diane Wondisford general director, in cooperation with Berkshire Theater Festival.
Sam .... Caroline Kava
Jude .... Priscilla Shanks
Harris .... Ed Blunt
Ruth .... Brenda Currin
David .... Tibor Feldman

No intermission.

STARR'S LAST TAPE. Solo performance by Brian Reddy as Kenneth Starr; written by Richard Lingeman and Victor Navasky. August 24, 1999. Director, Eric Hill; scenery, Jessica Wade; cos-

SEATTLE—Naama Potok and Andrew Traister in the Donald Margulies adaptation of Sholom Asch's *God of Vengeance* at A Contemporary Theater

tumes, Toni Wright; lighting, Tammy Owens Slauson; sound, Richard M. Dionne.

Time: The indefinite future. Place: Kenneth Starr's secret command post, an absolutely secure office-cum-vault where are stored all the materials accumulated during four years as Independent Counsel.

Teaneck, N.J.: American Stage Company

(James N. Vagias artistic director)

O. HENRY'S LOVERS. Musical with book and lyrics by Joe DiPietro; music by Michael Valenti. October 9, 1999. Director and choreographer, Chet Walker; musical direction, Jeffrey Buchsbaum; scenery, Michael Anania; costumes, Dale Dibernardo; lighting, Ted Mather; orchestrations, William R. Cox.

Porter .... Andy Gale
Barbara Ross .... Donna English
Gilbert .... Clif Thorn
Johnny .... Angela Christian
Sue .... Jessica Frankel
Dr. Jerome Ross .... Mitchell Greenberg
Nevada .... Kelli Rabke

One intermission.

MUSICAL NUMBERS: "So Beautiful," "It's Not Working," "When We Danced," "Lovely," "Johnsy's Dance," "East Meets West," "The Doctor Is Out," "Daddy, What Should Your Daughter Do?", "How Can Love Be Wrong?", "Rest, My Love, Rest," "Will the Rain Fall?", "What Would You Do?", "I Must Write Her," "The Song of Kate," "She Is My Love," "A Woman Knows."

Tucson: Arizona Theater Company

(David Ira Goldstein artistic director; Jessica L. Andrews managing director)

THE FIRST HUNDRED YEARS. By Geoff Hoyle; developed by Geoff Hoyle and Tony Taccone. April 14, 2000. Director, Tony Taccone; scenery, Christopher Barreca; costumes, masks, puppets, Peggy Snider; lighting, Peter Maradudin; sound, Matthew Spiro; produced in association with Berkeley Repertory Theater, Tony Taccone artistic director.

Jack Proust .... Geoff Hoyle
The Kid .... Rosalie Ward

Time: The present. Place: Liberty Theater. No intermission.

Staged Reading

BEFORE DEATH COMES FOR THE ARCHBISHOP. By Elaine Romero. December 10, 1999. Director, Amy Mueller.

Washington, D.C.: Arena Stage

(Molly Smith artistic director; Stephen Richard executive director; Zelda Fichandler founding director)

BLUE. By Charles Randolph-Wright; music by Nona Hendryx; lyrics by Nona Hendryx and Charles Randolph-Wright. April 15, 2000. Director, Sheldon Epps; scenery, James Leonard Joy; costumes, Debra Bauer; lighting, Michael Gilliam; sound, Timothy M. Thompson.

Reuben Clark (Adult) .... Michael Wiggins
Reuben Clark
(Young) .... Brandon Troy McMickens
Peggy Clark .... Phylicia Rashad
Blue Williams .... Arnold McCuller
Sam Clark III .... Howard W. Overshown
LaTonya Dinkins .... Messeret Stroman
Samuel Clark Jr. .... Randall Sheppard
Tillie Clark .... Jewell Robinson

Place: Kent, a fictional small town in South Carolina. Act I: The late Seventies. Act II: Fifteen years later. Epilogue: Later.

Washington, D.C.: Source Theater Company

(Joe Banno artistic director)

INNS & OUTS. By Caleen Sinnette Jennings. December 4, 1999. Director, Lisa Rose Middleton; scenery, Jordana Adelman; costumes, Susan Chiang; lighting, Dan Covey; sound, David Lamont Wilson.

Memorial Day:
Larry .... Scott Fortune
Robbie .... Lynn Chavis
Independence Day:
Paula .... Jewell Robinson
Denise .... Lynn Chavis
Leon .... David Lamont Wilson
Labor Day:
Logan .... Stephanie Johnson
Gene .... Gary Telles
Sherry .... Beverly Cosham
Roy .... Doug Brown
Christmas:
Crystal .... Strawberry Catubo
Chet .... Scott Fortune
Dot .... Lynn Chavis
New Year's Eve:
Vita .... Jewell Robinson
Louise .... Beverly Cosham
Joanie .... Lynn Chavis
Claude .... David Lamont Wilson
Bill .... Scott Fortune
Lisa .... Strawberry Catubo
Myra .... Stephanie Johnson
Jack .... Gary Telles
Sam .... Doug Brown

Time: The present. Place: A New England Inn.

Waterbury, Conn.: Seven Angels Theater

(Semina De Laurentis artistic director)

RANT & RAVE. By Pat Cooper and Rob Bartlett. November 7, 1999. Director, Peter Bennett; design, David O'Connor, Asa Wember; produced in association with Gary Grant Productions and Jamison Communications.

With Pat Cooper, Rob Bartlett.

MARCH TALE. By Tim Slover. March 4, 2000. Director, Don Amendolia; scenery, David Korins; costumes, Jennifer Emerson; lighting, David O'Connor; sound, Asa Wember; original music, Lou Romao; produced in association with Playwrights Kitchen Ensemble.

Elizabeth I .... Lee Bryant
Tom .... Matt Daniels
Emilia .... Kate Dawson
William Shakespeare .... Ted deChatelet
Robert Armin .... Hans Friedrichs
Richard Burbage .... Jerold Goldstein
Celia .... Sybil Ann Haggard

John Heminge .... Rick Lohman
William Kemp .... Anthony Santelmo Jr.
Robert Cecil .... Stephen Simon
Anne Hathaway Shakespeare .... Belinda Wolfe

MEXICAN STANDOFF AT FAT SQUAW SPRINGS. By Matthew Cowles. April 1, 2000. Director, Larry Hunt; scenery, David Regan; costumes, Jennifer Emerson; lighting, David O'Connor; sound, Asa Wember.

Anastazia Duchesne .... Judith Annozine
Loodie Duchesne .... Rosemarie Cepeda
Chicky Fennelli .... Matthew Cowles
John Fennel .... Matt Daniels
Chris .... Robert English
Mother Maria Immaculata ...... Cecelia Riddett

Waterford, Conn.: Eugene O'Neill Theater Center

(George C. White founder and chairman of the board; Lloyd Richards artistic director, Mary f. McCabe managing director, Tom Aberger production manager, National Playwrights Conference; Paulette Haupt artistic director, Steve Wood president, National Music Theater Conference)

National Playwrights Conference
Staged Readings, July 4–31

THE FALLS. By Hilary Bell.

BUCKLEY'S HOPE. By Ernie Blackmore.

THE WINNING STREAK. By Lee Blessing.

THE WOMEN OF LOCKERBIE. By Deborah Baley Brevoort.

SURVIVOR'S RITES. By Norman A. Caito.

DREAM HOUSE. By Carl Capotorto.

FREE LESSONS. By Jackob Aaron Estes.

MOTHER'S DAY. By Herman Daniel Farrell III.

CYCLONE. By Ron Fitzgerald.

LAST STAND OF THE COMANCHE RIDERS. By Elise Forier.

ROYALTY AND ROGUES. By Miro Gavran.

PORK PIE. By Michael Genet.

THE HUNGER EDUCATION. By Jessica Goldberg.

JOSEPHINE 65. By Kirsten Greenidge.

THE ELEPHANT'S CRY. By Farid Nagim.

Directors: Julie Boyd, Israel Hicks, Vadim Petrovich Kondratiev, Paul McCrane, David Milroy, William Partlan, Amy Saltz. Designers: Scenery, G. W. Mercier; lighting, Tina Charney.

National Music Theater Conference
Staged Concert Readings, July 28-Aug. 9

THE WILD PARTY. Musical-in-progress with book, music and lyrics by Andrew Lippa; based on *The Wild Party* by Joseph Moncure March.

RICHARD CORY. Musical-in-progress with book, music and lyrics by Ed Dixon; adapted from the play by A.R. Gurney.

Directors: Gabriel Barre, Kent Gash. Music directors: Jeff Halpern, David Loud.

Westport, Conn.: Westport Country Playhouse

(James B. McKenzie executive producer; Eric Friedheim associate producer)

CHASING MONSTERS. By Kevin Rehac. August 2, 1999. Director, Sabin Epstein; scenery, Richard Ellis; costumes, Randy Blair; lighting, Susan Roth; sound, Bruce Ellman.

Carolyn Nast .... Jenna Stern
Jack Carlson .... Ralph Waite
Margery Kendall .... Michael Learned
Allan Nast .... Victor Slezak

Time: A Friday in June. Place: Margery Kendall's lakeside home in the Andirondacks of Upstate New York. One intermission.

Williamstown, Mass: Williamstown Theater Festival

(Michael Ritchie producer)

CLIMMER BROTHERS. By Warren Leight. July 14, 1999. Director, Scott Ellis; scenery, Allen Moyer; costumes, Jennifer von Mayrhauser; lighting, Kenneth Posner; sound, Matthew Spiro.

Martin .... John Spencer
Jordan .... David Schwimmer
Delia .... Kim Raver
Daniel .... Terry Beaver

Orderlies: Frank Church, Brendan Murphy, Kristen Napiorkowski, Craig Pattison.

FACTORY GIRLS. By Frank McGuinness. July 14, 1999. Director, Nye Heron. Produced in association with Bay Street Theater, Sybil Christopher and Emma Walton artistic directors; see its entry in the Sag Harbor listing in this section.

CHAUCER IN ROME. By John Guare. July 28, 1999. Director, Nicholas Martin; scenery, Alexander Dodge; costumes, Deb Millison; lighting, Jeff Nellis; sound, Jerry Yager.

Matt .... B.D. Wong
Sarah .... Kali Rocha
Father Schapiro; Doctor; Joe;
Charlie .... Lee Wilkof
Pete .... Bruce Norris
Ron .... Jerry Hardin
Dolo .... Polly Holliday
Renzo .... Ethan Sandler

Pilgrims: Connor Barrett, Kathleen Carthy, Dara Fisher, Kathryn Hahn.

THE WAVERLY GALLERY. By Kenneth Lonergan. August 11, 1999. Director, Scott Ellis; scenery, Derek McLane; costumes, Michael Krass; lighting, Kenneth Posner; sound, Kurt B. Kellenberger.

Gladys Green .... Eileen Heckart
Daniel Fine .... Josh Hamilton
Ellen Fine .... Maureen Anderman
Howard Fine .... Mark Blum
Don Bowman .... Anthony Arkin
Alan George .... Stephen Mendillo

QUARK VICTORY. Musical with book and lyrics by Willie Reale; music by Robert Reale. July 22, 1999. Director, Jonathan Bernstein; choreography, Andy Blankenbuehler; musical direction, James Sampliner; scenery, Michael Brown; costumes, Mimi O'Donnell; lighting, Jeff Nellis; sound, One Dream Sound, Matthew Burton; orchestrations, Irwin Fisch.

Mother Fitzwater .... Allison Kate Cherkis
Herb Fitzwater .... John Hickok
Russell Fishman .... David Wohl
Penelope Fitzwater .... Karen Ziemba
Samantha Fitzwater .... Jessica Boevers
Newt .... Charlie Day
Scooter .... Wilson Jermaine Heredia
Cookie .... Shannon Walker Williams
Eileen .... Elisa Bocanegra
Beezer .... Anna Belknap
Billy Winsome .... Sterling Brown
Shimmie Heckleman;
Mannie the Muon .... Stephen DeRosa
Tiberious .... David Hornsby
Artiba .... Jimmi Simpson
Agnes .... Jane Bodle

Dance Ensemble: Brad Bilanin, Lee Fitzpatrick, Haley Fuller, Hana Nora McGrath, Catia Ojeda, Britt Shubow, David D. Turner.

MUSICAL NUMBERS, ACT I: "Suddenly Alive," "One Small Adjustment," "23 Skidoo," "Turn on the Charm," "Verbs," "Where Dreams Live."

ACT II: "It's Love," "Being Different," "The Muon Voodoo Swing," "Make a Wish," "Finally Alive."

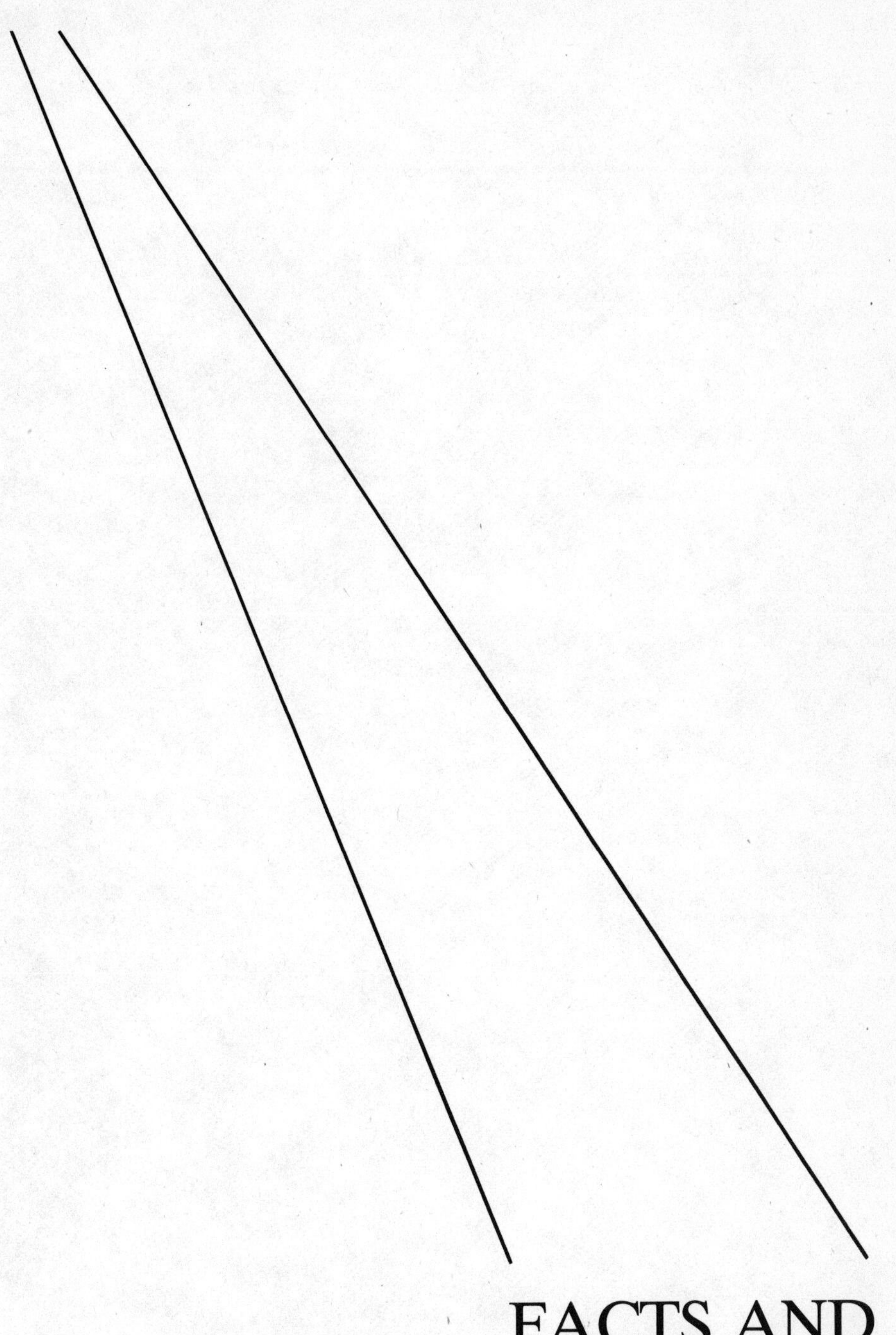

FACTS AND FIGURES

LONG RUNS ON BROADWAY

The following shows have run 500 or more continuous performances in a single production, usually the first, not including previews or extra non-profit performances, allowing for vacation layoffs and special one-booking engagements, but not including return engagements after a show has gone on tour. In all cases, the numbers were obtained directly from the show's production offices. Where there are title similarities, the production is identified as follows: (p) straight play version, (m) musical version, (r) revival, (tr) transfer.

THROUGH MAY 31, 2000

(PLAYS MARKED WITH ASTERISK WERE STILL PLAYING JUNE 1, 2000)

Plays	*Number Performances*
*Cats	7,367
A Chorus Line	6,137
Oh! Calcutta! (r)	5,959
*Les Misérables	5,442
*The Phantom of the Opera	5,154
*Miss Saigon	3,820
42nd Street	3,486
Grease	3,388
Fiddler on the Roof	3,242
Life With Father	3,224
Tobacco Road	3,182
Hello, Dolly!	2,844
My Fair Lady	2,717
*Beauty and the Beast	2,483
Annie	2,377
Man of La Mancha	2,328
Abie's Irish Rose	2,327
Oklahoma!	2,212
Smokey Joe's Cafe	2,036
Pippin	1,944
South Pacific	1,925
The Magic Show	1,920
Deathtrap	1,793
Gemini	1,788
Harvey	1,775
Dancin'	1,774
La Cage aux Folles	1,761
Hair	1,750
*Rent	1,707
The Wiz	1,672
Born Yesterday	1,642
The Best Little Whorehouse in Texas	1,639
Crazy for You	1,622
Ain't Misbehavin'	1,604
Mary, Mary	1,572
Evita	1,567
The Voice of the Turtle	1,557
Barefoot in the Park	1,530
Brighton Beach Memoirs	1,530
Dreamgirls	1,522
Mame (m)	1,508
Grease (r)	1,503
*Chicago (m)(r)	1,476
Same Time, Next Year	1,453
Arsenic and Old Lace	1,444
The Sound of Music	1,443
Me and My Girl	1,420
How to Succeed in Business Without Really Trying	1,417
Hellzapoppin	1,404
The Music Man	1,375
Funny Girl	1,348
Mummenschanz	1,326
Angel Street	1,295
Lightnin'	1,291
*Jekyll & Hyde	1,290
Promises, Promises	1,281
The King and I	1,246
Cactus Flower	1,234
Sleuth	1,222
Torch Song Trilogy	1,222
1776	1,217
Equus	1,209
Sugar Babies	1,208
Guys and Dolls	1,200
Amadeus	1,181
Cabaret	1,165
Mister Roberts	1,157
Annie Get Your Gun	1,147

Plays	*Number Performances*
Guys and Dolls (r)	1,144
The Seven Year Itch	1,141
Bring in 'da Noise Bring in 'da Funk	1,130
Butterflies Are Free	1,128
Pins and Needles	1,108
*The Lion King	1,098
Plaza Suite	1,097
They're Playing Our Song	1,082
Grand Hotel (m)	1,077
Kiss Me, Kate	1,070
Don't Bother Me, I Can't Cope	1,065
The Pajama Game	1,063
Shenandoah	1,050
The Teahouse of the August Moon	1,027
Damn Yankees	1,019
Never Too Late	1,007
Big River	1,005
The Will Rogers Follies	983
Any Wednesday	982
Sunset Boulevard	977
A Funny Thing Happened on the Way to the Forum	964
The Odd Couple	964
Anna Lucasta	957
Kiss and Tell	956
Show Boat (r)	949
Dracula (r)	925
Bells Are Ringing	924
The Moon Is Blue	924
Beatlemania	920
The Elephant Man	916
Kiss of the Spider Woman	906
Luv	901
The Who's Tommy	900
Chicago (m)	898
Applause	896
Can-Can	892
Carousel	890
I'm Not Rappaport	890
Hats Off to Ice	889
Fanny	888
Children of a Lesser God	887
Follow the Girls	882
*Cabaret (r)	881
City of Angels	878
Camelot	873
I Love My Wife	872
The Bat	867

Plays	*Number Performances*
My Sister Eileen	864
No, No, Nanette (r)	861
Ragtime	861
Song of Norway	860
Chapter Two	857
A Streetcar Named Desire	855
Barnum	854
Comedy in Music	849
Raisin	847
Blood Brothers	839
You Can't Take It With You	837
La Plume de Ma Tante	835
Three Men on a Horse	835
The Subject Was Roses	832
Black and Blue	824
The King and I (r)	807
Inherit the Wind	806
Anything Goes (r)	804
Titanic	804
No Time for Sergeants	796
Fiorello!	795
Where's Charley?	792
The Ladder	789
Forty Carats	780
Lost in Yonkers	780
The Prisoner of Second Avenue	780
M. Butterfly	777
Oliver!	774
The Pirates of Penzance (1980 r)	772
Woman of the Year	770
My One and Only	767
Sophisticated Ladies	767
Bubbling Brown Sugar	766
Into the Woods	765
State of the Union	765
Starlight Express	761
The First Year	760
Broadway Bound	756
You Know I Can't Hear You When the Water's Running	755
Two for the Seesaw	750
Joseph and the Amazing Technicolor Dreamcoat (r)	747
Death of a Salesman	742
For Colored Girls, etc.	742
Sons o' Fun	742
Candide (m, r)	740
Gentlemen Prefer Blondes	740
The Man Who Came to Dinner	739
Nine	739

Plays	*Number Performances*
Call Me Mister	734
Victor/Victoria	734
West Side Story	732
High Button Shoes	727
Finian's Rainbow	725
Claudia	722
The Gold Diggers	720
Jesus Christ Superstar	720
Carnival	719
The Diary of Anne Frank	717
A Funny Thing Happened on the Way to the Forum (r)	715
I Remember Mama	714
Tea and Sympathy	712
Junior Miss	710
Last of the Red Hot Lovers	706
The Secret Garden	706
Company	705
Seventh Heaven	704
Gypsy (m)	702
The Miracle Worker	700
That Championship Season	700
Da	697
Cat on a Hot Tin Roof	694
Li'l Abner	693
The Children's Hour	691
Purlie	688
Dead End	687
The Lion and the Mouse	686
White Cargo	686
Dear Ruth	683
East Is West	680
Come Blow Your Horn	677
The Most Happy Fella	676
Defending the Caveman	671
The Doughgirls	671
*Footloose	670
The Impossible Years	670
Irene	670
Boy Meets Girl	669
The Tap Dance Kid	669
Beyond the Fringe	667
Who's Afraid of Virginia Woolf?	664
Blithe Spirit	657
A Trip to Chinatown	657
The Women	657
Bloomer Girl	654
The Fifth Season	654
Rain	648
Witness for the Prosecution	645
Call Me Madam	644
Janie	642
The Green Pastures	640
Auntie Mame (p)	639
A Man for All Seasons	637
Jerome Robbins' Broadway	634
The Fourposter	632
The Music Master	627
Two Gentlemen of Verona (m)	627
The Tenth Man	623
The Heidi Chronicles	621
Is Zat So?	618
Anniversary Waltz	615
The Happy Time (p)	614
Separate Rooms	613
Affairs of State	610
Oh! Calcutta! (tr)	610
Star and Garter	609
The Mystery of Edwin Drood	608
The Student Prince	608
Sweet Charity	608
Bye Bye Birdie	607
Irene (r)	604
Sunday in the Park With George	604
Adonis	603
Broadway	603
Peg o' My Heart	603
Master Class	601
Street Scene (p)	601
Flower Drum Song	600
Kiki	600
A Little Night Music	600
Art	600
Agnes of God	599
Don't Drink the Water	598
Wish You Were Here	598
Sarafina!	597
A Society Circus	596
Absurd Person Singular	592
A Day in Hollywood/A Night in the Ukraine	588
The Me Nobody Knows	586
The Two Mrs. Carrolls	585
*Fosse	584
Kismet (m)	583
Gypsy (m, r)	582
Brigadoon	581
Detective Story	581
No Strings	580
Brother Rat	577

Plays	Number Performances
Blossom Time	576
Pump Boys and Dinettes	573
Show Boat	572
The Show-Off	571
Sally	570
Jelly's Last Jam	569
Golden Boy (m)	568
One Touch of Venus	567
The Real Thing	566
Happy Birthday	564
Look Homeward, Angel	564
Morning's at Seven (r)	564
The Glass Menagerie	561
I Do! I Do!	560
Wonderful Town	559
The Last Night of Ballyhoo	557
Rose Marie	557
Strictly Dishonorable	557
Sweeney Todd, the Demon Barber of Fleet Street	557
The Great White Hope	556
A Majority of One	556
The Sisters Rosensweig	556
Sunrise at Campobello	556
Toys in the Attic	556
Jamaica	555
Stop the World—I Want to Get Off	555
Florodora	553
Noises Off	553
Ziegfeld Follies (1943)	553
Dial "M" for Murder	552
Good News	551
Peter Pan (r)	551
How to Succeed in Business Without Really Trying (r)	548
Let's Face It	547
Milk and Honey	543
Within the Law	541
Pal Joey (r)	540
The Sound of Music (r)	540
What Makes Sammy Run?	540
The Sunshine Boys	538
What a Life	538
Crimes of the Heart	535
Damn Yankees (r)	533
The Unsinkable Molly Brown	532
The Red Mill (r)	531
Rumors	531
A Raisin in the Sun	530
Godspell (tr)	527
Fences	526
The Solid Gold Cadillac	526
Biloxi Blues	524
Irma La Douce	524
The Boomerang	522
Follies	521
Rosalinda	521
*Annie Get Your Gun (r)	520
The Best Man	520
Chauve-Souris	520
Blackbirds of 1928	518
The Gin Game	517
Sunny	517
Victoria Regina	517
Fifth of July	511
Half a Sixpence	511
The Vagabond King	511
The New Moon	509
The World of Suzie Wong	508
The Rothschilds	507
On Your Toes (r)	505
Sugar	505
Shuffle Along	504
Up in Central Park	504
Carmen Jones	503
The Member of the Wedding	501
Panama Hattie	501
Personal Appearance	501
Bird in Hand	500
Room Service	500
Sailor, Beware!	500
Tomorrow the World	500

LONG RUNS OFF BROADWAY

Plays	Number Performances
*The Fantasticks	16,594
*Perfect Crime	5,420
*Tony 'n' Tina's Wedding	4,109
*Tubes	4,061

Plays	*Number Performances*
Nunsense	3,672
*Stomp	2,633
The Threepenny Opera	2,611
Forbidden Broadway 1982–87	2,332
Little Shop of Horrors	2,209
Godspell	2,124
Vampire Lesbians of Sodom	2,024
Jacques Brel	1,847
Forever Plaid	1,811
Vanities	1,785
*I Love You, You're Perfect, Now Change	1,598
You're a Good Man Charlie Brown	1,597
The Blacks	1,408
One Mo' Time	1,372
Grandma Sylvia's Funeral	1,360
Let My People Come	1,327
Driving Miss Daisy	1,195
The Hot l Baltimore	1,166
I'm Getting My Act Together and Taking It on the Road	1,165
Little Mary Sunshine	1,143
Steel Magnolias	1,126
El Grande de Coca-Cola	1,114
The Proposition	1,109
Beau Jest	1,069
Tamara	1,036
One Flew Over the Cuckoo's Nest (r)	1,025
The Boys in the Band	1,000
Fool for Love	1,000
Other People's Money	990
Cloud 9	971
Secrets Every Smart Traveler Should Know	953
Sister Mary Ignatius Explains It All for You & The Actor's Nightmare	947
Your Own Thing	933
Curley McDimple	931
Leave It to Jane (r)	928
Hedwig and the Angry Inch	857
Forbidden Broadway Strikes Back	850
When Pigs Fly	840
The Mad Show	871
Scrambled Feet	831
The Effect of Gamma Rays on Man-in-the-Moon Marigolds	819
*Late Nite Catechism	796
*De La Guarda	794

Plays	*Number Performances*
A View From the Bridge (r)	780
The Boy Friend (r)	763
True West	762
Isn't It Romantic	733
Dime a Dozen	728
The Pocket Watch	725
The Connection	722
The Passion of Dracula	714
Adaptation & Next	707
Oh! Calcutta!	704
Scuba Duba	692
*Over the River and Through the Woods	691
The Foreigner	686
The Knack	685
The Club	674
The Balcony	672
Penn & Teller	666
America Hurrah	634
Oil City Symphony	626
Hogan's Goat	607
Beehive	600
The Trojan Women	600
The Dining Room	583
Krapp's Last Tape & The Zoo Story	582
Three Tall Women	582
The Dumbwaiter & The Collection	578
Forbidden Broadway 1990	576
Dames at Sea	575
The Crucible (r)	571
The Iceman Cometh (r)	565
The Hostage (r)	545
Wit	545
What's a Nice Country Like You Doing in a State Like This?	543
Forbidden Broadway 1988	534
Gross Indecency: The Three Trials of Oscar Wilde	534
Frankie and Johnny in the Clair de Lune	533
Six Characters in Search of an Author (r)	529
All in the Timing	526
Oleanna	513
Making Porn	511
The Dirtiest Show in Town	509
Happy Ending & Day of Absence	504
Greater Tuna	501
A Shayna Maidel	501
The Boys From Syracuse (r)	500

NEW YORK DRAMA CRITICS CIRCLE AWARDS 1935–1936 TO 1999–2000

Listed below are the New York Drama Critics Circle Awards from 1935–1936 through 1999–2000 classified as follows: (1) Best American Play, (2) Best Foreign Play, (3) Best Musical, (4) Best, Regardless of Category (this category was established by new voting rules in 1962–63 and did not exist prior to that year).

1935–36—(1) Winterset
1936–37—(1) High Tor
1937–38—(1) Of Mice and Men, (2) Shadow and Substance
1938–39—(1) No award, (2) The White Steed
1939–40—(1) The Time of Your Life
1940–41—(1) Watch on the Rhine, (2) The Corn Is Green
1941–42—(1) No award, (2) Blithe Spirit
1942–43—(1) The Patriots
1943–44—(2) Jacobowsky and the Colonel
1944–45—(1) The Glass Menagerie
1945–46—(3) Carousel
1946–47—(1) All My Sons, (2) No Exit, (3) Brigadoon
1947–48—(1) A Streetcar Named Desire, (2) The Winslow Boy
1948–49—(1) Death of a Salesman, (2) The Madwoman of Chaillot, (3) South Pacific
1949–50—(1) The Member of the Wedding, (2) The Cocktail Party, (3) The Consul
1950–51—(1) Darkness at Noon, (2) The Lady's Not for Burning, (3) Guys and Dolls
1951–52—(1) I Am a Camera, (2) Venus Observed, (3) Pal Joey (Special citation to Don Juan in Hell)
1952–53—(1) Picnic, (2) The Love of Four Colonels, (3) Wonderful Town
1953–54—(1) The Teahouse of the August Moon, (2) Ondine, (3) The Golden Apple
1954–55—(1) Cat on a Hot Tin Roof, (2) Witness for the Prosecution, (3) The Saint of Bleecker Street
1955–56—(1) The Diary of Anne Frank, (2) Tiger at the Gates, (3) My Fair Lady
1956–57—(1) Long Day's Journey Into Night, (2) The Waltz of the Toreadors, (3) The Most Happy Fella
1957–58—(1) Look Homeward, Angel, (2) Look Back in Anger, (3) The Music Man
1958–59—(1) A Raisin in the Sun, (2) The Visit, (3) La Plume de Ma Tante
1959–60—(1) Toys in the Attic, (2) Five Finger Exercise, (3) Fiorello!
1960–61—(1) All the Way Home, (2) A Taste of Honey, (3) Carnival
1961–62—(1) The Night of the Iguana, (2) A Man for All Seasons, (3) How to Succeed in Business Without Really Trying
1962–63—(4) Who's Afraid of Virginia Woolf? (Special citation to Beyond the Fringe)
1963–64—(4) Luther, (3) Hello, Dolly! (Special citation to The Trojan Women)
1964–65—(4) The Subject Was Roses, (3) Fiddler on the Roof
1965–66—(4) The Persecution and Assassination of Marat as Performed by the Inmates of the Asylum of Charenton Under the Direction of the Marquis de Sade, (3) Man of La Mancha
1966–67—(4) The Homecoming, (3) Cabaret
1967–68—(4) Rosencrantz and Guildenstern Are Dead, (3) Your Own Thing
1968–69—(4) The Great White Hope, (3) 1776
1969–70—(4) Borstal Boy, (1) The Effect of Gamma Rays on Man-in-the-Moon Marigolds, (3) Company
1970–71—(4) Home, (1) The House of Blue Leaves, (3) Follies
1971–72—(4) That Championship Season, (2) The Screens (3) Two Gentlemen of Verona (Special citations to Sticks and Bones and Old Times)
1972–73—(4) The Changing Room, (1) The Hot l Baltimore, (3) A Little Night Music
1973–74—(4) The Contractor, (1) Short Eyes, (3) Candide
1974–75—(4) Equus (1) The Taking of Miss Janie, (3) A Chorus Line
1975–76—(4) Travesties, (1) Streamers, (3) Pacific Overtures
1976–77—(4) Otherwise Engaged, (1) American Buffalo, (3) Annie
1977–78—(4) Da, (3) Ain't Misbehavin'
1978–79—(4) The Elephant Man, (3) Sweeney Todd, the Demon Barber of Fleet Street
1979–80—(4) Talley's Folly, (2) Betrayal, (3) Evita (Special citation to Peter Brook's Le Centre International de Créations Théâtrales for its repertory)
1980–81—(4) A Lesson From Aloes, (1) Crimes of the Heart (Special citations to Lena

Horne: The Lady and Her Music and the New York Shakespeare Festival production of The Pirates of Penzance)
1981–82—(4) The Life & Adventures of Nicholas Nickleby, (1) A Soldier's Play
1982–83—(4) Brighton Beach Memoirs, (2) Plenty, (3) Little Shop of Horrors (Special citation to Young Playwrights Festival)
1983–84—(4) The Real Thing, (1) Glengarry Glen Ross, (3) Sunday in the Park With George (Special citation to Samuel Beckett for the body of his work)
1984–85—(4) Ma Rainey's Black Bottom
1985–86—(4) A Lie of the Mind, (2) Benefactors (Special citation to The Search for Signs of Intelligent Life in the Universe)
1986–87—(4) Fences, (2) Les Liaisons Dangereuses, (3) Les Misérables
1987–88—(4) Joe Turner's Come and Gone, (2) The Road to Mecca, (3) Into the Woods
1988–89—(4) The Heidi Chronicles, (2) Aristocrats (Special citation to Bill Irwin for Largely New York)
1989–90—(4) The Piano Lesson, (2) Privates on Parade, (3) City of Angels
1990–91—(4) Six Degrees of Separation, (2) Our Country's Good, (3) The Will Rogers Follies (Special citation to Eileen Atkins for her portrayal of Virginia Woolf in A Room of One's Own)
1991–92—(4) Dancing at Lughnasa, (1) Two Trains Running
1992–93—(4) Angels in America: Millennium Approaches, (2) Someone Who'll Watch Over Me, (3) Kiss of the Spider Woman
1993–94—(4) Three Tall Women (Special citation to Anna Deavere Smith for her unique contribution to theatrical form)
1994–95—(4) Arcadia, (1) Love! Valour! Compassion! (Special citation to Signature Theater Company for outstanding artistic achievement)
1995–96—(4) Seven Guitars, (2) Molly Sweeney, (3) Rent
1996–97—(4) How I Learned to Drive, (2) Skylight, (3) Violet (Special citation to Chicago)
1997–98—(4) Art, (1) Pride's Crossing, (3) The Lion King (Special citation to the revival production of Cabaret)
1998–99—(4) Wit, (3) Parade, (2) Closer (Special citation to David Hare for his contributions to the 1998–99 theater season: Amy's View, Via Dolorosa and The Blue Room)
1999–00—(4) Jitney, (3) James Joyce's The Dead, (2) Copenhagen

NEW YORK DRAMA CRITICS CIRCLE VOTING 1999–2000

At their May 9, 2000 meeting the New York Drama Critics Circle voted two off-Broadway offerings the best play and best musical of the 1999–2000 theater season in New York, both on the third ballot: *Jitney* and *James Joyce's The Dead*. Having named an American play their best regardless of category, the critics then proceeded to give Broadway a slice of the awards pie by voting *Copenhagen* the year's best foreign play.

Eighteen members of the Circle were present, and two (Ben Brantley of the *Times* and Jack Kroll of *Newsweek)* voted by proxy. The first-ballot voting for best-of-bests was divided as follows: *Copenhagen* 8 (Clive Barnes, *Post;* Mary Campbell, AP; Robert Feldberg, *Bergen Record;* Charles Isherwood, *Variety;* Jack Kroll; Michael Kuchwara, AP; Jacques le Sourd, Gannett newspapers; Donald Lyons, *Post), Jitney* 6 (John Heilpern, *Observer;* Frank Scheck, *Christian Science Monitor;* David Sheward, *Backstage;* Sam Whitehead, *Time Out;* Linda Winer, *Newsday;* Richard Zoglin, *Time), Dinner With Friends* 3 (David Kaufman, *Daily News;* Ken Mandelbaum, Broadway.com; John Simon, *New York), Dirty Blonde* 2 (Ben Brantley; Michael Sommers, Newhouse group) and *In the Blood* 1 (Michael Feingold, *Village Voice).* No play having received enough votes to win by a majority on the first ballot, or the second, the Critics then proceeded to a third ballot on which only the top two contenders were eligible for consideration. On this ballot, all the votes which *Copenhagen* did not already possess went to *Jitney,* which won by 10 to 8, with the two absentee votes no longer counting. The Critics then proceeded to the voting for a best foreign play, which *Copenhagen* easily dominated with a large majority of 16 votes, against only 1 for *What You Get and What You Expect* (Feingold), *Waste* (Sommers) and *Waiting in the Wings* (Zoglin), with Scheck abstaining.

The contest for best musical also went to a third Critics ballot, after a first ballot dominated by the eventual runner-up, as follows: *Contact* 8 (Brantley, Feldberg, Isherwood, Kroll, Kuchwara, Lyons, Simon, Winer), New York Shakespeare Festival's *The Wild Party* 4 (Heilpern, Mandelbaum, Sheward, Sommers), Manhattan Theater Club's *The Wild Party* 3 (Barnes, Kaufman, Scheck), *James Joyce's The Dead* 2 (le Sourd, Whitehead) and 1 each for *Marie Christine* (Campbell), *Saturday Night* (Feingold) and *Aida* (Zoglin). On the second ballot, *James Joyce's The Dead* picked up enough votes to become one of the two contenders on the third ballot, which it won over *Contact* by a vote of 8 to 7, with three members (Feingold, Mandelbaum, Zoglin) abstaining and two absentees not counting. A 21st member of the Circle, Fintan O'Toole of the *Daily News,* was absent and not voting.

CHOICES OF SOME OTHER CRITICS

Critic	*Best Play*	*Best Musical*
Sherry Eaker *Backstage*	The Tale of the Allergist's Wife	The Wild Party (MTC)
Martin Gottfried N.Y. *Law Journal*	Dinner With Friends	The Wild Party (NYSF)
Ralph Howard WINS Radio	Copenhagen	James Joyce's The Dead
Alvin Klein N.Y. *Times Suburban*	Dinner With Friends	Marie Christine
Dick Schaap ABC *World News Tonight*	Dirty Blonde	Contact

PULITZER PRIZE WINNERS 1916–1917 TO 1999–2000

1916–17—No award
1917–18—Why Marry?, by Jesse Lynch Williams
1918–19—No award
1919–20—Beyond the Horizon, by Eugene O'Neill
1920–21—Miss Lulu Bett, by Zona Gale
1921–22—Anna Christie, by Eugene O'Neill
1922–23—Icebound, by Owen Davis
1923–24—Hell-Bent fer Heaven, by Hatcher Hughes
1924–25—They Knew What They Wanted, by Sidney Howard
1925–26—Craig's Wife, by George Kelly
1926–27—In Abraham's Bosom, by Paul Green
1927–28—Strange Interlude, by Eugene O'Neill
1928–29—Street Scene, by Elmer Rice

1929–30—The Green Pastures, by Marc Connelly
1930–31—Alison's House, by Susan Glaspell
1931–32—Of Thee I Sing, by George S. Kaufman, Morrie Ryskind, Ira and George Gershwin
1932–33—Both Your Houses, by Maxwell Anderson
1933–34—Men in White, by Sidney Kingsley
1934–35—The Old Maid, by Zoe Akins
1935–36—Idiot's Delight, by Robert E. Sherwood
1936–37—You Can't Take It With You, by Moss Hart and George S. Kaufman
1937–38—Our Town, by Thornton Wilder
1938–39—Abe Lincoln in Illinois, by Robert E. Sherwood
1939–40—The Time of Your Life, by William Saroyan
1940–41—There Shall Be No Night, by Robert E. Sherwood
1941–42—No award
1942–43—The Skin of Our Teeth, by Thornton Wilder
1943–44—No award
1944–45—Harvey, by Mary Chase
1945–46—State of the Union, by Howard Lindsay and Russel Crouse
1946–47—No award
1947–48—A Streetcar Named Desire, by Tennessee Williams
1948–49—Death of a Salesman, by Arthur Miller
1949–50—South Pacific, by Richard Rodgers, Oscar Hammerstein II and Joshua Logan
1950–51—No award
1951–52—The Shrike, by Joseph Kramm
1952–53—Picnic, by William Inge
1953–54—The Teahouse of the August Moon, by John Patrick
1954–55—Cat on a Hot Tin Roof, by Tennessee Williams
1955–56—The Diary of Anne Frank, by Frances Goodrich and Albert Hackett
1956–57—Long Day's Journey Into Night, by Eugene O'Neill
1957–58—Look Homeward, Angel, by Ketti Frings
1958–59—J.B., by Archibald MacLeish
1959–60—Fiorello!, by Jerome Weidman, George Abbott, Sheldon Harnick and Jerry Bock
1960–61—All the Way Home, by Tad Mosel
1961–62—How to Succeed in Business Without Really Trying, by Abe Burrows, Willie Gilbert, Jack Weinstock and Frank Loesser
1962–63—No award
1963–64—No award
1964–65—The Subject Was Roses, by Frank D. Gilroy
1965–66—No award
1966–67—A Delicate Balance, by Edward Albee
1967–68—No award
1968–69—The Great White Hope, by Howard Sackler
1969–70—No Place To Be Somebody, by Charles Gordone
1970–71—The Effect of Gamma Rays on Man-in-the-Moon Marigolds, by Paul Zindel
1971–72—No award
1972–73—That Championship Season, by Jason Miller
1973–74—No award
1974–75—Seascape, by Edward Albee
1975–76—A Chorus Line, by Michael Bennett, James Kirkwood, Nicholas Dante, Marvin Hamlisch and Edward Kleban
1976–77—The Shadow Box, by Michael Cristofer
1977–78—The Gin Game, by D.L. Coburn
1978–79—Buried Child, by Sam Shepard
1979–80—Talley's Folly, by Lanford Wilson
1980–81—Crimes of the Heart, by Beth Henley
1981–82—A Soldier's Play, by Charles Fuller
1982–83—'night, Mother, by Marsha Norman
1983–84—Glengarry Glen Ross, by David Mamet
1984–85—Sunday in the Park With George, by James Lapine and Stephen Sondheim
1985–86—No award
1986–87—Fences, by August Wilson
1987–88—Driving Miss Daisy, by Alfred Uhry
1988–89—The Heidi Chronicles, by Wendy Wasserstein
1989–90—The Piano Lesson, by August Wilson
1990–91—Lost in Yonkers, by Neil Simon
1991–92—The Kentucky Cycle, by Robert Schenkkan
1992–93—Angels in America: Millennium Approaches, by Tony Kushner
1993–94—Three Tall Women, by Edward Albee
1994–95—The Young Man From Atlanta, by Horton Foote
1995–96—Rent, by Jonathan Larson
1996–97—No award
1997–98—How I Learned to Drive, by Paula Vogel
1998–99—Wit, by Margaret Edson
1999–00—Dinner With Friends, by Donald Margulies

TONY AWARDS

The American Theater Wing's 54th annual Tony (Antoinette Perry) Awards are presented in recognition of distinguished achievement in the Broadway Theater. The League of American Theaters and Producers and the American Theater Wing present these awards, founded by the Wing in 1947. Legitimate theater productions opening in 37 eligible Broadway theaters during the present Tony season—April 28, 1999 to May 3, 2000—were considered by the Tony Awards Nominating Committee (appointed by the Tony Awards Administration Committee) for the awards in 21 regular and several special categories. The 1999–2000 Nominating Committee comprised Billie Allen, actress and director; Lisa Aronson, scenic designer; Mary Schmidt Campbell, educator; John Cunningham, actor; Merle Debuskey, publicist; Jerry Dominus, executive; Henry Guettel, administrator; Carol Hall, composer and lyricist; Geraldine Hammerstein, actress and writer; Jay Harnick, artistic director; Sheldon Harnick, lyricist; Allen Lee Hughes, lighting designer; Betty Jacobs, script consultant; Jack Lee, musical director; Stuart Little, writer and editor; Thomas Meehan, librettist; Joanna Merlin, actress and casting director; Jon Nakagawa, administrator; Peter Neufeld, general manager; Estelle Parsons, actress; Shirley Rich, casting director; Frances Sternhagen, actress; Arnold Weinstein, educator, and George White, artistic director.

The Tony Awards are voted from the list of nominees by members of the theater and journalism professions: the governing boards of the five theater artists' organizations—Actors' Equity Association, the Dramatists Guild, the Society of Stage Directors and Choreographers, the United Scenic Artists and the Casting Society of America—the members of the designated first night theater press, the board of directors of the American Theater Wing and the membership of the League of American Theaters and Producers. Because of fluctuation in these groups, the size of the Tony electorate varies from year to year. For the 1999–2000 season there were 705 qualified Tony voters.

The list of 1999–2000 nominees follows, with winners in each category listed in **bold face type**.

BEST PLAY (award goes to both author and producer). ***Copenhagen*** by **Michael Frayn,** produced by **Michael Codron, Lee Dean, The Royal National Theater, James M. Nederlander, Roger Berlind, Scott Rudin, Elizabeth I. McCann, Ray Larsen, Jon B. Platt, Byron Goldman, Scott Nederlander.** *Dirty Blonde* by Claudia Shear, produced by The Shubert Organization, Chase Mishkin, Ostar Enterprises, ABC Inc., New York Theater Workshop. *The Ride Down Mt. Morgan* by Arthur Miller, produced by The Shubert Organization, Scott Rudin, Roger Berlind, Spring Sirkin, ABC Inc., The Joseph Papp Public Theater/New York Shakespeare Festival/ George C. Wolfe. *True West* by Sam Shepard, produced by Ron Kastner.

BEST MUSICAL (award goes to the producer). ***Contact*** produced by **Lincoln Center Theater, Andre Bishop, Bernard Gersten.** *James Joyce's The Dead* produced by Gregory Mosher, Arielle Tepper, Playwrights Horizons, Tim Sanford. *Swing!* produced by Marc Routh, Richard Frankel, Steven Baruch, Tom Viertel, Lorie Cowen Levy/Stanley Shopkorn, Jujamcyn Theaters, BB Promotion, Dede Harris/Jeslo Productions, Libby Adler Mages/Mari Glick, Douglas L.

Meyer/James D. Stern, PACE Theatrical Group/SFX. *The Wild Party* produced by The Joseph Papp Public Theater/New York Shakespeare Festival, George C. Wolfe, Scott Rudin/Paramount Pictures, Roger Berlind, Williams/Waxman.

BEST BOOK OF A MUSICAL. *Contact* by John Weidman, ***James Joyce's The Dead*** by **Richard Nelson,** *Marie Christine* by Michael John LaChiusa, *The Wild Party* by Michael John LaChiusa and George C. Wolfe.

BEST ORIGINAL SCORE (music & lyrics) WRITTEN FOR THE THEATER. ***Aida,*** music by **Elton John,** lyrics by **Tim Rice;** *James Joyce's The Dead,* music by Shaun Davey, lyrics by Richard Nelson and Shaun Davey; *Marie Christine,* music and lyrics by Michael John LaChiusa; *The Wild Party,* music and lyrics by Michael John LaChiusa.

BEST REVIVAL OF A PLAY (award goes to the producer). *Amadeus,* produced by Kim Poster, PW Productions, Adam Epstein, SFX Theatrical Group, Center Theater Group/ Ahmanson Theater, Back Row Productions, Old Ivy Productions. *A Moon for the Misbegotten,* produced by Elliot Martin, Chase Mishkin, Max Cooper, Jujamcyn Theaters, Anita Waxman, Elizabeth Williams, The Goodman Theater. *The Price,* produced by David Richenthal. ***The Real Thing,*** produced by **Anita Waxman, Elizabeth Williams, Ron Kastner, Miramax Films, The Donmar Warehouse.**

BEST REVIVAL OF A MUSICAL (award goes to the producer). *Jesus Christ Superstar,* produced by The Really Useful Superstar Company Inc., The Nederlander Producing Company of America Inc., Terry Allen Kramer. ***Kiss Me, Kate,*** produced by **Roger Berlind, Roger Horchow.** *The Music Man,* produced by Dodger Theatricals, The John F. Kennedy Center for the Performing Arts, Elizabeth Williams/Anita Waxman, Kardana Swinsky Productions, Lorie Cowen Levy/ Dede Harris. *Tango Argentino,* produced by DG Producciones.

BEST PERFORMANCE BY A LEADING ACTOR IN A PLAY. Gabriel Byrne in *A Moon for the Misbegotten,* **Stephen Dillane** in *The Real Thing,* Philip Seymour Hoffmann and John C. Reilly in *True West,* David Suchet in *Amadeus.*

BEST PERFORMANCE BY A LEADING ACTRESS IN A PLAY. Jayne Atkinson in *The Rainmaker,* **Jennifer Ehle** in *The Real Thing,* Rosemary Harris in *Waiting in the Wings,* Cherry Jones in *A Moon for the Misbegotten,* Claudia Shear in *Dirty Blonde.*

BEST PERFORMANCE BY A LEADING ACTOR IN A MUSICAL. Craig Bierko in *The Music Man,* George Hearn in *Putting It Together,* **Brian Stokes Mitchell** in *Kiss Me, Kate,* Mandy Patankin in *The Wild Party,* Christopher Walken in *James Joyce's The Dead.*

BEST PERFORMANCE BY A LEADING ACTRESS IN A MUSICAL. Toni Collette in *The Wild Party,* **Heather Headley** in *Aida,* Rebecca Luker in *The Music Man,* Marin Mazzie in *Kiss Me,Kate,* Audra McDonald in *Marie Christine.*

BEST PERFORMANCE BY A FEATURED ACTOR IN A PLAY. Kevin Chamberlin and Bob Stillman in *Dirty Blonde,* Daniel Davis in *Wrong Mountain,* **Roy Dotrice** in *A Moon for the Misbegotten,* Derek Smith in *The Green Bird.*

BEST PERFORMANCE BY A FEATURED ACTRESS IN A PLAY. **Blair Brown** in *Copenhagen,* Frances Conroy in *The Ride Down Mt. Morgan,* Amy Ryan in *Uncle Vanya,* Helen Stenborg in *Waiting in the Wings,* Sarah Woodward in *The Real Thing.*

BEST PERFORMANCE BY A FEATURED ACTOR IN A MUSICAL. Michael Berresse, Michael Mulheren and Lee Wilkof in *Kiss Me, Kate,* **Boyd Gaines** in *Contact,* Stephen Spinella in *James Joyce's The Dead.*

BEST PERFORMANCE BY A FEATURED ACTRESS IN A MUSICAL. Laura Benanti and Ann Hampton Callaway in *Swing!,* Eartha Kitt in *The Wild Party,* Deborah Yates and **Karen Ziemba** in *Contact.*

BEST DIRECTION OF A PLAY. **Michael Blakemore** for *Copenhagen,* James Lapine

THE REAL THING—Stephen Dillane and Jennifer Ehle, both Tony winners for best leading performer, in a scene from their Tom Stoppard play, the winner for best revival

for *Dirty Blonde*, David Leveaux for *The Real Thing*, Matthew Warchus for *True West*.

BEST DIRECTION OF A MUSICAL. **Michael Blakemore** for *Kiss Me, Kate*, Susan Stroman for *Contact* and *The Music Man*, Lynne Taylor-Corbett for *Swing!*

BEST SCENIC DESIGN. **Bob Crowley** for *Aida*, Thomas Lynch for *The Music Man*, Robin Wagner for *Kiss Me, Kate*, Tony Walton for *Uncle Vanya*.

BEST COSTUME DESIGN. Bob Crowley for *Aida*, Constance Hoffmann for *The Green Bird*, William Ivey Long for *The Music Man*, **Martin Pakledinaz** for *Kiss Me, Kate*.

BEST LIGHTING DESIGN. Jules Fisher and Peggy Eisenhauer for *The Wild Party* and *Marie Christine*, Peter Kaczorowski for *Kiss Me, Kate*, **Natasha Katz** for *Aida*.

BEST CHOREOGRAPHY. Kathleen Marshall for *Kiss Me, Kate*, **Susan Stroman** for ***Contact*** and *The Music Man*, Lynne Taylor-Corbett for *Swing!*.

BEST ORCHESTRATIONS. Douglas Besterman for *The Music Man*, **Don Sebesky** for *Kiss Me, Kate*, Jonathan Tunick for *Marie Christine*, Harold Wheeler for *Swing!*.

SPECIAL TONY AWARDS. Live theatrical event: ***Dame Edna: The Royal Tour.*** Lifetime achievement in the theater: **T. Edward Hambleton,** founder of the Phoenix Theater.

TONY HONORS. For excellence in theater. **Eileen Heckart,** actress. **Sylvia Herscher,** agent and manager. ***Encores! Great American Musicals in Concert.***

REGIONAL THEATER. To a regional theater company that has displayed a continuous level of artistic achievement contributing to the growth of the theater nationally, recommended by the American Theater Critics Association: **The Utah Shakespearean Festival,** Cedar City, Utah.

TONY AWARD WINNERS, 1947–2000

Listed below are the Antoinette Perry (Tony) Award winners in the catgories of Best Play and Best Musical from the time these awards were established until the present.

1947—No play or musical award
1948—Mister Roberts; no musical award
1949—Death of a Salesman; Kiss Me, Kate
1950—The Cocktail Party; South Pacific
1951—The Rose Tattoo; Guys and Dolls
1952—The Fourposter; The King and I
1953—The Crucible; Wonderful Town
1954—The Teahouse of the August Moon; Kismet
1955—The Desperate Hours; The Pajama Game
1956—The Diary of Anne Frank; Damn Yankees
1957—Long Day's Journey Into Night; My Fair Lady
1958—Sunrise at Campobello; The Music Man
1959—J.B.; Redhead
1960—The Miracle Worker; Fiorello! and The Sound of Music (tie)
1961—Becket; Bye Bye Birdie
1962—A Man for All Seasons; How to Succeed in Business Without Really Trying
1963—Who's Afraid of Virginia Woolf?; A Funny Thing Happened on the Way to the Forum
1964—Luther; Hello, Dolly!
1965—The Subject Was Roses; Fiddler on the Roof
1966—The Persecution and Assassination of Marat as Performed by the Inmates of the Asylum of Charenton Under the Direction of the Marquis de Sade; Man of La Mancha
1967—The Homecoming; Cabaret
1968—Rosencrantz and Guildenstern Are Dead; Hallelujah, Baby!
1969—The Great White Hope; 1776
1970—Borstal Boy; Applause
1971—Sleuth; Company
1972—Sticks and Bones; Two Gentlemen of Verona
1973—That Championship Season; A Little Night Music
1974—The River Niger; Raisin
1975—Equus; The Wiz
1976—Travesties; A Chorus Line
1977—The Shadow Box; Annie
1978—Da; Ain't Misbehavin'
1979—The Elephant Man; Sweeney Todd, the Demon Barber of Fleet Street
1980—Children of a Lesser God; Evita
1981—Amadeus; 42nd Street
1982—The Life & Adventures of Nicholas Nickleby; Nine
1983—Torch Song Trilogy; Cats
1984—The Real Thing; La Cage aux Folles
1985—Biloxi Blues; Big River
1986—I'm Not Rappaport; The Mystery of Edwin Drood
1987—Fences; Les Misérables
1988—M. Butterfly; The Phantom of the Opera
1989—The Heidi Chronicles; Jerome Robbins' Broadway
1990—The Grapes of Wrath; City of Angels
1991—Lost in Yonkers; The Will Rogers Follies
1992—Dancing at Lughnasa; Crazy for You
1993—Angels in America, Part I: Millennium Approaches; Kiss of the Spider Woman
1994—Angels in America, Part II: Perestroika; Passion
1995—Love! Valour! Compassion!; Sunset Boulevard
1996—Master Class; Rent
1997—The Last Night of Ballyhoo; Titanic
1998—Art; The Lion King
1999—Side Man; Fosse
2000—Copenhagen; Contact

LUCILLE LORTEL AWARDS

The Lucille Lortel Awards for outstanding off-Broadway achievement were established in 1985 by a resolution of the League of Off-Broadway Theaters and Producers, which administers them and has presented them annually since 1986. Eligible for the 15th annual awards in 2000 were all off-Broadway productions which opened between March 31, 1999 and March 31, 2000 except any which had moved from an off-Broadway to a Broadway theater at the time of the selection. Winners were selected by a committee comprising Clive Barnes, Peter Filichia, John Heilpern, Charles Isherwood, Alvin Klein, Michael Kuchwara, Ken Mandelbaum, Emily Nunn, Donald Saddler, John Simon, Anna Strasberg, Sam Whitehead, John Willis and Linda Winer.

PLAY. ***Dinner With Friends*** by Donald Margulies.

MUSICAL. ***James Joyce's The Dead*** adapted by Richard Nelson from James Joyce's story, music by Shaun Davey, lyrics conceived and adapted by Richard Nelson and Shaun Davey.

REVIVAL. ***The Torch-Bearers*** by George Kelly, produced by The Drama Dept.

ACTOR. **Boyd Gaines** in *Contact.*

ACTRESS. **Eileen Heckart** in *The Waverly Gallery.*

DIRECTION. **Susan Stroman** for *Contact.*

SCENERY. **David Gallo** for *The Wild Party.*

COSTUMES. **Martin Pakledinaz** for *The Wild Party* and *Waste.*

LIGHTING. **Kenneth Posner** for *The Wild Party* and *Give Me Your Answer, Do!*

BODY OF WORK. **Eileen Heckart.**

LIFETIME ACHIEVEMENT. **Jason Robards.**

EDITH OLIVER AWARD. **Barry Grove.**

LORTEL AWARD WINNERS, 1986–2000

Listed below are the Lucille Lortel Award winners in the categories of Outstanding Play and Outstanding Musical from the time these awards were established until the present.

1986—Woza Africa!; no musical award
1987—The Common Pursuit; no musical award
1988—No play or musical award
1989—The Cocktail Hour; no musical award
1990—No play or musical award
1991—Aristocrats; Falsettoland
1992—Lips Together, Teeth Apart; And the World Goes 'Round
1993—The Destiny of Me; Forbidden Broadway
1994—Three Tall Women; Wings
1995—Camping With Henry & Tom; Jelly Roll!
1996—Molly Sweeney; Floyd Collins
1997—How I Learned to Drive; Violet
1998—Gross Indecency, and The Beauty Queen of Leenane (tie); no musical award
1999—Wit; no musical award
2000—Dinner With Friends; James Joyce's The Dead

ATCA PRINCIPAL CITATIONS AND NEW PLAY AWARD WINNERS, 1976–1999

Beginning with the season of 1976–77, the American Theater Critics Association (ATCA) has cited one or more outstanding new plays in cross-country theater; the principal ones, listed below, to be presented in script excerpts in *Best Plays* and—since 1985—to receive the ATCA New Play Award, in 2000 renamed the ATCA/Steinberg New Play Award (see the complete listing of 1999 ATCA citations in The Season Around the United States section of this volume).

1976—And the Soul Shall Dance, by Wakako Yamauchi
1977—Getting Out, by Marsha Norman
1978—Loose Ends, by Michael Weller
1979—Custer, by Robert E. Ingham
1980—Chekhov in Yalta, by John Driver and Jeffrey Haddow
1981—Talking With, by Jane Martin
1982—Closely Related, by Bruce MacDonald
1983—Wasted, by Fred Gamel
1984—Scheherazade, by Marisha Chamberlain
1985—Fences, by August Wilson
1986—A Walk in the Woods, by Lee Blessing
1987—Heathen Valley, by Romulus Linney
1988—The Piano Lesson, by August Wilson
1989—2, by Romulus Linney
1990—Two Trains Running, by August Wilson
1991—Could I Have This Dance?, by Doug Haverty
1992—Children of Paradise: Shooting a Dream, by Steven Epp, Felicity Jones, Dominique Serrand and Paul Walsh
1993—Keely and Du, by Jane Martin
1994—The Nanjing Race, by Reggie Cheong-Leen
1995—Amazing Grace, by Michael Cristofer
1996—Jack and Jill, by Jane Martin
1997—The Cider House Rules, Part II, by Peter Parnell
1998—Book of Days, by Lanford Wilson.
1999—Oo-Bla-Dee, by Regina Taylor

ADDITIONAL PRIZES AND AWARDS, 1999–2000

The following is a list of major prizes and awards for achievement in the theater this season. In all cases the names of winners appear in **bold face type**.

19th ANNUAL WILLIAM INGE FESTIVAL AWARD. For distinguished achievement in American theater. **A.R. Gurney.** New voice: **James Still.**

22d ANNUAL KENNEDY CENTER HONORS. For distinguished achievement by individuals who have made significant contributions to American culture through the arts. **Victor Borge, Sean Connery, Judith Jameson, Jason Robards, Stevie Wonder.**

3d ANNUAL KENNEDY CENTER-MARK TWAIN PRIZE. For American humor. **Carl Reiner.**

1999 NATIONAL MEDALS OF THE ARTS. For individuals and organizations who have made outstanding contributions to the excellence, growth, support and availability of the arts in the United States, selected by the President from nominees presented by the National Endowment. **Aretha Franklin, Harvey Lichtenstein, Odetta, The Juilliard School, Norman Lear, Rosetta LeNoire, Lydia Mendoza, Maria Tallchief.**

1999 ELIZABETH HULL-KATE WARRINER AWARD. To the playwright whose work dealt with controversial subjects involving the fields of political, religious or social mores of the time, selected by the Dramatists Guild Council. **Donald Margulies** for *Dinner With Friends.*

2000 HEWES DESIGN AWARDS (formerly American Theater Wing Design Awards). For design originating in the U.S., selected by a committee comprising Tish Dace (chairman), Mario Fratti, Mel Gussow, Henry Hewes, Jeffrey Eric Jenkins, and Joan Ungaro. Scenic design: **David Gallo** for *Jitney* and Manhattan Theater Club's *The Wild Party.* Costume design: **William Ivey**

Long for *Contact, The Music Man* and *Swing!*. Lighting design: **Peter Kaczorowski** for *Contact, Kiss Me, Kate* and *The Music Man.* Noteworthy unusual effect: **Steve O'Hearn** for the sets, puppets and costumes for *Squonk.*

22d ANNUAL SUSAN SMITH BLACKBURN PRIZE. For women who have written works of outstanding quality for the English-speaking theater. **Bridget Carpenter** for *Fall.*

GEORGE FREEDLEY MEMORIAL AWARD. For the best book about live theater published in the United States the previous year. ***Edward Albee: A Singular Journey: A Biography*** by **Mel Gussow.**

19th ANNUAL ASTAIRE AWARDS. For excellence in dance and choreography, administered by the Theater Development Fund and selected by a committee comprising Douglas Watt, Clive Barnes, Howard Kissel, Michael Kuchwara, Donald McDonagh, Richard Philp, Charles L. Reinhart and Linda Winer. Choreography: **Susan Stroman** for *Contact* and *The Music Man.* Female dancer: **Deborah Yates** in *Contact.* Male dancer: **Clyde Alves** in *The Music Man.*

2000 RICHARD RODGERS AWARDS. For production and staged reading of musicals in nonprofit theaters, administered by the American Academy of Arts and Letters and selected by a jury of its musical theater members comprising Stephen Sondheim (chairman), Lynn Ahrens, Jack Beeson, John Guare, Sheldon Harnick, R.W.B. Lewis, Richard Maltby Jr., Francis Thorne and Robert Ward. Richard Rodgers Production Awards: ***Bat Boy*** by Brian Flemming and Laurence O'Keefe; ***The Bubbly Black Girl Sheds Her Chameleon Skin*** by Kirsten Childs. Richard Rodgers Development Award: ***Suburb*** by Robert S. Cohen and David Javerbaum.

JOE A. CALLAWAY AWARD for excellence in the craft of direction, presented by the Stage Directors and Choreographers Foundation. **Trevor Nunn** for *Not About Nightingales.*

1999 GEORGE AND ELISABETH MARTON AWARD. To an American playwright, selected by a committee of Young Playwrights Inc. **Diana Son** for *Stop Kiss.*

65th ANNUAL DRAMA LEAGUE AWARDS. For distinguished achievement in the American theater. Play: ***Copenhagen***. Musical: ***Contact***. Revival of a play or musical: ***Kiss Me, Kate***. Distinguished performance: ***Eileen Heckart***.

2000 GEORGE OPPENHEIMER AWARD. To the best new American playwright, presented by *Newsday.* **Margaret Edson** for *Wit.*

2000 NEW DRAMATISTS LIFETIME ACHIEVEMENT AWARD. To an individual who has made an outstanding artistic contribution to the American theater. **Angela Lansbury.**

11th ANNUAL OSCAR HAMMERSTEIN AWARD. For lifetime achievement in musical theater. **John Kander** and **Fred Ebb.**

2000 *THEATER WORLD* AWARDS. For outstanding debut performers on Broadway or off Broadway during the 1999–2000 season, selected by a committee comprising John Willis, Clive Barnes, Peter Filichia, Alexis Greene, Harry Haun, Frank Scheck, Michael Sommers and Douglas Watt. **Craig Bierko** in *The Music Man,* **Everett Bradley** and **Ann Hampton Callaway** in *Swing!,* **Gabriel Byrne** in *A Moon for the Misbegotten,* **Toni Collette** in *The Wild Party,* **Henry Czerny** in *Arms and the Man,* **Stephen Dillane** and **Jennifer Ehle** in *The Real Thing,* **Philip Seymour Hoffman** in *True West,* **Hayley Mills** in *Noel Coward's Suite in 2 Keys,* **Cigdem Onat** in *The Time of the Cuckoo,* **Claudia Shear** in *Dirty Blonde.*

45th ANNUAL DRAMA DESK AWARDS. For outstanding achievement in the 1999–2000 season, voted by an association of New York drama reporters, editors and critics from nominations made by a committee. New play: ***Copenhagen***. New Musical: ***Contact.*** Revival of a play: ***The Real Thing.*** Revival of a musical: ***Kiss Me, Kate.*** Composer: **Andrew Lippa** for ***The Wild Party.*** Lyricist: **Stephen Sondheim** for ***Saturday Night.*** Actor in a play: **Stephen Dillane** in *The Real Thing.* Actress in a play: **Eileen Heckart** in *The Waverly Gallery.* Featured actor in a play: **Roy Dotrice** in *A Moon for the Misbegotten.* Featured actress in a play: **Marylouise Burke** in *Fuddy Meers.* Actor in a musical: **Brian Stokes Mitchell** in *Kiss Me, Kate.* Actress in a musical: **Heather Headley** in *Aida.* Featured actor in a musical: **Stephen Spinella** in *James Joyce's The Dead.* Featured actress in a musical: **Karen Ziemba** in *Contact.* Solo performance: **Barry Humphries** in ***Dame Edna: The Royal Tour.*** Director of a play: **Michael Blakemore** for *Copenhagen.* Director of a musical: **Michael Blakemore** for *Kiss Me, Kate.* Choreography: **Susan Stroman** for *Contact.* Orchestrations: **Don Sebesky** for *Kiss Me, Kate.* Set design of a play: **David Gallo** for *Jitney.* Set design of a musical: **Robin Wagner** for *Kiss Me, Kate.* Costume design: **Martin Pakledinaz** for *Kiss Me, Kate.* Lighting design: **Peter Kaczorowski** for *Contact.* Sound design: **Jamie Mereness** for *Charlie Victor Romeo.* Music in a play: **Jeanine Tesori** for *Twelfth Night.* Solo performance: **David Hare** in *Via Dolorosa.* Unique theatrical experience: ***Charlie Victor Romeo.***

50th ANNUAL OUTER CRITICS CIRCLE AWARDS. For outstanding achievement in the 1999–2000 season, voted by critics on out-of-town periodicals and media. Broadway play: ***Copenhagen***. Off-Broadway play: ***Dinner With Friends.*** Revival of a play: ***A Moon for the Misbegotten.*** Actor in a play: **Derek Jacobi** in *Uncle Vanya.* Actress in a play: **Eileen Heckart** in *The Waverly Gallery.* Featured actor in a play: **Roy Dotrice** in *A Moon for the Misbegotten.* Featured actress in a play: **Frances Conroy** in *The Ride Down Mt. Morgan.* Director of a play: **Daniel Sullivan** for *A Moon for the Misbegotten* and *Dinner With Friends.* Broadway musical: ***Contact***. Off-Broadway musical: ***The Wild Party.*** Revival of a musical: ***Kiss Me, Kate.*** Actor in a musical: **Brian Stokes Mitchell** in *Kiss Me, Kate.* Actress in a musical: **Marin Mazzie** in *Kiss Me, Kate.* Featured actor in a musical: **Stephen Spinella** in *James Joyce's The Dead.* Featured actress in a musical: **Karen Ziemba** in *Contact.* Director of a musical: **Susan Stroman** for *Contact* and *The Music Man.* Choreography: **Susan Stroman** for *Contact* and *The Music Man.* Scenic design: **Robin Wagner** for *Kiss Me, Kate.* Costume design: **Constance Hoffman** for *The Green Bird.* Lighting design: **Peter Kaczorowski** for *Contact.* Solo performance: **Olympia Dukakis** in *Rose* and **Mark Setlock** in *Fully Committed* (tie). John Gassner Playwriting Award: **Charles Busch** for *The Tale of the Allergist's Wife.* Special Achievement Award: **Barry Humphries** for *Dame Edna: The Royal Tour;* **Philip Seymour Hoffman** and **John C. Reilly** for *True West.*

45th ANNUAL *VILLAGE VOICE* OBIE AWARDS. For outstanding achievement in off- and off-off-Broadway theater. Playwriting: **Harley Granville-Barker** for *Waste.* Production: **Ben Katcho, Michael Gordon, David Lang, Julia Wolfe, Bob McGrath** for ***The Carbon Copy Building.*** Sustained achievement: **Ping Chong.** Performance: **Colm Meaney** in *The Cider House Rules, Part I,* **Lynne Thigpen** in *Jar the Floor,* **Elizabeth Marvel** and **Christopher Evan Welch** in *A Streetcar Named Desire,* **Charlayne Woodard** in *In the Blood,* **Lola Pashalinski** in *Gertrude and Alice,* **Dominique Dibbell** in *Jet Lag,* **Cynthia Hopkins** in *Another Telepathic Thing,* **Debra Monk** for *The Time of the Cuckoo,* **Eddie Korbich** for *Taking a Chance on Love,* **Byron Jennings** for *Waste,* **Eileen Heckart** for *The Waverly Gallery.* Ensemble performance: **The Cast** of *Jitney.* Direction: **Marion McClinton** for *Jitney.* Design: **Jan Hartley** for sustained excellence of projection design, **Mark Dendy** for *The Wild Party,* **Christopher Akerlind** for sustained excellence of lighting design, **David Gallo** for sustained excellence of set design, **Susan Hilferty** for sustained excellence of costume design.

Special citations: **Jan Lauwers/Needcompany** for *Morning Song,* **Sarah E. Johnson** for *Lava Love,* **Joe Mantello** and **Marc Wolf** for *Another American: Asking and Telling,* **The Builders Assn.** and **Diller + Scofidio** for *Jet Lag,* **Jesusa Rodriguez** and **Liliana Felipe** for *Las Horas de Belen—A Book of Hours,* **Bill Talen** for *The Reverend Billy,* **Maria Irene Fornes** for *Letters From Cuba,* **Deb Margolin** for sustained excellence of performance. Grants: **The Foundry** (The Ross Wetzsteon Grant), **Big Dance Theater, Circus Amok, Five Myles.**

10th ANNUAL CONNECTICUT CRITICS CIRCLE AWARDS. For outstanding achievement in Connecticut theater during the 1999–2000 season. Production of a play: **Hartford Stage** for *Enchanted April.* Production of a musical: **Downtown Cabaret Theater** for *Guys and Dolls.* Actress in a play: **Tovah Feldshuh** in *Tallulah Tonight.* Actor in a play: **Frank Ferrante** in *Groucho.* Actress in a musical: **Amy Eschman** in *Guys and Dolls.* Actor in a musical: **Anthony Santelmo Jr.** in *Guys and Dolls.* Direction of a play: **Michael Wilson** for *Camino Real* and *Enchanted April.* Direction of a musical: **Jamie Rocco** for *Guys and Dolls.* Choreography: **Stephen Terrell** for *No, No, Nanette.* Set design: **Ed Spires** for *The Beauty Queen of Leenane.* Lighting design: **Rui Rita** for *Enchanted April.* Costume design: **Jess Goldstein** for *Enchanted April.* Sound design: **John Gromada** for *Camino Real* and *Enchanted April.* Ensemble performance: **Starla Benford, Kim Gainer** and **Tonye Patano** in *From the Mississippi Delta.* Roadshow: **The Bushnell** for *Ragtime.*

Debut Award: **Kirsten Wyatt** in *Dames at Sea.* Lifetime Achievement Award for an innovative concept: **Long Wharf Theater** in association with **Cornerstone Theater Co.** for *The Good Person of New Haven.* Tom Killen Memorial Award: **Cory** and **Bob Donnalley**.

18th ANNUAL ELLIOT NORTON AWARDS. For outstanding contribution to the theater in Boston, voted by a Boston Theater Critics Association Selections Committee comprising Skip Ascheim, Terry Byrne, Carolyn Clay, Iris Fanger, Arthur Friedman, Joyce Kulhawik, Jon Lehman, Bill Marx, Ed Siegel and Caldwell Titcomb. Productions—Visiting company: ***Wit;*** Large resident company: ***Mary Stuart*** by Huntington Theater Company; Small resident company: ***The Old Settler*** by Lyric Stage Company; Local fringe company: ***St. Nicholas*** by Súgán Theater Company. Solo performance: **John Kuntz** in *Starfuckers.* Actor—Large company: **Will LeBow** in *Full Circle;* Small company: **Richard McElvain** in *St. Nicholas.* Actress—Large company: **Judith Light** in *Wit;* Small company: **Jacqui Parker** in *The Old Settler.* Musical performance: **Bridget Beirne** in *Violet.* Director—Large company: **Robert Woodruff** for *Full Circle;* Small company: **Rick Lombardo** for *Rosencrantz and Guildernstern Are Dead.* Designer: **Howard Jones** for *Cloud Tectonics.*

Special citations: **Arts/Boston Inc.** for 25 years of wide-ranging service to local theater companies and patrons. **Boston Theater Marathon** for enlivening local theater through the annual showcase of short plays at the Boston Playwrights' Theater.

15th ANNUAL HELEN HAYES AWARDS. In recognition of excellence in Washington, D.C. theater, presented by the Washington Theater Awards Society.

Resident productions—Play: ***Indian Ink*** produced by The Studio Theater. Musical: ***Animal Crackers*** produced by Arena Stage. Lead actress, musical: **Anne Kanengeiser** in *Eleanor: An American Love Story.* Lead actor, musical: **Anthony Cummings** in *Eleanor: An American Love Story.* Lead actress, play: **Isabel Keating** in *Indian Ink.* Lead actor, play: **Rick Foucheux** in *Edmond.* Supporting performer, musical: **Christopher Michael Bauer** in *Slam!.* Supporting actress, play: **June Hansen** in *Indian Ink.* Supporting actor, play: **Christopher Lane** in *Equus.* Director, play: **Joy Zinoman** for *Indian Ink.* Director, musical: **Douglas C. Wager** for *Animal Crackers.* Set design, play or musical: **Daniel Conway** for *Ambrosio.* Costume design, play or musical: **Helen Q. Huang** for *Indian Ink.* Lighting design, play or musical: **Jay A. Herzog** for *Ambrosio.* Sound design, play or musical: **Gil Thompson** and **Ronobir Lahiri** for *Indian Ink.* Musical direction, play or musical: **Kevin Campbell** for *The Dark Kalamazoo.* Choreography: **Irina Tsikurishvili** for *The Idiot.*

Non-resident productions—Production: ***Cabaret*** produced by The Warner Theater. Lead actress: **Angelica Torn** in *Side Man.* Lead actor: **Norbert Leo Butz** in *Cabaret.* Supporting performer: **Dick Latessa** in *Cabaret.* Charles MacArthur Award for outstanding new play: ***The Sins of Sor Juana*** by Karen Zacarias. American Express Tribute: **August Wilson.** KPMG Award for distinguished service to the Washington theater community: **Sunoco.** Washington *Post* Award for distinguished community service: **Winfred** and **Norman Portenoy** of the Max and Victoria Dreyfus Foundation.

31st ANNUAL JOSEPH JEFFERSON AWARDS. For achievement in Chicago theater during the 1998–99 season, selected by the Jefferson Awards Committee from 117 Equity productions offered by 50 producing organizations. Resident productions—New work: *Spinning Into Butter* by **Rebecca Gilman.** New Adaptation: *Metamorphoses* by **Mary Zimmerman.** Production of a play: **The Goodman Theater's** *Death of a Salesman.* Production of a musical: **Drury Lane Theater's** *La Cage aux Folles.* Production of a revue: **Drury Lane Theater's** *All Night Strut.* Director of a play: **Robert Falls** for *Death of a Salesman.* Director of a musical: **Marc Robin** for *La Cage aux Folles.* Director of a revue: **Marc Robin** for *All Night Strut.* Actor in a principal role, play: **Brian Dennehy** in *Death of a Salesman.* Actress in a principal role, play: **Carmen Roman** in *Master Class.* Actor in a supporting role, play: **Yasen Peyankov** in *Morning Star.* Actress in a supporting role, play: **Elizabeth Franz** in *Death of a Salesman.* Actor in principal role, musical: **James Hamms** in *La Cage aux Folles.* Actress in a principal role, musical: **Kathy Voytko** in *Crazy for You.* Actor in a supporting role, musical: **Guy Adkins** in *Floyd Collins.* Actress in a supporting role, musical: **Peggy Roeder** in *The Wizard of Oz.* Actor in a revue: **John Steven Crowley** in *Elvis Presley Was a Black Man.* Actress in a revue: **Hollis Resnik** in *Songs for a New World.* Ensemble: ***Are You Now or Have You Ever Been . . . ?*** Scenic design: **Stephanie Nelson** for *The Cut.* Costume design: **Virgil Johnson** for *Henry IV, Parts 1 & 2.* Lighting design, **T.J. Gerckens** for *Metamorphoses.* Sound design: **Lindsay Jones** for *Old Wicked Songs.* Choreography: **Sylvia Hernandez-DiStasi** for *The Baron in the Trees.* Original music: **Alaric Jans** for *Henry IV, Parts 1 & 2.* Musical direction: **Terry James** for *All Night Strut.* Non-resident productions—Production: **Pace Theatrical Group/SFX Entertainment's** *Ragtime.* Actor in a principal role: **Norbert Leo Butz** in *Cabaret.* Actress in a principal role: **Donna Bullock** in *Ragtime.* Actor in a supporting role: **Roger Bart** in *You're a Good Man, Charlie Brown.* Actress in a supporting role: **Kristin Chenoweth** in *You're a Good Man, Charlie Brown.*

Special Awards—**Chicago Shakespeare Theater** for combined vision and leadership resulting in the establishment of the company's landmark new home, the Chicago Shakespeare Theater on Navy Pier. **Joseph Drummond,** in recognition of his 25th anniversary with the Goodman Theater, through whose leadership and dedication to the artistic intentions of each production as stage manager has helped to make excellence in Chicago theater possible.

27th ANNUAL JOSEPH JEFFERSON CITATIONS WING AWARDS. For outstanding achievement in professional productions during the 1999–2000 season of Chicago area theaters not operating under union contracts. Productions: *The Crime of the Century* by **Circle Theater**, *A View From the Bridge* by **Raven Theater Company.** Ensembles: ***Laughter on the 23rd Floor, Lebens-***

raum, Stupid Kids. Directors: **Greg Kolack** for *The Crime of the Century,* **Michael Menendian** for *A View From the Bridge.* New work: **Penny Penniston** for *Now Then Again,* **David Rush** for *Police Deaf Near Far*. New adaptation: **Rebecca Gilman** for *The Crime of the Century.* Actresses in principal roles: **Bethanny Alexander** in *The Cover of Life,* **Janelle Snow** in *Suddenly Last Summer,* **Seema Sueko** in *The Crime of the Century*. Actor in a principal role: **Mike Vieau** in *A View From the Bridge.* Actresses in supporting roles: **Jennifer Fisk** in *The Cover of Life,* **Sharon Gopfert** in *Lebensraum.* Actors in supporting roles: **Woody Bolar** in *Get Ready,* **Ed Cunningham** in *A View From the Bridge,* **Eric Johnson** in *Lebensraum.* Scenic design: **Kevin Hagan** for *The Lower Depths.* Costume design: **Karen Kawa** for *The Lower Depths.* Lighting design: **Michael Rourke** for *Now Then Again,* **Michelle Smietana** for *A View From the Bridge.* Sound design: **Mike Creason** for *Measure for Measure.* Choreography: **Samantha Fitschen** for *Merrily We Roll Along.* Original music: **Mike Creason** for *Measure for Measure,* **David Pavkovic** for *Rachel's Love.* Musical direction: **Eugene Dizon** for *Merrily We Roll Along,* **Thomas Murray** for *Saturday Night.*

Special award: **John Ransford Watts** for lifetime achievement.

THE THEATER HALL OF FAME

The Theater Hall of Fame was created in 1971 to honor those who have made outstanding contributions to the American theater in a career spanning at least 25 years, with at least five major credits. Members are elected annually by the nation's drama critics and editors (names of those so elected in 1999 and inducted January 31, 2000 appear in ***bold face italics***).

George Abbott
Maude Adams
Viola Adams
Stella Adler
Edward Albee
Theoni V. Aldredge
Ira Aldridge
Jane Alexander
Winthrop Ames
Judith Anderson
Maxwell Anderson
Robert Anderson
Julie Andrews
Margaret Anglin
Jean Anouilh
Harold Arlen
George Arliss
Boris Aronson
Adele Astaire
Fred Astaire
Eileen Atkins
Brooks Atkinson
Lauren Bacall
Pearl Bailey
George Balanchine
William Ball
Anne Bancroft
Tallulah Bankhead
Richard Barr
Philip Barry
Ethel Barrymore
John Barrymore
Lionel Barrymore
Nora Bayes
Samuel Beckett
Brian Bedford
S.N. Behrman
Norman Bel Geddes
David Belasco
Michael Bennett
Richard Bennett
Robert Russell Bennett
Eric Bentley
Irving Berlin
Sarah Bernhardt
Leonard Bernstein
Earl Blackwell
Kermit Bloomgarden
Jerry Bock
Ray Bolger
Edwin Booth
Junius Brutus Booth
Shirley Booth
Philip Bosco
Alice Brady
Bertolt Brecht
Fannie Brice
Peter Brook
John Mason Brown
Billie Burke
Abe Burrows
Richard Burton
Mrs. Patrick Campbell
Zoe Caldwell
Eddie Cantor
Morris Carnovsky
Mrs. Leslie Carter
Gower Champion
Frank Chanfrau
Carol Channing
Ruth Chatterton
Paddy Chayefsky
Anton Chekhov
Ina Claire
Bobby Clark
Harold Clurman
Lee J. Cobb
Richard L. Coe
George M. Cohan
Alexander H. Cohen
Jack Cole
Cy Coleman
Constance Collier
Betty Comden
Marc Connelly
Barbara Cook
Katharine Cornell
Noel Coward
Jane Cowl
Lotta Crabtree
Cheryl Crawford
Hume Cronyn
Russel Crouse
Charlotte Cushman
Jean Dalrymple
Augustin Daly
E.L. Davenport
Gordon Davidson
Ossie Davis
Ruby Dee
Alfred de Liagre Jr.
Agnes DeMille
Colleen Dewhurst
Howard Dietz
Dudley Digges
Melvyn Douglas
Eddie Dowling
Alfred Drake
Marie Dressler
John Drew
Mrs. John Drew
William Dunlap
Mildred Dunnock
Charles Durning
Eleanora Duse
Jeanne Eagels
Fred Ebb
Florence Eldridge
Lehman Engel
Maurice Evans
Abe Feder
Jose Ferrer
Cy Feuer
Zelda Fichandler
Dorothy Fields
Herbert Fields
Lewis Fields
W.C. Fields
Jules Fisher

MINNIE MADDERN FISKE
CLYDE FITCH
GERALDINE FITZGERALD
HENRY FONDA
LYNN FONTANNE
HORTON FOOTE
EDWIN FORREST
BOB FOSSE
RUDOLF FRIML
CHARLES FROHMAN
JOHN GASSNER
GRACE GEORGE
GEORGE GERSHWIN
IRA GERSHWIN
JOHN GIELGUD
W.S. GILBERT
JACK GILFORD
WILLIAM GILLETTE
CHARLES GILPIN
LILLIAN GISH
JOHN GOLDEN
MAX GORDON
RUTH GORDON
ADOLPH GREEN
PAUL GREEN
CHARLOTTE GREENWOOD
JOEL GREY
JOHN GUARE
TYRONE GUTHRIE
UTA HAGEN
LEWIS HALLAM
OSCAR HAMMERSTEIN II
WALTER HAMPDEN
OTTO HARBACH
E.Y. HARBURG
SHELDON HARNICK
EDWARD HARRIGAN
JED HARRIS
JULIE HARRIS
ROSEMARY HARRIS
SAM H. HARRIS
REX HARRISON
KITTY CARLISLE HART
LORENZ HART
MOSS HART
TONY HART
HELEN HAYES
LELAND HAYWARD
BEN HECHT
EILEEN HECKART
THERESA HELBURN
LILLIAN HELLMAN
KATHARINE HEPBURN
VICTOR HERBERT
JERRY HERMAN
JAMES A. HERNE
AL HIRSCHFELD
RAYMOND HITCHCOCK
HAL HOLBROOK
CELESTE HOLM
HANYA HOLM
ARTHUR HOPKINS
DE WOLF HOPPER
JOHN HOUSEMAN
EUGENE HOWARD
LESLIE HOWARD
SIDNEY HOWARD
WILLIE HOWARD
BARNARD HUGHES
HENRY HULL
JOSEPHINE HULL
WALTER HUSTON
EARLE HYMAN
HENRIK IBSEN
WILLIAM INGE
BERNARD B. JACOBS
ELSIE JANIS
JOSEPH JEFFERSON
AL JOLSON
JAMES EARL JONES
MARGO JONES
ROBERT EDMOND JONES
TOM JONES
RAUL JULIA
JOHN KANDER
GARSON KANIN
GEORGE S. KAUFMAN
DANNY KAYE
ELIA KAZAN
GENE KELLY
GEORGE KELLY
FANNY KEMBLE
JEROME KERN
WALTER KERR
MICHAEL KIDD
RICHARD KILEY
SIDNEY KINGSLEY
FLORENCE KLOTZ
JOSEPH WOOD KRUTCH
BERT LAHR
BURTON LANE
LAWRENCE LANGNER
LILLIE LANGTRY
ANGELA LANSBURY
CHARLES LAUGHTON
ARTHUR LAURENTS
GERTRUDE LAWRENCE
JEROME LAWRENCE
EVA LE GALLIENNE
MING CHO LEE
ROBERT E. LEE
LOTTE LENYA
ALAN JAY LERNER
SAM LEVENE
ROBERT LEWIS
BEATRICE LILLIE
HOWARD LINDSAY
FRANK LOESSER
FREDERICK LOEWE
JOSHUA LOGAN
PAULINE LORD
LUCILLE LORTEL
ALFRED LUNT
CHARLES MACARTHUR
STEELE MACKAYE
ROUBEN MAMOULIAN
RICHARD MANSFIELD
ROBERT B. MANTELL
FREDRIC MARCH
JULIA MARLOWE
ERNEST H. MARTIN
MARY MARTIN
RAYMOND MASSEY
SIOBHAN MCKENNA
TERRENCE MCNALLY
HELEN MENKEN
BURGESS MEREDITH
ETHEL MERMAN
DAVID MERRICK
JO MIELZINER
ARTHUR MILLER
MARILYN MILLER
HELENA MODJESKA
FERENC MOLNAR
LOLA MONTEZ
VICTOR MOORE
ROBERT MORSE
ZERO MOSTEL
ANNA CORA MOWATT
PAUL MUNI
THARON MUSSER
GEORGE JEAN NATHAN
MILDRED NATWICK
NAZIMOVA
JAMES M. NEDERLANDER
MIKE NICHOLS
ELLIOT NORTON
SEAN O'CASEY
CLIFFORD ODETS

DONALD OENSLAGER
LAURENCE OLIVIER
EUGENE O'NEILL
JERRY ORBACH
GERALDINE PAGE
JOSEPH PAPP
OSGOOD PERKINS
BERNADETTE PETERS
MOLLY PICON
HAROLD PINTER
LUIGI PIRANDELLO
CHRISTOPHER PLUMMER
COLE PORTER
ROBERT PRESTON
HAROLD PRINCE
JOSE QUINTERO
ELLIS RABB
JOHN RAITT
TONY RANDALL
MICHAEL REDGRAVE
ADA REHAN
ELMER RICE
LLOYD RICHARDS
RALPH RICHARDSON
CHITA RIVERA
JASON ROBARDS
JEROME ROBBINS
PAUL ROBESON
RICHARD RODGERS
WILL ROGERS
SIGMUND ROMBERG
HAROLD ROME
LILLIAN RUSSELL
DONALD SADDLER
GENE SAKS
WILLIAM SAROYAN
JOSEPH SCHILDKRAUT
HARVEY SCHMIDT
ALAN SCHNEIDER
GERALD SCHOENFELD
ARTHUR SCHWARTZ
GEORGE C. SCOTT
MARIAN SELDES
IRENE SHARAFF
GEORGE BERNARD SHAW
SAM SHEPARD
ROBERT E. SHERWOOD
J.J. SHUBERT
LEE SHUBERT
HERMAN SHUMLIN
NEIL SIMON
LEE SIMONSON
EDMUND SIMPSON
OTIS SKINNER
MAGGIE SMITH
OLIVER SMITH
STEPHEN SONDHEIM
E.H. SOTHERN
KIM STANLEY
MAUREEN STAPLETON
FRANCES STERNHAGEN
ROGER L. STEVENS
ELLEN STEWART
DOROTHY STICKNEY
FRED STONE
TOM STOPPARD
LEE STRASBERG
AUGUST STRINDBERG
ELAINE STRITCH
JULE STYNE
MARGARET SULLAVAN
ARTHUR SULLIVAN
JESSICA TANDY
LAURETTE TAYLOR
ELLEN TERRY
TOMMY TUNE
GWEN VERDON
ROBIN WAGNER
NANCY WALKER
ELI WALLACH
JAMES WALLACK
LESTER WALLACK
TONY WALTON
DOUGLAS TURNER WARD
DAVID WARFIELD
ETHEL WATERS
CLIFTON WEBB
JOSEPH WEBER
MARGARET WEBSTER
KURT WEILL
ORSON WELLES
MAE WEST
ROBERT WHITEHEAD
OSCAR WILDE
THORNTON WILDER
BERT WILLIAMS
TENNESSEE WILLIAMS
LANFORD WILSON
P.G. WODEHOUSE
PEGGY WOOD
ALEXANDER WOOLLCOTT
IRENE WORTH
TERESA WRIGHT
ED WYNN
VINCENT YOUMANS
STARK YOUNG
FLORENZ ZIEGFELD
PATRICIA ZIPPRODT

THE THEATER HALL OF FAME FOUNDERS AWARD

Established in 1993 in honor of Earl Blackwell, James M. Nederlander, Gerard Oestreicher and Arnold Weissberger, The Theater Hall of Fame Founders Award is voted by the Hall's board of directors to an individual for his or her outstanding contribution to the theater.

1993 JAMES M. NEDERLANDER
1994 KITTY CARLISLE HART
1995 HARVEY SABINSON
1996 HENRY HEWES
1997 OTIS L. GUERNSEY JR.
1998 EDWARD COLTON
1999 NO AWARD

MARGO JONES CITIZEN OF THE THEATER MEDAL

Presented annually to a citizen of the theater who has made a lifetime commitment to the encouragement of the living theater in the United States and has demonstrated an understanding and affirmation of the craft of playwriting.

1961 Lucille Lortel
1962 Michael Ellis
1963 Judith Rutherford Marechal
George Savage (University Award)
1964 Richard Barr, Edward Albee & Clinton Wilder
Richard A. Duprey (University Award)
1965 Wynn Handman
Marston Balch (University Award)
1966 Jon Jory
Arthur Ballet (University Award)
1967 Paul Baker
George C. White (Workshop Award)
1968 Davey Marlin-Jones
Ellen Stewart (Workshop Award)
1969 Adrian Hall
Edward Parone & Gordon Davidson (Workshop Award)
1970 Joseph Papp
1971 Zelda Fichandler
1972 Jules Irving
1973 Douglas Turner Ward
1974 Paul Weidner
1975 Robert Kalfin
1976 Gordon Davidson
1977 Marshall W. Mason
1978 Jon Jory
1979 Ellen Stewart
1980 John Clark Donahue
1981 Lynne Meadow
1982 Andre Bishop
1983 Bill Bushnell
1984 Gregory Mosher
1985 John Lion
1986 Lloyd Richards
1987 Gerald Chapman
1988 No Award
1989 Margaret Goheen
1990 Richard Coe
1991 Otis L. Guernsey Jr.
1992 Abbot Van Nostrand
1993 Henry Hewes
1994 Jane Alexander
1995 Robert Whitehead
1996 Al Hirschfeld
1997 George C. White
1998 James Houghton
1999 George Keathley

1999–2000 PUBLICATION OF RECENTLY-PRODUCED NEW PLAYS AND NEW TRANSLATIONS/ADAPTATIONS

American Daughter, An. Wendy Wasserstein. Harcourt Brace (cloth edition, paperback), Dramatists Play Service (acting edition).
Among Friends. Kristine Thatcher. Dramatists Play Service (acting edition).
Ancestral Voices. A. R. Gurney. Broadway Play Publishing (spiral bound).
Art. Yasmina Reza. Dramatists Play Service (paperback).
Betty's Summer Vacation. Christopher Durang. Grove Press (paperback).
Bosoms and Neglect. John Guare. Dramatists Play Service (revised acting edition).
Boy Gets Girl. Rebecca Gilman. Faber & Faber (paperback).
Captain's Daughter, The: A Memoir for the Stage. Athol Fugard TCG (paperback).
Copenhagen: Revised. Michael Frayn. Methuen (paperback).
Countess, The. Gregory Murphy. Dramatists Play Service (acting edition).
Coyote on a Fence. Bruce Graham. Dramatists Play Service (acting edition).
Darlene and The Guest Lecturer. A. R. Gurney. Broadway Play Publishing (paperback).
Dispute, The. Marivaux, translated by Neil Bartlett. Absolute Press (paperback).
Exact Change. David Epstein. Dramatists Play Service (acting edition).
Experiment With an Air Pump, An. Shelagh Stephenson. Methuen (paperback).
Eyes for Consuela. Sam Shepard. Dramatists Play Service (acting edition).
Far East. A. R. Gurney. Broadway Play Publishing (paperback).
Frank Langella's Cyrano. Frank Langella. Broadway Play Publishing (paperback).
From Above. Tom Donaghy. Dramatists Play Service (acting edition).
Give Me Your Answer, Do! Brian Friel. New American Library (paperback).
Humana Festival '99—The Complete Plays. Michael Bigelow Dixon and Amy Wegener, editors. Smith & Kraus (paperback).
Impossible Marriage. Beth Henley. Dramatists Play Service (acting edition).
Knee Desires the Dirt, The. Julie Hebert. Dramatic Publishing (acting edition).
Mineola Twins, The. Paula Vogel. Dramatists Play Service (acting edition).
Over the River and Through the Woods. Joe DiPietro. Dramatists Play Service (acting edition).
Ride Down Mt. Morgan, The. Arthur Miller. Penguin (paperback), Dramatists Play Service (acting edition).
Rose. Martin Sherman. Methuen (paperback).
Shakespeare's R & J. Joe Calarco. Dramatists Play Service (acting edition).
Spring Storm. Tennessee Williams. New Directions (paperback).
Stop Kiss. Diana Son. Overlook (paperback).
Stray Cats. Warren Leight. Dramatists Play Service (acting edition).
Stupid Kids. John C. Russell. Dramatists Play Service (acting edition).
Things You Shouldn't Say Past Midnight. Peter Ackerman. Broadway Play Publishing (paperback).
This Is Our Youth. Kenneth Lonergan. Overlook Press (paperback), Dramatists Play Service (acting edition).
2 1/2 Jews. Alan Brandt. Broadway Play Publishing (paperback).
Uneasy Chair, The. Evan Smith. Dramatists Play Service (acting edition).
Valparaiso. Don DeLillo. Simon & Schuster (paperback).
Voices in the Dark. John Pielmeier. Broadway Play Publishing (acting edition).
Walking off the Roof. Anthony Clarvoe. Broadway Play Publishing (paperback).
Y2K. Arhur Kopit. Overlook Press (paperback).

A SELECTED LIST OF OTHER PLAYS PUBLISHED IN 1999–2000

American Plays of the New Woman. Keith Newlin editor. Ivan R. Dee (paperback).
Aristophanes Two. David R. Slavitt and Palmer Bovie editors. University of Pennsylvania (paperback).

Aristophanes, Three. David R. Slavitt and Palmer Bovie editors. University of Pennsylvania (paperback).
Arthur Schnitzler: Four Major Plays. Arthur Schnitzler. Smith & Kraus (paperback).
August Strindberg: Five Major Plays. Translated by C. R. Mueller. Smith & Kraus (paperback).
Beth Henley: Collected Plays Vol. II. Beth Henley. Smith & Kraus (paperback).
Boulevard Comedies. Charles Marowitz. Smith & Kraus (paperback).
Brian Friel: Plays 2. Brian Friel. Faber & Faber (paperback).
Bungler, The. Molière, Translated by Richard Wilbur. Dramatists Play Service (acting edition).
Chorus Line, A. James Kirkwood and Nicholas Dante. Applause (cloth edition, paperback).
Collected Plays—Volume III. Horton Foote, introduction by James Houghton. Smith & Kraus (paperback).
Collected Plays: Six. Noel Coward. Methuen (paperback).
Collected Plays: Seven. Noel Coward. Methuen (paperback).
Complete Plays. Everyman Edition, The. Christopher Marlowe. Everyman's Classic (paperback).
Crowtet 1. Mac Wellman. Green Integer (paperback).
De Musset, Three Plays. Alfred De Musset, translated by Declan Donnellan and Peter Meyer. Absolute Press (paperback).
Drama for a New South Africa: 7 Plays. David Graver editor. Indiana University Press (paperback).
Eight Twentieth-Century Russian Plays. Translation and introduction by Timothy Langen and Justin Weir. Northwestern University (paperback).
Euripides, 4. Euripides. University of Pennsylvania (paperback).
Extreme Exposure. Jo Bonney editor. TCG (paperback).
Four by Sondheim. Wheeler, Lapine, Shevelove & Gelbart. Applause (libretti).
General of Hot Desire & Other Plays. John Guare. Dramatists Play Service (acting edition).
Herb Gardner: The Collected Plays. Herb Gardner. Applause (cloth edition).
Hercules. Seneca, adapted by Ranjit Bolt. Oberon (paperback).
Hollywood Pinafore. George S. Kaufman, libretto. Dramatists Play Service (acting edition).
Little Tragedies, The. Alexander Pushkin, translated by Nancy K. Anderson. Yale (paperback).
Marivaux: Three Plays. Marivaux, translated and adapted by Stephen Wadsworth. Smith & Kraus (paperback).
Mexico: A Play. Gertrude Stein. Green Integer (paperback).
New Playwrights—The Best Plays of 1998, edited by Marisa Smith. Smith & Kraus (paperback).
Oresteia of Aeschylus, The. Aeschylus, translated by Ted Hughes. Farrar Straus Giroux (acting edition).
Paul Sills' Story Theater—Four Shows. Paul Sills. Applause (cloth edition).
Plays by Janet Neipris. Broadway Play Publishing (paperback).
Plays by Richard Nelson—Volume Three—Early Plays. Broadway Play Publishing (paperback).
Plays by Rochelle Owens. Broadway Play Publishing (paperback).
Plays One. John Bowen. Oberon (paperback).
Political Plays of Langston Hughes, The. Southern Illinois University Press (paperback).
Richard Nelson: Plays I. Faber & Faber (paperback).
Seven One-Act Plays by Wendy Wasserstein. Dramatists Play Service (acting edition).
Theater of the Holocaust: Vol. 2—Six Plays, The. Edited and introduction by Robert Skloot (paperback).
Three Days of Rain & Other Plays. Richard Greenberg. Grove Press (paperback).
Trojan Women, The. Euripides, translated by Nicholas Rudall. Ivan R. Dee (paperback).
Twelve Plays of Christmas, The. Lowell Sdwortzell editor. Applause (cloth).
What I Meant Was—New Plays and Selected One Acts. Craig Lucas (paperback).
Women Beware Women and Other Plays. Thomas Middleton, edited and introduction by Richard Dutton. Oxford (paperback).
Women Playwrights: The Best Plays of 1998. Marisa Smith editor, introduction by Carol Rocamora (paperback).

NECROLOGY
MAY 1999–MAY 2000

PERFORMERS

Adams, Joey (88)—December 2, 1999
Adams, Peter (61)—December 13, 1999
Adele, Jan (64)—February 27, 2000
Allen, Rex (77)—December 17, 1999
Alma, Linda (73)—August 2, 1999
Arnold, Newt (72)—February 12, 2000
Bannen, Ian (71)—November 3, 1999
Bartel, Paul (61)—May 13, 2000
Batcheller, Betty Macdonald (92)—January 15, 2000
Bedford, Patrick (67)—November 20, 1999
Benedict, William (82)—November 25, 1999
Blum, Anthony (61)—December 28, 1999
Brooke, Bunney (80)—April 2, 2000
Brooke, Hillary (84)—May 25, 1999
Brown, Vanessa (71)—May 21, 1999
Burr, Robert (78)—May 13, 2000
Cary, Christopher (65)—April 1, 2000
Chapman, Marguerite (82)—August 31, 1999
Chater, Gordon (77)—December 13, 1999
Chiaki, Minoru (82)—November 2, 1999
Cirillo, Charles (91)—December 4, 1999
Colicos, John (71)—March 6, 2000
Collier, Richard (80)—March 11, 2000
Crisp, Quentin (90)—November 21, 1999
Curley, Wilma (62)—October 16, 1999
Drake, Frances (91)—January 17, 2000
Elliot, Ross (82)—August 12, 1999
Elvira, Pablo (62)—February 5, 2000
Emmett, Robert (78)—April 8, 2000
Esambayev, Makhmud (75)—January 7, 2000
Everett, Francine (80s)—May 27, 1999
Everhart, Rex (79)—March 13, 2000
Fairbanks, Douglas Jr. (90)—May 7, 2000
Ferraro, Margaret Hart (84?)—January 26, 2000
Forrest, Helen (82)—July 11, 1999
Francine, Anne (82)—December 3, 1999
French, Kenneth N. (73)—March 22, 2000
Garland, Mignon (91)—September 15, 1999
Gielgud, John (96)—May 21, 2000
Gould, Sandra (73)—July 20, 1999
Gray, Charles (71)—March 7, 2000
Guild, Nancy (73)—August 16, 1999
Guízar, Tito (91)—December 24, 1999
Haddy, Anne (71)—June 6, 1999
Hairston, Jester (98)—January 18, 2000
Harris, Vivian (97)—February 18, 2000
Hemphill, Shirley (52)—December 10, 1999
Henning, Doug (52)—February 7, 2000
Herman, Gilbert O. (80)—September 6, 1999
Hicks, Maxine Elliott (95)—January 10, 2000
Howard, Jean (89)—March 21, 2000
James, Brion (54)—August 7, 1999
Jameson, Brian (42)—April 28, 2000
Johnson, Strech (85)—May 28, 2000
Kahn, Madeline (57)—December 3, 1999
Karns, Todd (79)—February 5, 2000
Kedrova, Lila (82)—February 16, 2000
Kelley, DeForest (79)—June 11, 1999
King, Mabel (66)—November 9, 1999
Kirby, Durward (88)—March 15, 2000
Kraus, Alfredo (71)—September 10, 1999
Lafferty, Frances (79)—September 15, 1999
Lamarr, Hedy (86)—January 19, 2000
Laubin, Reginald (96)—April 5, 2000
Lederer, Francis (100)—May 23, 2000
Leslie, Bethel (70)—November 28, 1999
Lewis, Mary Jane Croft (83)—August 24, 1999
Linville, Larry (60)—April 10, 2000
Llewelyn, Desmond (85)—December 19, 1999
MacKenzie, Kenneth (79)—September 23, 1999
Manos, Glenn Ryman (66)—November 3, 1999
Martin, Helen (90)—February 25, 2000
Mature, Victor (86)—August 4, 1999
McCann, Donal (56)—July 18, 1999
McDonald, Grace (81)—October 30, 1999
Meredith, Morley (77)—February 3, 2000
Mills, Donald (84)—November 13, 1999
Moore, Clayton (85)—December 28, 1999
Morse, Ella Mae (75)—October 16, 1999
Newland, John (82)—January 10, 2000
North, Alan (79)—January 19, 2000
O'Farrell, Bernadette (75)—September 1999
Pagan, Peter (77)—June 2, 1999
Parker, Chan Richardson (74)—September 9, 1999
Patterson, Dick (70)—September 20, 1999
Peverett, Dave (56)—February 7, 2000
Rayburn, Gene (81)—November 29, 1999
Reed, Janet (83)—February 28, 2000
Reeves, Steve (74)—May 1, 2000
Reid, Rex (79)—March 21, 2000
Richardson, Lee (73)—October 2, 1999
Roberts, Stephen (82)—October 26, 1999
Robinson, Vicki Sue (46)—April 27, 2000
Roman, Ruth (75)—September 9, 1999
Sax, Ted (73)—February 8, 2000
Schoop, Trudi (95)—July 14, 1999
Scott, George Campbell (71)—September 22, 1999
Shacklock, Constance (86)—June 29, 1999
Sherwood, Roberta (86)—July 5, 1999

Shull, Richard (70)—October 4, 1999
Sidney, Sylvia (88)—July 1, 1999
Stevens, Craig (81)—May 10, 2000
Stone, Robert (81)—May 11, 2000
Taylor, Johnnie (62)—May 31, 2000
Thompson, Peter (65)—April 24, 2000
Thomson, Norman (84)—February 3, 2000
Thornton, Teri (65)—May 2, 2000
Torme, Mel (73)—June 5, 1999
Trevor, Claire (91)—April 8, 2000
Tripp, Ruth Enders (79)—July 28, 1999
Tyrell, David (86)—July 5, 1999
Varney, Jim (50)—February 10, 2000
Vaughan, Frankie (71)—September 17, 1999
Von Scherler, Sasha (65)—April 15, 2000
Walker, Randolph (71)—May 22, 2000
Watson, Bobs (68)—June 26, 1999
Welting, Ruth (51)—December 16, 1999
Wessely, Paula (93)—May 11, 2000
White, Joan (89)—June 8, 1999
Williams, Megan (44)—April 17, 2000
Yefremov, Oleg (72)—May 24, 2000
Zeigler, Ted (73)—December 12, 1999

PRODUCERS, DIRECTORS CHOREOGRAPHERS

Allen, Lewis (94)—May 3, 2000
Autant-Lara, Claude (98)—February 5, 2000
Belsky, Igor (74)—July 3, 1999
Benson, Hugh (82)—October 28, 1999
Bergman, Jan (54)—March 2000
Bernds, Edward L. (94)—May 20, 2000
Berry, John (82)—November 29, 1999
Bresson, Robert (98)—December 18, 1999
Carr, Allan (62)—June 29, 1999
Cohen, Alexander H. (79)—April 22, 2000
Craigie, Jill (85)—December 13, 1999
Crichton, Charles (89)—September 14, 1999
Cullberg, Birgit (91)—September 8, 1999
Dmytryk, Edward (90)—July 1, 1999
Farber, Viola (67)—December 1999
Freberg, Donna Andresen (69)—May 12, 2000
Fried, Martin (62)—March 28, 2000
Fryer, Robert (79)—May 28, 2000
Goldman, Byron (78)—March 31, 2000
Green, Douglas Edward Sr. (78)—April 11, 2000
Green, Joseph (71)—September 1, 1999
Hujer, Flower (92)—May 1, 1999
Jackson, George (42)—February 10, 2000
Jones, Derek Anson (38)—January 18, 2000
Marshall, Anthony W. (93)—July 12, 1999
McCormick, Elizabeth (89)—August 15, 1999
McDonnell, M.J. (47)—January 22, 2000
Merrick, David (88)—April 25, 2000
Ockrent, Mike (53)—December 2, 1999
Polonsky, Abraham (88)—October 26, 1999
Rapper, Irving (101)—December 20, 1999
Seale, Douglas (85)—June 13, 1999
Siders, Irving (81)—October 13, 1999
Sircar, Ranjabati (36)—October 23, 1999
Sokolow, Anna (90)—March 29, 2000
Thompson, Michael (54)—September 24, 1999
Vadim, Roger (72)—February 11, 2000
Weed, Gene (64)—August 5, 1999
Weintraub, Sy (76)—April 4, 2000
Woolf, John (86)—June 28, 1999

PLAYWRIGHTS

Brodziak, Kenn (86)—June 3, 1999
Buero Vallejo, Antonio (83)—April 28, 2000
Davis, Jack (83)—March 17, 2000
Gomes, Dias (76)—May 18, 1999
Greenbaum, Everett (79)—July 11, 1999
MacIver, Joyce (95)—June 15, 1999
McCleery, William (88)—January 16, 2000
Shaber, David (70)—November 4, 1999
Simon, Howard (37)—April 12, 2000
Taylor, Samuel (87)—May 26, 2000
Tunstrom, Goran (62)—February 5, 2000
West, Morris (83)—October 9, 1999
Wexler, Norman (73)—August 23, 1999

COMPOSERS, LYRICISTS SONG WRITERS

Ariel, Meir (57)—July 18, 1999
Axton, Hoyt (61)—October 26, 1999
Brooks, John Benson (82)—November 13, 1999
Childs, Barney (73)—January 11, 2000
Clayton-Felt, Josh (32)—January 19, 2000
Collins, Tommy (69)—March 14, 2000
Dant, Charles G. (92)—October 31, 1999
Durden, Thomas (79)—October 17, 1999
Dury, Ian (57)—March 27, 2000
Ferguson, Howard (91)—November 1, 1999
Ferris, William (63)—May 16, 2000
Fine, Vivian (86)—March 20, 2000
Forrest, George (84)—October 10, 1999
Gilkyson, Hamilton H. III (83)—October 13, 1999
Grouya, Ted (89)—April 14, 2000
Gulda, Friedrich (69)—January 27, 2000
Harris, Don (61)—December 1, 1999
Heiden, Bernhard (89)—April 30, 2000
Kohs, Ellis (84)—May 17, 2000
Landowski, Marcel (84)—December 22, 1999
Levinsky, Walt (70)—December 14, 1999
Linn, Robert (74)—October 28, 1999
Litkei, Ervin (78)—February 8, 2000

Maxwell, Eddie (87)—November 21, 1999
Mayfield, Curtis (57)—December 26, 1999
McCurdy, Ed (81)—March 23, 2000
Moore, Frank Ledlie (75)—September 26, 1999
Morton, Arthur (91)—April 15, 2000
Parris, Robert (75)—December 5, 1999
Ralke, Don (80)—January 26, 2000
Reed, Nancy B. (75)—February 26, 2000
Rodrigo, Joaquin (97)—July 6, 1999
Roseman, Ronald (66)—February 10, 2000
Smit, Leo (78)—December 12, 1999
Snow, Hank (85)—December 20, 1999
Sturns, Arnolds (87)—November 7, 1999
Waldrop, Gideon (80)—May 19, 2000
Wilkins, Ernie (79)—June 5, 1999
Wynn, Larry (89)—September 28, 1999
Zayde, Jascha (87)—September 3, 1999

DESIGNERS

Balkan, Adele (92)—November 20, 1999
Berman, David (90)—March 2, 2000
Cunningham, Cliff (56)—April 18, 2000
Duguette, Anthony (85)—September 9, 1999
Eckart, William (80)—January 24, 2000
Elson, Charles (90)—March 30, 2000
Gallo, Suzanne (46)—February 19, 2000
Gorey, Edward (75)—April 15, 2000
Harris, Margaret (95)—May 10, 2000
Kurth, Henry J. (81)—June 6, 1999
Leigh, Douglas (92)—December 14, 1999
Leve, Sam (91)—December 6, 1999
Riva, William (79)—July 3, 1999
Simmons, Stanley (71)—September 4, 1999
Toms, Carl (72)—August 4, 1999
Thomas, Bill (79)—May 30, 2000
White, Miles (85)—February 17, 2000
Zipprodt, Patricia (74)—July 17, 1999

CRITICS

Berendt, Joachim-Ernst (77)—February 4, 2000
Betrock, Alan (49)—April 9, 2000
Ehrmann, Hans (74)—August 21, 1999
Fadiman, Clifton (95)—June 20, 1999
Frankel, Haskel (73)—November 3, 1999
Harris, Mike (64)—August 7, 1999
Jaehne, Karen (51)—January 21, 2000
Kroll, Jack (74)—June 8, 2000
Katz, Richard (33)—September 28, 1999
Parmenter, Ross (88)—October 18, 1999
Pleasants, Henry (89)—January 4, 2000
Quinn, John (88)—July 3, 1999

MUSICIANS

Adderley, Nat (68)—January 2, 2000
Baldwin, John Low (76)—December 31, 1999
Beneke, Gordon "Tex" (86)—May 30, 2000
Bolet, Alberto (94)—November 10, 1999
Bowie, Lester (58)—November 8, 1999
Burt, Heinz (57)—April 11, 2000
Byrd, Charlie (74)—November 30, 1999
Carson, Donald Tecumseh (70)—February 13, 2000
Carter, Anita (66)—July 29, 1999
Danell, Dennis (38)—February 29, 2000
de Coteau, Denis (70)—July 23, 1999
Drootin, Buzzy (80)—May 14, 2000
Duning, George (92)—February 27, 2000
Earland, Charles (58)—December 11, 1999
Edison, Harry (83)—July 27, 1999
Farmer, Art (71)—October 4, 1999
Fleming, Amaryllis (73)—July 27, 1999
Ford, Fred (69)—November 26, 1999
Frost, Frank Otis (63)—October 12, 1999
Glick, Jacob (73)—November 1, 1999
Gorbaty, Jan (84)—September 6, 1999
Grey, Al (74)—March 24, 2000
Hardin, Louis "Moondog" (83)—September 8, 1999
Harris, Gene (66)—January 16, 2000
Harris, Margaret Rosezarian (56)—March 7, 2000
Hayes, Evelyn Swarthout (87)—March 24, 2000
Jones, Jonah (91)—April 30, 2000
Jones, Philip (71)—January 17, 2000
Privin, Bernie (80)—October 8, 1999
Puente, Tito (77)—May 31, 2000
Puma, Joe (72)—May 31, 2000
Raileanu, Eufrosina (39)—November 20, 1999
Rampal, Jean-Pierre (78)—May 20, 2000
Sanders, Samuel (62)—July 9, 1999
Sandman, Mark (47)—July 3, 1999
Siravo, George (83)—February 28, 2000
Sorel, Claudette (66)—August 6, 1999
Talbot, Joe (72)—March 24, 2000
Washington, Grover Jr. (56)—December 17, 1999
Webster, Beveridge (91)—June 30, 1999
Wood, Bill (75)—April 30, 2000

OTHERS

Agronsky, Martin (84)—July 25, 1999
Broadcast journalist
Bergman, Mary Kay (38)—November 11, 1999
Voice of Snow White
Bowles, Paul (88)—November 18, 1999
Novelist

Brainard, Ingrid G. (74)—February 18, 2000
Dance historian
Cage, Betty (82)—December 19, 1999
New York City Ballet
Card, James (84)—January 16, 2000
Film preservationist
Converse, Veronica Cooper (86)—February 16, 2000
Gary Cooper's widow
Crohan, John F. (69)—July 25, 1999
New England Broadcasters
Cullman, Marguerite W. (94)—July 26, 1999
Stage magazine
Davis, Marc (86)—January 12, 2000
Disney animator
Davis, Martin (72)—October 4, 1999
Paramount Communications
Funt, Allen (84)—September 5, 1999
Candid Camera
Gayles, Juggy (86)—January 17, 2000
Music publisher
Goldenson, Leonard H. (94)—December 27, 1999
ABC Inc.
Graff, Herb (74)—January 9, 2000
Film preservationist
Heller, Joseph (76)—December 12, 1999
Novelist
Hillman, Bill (76)—August 3, 1999
AFTRA
Jaffe, Sam (98)—January 10, 2000
Talent agent
Jensen, Jim (73)—October 15, 1999
WCBS-TV
Kelly, Fred (83)—March 15, 2000
Gene Kelly's brother
Kraft, Gilman (73)—June 27, 1999
Playbill
Lustgarten, Marc A. (52)—August 30, 1999
Madison Square Garden
Lustig, Jo (74)—May 29, 1999
Publicist
MacDonald, Angus (60)—June 25, 1999
Elizabeth II's bagpiper
Margulies, Ed (48)—November 16, 1999
Columnist
Merrill, David (38)—February 13, 2000
Publicist
Mickelson, Sig (86)—March 24, 2000
CBS News
Mishkin, Meyer (87)—October 9, 1999
Agent
Moore, George S. (95)—April 12, 2000
Metropolitan Opera
Morrison, Hobe (95)—January 22, 2000
Variety
Murray, Kathryn (92)—August 6, 1999
Arthur Murray's widow
Patterson, Neil (50)—March 25, 2000
ABC News
Piercy, George T. (84)—March 30, 2000
Public TV
Rogers, Jim (84)—April 28, 2000
Will Rogers's son
Rothman, Frank (73)—April 25, 2000
MGM
Rudin, Milton A. (79)—December 13, 1999
Attorney
Schoen, Judy (57)—October 29, 1999
Agent
Schubart, Mark (81)—January 26, 2000
Lincoln Center Institute
Schulz, Charles (77)—February 12, 2000
Cartoonist
Seelen, Arthur (76)—February 7, 2000
Drama Book Shop
Segal, Jack (98)—January 12, 2000
Agent
Sherman, Barry L. (47)—May 2, 2000
Peabody Awards
Silverstein, Maurice (89)—September 6, 1999
MGM International
Steinberg, Herb (78)—May 8, 2000
Publicist
Wolfson, Joe (89)—February 1, 2000
Agent

THE BEST PLAYS, 1894–1996; THE MAJOR PRIZEWINNERS, 1997–1999

Listed in alphabetical order below are all those works selected as Best Plays in previous volumes of the *Best Plays* series through 1995–96, and the major prizewinners and special *Best Plays* citation in 1996–99. Opposite each title is given the volume in which the play appears, its opening date and its total number of performances. Two separate opening-date and performance-number entries signify two separate engagements off Broadway and on Broadway when the original production was transferred from one area to the other, usually in an off-to-on direction. Those plays marked with an asterisk (*) were still playing on June 1, 2000 and their number of performances was figured through May 31, 2000. Adaptors and translators are indicated by (ad) and (tr), the symbols (b), (m) and (l) stand for the author of the book, music and lyrics in the case of musicals and (c) signifies the credit for the show's conception, (i) for its inspiration. Entries identified as 94–99 and 99–09 are 19th century plays from one of the retrospective volumes. 94–95, 95–96, 96–97, 97–98 and 98–99 are late 20th century plays.

PLAY	VOLUME	OPENED	PERFS
ABE LINCOLN IN ILLINOIS—Robert E. Sherwood	38–39	Oct. 15, 1938	472
ABRAHAM LINCOLN—John Drinkwater	19–20	Dec. 15, 1919	193
ACCENT ON YOUTH—Samson Raphaelson	34–35	Dec. 25, 1934	229
ADAM AND EVA—Guy Bolton, George Middleton	19–20	Sept. 13, 1919	312
ADAPTATION—Elaine May; and NEXT—Terrence McNally	68–69	Feb. 10, 1969	707
AFFAIRS OF STATE—Louis Verneuil	50–51	Sept. 25, 1950	610
AFTER THE FALL—Arthur Miller	63–64	Jan. 23, 1964	208
AFTER THE RAIN—John Bowen	67–68	Oct. 9, 1967	64
AFTER-PLAY—Anne Meara	94–95	Jan. 31, 1995	400
AGNES OF GOD—John Pielmeier	81–82	Mar. 30, 1982	599
AH, WILDERNESS!—Eugene O'Neill	33–34	Oct. 2, 1933	289
AIN'T SUPPOSED TO DIE A NATURAL DEATH—(b, m, l) Melvin Van Peebles	71–72	Oct. 20, 1971	325
ALIEN CORN—Sidney Howard	32–33	Feb. 20, 1933	98
ALISON'S HOUSE—Susan Glaspell	30–31	Dec. 1, 1930	41
ALL MY SONS—Arthur Miller	46–47	Jan. 29, 1947	328
ALL IN THE TIMING—David Ives	93–94	Feb. 17, 1994	526
ALL OVER TOWN—Murray Schisgal	74–75	Dec. 29, 1974	233
ALL THE WAY HOME—Tad Mosel, based on James Agee's novel *A Death in the Family*	60–61	Nov. 30, 1960	333
ALLEGRO—(b, l) Oscar Hammerstein II, (m) Richard Rodgers	47–48	Oct. 10, 1947	315
AMADEUS—Peter Shaffer	80–81	Dec. 17, 1980	1,181
AMBUSH—Arthur Richman	21–22	Oct. 10, 1921	98
AMERICA HURRAH—Jean-Claude van Itallie	66–67	Nov. 6, 1966	634
AMERICAN BUFFALO—David Mamet	76–77	Feb. 16, 1977	135
AMERICAN ENTERPRISE—Jeffrey Sweet (special citation)	93–94	Apr. 13, 1994	15
AMERICAN PLAN, THE—Richard Greenberg	90–91	Dec. 16, 1990	37

PLAY	VOLUME	OPENED	PERFS
AMERICAN WAY, THE—George S. Kaufman, Moss Hart	38–39	Jan. 21, 1939	164
AMPHITRYON 38—Jean Giraudoux, (ad) S.N. Behrman	37–38	Nov. 1, 1937	153
AND A NIGHTINGALE SANG—C.P. Taylor	83–84	Nov. 27, 1983	177
ANDERSONVILLE TRIAL, THE—Saul Levitt	59–60	Dec. 29, 1959	179
ANDORRA—Max Frisch, (ad) George Tabori	62–63	Feb. 9, 1963	9
ANGEL STREET—Patrick Hamilton	41–42	Dec. 5, 1941	1,295
ANGELS FALL—Lanford Wilson	82–83	Oct. 17, 1982	65
	82–83	Jan. 22, 1983	64
ANGELS IN AMERICA, PART I: MILLENNIUM APPROACHES—Tony Kushner	92–93	May 4, 1993	367
ANGELS IN AMERICA, PART II: PERESTROIKA—Tony Kushner	93–94	Nov. 23, 1994	216
ANIMAL KINGDOM, THE—Philip Barry	31–32	Jan. 12, 1932	183
ANNA CHRISTIE—Eugene O'Neill	21–22	Nov. 2, 1921	177
ANNA LUCASTA—Philip Yordan	44–45	Aug. 30, 1944	957
ANNE OF THE THOUSAND DAYS—Maxwell Anderson	48–49	Dec. 8, 1948	286
ANNIE—(b) Thomas Meehan, (m) Charles Strouse, (l) Martin Charnin, based on Harold Gray's comic strip *Little Orphan Annie*	76–77	Apr. 21, 1977	2,377
ANOTHER LANGUAGE—Rose Franken	31–32	Apr. 25, 1932	344
ANOTHER PART OF THE FOREST—Lillian Hellman	46–47	Nov. 20, 1946	182
ANTIGONE—Jean Anouilh, (ad) Lewis Galantiere	45–46	Feb. 18, 1946	64
APPLAUSE—(b) Betty Comden and Adolph Green, (m) Charles Strouse, (l) Lee Adams, based on the film *All About Eve* and the original story by Mary Orr	69–70	Mar. 30, 1970	896
APPLE TREE, THE—(b, l) Sheldon Harnick, (b, m) Jerry Bock, (add'l b) Jerome Coopersmith, based on stories by Mark Twain, Frank R. Stockton and Jules Feiffer	66–67	Oct. 18, 1966	463
ARCADIA—Tom Stoppard	94–95	Mar. 30, 1995	173
ARISTOCRATS—Brian Friel	88–89	Apr. 25, 1989	186
ARSENIC AND OLD LACE—Joseph Kesselring	40–41	Jan. 10, 1941	1,444
ART—Yasmina Reza	97–98	Mar. 1, 1998	600
AS HUSBANDS GO—Rachel Crothers	30–31	Mar. 5, 1931	148
AS IS—William M. Hoffman	84–85	Mar. 10, 1985	49
	84–85	May 1, 1985	285
ASHES—David Rudkin	76–77	Jan. 25, 1977	167
AUNT DAN AND LEMON—Wallace Shawn	85–86	Oct. 1, 1985	191
AUTUMN GARDEN, THE—Lillian Hellman	50–51	Mar. 7, 1951	101
AWAKE AND SING—Clifford Odets	34–35	Feb. 19, 1935	209
BAD MAN, THE—Porter Emerson Browne	20–21	Aug. 30, 1920	350
BAD HABITS—Terrence McNally	73–74	Feb. 4, 1974	273
BAD SEED—Maxwell Anderson, based on William March's novel	54–55	Dec. 8, 1954	332
BARBARA FRIETCHIE—Clyde Fitch	99–09	Oct. 23, 1899	83
BAREFOOT IN ATHENS—Maxwell Anderson	51–52	Oct. 31, 1951	30
BAREFOOT IN THE PARK—Neil Simon	63–64	Oct. 23, 1963	1,530
BARRETTS OF WIMPOLE STREET, THE—Rudolf Besier	30–31	Feb. 9, 1931	370
BEAUTY QUEEN OF LEENANE, THE—Martin McDonagh	97–98	Feb. 26, 1998	46
	97–98	Apr. 23, 1998	372
BECKET—Jean Anouilh, (tr) Lucienne Hill	60–61	Oct. 5, 1960	193

PLAY	VOLUME	OPENED	PERFS
BEDROOM FARCE—Alan Ayckbourn	78–79	Mar. 29, 1979	278
BEGGAR ON HORSEBACK—George S. Kaufman, Marc Connelly	23–24	Feb. 12, 1924	224
BEHOLD THE BRIDEGROOM—George Kelly	27–28	Dec. 26, 1927	88
BELL, BOOK AND CANDLE—John van Druten	50–51	Nov. 14, 1950	233
BELL FOR ADANO, A—Paul Osborn, based on John Hersey's novel	44–45	Dec. 6, 1944	304
BENEFACTORS—Michael Frayn	85–86	Dec. 22, 1985	217
BENT—Martin Sherman	79–80	Dec. 2, 1979	240
BERKELEY SQUARE—John L. Balderston	29–30	Nov. 4, 1929	229
BERNARDINE—Mary Chase	52–53	Oct. 16, 1952	157
BEST LITTLE WHOREHOUSE IN TEXAS, THE—(b) Larry L. King, Peter Masterson, (m, l) Carol Hall	77–78	Apr. 17, 1978	64
	78–79	June 19, 1978	1,639
BEST MAN, THE—Gore Vidal	59–60	Mar. 31, 1960	520
BETRAYAL—Harold Pinter	79–80	Jan. 5, 1980	170
BEYOND THE HORIZON—Eugene O'Neill	19–20	Feb. 2, 1920	160
BIG FISH, LITTLE FISH—Hugh Wheeler	60–61	Mar. 15, 1961	101
BILL OF DIVORCEMENT, A—Clemence Dane	21–22	Oct. 10, 1921	173
BILLY BUDD—Louis O. Coxe, Robert Chapman, based on Herman Melville's novel	50–51	Feb. 10, 1951	105
BILOXI BLUES—Neil Simon	84–85	Mar. 28, 1985	524
BIOGRAPHY—S.N. Behrman	32–33	Dec. 12, 1932	267
BLACK COMEDY—Peter Shaffer	66–67	Feb. 12, 1967	337
BLITHE SPIRIT—Noel Coward	41–42	Nov. 5, 1941	657
BOESMAN AND LENA—Athol Fugard	70–71	June 22, 1970	205
BORN IN THE R.S.A.—Barney Simon in collaboration with the cast	86–87	Oct. 1, 1986	8
BORN YESTERDAY—Garson Kanin	45–46	Feb. 4, 1946	1,642
BOTH YOUR HOUSES—Maxwell Anderson	32–33	Mar. 6, 1933	72
BOY MEETS GIRL—Bella and Samuel Spewack	35–36	Nov. 27, 1935	669
BOY FRIEND, THE—(b, m, l) Sandy Wilson	54–55	Sept. 30, 1954	485
BOYS IN THE BAND, THE—Mart Crowley	67–68	Apr. 15, 1968	1,000
BRIDE OF THE LAMB, THE—William Hurlbut	25–26	Mar. 30, 1926	109
BRIEF MOMENT—S.N. Behrman	31–32	Nov. 9, 1931	129
BRIGADOON—(b, l) Alan Jay Lerner, (m) Frederick Loewe	46–47	Mar. 13, 1947	581
BROADWAY—Philip Dunning, George Abbott	26–27	Sept. 16, 1926	603
BROADWAY BOUND—Neil Simon	86–87	Dec. 4, 1986	756
BURLESQUE—George Manker Watters, Arthur Hopkins	27–28	Sept. 1, 1927	372
BUS STOP—William Inge	54–55	Mar. 2, 1955	478
BUTLEY—Simon Gray	72–73	Oct. 31, 1972	135
BUTTER AND EGG MAN, THE—George S. Kaufman	25–26	Sept. 23, 1925	243
BUTTERFLIES ARE FREE—Leonard Gershe	69–70	Oct. 21, 1969	1,128
CABARET—(b) Joe Masteroff, (m) John Kander, (l) Fred Ebb, based on John van Druten's play *I Am a Camera* and stories by Christopher Isherwood	66–67	Nov. 20, 1966	1,165
CACTUS FLOWER—Abe Burrows, based on a play by Pierre Barillet and Jean-Pierre Gredy	65–66	Dec. 8, 1965	1,234
CAGE AUX FOLLES, LA—(see *La Cage aux Folles*)			

PLAY	VOLUME	OPENED	PERFS
CAINE MUTINY COURT-MARTIAL, THE—Herman Wouk, based on his novel	53–54	Jan. 20, 1954	415
CALIFORNIA SUITE—Neil Simon	76–77	June 10, 1976	445
CALIGULA—Albert Camus, (ad) Justin O'Brien	59–60	Feb. 16, 1960	38
CALL IT A DAY—Dodie Smith	35–36	Jan. 28, 1936	194
CAMPING WITH HENRY & TOM—Mark St. Germain	94–95	Feb. 20, 1995	88
CANDIDE—(b) Lillian Hellman, based on Voltaire's satire (l) Richard Wilbur, John Latouche, Dorothy Parker, (m) Leonard Bernstein	56–57	Dec. 1, 1956	73
CANDLE IN THE WIND—Maxwell Anderson	41–42	Oct. 22, 1941	95
CARETAKER, THE—Harold Pinter	61–62	Oct. 4, 1961	165
CASE OF REBELLIOUS SUSAN, THE—Henry Arthur Jones	94–99	Dec. 20, 1894	80
CAT ON A HOT TIN ROOF—Tennessee Williams	54–55	Mar. 24, 1955	694
*CATS—(m) Andrew Lloyd Webber, based on T.S. Eliot's *Old Possum's Book of Practical Cats,* (add'l l) Trevor Nunn, Richard Stilgoe	82–83	Oct. 7, 1982	7,367
CELEBRATION—(b, l) Tom Jones, (m) Harvey Schmidt	68–69	Jan. 22, 1969	109
CHALK GARDEN, THE—Enid Bagnold	55–56	Oct. 26, 1955	182
CHANGELINGS, THE—Lee Wilson Dodd	23–24	Sept. 17, 1923	128
CHANGING ROOM, THE—David Storey	72–73	Mar. 6, 1973	192
CHAPTER TWO—Neil Simon	77–78	Dec. 4, 1977	857
CHICAGO—Maurine Dallas Watkins	26–27	Dec. 30, 1926	172
CHICAGO—(b) Fred Ebb, Bob Fosse, (m) John Kander, (l) Fred Ebb, based on the play by Maurine Dallas Watkins	75–76	June 3, 1975	898
CHICKEN FEED—Guy Bolton	23–24	Sept. 24, 1923	144
CHILDREN OF A LESSER GOD—Mark Medoff	79–80	Mar. 30, 1980	887
CHILDREN'S HOUR, THE—Lillian Hellman	34–35	Nov. 20, 1934	691
CHILD'S PLAY—Robert Marasco	69–70	Feb. 17, 1970	342
CHIPS WITH EVERYTHING—Arnold Wesker	63–64	Oct. 1, 1963	149
CHORUS LINE, A—(c) Michael Bennett, (b) James Kirkwood, Nicholas Dante, (m) Marvin Hamlisch, (l) Edward Kleban	74–75	Apr. 15, 1975	101
	75–76	July 25, 1975	6,137
CHRISTOPHER BLAKE—Moss Hart	46–47	Nov. 30, 1946	114
CIRCLE, THE—W. Somerset Maugham	21–22	Sept. 12, 1921	175
CITY OF ANGELS—(b) Larry Gelbart, (m) Cy Coleman, (l) David Zippel	89–90	Dec. 11, 1989	878
CLARENCE—Booth Tarkington	19–20	Sept. 20, 1919	306
CLAUDIA—Rose Franken	40–41	Feb. 12, 1941	722
CLEARING IN THE WOODS, A—Arthur Laurents	56–57	Jan. 10, 1957	36
CLIMATE OF EDEN, THE—Moss Hart, based on Edgar Mittleholzer's novel *Shadows Move Among Them*	52–53	Nov. 13, 1952	20
CLIMBERS, THE—Clyde Fitch	99–09	Jan. 21, 1901	163
CLOSER—Patrick Marber	98–99	Aug. 22, 1999	172
CLOUD 9—Caryl Churchill	80–81	May 18, 1981	971
CLUTTERBUCK—Benn W. Levy	49–50	Dec. 3, 1949	218
COCKTAIL HOUR, THE—A.R. Gurney	88–89	Oct. 20, 1988	351
COCKTAIL PARTY, THE—T.S. Eliot	49–50	Jan. 21, 1950	409
COLD WIND AND THE WARM, THE—S.N. Behrman	58–59	Dec. 8, 1958	120
COLLECTION, THE—Harold Pinter	62–63	Nov. 26, 1962	578
COME BACK, LITTLE SHEBA—William Inge	49–50	Feb. 15, 1950	191

PLAY	VOLUME	OPENED	PERFS
COMEDIANS—Trevor Griffiths	76–77	Nov. 28, 1976	145
COMMAND DECISION—William Wister Haines	47–48	Oct. 1, 1947	408
COMPANY—(b) George Furth, (m, l) Stephen Sondheim	69–70	Apr. 26, 1970	705
COMPLAISANT LOVER, THE—Graham Greene	61–62	Nov. 1, 1961	101
CONDUCT UNBECOMING—Barry England	70–71	Oct. 12, 1970	144
CONFIDENTIAL CLERK, THE—T.S. Eliot	53–54	Feb. 11, 1954	117
CONNECTION, THE—Jack Gelber (supplement)	60–61	Feb. 22, 1961	722
CONSTANT WIFE, THE—W. Somerset Maugham	26–27	Nov. 29, 1926	295
CONTRACTOR, THE—David Storey	73–74	Oct. 17, 1973	72
CONVERSATIONS WITH MY FATHER—Herb Gardner	91–92	Mar. 29, 1992	402
COQUETTE—George Abbott, Ann Preston Bridgers	27–28	Nov. 8, 1927	366
CORN IS GREEN, THE—Emlyn Williams	40–41	Nov. 26, 1940	477
COUNTRY GIRL, THE—Clifford Odets	50–51	Nov. 10, 1950	235
COUNTY CHAIRMAN, THE—George Ade	99–09	Nov. 24, 1903	222
CRADLE SONG, THE—Gregorio & Maria Martinez Sierra, (tr) John Garrett Underhill	26–27	Jan. 24, 1927	57
CRAIG'S WIFE—George Kelly	25–26	Oct. 12, 1925	360
CRAZY FOR YOU—(b) Ken Ludwig, (m) George Gershwin, (l) Ira Gershwin, (c) Ken Ludwig, Mike Ockrent, (i) Guy Bolton, John McGowan	91–92	Feb. 19, 1992	1,622
CREATION OF THE WORLD AND OTHER BUSINESS, THE—Arthur Miller	72–73	Nov. 30, 1972	20
CREEPS—David E. Freeman	73–74	Dec. 4, 1973	15
CRIMES OF THE HEART—Beth Henley	80–81	Dec. 9, 1980	35
	81–82	Nov. 4, 1981	535
CRIMINAL CODE, THE—Martin Flavin	29–30	Oct. 2, 1929	173
CRUCIBLE, THE—Arthur Miller	52–53	Jan. 22, 1953	197
CRYPTOGRAM, THE—David Mamet	94–95	Apr. 13, 1995	62
CURTAINS—Stephen Bill	95–96	May 21, 1996	64
CYNARA—H.M. Harwood, R.F. Gore-Browne	31–32	Nov. 2, 1931	210
DA—Hugh Leonard	77–78	May 1, 1978	697
DAISY MAYME—George Kelly	26–27	Oct. 25, 1926	112
DAMASK CHEEK, THE—John van Druten, Lloyd Morris	42–43	Oct 22, 1942	93
DANCE AND THE RAILROAD, THE—David Henry Hwang	81–82	July 16, 1981	181
DANCING AT LUGHNASA—Brian Friel	91–92	Oct. 24, 1991	421
DANCING MOTHERS—Edgar Selwyn, Edmund Goulding	24–25	Aug. 11, 1924	312
DARK AT THE TOP OF THE STAIRS, THE—William Inge	57–58	Dec. 5, 1957	468
DARK IS LIGHT ENOUGH, THE—Christopher Fry	54–55	Feb. 23, 1955	69
DARKNESS AT NOON—Sidney Kingsley, based on Arthur Koestler's novel	50–51	Jan. 13, 1951	186
DARLING OF THE GODS, THE—David Belasco, John Luther Long	99–09	Dec. 3, 1902	182
DAUGHTERS OF ATREUS—Robert Turney	36–37	Oct. 14, 1936	13
DAY IN THE DEATH OF JOE EGG, A—Peter Nichols	67–68	Feb. 1, 1968	154
DEAD END—Sidney Kingsley	35–36	Oct. 28, 1935	687
DEADLY GAME, THE—James Yaffe, based on Friedrich Duerrenmatt's novel	59–60	Feb. 2, 1960	39
DEAR RUTH—Norman Krasna	44–45	Dec. 13, 1944	683
DEATH OF A SALESMAN—Arthur Miller	48–49	Feb. 10, 1949	742

PLAY	VOLUME	OPENED	PERFS
Death Takes a Holiday—Alberto Casella, (ad) Walter Ferris	29–30	Dec. 26, 1929	180
Deathtrap—Ira Levin	77–78	Feb. 26, 1978	1,793
Deburau—Sacha Guitry, (ad) Harley Granville Barker	20–21	Dec. 23, 1920	189
Decision—Edward Chodorov	43–44	Feb. 2, 1944	160
Declassee—Zoë Akins	19–20	Oct. 6, 1919	257
Deep Are the Roots—Arnaud d'Usseau, James Gow	45–46	Sept. 26, 1945	477
Delicate Balance, A—Edward Albee	66–67	Sept. 22, 1966	132
Deputy, The—Rolf Hochhuth, (ad) Jerome Rothenberg	63–64	Feb. 26, 1964	109
Design for Living—Noel Coward	32–33	Jan. 24, 1933	135
Desire Under the Elms—Eugene O'Neill	24–25	Nov. 11, 1924	208
Desperate Hours, The—Joseph Hayes, based on his novel	54–55	Feb. 10, 1955	212
Destiny of Me, The—Larry Kramer	92–93	Oct. 20, 1992	175
Detective Story—Sidney Kingsley	48–49	Mar. 23, 1949	581
Devil Passes, The—Benn W. Levy	31–32	Jan. 4, 1932	96
Devil's Advocate, The—Dore Schary, based on Morris L. West's novel	60–61	Mar. 9, 1961	116
Dial "M" for Murder—Frederick Knott	52–53	Oct. 29, 1952	552
Diary of Anne Frank, The—Frances Goodrich, Albert Hackett, based on Anne Frank's *The Diary of a Young Girl*	55–56	Oct. 5, 1955	717
Dining Room, The—A.R. Gurney	81–82	Feb. 24, 1982	583
Dinner at Eight—George S. Kaufman, Edna Ferber	32–33	Oct. 22, 1932	232
Disenchanted, The—Budd Schulberg, Harvey Breit, based on Mr. Schulberg's novel	58–59	Dec. 3, 1958	189
Disraeli—Louis N. Parker	09–19	Sept. 18, 1911	280
Distaff Side, The—John van Druten	34–35	Sept. 25, 1934	177
Dodsworth—Sidney Howard, based on Sinclair Lewis's novel	33–34	Feb. 24, 1934	315
Doubles—David Wiltse	84–85	May 8, 1985	277
Doughgirls, The—Joseph Fields	42–43	Dec. 30, 1942	671
Dover Road, The—A.A. Milne	21–22	Dec. 23, 1921	324
Dream Girl—Elmer Rice	45–46	Dec. 14, 1945	348
Dresser, The—Ronald Harwood	81–82	Nov. 9, 1981	200
Drinking in America—Eric Bogosian	85–86	Jan. 19, 1986	94
Driving Miss Daisy—Alfred Uhry	86–87	Apr. 15, 1987	1,195
Drood—(see *The Mystery of Edwin Drood*)			
Duel of Angels—Jean Giraudoux's *Pour Lucrèce,* (ad) Christopher Fry	59–60	Apr. 19, 1960	51
Dulcy—George S. Kaufman, Marc Connelly	21–22	Aug. 13, 1921	246
Dybbuk, The—S. Ansky, (ad) Henry G. Alsberg	25–26	Dec. 15, 1925	120
Dylan—Sidney Michaels	63–64	Jan. 18, 1964	153
Easiest Way, The—Eugene Walter	09–19	Jan. 19, 1909	157
Eastern Standard—Richard Greenberg	88–89	Oct. 27, 1988	46
	88–89	Mar. 25, 1989	92
Eastward in Eden—Dorothy Gardner	47–48	Nov. 18, 1947	15
Edward, My Son—Robert Morley, Noel Langley	48–49	Sept. 30, 1948	260
Effect of Gamma Rays on Man-in-the-Moon Marigolds, The—Paul Zindel	69–70	Apr. 7, 1970	819

PLAY	VOLUME	OPENED	PERFS
EGG, THE—Felicien Marceau, (ad) Robert Schlitt	61–62	Jan. 8, 1962	8
ELEPHANT MAN, THE—Bernard Pomerance	78–79	Jan. 14, 1979	73
	78–79	Apr. 19, 1979	916
ELIZABETH THE QUEEN—Maxwell Anderson	30–31	Nov. 3, 1930	147
EMERALD CITY—David Williamson	88–89	Nov. 30, 1988	17
EMPEROR JONES, THE—Eugene O'Neill	20–21	Nov. 1, 1920	204
EMPEROR'S CLOTHES, THE—George Tabori	52–53	Feb. 9, 1953	16
ENCHANTED, THE—Maurice Valency, based on Jean Giraudoux's play *Intermezzo*	49–50	Jan. 18, 1950	45
END OF SUMMER—S.N. Behrman	35–36	Feb. 17, 1936	153
ENEMY, THE—Channing Pollock	25–26	Oct. 20, 1925	203
ENOUGH, FOOTFALLS AND ROCKABY—Samuel Beckett	83–84	Feb. 16, 1984	78
ENTER MADAME—Gilda Varesi, Dolly Byrne	20–21	Aug. 16, 1920	350
ENTERTAINER, THE—John Osborne	57–58	Feb. 12, 1958	97
EPITAPH FOR GEORGE DILLON—John Osborne, Anthony Creighton	58–59	Nov. 4, 1958	23
EQUUS—Peter Shaffer	74–75	Oct. 24, 1974	1,209
ESCAPE—John Galsworthy	27–28	Oct. 26, 1927	173
ETHAN FROME—Owen and Donald Davis, based on Edith Wharton's novel	35–36	Jan. 21, 1936	120
EVE OF ST. MARK, THE—Maxwell Anderson	42–43	Oct. 7, 1942	307
EXCURSION—Victor Wolfson	36–37	Apr. 9, 1937	116
EXECUTION OF JUSTICE—Emily Mann	85–86	Mar. 13, 1986	12
EXTRA MAN, THE—Richard Greenberg	91–92	May 19, 1992	39
EXTREMITIES—William Mastrosimone	82–83	Dec. 22, 1982	325
FAIR COUNTRY, A—Jon Robin Baitz	95–96	Oct. 29, 1995	153
FALL GUY, THE—James Gleason, George Abbott	24–25	Mar. 10, 1925	176
FALSETTOLAND—William Finn, James Lapine	90–91	June 28, 1990	215
FAMILY BUSINESS—Dick Goldberg	77–78	Apr. 12, 1978	438
FAMILY PORTRAIT—Lenore Coffee, William Joyce Cowen	38–39	May 8, 1939	111
FAMOUS MRS. FAIR, THE—James Forbes	19–20	Dec. 22, 1919	344
FAR COUNTRY, A—Henry Denker	60–61	Apr. 4, 1961	271
FARMER TAKES A WIFE, THE—Frank B. Elser, Marc Connelly, based on Walter D. Edmonds's novel *Rome Haul*	34–35	Oct. 30, 1934	104
FATAL WEAKNESS, THE—George Kelly	46–47	Nov. 19, 1946	119
FENCES—August Wilson	86–87	Mar. 26, 1987	526
FIDDLER ON THE ROOF—(b) Joseph Stein, (l) Sheldon Harnick, (m) Jerry Bock, based on Sholom Aleichem's stories	64–65	Sept. 22, 1964	3,242
5TH OF JULY, THE—Lanford Wilson (also called *Fifth of July*)	77–78	Apr. 27, 1978	159
FIND YOUR WAY HOME—John Hopkins	73–74	Jan. 2, 1974	135
FINISHING TOUCHES—Jean Kerr	72–73	Feb. 8, 1973	164
FIORELLO!—(b) Jerome Weidman, George Abbott, (l) Sheldon Harnick, (m) Jerry Bock	59–60	Nov. 23, 1959	795
FIREBRAND, THE—Edwin Justus Mayer	24–25	Oct. 15, 1924	269
FIRES IN THE MIRROR—Anna Deavere Smith	91–92	May 12, 1992	109
FIRST LADY—Katherine Dayton, George S. Kaufman	35–36	Nov. 26, 1935	246

PLAY	VOLUME	OPENED	PERFS
FIRST MONDAY IN OCTOBER—Jerome Lawrence, Robert E. Lee	78–79	Oct. 3, 1978	79
FIRST MRS. FRASER, THE—St. John Ervine	29–30	Dec. 28, 1929	352
FIRST YEAR, THE—Frank Craven	20–21	Oct. 20, 1920	760
FIVE FINGER EXERCISE—Peter Shaffer	59–60	Dec. 2, 1959	337
FIVE-STAR FINAL—Louis Weitzenkorn	30–31	Dec. 30, 1930	175
FLIGHT TO THE WEST—Elmer Rice	40–41	Dec. 30, 1940	136
FLOATING LIGHT BULB, THE—Woody Allen	80–81	Apr. 27, 1981	65
FLOWERING PEACH, THE—Clifford Odets	54–55	Dec. 28, 1954	135
FOLLIES—(b) James Goldman, (m, l) Stephen Sondheim	70–71	Apr. 4, 1971	521
FOOL, THE—Channing Pollock	22–23	Oct. 23, 1922	373
FOOL FOR LOVE—Sam Shepard	83–84	May 26, 1983	1,000
FOOLISH NOTION—Philip Barry	44–45	Mar. 3, 1945	104
FOREIGNER, THE—Larry Shue	84–85	Nov. 1, 1984	686
FORTY CARATS—Pierre Barillet, Jean-Pierre Gredy, (ad) Jay Allen	68–69	Dec. 26, 1968	780
42ND STREET—(b) Michael Stewart, Mark Bramble, (m, l) Harry Warren, Al Dubin, (add'l l) Johnny Mercer, Mort Dixon, based on the novel by Bradford Ropes	80–81	Aug. 25, 1980	3,486
*FOSSE—(choreography) Robert Fosse, (c) Richard Maltby Jr., Chet Walker, Ann Reinking	98–99	Jan. 14, 1999	584
FOURPOSTER, THE—Jan de Hartog	51–52	Oct. 24, 1951	632
FOXFIRE—Susan Cooper, Hume Cronyn, (m) Jonathan Holtzman; based on materials from the *Foxfire* books	82–83	Nov. 11, 1982	213
FRONT PAGE, THE—Ben Hecht, Charles MacArthur	28–29	Aug. 14, 1928	276
GENERATION—William Goodhart	65–66	Oct. 6, 1965	299
GEORGE WASHINGTON SLEPT HERE—George S. Kaufman, Moss Hart	40–41	Oct. 18, 1940	173
GETTING OUT—Marsha Norman	78–79	Oct. 19, 1978	259
GIDEON—Paddy Chayefsky	61–62	Nov. 9, 1961	236
GIGI—Anita Loos, based on Colette's novel	51–52	Nov. 24, 1951	219
GIMME SHELTER—Barrie Keefe (*Gem, Gotcha* and *Getaway*)	78–79	Dec. 10, 1978	17
GIN GAME, THE—D.L. Coburn	77–78	Oct. 6, 1977	517
GINGERBREAD LADY, THE—Neil Simon	70–71	Dec. 13, 1970	193
GIRL ON THE VIA FLAMINIA, THE—Alfred Hayes, based on his novel	53–54	Feb. 9, 1954	111
GLASS MENAGERIE, THE—Tennessee Williams	44–45	Mar. 31, 1945	561
GLENGARRY GLEN ROSS—David Mamet	83–84	Mar. 25, 1984	378
GOBLIN MARKET—(ad) Peggy Harmon, Polly Pen from the poem by Christina Rosetti, (m) Polly Pen (special citation)	85–86	Apr. 13, 1986	89
GOLDEN APPLE, THE—(b, l), John Latouche, (m) Jerome Moross	53–54	Apr. 20, 1954	125
GOLDEN BOY—Clifford Odets	37–38	Nov. 4, 1937	250
GOOD—C.P. Taylor	82–83	Oct. 13, 1982	125
GOOD DOCTOR, THE—(ad) Neil Simon and suggested by stories by Anton Chekhov	73–74	Nov. 27, 1973	208
GOOD GRACIOUS ANNABELLE—Clare Kummer	09–19	Oct. 31, 1916	111
GOOD TIMES ARE KILLING ME, THE—Lynda Barry	90–91	May 21, 1991	207

PLAY	VOLUME	OPENED	PERFS
GOODBYE, MY FANCY—Fay Kanin	48–49	Nov. 17, 1948	446
GOOSE HANGS HIGH, THE—Lewis Beach	23–24	Jan. 29, 1924	183
GRAND HOTEL—Vicki Baum, (ad) W. A. Drake	30–31	Nov. 13, 1930	459
GRAND HOTEL: THE MUSICAL—(b) Luther Davis, (m, l) Robert Wright, George Forrest, (add'l m, l) Maury Yeston, based on Vicki Baum's *Grand Hotel*	89–90	Nov. 12, 1989	1,077
GRAPES OF WRATH, THE—(ad) Frank Galati from the novel by John Steinbeck	89–90	Mar. 22, 1990	188
GREAT DIVIDE, THE—William Vaughn Moody	99–09	Oct. 3, 1906	238
GREAT GOD BROWN, THE—Eugene O'Neill	25–26	Jan. 23, 1926	271
GREAT WHITE HOPE, THE—Howard Sackler	68–69	Oct. 3, 1968	556
GREEN BAY TREE, THE—Mordaunt Shairp	33–34	Oct. 20, 1933	166
GREEN GODDESS, THE—William Archer	20–21	Jan. 18, 1921	440
GREEN GROW THE LILACS—Lynn Riggs	30–31	Jan. 26, 1931	64
GREEN HAT, THE—Michael Arlen	25–26	Sept. 15, 1925	231
GREEN JULIA—Paul Abelman	72–73	Nov. 16, 1972	147
GREEN PASTURES, THE—Marc Connelly, based on Roark Bradford's *Ol' Man Adam and His Chillun*	29–30	Feb. 26, 1930	640
GROSS INDECENCY: THE THREE TRIALS OF OSCAR WILDE—Moisés Kaufman	97–98	June 5, 1997	534
GUS AND AL—Albert Innaurato	88–89	Feb. 27, 1989	25
GUYS AND DOLLS—(b) Jo Swerling, Abe Burrows, based on a story and characters by Damon Runyon, (m, l) Frank Loesser	50–51	Nov. 24, 1950	1,200
GYPSY—Maxwell Anderson	28–29	Jan. 14, 1929	64
HADRIAN VII—Peter Luke, based on works by Fr. Rolfe	68–69	Jan. 8, 1969	359
HAMP—John Wilson, based on an episode from a novel by J.L. Hodson	66–67	Mar. 9, 1967	101
HAPGOOD—Tom Stoppard	94–95	Dec. 4, 1994	129
HAPPY TIME, THE—Samuel Taylor, based on Robert Fontaine's book	49–50	Jan. 24, 1950	614
HARRIET—Florence Ryerson, Colin Clements	42–43	Mar. 3, 1943	377
HARVEY—Mary Chase	44–45	Nov. 1, 1944	1,775
HASTY HEART, THE—John Patrick	44–45	Jan. 3, 1945	207
HE WHO GETS SLAPPED—Leonid Andreyev, (ad) Gregory Zilboorg	21–22	Jan. 9, 1922	308
HEART OF MARYLAND, THE—David Belasco	94–99	Oct. 22, 1895	240
HEIDI CHRONICLES, THE—Wendy Wasserstein	88–89	Dec. 11, 1988	81
	88–89	Mar. 9, 1989	621
HEIRESS, THE—Ruth and Augustus Goetz, suggested by Henry James's novel *Washington Square*	47–48	Sept. 29, 1947	410
HELL-BENT FER HEAVEN—Hatcher Hughes	23–24	Jan. 4, 1924	122
HELLO, DOLLY!—(b) Michael Stewart, (m, l) Jerry Herman, based on Thornton Wilder's *The Matchmaker*	63–64	Jan. 16, 1964	2,844
HER MASTER'S VOICE—Clare Kummer	33–34	Oct. 23, 1933	224
HERE COME THE CLOWNS—Philip Barry	38–39	Dec. 7, 1938	88
HERO, THE—Gilbert Emery	21–22	Sept. 5, 1921	80
HIGH TOR—Maxwell Anderson	36–37	Jan. 9, 1937	171
HOGAN'S GOAT—William Alfred	65–66	Nov. 11, 1965	607

PLAY	VOLUME	OPENED	PERFS
HOLIDAY—Philip Barry	28–29	Nov. 26, 1928	229
HOME—David Storey	70–71	Nov. 17, 1970	110
HOME—Samm-Art Williams	79–80	Dec. 14, 1979	82
	79–80	May 7, 1980	279
HOMECOMING, THE—Harold Pinter	66–67	Jan. 5, 1967	324
HOME OF THE BRAVE—Arthur Laurents	45–46	Dec. 27, 1945	69
HOPE FOR A HARVEST—Sophie Treadwell	41–42	Nov. 26, 1941	38
HOSTAGE, THE—Brendan Behan	60–61	Sept. 20, 1960	127
HOT L BALTIMORE, THE—Lanford Wilson	72–73	Mar. 22, 1973	1,166
HOUSE OF BLUE LEAVES, THE—John Guare	70–71	Feb. 10, 1971	337
HOUSE OF CONNELLY, THE—Paul Green	31–32	Sept. 28, 1931	91
HOW I LEARNED TO DRIVE—Paula Vogel	96–97	May 4, 1997	400
HOW TO SUCCEED IN BUSINESS WITHOUT REALLY TRYING—(b) Abe Burrows, Jack Weinstock, Willie Gilbert, based on Shepherd Mead's novel, (m, l) Frank Loesser	61–62	Oct. 14, 1961	1,417
HURLYBURLY—David Rabe	84–85	June 21, 1984	45
	84–85	Aug. 7, 1984	343
I AM A CAMERA—John van Druten, based on Christopher Isherwood's Berlin stories	51–52	Nov. 28, 1951	214
I KNOW MY LOVE—S.N. Behrman, based on Marcel Achard's *Auprès de Ma Blonde*	49–50	Nov. 2, 1949	246
I NEVER SANG FOR MY FATHER—Robert Anderson	67–68	Jan. 25, 1968	124
I OUGHT TO BE IN PICTURES—Neil Simon	79–80	Apr. 3, 1980	324
I REMEMBER MAMA—John van Druten, based on Kathryn Forbes's book *Mama's Bank Account*	44–45	Oct. 19, 1944	714
ICEBOUND—Owen Davis	22–23	Feb. 10, 1923	171
ICEMAN COMETH, THE—Eugene O'Neill	46–47	Oct. 9, 1946	136
IDIOT'S DELIGHT—Robert E. Sherwood	35–36	Mar. 24, 1936	300
IF I WERE KING—Justin Huntly McCarthy	99–09	Oct. 14, 1901	56
I'M NOT RAPPAPORT—Herb Gardner	85–86	June 6, 1985	181
	85–86	Nov. 18, 1985	890
IMMORALIST, THE—Ruth and Augustus Goetz, based on André Gide's novel	53–54	Feb. 8, 1954	96
IN ABRAHAM'S BOSOM—Paul Green	26–27	Dec. 30, 1926	116
IN THE MATTER OF J. ROBERT OPPENHEIMER—Heinar Kipphardt, (tr) Ruth Speirs	68–69	Mar. 6, 1969	64
IN THE SUMMER HOUSE—Jane Bowles	53–54	Dec. 29, 1953	55
IN TIME TO COME—Howard Koch, John Huston	41–42	Dec. 28, 1941	40
INADMISSABLE EVIDENCE—John Osborne	65–66	Nov. 30, 1965	166
INCIDENT AT VICHY—Arthur Miller	64–65	Dec. 3, 1964	99
INDIANS—Arthur L. Kopit	69–70	Oct. 13, 1969	96
INHERIT THE WIND—Jerome Lawrence, Robert E. Lee	54–55	Apr. 21, 1955	806
INNOCENTS, THE—William Archibald, based on Henry James's *The Turn of the Screw*	49–50	Feb. 1, 1950	141
INNOCENT VOYAGE, THE—Paul Osborn, based on Richard Hughes's novel *A High Wind in Jamaica*	43–44	Nov. 15, 1943	40
INSPECTOR CALLS, AN—J.B. Priestley	47–48	Oct. 21, 1947	95
INTO THE WOODS—(b) James Lapine, (m, l) Stephen Sondheim	87–88	Nov. 5, 1987	765

PLAY	VOLUME	OPENED	PERFS
ISLAND, THE—Athol Fugard, John Kani, Winston Ntshona	74–75	Nov. 24, 1974	52
"IT'S A BIRD IT'S A PLANE IT'S SUPERMAN"—(b) David Newman and Robert Benton, (l) Lee Adams, (m) Charles Strouse, based on the comic strip "Superman"	65–66	Mar. 29, 1966	129
IT'S ONLY A PLAY—Terrence McNally	85–86	Jan. 12, 1986	17
J.B.—Archibald MacLeish	58–59	Dec. 11, 1958	364
JACOBOWSKY AND THE COLONEL—S.N. Behrman, based on Franz Werfel's play	43–44	Mar. 14, 1944	417
JANE—S.N. Behrman, suggested by W. Somerset Maugham's story	51–52	Feb. 1, 1952	100
JANE CLEGG—St. John Ervine	19–20	Feb. 23, 1920	158
JEFFREY—Paul Rudnick	92–93	Mar. 6, 1993	365
JASON—Samson Raphaelson	41–42	Jan. 21, 1942	125
JEROME ROBBINS' BROADWAY—(c) Jerome Robbins (special citation)	88–89	Feb. 26, 1989	634
JESSE AND THE BANDIT QUEEN—David Freeman	75–76	Oct. 17, 1975	155
JEST, THE—Sem Benelli, (ad) Edward Sheldon	19–20	Sept. 19, 1919	197
JOAN OF LORRAINE—Maxwell Anderson	46–47	Nov. 18, 1946	199
JOE EGG—(see *A Day in the Death of Joe Egg*)			
JOE TURNER'S COME AND GONE—August Wilson	87–88	Mar. 27, 1988	105
JOHN FERGUSON—St. John Ervine	09–19	May 13, 1919	177
JOHN LOVES MARY—Norman Krasna	46–47	Feb. 4, 1947	423
JOHNNY JOHNSON—(b, l) Paul Green, (m) Kurt Weill	36–37	Nov. 19, 1936	68
JOINED AT THE HEAD—Catherine Butterfield	92–93	Nov. 15, 1992	41
JOURNEY'S END—R.C. Sherriff	28–29	Mar. 22, 1929	485
JUMPERS—Tom Stoppard	73–74	Apr. 22, 1974	48
JUNE MOON—Ring W. Lardner, George S. Kaufman	29–30	Oct. 9, 1929	273
JUNIOR MISS—Jerome Chodorov, Joseph Fields	41–42	Nov. 18, 1941	710
K2—Patrick Meyers	82–83	Mar. 30, 1983	85
KATAKI—Shimon Wincelberg	58–59	Apr. 9, 1959	20
KENTUCKY CYCLE, THE—Robert Schenkkan	93–94	Nov. 14, 1993	34
KEY LARGO—Maxwell Anderson	39–40	Nov. 27, 1939	105
KILLING OF SISTER GEORGE, THE—Frank Marcus	66–67	Oct. 5, 1966	205
KINGDOM OF GOD, THE—G. Martinez Sierra, (ad) Helen and Harley Granville Barker	28–29	Dec. 20, 1928	92
KISS AND TELL—F. Hugh Herbert	42–43	Mar. 17, 1943	956
KISS OF THE SPIDER WOMAN—(b) Terrence McNally, (m) John Kander, (l) Fred Ebb, based on the novel by Manuel Puig	92–93	May 3, 1993	906
KISS THE BOYS GOODBYE—Clare Boothe	38–39	Sept. 28, 1938	286
KNOCK KNOCK—Jules Feiffer	75–76	Jan. 18, 1976	41
	75–76	Feb. 24, 1976	152
KVETCH—Steven Berkoff	86–87	Feb. 18, 1987	31
LA BETE—David Hirson (special citation)	90–91	Feb. 10, 1991	25
LA CAGE AUX FOLLES—(b) Harvey Fierstein, (m, l) Jerry Herman, based on the play by Jean Poiret	83–84	Aug. 21, 1983	1,761

PLAY	VOLUME	OPENED	PERFS
LA TRAGEDIE DE CARMEN—(ad) Peter Brook, Jean-Claude Carrière, Marius Constant from Georges Bizet's opera *Carmen* (special citation)	83–84	Nov. 17, 1983	187
LADY FROM DUBUQUE, THE—Edward Albee	79–80	Jan. 31, 1980	12
LADY IN THE DARK—(b) Moss Hart, (l) Ira Gershwin, (m) Kurt Weill	40–41	Jan. 23, 1941	162
LARGO DESOLATO—Vaclav Havel, (tr) Marie Winn	85–86	Mar. 25, 1986	40
LARK, THE—Jean Anouilh, (ad) Lillian Hellman	55–56	Nov. 17, 1955	229
LAST MEETING OF THE KNIGHTS OF THE WHITE MAGNOLIA, THE—Preston Jones	76–77	Sept. 22, 1976	22
LAST MILE, THE—John Wexley	29–30	Feb. 13, 1930	289
LAST NIGHT OF BALLYHOO, THE—Alfred Uhry	96–97	Feb. 27, 1997	557
LAST OF MRS. CHEYNEY, THE—Frederick Lonsdale	25–26	Nov. 9, 1925	385
LAST OF THE RED HOT LOVERS—Neil Simon	69–70	Dec. 28, 1969	706
LATE CHRISTOPHER BEAN, THE—(ad) Sidney Howard from the French of Rene Fauchois	32–33	Oct. 31, 1932	224
LATE GEORGE APLEY, THE—John P. Marquand, George S. Kaufman, based on John P. Marquand's novel	44–45	Nov. 23, 1944	385
LATER LIFE—A.R. Gurney	92–93	May 23, 1993	126
LAUGHTER ON THE 23RD FLOOR—Neil Simon	93–94	Nov. 22, 1993	320
LEAH KLESCHNA—C.M.S. McLellan	99–09	Dec. 12, 1904	131
LEFT BANK, THE—Elmer Rice	31–32	Oct. 5, 1931	242
LEND ME A TENOR—Ken Ludwig	88–89	Mar. 2, 1989	481
LES LIAISONS DANGEREUSES—Christopher Hampton, based on Choderlos de Laclos's novel	86–87	Apr. 30, 1987	148
*LES MISERABLES—(b) Alain Boublil, Claude-Michel Schönberg, (m) Claude-Michel Schönberg, (l) Herbert Kretzmer, add'l material James Fenton, based on Victor Hugo's novel	86–87	Mar. 12, 1987	5,442
LESSON FROM ALOES, A—Athol Fugard	80–81	Nov. 17, 1980	96
LET US BE GAY—Rachel Crothers	28–29	Feb. 19, 1929	353
LETTERS TO LUCERNE—Fritz Rotter, Allen Vincent	41–42	Dec. 23, 1941	23
LIFE, A—Hugh Leonard	80–81	Nov. 2, 1980	72
LIFE & ADVENTURES OF NICHOLAS NICKLEBY, THE—(ad) David Edgar from Charles Dickens's novel	81–82	Oct. 4, 1981	49
LIFE IN THE THEATER, A—David Mamet	77–78	Oct. 20, 1977	288
LIFE WITH FATHER—Howard Lindsay, Russel Crouse, based on Clarence Day's book	39–40	Nov. 8, 1939	3,224
LIFE WITH MOTHER—Howard Lindsay, Russel Crouse, based on Clarence Day's book	48–49	Oct. 20, 1948	265
LIGHT UP THE SKY—Moss Hart	48–49	Nov. 18, 1948	216
LILIOM—Ferenc Molnar, (ad) Benjamin Glazer	20–21	Apr. 20, 1921	300
LION IN WINTER, THE—James Goldman	65–66	Mar. 3, 1966	92
*LION KING, THE—(b) Roger Allers, Irene Mecchi, (m, l) Elton John, Tim Rice, (add'l m, l) Lebo M, Mark Mancina, Jay Rifkin, Julie Taymore, Hans Zimmer	97–98	Nov. 13, 1997	1,098
LIPS TOGETHER, TEETH APART—Terrence McNally	91–92	June 25, 1991	406
LITTLE ACCIDENT—Floyd Dell, Thomas Mitchell	28–29	Oct. 9, 1928	303
LITTLE FOXES, THE—Lillian Hellman	38–39	Feb. 15, 1939	410
LITTLE MINISTER, THE—James M. Barrie	94–99	Sept. 27, 1897	300

PLAY	VOLUME	OPENED	PERFS
LITTLE NIGHT MUSIC, A—(b) Hugh Wheeler, (m, l) Stephen Sondheim, suggested by Ingmar Bergman's film *Smiles of a Summer Night*	72–73	Feb. 25, 1973	600
LIVING ROOM, THE—Graham Greene	54–55	Nov. 17, 1954	22
LIVING TOGETHER—Alan Ayckbourn	75–76	Dec. 7, 1975	76
LOMAN FAMILY PICNIC, THE—Donald Margulies	89–90	June 20, 1989	16
LONG DAY'S JOURNEY INTO NIGHT—Eugene O'Neill	56–57	Nov. 7, 1956	390
LOOK BACK IN ANGER—John Osborne	57–58	Oct. 1, 1957	407
LOOK HOMEWARD, ANGEL—Ketti Frings, based on Thomas Wolfe's novel	57–58	Nov. 28, 1957	564
LOOSE ENDS—Michael Weller	79–80	June 6, 1979	284
LOST HORIZONS—Harry Segall, revised by John Hayden	34–35	Oct. 15, 1934	56
LOST IN THE STARS—(b, l) Maxwell Anderson, based on Alan Paton's novel *Cry, the Beloved Country,* (m) Kurt Weill	49–50	Oct. 30, 1949	273
LOST IN YONKERS—Neil Simon	90–91	Feb. 21, 1991	780
LOVE LETTERS—A.R. Gurney	89–90	Aug. 22, 1989	64
	89–90	Oct. 31, 1989	96
LOVE OF FOUR COLONELS, THE—Peter Ustinov	52–53	Jan. 15, 1953	141
LOVE! VALOUR! COMPASSION!—Terrence McNally	94–95	Nov. 1, 1994	72
	94–95	Feb. 14, 1995	249
LOVERS—Brian Friel	68–69	July 25, 1968	148
LOYALTIES—John Galsworthy	22–23	Sept. 27, 1922	220
LUNCH HOUR—Jean Kerr	80–81	Nov. 12, 1980	262
LUTE SONG—(b) Sidney Howard, Will Irwin from the Chinese classic *Pi-Pa-Ki,* (l) Bernard Hanighen, (m) Raymond Scott	45–46	Feb. 6, 1946	385
LUTHER—John Osborne	63–64	Sept. 25, 1963	211
LUV—Murray Schisgal	64–65	Nov. 11, 1964	901
M. BUTTERFLY—David Henry Hwang	87–88	Mar. 20, 1988	777
MA RAINEY'S BLACK BOTTOM—August Wilson	84–85	Oct. 11, 1984	275
MACHINAL—Sophie Treadwell	28–29	Sept. 7, 1928	91
MAD FOREST—Caryl Churchill	91–92	Dec. 4, 1991	54
MADNESS OF GEORGE III, THE—Alan Bennett	93–94	Sept. 28, 1993	17
MADWOMAN OF CHAILLOT, THE—Jean Giraudoux, (ad) Maurice Valency	48–49	Dec. 27, 1948	368
MAGIC AND THE LOSS, THE—Julian Funt	53–54	Apr. 9, 1954	27
MAGNIFICENT YANKEE, THE—Emmet Lavery	45–46	Jan. 22, 1946	160
MAHABHARATA, THE—Jean-Claude Carrière, (ad) Peter Brook	87–88	Oct. 13, 1987	25
MALE ANIMAL, THE—James Thurber, Elliott Nugent	39–40	Jan. 9, 1940	243
MAMMA'S AFFAIR—Rachel Barton Butler	19–20	Jan. 29, 1920	98
MAN FOR ALL SEASONS, A—Robert Bolt	61–62	Nov. 22, 1961	637
MAN FROM HOME, THE—Booth Tarkington, Harry Leon Wilson	99–09	Aug. 17, 1908	406
MAN IN THE GLASS BOOTH, THE—Robert Shaw	68–69	Sept. 26, 1968	268
MAN OF LA MANCHA—(b) Dale Wasserman, suggested by the life and works of Miguel de Cervantes y Saavedra, (l) Joe Darion, (m) Mitch Leigh	65–66	Nov. 22, 1965	2,328
MAN WHO CAME TO DINNER, THE—George S. Kaufman, Moss Hart	39–40	Oct. 16, 1939	739

PLAY	VOLUME	OPENED	PERFS
MARAT/SADE—(see *The Persecution and Assassination of Marat,* etc.)			
MARGIN FOR ERROR—Clare Boothe	39–40	Nov. 3, 1939	264
MARRIAGE OF BETTE AND BOO, THE—Christopher Durang	84–85	May 16, 1985	86
MARVIN'S ROOM—Scott McPherson	91–92	Dec. 5, 1991	214
MARY, MARY—Jean Kerr	60–61	Mar. 8, 1961	1,572
MARY OF SCOTLAND—Maxwell Anderson	33–34	Nov. 27, 1933	248
MARY ROSE—James M. Barrie	20–21	Dec. 22, 1920	127
MARY THE 3RD—Rachel Crothers	22–23	Feb. 5, 1923	162
MASS APPEAL—Bill C. Davis	81–82	Nov. 12, 1981	214
MASTER CLASS—Terrence McNally	95–96	Nov. 5, 1995	601
MASTER HAROLD . . . AND THE BOYS—Athol Fugard	81–82	May 4, 1982	344
MATCHMAKER, THE—Thornton Wilder, based on Johann Nestroy's *Einen Jux Will Er Sich Machen,* based on John Oxenford's *A Day Well Spent*	55–56	Dec. 5, 1955	486
ME AND MOLLY—Gertrude Berg	47–48	Feb. 26, 1948	156
MEMBER OF THE WEDDING, THE—(ad) Carson McCullers, from her novel	49–50	Jan. 5, 1950	501
MEN IN WHITE—Sidney Kingsley	33–34	Sept. 26, 1933	351
MERRILY WE ROLL ALONG—George S. Kaufman, Moss Hart	34–35	Sept. 29, 1934	155
MERTON OF THE MOVIES—George S. Kaufman, Marc Connelly, based on Harry Leon Wilson's novel	22–23	Nov. 13, 1922	381
MICHAEL AND MARY—A.A. Milne	29–30	Dec. 13, 1929	246
MILK TRAIN DOESN'T STOP HERE ANYMORE, THE—Tennessee Williams	62–63	Jan. 16, 1963	69
MINICK—George S. Kaufman, Edna Ferber	24–25	Sept. 24, 1924	141
MISERABLES, LES—(see *Les Misérables*)			
MISS FIRECRACKER CONTEST, THE—Beth Henley	83–84	May 1, 1984	131
*MISS SAIGON—(b) Alain Boublil, Claude-Michel Schönberg (m) Claude-Michel Schönberg, (l) Richard Maltby Jr., Alain Boublil, (add'l material) Richard Maltby Jr.	90–91	Apr. 11, 1991	3,820
MISTER ROBERTS—Thomas Heggen, Joshua Logan, based on Thomas Heggen's novel	47–48	Feb. 18, 1948	1,157
MOLLY SWEENEY—Brian Friel	95–96	Jan. 7, 1996	145
MOON FOR THE MISBEGOTTEN, A—Eugene O'Neill	56–57	May 2, 1957	68
MOON IS DOWN, THE—John Steinbeck	41–42	Apr. 7, 1942	71
MOONCHILDREN—Michael Weller	71–72	Feb. 21, 1972	16
MORNING'S AT SEVEN—Paul Osborn	39–40	Nov. 30, 1939	44
MOTHER COURAGE AND HER CHILDREN—Bertolt Brecht, (ad) Eric Bentley	62–63	Mar. 28, 1963	52
MOURNING BECOMES ELECTRA—Eugene O'Neill	31–32	Oct. 26, 1931	150
MR. AND MRS. NORTH—Owen Davis, based on Frances and Richard Lockridge's stories	40–41	Jan. 12, 1941	163
MRS. BUMSTEAD-LEIGH—Harry James Smith	09–19	Apr. 3, 1911	64
MRS. KLEIN—Nicholas Wright	95–96	Oct. 24, 1995	280
MRS. MCTHING—Mary Chase	51–52	Feb. 20, 1952	350
MRS. PARTRIDGE PRESENTS—Mary Kennedy, Ruth Hawthorne	24–25	Jan. 5, 1925	144
MY CHILDREN! MY AFRICA!—Athol Fugard	89–90	Dec. 18, 1989	28
MY FAIR LADY—(b, l) Alan Jay Lerner, based on George Bernard Shaw's *Pygmalion,* (m) Frederick Loewe	55–56	Mar. 15, 1956	2,717

PLAY	VOLUME	OPENED	PERFS
MY ONE AND ONLY—(b) Peter Stone, Timothy S. Mayer, (m) George Gershwin from *Funny Face* and other shows, (l) Ira Gershwin	82–83	May 1, 1983	767
MY SISTER EILEEN—Joseph Fields, Jerome Chodorov, based on Ruth McKenney's stories	40–41	Dec. 26, 1940	864
MY 3 ANGELS—Samuel and Bella Spewack, based on Albert Husson's play *La Cuisine des Anges*	52–53	Mar. 11, 1953	344
MYSTERY OF EDWIN DROOD, THE—(b, m, l) Rupert Holmes (also called *Drood*)	85–86	Aug. 4, 1985	24
	85–86	Dec. 12, 1985	608
NATIONAL HEALTH, THE—Peter Nichols	74–75	Oct. 10, 1974	53
NATIVE SON—Paul Green, Richard Wright, based on Mr. Wright's novel	40–41	Mar. 24, 1941	114
NEST, THE—(ad) Grace George, from Paul Geraldy's *Les Noces d'Argent*	21–22	Jan. 28, 1922	152
NEVIS MOUNTAIN DEW—Steve Carter	78–79	Dec. 7, 1978	61
NEW ENGLAND—Richard Nelson	95–96	Nov. 7, 1995	54
NEXT (see *Adaptation*)			
NEXT TIME I'LL SING TO YOU—James Saunders	63–64	Nov. 27, 1963	23
NICE PEOPLE—Rachel Crothers	20–21	Mar. 2, 1921	247
NICHOLAS NICKLEBY—(see *The Life & Adventures of Nicholas Nickleby*)			
NIGHT AND HER STARS—Richard Greenberg	94–95	Apr. 26, 1995	39
NIGHT OF THE IGUANA, THE—Tennessee Williams	61–62	Dec. 28, 1961	316
'NIGHT, MOTHER—Marsha Norman	82–83	Mar. 31, 1983	380
	83–84	Apr. 14, 1984	54
NINE—(b) Arthur L. Kopit, (m, l) Maury Yeston, (ad) Mario Fratti from the Italian	81–82	May 9, 1982	739
NO MORE LADIES—A.E. Thomas	33–34	Jan. 23, 1934	162
NO PLACE TO BE SOMEBODY—Charles Gordone	68–69	May 4, 1969	250
NO TIME FOR COMEDY—S.N. Behrman	38–39	Apr. 17, 1939	185
NO TIME FOR SERGEANTS—Ira Levin, based on Mac Hyman's novel	55–56	Oct. 20, 1955	796
NOEL COWARD IN TWO KEYS—Noel Coward (*Come Into the Garden Maud* and *A Song at Twilight*)	73–74	Feb. 28, 1974	140
NOISES OFF—Michael Frayn	83–84	Dec. 11, 1983	553
NORMAN CONQUESTS, THE—(see *Living Together, Round and Round the Garden* and *Table Manners*)			
NOT ABOUT NIGHTINGALES—Tennessee Williams	98–99	Feb. 25, 1999	125
NUTS—Tom Topor	79–80	Apr. 28, 1980	96
O MISTRESS MINE—Terence Rattigan	45–46	Jan. 23, 1946	452
ODD COUPLE, THE—Neil Simon	64–65	Mar. 10, 1965	964
OF MICE AND MEN—John Steinbeck	37–38	Nov. 23, 1937	207
OF THEE I SING—(b) George S. Kaufman, (m) George Gershwin, Morrie Ryskind, (l) Ira Gershwin	31–32	Dec. 26, 1931	441
OH DAD, POOR DAD, MAMA'S HUNG YOU IN THE CLOSET AND I'M FEELIN' SO SAD—Arthur L. Kopit	61–62	Feb. 26, 1962	454
OHIO IMPROMPTU, CATASTROPHE AND WHAT WHERE—Samuel Beckett	83–84	June 15, 1983	350

PLAY	VOLUME	OPENED	PERFS
OKLAHOMA!—(b, l) Oscar Hammerstein II, based on Lynn Riggs's play *Green Grow the Lilacs,* (m) Richard Rodgers	42–43	Mar. 31, 1943	2,212
OLD MAID, THE—Zoe Akins, based on Edith Wharton's novel	34–35	Jan. 7, 1935	305
OLD SOAK, THE—Don Marquis	22–23	Aug. 22, 1922	423
OLD TIMES—Harold Pinter	71–72	Nov. 16, 1971	119
OLD WICKED SONGS—Jon Marans	96–97	Sept. 5, 1996	210
OLDEST LIVING GRADUATE, THE—Preston Jones	76–77	Sept. 23, 1976	20
OLEANNA—David Mamet	92–93	Oct. 25, 1992	513
ON BORROWED TIME—Paul Osborn, based on Lawrence Edward Watkin's novel	37–38	Feb. 3, 1938	321
ON GOLDEN POND—Ernest Thompson	78–79	Sept. 13, 1978	30
	78–79	Feb. 28, 1979	126
ON TRIAL—Elmer Rice	09–19	Aug. 19, 1914	365
ONCE IN A LIFETIME—Moss Hart, George S. Kaufman	30–31	Sept. 24, 1930	406
ONCE ON THIS ISLAND—(b, l) Lynn Ahrens, (m) Stephen Flaherty, based on the novel *My Love My Love* by Rosa Guy	89–90	May 6, 1990	24
	90–91	Oct. 18, 1990	469
ONE SUNDAY AFTERNOON—James Hagan	32–33	Feb. 15, 1933	322
ORPHEUS DESCENDING—Tennessee Williams	56–57	Mar. 21, 1957	68
OTHER PEOPLE'S MONEY—Jerry Sterner	88–89	Feb. 16, 1989	990
OTHERWISE ENGAGED—Simon Gray	76–77	Feb. 2, 1977	309
OUR COUNTRY'S GOOD—Timberlake Wertenbaker	90–91	Apr. 29, 1991	48
OUTRAGEOUS FORTUNE—Rose Franken	43–44	Nov. 3, 1943	77
OUR TOWN—Thornton Wilder	37–38	Feb. 4, 1938	336
OUTWARD BOUND—Sutton Vane	23–24	Jan. 7, 1924	144
OVER 21—Ruth Gordon	43–44	Jan. 3, 1944	221
OVERTURE—William Bolitho	30–31	Dec. 5, 1930	41
P.S. 193—David Rayfiel	62–63	Oct. 30, 1962	48
PACIFIC OVERTURES—(b) John Weidman, (m, l) Stephen Sondheim, (add'l material) Hugh Wheeler	75–76	Jan. 11, 1976	193
PACK OF LIES—Hugh Whitemore	84–85	Feb. 11, 1985	120
PAINTING CHURCHES—Tina Howe	83–84	Nov. 22, 1983	206
PARADE—(b) Alfred Uhry, (m,l) Jason Robert Brown	98–99	Dec. 17, 1998	85
PARIS BOUND—Philip Barry	27–28	Dec. 27, 1927	234
PASSION—(b) James Lapine, (m) Stephen Sondheim, based on the film *Passione D'Amore*	93–94	May 9, 1994	280
PASSION OF JOSEPH D., THE—Paddy Chayevsky	63–64	Feb. 11, 1964	15
PATRIOTS, THE—Sidney Kingsley	42–43	Jan. 29, 1943	173
PERFECT GANESH, A—Terrence McNally	93–94	June 27, 1993	124
PERFECT PARTY, THE—A.R. Gurney	85–86	Apr. 2, 1986	238
PERIOD OF ADJUSTMENT—Tennessee Williams	60–61	Nov. 10, 1960	132
PERSECUTION AND ASSASSINATION OF MARAT AS PERFORMED BY THE INMATES OF THE ASYLUM OF CHARENTON UNDER THE DIRECTION OF THE MARQUIS DE SADE, THE—Peter Weiss, English version by Geoffrey Skelton, verse (ad) Adrian Mitchell	65–66	Dec. 27, 1965	144
PETRIFIED FOREST, THE—Robert E. Sherwood	34–35	Jan. 7, 1935	197

PLAY	VOLUME	OPENED	PERFS
*PHANTOM OF THE OPERA, THE—(b) Richard Stilgoe, Andrew Lloyd Webber, (m) Andrew Lloyd Webber, (l) Charles Hart, (add'l l) Richard Stilgoe, adapted from the novel by Gaston Leroux (special citation)	87–88	Jan. 26, 1988	5,154
PHILADELPHIA, HERE I COME!—Brian Friel	65–66	Feb. 16, 1966	326
PHILADELPHIA STORY, THE—Philip Barry	38–39	Mar. 28, 1939	417
PHILANTHROPIST, THE—Christopher Hampton	70–71	Mar. 15, 1971	72
PHYSICISTS, THE—Friedrich Duerrenmatt, (ad) James Kirkup	64–65	Oct. 13, 1964	55
PIANO LESSON, THE—August Wilson	89–90	Apr. 16, 1990	329
PICK UP GIRL—Elsa Shelley	43–44	May 3, 1944	198
PICNIC—William Inge	52–53	Feb. 19, 1953	477
PLAY'S THE THING, THE—Ferenc Molnar, (ad) P.G. Wodehouse	26–27	Nov. 3, 1926	260
PLAZA SUITE—Neil Simon	67–68	Feb. 14, 1968	1,097
PIGEONS AND PEOPLE—George M. Cohan	32–33	Jan. 16, 1933	70
PLEASURE OF HIS COMPANY, THE—Samuel Taylor, Cornelia Otis Skinner	58–59	Oct. 22, 1958	474
PLENTY—David Hare	82–83	Oct. 21, 1982	45
	82–83	Jan. 6, 1983	92
PLOUGH AND THE STARS, THE—Sean O'Casey	27–28	Nov. 28, 1927	32
POINT OF NO RETURN—Paul Osborn, based on John P. Marquand's novel	51–52	Dec. 13, 1951	364
PONDER HEART, THE—Joseph Fields, Jerome Chodorov, based on Eudora Welty's story	55–56	Feb. 16, 1956	149
POOR BITOS—Jean Anouilh, (tr) Lucienne Hill	64–65	Nov. 14, 1964	17
PORGY—Dorothy and DuBose Heyward	27–28	Oct. 10, 1927	367
POTTING SHED, THE—Graham Greene	56–57	Jan. 29, 1957	143
PRAYER FOR MY DAUGHTER, A—Thomas Babe	77–78	Dec. 27, 1977	127
PRELUDE TO A KISS—Craig Lucas	89–90	Mar. 14, 1990	33
	89–90	May 1, 1990	440
PRICE, THE—Arthur Miller	67–68	Feb. 7, 1968	429
PRIDE AND PREJUDICE—Helen Jerome, based on Jane Austen's novel	35–36	Nov. 5, 1935	219
PRIDE'S CROSSING—Tina Howe	97–98	Dec. 7, 1997	137
PRISONER OF SECOND AVENUE, THE—Neil Simon	71–72	Nov. 11, 1971	780
PROLOGUE TO GLORY—E.P. Conkle	37–38	Mar. 17, 1938	70
QUARTERMAINE'S TERMS—Simon Gray	82–83	Feb. 24, 1983	375
R.U.R.—Karel Capek	22–23	Oct. 9, 1922	184
RACKET, THE—Bartlett Cormack	27–28	Nov. 22, 1927	119
RAGTIME—(b) Terrence McNally, (m) Stephen Flaherty, (l) Lynn Ahrens, based on E.L. Doctorow's novel	97–98	Jan. 18, 1998	861
RAIN—John Colton, Clemence Randolph, based on the story by W. Somerset Maugham	22–23	Nov. 7, 1922	648
RAISIN IN THE SUN, A—Lorraine Hansberry	58–59	Mar. 11, 1959	530
RATTLE OF A SIMPLE MAN—Charles Dyer	62–63	Apr. 17, 1963	94
REAL ESTATE—Louise Page	87–88	Dec. 1, 1987	55
REAL THING, THE—Tom Stoppard	83–84	Jan. 5, 1984	566
REBEL WOMEN—Thomas Babe	75–76	May 6, 1976	40
REBOUND—Donald Ogden Stewart	29–30	Feb. 3, 1930	114

PLAY	VOLUME	OPENED	PERFS
Red Diaper Baby—Josh Kornbluth	92–93	June 12, 1992	59
Rehearsal, The—Jean Anouilh, (ad) Pamela Hansford Johnson, Kitty Black	63–64	Sept. 23, 1963	110
Remains To Be Seen—Howard Lindsay, Russel Crouse	51–52	Oct. 3, 1951	199
*Rent—(b,m,l) Jonathan Larson	95–96	Feb. 13, 1996	56
	95–96	Apr. 29, 1996	1707
Requiem for a Nun—Ruth Ford, William Faulkner, adapted from William Faulkner's novel	58–59	Jan. 30, 1959	43
Reunion in Vienna—Robert E. Sherwood	31–32	Nov. 16, 1931	264
Rhinoceros—Eugene Ionesco, (tr) Derek Prouse	60–61	Jan. 9, 1961	240
Ritz, The—Terrence McNally	74–75	Jan. 20, 1975	400
River Niger, The—Joseph A. Walker	72–73	Dec. 5, 1972	120
	72–73	Mar. 27, 1973	280
Road—Jim Cartwright	88–89	July 28, 1988	62
Road to Mecca, The—Athol Fugard	87–88	Apr. 12, 1988	172
Road to Rome, The—Robert E. Sherwood	26–27	Jan. 31, 1927	392
Rockaby—(see *Enough, Footfalls* and *Rockaby*)			
Rocket to the Moon—Clifford Odets	38–39	Nov. 24, 1938	131
Romance—Edward Sheldon	09–19	Feb. 10, 1913	160
Rope Dancers, The—Morton Wishengrad	57–58	Nov. 20, 1957	189
Rose Tattoo, The—Tennessee Williams	50–51	Feb. 3, 1951	306
Rosencrantz and Guildenstern Are Dead—Tom Stoppard	67–68	Oct. 16, 1967	420
Round and Round the Garden—Alan Ayckbourn	75–76	Dec. 7, 1975	76
Royal Family, The—George S. Kaufman, Edna Ferber	27–28	Dec. 28, 1927	345
Royal Hunt of the Sun—Peter Shaffer	65–66	Oct. 26, 1965	261
Rugged Path, The—Robert E. Sherwood	45–46	Nov. 10, 1945	81
Runner Stumbles, The—Milan Stitt	75–76	May 18, 1976	191
St. Helena—R.C. Sheriff, Jeanne de Casalis	36–37	Oct. 6, 1936	63
Same Time, Next Year—Bernard Slade	74–75	Mar. 13, 1975	1,453
Saturday's Children—Maxwell Anderson	26–27	Jan. 26, 1927	310
Screens, The—Jean Genet, (tr) Minos Volanakis	71–72	Nov. 30, 1971	28
Scuba Duba—Bruce Jay Friedman	67–68	Oct. 10, 1967	692
Sea Horse, The—Edward J. Moore (James Irwin)	73–74	Apr. 15, 1974	128
Searching Wind, The—Lillian Hellman	43–44	Apr. 12, 1944	318
Seascape—Edward Albee	74–75	Jan. 26, 1975	65
Season in the Sun—Wolcott Gibbs	50–51	Sept. 28, 1950	367
Season's Greetings—Alan Ayckbourn	85–86	July 11, 1985	20
Second Threshold—Philip Barry, revisions by Robert E. Sherwood	50–51	Jan. 2, 1951	126
Secret Service—William Gillette	94–99	Oct. 5, 1896	176
Separate Tables—Terence Rattigan	56–57	Oct. 25, 1956	332
Serenading Louie—Lanford Wilson	75–76	May 2, 1976	33
Serpent: A Ceremony, The—Jean-Claude van Itallie	69–70	May 29, 1973	3
Seven Guitars—August Wilson	95–96	Mar. 28, 1996	187
Seven Keys to Baldpate—(ad) George M. Cohan, from the novel by Earl Derr Biggers	09–19	Sept. 22, 1913	320
1776—(b) Peter Stone, (m, l) Sherman Edwards, based on a conception by Sherman Edwards	68–69	Mar. 16, 1969	1,217
Sex, Drugs, Rock & Roll—Eric Bogosian	89–90	Feb. 8, 1990	103
Shadow and Substance—Paul Vincent Carroll	37–38	Jan. 26, 1938	274

PLAY	VOLUME	OPENED	PERFS
SHADOW BOX, THE—Michael Cristofer	76–77	Mar. 31, 1977	315
SHADOW OF HEROES—(see *Stone and Star*)			
SHADOWLANDS—William Nicholson	90–91	Nov. 11, 1990	169
SHE LOVES ME—(b) Joe Masteroff, based on Miklos Laszlo's play *Parfumerie,* (l) Sheldon Harnick, (m) Jerry Bock	62–63	Apr. 23, 1963	301
SHINING HOUR, THE—Keith Winter	33–34	Feb. 13, 1934	121
SHIRLEY VALENTINE—Willy Russell	88–89	Feb. 16, 1989	324
SHORT EYES—Miguel Piñero	73–74	Feb. 28, 1974	54
	73–74	May 23, 1974	102
SHOW-OFF, THE—George Kelly	23–24	Feb. 5, 1924	571
SHRIKE, THE—Joseph Kramm	51–52	Jan. 15, 1952	161
SIDE MAN—Warren Leight	98–99	June 25, 1998	458
SIGHT UNSEEN—Donald Margulies	91–92	Jan. 20, 1992	263
SILVER CORD, THE—Sidney Howard	26–27	Dec. 20, 1926	112
SILVER WHISTLE, THE—Robert E. McEnroe	48–49	Nov. 24, 1948	219
SISTERS ROSENSWEIG, THE—Wendy Wasserstein	92–93	Oct. 22, 1992	149
	92–93	Mar. 18, 1993	556
SIX CYLINDER LOVE—William Anthony McGuire	21–22	Aug. 25, 1921	430
SIX DEGREES OF SEPARATION—John Guare	90–91	June 14, 1990	155
	90–91	Nov. 8, 1990	485
6 RMS RIV VU—Bob Randall	72–73	Oct. 17, 1972	247
SKIN GAME, THE—John Galsworthy	20–21	Oct. 20, 1920	176
SKIN OF OUR TEETH, THE—Thornton Wilder	42–43	Nov. 18, 1942	359
SKIPPER NEXT TO GOD—Jan de Hartog	47–48	Jan. 4, 1948	93
SKRIKER, THE—Caryl Churchill	95–96	May 12, 1996	17
SKYLARK—Samson Raphaelson	39–40	Oct. 11, 1939	256
SKYLIGHT—David Hare	96–97	Sept. 19, 1996	116
SLEUTH—Anthony Shaffer	70–71	Nov. 12, 1970	1,222
SLOW DANCE ON THE KILLING GROUND—William Hanley	64–65	Nov. 30, 1964	88
SLY FOX—Larry Gelbart, based on *Volpone* by Ben Jonson	76–77	Dec. 14, 1976	495
SMALL CRAFT WARNINGS—Tennessee Williams	71–72	Apr. 2, 1972	192
SOLDIER'S PLAY, A—Charles Fuller	81–82	Nov. 20, 1981	468
SOLDIER'S WIFE—Rose Franken	44–45	Oct. 4, 1944	253
SPEED-THE-PLOW—David Mamet	87–88	May 3, 1988	278
SPIC-O-RAMA—John Leguizamo	92–93	Oct. 27, 1992	86
SPLIT SECOND—Dennis McIntyre	84–85	June 7, 1984	147
SQUAW MAN, THE—Edward Milton Royle	99–09	Oct. 23, 1905	222
STAGE DOOR—George S. Kaufman, Edna Ferber	36–37	Oct. 22, 1936	169
STAIRCASE—Charles Dyer	67–68	Jan. 10, 1968	61
STAR-WAGON, THE—Maxwell Anderson	37–38	Sept. 29, 1937	223
STATE OF THE UNION—Howard Lindsay, Russel Crouse	45–46	Nov. 14, 1945	765
STEAMBATH—Bruce Jay Friedman	70–71	June 30, 1970	128
STEEL MAGNOLIAS—Robert Harling	87–88	June 19, 1987	1,126
STICKS AND BONES—David Rabe	71–72	Nov. 7, 1971	121
	71–72	Mar. 1, 1972	245
STONE AND STAR—Robert Ardrey (also called *Shadow of Heroes*)	61–62	Dec. 5, 1961	20
STOP THE WORLD—I WANT TO GET OFF—(b, m, l) Leslie Bricusse, Anthony Newley	62–63	Oct. 3, 1962	555
STORM OPERATION—Maxwell Anderson	43–44	Jan. 11, 1944	23
STORY OF MARY SURRATT, THE—John Patrick	46–47	Feb. 8, 1947	11

PLAY	VOLUME	OPENED	PERFS
Strange Interlude—Eugene O'Neill	27–28	Jan. 30, 1928	426
Streamers—David Rabe	75–76	Apr. 21, 1976	478
Street Scene—Elmer Rice	28–29	Jan. 10, 1929	601
Streetcar Named Desire, A—Tennessee Williams	47–48	Dec. 3, 1947	855
Strictly Dishonorable—Preston Sturges	29–30	Sept. 18, 1929	557
Subject Was Roses, The—Frank D. Gilroy	64–65	May 25, 1964	832
Substance of Fire, The—Jon Robin Baitz	90–91	Mar. 17, 1991	120
SubUrbia—Eric Bogosian	93–94	May 22, 1994	113
Sugar Babies—(ad) Ralph G. Allen from traditional material (special citation)	79–80	Oct. 8, 1979	1,208
Sum of Us, The—David Stevens	90–91	Oct. 16, 1990	335
Summer of the 17th Doll—Ray Lawler	57–58	Jan. 22, 1958	29
Sunday in the Park With George—(b) James Lapine, (m, l) Stephen Sondheim	83–84	May 2, 1984	604
Sunrise at Campobello—Dore Schary	57–58	Jan. 30, 1958	556
Sunset Boulevard—(b, l) Don Black, Christopher Hampton, (m) Andrew Lloyd Webber, based on the film by Billy Wilder	94–95	Nov. 17, 1994	977
Sunshine Boys, The—Neil Simon	72–73	Dec. 20, 1972	538
Sun-Up—Lula Vollmer	22–23	May 25, 1923	356
Susan and God—Rachel Crothers	37–38	Oct. 7, 1937	288
Swan, The—Ferenc Molnar, (tr) Melville Baker	23–24	Oct. 23, 1923	255
Sweeney Todd, the Demon Barber of Fleet Street—(b) Hugh Wheeler, (m, l) Stephen Sondheim, based on a version of *Sweeney Todd* by Christopher Bond	78–79	Mar. 1, 1979	557
Sweet Bird of Youth—Tennessee Williams	58–59	Mar. 10, 1959	375
Table Manners—Alan Ayckbourn	75–76	Dec. 7, 1975	76
Table Settings—James Lapine	79–80	Jan. 14, 1980	264
Take a Giant Step—Louis Peterson	53–54	Sept. 24, 1953	76
Taking of Miss Janie, The—Ed Bullins	74–75	May 4, 1975	42
Talley's Folley—Lanford Wilson	78–79	May 1, 1979	44
	79–80	Feb. 20, 1980	277
Tarnish—Gilbert Emery	23–24	Oct. 1, 1923	248
Taste of Honey, A—Shelagh Delaney	60–61	Oct. 4, 1960	376
Tchin-Tchin—Sidney Michaels, based on François Billetdoux's play	62–63	Oct. 25, 1962	222
Tea and Sympathy—Robert Anderson	53–54	Sept. 30, 1953	712
Teahouse of the August Moon, The—John Patrick, based on Vern Sneider's novel	53–54	Oct. 15, 1953	1,027
Tenth Man, The—Paddy Chayefsky	59–60	Nov. 5, 1959	623
That Championship Season—Jason Miller	71–72	May 2, 1972	144
	72–73	Sept. 14, 1972	700
There Shall Be No Night—Robert E. Sherwood	39–40	Apr. 29, 1940	181
They Knew What They Wanted—Sidney Howard	24–25	Nov. 24, 1924	414
They Shall Not Die—John Wexley	33–34	Feb. 21, 1934	62
Thousand Clowns, A—Herb Gardner	61–62	Apr. 5, 1962	428
Three Postcards—(b) Craig Lucas, (m, l) Craig Carnelia	86–87	May 14, 1987	22
Three Tall Women—Edward Albee	93–94	Apr. 5, 1994	582
Threepenny Opera—(b, l) Bertolt Brecht, (m) Kurt Weill, (tr) Ralph Manheim, John Willett	75–76	Mar. 1, 1976	307

PLAY	VOLUME	OPENED	PERFS
THURBER CARNIVAL, A—James Thurber	59–60	Feb. 26, 1960	127
TIGER AT THE GATES—Jean Giraudoux's *La Guerre de Troie n'Aura Pas Lieu,* (tr) Christopher Fry	55–56	Oct. 3, 1955	217
TIME OF THE CUCKOO, THE—Arthur Laurents	52–53	Oct. 15, 1952	263
TIME OF YOUR LIFE, THE—William Saroyan	39–40	Oct. 25, 1939	185
TIME REMEMBERED—Jean Anouilh's *Léocadia,* (ad) Patricia Moyes	57–58	Nov. 12, 1957	248
TINY ALICE—Edward Albee	64–65	Dec. 29, 1964	167
TITANIC—(b) Peter Stone, (m, 1) Maury Yeston	96–97	Apr. 23, 1997	804
TOILET, THE—LeRoi Jones (a.k.a. Amiri Baraka)	64–65	Dec. 16, 1964	151
TOMORROW AND TOMORROW—Philip Barry	30–31	Jan. 13, 1931	206
TOMORROW THE WORLD—James Gow, Arnaud d'Usseau	42–43	Apr. 14, 1943	500
TORCH SONG TRILOGY—Harvey Fierstein (*The International Stud, Fugue in a Nursery, Widows and Children First*)	81–82	Jan. 15, 1982	117
	82–83	June 10, 1982	1,222
TOUCH OF THE POET, A—Eugene O'Neill	58–59	Oct. 2, 1958	284
TOVARICH—Jacques Deval, (tr) Robert E. Sherwood	36–37	Oct. 15, 1936	356
TOYS IN THE ATTIC—Lillian Hellman	59–60	Feb. 25, 1960	556
TRACERS—John DiFusco (c); Vincent Caristi, Richard Chaves, John DiFusco, Eric E. Emerson, Rick Gallavan, Merlin Marston, Harry Stephens with Sheldon Lettich	84–85	Jan. 21, 1985	186
TRAGEDIE DE CARMEN, LA—(see *La Tragédie de Carmen*)			
TRANSLATIONS—Brian Friel	80–81	Apr. 7, 1981	48
TRAVESTIES—Tom Stoppard	75–76	Oct. 30, 1975	155
TRELAWNY OF THE WELLS—Arthur Wing Pinero	94–99	Nov. 22, 1898	131
TRIAL OF THE CATONSVILLE NINE, THE—Daniel Berrigan, Saul Levitt	70–71	Feb. 7, 1971	159
TRIBUTE—Bernard Slade	77–78	June 1, 1978	212
TUNA CHRISTMAS, A—Jaston Williams, Joe Sears, Ed Howard	94–95	Dec. 15, 1994	20
TWILIGHT: LOS ANGELES, 1992—Anna Deavere Smith	93–94	Mar. 23, 1994	13
	93–94	Apr. 17, 1994	72
TWO BLIND MICE—Samuel Spewack	48–49	Mar. 2, 1949	157
TWO TRAINS RUNNING—August Wilson	91–92	Apr. 13, 1992	160
UNCHASTENED WOMAN, THE—Louis Kaufman Anspacher	09–19	Oct. 9, 1915	193
UNCLE HARRY—Thomas Job	41–42	May 20, 1942	430
UNDER MILK WOOD—Dylan Thomas	57–58	Oct. 15, 1957	39
VALLEY FORGE—Maxwell Anderson	34–35	Dec. 10, 1934	58
VALLEY SONG—Athol Fugard	95–96	Dec. 12, 1995	96
VENUS OBSERVED—Christopher Fry	51–52	Feb. 13, 1952	86
VERY SPECIAL BABY, A—Robert Alan Aurthur	56–57	Nov. 14, 1956	5
VICTORIA REGINA—Laurence Housman	35–36	Dec. 26, 1935	517
VIEW FROM THE BRIDGE, A—Arthur Miller	55–56	Sept. 29, 1955	149
VIOLET—(b,1) Brian Crawley, (m) Jeanine Tesori, based on *The Ugliest Pilgrim* by Doris Betts	96–97	Mar. 11, 1997	32
VISIT, THE—Friedrich Duerrenmatt, (ad) Maurice Valency	57–58	May 5, 1958	189
VISIT TO A SMALL PLANET—Gore Vidal	56–57	Feb. 7, 1957	388
VIVAT! VIVAT REGINA!—Robert Bolt	71–72	Jan. 20, 1972	116

PLAY	VOLUME	OPENED	PERFS
VOICE OF THE TURTLE, THE—John van Druten	43–44	Dec. 8, 1943	1,557
WAGER, THE—Mark Medoff	74–75	Oct. 21, 1974	104
WAITING FOR GODOT—Samuel Beckett	55–56	Apr. 19, 1956	59
WALK IN THE WOODS, A—Lee Blessing	87–88	Feb. 28, 1988	136
WALTZ OF THE TOREADORS, THE—Jean Anouilh, (tr) Lucienne Hill	56–57	Jan. 17, 1957	132
WATCH ON THE RHINE—Lillian Hellman	40–41	Apr. 1, 1941	378
WE, THE PEOPLE—Elmer Rice	32–33	Jan. 21, 1933	49
WEDDING BELLS—Salisbury Field	19–20	Nov. 12, 1919	168
WEDNESDAY'S CHILD—Leopold Atlas	33–34	Jan. 16, 1934	56
WENCESLAS SQUARE—Larry Shue	87–88	Mar. 2, 1988	55
WHAT A LIFE—Clifford Goldsmith	37–38	Apr. 13, 1938	538
WHAT PRICE GLORY?—Maxwell Anderson, Laurence Stallings	24–25	Sept. 3, 1924	433
WHAT THE BUTLER SAW—Joe Orton	69–70	May 4, 1970	224
WHEN LADIES MEET—Rachel Crothers	32–33	Oct. 6, 1932	191
WHEN YOU COMIN' BACK, RED RYDER?—Mark Medoff	73–74	Dec. 6, 1973	302
WHERE HAS TOMMY FLOWERS GONE?—Terrence McNally	71–72	Oct. 7, 1971	78
WHITE HOUSE MURDER CASE, THE—Jules Feiffer	69–70	Feb. 18, 1970	119
WHITE STEED, THE—Paul Vincent Carroll	38–39	Jan. 10, 1939	136
WHO'S AFRAID OF VIRGINIA WOOLF?—Edward Albee	62–63	Oct. 13, 1962	664
WHO'S TOMMY, THE—(b) Pete Townshend, Des McAnuff, (m, l) Pete Townshend, (add'l m, l) John Entwistle, Keith Moon (special citation)	92–93	Apr. 22, 1993	900
WHOSE LIFE IS IT ANYWAY?—Brian Clark	78–79	Apr. 17, 1979	223
WHY MARRY?—Jesse Lynch Williams	09–19	Dec. 25, 1917	120
WHY NOT?—Jesse Lynch Williams	22–23	Dec. 25, 1922	120
WIDOW CLAIRE, THE—Horton Foote	86–87	Dec. 17, 1986	150
WILD BIRDS—Dan Totheroh	24–25	Apr. 9, 1925	44
WILD HONEY—Michael Frayn, from an untitled play by Anton Chekhov	86–87	Dec. 18, 1986	28
WINGED VICTORY—Moss Hart, (m) David Rose	43–44	Nov. 20, 1943	212
WINGS—Arthur L. Kopit	78–79	June 21, 1978	15
	78–79	Jan. 28, 1979	113
WINGS—(b, l) Arthur Perlman, (m) Jeffrey Lunden, based on the play by Arthur L. Kopit	92–93	Mar. 9, 1993	47
WINGS OVER EUROPE—Robert Nichols, Maurice Browne	28–29	Dec. 10, 1928	90
WINSLOW BOY, THE—Terence Rattigan	47–48	Oct. 29, 1947	215
WINTER SOLDIERS—Daniel Lewis James	42–43	Nov. 29, 1942	25
WINTERSET—Maxwell Anderson	35–36	Sept. 25, 1935	195
WISDOM TOOTH, THE—Marc Connelly	25–26	Feb. 15, 1926	160
WISTERIA TREES, THE—Joshua Logan, based on Anton Chekhov's *The Cherry Orchard*	49–50	Mar. 29, 1950	165
WIT—Margaret Edson	98–99	Oct. 6, 1998	545
WITCHING HOUR, THE—Augustus Thomas	99–09	Nov. 18, 1907	212
WITNESS FOR THE PROSECUTION—Agatha Christie	54–55	Dec. 16, 1954	645
WOMEN, THE—Clare Boothe	36–37	Dec. 26, 1936	657
WONDERFUL TOWN—(b) Joseph Fields, Jerome Chodorov, based on their play *My Sister Eileen* and Ruth McKenney's stories, (l) Betty Comden, Adolph Green, (m) Leonard Bernstein	52–53	Feb. 25, 1953	559

PLAY	VOLUME	OPENED	PERFS
WORLD WE MAKE, THE—Sidney Kingsley, based on Millen Brand's novel *The Outward Room*	39–40	Nov. 20, 1939	80
YEARS AGO—Ruth Gordon	46–47	Dec. 3, 1946	206
YES, MY DARLING DAUGHTER—Mark Reed	36–37	Feb. 9, 1937	405
YOU AND I—Philip Barry	22–23	Feb. 19, 1923	178
YOU CAN'T TAKE IT WITH YOU—Moss Hart, George S. Kaufman	36–37	Dec. 14, 1936	837
YOU KNOW I CAN'T HEAR YOU WHEN THE WATER'S RUNNING—Robert Anderson	66–67	Mar. 13, 1967	755
YOUNG MAN FROM ATLANTA, THE—Horton Foote	94–95	Jan. 27, 1995	24
YOUNG WOODLEY—John van Druten	25–26	Nov. 2, 1925	260
YOUNGEST, THE—Philip Barry	24–25	Dec. 22, 1924	104
YOUR OWN THING—(b) Donald Driver, (m, l) Hal Hester and Danny Apolinar, suggested by William Shakespeare's *Twelfth Night*	67–68	Jan. 13, 1968	933
YOU'RE A GOOD MAN CHARLIE BROWN—(b, m, l) Clark Gesner, based on the comic strip *Peanuts* by Charles M. Schulz	66–67	Mar. 7, 1967	1,597
ZOOMAN AND THE SIGN—Charles Fuller	80–81	Dec. 7, 1980	33

INDEX

Play titles appear in **bold face.** ***Bold face italic*** page numbers refer to those pages where cast and credit listings may be found.